BIG ISLAND OF HAWAI'I

BREE KESSLER

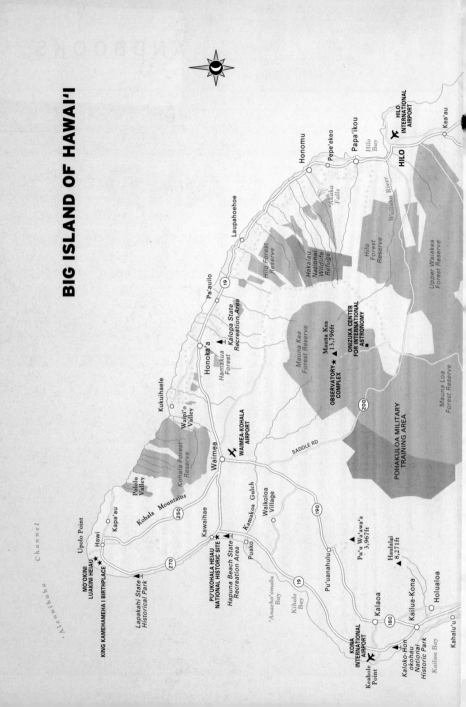

BIG ISLAND OF HAWAI'I

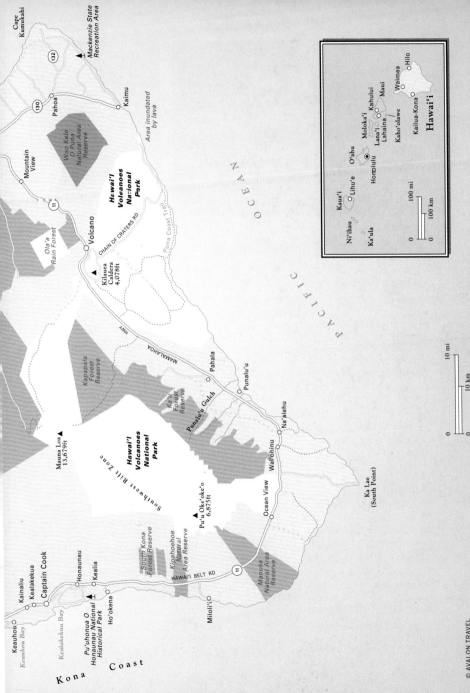

Cape
Kumukahi

132

Mackenzie State
Recreation Area

130   Pahoa

Kaimu

Mountain
View

Wao Kele
O Puna
Natural Area
Reserve

Area inundated
by lava

11   Volcano

Hawai'i
Volcanoes
Na-ional
Park

Ola'a
Rain Forest

CHAIN OF CRATERS RD

Kilauea
Caldera
4,078ft

Puna Coast Trail

PACIFIC   OCEAN

Kapapala
Forest
Reserve

MAMALAHOA   HWY

Pahala

Punalu'u

Ka'u
Forest
Reserve

Punalu'u Gulch

Na'alehu

Mauna Loa
13,679ft

Hawai'i
Volcanoes
National
Park

Wai'ohinu

Southwest Rift Zone

Pu'u Oke'oke'o
6,875ft

Ocean View

Ka Lae
(South Point)

Keauhou

Kainaliu
Keauhou Bay
Kealakekua

Captain Cook

Honaunau
Kealia

South Kona
Forest Reserve

Kipahoehoe
Natural
Area Reserve

HAWAI'I BELT RD

Manuka
Natural Area
Reserve

11

Pu'uhonua O
Honaunau National
Historical Park

Ho'okena

Milioli'i

Keauhou Bay

Kona   Coast

Hawai'i

Hilo

Waimea

Kahului
Maui
Lahaina
Kaho'olawe

Kailua-Kona

Moloka'i
Lana'i

O'ahu
Honolulu

Lihu'e

Kaua'i

Ni'ihau

Ka'ula

0   100 mi

0   100 km

0   10 mi

0   10 km

© AVALON TRAVEL

Contents

Discover the Big Island of Hawai'i

Everyone knows the Big Island of Hawai'i has beaches and sunshine. But it's so much more than its unbelievably good weather. It's not so hard to get off the beaten path, since the majority of the Big Island offers seclusion and adventure with easy access.

The Big Island of Hawai'i is the newest island, geologically speaking, in the chain of islands that make up the state of Hawaii. While lava formed the island's physical structure, it is the sugar plantation industry, established in the mid-1800s, that is credited for creating the Big Island's culture, through bringing numerous immigrants to work the island's land. Much of the island's modern-day customs, from language (Hawaiian pidgin, or *da' kine*) to food (like the *loco moco* or Spam *musubi*) to clothing (the classic aloha shirt), reflect this merging of Chinese, Filipino, Japanese, Polynesian, Portuguese, as well as Mainland American cultures.

It's sometimes hard to tell locals from visitors – the only real way to confirm a true local is by checking for the Local brand *slippahs* (flip-flops) on someone's feet. These preferred shoes, which anyone can pick up for $3.99 at nearly every grocery or drug store, embody the Hawaiian notion of *aloha*, the laid-back way of life in Hawaii that attracts new residents and visitors every year. (Your first order of business when arriving to the island should be picking up a pair yourself.)

Many visitors are beckoned by the Big Island's warm weather and well-known spectacular landscape – including pristine Hapuna Beach, picture-perfect Waipi'o Valley, and the lava flow rush into the ocean in Pahoa. Of course the island provides an array of activities for outdoor lovers, from "fluming the ditch" (kayaking through an old plantation-era ditch in Kohala) to surfing the popular Honoli'i Beach Park; from night snorkeling with the manta rays in Keauhou Bay to stargazing at the Mauna Kea Observatory. And you're never more than 10–20 minutes away from a gorgeous beach.

The Big Island doesn't offer just one kind of experience. When the weather gets too hot seaside, drive upcountry to Waimea, the cool interior part of the island, where a fireside meal will be waiting for you. Or spend an early Sunday morning at one of the island's numerous farmers markets adorned with tropical fruits, *malasadas* (Portuguese doughnuts), and food carts with mouthwatering *huli huli* chicken and smoked fish.

When your visit is over, say *"a hui hou"* (until we meet again). You'll want to come back.

Planning Your Trip

What makes the Big Island so great is also what makes it so difficult for trip planning. Every nook and cranny of the island is so unique that it's hard to not want to experience it all. The Big Island isn't the kind of place where you can say, "Well, the beaches on the east side are probably the same as here." They aren't. And the interior part of the island is worlds away from the coast, while actually only being 15 minutes away. Don't worry, though. Just take a deep breath—you can see it all.

▶ WHERE TO GO

Kona

Kona is dry, sunny, and brilliant—most visitors' introduction to the island. When watered, the rich soil blossoms, as in the small artists' enclave of Holualoa and South Kona, renowned for its diminutive coffee plantations. As the center of this region, Kailua-Kona boasts an array of art and designer shops, economical accommodations, great restaurants, and plenty of historical and cultural sites like Moku'aikaua Church, a legacy of the very first packet of missionaries to arrive in the islands, and Hulihe'e Palace, vacation home of the Hawaiian royalty. Kealakekua Bay, one of the first points of contact with foreigners, is also one of the best snorkel sites that Hawai'i has to offer. Nearby is Pu'uhonua O Honaunau National

Kealakekua Bay

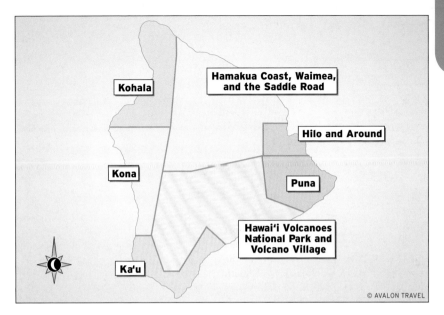

© AVALON TRAVEL

Historical Park, the location of a traditional Hawaiian safe refuge.

Kohala

North of Kailua-Kona, otherworldly black lava bleeds north into Kohala. Up the coast is Hapuna Beach, one of the best on the island. In 1965, Laurance Rockefeller opened the Mauna Kea Beach Hotel near there. Since then, other expansive resorts have been added, making this the island's luxury resort area, barren lava turned into oases of green. Peppered among these resorts are petroglyph fields left by ancient Hawaiians. As you travel north on Highway 19 it becomes Highway 270 and you'll find yourself in the hilly peninsular thumb at the northern extremity of the island. The Kohala Mountains sweep down to the west to a warm and largely uninhabited coast, and to the east tumble into deep valleys cut by wind and rain. Several isolated beach parks dot the coast, and here and there are cultural sites, including a modern-day ruin at

Mahukona Beach Park. The main town up this way is sleepy Hawi, holding on after sugar left. At road's end is the overlook of stunning Pololu Valley.

Ka'u

One of the best scenic drives on the island, the "underdeveloped" southernmost region of the island is primarily an arid coastal region with a few towns at the base of Mauna Loa and the recognizable Ka Lae, also known as South Point, the most southerly piece of real estate in the United States. Below the ranches, macadamia nut farms, and coffee fields are lovely beaches, some of which can only be reached by harsh four-wheel-drive roads like the Road to the Sea. Or skip the four-wheel driving and take an hour-long stroll to the Green Sand Beach, which truly has green-tinted sand (it's from olivine), or an easy paved drive to the Punalu'u Black Sand Beach, where you're almost guaranteed to see turtles lounging in the sand.

the spatter cone of Kilauea Iki in Hawai'i Volcanoes National Park

Hawai'i Volcanoes National Park and Volcano Village

The greatest lava fields that have spewed from Kilauea dominate the heart of Hawai'i Volcanoes National Park. While miles of hiking trails crisscross the park, most see it by car (but some by bike) along the rim drive that brings you up close to sights like the impressive Halema'uma'u Crater, the mythical home of Madame Pele, the fire goddess. Chain of Craters Road spills off the *pali* through a forbidding yet vibrant wasteland of old and new lava to where this living volcano fumes and throbs. Nights in Volcano Village can be cold, but you'll be so distracted by watching the lava glow from the Thomas A. Jaggar Museum and then singing karaoke alongside park employees at Kilauea Military Camp that you'll hardly notice the drop in temperature at all.

Puna

Puna lies south of Hilo and makes up the majority of the southeast coast. It is one of the last bastions of tropical old Hawaii, a place of "independent-minded" people willing to live on the edge and off the grid. While it once grew sugarcane, it's now best known for anthuriums, orchids, and papayas. Recent lava flows cover this region. One embraced a forest in its fiery grasp, entombing trees that stand like sentinels today in Lava Tree State Monument. Another formed Cape Kumukahi in 1868, becoming the easternmost point in Hawaii. The Kapoho tide pools anchor the eastern end of this coast, and from there a string of ebony-black beaches dot the shoreline, including Kehena Beach, where on Sundays locals come to beat drums and sun their naked bodies. The coastal road dead-ends where it's been covered by lava at the small village of Kaimu, and if you're lucky, at night you can see the orange and red lava flow across the field from the viewing area of the south part of Hawai'i Volcanoes National Park.

Hilo and Around

Hilo is the oldest port of entry and the only major city on the island's windward (east) coast. This is where it feels like old Hawaii. The city is one tremendous greenhouse where exotic flowers and tropical plants are a normal part of the landscape. The town boasts Japanese gardens, Honoli'i Beach (the best place to watch surfing), the Lyman Museum and Mission House, the Pacific Tsunami Museum, and a profusion of natural phenomena, including Rainbow Falls and Boiling Pots as well as black-sand beaches on the east side of town. Drive 20 minutes west of town to the mesmerizing 'Akaka Falls. As the focus of tourism has shifted to the Kona side, Hilo is a place where there are deals to be had.

Hamakua Coast, Waimea, and the Saddle Road

Hamakua refers to the northeast coast above Hilo, where streams, wind, and pounding surf have chiseled the lava into cliffs and precipitous valleys. The road north from one-street Honoka'a dead-ends at the lookout at Waipi'o Valley, the most spectacular and enchanted valley on the island. Upcountry is Waimea, the heart of Hawaiian cowboy country and

Rainbow Falls

home to the Hawaii Regional Cuisine movement. From Waimea one can traverse the island via the Saddle Road separating the mountains of Mauna Loa and Mauna Kea. Along the Saddle Road are long stretches of native forest, barren lava flow, and rangeland, plus a number of worthy spots for a stretch. From the Saddle Road, a spur road heads up to the top of Mauna Kea, where, at 13,796 feet, observatories peer into the heavens through the clearest air on earth. Heading south, another road zigzags up the slope to an atmospheric observatory, from where a hiking trail for the hale and hearty heads to the top of Mauna Loa.

▶ WHEN TO GO

As with all of the Hawaiian Islands, the prime tourist season for the Big Island starts two weeks before Christmas and lasts until Easter. It picks up again with summer vacation in early June and ends once more in late August. Everything is more heavily booked and prices are higher. Hotel, airline, and car reservations are a must at this time of year. You can generally save substantially and avoid a lot of hassle if you travel in the off-season—September to early December and mid-April (after Easter) until late May.

a coffee plant growing on a Kona hillside

Recently, the drop in numbers of tourists during the off-season has not been nearly as substantial as in years past, indicating the increasing popularity of the island at all times of the year, but you'll still find the prices better and the beaches, trails, activities, and even restaurants less crowded.

The weather in Hawaii is moderate all year round, and any time can be pleasant. Rains come and go—more so in winter—and are seldom sustained, so usually you can move a few miles down the coast to a sunny spot or wait for the warm breezes to blow away the clouds and dry things up.

While nearly all activities are available throughout the year, there are some exceptions. For instance, if you intend to see humpback whales, you must visit from late winter through spring, as these lovable giants of the sea are in Hawaiian waters only from December through April. Plenty of coffee is grown on the Big Island, and if you intend to view its harvesting and processing, it's best

to go from September through January when the bulk of that job is done.

How Long to Stay

The Big Island can be "seen" in a few days, but there is much more to see and do than even a week or 10 days will give you time for. The island is relatively large, and it takes hours to drive straight around. At a minimum for sightseeing, spend one day each in Kona and Hilo, another day at Hawai'i Volcanoes National Park, a day up the Hamakua Coast, and a day in Waimea and the North Kohala area. For those with more time, a trip up to the top of Mauna Kea would be rewarding, or a cultural tour of historical sites up and down the Kona and Kohala Coasts might be worth your time. Then there are the activities, most of which are half-day or full-day affairs. Remember that some activities should not be coupled with others on the same day, like scuba diving and a helicopter ride. Leave them for different days.

Best of the Big Island

The Big Island is big—at least in relation to the other Hawaiian Islands. While it's possible to "do" the island in a few days, it is preferable to go at a more leisurely pace. As the average visitor from the Mainland spends nine days on a vacation in Hawaii, this time frame is a good choice for an all-encompassing Best of the Big Island tour. If you like to take it slow or build in at least some beach time into each day, you can easily expand this itinerary to 10 or even 14 days.

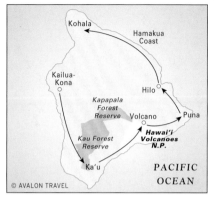

Day 1

Fly into Kona, knowing that the bleak, black lavascape that you come in over will not be how the entire island looks. Pick up your rental car and, if you are staying in Kailua or Keauhou, head into town and take the shoreline route down Ali'i Drive to your hotel. Settle in, have a look around the property, and take a leisurely stroll along the beach or on Ali'i Drive after dinner in Kailua.

Day 2

Pre-book a morning kayak tour of Kealakekua Bay and spend a few hours cruising around watching the dolphins or watching (via snorkel or diving) an out-of-this-world underworld. Dry off and head to Pu'uhonua O Honaunau National Historical Park and try to catch an extremely informative tour

Pu'uhonua O Honaunau National Historical Park

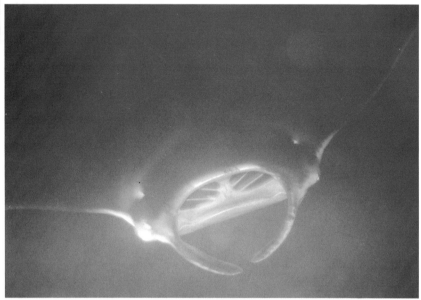

manta ray

with a ranger. If you want to get back in the water, snorkel Two Step located next to the national historical park or even catch some sun at the tide pools in the park itself. In the later afternoon travel uphill to the quaint town of Holualoa to peruse the galleries and eat dinner. Or the serious water lovers will want to book themselves on a night manta ray snorkel tour in Keauhou Bay. Those who want to remain dry can watch the manta rays (and the snorkelers) from the bar at the Sheraton Keauhou Bay Resort and Spa.

Day 3

Head to Ka'u, where you'll take a quick morning tour of the private lava tubes at Kula Kai Caverns. Then drive to the southernmost point in the United States of America, Ka Lae, also called South Point, where you can try out your amateur cliff diving skills (it's quite the drop to the ocean)

or just shake your head as others fall from the point. From South Point, walk to Green Sand Beach—because where else are you going to see a beach with a green tint? Then drive to the Punalu'u Bake Shop, the southernmost bakery (you'll also pass the southernmost restaurant and southernmost bar), to fill your belly with multiple *malasadas*. Then get to Punalu'u Black Sand Beach for a sunset you'll share with a bunch of turtles hanging around the beach. Consider spending the night at one of several unique lodgings that Ka'u has to offer (like a Buddhist temple or a Volkswagen bus) or drive back to your hotel in Kona.

Day 4

Wake up early! This is the day for Hawai'i Volcanoes National Park. From Ka'u it's a 30-minute drive, from Hilo it's an hour's drive, from Kona it's perhaps twice that. Make your first stop at the Kilauea Visitor Center

the brightly burning glow from Halema'uma'u Crater

for a quick introduction to the wonders of the park. For the best overall tour, travel the open sections of the Crater Rim Drive, stopping at all the marked sites. Be sure to spend time at the Thomas A. Jaggar Museum to learn more about the geology of the park. Pay your respects at Halema'uma'u Crater, the home of the Hawaiian goddess Pele, before heading down the Chain of Craters Road to the ever-changing landscape at the shore. Spend the night in Volcano Village so that you can come back at night and watch the lava glow (you'll never forget it).

Day 5

Finally, a day at the beach. Travel to the southern part of Puna (about an hour from Volcano Village or Hilo) and leave your worries (and cell phone reception) behind. Follow the Red Road as it curves around the southeast part of the island, stopping for top-notch snorkeling at the Kapoho tide pools.

Then warm up at the Ahalanui Beach Park warm ponds or the semi-secret warm pond secluded in the trees of Isaac Hale Beach Park. If it's a Saturday visit the SPACE market to catch a true glimpse of lower Puna's culture while munching on raw vegan treats. If it it's a Sunday you'll hear the drumming (and see the cars lined up) down the road from Kehena Beach. You'll know you've gotten to the end of the road because it's covered with lava (and your cell phone reception has magically returned). Take a leisurely walk out to Kaimu Beach to get a sense of what the area was once and to see how locals are re-planting it to transform it back to its original glory. If the lava is flowing, end your day around sunset at the viewing area just north of Kaimu Beach where, if conditions are right, visitors can walk a mile across the lava field to watch (from a safe distance) the grandeur of lava curving its way into the ocean. Drive back to Volcano Village to sleep.

'Akaka Falls

Day 6

Spend the morning on a walking tour of downtown Hilo. Visit the Lyman Museum and Mission House and don't miss the Pacific Tsunami Museum, as it tells the story of the two deadly tsunamis that wreaked havoc on this city during living memory. Stroll along Banyan Drive, or walk through the bayside Lili'uokalani Gardens and then watch the surfers do their thing at Honoli'i Beach Park. Natural sites only a few minutes from the center of town are Rainbow Falls and Boiling Pots. Hilo is a foodie town, so make plenty of time (and space) to eat at least several meals there (even if you just have one day, really). Excellent options include Hilo Lunch Shop, Ken's House of Pancakes, Puka Puka Kitchen, and Sombat's Fresh Thai Cuisine. Stay in Volcano Village or book a room in Hilo (they're a great deal).

Day 7

The Hamakua Coast is deeply cut by "gulches," and many waterfalls and scenic points abound along the way. As you leave Hilo, turn off the main highway and take the Onomea Scenic Route, stopping at the Hawaii Tropical Botanical Garden or hiking down to Onomea Bay. Soon after, back on the highway, you'll pass the turnoff for 'Akaka Falls, which is really two falls, and a must-see sight for even non-nature lovers (it might convert you). Continue on Highway 19 toward Honoka'a enjoying the top scenic drive on the island, but you might have to hurry to ensure that you get to Waipi'o Valley in time for your afternoon horseback riding or ATV or carriage tour of the valley. If you'd rather do it yourself without the tour enjoy the nearly vertical hike down to the beach. Bring plenty of water and a good spirit. If you make it back up travel

Pololu Valley

20 minutes to the "upcountry" of Waimea for dinner. The hardest part of your day will be deciding at which excellent restaurant to dine. If you still have energy, take yourself (and your loved one) dancing at the open-air Blue Dragon Coastal Cuisine & Musiquarium. It's one of few places on the island where people get dressed up for a night out. Spend the night in Waimea or on the Kohala Coast.

Day 8

You probably need some rest by now so pick any one of the stunning beaches on the Kohala Coast and enjoy the morning basking away in the sun. If you need a little adventure with your beach-going, trek the Ala Kahakai National Historic Trail, parts of which are part of the historical King's Trail linking together several beaches (some hidden since they don't have easy access!). Make a quick trip to the Hamakua Macadamia Nut Company on your way to the artist towns of Hawi and Kapaʻau. Make sure to eat at least a lunch or dinner (or both) in Hawi. This small town is a culinary mecca. Sushi Rock is a real treat. Where Highway 270 ends you'll find yourself at Pololu Valley (the other side of Waipiʻo Valley). Hike down to the beach at the bottom if you have time (the hike down isn't so bad, but the hike up is another story). In the later afternoon, take a self-guided or prearranged guided tour to the top of Mauna Kea for a sunset spectacle and for stargazing after sundown. Spend the night in Waimea or on the Kohala Coast.

Day 9

This will be your last day on the Big Island and your last chance for another dip in the ocean or to pick up gifts before heading to the airport for your trip home.

Best Beaches

This is why you left home and came to the Big Island: the fabulous beaches. Some of these beaches do take a little work to get to (either by a short walk or rough four-wheel-drive road), but to get to sheer beauty, sometimes you have to do a little work.

Kona

MAKALAWENA BEACH (page 40)

It's a bit of walk over a desolate lava field to the Makalawena Beach part of Kekaha Kai State Park, but the payoff is worth it: a nearly uninhabited white silky sand beach, with truly nothing around you but sun and ocean.

MANINI'OWALI BEACH (page 39)

If a sweltering walk isn't your idea of a vacation, no worries—Makalawena has a sister beach, Manini'owali Beach, in the Kua Bay section of Kekaha Kai State Park. Remember, though, when you've got it this good (beautiful white-sand beach, great snorkeling and body boarding, close parking, bathrooms), it can get very crowded.

Kohala

HAPUNA BEACH STATE RECREATION AREA (page 76)

Locals swear that Hapuna Beach is ranked one of the top 20 beaches in the world. A smooth and wide white-sand beach that's welcoming to swimmers, body boarders, and snorkelers, Hapuna draws huge weekend crowds—a good indication of just how nice this beach really is.

KAUNA'OA BEACH (MAUNA KEA BEACH) (page 77)

If you can procure a parking pass from the guard at the gate of the Mauna Kea Beach Hotel—the beach is public but the parking lot is private—you can take pleasure in the same five-star white-sand beach as guests of the five-star hotel.

Ka'u

MANUKA BAY (page 100)

The rough drive on the unmarked road to Manuka Bay will take you almost 45 minutes, but when you finally arrive, you'll think that you've transported yourself to a beach

Punalu'u Black Sand Beach

in Mexico. You've got a small beach shack behind you, crabs strolling around, and blue water all to yourself.

PUNALU'U BLACK SAND BEACH
(page 103)

Easy to access, this black-sand beach is popular with tourists and turtles—you're almost certain to see turtles lolling in the sun here.

Hawai'i Volcanoes National Park
HALAPE (page 132)

Although the park borders the ocean, there isn't very good access to it now, thanks to the lava flow that has essentially covered this area. One exception is Halape, an unspoiled beach with swaying coconut trees on the southern coast of the park. The bad news: The hike there is grueling. The good news: The park limits the number of visitors (you have to get a permit to camp there), guaranteeing that the beach will retain an untouched feel.

Puna
SECRET BLACK SAND BEACH
(page 152)

There are plenty of places to get in the water in Puna. But that's just it—you can only get in the water at these locations because there is little sand to lie on. If basking in the sun on a towel perched on the sand is your delight, then head to this small black-sand beach with hidden tide pools set behind a coastal forest. It's only a few minutes' walk from the road, so this beach likely won't remain a secret for long.

Hilo
RICHARDSON'S BEACH PARK
(page 175)

There are drive-up beaches galore on Kalaniana'ole Avenue, all with something different to offer the beachgoer. This is one of the favorites for its shade, full facilities, and clear blue water perfect for swimming and snorkeling.

Hamakua Coast
WAIPI'O BEACH (page 209)

You have to hike down a nearly vertical road before you arrive at the beach at Waipi'o Valley, but with black sand and a waterfall (far) behind you, you can't really argue with its appeal. And given the effort it takes to get here, you might as well stay the whole day and explore the valley.

Manuka Bay

Hapuna Beach State Recreation Area

Best Cultural and Historical Sites

While the entire island was inhabited by the Hawaiians, most of the readily accessible pre-contact and early postcontact historical remains are found on the Big Island's dry side. The island is also home to unofficial modern archaeological sites—discarded machinery and buildings from the plantation days, mainly located on the Hamakua Coast.

Kona

KEALAKEKUA BAY STATE HISTORICAL PARK AND CAPTAIN COOK MONUMENT (page 41)

Kealakekua Bay was the site of the first significant and sustained contact between Hawaiians and Europeans. While it started off well, the relationship deteriorated, ending in the death of many Hawaiians, Captain James Cook, and several of his crewmembers. Across the bay is a white obelisk memorial to Cook, marking the spot where he fell.

KALOKO-HONOKOHAU NATIONAL HISTORICAL PARK (page 49)

Just north of Kailua, this park contains many relics of an old Hawaiian community and is one of the largest concentrations of such relics in the state. Points of interest include a *heiau*, home sites, petroglyphs, and fishponds.

HISTORICAL KAILUA (page 50)

King Kamehameha lived his last years at Kamakahonu Beach, using Ahu'ena Heiau for governing purposes. Later rulers built Hulihe'e Palace, an escape from the affairs of state in Honolulu. Land was given to the first missionaries to put up Moku'aikaua Church across the street from the palace.

PU'UHONUA O HONAUNAU NATIONAL HISTORICAL PARK (PLACE OF REFUGE) (page 53)

South of Kealakekua Bay is the state's best-known temple of refuge, a safe haven for wrongdoers, *kapu*-breakers, and defeated warriors in ancient times. Outside its walls is a reconstructed royal village site.

Kohala

MAHUKONA BEACH PARK (page 78)

Discover the unofficial underwater museum

Pu'uhonua O Honaunau National Historical Park (Place of Refuge)

of debris left from the plantation and railroad days (it makes for excellent snorkeling). Or peek through the trees at the charming, nearly intact Hawaiian Railroad Company building, which shut down in 1945.

PU'UKOHOLA HEIAU NATIONAL HISTORIC SITE (page 83)

As part of a prophecy regarding his domination of the islands, Kamehameha I was told to build a temple to the war god Ku. Sitting high on the hill overlooking Kawaihae Harbor, this commanding stone structure was the last large *heiau* built before the dissolution of the Hawaiian religious system.

LAPAKAHI STATE HISTORICAL PARK (page 84)

The North Kohala Coast was inhabited by scattered fishing communities. The site of Lapakahi is one of these, and it contains numerous home sites and other stone remains that have been partially restored to better give a sense of the place.

KOHALA HISTORICAL SITES STATE MONUMENT (page 85)

The island's remote northern tip has two remarkable sites drawn together to form this state monument. The Kamehameha 'Akahi 'Aina Hanau marks the spot assumed to be that where Hawaii's most well-known historical figure was born. A short stride away and much, much older is Mo'okini Luakini Heiau, a sacrificial temple, one of the oldest *heiau* on the island.

Hilo and Around

GLASS FROM THE PAST (page 188)

In the town of Honomu, north of Hilo, is this store filled with glass bottles and other found objects from the plantation towns. Each town had its own bottling works and each bottle tells a different story.

Hamakua Coast

HAKALAU BAY (page 219)

This untouched modern-day archaeology site is filled with the plantation-era ruins of Hakalau Mill, destroyed in the tsunami of 1946.

LAUPAHOEHOE TRAIN MUSEUM (page 220)

You can't miss this museum—there is a full-size train car on the side of the road. The museum houses an impressive photo archive of the Big Island in the early 20th century.

Captain Cook Monument   Laupahoehoe Train Museum

Best Outdoor Adventures

The Big Island offers great options for both the novice who wants to try something new and the serious thrillseeker who wants to experience some of the most extreme outdoor adventures in the world.

Kona

KAYAKING AND SNORKELING (page 42)

While you can just head to the water at any number of good snorkel spots along this coast, an organized kayak trip to Kealakekua Bay not only gets you to the best snorkel location on the island but gives you a tour of this largely undeveloped and inaccessible coast. One of the most exhilarating things you can do on the Big Island is night diving/snorkeling with the manta rays in Keauhou Bay.

SPORTFISHING (page 46)

Hop aboard a deep-sea fishing boat at Honokohau Harbor for a day of pursuing the big one. The waters off the Kona Coast are some of the best sportfishing waters in the world.

Kohala

DITCH FLOAT (page 81)

Try "fluming the ditch," where you float a specially designed kayak down several miles of the Kohala Ditch, a former sugar plantation flume, in and out of tunnels and across ravines.

ATV TOURING AND ZIPLINING (page 81)

Take an ATV tour of the rocky coast or go ziplining in the inland forest in the area.

BIKING THE IRONMAN COURSE (page 80)

Rent a bike and follow all or parts of the 112-mile Ironman course, a loop around the Kohala Coast. The ride officially takes place in October, but you can do it anytime of year.

Ka'u

CAVING IN A LAVA TUBE (page 104)

Book the extended cave tour at the Kula Kai Caverns, a thousand-year-old lava tube, and spend some time exploring this labyrinth on your hands and knees.

JUMPING OFF A CLIFF (page 105)

Travel to Ka Lae (South Point) and get your

Kilauea Volcano in Hawai'i Volcanoes National Park

adrenaline really going when you leap off the point 50 feet into the ocean.

Hawai'i Volcanoes National Park and Volcano Village
BACKCOUNTRY HIKING AND CAMPING (page 132)
Get off the beaten path and head to Halape, one of the island's most remote and pristine beaches, located in the national park (this is at least an overnight trip).

BIKING IN THE PARK (page 135)
A biking trip of Hawai'i Volcanoes National Park is not the most extreme biking adventure on the island, but it's a superb way to see the park.

Hilo
HELICOPTER TOUR (page 178)
Hop on a helicopter for a flight over Kilauea Volcano and the current lava flow. While helicopters also fly to the volcano from the Kona side, it's shorter and less expensive from Hilo, and these flights usually include views of some of the wet-side waterfalls.

SURFING (page 176)
If you have any experience surfing (read: this

isn't for novices), grab a board and head to Honoli'i Beach Park to surf with the locals.

Hamakua Coast
EXPLORING WAIPI'O VALLEY (page 215)
Head down into the valley for a horseback or ATV ride that ambles through this wet and steamy vale.

The Saddle Road
STARGAZING ON MAUNA KEA (page 224)
Late in the afternoon, hop on a van that takes you on a sunset and stargazing tour on Mauna Kea. Or travel to the summit on your own and add a hike to Lake Waiau, the country's third highest lake, on your way up. A sunset from the top of the mountain is awe-inspiring. After sunset, telescopes are set up for viewing the heavens.

HIKING ON MAUNA LOA (page 213)
One of the most extreme hikes on the island (if not the most, due to altitude and weather) is the hike to the summit of Mauna Loa. This hike has two access points (the other is in Volcano near the park); however, it's a closer hike if you begin from near the Mauna Loa observatory on the Saddle Road.

Kealakekua Bay   Mauna Loa

Best Finds for Foodies

The Big Island is an underrated foodie paradise, and how could it not be, given the immense amount of tropical produce grown here, fresh fish, and Big Island beef. On top of availability of ingredients, the Big Island has rich and layered food traditions: a conglomeration of foods from Polynesia, foods that arrived to the islands with immigrants working the plantations, and foods that are making a comeback due to the Hawaii Regional Cuisine movement and inundation of farmers markets on the island. Make sure to try these foods, which epitomize the essence of eating in Hawaii:

Kalua Pork

Usually served as shredded pork, this is the best and most popular item made in an *imu,* a pit oven (it's the device used to cook pigs for *lu'au*). *Kalua* pig makes for a great topping for nachos, or try it cooked into a breakfast hash at Hawaiian Style Café (in Waimea, page 234).

Li Hing Mui

Li hing mui is salted dried plum, a specialty flavoring in Hawaii that originates from China. Try it as a cold beverage at the Kona Pacific Farmers Cooperative (in Captain Cook, page 55) or as the rim of your margarita

at the Kilauea Lodge (in Volcano Village, page 140).

Loco Moco

Originating from Hilo in the late 1940s, *loco moco* started as a way to use leftover food and offer a cheap dish to workers. There are variations, but the standard is two scoops of white rice, a hamburger patty, one fried egg, and brown gravy. At Cafe 100 (in Hilo, page 193), you can get a near infinite variety of *loco moco,* changing with the seasons and holidays.

Malasadas

Portuguese doughnuts, but without a hole,

mochi

malasadas are often filled with flavored crèmes such as chocolate, guava, or *liliko'i* (passion fruit). The top contenders: Baker Tom's (in Papa'ikou outside of Hilo, page 198), Tex Drive In (in Honoka'a, page 231), and Punalu'u Bake Shop (in Na'alehu, page 108).

Mochi

A Japanese delicacy made of sweet rice flour, these treats are an art form. *Mochi* is available at the grocery store, but the best place to experience one is at the Two Ladies Kitchen (in Hilo, page 196).

Poke

Cubed raw fish (usually ahi tuna) marinated with sea salt, soy sauce, sesame oil, and seaweed—this is the quintessential pupu (appetizer). There are other variations, such as *poke* made with octopus or raw salmon or with other seasonings, such as spicy wasabi *poke* that can be purchased at KTA (throughout the island). A good place for a novice *poke* eater is Da Poke Shack (in Kailua, page 61), where the staff allows you to make your own variety or try the ones they've already put together.

Shave Ice

Shave ice is a dessert made from the careful shaving of blocks of ice followed by the addition of liquid flavoring, encompassing local flavors such as guava, mango, and *li hing mui*. Locals always have their favorite spots for shave ice. A good starter place is Wilson's by the Bay (in Hilo, page 193).

Spam *Musubi*

This island classic originated from the Japanese tradition of *onigiri*. It's like a big sushi roll, but the inside is Spam. And it's delicious, filling, and cheap ($1–3). You can get it at any convenience store—try 7-Eleven (throughout the island) for Spam *musubi* with egg in the middle, making the perfect breakfast sandwich. Or head to Hilo Lunch Shop (in Hilo, page 196), but go early, as they sell out of everything quickly. Or avoid Spam altogether and try a salmon *musubi* at Island Naturals Market and Deli (locations in Kailua, page 63; Pahoa, page 164; and Hilo, page 198).

kalua pork

shave ice

Best for Honeymooners

For those looking to really go above and beyond to treat a special someone to something extraordinary, here are suggestions for the Big Island's most romantic hotels, restaurants, sights, and sunsets.

Kona

Book a manta ray night dive/snorkel trip (page 43) and hold hands underwater as you (and 30 other people) try to stay afloat in order not to accidentally kick a manta ray (much harder than you'd think).

Stay at the Holualoa Inn (page 248) so that when the night is over you can warm up in your private heart-shaped hot tub secluded in the garden overlooking Kailua-Kona.

Kohala

Take a sunset cruise with champagne toast with Ocean Sports (page 79).

Book a room at The Fairmont Orchid (page 260), the epitome of elegance. Or play house (really upscale house) at Puakea Ranch (page 262) and relax in the antique copper tub or your private pool.

Put something nice on and take your sweetie to the Blue Dragon Coastal Cuisine & Musiquarium (page 89) for dinner and some big band dancing.

Ka'u

Wake up before dawn and drive to the Green Sand Beach (page 101) for sunrise—there is nothing more spectacular than watching the pink hues of sunrise spread across the greenish sand. Stop at Ka Lae (South Point) (page 105) and make the big leap off the cliff together.

Share a slice of macadamia nut pie at Hana Hou (page 108).

And if love for you is about surviving small spaces together, or maybe trying something new and different, spend a night at Lova Lava Land Eco-Resort (page 263) in one of their Volkswagen camper vans. Pop the roof and watch the stars as you drift off to sleep.

snorkeling off the Kona Coast

Lova Lava Land Eco-Resort

Hawai'i Volcanoes National Park and Volcano Village

Stop at the Volcano Winery (page 138) for a free tasting or private tour, and purchase a bottle of wine or mead.

Make a reservation at the Kilauea Lodge (page 140) for a table near the fireplace. If you call ahead, they will put your name on the menu with congratulations or a message (they are printed daily).

Once it's dark, drive into Hawai'i Volcanoes National Park to watch the lava glow from the Thomas A. Jaggar Museum (page 122). Bring a blanket for snuggling and

that bottle of wine you picked up earlier from the winery.

Puna

Learn how to give a real massage by taking the half-day couples massage class with Living Love Hawaii Retreats and Tours (page 155).

Visit nearby Kehena Beach (page 153), where clothing is optional, or the secluded jungle-like warm ponds in Isaac Hale Beach Park (page 152), where you should definitely keep your clothes on (there are kids around, please!).

Green Sand Beach

Mauna Kea

Hamakua Coast

The views of Waipi'o Valley (page 221) are so beyond incredible that it doesn't matter much what you do here with your loved one. For those who have always had a *Bridges of Madison County*–like fantasy, I recommend a horseback riding trip (page 216) of the valley. For those who have some anger issues to work through with said partner, I recommend an off-roading ATV trip (page 215) of the valley.

Book a room at Waipi'o Rim (page 282). Several successful engagements have started on the balcony of this bed-and-breakfast.

Mauna Kea

Pack a picnic, blankets, and lots of warm clothes and drive the Saddle Road to Mauna Kea—sunset on top of the summit (page 224) is mystical.

After sunset, drive back down to the visitors center for some stargazing (page 224). You'll see things you never thought possible, like the rings around Saturn. Pull yourself away from the telescope and head down the hill a little more. Park your car, take out your blanket and picnic, and enjoy feeling like you're the only ones on earth with the huge sky above you.

Waipi'o Valley

KONA

Kona can feel like the hottest place on the island, not just due to the warm temperatures, but because there is always something going on here, from frequent festivals (celebrating everything from coffee to chocolate to beer to fishing) to serious nightlife (which locals will tell you means anything open later than 9 P.M.). It's no wonder that most visitors spend the majority of their time on the Kona side, as it is called. Although Kona is talked about as if it were a city, it is actually a large district (a region) and an important one in Hawaiian history as well as modern-day Hawaii due to economic importance resulting from the coffee and tourism industries. From national historical parks (two of them!) to some of the very best white-sand beaches on the island to nearly every ocean activity possible (snorkeling, kayaking, surfing, and paddling), Kona is a microcosm of what the larger island has to offer.

In March 2011 Kona was affected by a tsunami resulting from a large earthquake in Japan. Damage to some oceanfront areas was significant, with beaches completely changing overnight, and in some cases buildings were destroyed from the force of the wave. The reviews of beaches in this guide were conducted both before and after the tsunami hit, but as rebuilding continues it is possible that some locations will differ in appearance from what is written here.

ORIENTATION
North of the Airport: North Kona

This is what you were imagining when you booked your trip to Hawaii: turquoise waters

© COLLETTE MURPHY/WWW.123RF.COM

KONA

HIGHLIGHTS

LOOK FOR ◖ TO FIND RECOMMENDED SIGHTS, ACTIVITIES, DINING, AND LODGING.

◖ **Kikaua Point Park Beach:** Bring a picnic to this uncrowded beach – the water tends to remain calm here, making it a perfect spot for kids (page 38).

◖ **Maniniʻowali Beach (Kua Bay):** This small white-sand beach in the Kua Bay section of Kekaha Kai State Park offers close parking and clear waters that are excellent for body boarding and snorkeling (page 39).

◖ **Kealakekua Bay State Historical Park and Captain Cook Monument:** Tourists flock here for novice-friendly kayaking and stellar snorkeling. Depending on the season, it's common to see dolphins swimming up next to you (page 41).

◖ **Diving and Snorkeling:** Nearly the entire coast presents ideal snorkeling conditions given how close the reef is to the shoreline. The best spots are Kealakekua Bay and Pawai Bay during the day and Keauhou Bay at night for the manta ray sightings (page 43).

◖ **Puʻuhonua O Honaunau National Historical Park (Place of Refuge):** Get a glimpse of ancient Hawaii at this restored temple of refuge, a safe haven for defeated chiefs and *kapu*-breakers. It's especially magical at sunrise (page 53).

◖ **Annual Kona Brewers Festival:** Over 40 Hawaii and Mainland breweries offer samplings of their craft beers at this March festival, and the island's top chefs serve up unlimited samples of their best dishes to pair with the drinks (page 59).

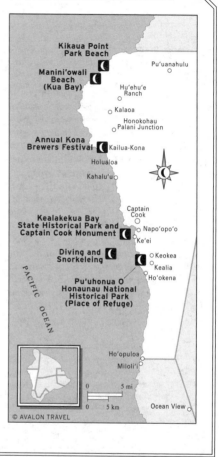

© AVALON TRAVEL

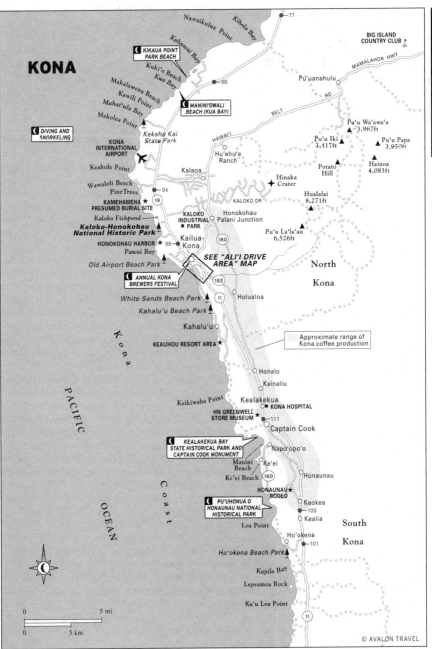

KONA

Nawaikulua Point
Kiholo Bay
77

Kahuwai Bay

BIG ISLAND
COUNTRY CLUB

MAMALAHOA HWY

KIKAUA POINT
PARK BEACH

Kuki'o Beach
Kua Bay

86

Pu'uanahulu

RD

Makalawena Beach

MANINI'OWALI
BEACH (KUA BAY)

BELT

Pu'u Wa'awa'a
3,967ft

Kawili Point

Mahai'ula Bay

HAWAI'I

Pu'u Iki
3,417ft

Pu'u Papa
3,950ft

Makolea Point

Kekaha Kai
State Park

DIVING AND
SNORKELING

Hu'ehu'e
Ranch

Potato
Hill

Hainoa
4,083ft

KONA
INTERNATIONAL
AIRPORT

Kalaoa

Hinaka
Crater

Keahole Point

KALOKO DR.

Hualalai
8,271ft

Wawaloli Beach
PineTrees

94

KALOKO
INDUSTRIAL
PARK

KAMEHAMEHA
PRESUMED BURIAL SITE

19

Honokohau
Palani Junction

Kaloko Fishpond

**Kaloko-Honokohau
National Historic Park**

Pu'u La'la'au
6,526ft

Kailua-
Kona

HONOKOHAU HARBOR

180

98

Pawai Bay

**SEE "ALI'I DRIVE
AREA" MAP**

North

Old Airport Beach Park

**ANNUAL KONA
BREWERS FESTIVAL**

Kona

182

White Sands Beach Park

11

Holualoa

Kahalu'u Beach Park

K
o
n
a

Kahalu'u

KEAUHOU RESORT AREA

Approximate range of
Kona coffee production

PACIFIC

Honalo

Kainaliu

Keikiwaha Point

Kealakekua

KONA HOSPITAL

HN GREENWELL
STORE MUSEUM

111

Captain Cook

C
o
a
s
t

**KEALAKEKUA BAY
STATE HISTORICAL PARK AND
CAPTAIN COOK MONUMENT**

Napo'opo'o

Manini
Beach

Ke'ei

160

Ke'ei Beach

Honaunau

HONAUNAU
RODEO

**PU'UHONUA O
HONAUNAU NATIONAL
HISTORICAL PARK**

Keokea

103

OCEAN

Kealia

South

Loa Point

Ho'okena

101

Kona

Ho'okena Beach Park

Kapilo Bay

Lepeamoa Rock

Ka'u Loa Point

11

0   5 mi

0   5 km

© AVALON TRAVEL

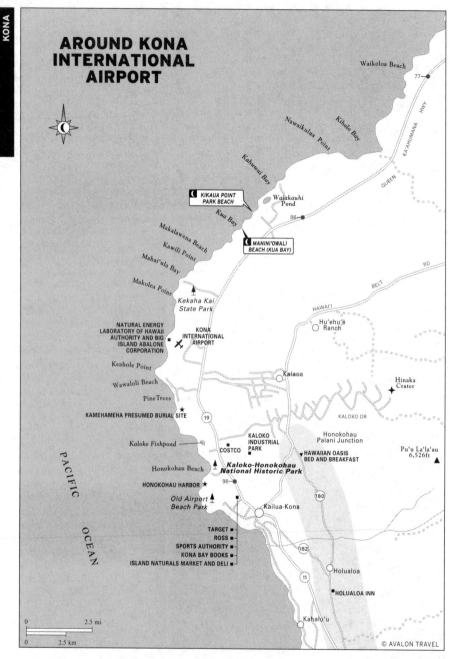

AROUND KONA INTERNATIONAL AIRPORT

Waikoloa Beach

77

QUEEN KA'AHUMANU HWY

Kiholo Bay

Nawaikulua Point

Kahuwai Bay

KIKAUA POINT PARK BEACH

Kua Bay

Waiakauhi Pond

86

Makalawena Beach

MANINI'OWALI BEACH (KUA BAY)

Kawili Point

Mahai'ula Bay

BELT RD

Makolea Point

Kekaha Kai State Park

HAWAI'I

Hu'ehu'e Ranch

NATURAL ENERGY LABORATORY OF HAWAII AUTHORITY AND BIG ISLAND ABALONE CORPORATION

KONA INTERNATIONAL AIRPORT

Keahole Point

Kalaoa

Hinaka Crater

Wawaloli Beach

PineTrees

KAMEHAMEHA PRESUMED BURIAL SITE

KALOKO DR

19

Kaloko Fishpond

KALOKO INDUSTRIAL PARK

Honokohau Palani Junction

Pu'u La'la'au 6,526ft

COSTCO

HAWAIIAN OASIS BED AND BREAKFAST

Honokohau Beach

Kaloko-Honokohau National Historic Park

HONOKOHAU HARBOR

98

Old Airport Beach Park

180

Kailua-Kona

PACIFIC

TARGET
ROSS
SPORTS AUTHORITY
KONA BAY BOOKS
ISLAND NATURALS MARKET AND DELI

182

OCEAN

11

Holualoa

HOLUALOA INN

Kahalu'u

0   2.5 mi

0   2.5 km

© AVALON TRAVEL

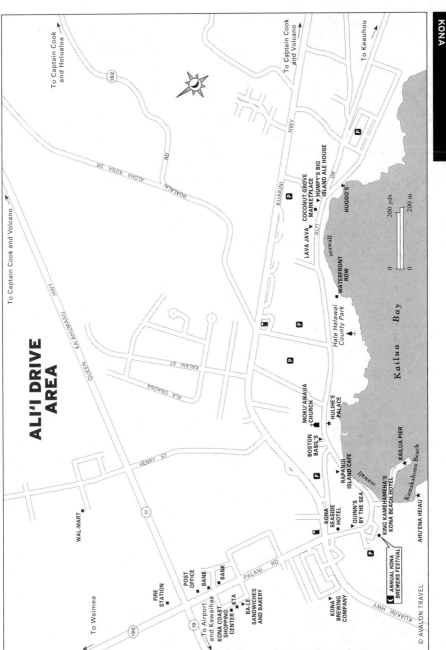

KONA

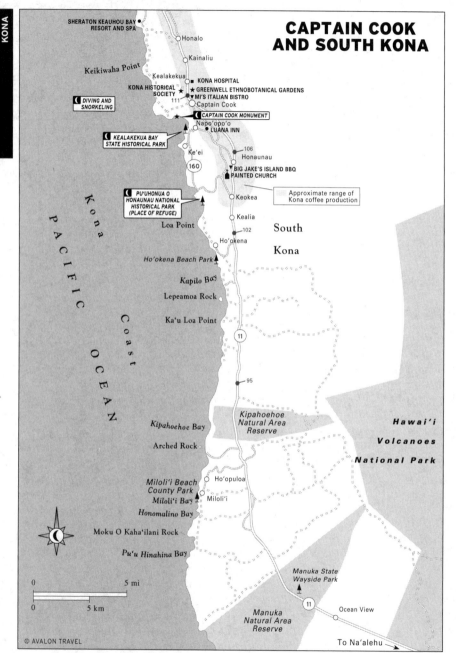

SHERATON KEAUHOU BAY
RESORT AND SPA ●
○ Honalo

Keikiwaha Point
○ Kainaliu
Kealakekua ○
■ KONA HOSPITAL
KONA HISTORICAL   ★ GREENWELL ETHNOBOTANICAL GARDENS
SOCIETY ★   ▼ MI'S ITALIAN BISTRO
111   ○ Captain Cook

◖ DIVING AND
SNORKELING

★ ◖ CAPTAIN COOK MONUMENT
▲ ○ Napo'opo'o
● LUANA INN

◖ KEALAKEKUA BAY
STATE HISTORICAL PARK

Ke'ei ○
● 106
Honaunau
160   ▼ BIG JAKE'S ISLAND BBQ
▲ PAINTED CHURCH

◖ PU'UHONUA O
HONAUNAU NATIONAL
HISTORICAL PARK
(PLACE OF REFUGE)   ▲

○ Keokea

Approximate range of
Kona coffee production

Loa Point
○ Kealia
● 102
○ Ho'okena

South

Kona

Ho'okena Beach Park ▲

**CAPTAIN COOK
AND SOUTH KONA**

Kona

P A C I F I C

Coast

O C E A N

Kapilo Bay
Lepeamoa Rock

Ka'u Loa Point

11

● 95

Hawai'i

Volcanoes

National Park

Kipahoehoe Bay
Kipahoehoe
Natural Area
Reserve

Arched Rock

*Miloli'i Beach
County Park*   ○ Ho'opuloa
Miloli'i Bay ▲ ● Miloli'i
Honomalino Bay

Moku O Kaha'ilani Rock

Pu'u Hinahina Bay

Manuka State
Wayside Park

▲

0   5 mi
0   5 km

Manuka
Natural Area
Reserve

11   ○ Ocean View

To Na'alehu ➤

beside long stretches of white-sand beaches. Amazingly, there are several very good options for these types of beaches within 20 minutes of Kona International Airport—and they are all public places! What might surprise you the most is that parts of this area look like they were hit by a bomb: It is completely desolate. The landscape is made up of lava fields, and in recent years, the black rocks have become dotted with white stones that spell out names of favorite teams and loved ones (and in some cases proposals). Don't be thrown off by the lack of infrastructure in the area. The ocean and beaches lurking behind the lava fields are some of the most magical the island has to offer for those looking for white-sand beaches and astonishing underwater life.

South of the Airport

To be honest, the small area south of the international airport looks a lot like any other place in suburban America (except that you can see the ocean from the road). What is notable here is that it is a significant wayfinding point. Many hotels and bed-and-breakfast establishments use this area—specifically Costco (which can be seen like a beacon of light up above off of Hina Lani Street) and Target (off of Makala Boulevard in the Kona Commons shopping center) to give directions. You'll likely use this area to get from one place to another and for its resource-laden shops (again, Costco and Target), but don't miss out on Pine Trees, one of the best surfing spots on the island and some significant sites such as Natural Energy Laboratory of Hawaii Authority (NELHA), Kaloko-Honokohau National Historical Park, and the small boat harbor all located in this area.

Ali'i Drive: Kailua and Keauhou

The heart of Kona, Ali'i Drive is the north–south thoroughfare stretching from the Keauhou resort area (the south end) through downtown Kailua and ending in the north near where Highway 11 becomes Highway 19 (and the counting of the mile markers starts all over again—actually, it starts backward). Starting at the very south end of Ali'i Drive

A ROAD BY ANY OTHER NAME

Highway 11 and Highway 19 are the main routes in the Kona region. Highway 11 has several names: Kuakini Highway, Hawai'i Belt Road, Queen Ka'ahumanu Highway, Mamalahoa Highway. These names are sometimes used in addresses, but sometimes businesses simply use Highway 11. Highway 19 on some maps and in some addresses is also called Hawai'i Belt Road, Queen Ka'ahumanu Highway, and Mamalahoa Highway (when it runs through Waimea). Remember that in Kailua town Highway 11 and Highway 19 merge, and thus, it is important to note which highway you are on when looking for the mile marker (i.e., there is a mile marker 100 on Highway 11 and another on Highway 19). Using the mile markers is a great way to gauge how far you must travel.

(*ali'i* is Hawaiian for royalty) are a few larger resorts (such as the Sheraton Keauhou Bay Resort and Spa and Outrigger Keauhou Beach Resort). There are really only two big resort areas on the Big Island, and Keauhou is one of them (the other is the Kohala "Gold" Coast). Since Keauhou is designed as a resort area it is constructed so that a visitor never really has to leave its proximity. The beach access here from the hotels and Keauhou Bay is rocky and the water can get rough. Most visitors use their hotel's or condo's pools (which often overlook the ocean) and save a dip in the water for an evening excursion to view the manta rays that hang out in the bay (and near the Sheraton).

As you drive north you'll pass by a slew of vacation rentals and crowded small urban beaches. The downtown area, which is Kailua, is a combination of Bourbon Street (as in New Orleans) and Florida. This is the area where the cruise ships dock (usually on Wednesdays), and you'll see passengers running ashore to shop. At night there is street life on Ali'i, so if you're looking to "go out" (maybe even until after

YOUR BEST DAY IN KONA

- Visit **Pu'uhonua O Honaunau National Historical Park** in the early morning when you'll have the place to yourself.

- Join a guided **kayaking** tour of **Kealakekua Bay**, where you'll be side-by-side with the dolphins and experience some of the best **snorkeling** on the island.

- After a busy morning, relax at the white-sand **Manini'owali Beach/Kua Bay** in Kekaha Kai State Park (or really any number of gorgeous white-sand beaches north of the Kona airport).

- In the late afternoon cool off by heading up the mountain to gallery-filled **Holualoa**, also

home of the fabulous **Holuakoa Gardens and Café**, where a dinner reservation is a must.

- Finish this long day bar-hopping or dancing on **Ali'i Drive.**

RAINY DAY ALTERNATIVE
It doesn't often happen in Kona, but every once in a while you'll catch yourself in less-than-perfect weather. If so, visit the **Natural Energy Laboratory of Hawaii Authority (NELHA)** for an indoor talk on natural energy technology and efforts in Hawaii and a tour and tasting at an abalone farm (you'll like them so much that you will likely buy some to bring back for dinner).

---

midnight!) this is where you go. Especially on the weekends there is music blasting from the bars overhead (most of them are open-air establishments), local kids cruising and parking in their rigged-up trucks, and tourists strolling from shop to shop. There are many stores in the downtown Ali'i section—but it's a lot of the same T-shirt shops, jewelry stores, and tour agents hocking *lu'au* and kayak adventures.

Captain Cook Area: South Kona
Captain Cook is an actual town, named for the explorer James Cook, who in 1778 was the first European to have contact with the Hawaiian Islands. An obelisk of Cook adorns Kealakekua Bay (it's the white structure seen in the distance), where he was killed (yes, it's where he landed and where he was killed), and the rumor is that the very small area surrounding the obelisk is considered British territory. There are several other little towns in the area, like Kainaliu and Kealakekua (all off of Highway 11), but the area generally is referred to as "Captain Cook" or even South Kona.

A visit to the Kona area would not be complete without spending as much time as possible in this area, where kayak trips and snorkeling adventures are plentiful and the beaches are easily accessible (for the most part). If you are water-logged and looking for some drive time head to the main road for a bit of antiquing or to try one of several excellent restaurants in the area.

PLANNING YOUR TIME
There is probably more to do in the Kona district than any other place on the Big Island, but the good news is that even though the district is split into smaller sections (as it is here), nothing is actually that far from anything else. If there is no traffic (and there can be in Kona) you can make it from the airport to the town of Captain Cook in about 40 minutes.

It's best to treat the Kona region like a mini road trip starting either north or south. The **Kealakekua Bay** to the south should not be missed. The water here is perfection for nearly every water activity, and there are abundant tours to choose from to assist you in exploring the grandeur that exists underwater. If you feel like staying dry for a bit, there are several nearby historical sites well worth exploring—including a stop at the **Kona Pacific Farmers Cooperative** for regional culinary delights.

In many cases, the bulk of your day will occur before lunchtime (which won't be a problem if you are jet lagged), as early morning is when you'll venture out on kayaking, snorkeling, dolphin-swimming, and deep-sea fishing tours. The warm afternoons are a perfect time to relax, with little effort, on a nearby beach, such as **Kikaua Point Park Beach** or **Manini'owali Beach** in north Kona. If it's just too hot out, head north up the hill (only a few minutes, really) to **Holualoa**, where the weather is cooler than down below and the street is lined with art galleries. The

late afternoon presents the best time to hike to one of the beaches, like **Makalawena,** that does require some walking—usually over an open lava field.

Kona is one of few places on the island with nightlife. Many first-time visitors arrange to see a *lu'au* at one of the hotels or take a stroll on Ali'i Drive to people-watch. On the weekends or holidays, the open-air Ali'i Drive bars can become quite bustling when the cover bands come out to play.

Beaches

Many of the best Kona beaches require some work to get to them. Keep in mind that it's often the destination, not the journey (you'll want to repeat this over and over while you are extremely hot making your way to the beach on a not very scenic trail). The majority of routes to the beaches can be accomplished in a good pair of sandals, but the walk, which is usually over uneven lava, can be difficult for some. There are equal amounts of beaches that don't require any walking beyond from

the parking lot to the sand, so don't fret if you opt out of the beaches that require more effort to get to them.

NORTH OF THE AIRPORT: NORTH KONA
Kiholo Bay

If you stop at the scenic point near mile marker 82 you get a great panoramic of Kiholo Bay (Hwy. 19 near mile marker 81 and also between mile markers 82 and 83, gate open

Although the beach at Kiholo Bay is surrounded by exclusive homes, it's not off limits to beachgoers.

7 A.M.–7 P.M.), and chances are you'll want to get closer to it to see what looks like completely untouched paradise: a deserted beach with turquoise water and what appears to be an island off the bay (it's not really an island, though). If you start your journey at the south end of the beach, you'll find a cold freshwater lava tube bath called the **Queen's Bath** (Keanalele Waterhole). It is a sacred site, so please be respectful. A sign there asks people to take care to respect the water by not using it for bathing. As you continue on the shoreline you'll see very fancy homes with private property signs (some famous people built these homes, including country singer Loretta Lynn). If you continue walking north on the shoreline, you'll see turtles nesting nearby. Feel free to jump in and take a dip with them. This also is a good place for snorkeling when the water is clear. The beach ends and then you need to walk over the lava rock around the bend to a wonderful little shaded cove (you're still on the lava rock). From here you can swim out to that "island" (it's attached to the landmass on its north side). Be careful of the many turtles you are likely to see in this area as some people have kicked them when swimming out to the island.

To drive to the south end of the bay, look for the stick with the yellow reflector on it on the *makai* side of the road between mile markers 82 and 83. If you're driving north on Highway 19 and you passed the blue scenic point sign, you went too far. The road you turn onto is gravel, but a rental car can make it to the end, where there are portable bathrooms. If you decide to walk all the way from Highway 19 to the beach, the makeshift parking lot is right before mile marker 81. Usually there are other cars parked on the side of the road. The trail, which will take you about 20 sweaty minutes to walk, starts to the left of the parking lot and veers left as you're walking. The benefit in walking and not driving down is that the walk will get you much closer to the bay. If you drive, you end up on the south side of the bay and need to walk around it about 15 minutes.

Kuki'o Beach (Four Seasons Resort Beach)

The wonderful thing about Hawaii is that the entire shoreline is public—so even when the beach is at a five-star hotel, as it is in this case with Kuki'o Beach (Hwy. 19 between mile markers 86 and 87), the public must have access to it. The beach usually offers calm water for swimming and has a pleasant, unshaded, small white-sand area off of a paved path that makes for an excellent oceanfront jogging trail. The path is part of the historical *ala loa* (long path) route that ancestors would use for a nightly procession. Given that the beach actually is maintained by the Four Seasons Resort and since they don't want "the public" sneaking off into the hotel to use facilities, they have provided bathrooms, showers, and drinking water for the public here, and they are nice (I mean, it is the Four Seasons). There is no lifeguard on duty. This bay is a fisheries management area, which means that you can fish here but a board alerts you to how many fish you can catch of each type (there is talk of making it a complete "no take" zone in the future).

To get to Kuki'o Beach, you are required to stop at the Four Seasons Resort gate and alert the guard that you are going to the public access beach. Note: The resort is open to the public, so you can also say you are visiting it and go take a peek if you want. Follow the signs to the "public access" and park in the lot where the road ends.

◖ Kikaua Point Park Beach

Kikaua Point Park Beach (Kuki'o Nui Dr., off Hwy. 19 between mile markers 87 and 88) is perfect in so many ways. Perhaps due to the fact that entry is limited (passes are handed out at the security gate), it's never as crowded as you'd expect it to be. The water is glorious, and even when there are waves other places on the same shoreline, it tends to remain calm here, making it a perfect spot for kids (and there are lots of them here), although there is not a lifeguard on duty. Bring a picnic—locals tend to bring pizza from Costco—and head to the grassy area shaded by the coconut trees (face the ocean so that you don't gawk at the huge houses behind you). Bathroom, shower, and drinking water are available and they are lovely facilities due to the fact that they are maintained privately.

To get to Kikaua Point Park Beach, turn *makai* onto Kuki'o Nui Drive and proceed to the security booth. The guards only hand out 28 passes per day, but the turnover is pretty high, so if you wait around long enough, and people do, you'll likely end up with a pass. Another option is to park at the Kuki'o Beach parking lot near the Four Seasons Resort and walk south to Kikaua—it's only a 10-minute walk. Don't get tricked in the parking lot with the Beach Access sign pointing to the left— this is only the tide pool area. Take the paved path straight back (about a five-minute walk) to the sandy portion. When you're done with the best beach day ever, don't forget to return your access card to the security guard so that someone else can enjoy the beach.

◖ Manini'owali Beach (Kua Bay)

Before about 15 years ago there wasn't a good road (or any road) to get to Manini'owali Beach (Hwy. 19 between mile markers 88 and 89, daily 9 A.M.–7 P.M.) in the Kua Bay section of **Kekaha Kai State Park.** One had to really want to get there by hiking or finding a four-wheel-drive way. And even with all those barriers, people still went—so you know it has to be good. It's a small white-sand beach with turquoise water that is excellent for body boarding (and the kids do it in droves here) and snorkeling. There is not much shade, but if you're aching for sun this is a perfect place to spend the day absorbing some rays. Nowadays, the state has made it easier to get here. A lovely paved road reaches a parking lot (which is always overflowing) and full facilities. It's getting so crowded that now there is a security guard at the entrance to the beach itself (he doesn't seem to do much besides protect the beauty of the place). To get there from Highway 19, look

© MARK WASSER

It's about a 30-minute walk to get here, but Makalawena Beach is worth the effort for its soft white sand and swimmable ocean.

for the Kehaha Kai Park sign and turn *makai* across from West Hawaii Veterans Cemetery.

Makalawena Beach

In the state beach section of **Kekaha Kai State Park,** Makalawena (Hwy. 19 between mile markers 90 and 91, daily 9 A.M.–7:30 P.M.) is a favorite beach of many locals, probably because it's an authentic Big Island experience given that it requires a little bit of hiking to get there. You'll be rewarded by the isolated white-sand beach and turquoise water if you make the 30-minute trek to the beach. Given the walk, Makalawena is often fairly deserted and truly offers that "I am on a beautiful beach alone" experience (that also means alone with no facilities). The beach itself is made up of three crescent-shaped white-sand areas that are backed by trees (there isn't too much shade). Body boarding and snorkeling are possible.

Before you get excited about coming here, you should know that while you can do it in a standard rental car (non-four-wheel drive), it's a slow-going 20-minute drive and then there is a 30-minute walk over a lava field. From Highway 19, look for the Kekaha Kai Park sign and turn *makai*. The initial road starts off paved but then quickly becomes uneven lava (again, high clearance isn't required, but you must go slow).

To get to Makalawena, walk from the parking lot through the first beach, **Mahai'ula,** where the bathrooms are located, and then through the lava field (it's not really worth driving the read just to go to Mahai'ula). When you start coming to sand again, you're very close. You might want to wear good shoes on the walk, as the lava field can be tricky to navigate.

SOUTH OF THE AIRPORT
Pine Trees

Although famous with surfers and the site of many competitions, Pine Trees (Hwy. 19 near mile marker 95, access road gate open daily 7 A.M.–7 P.M.) is not a good swimming beach (and not a good place to see pine trees as there are none here). There are a few one-towel coves along the rocky shoreline where you can gain access to the water, but mostly it's a place from which to observe the action. To get to Pine Trees, turn *makai* where you see the sign for the Natural Energy Laboratory of Hawaii Authority (NELHA). You can also follow the road toward the NELHA facility a short way to **Wawaloli Beach,** a small public beach of sand and crushed coral, fronted by plenty of rock near the south end of the airport runway. There are a few restrooms and some picnic tables.

Old Airport Beach Park and Pawai Bay

We should thank whatever politician decided to take this old abandoned airport (it closed in 1970) and turn it into Old Airport Beach Park (Hwy. 19 between mile markers 99 and 100). Don't you wish they would do that with more airports (both abandoned ones and ones still in use)? There are nicely kept picnic areas that get busy, and the facilities (restroom and showers) are placed between the parking lot and sandy area, which doesn't make for an ideal beach (especially when there are so many spectacular ones around). The runway is now utilized as a jogging area, but if you're looking for some beach jogging head north on the sand toward Pawai Bay (beware of the tide). Since you are near a reef here, the little bay with sand is the best place to get in the water for some excellent snorkeling (as a result it's also a place where dive shops take their tours). Locals will tell you that you can camp here, but I don't recommend it (the police seem to be monitoring the situation more closely these days).

ALI'I DRIVE: KAILUA AND KEAUHOU
Kahalu'u Beach Park

With a large covered picnic pavilion, barbecue pits, a guy sitting around playing ukulele on a bench, and locals drinking from the backs of their trucks in the parking lot, Kahalu'u Beach Park (Ali'i Dr. near the Outrigger Keauhou Beach Resort between mile markers 3.5 and 4, daily 6 A.M.–11 P.M.) has all the makings of a quintessential urban beach park. Although there is a small sandy beach area (and a life-guard on duty), it's not so much a place to lay out (it's sort of loud given the road is directly behind it). But it is a good spot for snorkeling and ideal for kids since the water is shallow and calm. Bathroom and shower facilities are available.

White Sands Beach (La'aloa Beach Park)

Even though White Sands Beach (Ali'i Dr. between mile markers 3.5 and 4, daily 7 A.M.–11 P.M., gate closes at 8 P.M.) is also right off the road, it still retains a peaceful feel to it. Officially known as La'aloa (Very Sacred) Beach Park and nicknamed Disappearing Sands Beach, it is very popular for body boarding, surfing, and sunning (there is little shade here). Grab your towel and head out early because this beach gets very crowded on weekends. Bathroom and shower facilities available, and there is a lifeguard on duty.

Parking can be tricky (the lot is tiny), but locals park on the *makai* side of the road (where it says No Parking) or in a small lot across the street (it doesn't say no parking there).

CAPTAIN COOK AREA: SOUTH KONA
◖ Kealakekua Bay State Historical Park and Captain Cook Monument

Tourists flock to Kealakekua Bay State Historical Park and Captain Cook Monument (Beach Rd. off of Hwy. 160, daylight hours) to kayak, go on kayak tours to the monument, or to simply snorkel. The park is exactly at the intersection where Beach Road intersects with Napo'opo'o Road. There is a parking lot with a boat launch right at the intersection, and a few yards away is the historical park with bathrooms, showers, picnic areas, drinking water, and an ample parking area.

Given the proximity to the reef, the snorkeling here is excellent, and depending on the season, it's common to see dolphins swimming up next to you. The kayaking here is some of the easiest ocean kayaking, so it's suitable for novices.

After some recent controversy, it is now required that you obtain a permit (go to www.hawaiistateparks.org/parks/hawaii and click on Kealakekua Bay State Historical Park) to land at the monument across the bay (there is an actual landing there). You don't need a permit if you're just going to paddle around and not land. The controversy has ensued, however, because there is no regulation of the permits and many of them are taken by the tour operating companies. If you make it across the bay and "permit" yourself to get out, a trail heads uphill from the statue.

Manini Beach

Manini Beach (off of Hwy. 160) is a prime snorkeling and kayaking area with great views of the Captain Cook Monument in the distance, but it was greatly affected by the tsunami in March 2011, which forced two beachfront homes into the ocean. Currently, the beach area is slowly being restored, and locals think it will be an even nicer beach now that it will be less rocky. Instead there will be more sand and a larger open area (the tsunami knocked down a lot of the trees that shaded the area). There are very few places to park here so it may be hard to find a spot, but the good news is that the water never gets too crowded. From Highway 160, also called Pu'uhonua Road, turn *makai* onto Kahauloa Road and then right onto Manini Beach Road—follow it around for 0.2 mile until you see cars parked and a bay.

Ke'ei Bay Beach

A real local place, Ke'ei Bay Beach (off Hwy. 160) has a lovely beach, and it can get surprisingly busy given how you have to be in the know to get here (and have a suitable car to get here). There is white sand and the water is calm for swimming or snorkeling. Since you're staring at prime real estate you'll likely be surprised by the small, somewhat underdeveloped homes (reminiscent in ways of central America) surrounding the area. The land is owned by Kamehameha Schools trust (if you look, you'll see a lot of other beachfront land around the island with signs indicating that it is owned by this trust), and long-term leases are given for less than market value to native Hawaiians.

From Highway 160, also called Pu'uhonua Road, turn onto an unmarked dirt on the *makai* side between Ke'ei transfer station and Keawaiki Road, which it is gated. Four-wheel drives are best for this road to the beach, but you can reach it in a standard car with some careful slow driving. Drive toward the ocean (or you can walk about 15 minutes) until you can't drive anymore. Park in the semi-designated lot in front of the houses.

Ho'okena Beach Park

The road down to Ho'okena Beach Park (Hwy. 11 near mile marker 101) is worth the trip; it has excellent views of the coastline and the surrounding area, and if you are an advanced biker you might want to try this route for a challenge (it's a pretty big hill). There is an actual sandy beach here (not just a rocky coastline), and it makes for a nice place to bring a towel and sit the day away. There is even some shade.

The water here is not too rough, so it's a nice place to swim, snorkel, or kayak (rentals are available at the beach or by calling 808/328-8430, $20 for a single kayak for two hours or $25 for a tandem). If you get there early you might see a spinner dolphin, as this area is one of their habitats. Facilities such as showers, bathrooms, barbecues, and a large covered picnic area are available. Camping is allowed is designated areas, and permits can be obtained starting at 9 A.M. at the beach from the attendant or online (http://hookena.org/camping.html). There is also a separate area to park if you're camping here (to the left of the main parking lot). Note: The area is popular with locals and can get crowded and rowdy at night, so it might not be the best place if you're camping with kids or looking for a very peaceful evening.

From Highway 11 it is a two-mile paved windy road (car-sickness alert) to the entrance. Where the road splits when you are almost at the ocean, fork to the left—don't go straight—where there is usually a sign for kayak rentals, and head on the one-lane road into the parking lot. You will see the sign for Ho'okena on the ocean side of the road.

Water Sports

CANOEING AND KAYAKING

Kealakekua Bay is the perfect place to canoe or kayak given the calm water, the abundance of nearby dolphins, and the lure of boating toward a destination (the Captain Cook Monument); however, there are a lot of politics around this activity. It is now required to obtain a permit (go to www.hawaiistateparks.org/parks/hawaii and click on Kealakekua Bay State Historical Park) to land your boat at the monument (you can just float around it without a permit). Only a few permits are given each day, and it seems that the big tour operators have pre-reserved them, leaving the small operators without permits.

If you drive down to the bay you'll see many locals renting boats out by the hour. As the day goes on it's easy to haggle down the price (usually $20–30 per boat). The large tour operators do not like these "rental agencies," as they aren't insured and do not take care to *malama 'aina* (take care of the environment). But they have cheap boats that are at the bay and don't require any additional transport besides putting them in the water. All the larger companies rent single and double kayaks by the day (prices vary but are all around the same range of $40), which are generally newer, better boats than the ones you'd pick up at the bay, and the companies will assist you in putting the kayak on your car (they will put it on anything—I've seen them on convertibles!).

The larger companies offer essentially the same tour of the bay, which includes four-hour morning or afternoon combination trips of kayaking, snorkeling, looking for dolphins, and paddling to the Captain Cook Monument. The differences between the tours are the quality of the boats and expertise of the tour guides.

Ancient Hawaiians traveled to Puʻuhonua O Honaunau to escape death, while modern-day kayakers visit the area for more benign reasons, such as its calm waters and excellent snorkeling opportunities.

The preferred company for the Kealakekua kayak tour, because of its quality of tours and equipment, is **Kona Boys** (79-7539 Mamalahoa Hwy./Hwy. 11, 808/328-1234, www.konaboys.com, $125 per person). Kona Boys also offers kayak tours to Pawai Bay (near the Old Airport Beach Park with the fantastic snorkeling). In addition, a trip in an old-style canoe leaves from the Kailua dock (1 hour, $50); someone boats you around the bay while giving you the history of the coastline.

Other choices for kayak tours include: **Aloha Kayak Company** (Hwy. 11 between mile markers 113 and 114, 808/322-2868, www. alohakayak.com, $109 adults, $59 children), a capable company with a storefront that should be updated to make it appear more professional.

For a different kind of kayak adventure (and one that might be a little less crowded), try **Ocean Safaris** (on Keauhou Bay, 808/326-4699, www.oceansafariskayaks.com, Mon.– Sat., 3.5-hour morning tour, $64). Unlike the majority of kayaking in the area, this tour starts in Keauhou Bay and journeys to a sea cave in Kuamoo Bay. You'll snorkel on the way in an effort to view dolphins and turtles.

🄲 DIVING AND SNORKELING

Nearly every kayak trip or boating trip includes snorkeling, but if you're simply looking to rent gear on your own, there are several longstanding shops in the area. Nearly the entire coast presents ideal snorkeling conditions given how close the reef is to the shoreline; however, some areas are harder to access due to the rocky coast. Beginners can easily start at Two Step or Puʻuhonua O Honaunau National Historical Park. The best spots are Kealakekua Bay and Pawai Bay during the day and Keauhou Bay at night for the manta ray sightings.

Big Island Divers (74-5467 Kaiwi St., 808/329-6068, www.bigislanddivers.com) offers a similar deal to other providers in the area. A two-tank guided tour ($130 per person or $80 for snorkeling includes lunch) is offered most days (8 A.M.–1:30 P.M.), and most

WATCHING MANTA RAYS FROM SEA OR SHORE

Many say that Kona is the number one place in the world to see manta rays, partly because they have become conditioned over time to feed at night in Keauhou Bay (they come to eat the plankton that is attracted to the light at the Sheraton hotel). Snorkeling companies offer nighttime excursions into the bay so that you can snorkel with the manta rays (try not to kick them!).

Manta rays are completely harmless (the first question always asked about them). Although their wingspan averages 5–8 feet, they have no teeth or stinger – but given their large size, seeing a manta ray close up is completely terrifying and exhilarating and well worth this

unique experience. That said, if you are apt to get seasick, this might not be the best trip for you. Even though the tour boats truly do not travel very far out in the bay (you can easily see the shore from the boat), at night the water can be very rough, and once one person gets sick, it seems like several more people follow.

While you won't be up close and personal with the manta rays, an alternative is simply to watch them from the Sheraton Keauhou Resort and Spa. The aptly named **Manta Ray Bar and Grill** (5:30–11 P.M. with a good happy hour 5:30–6:30 P.M.) has a viewing area and offers complimentary manta talks every day but Sunday at sunset.

---

nights they offer manta ray night dives and snorkeling trips ($100–135 per person diving or $80–90 snorkeling) with several different combinations of options, from one tank to two tanks and depending on the length of trip (some trips are solely for the manta rays and others allow for more nighttime exploration). The best thing about this company is that it offers discounts for the more you dive—so if you think you'll go out at least twice, Big Island Divers is a good deal for you.

Body Glove Cruises (75-5629 Kuakini Hwy., check in at Kailua Pier, 800/551-8911, www.bodyglovehawaii.com) is one of the larger companies with a big boat (the kind of boat with bathrooms and a bar). The 4.5-hour deluxe snorkel and dolphin-viewing tour ($120 adults, $78 children 6–17) is a full-service excursion with breakfast, lunch, snacks, cash bar, snorkel gear, and instruction. However, given the immense amount of time that you're eating and drinking, the water time is only about half the time that you're on the boat. The same goes for the non-deluxe shorter three-hour excursion ($78 adults, $58 children 6–17); only half the time is in the water and the other half is spent snacking and drinking.

Captain Zodiac (Honokohau Harbor, 808/329-3199, www.captainzodiac.com) offers a four-hour snorkel and dolphin-watching

tour, but does it from a Zodiac boat and leaves from the harbor near Kailua, although the tour travels to Kealakekua Bay ($104 per adult, $84 per child with online discount). This is an extremely professional and dedicated company that truly values customer service. Also, Zodiacs are a good option if you don't want to paddle around yourself but still want to be close to the dolphin and snorkeling action.

Fair Wind (78-7130 Kaleiopapa St., Keauhou Bay, 808/322-2788, www.fair-wind.com, snorkel and dive tour $165 plus tax per person, manta ray diving $89 per person, discount if booked online) is your first-class deluxe option for snorkeling and diving tours. Fair Wind offers a five-hour morning snorkel and dive (although you have to pay extra if you want to dive) that includes breakfast and lunch. The boat, the *Hula Kai,* is comfortable (it has two bathrooms!), and staff is undoubtedly there to meet your every need (including holding your hair back if you get seasick). The manta ray night snorkel (they say dive, but I don't that's really an option) 6:30–8:30 P.M. includes all gear and a snack. Other places offer manta ray night tours, but Fair Wind's tour is set apart because of the service (they essentially light up the ocean for you for easy viewing) and the fact that they have a manta ray expert on board who films the entire experience (with a special camera down below) for purchase after the trip.

A longtime favorite of locals, **Jack's Diving Locker** (75-5813 Ali'i Dr., 808/329-7585, www.jacksdivinglocker.com) offers two-tank morning dives (8:30 A.M., $125 per person plus gear rental or $55 for snorkeling; all prices include lunch) and manta ray night trips ($145 per person plus gear rental and $95 per person for snorkeling, not offered Sun. or Tues.). A four-day open-water PADI certification course ($550, minimum two students) is also available.

Kona Honu Divers (74-5583 Luhia St., 808/324-4668, konahonudivers.com) is another outfitter with a good reputation for service and luxury, and this one really specializes in diving (not just snorkeling). They offer a few different types of tours, from a manta ray night dive ($95 for one tank and $130 for two tanks) to manta ray night snorkeling ($80 per person) to two-tank daytime dives for beginners to advanced divers ($130–170 per person). On Wednesday they have a black-water night dive that occurs after the manta ray dive for those who really want to experience the ocean by night ($150 just for the dive or $230 plus tax with the manta ray dive).

Kona Boys (79-7539 Mamalahoa Hwy./ Hwy. 11, 808/328-1234, www.konaboys.com) rents snorkeling gear and offers discounts if you rent for several days (or if you keep coming back over several years).

Sandwich Isle Divers (75-5729 Ali'i Dr., 808/329-9188, www.sandwichisledivers.com, daily 8 A.M.–6 P.M.) is a reputable company that offers a slew of services, from rentals to charters (two tanks, two locations runs $120–165 per person depending on level of instruction and equipment needed). In addition to their daily dives and manta ray night dives, they also offer a four-day open-water PADI certification course ($550).

SURFING AND STAND-UP PADDLE-BOARDING

Surfing is not as significant a sport on the Big Island as on the other islands. Proportionally for the size of the island and in terms of real

numbers, there are fewer good surfing spots on this island, and many of the traditional surfing sites are just not easy to access. Whether this is due to the lack of the underwater environment necessary to create the right kind of waves or for some other reason, conditions seem to be lacking for great surf that the other islands have in abundance. However, a few local sites on the Kona side do draw the faithful. Perhaps the most popular is the break along the reef at **Kahalu'u Bay** in front of the beach park. Two alternative spots are **Banyans** near White Sands Beach (a.k.a. Disappearing Sands Beach) and **Pine Trees,** north of town near the airport. Any of the shops that sell or rent boards can give you current information about surfing conditions and sites, so be sure to ask.

Stand-up paddle-boarding is the newest and hottest sport around. In many cases, the paddle boarders can be found where the surfers are (and vice versa). However, you'll also see paddle boarders out with boogie boarders since smaller waves are much more practical for the stand-up paddle board and essential for novices (and those who have a hard time admitting that stand-up paddle-boarding is really hard!). If you are just beginning, try a lesson or rent a board and test it out on some flat waters (I am telling you, it's harder than it looks). Most places that rent surfboards also rent stand-up paddle boards.

If you need a rental, oftentimes there will be beachfront peddlers hocking boards at hourly rates (you can bargain). Many of the tour outfitters, such as the ones located near the Kailua Pier, rent boards out by the day or week. **Kona Boys** (79-7539 Mamalahoa Hwy./Hwy. 11, 808/328-1234, www.konaboys.com) is one of few providers in Kona that provide stand-up paddle-board instruction ($75 per person for 1.5-hour group class, minimum two people, or $175 for private instruction). They also rent stand-up paddle boards ($25 per hour or $67 per day). If you're looking for surf instruction, contact **Ocean Eco Tours** (Honokohau Harbor off of Hwy. 19, 808/324-7873, www.oceanecotours.com, 8:30 A.M. or 11:30 A.M. check in, group lessons $95, private $150 for 2 hours), which holds the first permit to operate in Kaloko-Honokohau Park boundaries.

DOLPHIN SWIMS AND WHALE-WATCHING

Many of the kayaking and snorkeling trips offer dolphin options (both viewing and swimming with dolphins), since Kealakekua Bay has it all and the majority of boat trips will state that whale viewing is available during the winter season (since the whales can be sighted anywhere). Listed here are outfitters and excursions that are fully dedicated to dolphin and/or whale swims and watches. If you want to swim with the dolphins it's best to join an organized trip so that you have some instruction and assistance with this undertaking.

Dan McSweeney's Whale Watching Learning Adventures (Honokohau Harbor off of Hwy. 19, 888/942-5376, http://ilove-whales.com, Dec.–Mar. only, $90 adults, $80 children). Dan McSweeney loves whales and wants you to love them too. He personally conducts each tour and guarantees that you will see whales. If you're interested in learning about whales (more than just learning about them while there so happens to be an open bar on the boat), this tour is for you (there is no open bar on the boat). Morning and afternoon departures are available and the tour lasts three hours.

One Love One Spirit (808/987-0359, www.oneloveonespirit.com/boat.html, 4-hour tour $185 plus tax per person)—the name gives it away (doesn't it?). Phillipa, the company owner, runs morning tours, mini-retreats, and week-long retreats training visitors how to connect with the dolphins. This company is all about communing with spinner dolphins in the most respectful manner possible—but this is a good thing. Of course there is some touchy-feely stuff that goes along with the swimming, but you can be sure to really "get" dolphins when you're done.

Sunlight on Water (Honokohau Harbor off of Hwy. 19, 808/896-2480, sunlightonwater.com) offers whale-watching tours (afternoons daily during winter, $75 per person), a three-hour tour to swim with spinner dolphins (mornings daily, $110 per person if booked online, includes snorkel gear) and manta ray swims (nightly, $71 per person if booked online). The good deal here is that they will offer you a discount if you book more than one trip with them. They are highly recommended for the dolphin swim since that is their real passion, but other companies might be better for whale-watching and manta ray trips.

SPORTFISHING

The fishing around the Big Island's Kona Coast ranges from excellent to outstanding! It's legendary for marlin fishing, but there are other fish in the sea. The best time of year for big blues is July–September; August is the optimum month. Rough seas can keep boats in for a few days during December and early January, but by February all are generally out. A large fleet of charter boats with skilled captains and tested crews is ready, willing, and competent to take you out. Most of the island's 80 charter boats are berthed at Honokohau Harbor off Hwy. 19, about midway between downtown Kailua and Kona airport. When the big fish are brought in, they're weighed in at the fuel dock, usually around 11:30 A.M. and 3:30 P.M. Honokohau Harbor has far eclipsed Kailua pier, which is now tamed and primarily for swimmers, triathletes, and body boarders.

There is some correlation between the amount you pay for your charter or tour and the experience you have. What you want to check for when booking a tour is if there is a minimum requirement of passengers if you are signing up for a shared boat (if the boat doesn't meet the minimum you'll get canceled). But not all boats even have the shared option and instead require you to charter the entire boat (which can be expensive). Also, for larger companies that have multiple boats and captains, you might want to check what boat/captain you'll be joining and what their success rate is out at sea. If you simply visit the **Honokohau Harbor** (on Kealakehe Pkwy. off Hwy. 19 between mile markers 97 and 98) and walk around the dock, you'll surely find someone eager to get you onto their boat early the next morning. Here are some places to get started for booking your fishing excursion.

Kona Billfish Charter (808/329-2840) has a few different boats, including the *Wild Hooker* boat with Captain Randy Parker. Randy is the son of George Parker, who is well known in Kona as the father of sportfishing. Other boats are: *The Silky* (808/938-0706, silkysportfishing@msn.com), *Hapa Laka* (808/322-2229, www.hapalakafishingcharters.com), and *Sea Wife II* (808/329-1806, seawifecharters.com, shared charter $95 per person for 4 hours). **Bite Me** (808/936-3442, www.bitemesportfishing.com) is a well-known corporate option with many boats and captains, and *The Camelot* (www.camelotsportfishing.com), which touts itself as family run, is an excellent option. They only offer shared boat options if others call for the same day (it rarely happens), but their charters are reasonably priced, their boat is in good shape, and the family that operates the boat is experienced with a good track record.

BOAT TOURS

Boat tours are more popular during the winter season when whale-watching is at its prime; nevertheless, off-season an evening (or day) on the water can still be a fun experience, and don't fret—the dolphins are available year-round.

Kailua Bay Charter (Kailua Harbor in front of Courtyard King Kamehameha's Kona Beach Hotel, 808/324-1749, www.konaglassbottomboat.com, daily 10:30 A.M., 11:30 A.M., and 12:30 P.M., $40 adults, $20 children under 12) offers the unique experience of an hour-long glass bottom boat cruise. It's sort of like snorkeling but on a boat—you get to see wonderful marine life without getting wet. It's a nice way to see coral and tropical fish—and an especially easy way to show young children what lies beneath the ocean—but for the hour-long excursion your money and time might be better used elsewhere, since at times it can be difficult to actually see anything from above the glass.

What is most notable about **Body Glove Cruises** (75-5629 Kuakini Hwy., check in at Kailua Pier, 800/551-8911, www.bodyglovehawaii.com) is that they can accommodate wheelchairs on their boat (this is somewhat rare in the world of boating). Body Glove will also accommodate gluten-free and vegan dietary restrictions with 48 hours notice (also notable). They offer two types of dining cruises with very different vibes. The first tour is the historical dinner cruise ($94 adults, $58 children), which includes a full dinner, one complimentary cocktail, live entertainment, and the highlight—a tour with instruction of historical sites on the coast. The sunset cocktail cruise is the same price as the historical dinner cruise but only serves heavy appetizers (not dinner), although you won't mind since there is a full open bar and live entertainment. Both tours offer whale-watching opportunities during the winter months.

Hiking and Biking

HIKING

If serious hiking is what you're looking for, you'll want to visit other regions of the islands. Instead, the Kona area offers a lot of moderate trails that are almost always the means to getting to some awesome beach.

For instance, you can hike to **Captain Cook Monument** via the inland trail (otherwise you can kayak there). It's not the most exciting hike ever, but the destination is the goal (like swimming in the bay). The trail starts on Napo'opo'o Road just 500 feet below where it drops off Highway 11 (between mile markers 110 and 111). Look for a group of three coconut trees right near a telephone pole. The trailhead will be obvious as it is worn there. It will take you 60–90 minutes to descend and much longer to return to the top. While on the trail, if you see any side paths, just keep to the left always (and keep right on your way up).

If you are looking for something more organized, try **Hawaii Forest and Trails** (74-5035B Queen Ka'ahumanu Hwy./Hwy. 19, 808/331-8505, www.hawaii-forest.com). Generally speaking, although their headquarters is in the heart of Kona, their tours are outside this region (mainly to Kohala and Volcano). It is a wonderful company with an excellent environmental ethic—the tours are highly recommended.

BIKING

Home to the famous Ironman World Championship, Kona takes biking very seriously. On any given day you'll easily see many serious bikers riding along Highway 19, sometimes faster than the cars. Some areas have semi-designated bike lanes (meaning it's usually the shoulder of the road but it says Bike Lane on it). Generally, Highway 19 is an ideal ride as it smooth and flat and you can ride uninterrupted for many miles. Check out PATH (www.pathhawaii.org) to learn more about efforts in Hawaii to develop bike lanes.

Since Kona is a bike town, there are many shops that build custom bikes for elite athletes. If you're just looking for a rental visit **Cycle Station** (73-5619 Kauhola St., 808/327-0087, www.cyclestationhawaii.com or www.konabikerentals.com, Mon.–Fri. 10 A.M.–6 P.M., Sat. 10 A.M.–5 P.M., Sun. 10 A.M.–4 P.M., $20–75 a day). The website has an extensive list of what bikes are available, ranging from hybrid to luxury bikes. Another option with online booking options is **Bike Works** (74-5583 Luhia St., 808/326-2453, http://bikeworkskona.com, Mon.–Sat. 9 A.M.–6 P.M., Sun. 10 A.M.–4 P.M., $40–60).

If a guided or group riding tour is what you're aching for (and you will ache when you're done), **Orchid Isle Bicycling** (808/327-0087, www.cyclekona.com, $125–145 per person) offers four different trips. Some trips are for beginners while others are for more experienced riders (and those who want to fulfill a dream of riding part of the Ironman course)—like the ride up the Kohala Mountain Range. Orchid Isle also offers week-long bicycling tours that include accommodations ($3,000) for those who want to cycle around the entire island.

Golf

Sometimes it seems that half of available land on the Big Island is dedicated to golf courses (that's not a real statistic, it just seems that way). With perfect weather for the sport, the Kona side does a good job creating courses to meet the demand of visitors. The majority of resorts have their own courses (or courses that they partner with to offer discounts). However, some truly public courses do exist and usually offer lower prices than those at the resorts. If the greens fees seem a little much for you, wait until midafternoon when the fees tend to drop substantially.

The **Kona Country Club** (78-7000 Ali'i Dr., 808/322-2595, www.konagolf.com) is a lovely golf course near the end of Ali'i Drive in Keauhou that has 18-hole ocean and mountain courses, with grand views over this eminently rocky coast. Greens fees run $145 for

the mountain course and $165 for the ocean course, with senior and "twilight" discounts available. The pro shop is open daily, and the adjacent Vista Restaurant at the clubhouse serves breakfast and lunch (daily 8 A.M.–3 P.M., lounge open till 6:30 P.M.).

A little farther afield but still close enough to Kailua to make a good play date are Big Island Country Club and Makalei Hawaii Country Club—both are along Mamalahoa Highway heading toward Waimea. The **Big Island Country Club** (Hwy. 190 at mile marker 20, 808/325-5044, www.bigislandcountryclub. net) is a rolling, challenging course with wonderful vistas over the Kohala Coast. Greens fees run $69 for morning play and $55 in the afternoon (*kama'aina* discount available). Carved from ranchland up on the steep

KONA

hillside closer to Kailua is the equally challenging **Makalei Hawaii Country Club** (72-3890 Hawai'i Belt Rd., 808/325-6625, www.

makalei.com), where play costs $85 before 11 A.M., $65 11 A.M.–1 P.M., or $55 after that. A nice *kama'aina* discount is available.

Sights

SOUTH OF THE AIRPORT
Natural Energy Laboratory of Hawaii Authority (NELHA)

Ever wonder what the building with all the solar panels is that you passed when driving south from the airport? It is the Natural Energy Laboratory of Hawaii Authority (NELHA, 73-4460 Queen Ka'ahumanu Hwy. #101/Hwy. 19 near mile marker 95, 808/329-7341, http://nelha.org, Mon.–Thurs. 10–11:30 A.M., $8 adults, $5 for students and seniors). The fascinating 90-minute talk will teach you about current alternative energy efforts and technology in Hawaii. For an additional $10 per person you can join the **Big Island Abalone Corporation** tour (NELHA complex, 808/334-0034, www.bigislandabalone.

com, Mon., Wed., Thurs. at noon), a deep seawater aquaculture company raising abalone (they kind of look like snails) in the NELHA complex. You'll tour their facilities and learn how they are trying to produce abalone in a sustainable way (this includes the abalone eating seaweed from their aqua farm). The tour ends with an abalone tasting and tips for how to cook abalone at home or even in your hotel room sink!

Kaloko-Honokohau National Historical Park

Looking to learn more about the lives of ancient Hawaiians? Well, look no further. Kaloko-Honokohau National Historical Park (Hwy. 19 between mile markers 97

© HAWAII'S BIG ISLAND VISITOR BUREAU (BIVB)

Most tourists only know Kaloko-Honokohau as a national historical park, but don't let the prospect of absorbing some culture deter you from visiting the park's lovely white-sand beach.

and 98, 808/326-9057, www.nps.gov/kaho, 8:30 A.M.–4 P.M.) houses fishponds that highlight the engineering skills of ancient Hawaiians. These fishponds are home to birds migrating for the winter as well as endangered Hawaiian stilts and coots. Take a walk around the fishponds to **Honokohau Beach,** where on any given day you'll see plenty of sea turtles lounging in the sand. If you're lucky you might also see a monk seal. Continue on the beach and visit the *heiau* (temple) that sits on the south end of the beach and then follow the well-marked trail back over the lava field to the visitors center near the restrooms and parking lot.

The park is very serious about locking the gate at 4 P.M. (take it from someone who has been locked in). Another option for accessing the park is through the **Honokohau Harbor** (on Kealakehe Pkwy. off of Hwy. 19 between mile markers 97 and 98), where there is a parking lot and restroom area (and not a gate to lock you in). Although this is a national historical park, quite a few people use it solely as a beach spot. It's a nice enough beach, usually not that crowded and with calm waters, but it is at the small boat harbor and essentially right next to the airport, making the water a bit murky.

ALI'I DRIVE: KAILUA AND KEAUHOU
Historical Kailua

In reality, Kailua proper extends farther than Ali'i Drive, but commonly (or to the business improvement district) Kailua refers to the historical area, which is the north end of Ali'i Drive with the shops. For instance, Ali'i Drive is the location for the Hulihe'e Palace—the last royal palace in the United States of America and where King Kamehameha spent his last days. If historical Kailua is truly what you are seeking, contact the **Kona Historical Society** (808/938-8825, khs@konahistorical. org). Generally, the society's 90-minute tours are given only to groups of 10 or more, but likely you'll be able to get your hands on an extensive pamphlet that outlines the historical relevance of the area.

Also, **Body Glove Cruises** offers historical sunset dinner cruises (808/326-7122 or 800/551-8911, www.bodyglovehawaii.com, Tues., Thurs., Sat., adults $94, youth 6–17 $58, under 6 free) that will take you to some of the coastal historical sights, and part of the proceeds from this two-hour sunset cruise go to support the Kona Historical Society. Price includes dinner, dessert, and complimentary cocktail. You'll cruise around the bay in this "you'll do it all tour" that combines food, entertainment, a historical spiel, and the promise of seeing dolphins and/or whales depending on the season. It's sort of a *lu'au* on the water but a good way to check lots of "must do" activities off your list at once.

AHU'ENA HEIAU

Directly seaward of Courtyard King Kamehameha's Kona Beach Hotel (75-5660 Palani Rd.), at the north end of "downtown" Kailua, is the restored Ahu'ena Heiau. Built on an artificial island in Kamakahonu (Eye of the Turtle) Beach, it's in a very important historical area. Kamehameha I, the great conqueror, came here to spend the last years of his life, settling down to a peaceful existence after many years of war and strife. The king, like all Hawaiians, reaffirmed his love of the *'aina* (land) and tended his own royal taro patch on the slopes of Mount Hualalai. After he died, his bones were prepared according to ancient ritual on a stone platform within the temple, then taken to a secret burial place, which is believed to be just north of town somewhere near Wawahiwa'a Point—but no one knows for sure. It was Kamehameha who initiated the first rebuilding of Ahu'ena Heiau, a temple of peace and prosperity dedicated to Lono, god of fertility.

The tallest structure on the temple grounds is the *'anu'u* (oracle tower), where the chief priest, in deep trance, received messages from the gods. Throughout the grounds are superbly carved *kia akua* (temple image posts) in the distinctive Kona style, considered some of the finest of all Polynesian art forms. The spiritual focus of the *heiau* was humanity's higher nature, and the tallest figure, crowned with an image of the golden plover, was that of Koleamoku, a god of healing. Another interesting structure is a small thatched hut of sugarcane leaves, Hale Nana Mahina, which means "house from which to watch the farmland." Kamehameha would come here to meditate while a guard kept watch from a nearby shelter. The commanding view from the doorway affords a sweeping panorama from the sea to the king's plantations on the slopes of Mount Hualalai. Though the temple grounds, reconstructed under the auspices of the Bishop Museum, are impressive, they are only one-third their original size. The *heiau* itself is closed to visitors, but you can get a good look at it from the shore.

KAILUA PIER

While in the heart of downtown, make sure to visit Kailua Pier, which is directly in front of Ahu'ena Heiau. Tour boats and the occasional fishing boat use this facility, so there is some activity on and off all day. Shuttle boats also use this pier to ferry passengers from cruise ships to town for land excursions. While it varies throughout the year, more of these large ships make Kailua a port of call during the late spring and autumn months than the rest of the year, and interisland cruise ships make regular stops here throughout the week. When periodic canoe races and the swimming portion of the Ironman Triathlon competition are held in the bay, the pier is crowded with plenty of onlookers.

MOKU'AIKAUA CHURCH

Kailua is one of those towns that would love to contemplate its own navel if it could only find it. It doesn't really have a center, but if you had to pick one, it would be the 112-foot steeple of Moku'aikaua Church (75-5713 Ali'i Dr., www.mokuaikaua.org, daily dawn–dusk). This highest structure in town has been a landmark for travelers and seafarers ever since the church was completed in January 1837. Established in 1820, the church claims to be the oldest house of Christian worship in Hawaii. The

site was given by King Liholiho to the first Congregationalist missionaries, who arrived on the brig *Thaddeus* in the spring of that year. Taking the place of two previous grass structures, the construction of this building was undertaken in 1835 by the Hawaiian congregation under the direction of Rev. Asa Thurston. Much thought was given to the orientation of the structure, designed so the prevailing winds blow through the entire length of the church to keep it cool and comfortable. The walls of the church are fashioned from massive, rough-hewn lava stone, mortared with plaster made from crushed and burned coral that was bound with *kukui* nut oil. The huge cornerstones are believed to have been salvaged from a *heiau* built in the 15th century by King Umi that had occupied this spot. The masonry is crude but effective—still sound after more than 170 years.

Inside, the church is extremely soothing, expressing a feeling of strength and simplicity. The pews, railings, pulpit, and trim are all fashioned from koa, a rich brown, lustrous wood that begs to be stroked. Although the church is still used as a house of worship, it also has the air of a museum, housing paintings of historical personages instrumental in Hawaii's Christian past. The crowning touch is an excellent model of the brig *Thaddeus*, painstakingly built by the men of the Pacific Fleet Command in 1934 and presented to the church in 1975.

HULIHE'E PALACE

Go from the spiritual to the temporal by walking across the street from Moku'aikaua Church and entering Hulihe'e Palace (75-5718 Ali'i Dr., 808/329-1877, www.huliheepalace.com, Mon.–Sat. 9 A.M.–4 P.M. and Sun. 10 A.M.–4 P.M., except major holidays. You can look around on your own or ask the staff for a tour, which usually lasts 45 minutes. Admission is $6 adults, $4 seniors, $1 students. This two-story Victorian structure commissioned by Hawaii's second royal governor, John Kuakini, dates from 1838. A favorite summer getaway for all the Hawaiian monarchs who

COOLING OFF IN HOLUALOA

Want to get away from the beach for a few hours? The village of Holualoa (www.holualoahawaii.com), on the mountainside above Kailua-Kona, is quaint, and the views of Kona below are unbelievable. Plan a visit to Holualoa, where the weather is cooler, for an hour or two – or overnight as there are some choice bed-and-breakfasts here – to stroll the upscale galleries (not too upscale) and to have a meal at Holuakoa Gardens and Café. Holualoa is on Highway 180, which breaks off from Highway 11 to the south and connects to Highway 190 to the north.

Holuakoa Gardens and Café (76-5901 Mamalahoa Hwy., 808/322-2233, brunch Tues.-Fri. 10 A.M.-2:30 P.M., Sat.-Sun. 9 A.M.-2:30 P.M., $12-15; dinner Tues.-Sat. 5:30-8:30 P.M., reservations recommended, $18-28; café Mon.-Fri. 6:30 A.M.-3 P.M., Sat.-Sun. 8 A.M.-3 P.M.) is a restaurant where people actually do dress up (but you don't have to). The seating is all outdoors (but covered) in a lovely garden, and the wait staff is attentive. The menu changes daily, the meat and greens are local when available, and the choices aren't the same old dish (like the ubiquitous macadamia-nut-crusted anything seen on most menus in Hawaii). There are vegetarian and gluten-free options (including a very tasty flourless chocolate cake). The wine list is extensive wine list.

If you're in Holualoa during the day, be sure to check out **Holualoa Ukulele Gallery** (Hwy. 180, 808/324-4100, www.konaweb.com/ukegallery/index.html, Tues.-Sat. 11 A.M.-5:30 P.M.). The building was the original town post office, and the current store owner refurbished the exterior with original postal boxes (not from the Holualoa post office, just from the same era). It is truly beautiful and a great photo opportunity. Contact the owner, Sam Rosen, to learn more about his private workshops (from a few days to a week), where you can make your own ukulele!

Also in town is the **Donkey Mill Art Center** (78-6670 Hwy. 180, 808/322-3362, www.donkeymillartcenter.org, Tues.-Sat. 11 A.M.-4 P.M.); check the website to see what one-day or weekend workshops the center is offering. The selections range from painting to woodcarving to silk screening.

followed, especially King Kalakaua, it was used as such until 1914. At first glance, the outside is unimpressive, but the more you look the more you realize how simple and grand it is. The architectural lines are those of an English country manor, and indeed Great Britain was held in high esteem by the Hawaiian royalty. Inside, the palace is bright and airy. Most of the massive furniture is made from koa. Many pieces were constructed by foreigners, including Wilhelm Fisher, a German. The most magnificent pieces include a huge formal dining table, 70 inches in diameter, fashioned from one solid koa log. Upstairs is a tremendous four-poster bed that belonged to Queen Kapi'olani, and two magnificent cabinets built by a Chinese convict serving a life sentence for smuggling opium. King Kalakaua heard of his talents and commissioned him to build the cabinets. They proved to be so wonderfully crafted that after they were completed the king pardoned the craftsman.

Prince Kuhio, who inherited the palace from his uncle, King Kalakaua, was the first Hawaiian delegate to Congress. He decided to auction off all the furniture and artifacts to raise money, supposedly for the benefit of the Hawaiian people. Providentially, the night before the auction each piece was painstakingly numbered by the royal ladies of the palace, and the name of the person bidding for the piece was dutifully recorded. In the years that followed, the **Daughters of Hawai'i,** who now operate the palace as a museum, tracked down the owners and convinced many to return the items for display. Most of the pieces are privately owned, and because each is unique, the owners wish no duplicates to be made. It is for this reason, coupled with the fact that flashbulbs can fade the wood, that a strict *no* *photography* policy is enforced. The palace was opened as a museum in 1928. In 1973, Hulihe'e Palace was added to the National Register of Historic Sites.

Historical artifacts are displayed in a downstairs room. Delicate and priceless heirlooms on display include a tiger-claw necklace that belonged to Kapi'olani. You'll also see a portrait gallery of Hawaiian monarchs. Personal and mundane items are on exhibit as well—there's an old report card showing a 68 in philosophy for King Kalakaua—and lining the stairs is a collection of spears reputedly belonging to the great Kamehameha himself.

CAPTAIN COOK AREA: SOUTH KONA
H.N. Greenwell Store Museum

It's *Little House on the Prairie* meets Hawaii. Constructed in the 1870s to make supplies available to the Euro-American immigrant community, the H.N. Greenwell Store Museum (Hwy. 11 between mile markers 111 and 112, 808/323-3222, www.konahistorical.org, Mon.–Thurs. 10 A.M.–2 P.M., $7 adults, $3 children 5–12) is the oldest surviving store in Kona and one of the oldest buildings in the area. A great experience for kids or history buffs, the volunteer-led tour of the building filled with historical pictures and relics of the area takes about a half hour and occurs on demand (as soon as a few people show up). Foodies will want to visit around 10 A.M. on Thursdays, when you can assist in baking Portuguese bread in the stone oven located behind the building. If you're just passing by on a Thursday, stop and pick up a loaf ($7)—but they go fast and are usually sold out by 2 P.M.

Amy B.H. Greenwell Ethnobotanical Garden

Ethnobotany is the study of how plants are used by different cultures (hey, don't be embarrassed if you didn't know). Amy B.H. Greenwell Ethnobotanical Garden (Hwy. 11 at mile marker 110, 808/323-3318, www.bishopmuseum.org/greenwell, Mon.–Fri.

COFFEE FARM TOURS

The upland Kona district is a splendid area for raising coffee, and Kona coffee has long been accepted as gourmet quality and is sold in the better restaurants throughout Hawaii and in fine coffee shops around the world. It's a dark, full-bodied coffee with a rich aroma.

There are a lot of options for tours of working coffee farms, and many include quick coffee tastings followed by a brief nudge for you to buy their product. One of the better, non-pushy tours is at **Greenwell Farms** (81-6581 Mamalahoa Hwy./Hwy. 11, Kealakekua, between mile markers 111 and 112, 808/323-2275, www.greenwellfarms.com, daily 8:30 A.M.–5 P.M., last tour at 4:30 P.M.). They offer a free 20-minute walking tour through their coffee farm, discussing the roasting and processing of coffee and ending with some coffee sampling.

8:30 A.M.–5 P.M., $5 suggested donation), a 15-acre garden dedicated to the pursuit of ethnobotany, showcases over 275 rare species of native plants grown in Kona before Western contact. The placards labeling the plants throughout the garden offer detailed descriptions of how the plant arrived to the island (many plants although native to Hawaii were brought by Polynesians) and how Hawaiians traditionally used them. One can spend anywhere from 30 minutes to an hour walking around the loop learning this interesting botanical history. One-hour guided tours are offered Monday and Wednesday at 1 P.M. and on the second Saturday of the month at 10 A.M. ($5).

🅒 Pu'uhonua O Honaunau National Historical Park (Place of Refuge)

If you are going to do one historical activity while on the Big Island, do Pu'uhonua O

© MARK WASSER

Pu'uhonua O Honaunau National Historical Park, also known as "Place of Refuge," features original structures as well as replicas.

Honaunau National Historical Park (off Hwy. 11 on Hwy. 160, 808/328-2326, www.nps.gov/puho). The gate is open daily 7 A.M.–7 P.M., while visitors center hours are daily 8:45 A.M.–5:30 P.M. Admission is $5 per car, $3 to walk in, free with a national park pass, or included in the $25 pass for three national parks on the Big Island. To get there from Highway 11, between mile markers 103 and 104 turn onto Highway 160 and travel down the hill a few miles to the entrance on the *makai* side.

This is where you see old Hawaii (not like 1950s Hawaii, but Hawaii circa the 1600s). A park ranger explains that there is a calming feeling here because it is a religious site dedicated to the god Lono, who was a god of life. No killing or wars occurred at Pu'uhonua O Honaunau—it was, as it is sometimes called, a place of refuge or the Camp David for Hawaiian chiefs. During times of war, women and children would seek safety on the grounds, and if defeated chiefs or those accused of sins could make it to the shore (by swimming across the bay), then they would be absolved of their sins and given a second chance. In fact there were 30 such places like Pu'uhonua O Honaunau across the islands (places where redemption could be sought), but this site is the only one that remains. It's sort of a bonus that it's actually at the beach.

Some of the structures in place at the park are original, but many are replicas (the originals are in places like the British Museum in London). Kids tend to be particularly impressed by the imposing structures and sculptures of ancient times. The best time to visit the park is early morning—even before the gate opens (you can park outside the gate). There is a wonderful sense of peace that overtakes the area around and just after sunrise. Tours with the knowledgeable staff are free and offered daily at 10:30 A.M. and 2:30 P.M., and are highly recommended. Otherwise, pamphlets are provided for your self-guided tours, which would take a half hour if you just walked straight through, or you can do a self-guided audio cell phone tour by calling 808/217-9279.

Snorkeling is not possible in the area directly

SCENIC DRIVE FROM PU'UHONUA O HONAUNAU TO KEALAKEKUA BAY AND AROUND

This scenic drive is definitely a full, fun-packed day. Begin at the junction of Highway 11 and Highway 160 by turning onto Ke Ala O Keawe Road (Hwy. 160) toward Honaunau. Your first stop will be at **Pu'uhonua O Honaunau National Historical Park** as early as you can manage to get up (hopefully before the crowds get there). Either snorkel at **Two Step** or leave the park and turn left back onto Highway 160 and travel about 10 minutes (enjoying the ocean views) to **Manini Beach** for snorkeling.

Your next stop should be **Kealakekua Bay** for kayaking to the **Cook Monument.** Afterward, backtrack to the intersection (right before the Dead End sign) and head left (or *mauka*) on Highway 160, which is also called Napo'opo'o Road. Travel up the hill until you see the **Kona Pacific Farmers Cooperative** (82-5810 Napo'opo'o Rd., 808/328-8985, www.kpfc.com, daily 9 A.M.-4 P.M.). Stop in for a treat and a self-guided coffee tour and tour of their fruit orchard.

When you leave, continue up the hill (north) and make a right turn at the next right onto Middle Ke'ei Road (it's where the road forks). From Middle Ke'ei Road make the next right onto Painted Church Road. Look for **Paleaku Gardens Peace Sanctuary** (83-5401 Painted Church Rd., 808/328-8084, www.paleaku.com, Tues.-Sat. 9 A.M.-4 P.M., self guided tours $5 adults, $3 children 6-12). One of the innkeepers described these gardens as a "mishmash of shrines dedicated to different traditions." It's actually seven acres of manicured gardens with the highlight being the Galaxy Garden, the world's first walk-through model of the Milky Way formed by flowering plants. It truly is peaceful there, with a grand view of Kealakekua Bay – an ideal place to sit and eat lunch or meditate or practice yoga (which is offered Tues. and Fri. 9:30-11 A.M. for $12).

Farther along Painted Church Road you'll ar-

rive at the (wait for it) **Painted Church** (84-5140 Painted Church Rd., *mauka* side, 808/328-2227, www.thepaintedchurch.org, daylight hours). The church, erected in 1899 by Father John Velghe, offers beautiful detailed paintings of scenes from the Bible painted onto wood (there are some bits of Hawaiian words intermixed). It's not a must-see, but if you go you will spend a few minutes investigating the photos and the small church (with its musty smell). From the Painted Church you are less than a mile from Highway 160 where you started; when you get to the intersection of Painted Church and Highway 160, turn left to get back to Highway 11.

in the middle of the park (it's roped off), but you can swim, snorkel, and fish anywhere else. Head to the picnic areas (the road is to the left of the visitors center)—where there are barbecues, shaded picnic tables, and portable bathroom facilities—to explore the tide pools situated between lava rocks (most visitors don't know that this area is even here!).

The majority of tourists head straight to **Two Step** (turn *makai* off of Hwy. 160 where you see the Pu'uhonua O Honaunau park sign, and instead of driving straight into the gate turn right onto the road directly before the gate), called such because of the lava shelf that requires you to take two steps down into the water. It's an incredibly popular (read: crowded) area because it does have great snorkeling (everything is just right there—you don't have to swim very far), and it's shallow so it's popular with non-experts and kids. There are no facilities, so it is recommended that you park in Pu'uhonua O Honaunau's lot, where there are bathrooms (and proper parking spots), and walk to the two minutes to the right back to Two Step.

Shopping

SOUTH OF THE AIRPORT
Kona Commons (Target) and Costco

The old industrial area has grown into a strip shopping mall called Kona Commons with a huge **Target** (74-5455 Makala Blvd., 808/334-4020, Mon.–Sat. 8 A.M.–10 P.M., Sun. 8 A.M.–9 P.M.), **Ross Dress for Less** (74-5454 Makala Blvd., 808/327-2160, Mon.–Thurs. 9 A.M.–9:30 P.M., Fri.–Sat. 9 A.M.–10 P.M., Sun. 10 A.M.–9:30 P.M.), and **Sports Authority** (74-5444 Makala Blvd., 808/327-6070, Mon.–Sat. 9 A.M.–9:30 P.M., Sun. 9 A.M.–9 P.M.)—one of few resources if you're in need of supplies for camping (like small propane tanks).

In the actual old industrial area behind Target, you'll find a wonderful "near used" book, CD, and DVD store, **Kona Bay Books** (74-5487 Kaiwi St., 808/326-7790, www.konabaybooks.com, daily 10 A.M.–6 P.M.), which has nearly everything possible (it also has air-conditioning). This is one of very few bookstores available on the island since the closing of all the Borders stores. In the same complex you'll find a branch of **Island Naturals Market and Deli** (74-5487 Kaiwi St., 808/326-1122, www.islandnaturals.com, Mon.–Sat. 7:30 A.M.–8 P.M., Sun. 9 A.M.–7 P.M.).

Costco (73-5600 Maiau St., 808/331-4800, Mon.–Fri. 10 A.M.–8:30 P.M., Sat. 9:30 A.M.–6 P.M., Sun. 10 A.M.–6 P.M.) is truly a wayfinding point in Kona (many bed-and-breakfast locations will give their directions using Costco as a mark to where to turn). What is most notable here is the gas (gas hours Mon.–Fri. 6 A.M.–9:30 P.M., Sat. 6 A.M.–8 P.M., Sun. 6 A.M.–7 P.M.). If you're a member of Costco you are able to access their gas, which is significantly cheaper than anywhere else (sometimes by 30 cents a gallon).

ALI'I DRIVE: KAILUA AND KEAUHOU
Ali'i Drive

The shops that line Ali'i Drive are tchotchke central. There are many gift shops—the kinds with the "My grandmother went to Hawaii and all I got was . . ." T-shirts and assorted items like snorkel equipment and sunscreen needed for a day at the beach. There are also local non-chain jewelry stores selling the island specialty of black pearls. The quality of goods at these shops tends to be low, so buyer beware.

.Keauhou

If you need to escape the heat during the day, there is the **Keauhou Shopping Center** (78-6831 Ali'i Dr.). The shopping itself is not really worthwhile (actually, there is very little shopping to speak of here), but there is **Regal Theaters Keauhou 7** (808/324-0172), one of only three multiplexes on the island; a good independent bookstore, **Kona Stories** (808/324-0350, www.konastories.com, Mon.–Sat.

10 A.M.–6 P.M., Sun. 11 A.M.–4 P.M.), which has a significant stock of new books (and some are very discounted); a **Longs Drugs,** which is actually owned by CVS (808/322-5122, Mon.–Sat. 8 A.M.–9 P.M., Sun. 8 A.M.–6 P.M.); and **KTA** (808/322-2311, daily 7 A.M.–10 P.M.).

Restaurants seem to go in and out here, a new and notable one (actually, it is old but trying to make a return) is **Bianelli's Gourmet Pizza and Pasta** (808/322-0377, http://bianellis.com, Mon.–Sat. 11 A.M.–9 P.M., happy hour 4–6 P.M., $15 for large pizza). With beer on draft, sandwiches, salads, a signature pink sauce (a white wine mushroom sauce mixed with marinara pasta sauce), and gluten-free as well as vegan pizza options, this place is a real winner (unless you're used to local New York and Chicago pizza places). If you happen to be in the area and hungry weekdays 4:30–6:30 P.M., try **Kenichi Pacific** (808/322-6400, www.kenichihawaii.com) for an excellent happy hour of half-price sushi and drink specials. At other times this restaurant isn't worth the stop. On Saturdays stop by the **Keauhou Farmers Market** (8 A.M.–noon) near the movie theater and Longs Drugs.

CAPTAIN COOK AREA: SOUTH KONA
Kainaliu
It's only about a city block long, but Kainaliu (Mamalahoa Hwy./Hwy. 11 between mile markers 113 and 114) makes for a pleasant stroll given there are so few walkable towns on the island where you can stroll from store to store. There are also several good restaurants if you get hungry while you're shopping.

Yoganics (79-7401 Mamalahoa Hwy. Ste. C, 808/322-0714, www.yoganicshawaii.com, Mon.–Sat. 10 A.M.–5 P.M.) is an eco boutique to go to if you forgot your organic or hemp yoga pants at home. Aside from the somewhat pricey exercise and yoga wear there is jewelry and nice smelling locally made bath products. Check the website or call for the schedule of yoga classes, which are offered in-store nearly every day.

Next door to Yoganics is **Kiernan Music** (808/322-4939, www.kiernanmusic.com, Tues.–Sat. 11 A.M.–6 P.M.), the best place to buy that ukulele you promise you'll learn to play (they also have guitars). The instruments are beautifully crafted, some are vintage, and they also do custom made. If you don't have enough room to put one in your suitcase, no worries, they'll ship your uke home for you for a reasonable price.

Antique Row
In Kealakekua (South Kona) between mile markers 111 and 112 you'll come upon a slew of antiques shops that are definitely worth a browsing. They tend to be a mix of Hawaiiana (like old airline advertisements for Hawaii), old bottles, and beautiful furniture made of koa wood. All the shops essentially are within walking distance from one another so park your car and take a stroll.

Entertainment and Events

ENTERTAINMENT
Lu'au
There are two main *lu'au* in the Kona area: at **Courtyard King Kamehameha's Kona Beach Hotel** (in Kailua-Kona) and at the **Sheraton Keauhou Bay Resort and Spa** (in Keauhou). They are both produced by the same company (they are huge productions), Island Breeze (http://ibphawaii.com/luaus/), and tickets can be purchased through the website. You'll likely pick which *lu'au* to attend purely on what day of the week you want to go because they aren't offered every day of the week at each hotel.

Live Music and Theater
Live music often tends to pop up on weekend nights at numerous bars and restaurants on Ali'i Drive. You don't have to go too far to find it (or hear it). The majority of hotels also

KONA

IS IT WORTH GOING TO A *LU'AU*?

Answer: How much do you like watching musicals or theater? A *lu'au* might not be what you think it is. Gone are the days of roasting a pig as onlookers watch in awe. For the most part, attending a *lu'au* is like going to dinner theater. It's a good opportunity to try a lot of local foods at once, but nearly all the buffets are only mediocre tasting (that's what tends to happen when you cook in bulk). If the food is what you're most interested in, it would be better to go to a restaurant (like Jackie Rey's in Kona) instead of spending $100 (the average price for most *lu'au*), although drinkers may get their money's worth – nearly all the *lu'au* offer an open bar.

If you really enjoy a good Broadway show, then you might enjoy a *lu'au*, and kids seem to love them. The productions vary, but **Island Breeze** (http://ibphawaii.com/luaus), the company that puts on *lu'au* at the Courtyard King Kamehameha's Kona Beach Hotel (in Kailua-Kona), the Sheraton Keauhou Bay Resort and Spa (in Keauhou), and The Fairmont Orchid (in Kohala) tends to offer the best show. For a traditional *lu'au* with lots of hula try the King Kamehameha version. For a more Cirque de Soleil experience (with more modern dance and less hula) head to The Fairmont Orchid, which does offer a more pricey experience – but the food is better here than at other *lu'au*. Lastly, all *lu'au* offer preferred seating options, meaning that you pay about $20 per person extra to sit closer but you are still eating the same food as everyone else (although you get to visit the buffet line first). Unless you have some extra money to spend, preferred seating isn't really worth the splurge in this author's opinion.

offer live music in their cocktail lounges—but nothing too notable.

If you're looking for something a little different from the standard cover band (mostly what you'll hear at the bars), stop by **Boston Basil's** (75-5707 Ali'i Dr., Kailua, 808/326-7836, www.bostonbasils.com, daily 11 A.M.–9:30 P.M.), where the upstairs (not the downstairs pizzeria, which gets mixed reviews) books fairly good bands from jazz to bluegrass.

The town of Kainaliu is home to the **Aloha Theatre** (79-7384 Mamalahoa Hwy., Kainaliu, 808/322-2323, www.apachawaii.org), constructed beginning in 1929 by a Japanese family who owned a few other theaters on the island. It is currently one of few old theaters on the island that are still functioning not as movie theaters but as community theaters and concert venues. The building itself is lovely (and worth checking out for architecture buffs), and shows here tend to be inexpensive. So if you're looking for a night out on the town check out their schedule, which includes anything from *Mary Poppins* to reggae bands.

Movies
If you think you'll ache to see a movie while on the Big Island, this is one of your few chances. The island boasts only a few multiplexes, and the Kona area wins out with two of them! (I guess maybe you don't need movies when you live next to gorgeous beaches.) Note: If you're searching for movie showtimes, the Kona zip code is 96740.

In Kailua, see movies at the 12-screen multiplex **Makalapua Stadium Cinemas** (74-5469 Kamakaeha, Kailua, 808/327-0444).

The **Regal Theaters Keauhou 7** (78-6831 Ali'i Dr., Keauhou, 808/324-0172) at the Keauhou Shopping Center also shows first-run movies.

EVENTS
It seems like nearly every week there is some new "annual festival" planned on the Big Island. These listings are for festivals that have been around year after year. To check for new listings (and surely there are some), go to www.konaweb.com/calendar, a comprehensive website with Big Island events listed by month.

Annual Hawaii Avocado Festival

If you love your guacamole, you'll love the Annual Hawaii Avocado Festival (at the Amy B.H. Greenwell Ethnobotanical Gardens, Hwy. 11 at mile marker 110, Kealakekua, 808/323-3318, www.bishopmuseum.org/greenwell). Held in February, this free one-day event includes: tastings of the numerous varieties of avocados grown on the Big Island, a recipe contest, live music, as well as arts and crafts booths. In addition to the festival, there is an avocado-inspired dinner at the Outrigger Keauhou Beach Resort.

◖ Annual Kona Brewers Festival

People come from the Mainland specifically to sample craft beers at the Annual Kona Brewers Festival (Courtyard King Kamehameha's Kona Beach Hotel, Kailua, www.konabrewersfestival.com, $55) in March, and thus tickets sell out very fast (you'll want to get them the week they are released). There are a few days of pre-events (golf outings, a three-course beer-themed dinner), but the main event takes place on the Saturday of the festival, when the beer sampling begins (there are over 40 breweries from both the Mainland and Hawaii), and if you thought it couldn't get any better, the top chefs on the island serve up unlimited samples of their best dishes to pair with the drinks. The biggest challenge becomes having enough room to eat and drink all afternoon. Luckily, there is live music ongoing through the afternoon to let you work off some of the food and get hungry and thirsty enough to go back for more.

Kona Music Festival

Previously known as the Kona Jazz festival, the re-envisioned Kona Music Festival (Outrigger Keauhou Beach Resort, Keauhou, www.konamusicfestival.com, $50) is a day-long event held in April highlighting local musicians of various genres. With an open bar and views of the ocean from the event space this festival offers a good way to get to know Big Island music.

Hawaiian International Billfish Tournament

For over 50 years, teams from around the world have come to Kona to fish for Pacific blue marlin. Even if you don't fish (or care for fishing), you'll still want to head down to Kailua Pier to watch the weigh-ins that take place during the weekend Hawaiian International Billfish Tournament (HIBT, Kailua Pier, www.hibt-fishing.com), also known as "grandfather of all big game fishing tournaments," held in July or August.

Annual Don the Beachcomber Mai Tai Festival

I probably had you at mai tai, but still, the one-day Annual Don the Beachcomber Mai Tai Festival (Royal Kona Resort, Kailua, 808/214-8133, www.donsmaitaifest.com) in August brings bartenders from around the country to compete for mixing the best mai tai. The competition is judged by celebrities. As if that weren't enough, there is also a competition between local chefs for the title of the world's best barbecue (although shouldn't it be Hawaii's best barbecue?). On top of this there is a DJ poolside during the competition (yes, some sampling occurs), and the night tops off with some bigger name Mainland band (in 2011 it was the Spin Doctors).

Queen Liliʻuokalani Canoe Race

Paddlers from all over the world converge over Labor Day weekend to participate in the Queen Liliʻuokalani Canoe Race (Kailua, www.queenliliorace.com)—the world's largest long-distance canoe race. Even if you're not participating, it's fascinating to watch the teams paddle back and forth along the bay during the two days of races. In addition to the racing events there is also a craft fair and a torchlight parade on Aliʻi Drive, and a dance on Saturday night. Beware: After the dance, the bars on Aliʻi Drive are alive with post-race paddlers.

Ironman Triathlon World Championship

With over 1,500 of the world's top triathletes coming to compete to earn the top title, the Ironman Triathlon World Championship

(Kona, www.ironmanworldchampionship. com) is a big deal in Kona. Even though it only takes place one weekend in October (usually the second weekend of the month), you can see visages of it throughout the year. The roads throughout the region are generally closed off during the race (traffic is terrible!), but if you want to be part of the action without participating in the 2.4-mile ocean swim, 112-mile bike course, and 26.2-mile run, contact the Ironman committee, which seems to always be desperately seeking volunteers for the event.

Kona Coffee Cultural Festival

Over 40 years old, November's Kona Coffee Cultural Festival (Kona-wide, www.konacoffeefest.com) promotes Kona's centuries-old coffee heritage. With 10 days of events ranging from coffee samplings (and competitions) to art exhibitions to hands-on courses, there truly is something for everyone during this festival. Some events charge a fee, but many are free, so check the festival's listings and you are sure to find something that suits your taste.

Holualoa Village Coffee Tasting and Art Stroll

Although in conjunction with the larger Kona Coffee Cultural Festival, the Holualoa Village Coffee Tasting and Art Stroll (Holualoa, www.holualoahawaii.com) tends to stand on its own. If you haven't visited the lovely town of Holualoa, this November festival presents an excellent opportunity to stroll its street lined with art galleries, test out coffee from local farms, and witness the children's art contest—all while listening to live music. It's a great event for the entire family.

Food

ALI'I DRIVE: KAILUA AND KEAUHOU

While there are many restaurants on Ali'i Drive, most of them cater to tourists and lack quality service. So beware; even a crowded restaurant (a usual sign that a restaurant is good) is no indication on Ali'i Drive!

◖ Rapanui Island Café (75-5695 Ali'i Dr., Kailua, 808/329-0511, lunch Tues.–Fri. 11 A.M.–2 P.M. and dinner Mon.–Sat. 5–9 P.M., $12–20) offers cuisine from New Zealand and with it a lesson on what is cuisine of New Zealand. The restaurant's location is a bit odd—across from a hair salon in a strip of shops—but one can still hear the ocean breeze just across the street. Most dishes involve meat and/or fish skewers served over house-made coconut rice and well-flavored sauces. The lunch specials are a real bargain, and locals run to order the lamb burger (it has a hint of mint in it) when it is available. Overall, the portions are generous, but save room for dessert: peanut butter rolled in chocolate and coconut with a hint of wasabi inside. You'll want to order one (maybe two) per person.

With a great oceanfront view (the majority

WHERE TO PARK ON ALI'I DRIVE

Parking is no fun on Ali'i Drive. But luckily, it's probably the only place on Hawai'i where you can't find parking. There are very few spaces on the actual street itself, only a handful of free public lots, and then you have the option to pay for parking. If you are spending a night on the town, try the Coconut Grove parking lot (people sometimes refer to it as the one with Outback Steakhouse); usually parking is plentiful there and you can avoid the nighttime traffic of Ali'i Drive (it moves *slowly*) since you get to this parking lot via Kuakini Highway, which parallels Ali'i Drive.

of seating is outside), **Lava Java** (75-5799 Ali'i Dr. next to the Coconut Grove shopping area, Kailua, 808/327-2161, www.islandlavajava. com, daily breakfast 6:30–9:30 A.M., lunch 9:30 A.M.–5 P.M., dinner 5–9 P.M., coffee anytime, $12–20) keeps busy. In fact, sometimes it's even hard to get a table at 7 A.M. for breakfast. The service can be slow at times (perhaps because they are crowded), but the food is consistently good and the portions are large. If you're in a rush for breakfast you can grab a pastry (from inside) to go. The non-breakfast cuisine is mostly pizzas, salads, and burgers, but vegetarian options are available and the sandwiches are highly recommended.

The original restaurant is in Anchorage, and this **Humpy's Big Island Ale House** (75-5815 Ali'i Dr., Kailua, 808/324-2337, www.humpys.com/kona, bar daily 8 A.M.–2 A.M.), kitchen daily 8 A.M.–midnight, happy hour daily 3–6 P.M.), $12–28) is their second location. Humpy's is where to go to watch sports, to drink, and to eat breakfast (you have to remember that a lot of Mainland games are actually on during breakfast time in Hawaii). At night, this place gets packed upstairs, where sometimes there is a live band. Downstairs is a bit calmer and cooler, and you can enjoy drinks on the patio facing the ocean. Lunch and dinner are good enough—they have the usual bar food (pizza, burgers, and a few "healthy options"). Try the *lu'au* feast ($28) with all the kinds of foods you'd find at a *lu'au* (but for half the price). The real winner here is breakfast. The blackened halibut Benedict ($14) is fantastic. For the smaller appetite, I recommend ordering a side of it ($6 for essentially a half portion), which also comes with potatoes.

Right on the oceanfront, **Huggo's** (75-5828 Kahakai Rd., entrance on Ali'i Dr., Kailua, 808/329-1493, www.huggos.com, dinner Sun.–Thurs. 5:30–9 P.M.), Fri.–Sat. 5:30–10 P.M., brunch Sun. 10 A.M.–1 P.M., $22–37) is a great spot if you're looking for a romantic dinner (try getting there for the sunset). The food isn't trendy—there aren't many complex flavors. Instead, it's simple dishes plated to look elegant. But perhaps sticking with what they know has allowed Huggo's to survive in the same location for the last 40 years (while other restaurants on the strip come and go). The fish, especially the fresh catch of the day ($36) cooked in different ways, is recommended given the restaurant's close relationship with

local fishers (you know the fish is really the "fresh catch"). Here is also a good opportunity to try a local delicacy, *ulu* (breadfruit) in a familiar way—they make them into french fries. Note: Huggo's has parking in a small lot right in front of the restaurant.

With at least a dozen variations of fish, seasonings, sauces, and the make-your-own option, **Da Poke Shack** (76-6246 Ali'i Dr., Kailua, 808/333-7380, daily 10 A.M.–6 P.M.) is a *poke* dream come true. If you're not sure what to get (or a little nervous about eating *poke* in general) the friendly staff will let you sample as many kinds as you need to convince you that *poke* is for you. There isn't really anywhere to sit here, but it's not that kind of place. Grab a to-go container and bring it with you to the beach (but do eat it quickly; I mean, it's raw fish).

Near Ali'i Drive

The portions are huge and inexpensive, and for a restaurant close to Ali'i Drive, that alone makes **Quinn's Almost By The Sea** (75-5655A Palani Rd., Kailua, 808/329-3822, daily 11 A.M.–11 P.M., $11–24) notable. Whereas many other restaurants in the area cater to tourists, Quinn's keeps it local and casual. As the restaurant's name indicates, there aren't any views here, just an outdoor covered area bordering a parking lot and an inside bar scene (and with it a full bar including several beers on tap and reasonably priced cocktails). The fish and chips are fresh and one of the more popular dishes—but also try the short ribs (again, it's a huge portion). A few vegetarian options also are available.

A craft beer lover's fantasy, **Kona Brewing Company** (75-5629 Kuakini Hwy., 808/334-2739, http://konabrewingco.com, Sun.–Thurs. 11 A.M.–10 P.M., Fri.–Sat. 11 A.M.–11 P.M., happy hour Mon.–Fri. 3–6 P.M., brewery tours daily at 10:30 A.M. and 3 P.M., $9–18) offers not only supreme beer on tap (with a slew of rotating specials) but also pretty good food. The "brew your own" pizza allows you to pick your toppings and sauces, and there are fish and salad options (the salads should be avoided as they sound much better on the menu than they appear in person). The restaurant can get

KAVA: A NATURAL RELAXANT

Even though the kava plant has existed on the Hawaiian Islands for centuries, Zachary and Johanna Gibson, of Pu'u'ala Farm and Ranch on the Big Island, are helping it to make a big comeback. It was first used in fishing as bait to sedate fish, and Hawaiians then began utilizing the plant, which is part of the pepper family, for ceremonial and medicinal purposes.

The Gibsons, who started growing organic kava (or 'awa in Hawaiian) almost 15 years ago and now are the largest producer of kava on the islands, explain that it takes about 3-4 years before a plant can be harvested. The plant is then dug up and the leaves are discarded, because it is actually the root of the plant that holds the therapeutic elements. Then, along with the help of some 15 volunteers on the farm, the kava root is cleaned and ground into a paste. The last step of the process is to insert the paste into a cheesecloth bag, which soaks in a bowl of liquid that absorbs the kava.

Jason Nice, a volunteer at the farm, firmly believes "kava is a spiritual thing here in Hawaii." In liquid form kava is thought to reduce anxiety, to relax muscles, and to act as a diuretic when large quantities are consumed. Ancient Hawaiians also used the paste to cure skin diseases and chewed the roots for their calming effect. At the Gibsons' bar, **Kanaka Kava** (75-5803 Ali'i Dr., Kailua, 866/327-1660) in Kona, several different types of kava, all with relaxing properties, are mixed together and served, as is the custom, in bowls. With a gritty flavor, the drink, when solely mixed with water, does not always go down smoothly, so at Kanaka Kava it can be ordered mixed with either coconut water or juice. For some, the most important part of drinking is not for its health benefits, but for the ritual surrounding it. The etiquette, created by Chief Pahoa, says Zachary Gibson, "is to serve others and not yourself." Gibson's advice for getting the most out of a kava experience: "Get yourself a bowl and enjoy with a friend."

very crowded on the weekends, so call ahead or expect to wait for a bit. If you're going to be in town awhile pick up a growler (full growler $22, refill $13.50) and save some money on beer (to use for surfing or snorkeling).

At **Ba-Le Sandwiches and Bakery** (74-5588 Palani Rd., Kona Coast Shopping Center, Kailua, 808/327-1212, Mon.–Sat. 10 A.M.–9 P.M., Sun. 11 A.M.–7 P.M., $9) you'll find the classic *banh mi* sandwich on french rolls baked daily—the spicy lemongrass chicken (or its tofu counterpart) is the most popular selection. They also offer *pho* (rice noodle soups—an excellent gluten-free option) and vegetarian selections. If you're not too hungry order off the $5 mini menu, which has on it short ribs, *pho,* and the lemongrass chicken and tofu sandwiches. The mini menu, which is available all day, is an unbelievable deal given the relatively big portions. The ambiance only reflects the food in the sense that its lack of ambiance makes it reminiscent of any soup shop in any Chinatown.

This is old school Kona at its finest: A great family restaurant, **Jackie Rey's Ohana Grill** (75-5995 Kuakini Hwy., Kailua, 808/327-0209, www.jackiereys.com, lunch Mon.–Fri. 11 A.M.–2 P.M., appetizers Mon.–Fri. 2–5 P.M., happy hour Mon.–Fri. 3–5 P.M., dinner daily 5–9 P.M., lunch $12–14, dinner $16–28) has a well-deserved excellent reputation. The restaurant itself has a casual atmosphere with butcher paper lining the tables (and crayons to color with, of course), but the food is consistently good and the service usually attentive (although they can rush you a bit if they're getting busy). Most dishes are either fish or meat (not the best place for a vegetarian or vegan) served in a way that makes them local style—either by including fruit salsas or macadamia nuts or local sweet potatoes. A good gluten-free option is the *mochiko*-crusted fish (*mochiko* is sweet rice flour). There is a children's menu available as well as a full wine list (not related to the kids' menu). If you like cocktails try the Ling Mui martini (*li hing mui,* a salted dried plum, is a specialty flavoring in Hawaii).

Markets

One of the larger locations of **Island Naturals Market and Deli** (74-5487 Kaiwi St., Kailua, 808/326-1122, www.islandnaturals.com, Mon.–Sat. 7:30 A.M.–8 P.M., Sun. 9 A.M.–7 P.M.), a local chain natural foods grocery store, is in Kailua. It has a coffee and smoothie bar as well as an excellent hot bar (they charge per pound) with many gluten-free and vegan options. Beer and wine (non-organic and organic varieties) are available and on sale for 20 percent off every Friday (what a deal!).

Part of the local chain of grocery stores, **KTA** (74-5594 Palani Rd., Kona Coast Shopping Center, Kailua, 808/329-1677, www.ktasuperstores.com, daily 5 A.M.–11 P.M.) offers tons of local products (coffee, macadamia nuts, honey, etc.) and has an excellent fish and meat department (with Big Island beef). Pick up marinated short ribs for your barbecue—they are better than the same dish at some of the fancier restaurants.

Owed by the Mainland chain Foodland, **Sack N Save Kona** (75-5595 Palani Rd., 808/326-2729, Kailua, www.foodland.com, 5 A.M.–midnight) has everything you need including fish and meat departments.

Although the hours are posted, it always seems that the **Kailua Village Market–Kona Farmers Market** (in the parking lot next to the Kona Public Library, at Hualalai Rd. and Ali'i Dr., across from Waterfront Row, Kailua, www.konafarmersmarket.com, Wed.–Sat. 9 A.M.–noon) stays open later and that the crafts vendors (unlike the food vendors) are there at all times. Beware; not all the produce and food items sold at the market are in fact locally grown.

CAPTAIN COOK AREA: SOUTH KONA

The best barbecue on the island, **⊂ Big Jake's Island BBQ** (Hwy. 11 near mile marker 106, *mauka* side, Honaunau, 808/328-1227, daily 11 A.M.–6 P.M.) will make you feel like you're at home in Memphis (even if that's not your home).

The portions are huge, mouthwatering, and slow-cooked with on local keawe wood. The plates ($11–25 for a full rack of ribs) all come with rice, coleslaw, and beans. For a bit of Hawaiian fusion (or a gluten-free option) try their barbecue bowls of pulled chicken or pork over rice ($7). There is only outdoor picnic style seating, so it's not the best place if it's raining outside. BYOB is encouraged and you can grab a beer from the store next door while you wait. Call ahead because hours are variable due to catering.

Directly across from Big Jake's BBQ, **Coffees n' Epicurea** (Hwy. 11 near mile marker 106, *makai* side, Honaunau, 808/328-0322, www.coffeeepicurea.com, daily 6:30 A.M.–6 P.M.) is a proper coffee shop with a few tables and outdoor seating. They brew ice coffee (it takes nearly 24 hours to do this in a really neat-looking device) and bake their own pastries, which are more European style (like croissants, scones, and danishes) than local style. They run out of pastries early and some days coffee too (and soy milk). It's a nice place to stop and grab something to go early in the morning on your way out of town.

The killer view of Kealakekua Bay from the balcony of **The Coffee Shack** (Hwy. 11 between mile markers 108 and 109, *makai* side, Captain Cook, 808/328-9555, www.coffeeshack.com, daily 7:30 A.M.–3 P.M., breakfast mains $11, lunch $10–13) send tourists flocking here. It can get quite crowded, especially on the weekend. The food is good but not impressive. There are egg dishes (from Benedict to omelets) and sandwiches but the view is what you are paying for (actually, that is what you tell yourself while you're eating because the food seems overpriced). You can get the same food (and coffee) cheaper other places, but then you'd miss the view.

⊂ Mi's Italian Bistro (81-6372 Mamalahoa Hwy. between mile markers 110 and 111, *mauka* side, Kealakekua, 808/323-3880, www.misitalianbistro.com, Tues.–Sun. 4:30–8:30 P.M., reservations recommended, $19–32) is up there as one of the better restaurants on the island. Even though the location doesn't seem ideal (it's in a small strip mall), the restaurant itself feels quaint and romantic. Service is attentive. The chef waits on you (and serves you the food), ensuring that you order the perfect dish (and assisting if you require gluten-free or vegetarian options) and pair it with the right wine. For appetizers try the marinated beets with candied macadamia nuts. The mains are good-size portions. Try a dish with local veal or beef (the fish here is good but not their specialty), but save room for their award-winning tiramisu or flourless chocolate torte.

A hole-in-the-wall serving up pizza and *malasadas* (Portuguese doughnuts) that contend with those of the island's best bakers, **Patz Pies** (81-6596 Mamalahoa Hwy./ Hwy. 11 between mile markers 111 and 112, Captain Cook, 808/323-8100, $3 per slice) is a new foodie favorite. The pizza is thin-crust style and served with top-notch vegetables and meats. Salads are also available. Although you may be full, don't forget to pick up a hot *malasada* to go (otherwise how will you be able to fairly judge who makes the best *malasadas* on the island?).

Their slogan is "our only additive is *aloha*," and that pretty much tells all you need to know about **The Nasturtium Café** (Hwy. 11 between mile markers 112 and 113, *mauka* side, Kealakekua, 808/322-5083, Mon. 9 A.M.–3 P.M., Tues.–Fri. 9 A.M.–7:30 P.M., breakfast $8, lunch/dinner $11–15). The restaurant is small with only six tables, but the menu has a lot to offer and is perfect for vegetarians, vegans, and gluten-free individuals (and still good for "normal eaters"). Breakfast includes wraps (with tofu or turkey sausage), whole grain pancakes, and an assortment of egg dishes. Lunch offers a soup of the day with a tasty homemade spelt biscuit and salad combo or sandwiches with flavorful sauces and locally made cheeses. The dinner menu is rotating and there is a $10 BYOB fee—or try the *mamaki* lemongrass herbal tea (a homeopathic treat).

A good foodie choice is **Annie's Island Fresh Burgers** (79-7460 Mamalahoa Hwy./ Hwy. 11 between mile markers 112 and 113, 808/324-6000, www.anniesislandfreshburgers.

com, Kealakekua, daily 11 A.M.–6 P.M., $11). The meat is local, the salads have local organic lettuce and local vine-ripe tomatoes, and there are vegan options (a chickpea patty) in addition to the numerous local beef hamburgers with all kinds of toppings and savory sauces. The french fries (not included with burgers) are a must-try. Beer on draft is available.

Mostly known for breakfast (but some will argue it's overpriced), **Aloha Theatre Café** (79-7384 Mamalahoa Hwy./Hwy. 11 between mile markers 113 and 114, 808/322-3383, www.alohatheatrecafe.com, Kainaliu, daily 8 A.M.–3 P.M., dinner Mon.–Fri. 5–8:30 P.M., lunch $11–14 dinner $16). The restaurant has a good atmosphere (it is an old theater) and serves large portions of plates from local-style pupu (appetizers) to burgers to "south of the border" (Mexican) cuisine. Mixed drinks, wine, and beer are available (better than paying their $9 cork fee if you BYOB), as are vegetarian options.

Donkey Balls and Surfin Ass Coffee Company (79-7411 Mamalahou Hwy. between mile markers 113 and 114, *mauka* side, Kainaliu, 808/322-1475, www.aloha-hawaiianstore.com, daily 8 A.M.–6 P.M.) are not the same donkey balls as the stores you see throughout Kailua. These donkey balls are better. Donkey balls are dark/white/milk chocolate covered coffee beans, and they are addictive! Buy a few bags ($13 each) to take with you as a snack or to bring home. There are samples available and the staff is friendly. The coffee drinks are fantastic (especially the ones that seem like they are really ice cold milk shakes) and huge, so order small.

The exterior of **Roadhouse Café** (79-7399 Mamalahoa Hwy. between mile markers 113 and 114, *mauka* side, Kainaliu, 808/322-0616, Mon.–Fri. 11 A.M.–4 P.M. or until out of food, $6.25) is very inviting with its old diner look. The inside of the diner is less inviting. The food is not local style (the owner, Cathy Haber, says she doesn't do local style). The flavorful sandwiches and specials that change daily are cheap ($6.25 for nearly everything), and all baking is done on premises. Some days vegan options are available (other days there are usually vegetarian options). The pastries are displayed beautifully in a case and are equally as good to taste. So-so gluten-free cookies and a flourless ganache chocolate cake are available.

An institution in town, **Teshima Restaurant** (79-7251 Mamalahoa Hwy./Hwy. 11 between mile markers 113 and 114, *mauka* side, Kainaliu, 808/322-9140, daily 6:30 A.M.–1:45 P.M. and 5–9 P.M., $8–17 for fresh catch, cash only) has been serving it up the same for years and it works well (so why change it?). It's a Japanese-style diner (very casual) run for generations by the Teshima family, who opened it as a general store in 1929 and then a restaurant in 1940. The most popular dish is the bento box ($8.25), which you can get to go or to stay (additional $1.25 if you stay as it then includes miso soup and tea). It comes with meat, egg roll, fried fish, and additional sides. In general, meals from fish to teriyaki beef come with a lot of extras (like a complimentary appetizer of sushi), ensuring that you'll leave completely satisfied—and I can almost guarantee that you will.

Markets

If you've never seen a cacao fruit—now you will. The **South Kona Fruit Stand** (84-4770 Mamalahoa Hwy./Hwy. 11 between mile markers 103 and 104, Honaunau, 808/328-8547, Mon.–Sat. 9 A.M.–6 P.M. for fruit, café 10 A.M.–4 P.M.) is like an exotic mini farmers market with organic produce all grown on their farm. It has the standard Hawaiian fruits (pineapples, apple bananas, papayas) but also fruits that you don't often see anywhere else in Hawaii—like figs! There is dried fruit and trail mix for sale (pick some up if you're on your way to Hawai'i Volcanoes National Park) as well as smoothies ($4.50) and local coffee ($2).

Choicemart (82-6066 Mamalahoa Hwy./Hwy. 11 near mile marker 109, Captain Cook, 808/323-3994, daily 5 A.M.–10 P.M.) is the only large grocery store in the area. The inside of the store doesn't look as nice as some of the grocery stores in the area (like KTA), but it has everything you'll need, and some locals argue that its prices are cheaper.

The second Kona location of natural foods chain **Island Naturals Market and Deli** (79-7460 Mamalahoa Highway, Kealakekua, 808/930-7550, Mon.–Sat. 7:30 A.M.–8 P.M., Sun. 8 A.M.–7 P.M.) has a coffee and smoothie bar as well as a small hot buffet with gluten-free and vegan options. Beer and wine (non-organic and organic varieties) are available and on sale for 20 percent off every Friday.

South Kona Green Market (Kealakekua Ranch Center behind ChoiceMart and Ace Hardware, Captain Cook, www.skgm.org, Sun. 9 A.M.–1 P.M.) offers local produce plus handicrafts. Check the schedule on the website for live music performances.

Information and Services

EMERGENCY SERVICES

The **Kona Community Hospital** (79-1019 Haukapila St., 808/322-9311) is in Kealakekua, about 10 miles south of central Kailua-Kona. Along with its many other departments, it offers 24-hour emergency care.

For minor emergencies and urgent care, try **Hualalai Urgent Care** (77-6447 Kuakini Hwy./Hwy. 11, Kailua, 808/327-4357, Mon.–Fri. 8 A.M.–5 P.M., Sat. 9 A.M.–5 P.M.).

For pharmacies, try **Longs Drugs** in Kailua (808/329-1632, pharmacy Mon.–Fri.

8 A.M.–8 P.M., Sat.–Sun. 8 A.M.–6 P.M.) and Keauhou (808/322-6627, pharmacy Mon.–Fri. 8 A.M.–6 P.M., Sat.–Sun. 9 A.M.–5 P.M.), **KTA Super Stores** in Keauhou (808/322-2511, pharmacy Mon.–Fri. 9 A.M.–6 P.M., Sat. 9 A.M.–1 P.M., closed Sun.), and **Kmart** (808/326-1707) at the Makalapua Center.

BANKS

The **First Hawaiian Bank, Bank of Hawaii,** and the **American Savings Bank** all have branches and ATMs at or next to the Lanihau

Center on Palani Road in Kailua. **Bank of Hawaii** also maintains a store office at the KTA Super Store in Keauhou.

POST OFFICES

Many of the small towns that you'll pass on the highway have small post offices (hypothetically, every town has one—you'll love how small and user-friendly they are). The larger ones include the **Kailua-Kona** post office (74-55 Palani Rd., Mon.–Fri. 8:30 A.M.–4:30 P.M., Sat. 9:30 A.M.– 1:30 P.M.) and the **Keauhou** branch, located in the Keauhou Shopping Center (78-6831 Ali'i Dr., Mon.–Fri. 9 A.M.–4 P.M., Sat. 10 A.M.–3 P.M.).

Getting There and Around

BY PLANE

The **Kona International Airport** (code KOA) is just north of Kailua-Kona on Highway 19. The drive from the airport to Kailua is only about 20 minutes. The airport is small and outdoors (just like a Hawaiian airport might be imagined to look like). However, although it is tiny, it can get very crowded due to the sheer number of travelers moving through it. So do arrive early as the check-in and security lines can get quite long. If you are dropping someone off or coming to the airport to pick someone up, it's free to park in the lot if you are there less than 20 minutes.

The airport is served by both **Hawaiian Airlines** (www.hawaiianair.com) and **Go!Mokulele** (www.iflygo.com). These interisland flights tend to board minutes before their scheduled departure times. There are many daily direct flights to Honolulu and a few to Maui; however, to get to the other islands, it is often necessary to travel through Honolulu.

From Kona, it is possible to fly directly to the Mainland (without stopping in Honolulu) on airlines such as Alaska Airlines, American Airlines, Delta Airlines, United Airlines, and US Airways.

BY BUS

Via **Hele-On Bus** (www.heleonbus.org, 808/961-8744, $1 per ride, $1 each for luggage, large backpacks, bikes) it is possible, with a little planning, to make it from the Kona side to the Hilo side and from Kona north to Kohala as far as Hawi. Check the website for bus stop locations.

From the Kona Side to the Hilo Side

If you are traveling from Honaunau to Hilo the bus leaves at 5:55 A.M. and arrives to Hilo at 9:45 A.M., making all stops north through Kohala, Waimea, and the Hamakua Coast. The bus returns on the same route, leaving Hilo at 1:30 P.M. and arriving to Honaunau at 5:20 P.M.

A second bus, following the same route as the first bus, leaves from Ali'i Drive at 6:30 A.M. arriving to Hilo at 9:40 A.M. It makes its return from Hilo at 3:50 P.M., arriving to Ali'i Drive at 6:35 P.M.

A third bus, again following the same route as the other two Kona to Hilo buses, leaves from Hilo at 9:15 A.M. and arrives at 11:50 A.M. to the Kona Commons (the strip mall across the parking lot from Target in the Old Industrial Area). It returns from the Kona Commons at 4 P.M., arriving to Hilo at 7 P.M.

North-South Kona Side Routes

If you want to get from Kohala to the south of Kona, a bus travels from Kapa'au in the north at 6:45 A.M., taking the inland route through Waimea and arriving at the Keauhou Shopping Center (78-6831 Ali'i Dr.) at 9:45 A.M. The return trip leaves at 1:35 P.M., arriving in Kapa'au at 4:55 P.M. Another bus makes the trip between Kapa'au and Keauhou along the ocean route (Hwy. 19 to Hwy. 11), leaving from Kapa'au at 9:15 A.M. and arriving at 11:45 A.M. in Keauhou, returning at 2:30 P.M. and arriving in Kapa'au at 4:35 P.M.

The Hele-On **Intra Kona Bus** runs almost every 1.5 hours beginning at 5:05 A.M. and ending at 6 P.M. It makes intermediate stops north on Highway 11 through Kailua and then turns north in town and makes its final stop at the Matsuyama Market (73-4354 Mamalahoa

Hwy.) in Holualoa (on Hwy. 180). The only time the bus makes its final stop at the airport is at 8:20 A.M. (it also picks people up at the time to drive back south through Kona toward Captain Cook).

TO AND FROM THE AIRPORT

If you're not renting a car, many of the resorts will arrange a pickup for you (for a fee). If you would like to schedule your own shared ride service, try **SpeediShuttle** (808/329-5433, www.speedishuttle.com, beginning at $12 per person for minimum 2 people). It is a shared ride although they charge more if you're not traveling with two people. For a private taxi (available outside the airport) you can expect to pay $25 to Kailua and upward of $60 to the Kohala resorts.

KOHALA

The Kohala district, also known as the Gold Coast, is the peninsular thumb in the northwestern portion of the Big Island. At its tip is Upolu Point, only 30 miles from Maui across the 'Alenuihaha Channel. Kohala was the first section of the Big Island to rise from beneath the sea. The long-extinct volcanoes of the Kohala Mountains running down its spine have been reduced by time and the elements from lofty, ragged peaks to rounded domes of 5,000 feet or so. Kohala is divided into North and South Kohala. North Kohala, an area of dry coastal slopes, former sugar lands, a string of sleepy towns, and deeply incised lush valleys, forms the northernmost tip of the island. South Kohala boasts *the* most beautiful swimming beaches on the Big Island, along with world-class hotels and resorts.

South Kohala is a region of contrast. It's dry, hot, tortured by wind, and scored by countless old lava flows. The predominant land color here is black, and this is counterpointed by scrubby bushes and scraggly trees, a seemingly semi-arid wasteland. This was an area that the ancient Hawaiians seemed to have traveled through to get somewhere else, yet Hawaiians did live here—along the coast—and numerous archaeological sites dot the coastal plain. Still, South Kohala is stunning with its palm-fringed white-sand pockets of beach, luxury resorts, green landscaped golf courses, a proliferation of colorful planted flowers, and its deep blue inviting water. You don't generally travel here to appreciate the stunning landscape, although it too has its attraction. You come here to settle into a sedate resort community, to be pampered

© BREE KESSLER

HIGHLIGHTS

LOOK FOR 🌙 TO FIND RECOMMENDED SIGHTS, ACTIVITIES, DINING, AND LODGING.

🌙 **Puako Tide Pools:** Teeming with sea life, this watery wonderland offers some of the best snorkeling and diving on the island (page 76).

🌙 **Hapuna Beach State Recreation Area:** With pristine white sands and turquoise waters perfect for snorkeling, body boarding, and swimming, this is one of the best beaches on the island (page 76).

🌙 **Mahukona Beach Park:** Here you'll find an underwater treasure of ruins from the plantation days, a good opportunity for beginning snorkelers (page 78).

🌙 **Hamakua Macadamia Nut Factory:** Nibble on sample macadamia nuts of every variety imaginable for free while you watch the workings of the factory (page 83).

🌙 **Pololu Valley Lookout and Beach:** The spectacular view of the coastline is worth driving to the road's end and simply staring for a few minutes, or taking a steep hike down to the secluded beach (page 86).

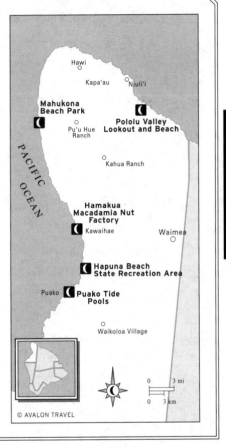

© AVALON TRAVEL

KOHALA

and pleased by the finer things that await at luxury resorts that are destinations in and of themselves. Of the many scattered villages that once dotted this coast, only two remain: Puako, now a sleepy beach hideaway, and Kawaihae, one of the principal commercial deepwater ports on the island. In Kawaihae, at the base of the North Kohala peninsula, Highway 19 turns east and coastal Route 270, known as the Akoni Pule Highway, heads north along the coast.

North Kohala was the home of Kamehameha the Great. From this fiefdom he launched his conquest of all the islands. The shores and lands of North Kohala are rife with historical significance, and with beach parks where only a few local people ever go. Among North Kohala's cultural treasures is Lapakahi State Historical Park, a must-stop offering a walk-through village and "touchable" exhibits that allow you to become actively involved in Hawaii's traditional past. Northward is Kamehameha's birthplace—the very spot—and within walking distance is

KOHALA

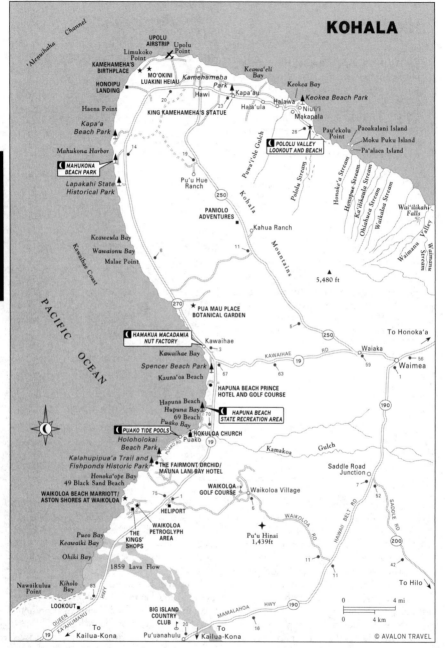

KOHALA

'Alenuihaha Channel

UPOLU AIRSTRIP
Upolu Point
Limukoko Point

KAMEHAMEHA'S BIRTHPLACE
MO'OKINI LUAKINI HEIAU
Kamehameha Park
Keawa'eli Bay

HONOIPU LANDING
Hawi
Kapa'au
Keokea Bay
Keokea Beach Park

Haena Point
KING KAMEHAMEHA'S STATUE
20
Hala'ula
Halawa
Niuli'i
Makapala

Kapa'a Beach Park
23
Pau'ekolu Point
Paoakalani Island
Moku Puku Island
Pa'alaea Island

Mahukona Harbor
14
28
POLOLU VALLEY LOOKOUT AND BEACH

MAHUKONA BEACH PARK
19

Lapakahi State Historical Park
Pu'u Hue Ranch

Honoke'a Stream
Homopue Stream
Ka'ilikaala Stream
Ohiahuea Stream
Waikaloa Stream
Wai'ilikahi Falls

250
PANIOLO ADVENTURES

Keaweula Bay
Kahua Ranch
Waimanu Valley
Waimanu Stream

Wawaionu Bay
Malae Point
6
11

Kawaihae Coast
Kohala Mountains

PACIFIC OCEAN
5,480 ft

270
PUA MAU PLACE BOTANICAL GARDEN

5
250
To Honoka'a

HAMAKUA MACADAMIA NUT FACTORY
Kawaihae
Waiaka
Waimea

Kawaihae Bay
3
KAWAIHAE RD
19
56

Spencer Beach Park
67
63
59
1

Kauna'oa Beach
HAPUNA BEACH PRINCE HOTEL AND GOLF COURSE

Hapuna Beach
Hupuna Bay
69 Beach
Puako Bay
70
HAPUNA BEACH STATE RECREATION AREA

PUAKO TIDE POOLS
Puako
HOKULOA CHURCH
190

Holoholokai Beach Park
19
Kamakoa Gulch

Kalahupipua'a Trail and Fishponds Historic Park
Saddle Road Junction

Honoka'ope Bay
49 Black Sand Beach
THE FAIRMONT ORCHID/ MAUNA LANI BAY HOTEL
7
52

WAIKOLOA BEACH MARRIOTT/ ASTON SHORES AT WAIKOLOA
WAIKOLOA GOLF COURSE
Waikoloa Village

75
1
6

HELIPORT
WAIKOLOA
HAWAII BELT RD
SADDLE RD

Pueo Bay
Keawaiki Bay
THE KINGS' SHOPS
WAIKOLOA PETROGLYPH AREA
Pu'u Hinai 1,439ft
200
To Hilo

Ohiki Bay
11
11
42

Nawaikulua Point
Kiholo Bay
1859 Lava Flow

LOOKOUT
83
HWY

QUEEN KA'AHUMANU
BIG ISLAND COUNTRY CLUB
MAMALAHOA HWY
190
0   4 mi
0   4 km

19
To Kailua-Kona
20
Pu'uanahulu
To Kailua-Kona
16

© AVALON TRAVEL

Mo'okini Luakini, one of the oldest *heiau* in Hawaii and still actively ministered by the current generation of a long line of *kahuna*.

Hawi, the main town in North Kohala, was a sugar settlement whose economy turned sour when the last of the seven sugar mills in the area stopped operations in the mid-1970s. Hawi is making a big comeback, along with this entire northern shore, which has seen an influx of small, boutique businesses and art shops. The main coastal road winds in and out of numerous small gulches, crosses some one-lane bridges, and ends at Pololu Valley lookout, where you can overlook one of the premier taro-growing valleys of old Hawaii. A walk down the steep *pali* into this valley is the Hawaii you imagined from movies and reruns of *Lost*.

ORIENTATION
South Kohala: Resort Area

A distinctive area for its abundance of large resorts and rental properties, white-sand beaches lined with coconut trees, and its proximity to the airport, the Waikoloa and Mauna Lani areas are geared to meet the needs of tourists. With the highly manicured landscapes one will never feel off the beaten track. Actually, it almost feels like Florida here. This small area holds enough beaches and restaurants to keep someone occupied for days, and with the three shopping centers within the resorts one really never has to leave the premises.

This coast's fabulous beaches are known not only for swimming and surfing, but for tide-pooling and awe-inspiring sunsets as well. There are little-disturbed and rarely visited archaeological sites, expressive petroglyph fields, and the best preserved portion of the Ala Kahakai National Historic Trail. Note: The Waikoloa Beach Resort area *(makai)* is drastically different than the Waikoloa Village area *(mauka)*. Waikoloa Village is where many of the workers from the resorts live. You won't find your hotel or beaches there!

Kawaihae

Kawaihae is just a pass-through port town with a gas station and some restaurants worthy of a

---

KOHALA MOUNTAIN ROAD

Route 250, the back road to Hawi, is a delightful country lane that winds through gloriously green grazing lands for almost 20 miles along the leeward side of the Kohala Mountains. It begins in the western outskirts of Waimea and ends in Hawi. One of the most picturesque roads on the island, it's lined with ironwood trees and dotted with mood-setting cactus, and herds of cattle graze in the pastures of the several ranches along the way. Vistas open to the west, and far below are expansive panoramas of rolling hills tumbling to the sea. Just outside Hawi, Route 250 splits; going right takes you to Kapa'au, left to Hawi.

KOHALA

---

stop. Some dive outfitters are based out of the harbor, but they often take their clients to the waters of South Kohala or Kona, although the nearby waters are just as nice and less crowded.

Hawi to the End of the Road

Located on the very northwest tip of the island, these communities are nearly perfect small towns offering walkable main streets filled with excellent restaurants, art galleries, and coffee shops. The beaches here are rocky but offer breathtaking views of the coast and, if you're lucky, of Maui too. Unlike the southern part of the Kohala district, northern Kohala doesn't look like a lava-filled landscape from outer space. Instead, although it is quite dry in this region, there are gorgeous large trees providing shade from the sun. Spend the day strolling the streets of Hawi, explore the backroads of Kohala on an ATV or kayak, watch the sunset at Pololu Valley, and then finish your day with dinner (and maybe drinks) at Sushi Rock or Bamboo Restaurant or live music at Luke's Place in Hawi.

PLANNING YOUR TIME

The only reason to plan your time in Kohala is so that you remember to leave that perfect

KOHALA

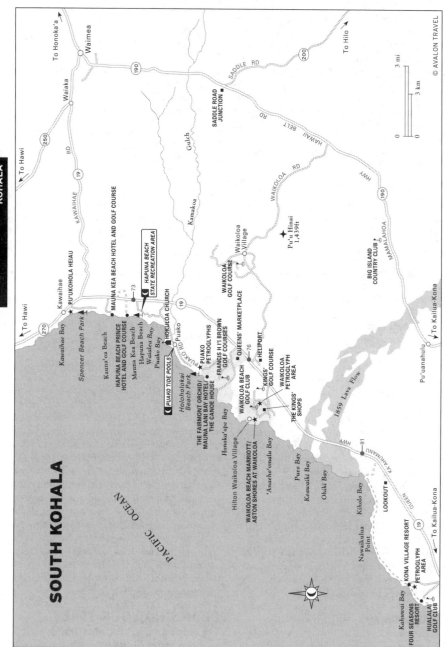

© AVALON TRAVEL

SOUTH KOHALA

PACIFIC OCEAN

NORTH KOHALA

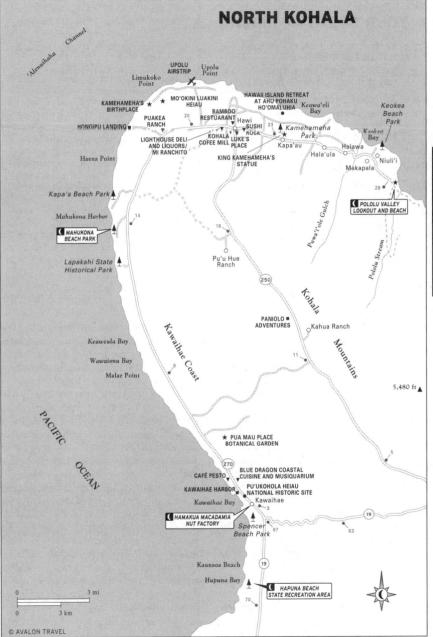

KOHALA

© AVALON TRAVEL

YOUR BEST DAY IN KOHALA

- Start your day on the **Ala Kahakai National Historic Trail.** Pick a point on the trail and go for a short walk, leaving plenty of time to stop at any number of beaches (especially the secret ones).

- Stop to sample all sorts of flavors of macadamia nuts and brittle at the **Hamakua Macadamia Nut Factory** on your way north to Hawi.

- Visit the galleries and shops in **Hawi** and eat lunch at one of the excellent restaurants in town.

- Try an adventure like **ziplining** or **"fluming the ditch"** (kayaking down an old irrigation ditch from the plantation days).

- Drive to the lookout at **Polulu Valley** to watch the sunset and witness one of the best views on the island (I guarantee you'll be amazed).

- Finish your day with dinner and dancing at the **Blue Dragon Coastal Cuisine & Musiquarium** in Kawaihae (make a reservation!).

RAINY DAY ALTERNATIVE

Most people come to Kohala and never leave the beach, so there aren't very many daytime indoor activities in the area. Thus, if it's raining in Kohala, take a peek to the south to Kona and then look *mauka* toward Waimea and see if you can spot any clouds in either direction – head to where there are no clouds. If it's simply raining everywhere on the island (and I am sorry to say it does happen every once in a while), your best bet is to drive the 15 minutes to nearby Waimea or Kona to spend some time inside one of the museums or movie theaters.

beach you've been lounging on for days. The afternoons in Kohala can cloud over (I said clouds, not rain), so depending on if you're looking to soak up the sun or if you want to avoid the rays plan your day accordingly. If you are spending an entire week in Kohala, as many do, take the time to explore the assorted beaches, such as the well-regarded (but crowded) Hapuna Beach State Recreation Area or a resort beach, which you are free to visit because all beaches must have public access points even for nonguests. When you are ready to get off the sand and into the water experienced divers and snorkelers should get themselves into the Puako tide pools for a multitude of sea life much more than you can imagine or to Mahukona Beach Park to discover the unofficial underwater museum of debris left from the plantation and railroad days.

For those who want to stay dry, there are some great trails (no hiking really necessary) best visited early morning or late afternoon—the short Kalahupipua'a Trail near the Mauna Lani Bay Hotel, the Malama Trail to view ancient petroglyphs, or the Ala Kahakai National Historic Trail, which spans most of the length of the Kohala region. If you need more breaks from the beach, hop in the car and take an extremely scenic drive up the coast (from Highway 19 to Highway 270), watching for whales peeking out from the ocean (only in the winter) on your way to the Pololu Valley for sunset. Even though the distance is short, you can take your time with this drive, stopping at the Hamakua Macadamia Nut Factory on the way and then wandering through the shops in Hawi. Or, use the afternoon (the hot or cloudy part of the day) for several short jaunts to the north for some of the best lunch places on the island or for ziplining and kayaking the ditches of plantation days or even for traveling to Waimea, which actually is only about 20 minutes away from the Kohala Coast and has significantly cooler weather.

Beaches

SOUTH KOHALA: RESORT AREA
Anaeho'omalu Bay (A Bay)

Once a long narrow strip of inviting salt-and-pepper sand, Anaeho'omalu Bay, or A Bay (Hwy. 19 at mile marker 76, daily 6 A.M.–7 P.M.), the beach that fronts hotels such as the Waikoloa Beach Marriott Resort and Hilton Waikoloa Village, was split into two parts by the March 2011 tsunami. Now the only option to walk the beach is via the walkway behind the sandy area where some ancient fishponds are located. Enter through Waikoloa Beach Resort area and park behind Queens' MarketPlace. Although the beach is used by the resort hotels, it is accessible for nonguests via a huge parking lot (where the Hele-On buses wait). All the standard water sports are possible here, and rentals for equipment are available from a kiosk in front of the Marriott.

© DMITRI KOTCHETOV/WWW.123RF.COM
Anaeho'omalu Bay is a popular spot for tourists and locals.

Also in front of the Marriott are lounge chairs that are open (and seemingly free) to the public. The public restrooms and showers are near the parking lot (which means that people tend to sneak into the Marriott for its facilities).

Holoholokai Beach Park and Malama Trail

A shaded park with a grassy area, Holoholokai Beach Park (Holoholokai Beach Park Rd., daily 6:30 A.M.–6:30 P.M.) makes a nice place to picnic (grills available) or to fish away the afternoon. There are better places to access to the ocean, but you might want to jump in after walking the Malama Trail to view the petroglyph site, approximately 3,000 individual rock carvings considered some of the finest and oldest in Hawaii. The trail is 1.4 miles round-trip (about a 45-minute walk), but avoid going midday when the unshaded trail can be extremely hot. Bathrooms and drinking fountains are available in the parking lot. To get there, from Highway 19 (between mile markers 73 and 74) turn onto Mauna Lani Drive, turn right at the first turn on the roundabout to North Kaniku Drive, and then turn right onto Holoholokai Beach Park Road.

Kalahupipua'a Trail and Fishponds Historic Park

The short paved Kalahupipua'a Trail (Mauna Lani Bay Hotel, daily 6:30 A.M.–6:30 P.M.), which can be connected with the larger shoreline trail system (the Ala Kahakai National Historic Trail), passes through ancient fishponds (still stocked with fish) and the Eva Parker Woods Cottage Museum, originally constructed in the 1920s as part of a larger oceanfront estate. To get there, from Highway 19 (between mile markers 73 and 74) turn onto Mauna Lani Drive and gain access through the Mauna Lani Bay Hotel, or for public access follow Mauna Lani Drive and turn left on Pauoa Road; look for the public access lot on the right side.

KOHALA

KOHALA

If you continue to walk south on the Kalahupipua'a Trail for a few more minutes, you'll end up at **Makaiwa Bay,** a white-sand beach that is a great spot for snorkeling, especially for beginners (the signage is so good here that there is a diagram indicating where to go snorkeling in the water based on your level of expertise). Behind the beach is the Mauna Lani Beach Club (the parking lot is not open to the public before 4:30 P.M., but you can walk there via the trail), housing the upscale restaurant **Napua** (1292 S. Kaniku Dr., 808/885-5022, daily 11 A.M.–4 P.M. and 5–9 P.M., lunch $12–16, dinner $28–36). If you walk through the beach and up the stairs at the end of the beach, you'll be on **Ala Kahakai National Historic Trail,** passing by some amazing-looking homes, and you can continue on this scenic path (it's uneven lava here) to 49 Black Sand Beach.

49 Black Sand Beach

A little known quiet beach with little shade, white sand, and calm water, 49 Black Sand Beach (Mauna Lani Resort) makes for a nice place to get away. The parking lot, including shower and bathroom facilities, is only a minute away from the beach, making this spot a good place to go if you don't want the hassle of parking and trekking far out to a beach.

To get there from Highway 19, between mile markers 73 and 74 turn onto Mauna Lani Drive; continue around the roundabout and turn right onto North Kaniku Drive, then left on Honokaope Place. Check in with the security guard to get a beach pass.

69 Beach (Waialea Bay)

The name of the beach is mostly what gets curious onlookers to visit it, but they are usually happy they made the trip. The 69 Beach on Waialea Bay (Hwy. 19 between mile markers 70 and 71, daily 7 A.M.–8 P.M.) is very pleasant: a long narrow stretch of white sand, lots of shade, and excellent snorkeling. Restroom and shower facilities are available as are several picnic areas. This isn't the best beach in the area (but in fairness, there is some steep

competition), but you won't be disappointed if you spend an afternoon here.

To get to 69 Beach from Highway 19, between mile markers 70 and 71 turn *makai* onto Puako Beach Drive and take the first right onto old Puako Road and then the first left after that; follow the road into the parking area.

◖ Puako Tide Pools

One of the most developed fringing reefs on the island, the Puako tide pools area (Puako Beach Dr., off Hwy. 19 between mile markers 70 and 71) is an underwater wonderland offering some of the best snorkeling and diving on the island. Once you are in the water, look for submerged lava tubes and garden eels (they won't hurt you) hiding under the sandy ocean bottom. There are no facilities or rental companies located here, so bring in what you need, including equipment (and snacks).

Access is available at several different points along the shorefront, but the easiest point may be right before the road dead-ends; from Highway 19 between mile markers 70 and 71 turn *makai* onto Puako Beach Drive and follow the road through the village—even though there is a Dead End sign—head toward the dead end and turn *makai* into the dirt parking area.

◖ Hapuna Beach State Recreation Area

Locals allege that the Hapuna Beach State Recreation Area (Hwy. 19 near mile marker 69, daily 7 A.M.–8 P.M.) is one of the top 20 beaches in the world, and that assertion might be true. Even on weekdays the large parking lot fills up early as locals and tourists alike rush to this white-sand beach to get a top spot (especially since there is little shade here). The turquoise waters are perfect for snorkeling, body boarding, and swimming. There is a lifeguard on duty, and the picnic areas, some of which are shaded, have great views of all the action on the beach (as well as, at times, Maui in the distance). If you forgot your snorkel gear, towels, boogie boards, or chairs you can rent from the **Hapuna Beach Grill** (on the grassy area

KOHALA

You can see both submerged lava tubes and garden eels at the Puako tide pools.

near the parking lot, 808/882-4447, grill daily 11 A.M.–3 P.M., $8, rentals daily 10 A.M.–4 P.M., cash only). The grill offers burgers, fries, ice cream, and fruit smoothies that are better than your usual beach shack foods.

Kauna'oa Beach (Mauna Kea Beach)

Since all beaches in Hawaii are public, it's just knowing how to access them that is the trick. The Mauna Kea Beach Hotel's beach, Kauna'oa Beach (Hwy. 19 near mile marker 68), is another example where you merely have to ask (beg) a security guard for a pass to park in the public lot at the hotel (passes can go quickly in the morning). Technically, there are even different bathroom and shower facilities for the public users versus the guests that are staying at the hotel, but since the beach is the same beach there seems to be a lot of intermingling, including public use of lounge chairs reserved for guests. But once you're in, you'll want to stay for the entire day. The water

is perfect for swimming and there is a long stretch of white sand as well as a grassy area ideal for a picnic or just lounging with a book.

To get to Kauna'oa Beach, from Highway 19 turn *makai* onto Mauna Kea Beach Drive near mile marker 68 and ask the guard if you can have a parking permit for the public beach.

Spencer Beach Park

A top family beach and one of the best camping spots on the Big Island (you need a permit), Spencer Beach Park (Hwy. 270 between mile markers 2 and 3, 6 A.M.–11 P.M.) gets very crowded on weekends and holidays. Enter through the entrance to Pu'ukohola Heiau National Historic Site. There are picnic pavilions with barbecues, lots of shade, a sandy beach with calm waters, restroom and shower facilities, and just a general congenial atmosphere. It's more popular among locals rather than tourists, probably given the fact that nearby Hapuna Beach provides a more idyllic beach setting.

HAWI TO THE END OF THE ROAD

◖ Mahukona Beach Park

There is no sand at this beach; instead, Mahukona Beach Park (Hwy. 270 between mile markers 14 and 15) is a modern-day ruin. It was a shipping port during the plantation days, and you can still see the decrepit structure of the Hawaii Railroad Company (from 1930) standing in the parking lot. History or archaeology buffs will want to take a quick detour just to see the ruins that are above ground. Snorkelers can delight in an underground adventure not so much for the fish, but for plantation and shipping artifacts scattered under the water. To enter the water, look for the ladder at the old dock. There are no facilities in this section of the beach park; instead, at the fork in the road veer left to the campground area, where there are portable bathrooms (you can also just walk here from the snorkeling parking lot—it's only a three-minute walk). It's not a great campsite, but the picnic area is nice and sheltered.

Kapaʻa Beach Park

A good place for a picnic, Kapaʻa Beach Park (Hwy. 270 near mile marker 16) is breezy with decent views. However, with only portable bathrooms, a run-down picnic shelter, and rocky beach access, it's not your best choice for a day at a beach or a campground (although camping is allowed here).

Water Sports

The Waikoloa resort area and Anaehoʻomalu Bay (A Bay) are not as much of an apex of ocean activities as other areas in the region (there are nicer beaches and better snorkeling and surfing in other spots). Each resort tends to offer ocean and beach equipment rental to its guests, and most also offer quick instruction for snorkeling and stand-up paddling. Fees for activities and rentals tend to be higher when purchased through hotels. You'd be better off to go directly to the source (most of the resorts actually contract out to Ocean Sports) to get a better price.

DIVING AND SNORKELING

Given that there is a harbor in Kawaihae it seems like a natural location for diving and snorkeling tours; however, there isn't much activity here as most tourists prefer Kona. There really is no reason to avoid diving and snorkeling here; in fact, the benefits are that it is less crowded than the Kona Coast and the water is just as full of remarkable marine life.

Those with experience snorkeling or diving should explore the Puako tide pools, one of the most developed fringing reefs on the island. One can spend the entire day surveying sea life. There aren't rental agencies here

so it is imperative to rent before you come. Alternatively, Mahukona Beach Park with its shallow water presents a good opportunity for beginners to get their feet wet and discover some nearby underwater treasure (or garbage, depending how you look at it).

If you want to join a tour, **Kohala Divers** (Hwy. 270 in Kawaihae Shopping Center, 808/882-7774, www.kohaladivers.com) has a great reputation for good service and quality equipment. Since this part of the coast is much less trafficked the dive sites are usually less worn and you won't have to worry about bumping into many divers down below. Kohala Divers offers a PADI open-water certification course ($600). Experienced divers can book a trip such as the popular two-tank morning charter ($130 per person), a two-tank night dive ($140), or a shorter one-tank dive ($100). Both diving and snorkeling equipment is available to rent.

The other option is **Mauna Lani Sea Adventures** (66-1400 Mauna Lani Dr., 808/885-7883, www.hawaiiseaadventures.com), but it doesn't specialize in scuba diving. For certified divers, two-tank dives with gear ($160 plus tax) are offered twice daily, and one-tank dives ($115 plus tax) with a minimum of two divers are offered three times daily. PADI-certified courses are available and more information is available upon request.

BODY-BOARDING, SURFING, AND STAND-UP PADDLE-BOARDING

The Kohala Coast is a good place to try out your stand-up body-boarding and paddle-boarding skills since the waves here tend not to be too big or rough. Conversely, these conditions are not ideal for surfing. Experienced surfers tend to try the beach at Pololu Valley, but you have to really want to surf there since a visit requires carrying your board down (and more importantly up) this steep trail.

Ocean Sports (Queens' MarketPlace and beach shack on Anaeho'omalu Bay, 808/886-6666) offers rentals for all your ocean needs. The individual ($50) or family plan ($140 for up to four people) includes unlimited use of equipment for a day, a great deal considering a stand-up paddle board is $50 for an hour. Where this might not be a good deal is that you must return at the end of each hour with your equipment and can only take it out again if no one else is waiting (some days this might be a problem). If you need some help getting started, they offer beach boys (who are like lifeguards) to aid you in short classes. Snorkeling is $30 for 45 minutes ($10 for an extra person), and stand-up paddling is $40 for 30 minutes of instruction.

WATER FITNESS

Even if you're not planning on signing up for a triathlon, **Ocean Sports** (Queens' MarketPlace and beach shack on Anaeho'omalu Bay, 808/886-6666, www.hawaiioceansports. com) has group exercise classes that are fun for all. They offer open-water courses (Mon. and Fri. 8 A.M., $5), a deep-water ocean jog course that uses foam jogging belts for floatation so you run without touching the bottom (Tues. and Thurs. 8 A.M., $5), and a swim stroke technique course (Thurs. 3:30 P.M., $15).

For a free option, visit **Kamehameha Park** (54-3853 Akoni Pule Hwy., Kapa'au, 808/889-6933), which has a full recreation area, including an Olympic-size pool, basketball courts, and weight rooms in the main building along with outside tennis courts with night lighting and a driving range. There are restrooms, picnic tables, and a kiddie area, all open to the public. Call ahead to check open-swim times.

BOAT TOURS

During the winter months Kawaihae Harbor is a prime location for whale-watching. Leaving from here (versus from Honokohau Harbor in Kona) will save you some time on the road, as this harbor is closer to the majority of resorts and also tends to be less crowded than Honokohau. Boat trips range from snorkeling and/or diving adventures to whale- and dolphin-watching rides (remember that whales are only around in the winter) to sunset open-bar cruises.

Extending their monopoly on the water, **Ocean Sports** (Whale Center in Kawaihae Harbor, 61-3657 Akoni Pule Hwy./Hwy. 270, 808/886-6666, www.hawaiioceansports.com) touts a champagne sunset cruise on a sailing catamaran. It is a good deal ($115 adults, $58 children, *kama'aina* rates available) for those who like to combine drinking with cruising. The open bar (including a sunset champagne toast) comes with lots of appetizers, and for only an extra $25 you can renew your vows on board! The Moku Nui Cocktail Sail (Sun., Tues., Thurs. only, $99 adults, $50 children) is similar to the champagne cruise, but with less food and no champagne. The champagne cruise might be worth the extra $16 if you don't have dinner plans afterward. In the summer months (April–November), Ocean Sports offers a 3.5-hour morning dolphin snorkel trip (Sun., Tues., Thurs., $138 adults, $69 children) complete with lunch and an open bar (that they assure is only available after the snorkeling is complete).

KOHALA

Hiking and Biking

HIKING

Guided hikes aren't a big business in Kohala as there aren't too many established trails here, but the Kohala Mountains do offer some splendid scenery if you decide to explore on your own or join **Hawaii Forest and Trail** (808/331-8505, www.hawaii-forest.com, adults $159 plus tax, children $129 plus tax). This top-rated tour company offers an all-day hiking experience along the Kohala Ditch trail to Kapoloa Waterfall at the back of the Pololu Valley and another hiking trek to other waterfalls in the area. It also takes guests on its six-wheel Pinzgauer vehicle into rugged former sugarcane lands for views of waterfalls and the coast. The hiking portion is pretty minimal (only 1.5 miles), making this tour accessible to anyone comfortable walking that distance over uneven terrain.

BIKING

Highway 19 extending north of the airport provides a nice flat (albeit very hot) stretch of road. It's an ideal place to ride fast, and you'll see many serious bikers doing just that. Otherwise, renting a bike simply to ride around the resort area can make for a nice afternoon. Riders wishing to follow the Kona **Ironman route** will want to continue from Highway 19 to Highway 270 north to Hawi to experience the steep climb. Beware: As you travel north on

ALA KAHAKAI NATIONAL HISTORIC TRAIL: THE KING'S TRAIL

A conglomeration of several trails, this system of trails stretching over half the island was formalized in 1847 as a way to increase access for missionaries and transportation of goods. But even before the trails became a more formalized system in the 1800s, these trails were the method ancient Hawaiians used to travel the island since they linked together the kingdom of Hawaii's major districts. Thus, the trails present sites of significant events in Hawaiian history from the arrival of the Polynesians to the islands to the arrival (and subsequent killing) of Captain Cook in Hawaii. Historically, the trail began in the northern part of Kohala (at Upolu Point) and extended into south Puna (at Waha'ula Heiau). Much of this route is not visible anymore due to modern-day construction and/or lava covering it up.

Nowadays, the trail is most visible and walkable between Kawaihae and Pu'uhonua O Honaunau (south of Captain Cook). The National Park Service is working on improving the usability of these trails even more, but for now, there is about a 15-mile section that one can easily follow. If you start at Spencer Beach Park, the trail can be followed south along the coast. Or another well-marked section starts at the Mauna Kea Beach Hotel (there is public access there), where you can travel south toward Hapuna Beach or north to a secret beach that can only be accessed by the trail. Since the trail is a combination of a historical shore trail and the *ala loa* (king's trail or long trail), you will see different signage depending on where you are (many of the signs read Ala Kahakai, though) and in some places it seems like there are two parallel trails (one on the shore and one more inland). One of the nicest sections of the trail starts near the Mauna Lani Bay Hotel and Bungalows and takes you through ancient fishponds to some beautiful beaches, and then passes by million-dollar homes. The trail can be easily accessed in sections for a stroll of an hour or two, or you can try a larger portion of the trail from Spencer Beach Park to Hapuna Beach (about three miles one-way) if you are looking for a half-day or a whole-day activity. This route will take you through two desolate hidden beaches (Mau'umae Beach and a beach literally called "secret beach") that make for excellent stops on your journey.

Highway 270 there is not much of a shoulder for bike riding.

For do-it-yourself rentals in the area, **Bikeworks Beach and Sport** (Queens' MarketPlace, 808/836-5000, www.bikeworkshawaii.com) has a nice selection of ultra-deluxe road bikes ($60 per day), deluxe bikes ($50), and cruisers ($25).

Alternatively, **Orchid Isle Bicycling** (808/327-0087, www.cyclekona.com, $125 plus tax) has a two- to three-hour 21-mile tour that starts at the summit of the Kohala mountain range and then continues downhill through Hawi, ending at the ocean. The tour includes equipment rental and snacks.

Adventure Sports and Tours

DITCH FLOATS AND ATV TOURS

There is little in the way of organized recreation along the north coast, but what there is can be exciting. Perhaps the most unusual activity is a kayak ride down a section of the Kohala Ditch. Completed in 1906 and considered a feat of engineering, this 22-mile-long irrigation system, with its 57 tunnels, supplied the Kohala sugar mills with a steady supply of water until the last plantation ceased business in 1975.

The ditch was damaged in 2006 during a big earthquake but after a long delay is finally repaired. **Kohala Ditch Adventures** (Hwy. 270 between mile markers 24 and 25, Kapa'au, 808/889-6000, www.kohaladitchadventures. com, $129 per person, $65 for children 5–12), the company that facilitates this journey down two miles of the ditch, recently reopened and is eager for guests to return to "flume the ditch." The specially designed five-person inflatable kayaks drift down the flume, into and out of 10 tunnels and over gullies. Prepare to get wet. The journey ends with an ATV ride through a macadamia nut orchard.

ATV Outfitters (Hwy. 270 between mile markers 24 and 25, 808/889-6000, www.atvoutfittershawaii.com, adults $129–149, children 5–11 $80–130) offers an equally extreme way to experience the Kohala backcountry, and the tours aren't limited to the just the ditches. There are three options of varying duration, each available twice daily: a historical tour (one hour), waterfall tour (two hours), waterfall and rainforest tour (three hours). Each will take you to out-of-the-way places along the coast and up into the rainforest on former Kohala sugar plantation land on rugged four-wheel motorcycles. You'll ride over backroads and fields, through lush gullies to waterfalls, come to the edge of ocean cliffs, or dip down to a pebble beach. These fully equipped machines let you get to places that you wouldn't be able to reach otherwise. Safe and reliable, the four-wheelers are easy to operate even for those who have had no experience on a motorcycle. Helmets, gloves, and goggles are supplied and instruction is given. Wear long pants and closed-toe shoes. Mention the website for a discount; reservations are recommended as the tours do get filled up quickly.

ZIPLINING

The ziplining business (also known as the business of suspending oneself on a line in the tree's canopy) is flourishing on the Big Island, with three new courses opening just in 2011. **Big Island Eco Adventures** (55-510 Hawi Rd., 808/889-5111, www.bigislandecoadventures. com, $169 per person plus tax) has a good reputation for not only their professionalism but also for having a more advanced course than other outfitters on the island. If you're keen on doing a zipline course (and really want something exciting), this course is your best bet. In addition to the four-hour zipline course, which consists of eight actual lines, guests are taken offroading on the way to and from the course the while guides provide excellent information about the history of the area and the surrounding natural environment. There are seven tours

KOHALA

daily beginning at 8 A.M. If you're on a tight schedule, book ahead of time because tours fill up; although you'll still probably be able to book a time, the options might be limited.

HELICOPTER TOURS

The majority of helicopter tours leave from the heliport just south of the Waikoloa resort area or from a heliport next to the Hilo airport. Companies tend to focus on tours to see lava at Hawai'i Volcanoes National Park, and the longer or deluxe tours will circle the island to get a glimpse of Waipi'o Valley and waterfalls in Kohala. These tours inevitably are expensive, but if you have the funds do it, people always say that it was their favorite part of the trip.

Sunshine Helicopters (808/882-1233 or 800/622-3144, www.sunshinehelicopters. com), one of the larger companies with service on each island, runs a 40-minute Kohala Mountain and Hamakua Valley tour ($170 per person with online discount) and a two-hour Volcano Deluxe tour that circles the island ($510 per person with online discount or $485 for the early-bird tour).

Another large operation with a spotless safety record, **Blue Hawaiian Helicopters** (808/886-1768 in Waikoloa, 800/786-2583, www.bluehawaiian.com) operates tours from both the Kona and Hilo sides with two helicopter options—the A-Star and the Eco-star. The difference between the helicopters is that the Eco-star is "the first touring helicopter of the 21st century," meaning that its seats are more comfortable, it is quieter, and it has larger windows for a less obstructed view than the A-Star. Most importantly, it costs more. From the Kona side, there are three tour options: a 90-minute Kohala Coast Adventure ($213 for A-Star, $259 for Eco-Star), the standard trip to see the waterfalls of the region; the two-hour Big Island Spectacular ($396, $495), an all-encompassing trip that circumvents the island to witness all its highlights; and the two-hour Big Island-Maui trip ($440, $495), a quick jaunt over to Maui to view Haleakala Crater and then a glimpse of the Kohala waterfalls on the way back. This particular tour has a six-person minimum.

Golf

The resorts in South Kohala offer half a dozen of the best golf courses in the state, and they are all within a few miles of each other.

Like rivers of green, the Waikoloa Scottish-links **Kings' Golf Course** (600 Waikoloa Beach Dr., 808/886-7888, http://waikoloa-beachgolf.com), designed by Tom Weiskopf and Jay Morrish, and the **Beach Golf Course** (808/886-6060), a Robert Trent Jones Jr. creation, wind their way around the hotels and condos of Waikoloa Beach Resort. Both have plenty of water and lava rock hazards, and each has its own clubhouse. Lessons, a golf clinic, and a half-day golf school can be arranged through both courses. Prices are reasonable (for the area), ranging $85–165. Off-property guests pay about $30 more per round than Waikoloa Beach Resort guests. Discounts are available

after 3 P.M. and for nine-hole rounds. Family golf days, where children under 17 play for a discounted rate (and with free rental), are a great deal.

Surrounding the Mauna Lani Bay Hotel are the marvelous **Francis H. I'i Brown North Course** and **Francis H. I'i Brown South Course,** whose artistically laid out fairways, greens, and sand traps make it a modern landscape sculpture. The 18-hole courses are carved from lava, with striking ocean views in every direction. Call the pro shop (808/885-6655) for information, tee times, clinics, and lessons. Discounts are available for booking online (www.maunalani.com/g_rates.htm). Guests pay $165, and non-resort guests can expect to pay at least $215 for a round.

The Mauna Kea's classic, trend-setting

Mauna Kea Golf Course (808/882-5400, www.princeresortshawaii.com/mauna-kea-golf-course/) was designed by the master, Robert Trent Jones Sr., and has been voted among America's 100 greatest courses and one of Hawaii's finest. Deceptive off the tee, it's demanding at the green. It lies near the ocean and has been joined by the more spread-out **Hapuna Golf Course** (808/880-3000, www.princeresortshawaii.com/hapuna-golf.php),

designed by Arnold Palmer and Ed Seay, which has been cut into the lava up above the hotels and highway. Both 18-hole courses give even the master players a challenge. Rates for the Mauna Kea course range $155–225 for resort guests depending on the time of day (discounts given for twilight play) and $250 for nonguests. The Hapuna course ranges $75–125 (discounts again for twilight play), and *kamaʻaina* discounts are also available.

Sights

KAWAIHAE
Puʻukohola Heiau National Historic Site

Whereas Puʻuhonua O Honaunau was (and is) the "city of refuge," Puʻukohola Heiau National Historic Site (Hwy. 270 between mile markers 2 and 3, 808/882-7218, www.nps.gov/puhe, gate hours 7:45 A.M.–4 P.M., park open 24 hours, free), which means "the temple on the hill of the whale," was a place of war. Present day, it is one of the best-preserved and most significant temple sites in Hawaii. A walk around the park will take you about 30–45 minutes, and if you want some additional information while walking around you can call 808/206-7056 for a self-guided cell phone audio tour or ask a ranger in the visitor center for a tour ($2 suggested donation) if one is available. You can also call ahead to reserve a tour, and I encourage you to do just that as the rangers are a true wealth of information about all things Hawaii. If you're bringing kids, ask the ranger for the Junior Ranger activity book, which offers fun activities to complete while visiting the park and it comes with a free Junior Ranger pin (they are available at all national parks so get ready to start your collection)!

The early morning is the best time to visit as that is when you have the best chance of seeing black tip reef sharks (and the chances are good); also keep a lookout for birds as the park ranger guarantees that you will see at least 10 different kinds during your visit.

◖ Hamakua Macadamia Nut Factory

The Hamakua Macadamia Nut Factory (Maluokalani St., off Hwy. 270 between mile markers 4 and 5, 808/882-1690, www.hawnnut.com, 9 A.M.–5:30 P.M.) might become your happy place (unless you have a tree nut allergy—then please don't go here). Imagine a room full of macadamia nuts of every variety imaginable (dark chocolate, Spam flavored, garlic, lightly salted, etc.), all available to sample for free. Candy corn, brittles, and coffee can be sampled as well. If you're planning on purchasing some nuts to take home the prices here are comparable to the local grocery stores. Or if you really love mac nuts, buy one of the four-pound bags—a good deal for about $32 depending on the variety. While nibbling on your samples you can also watch through a window the interior workings of the factory or try to crack a macadamia nut yourself at one of the interactive stations.

Pua Mau Place Botanical Garden

This 12-acre garden doesn't get much traffic, but it's quite a sight for plant enthusiasts. The one-hour self-guided tour through Pua Mau Place Botanical Garden (Ala Kahua Dr. off Hwy. 270 near mile marker 6, 808/882-0888, www.puamau.org, daily 9 A.M.–4 P.M., $8) takes you though the landscaped garden, an unlikely location here in arid Kohala. The focus here is on flowering plants, ones that

© HAWAII'S BIG ISLAND VISITOR BUREAU (BIVB)

The self-guided tour of the reconstructed village in Lapakahi State Historical Park is a favorite for kids and history buffs alike.

thrive and flourish in a windy and arid environment. While many plants have been established, some of the showiest are the hibiscus, plumeria, and date palm. With so much sunshine and so little rain, this is a harsh environment, and only certain types of plants survive. A greater challenge for the plants is that no pesticides are sprayed and brackish water is used for irrigation. Only the hardy make it, and those that do seem to love it. Heavy mulch guides you along the well-signed paths; plant numbers correspond to a book you take on your self-guided tour. A bit of whimsy is added by a fair number of giant bronze sculptures of insects that dot the garden here and there, the aviary, and the Magic Circle, a circle of stones reminiscent of megalithic stone monuments like Stonehenge. The garden is open for private functions such as weddings.

HAWI TO THE END OF THE ROAD
Lapakahi State Historical Park
Want to experience Hawaii as early settlers did 600 years ago? A visit to Lapakahi State Historical Park (Hwy. 270 between mile markers 13 and 14, daily 8 A.M.–4 P.M., gate closes 3:30 P.M.), a reconstructed historical village, is a good place for kids and history buffs. The self-guided tour is one of the better ones on the island because the pamphlet available at the small visitors center (if you can call it that) in the parking lot is user-friendly, and the trail is well marked and maintained (the trail is dirt but fairly even, and you can easily wear sandals on it). The trail, made up of two 0.5-mile loops, takes about 45 minutes. As you walk clockwise around the numbered stations, you pass canoe sheds and a fish shrine dedicated to Ku'ula, to whom the fishermen always dedicated a portion of their catch. A salt-making area demonstrates how the Hawaiians evaporated seawater by moving it into progressively smaller "pans" carved in the rock. There are numerous home sites along the wood-chip trail. Particularly interesting to children are exhibits of games like *konane* (Hawaiian checkers) and *'ulu maika* (a form of bowling using stones) that the children

are encouraged to try. Throughout the area, numerous trees, flowers, and shrubs are identified, and as an extra treat, migrating whales come close to shore December–April.

Upolu Airport Road Scenic Drive to Kohala Historical Sites State Monument

At mile marker 20, turn off Highway 270 down a one-lane road to Upolu airstrip. You'll know you're on Upolu Airport Road when you see the wind farm on your right. You really need a Jeep (but not a serious four-wheel-drive) to do the scenic drive. Follow the road until it reaches a dead end at the runway. Turn left onto a *very* rough dirt road (which may not be passable). This entire area is one of the most rugged and isolated on the Big Island, with wide windswept fields, steep sea cliffs, and pounding surf. Pull off at any likely spot along the road and keep your eyes peeled for signs of cavorting humpback whales, which frequent this coast November–May. After bumping down the road for about two miles (count on at least 45 minutes if you walk), turn and walk five minutes uphill to gain access to **Mo'okini Luakini Heiau.**

In 1962, Mo'okini Heiau was declared a national historic landmark. Legend says that the very first temple at Mo'okini was built as early as A.D. 480. This incredible date indicates that Mo'okini must have been built immediately upon the arrival of the first Polynesian explorers, who many scholars maintain arrived in large numbers a full two centuries later. Regardless of its age, the integrity of the remaining structure is remarkable and shows great skill in construction.

When you visit the *heiau* (temple), pick up a brochure from a box at the entrance (often empty); if none are available, a signboard nearby gives general information. The entire *heiau* is surrounded by a stone wall erected for its protection in 1981. In one corner of the enclosure is a traditional Hawaiian structure used in some of the temple ceremonies. On occasion, this building is blown down by the strong winds that lash this coast. Be aware of

the integration of its stone platform and notice how perfectly suited this thatched structure is to provide comfort against the elements in Hawaii. Look through the door at a timeless panorama of the sea and surf. Notice that the leeward stones of the *heiau* wall are covered in lichens, giving them a greenish cast and testifying to their age. A large, flat stone outside the wall was used to prepare victims for the sacrificial altar. Next to it and embedded in the ground is Kapakai, the guardian god in stone of the nearby King Kamehameha birth site. This stone was removed here in the mid-1900s for protection but will be returned to its original place when the time is right. The only entrance to the *heiau* itself is in the wall roughly facing southwest. Inside is an enclosure used by the person responsible for finding and catching the human sacrifices that were offered at the temple.

Once this was a closed temple only for the *ali'i,* but the *kapu* (restriction) was lifted in 1977 so that others may visit and learn. However, please be respectful as you walk around, as this temple is still in use, and stay on the designated paths, which are cordoned off by woven rope. Along the short wall closest to the sea is a "scalloped" altar where recent offerings of flowers are often seen. Inside the *heiau* are remnants of enclosures used by the *ali'i* and space set aside for temple priests. The floor of the temple is carpeted with well-placed stones and tiny green plants that give a natural mosaic effect.

A few minutes' walk south of the *heiau* along this coastal dirt track is **Kamehameha's birthplace,** called **Kamehameha 'Akahi 'Aina Hanau.** Rather unpretentious for being of such huge significance, the entrance to the area is at the back side, away from the sea. Inside the low stone wall, which always seems to radiate heat, are some large boulders believed to be the actual "birthing stones" where the high chiefess Kekuiapoiwa, wife of the warrior *ali'i* Keoua Kupuapaikalananinui, gave birth to Kamehameha sometime around 1758. There is much debate about the actual year and place of Kamehameha's birth, and some place it elsewhere in 1753, but it was to the Moʻokini Heiau nearby that he was taken for his birth rituals, and it was there that he performed his religious rituals until he completed Puʻu Kohola Heiau down the coast at Kawaihae around 1791. This male child, born as his father prepared a battle fleet to invade Maui, would grow to be the greatest of the Hawaiian chiefs—a brave, powerful, but lonely man, isolated like the flat plateau upon which he drew his first breath. The temple's ritual drums and haunting chants dedicated to Ku were the infant's first lullabies. He would grow to accept Ku as his god, and together they would subjugate all of Hawaii. In this expansive North Kohala area, Kamehameha was confronted with unencumbered vistas and sweeping views of neighboring islands, unlike most Hawaiians, whose outlooks were held in check by the narrow, confining, but secure walls of steep-sided valleys. Only this man with this background could rise to become "The Lonely One," high chief of a unified kingdom.

Together, Moʻokini Heiau, King Kamehameha's birthplace, and several other nearby historical sites make up the seven-acre **Kohala Historical Sites State Monument.**

In 2005, Kamehameha Schools bought a large tract of land surrounding Kamehameha's birthplace and Moʻokini Luakini Heiau in order to protect the environs from residential and commercial development that might disturb the sacred nature of these cultural sites.

Note: You'll have to return to Highway 270 the way you came because the road is closed off on the south end (but there is a small dirt turnaround there).

🄲 Pololu Valley Lookout and Beach

If you are looking for the *Lost* experience on the Big Island, the Pololu Valley lookout and beach (Hwy. 270 where the road ends) is it. Park your car in the lot at the end of the highway (there will be many other cars there catching the spectacular views of the coastline); grab your bathing suit, tent, some food and water; and hike the one-mile trail to the beach (about 30 minutes down and 45 minutes up for a novice hiker). If you're not interested in the hike, the view itself is worth driving to the road's end and simply staring for a few minutes. If you do walk down, the beach at the bottom

Enjoy the beautiful view at the Pololu Valley Lookout.

© MARK WASSER

has wonderful blackish sand, but the shoreline can be rocky and the waves hit hard depending on the day (you'll see surfers carrying boards down the trail—ask them about the conditions).

It's about 12 miles from Pololu Valley to Waipi'o Valley, with five deep-cut valleys in between, including the majestic Waimanu, the largest. It's not possible to drive to Waipi'o here (but we wish it were), but a super hiker could likely make it between the two.

Locals swear that you don't need a permit to stay here, and it's not patrolled at night—but don't worry, no safety issues ever have been reported. Pitch your tent on top of one of the small green hills (many already have fire pits left from previous campers) and it's likely that you will have the place to yourself, or you won't notice if anyone else is there. There are no facilities so make sure to bring enough food and water for your visit. Enjoy a nighttime dip in the ocean, but take care because the tide can be rough!

Shopping and Entertainment

SHOPPING
South Kohala: Resort Area

The two main shopping areas in Waikoloa, **Kings' Shops** and **Queens' MarketPlace,** are across the street from one another on Waikoloa Beach Drive. The Kings' Shops are more high-end restaurants and stores like Louis Vuitton, Coach, Tiffany's (if you need to propose to someone on vacation, for instance), and the tiniest Macy's that you will ever see (it is essentially just a room with cruise wear). Across the street, the Queens' MarketPlace offers more typical mall selections, such as Lids (hats), Claire's (jewelry), and Quicksilver (surfer clothing), as well as a food court (daily 7:30 A.M.–9:30 P.M. although individual restaurant times may vary) with Subway and Arby's.

Hawi to the End of the Road

Hawi and the adjoining Kapa'au epitomize the notion of "cute towns" with a small main street (it's actually Hwy. 270) lined with shops, galleries, and restaurants. It's definitely worth making a short detour here, parallel parking your car (there are so few occasions to do this on the Big Island!), and strolling from store to store. The entire walk will take you less than two hours (at most). Yes, there is some Hawaiiana here (check out the gift shop in the Bamboo Restaurant in Hawi), but this area has an artist colony feel to it, lending to goods that are higher quality than the standard kitsch you'll find in Kona or Hilo.

ENTERTAINMENT AND EVENTS
Entertainment

All the resort hotels in the area have bars with live music performances on the weekends and sometimes also weekday evenings. The Waikoloa Beach area hosts daily events at the Queens' MarketPlace, Kings' Shops, Hilton Waikoloa Village, and Waikoloa Beach Resort. Many of the events are free and can be found on the website (www.waikoloabeachresort.com). Many of the events are ideal for children—such as Hawaiian storytelling. One notable event is the weekly free concert with Big Island slack-key guitarist John Keawe. I highly urge you to attend that show. He plays other places on the island during the week, but you usually have to pay to see him.

For something a little bit more local style go to **Sansei Seafood Restaurant and Sushi Bar** (201 Waikoloa Beach Dr. in Queens' MarketPlace, 808/886-6286, www.dkrestaurants.com) for weekend karaoke coupled with cheap sushi and drink deals.

North of the resort area in Kawaihae, the **Blue Dragon Coastal Cuisine & Musiquarium** (Hwy. 270 between mile markers 3 and 4, 808/882-7771, www.bluedragon-hawaii.com) has the best of both worlds: live music and dancing. It's one of few places on the island where people get dressed up for a night out. No, it's not a club, it's more like an

KOHALA

old-timers' big band dance hall—classy and romantic with excellent (and kind of expensive) cocktails.

In Hawi, both **Bamboo Restaurant** (Hwy. 270, Hawi, 808/889-5555, www.bamboorestaurant.info) and **Luke's Place** (55-514 Hawi Rd., 808/889-1155, www.lukeskohala.com) have live music on the weekends. Bamboo's variety tends to be a little bit quieter (folks like John Keawe), while Luke's is a louder bar scene.

The larger resorts all hold *lu'au* on alternating days during the week (the Waikoloa Beach Resort calendar at www.waikoloabeachresort.com notes them). They mostly feel like factory *lu'au*—getting people in and out and fed quickly. While it is more convenient to simply attend a *lu'au* at your hotel, you might want to venture out for a more Cirque de Soleil experience (with more modern dance and less hula) at The Fairmont Orchid (www.fairmont.com/orchid). This *lu'au* is more expensive than its

counterparts, but the food is better than at other *lu'au* (which in some cases is downright terrible).

Events

There are numerous events in this area, many sponsored by the resort hotels and oftentimes involving golf. Some great resources so that you can become "in the know" are www.konaweb.com and the special events section of www.waikoloabeachresort.com.

One notable annual event for promising filmmakers and movie connoisseurs is the **Big Island Film Festival** (http://bigislandfilmfestival.com) in May at the Mauna Lani resort and The Fairmont Orchid. This celebration showcases narrative and short films from international filmmakers as well as Hawaii-based artists and was voted one of the "25 Coolest Film Festivals." Most screenings require a ticket, but some are shown free to the public, so check the schedule.

Food

SOUTH KOHALA: RESORT AREA

All the resorts in the area have at least one restaurant located on the premises. These restaurants, for the most part, are fine but not notable and tend to be more expensive than off-premises restaurants. If you don't want to travel too far away from your hotel or condo, but still want to eat out, there are some worthwhile options nearby.

This would be a number one spot on the Mainland, but given the immense amount of great sushi on the Big Island, **⬤ Sansei Seafood Restaurant and Sushi Bar** (201 Waikoloa Beach Dr., Queens' MarketPlace, 808/886-6286, www.dkrestaurants.com, dinner Sun.–Thurs. 5:30–10 P.M., Fri. and Sat. 5:30 P.M.–1 A.M., rolls $4–18, appetizers $3–14, entrées $18–48) is simply good. What is of note here is their amazing specials and the fact that it is open much later than almost any other restaurant around. The daily early-bird

special offers 25 percent off sushi, appetizers, and entrées 5–6 P.M., and locals get 50 percent off Sunday and Monday for early-bird dining. Friday and Saturday there is late night karaoke (free for 21 and over, 10 P.M.–1 A.M.) with drink specials and 50 percent off sushi and appetizers.

It's the **Starbucks** (201 Waikoloa Beach Dr., Queens' MarketPlace, www.starbucks.com, daily 5 A.M.–9:30 P.M.) you're familiar with from home, but it might save your life if you're jet-lagged and aching for coffee at 5 A.M. and nothing else is open. If you have a mild Starbucks addiction you might want to stock up here, as Starbucks shops on the Big Island are far and few between (there are only four other locations)! They also offer free wireless Internet (unlike many of the resorts in the area).

A fine restaurant by Peter Merriman, one of the well-known chefs of Hawaii Regional Cuisine, **Merriman's Market Café** (250 Waikoloa Beach Dr., Kings' Shops,

808/886-1700, daily 11:30 A.M.–9 P.M., happy hour 3–5:30 P.M., bar open till 9:30 P.M., $11–28) utilizes local ingredients to create standard dishes of fish, burgers, and salads. It isn't the same experience as Merriman's Waimea location, which is more upscale, but still a worthy choice especially given the children's menu, vegetarian options, and gluten-free accommodations.

If you're seeking something on the lighter side, **Juice 101** (68-1330 Mauna Lani Dr., The Shops at Mauna Lani, 808/887-2244, www. juicebar101.com, daily 7 A.M.–9 P.M.) is just what you're looking for. As their name implies, they have fresh juice squeezed from fruits and greens as well as smoothies ($6). Try the kale smoothie and *açai* bowl to energize you for the day. If that's not your thing, enjoy the breakfast bagels and a cup of coffee—just $1 if you bring your own mug. Lunch is available, and kid-friendly too, with options such as grilled cheese. It's more a takeout place than a dine-in joint, but they do have free wireless Internet.

Among the usual humdrum of resort restaurants, **◖ The Canoe House** (68-1400 Mauna Lani Dr., Mauna Lani Bay Hotel, 808/885-6622, www.maunalani.com/d_ch_overview. htm, $40) stands out. The menu is thoughtful, using local ingredients (as much as possible) to create beautiful well-thought-out dishes, and the wine list is extensive. I recommend any of the fresh fish or the rack of lamb. And the view! Right on the ocean, this restaurant makes for an ideal romantic evening (read: somewhere to get engaged or honeymoon or simply rekindle). Best of all, the chef is more than willing to accommodate food allergies.

Markets

Although slightly overpriced for the convenience of the location, the **Island Gourmet Market** (201 Waikoloa Beach Dr., Queens' MarketPlace, 808/886-3577, daily 7 A.M.–11 P.M.) has an excellent selection of local products (try the Kona brand chips), including local liquors and wines. It also houses a sushi bar, *poke* bar, and made-to-order sandwich bar. If you're looking to save some money while staying at a resort, this is where you should go to grab lunch or a steak to grill at your condo. Attached to the market is a **Wine Bar** with a good happy hour.

Foodland Farms (68-1330 Mauna Lani Dr., The Shops at Mauna Lani, 808/887-6101, daily 6 A.M.–11 P.M.) is the upscale version of the Foodland grocery chain, with a good selection of produce and in-house-made food to go, such as sushi, sandwiches, and prepared foods like chicken and short ribs. It also has an extensive liquor, wine, and beer section as well as a Redbox for DVD rental.

KAWAIHAE

There is a surprisingly large number of restaurants in this small place with not much going on. This area tends to attract the overflow of resort visitors seeking food outside the bounds of their hotel. Thus, the meal prices are somewhat higher than what you'd expect given the looks of the area. Since there is a harbor right in town many restaurants offer fresh seafood. If you visit a joint not listed here, you'd best order the fish with a simple preparation (like grilled or broiled) given that the restaurants tend to try to mask the fish with sauces that are not prepared well.

One of the most fun eating experiences on the Big Island, the **◖ Blue Dragon Coastal Cuisine & Musiquarium** (Hwy. 270 between mile markers 3 and 4, 808/882-7771, www.blue-dragonhawaii.com, Thurs.–Sun. 5:30–11 P.M., $30) is always crowded with locals and visitors alike dancing away the evening while breaking for bites of the coastal cuisine. The menu offers good choices of local fish and produce, and the online menu notes which items are gluten free, vegetarian, and/or vegan. The food is tasty and definitely highlights what the island has to offer—like the Hamakua mushroom dishes (so good!)—but the food can seem a bit overpriced and service can be slow when the place gets really bumping. Sometimes, however, you can find a coupon for the restaurant on the website or in the *Big Island Weekly* newspaper. What you're really paying for is the live entertainment, and it's worth it. Reservations are a must; however, if there are just one or two of you sometimes you can get a seat at the small bar. Kids are welcome (and there even is a *keiki* menu), but I would recommend bringing them early as the restaurant feels more like a club as it gets later.

The other choice close by is **Café Pesto** (Kawaihae Center, 808/882-1071, www.cafepesto.com, daily 11 A.M.–9 P.M., pizzas average $9, dinner mains $18–35), which feels entirely like your hometown Italian restaurant meets Hawaii. The menu is a little all over the place, from pizza and calzones to fish and Thai-style food. I'd stick with the Italian side of the menu. Vegetarian and gluten-free options are available. Reservations are recommended.

HAWI TO THE END OF THE ROAD

Hawi is the spot were ex-New Yorkers or ex-restaurateurs come to open restaurants, and you will reap the benefits of their decision. Nearly every restaurant in the area offers something better than the next. In fact, one of your biggest hardships in Hawaii will be finding time to eat everywhere in town.

Best known for their *liliko'i* (passion fruit) infused drinks, **Bamboo Restaurant** (Hwy. 270, Hawi, 808/889-5555, www.bamboorestaurant. info, Tues.–Sat. 11:30 A.M.–2 P.M. and 6–8 P.M., Sun. brunch 11:30 A.M.–2:30 P.M., happy hour Mon.–Fri. 4–6 P.M., $20) is a Hawi mainstream offering classic dishes like chicken, fish, and vegetarian options such as polenta with a hint of Hawaiiana—meaning that the standard dishes are seasoned with teriyaki sauce, coconut milk (making the food taste almost Thai-like), and of course passion fruit sauces galore. The food is good enough (yet slightly overrated by reviews), but the restaurant is located in an early 1900s building that provides a wonderful ambiance for a hot afternoon, and the overall experience (including their excellent cocktails and award-winning desserts) is worthwhile. Live music on Friday and Saturday nights.

A few doors down from Bamboo Restaurant, **Lighthouse Deli** (55-3419 Akoni Pule Hwy./Hwy. 270, Hawi, www.lighthousedelihi.com, 808/889-5757, Mon.–Sat. 10 A.M.–6 P.M., Sun.

9 A.M.–4 P.M., happy hour Mon.–Fri. 4–6 P.M., $12) is the Jewish deli you've been looking for in Hawaii. Classic deli sandwiches are served on locally made bread (many of their ingredients are local when available). They have wine and beer on draft, not to mention they own the **Lighthouse Liquors** store (808/889-0505, Sun.–Tues. noon–8 P.M., Wed.–Sat. 11 A.M.–10 P.M.) next door, which has an extensive wine and beer selection, and you're welcome to pick something up there to pair with your meal as well. Although there is a tasty mozzarella salad available, the vegetarian and gluten-free options are limited (this is really a meat lover's place). The Sunday brunch is a big hit in town, and likewise you'll want to come early to get a taste of their Benedict (with various meat and fish offerings). Limited seating is available inside, but the additional sidewalk seating makes for a wonderful people-watching spot (and kind of makes you feel like you're in New York).

Next door to Lighthouse Deli, one of few authentic Mexican restaurants on the island, **Mi Ranchito** (55-3419 Akoni Pule Hwy./Hwy. 270, Hawi, daily 11 A.M.–8 P.M., $9–16), is a true taquería and one of the best choices if you're looking for something a little less pricey than the majority of Hawi restaurants. The price is right and the portions are huge. Vegetarian and gluten-free options available. You won't see it from the street; it is in the interior of the building where Lighthouse Liquors is located (it's convenient, though; you can grab a beer to have with your meal).

If you're looking for a quick to-go treat while strolling the streets, stop in to **Kohala Coffee Mill** (55-3412 Akoni Pule Hwy./Hwy. 270, Hawi, 808/889-5577, Mon.–Fri. 6 A.M.–6 P.M., Sat.–Sun. 7 A.M.–6 P.M., $7–10) for an ice cream cone or a cookie or take a seat outdoors and listen to a live music performance that tends to pop up on any given day. This is a laid-back coffee shop with beverages like hot coffee and ice-cold chai as well as breakfast bagel sandwiches. Salads and hamburgers are available for lunch.

Originally opened in 1950 and now owned by Big Island Eco Adventures (your zipline outfitter), **Luke's Place** (55-514 Hawi Rd.,

Hawi, 808/889-1155, www.lukeskohala.com, 11:30 A.M.–9 P.M., happy hour 3–6 P.M., $12) serves up bar food that is better than the usual fare at reasonable prices for large portions. The burgers, which are made from Big Island beef, are flavorsome and have the usual fixings. A good vegetarian option is the veggie wrap. Many people eat here for convenience before or after their zipline trip, but there is better food in town if you're not in a rush or not on a budget. There is a nighttime scene here, so it is worth stopping by after dinner for drinks and live music. Drinks are 20 percent off all day Thursday for "Thirsty Thursdays," and the bar stays open until *pau* (when everyone is finished).

A real treat for those who love sushi and even those who do not, the rolls at ◖ **Sushi Rock**

(55-3435 Akoni Pule Hwy./Hwy. 270 in Hawi Town, 808/889-5900, www.sushirockrestaurant.net, daily noon–3 P.M. and 5:30–8 P.M., rolls $17) truly are a fusion of traditional sushi combinations and local ingredients, such as purple sweet potatoes with ahi and goat cheese. Don't forget to ask for the local wasabi grown in Volcano. It really tastes different (and so much better) than the green wasabi you're used to getting at sushi restaurants. Rolls can be ordered individually or by platter, such as the Ali'i ($64), which includes 32 premium rolls. Feel free to ask the chef to pick your rolls if you can't decide for yourself. The platters are a good deal but the larger platters are a better deal if you're with friends as it is a lot of sushi to eat. There are vegetarian and gluten-free options available.

Information and Services

EMERGENCY SERVICES

There are no major hospitals located in this region; for serious emergencies head to Kona or Waimea for the best care.

For minor emergencies, try the **Kohala Family Health Center** (53-3925 Akoni Pule Hwy./Hwy. 270, 808/889-6236, Mon.–Fri. 8 A.M.–7 P.M., Sat. 9 A.M.–1 P.M.) in Kapa'au just north of Hawi. This clinic is the only place in the area where there is a pharmacy, so it's better to pick up your prescriptions in Kona or Waimea, where the chain pharmacies are located.

BANKS

There are no bank branches in the resort areas of South Kohala. However, **First Hawaiian Bank** ATMs are available in the Queens' MarketPlace, Waikoloa Golf Course, The Fairmont Orchid, and in Kawaihae at the Minit Stop (like a 7-Eleven). A **Bank of Hawaii** branch (including an ATM) is located in the middle of Kapa'au town.

POST OFFICES

Sometimes it seems like there are post offices every few miles in Hawaii—that is not the case

DON'T FORGET TO GAS UP

If you're heading back to the airport from the Kohala Coast, the last gas station you'll pass before you get to the airport is the Shell station in the Kings' Shops in the Waikoloa resort area. The problem is that it's still about 20 miles from the airport, but if you top your tank off you should be okay. Likewise, there isn't a close gas station south of the airport either! The closest station is probably at Costco in Kailua and isn't open early in the morning or late at night. If you're heading north from Waikoloa, your next gas station is about 15 miles away in Kawaihae.

here, probably since the resort areas aren't actual towns. The closest post office to the resort area is up the hill in Waikoloa Village (68-1875 Pua Melia St.). If you have postal needs in northern Kohala go to the Hawi post office (55-515 Hawi Rd.), just off the main drag through town.

Getting There and Around

It is possible, with some good planning, to make it from the Kona side to the Hilo side and from Kona to Kohala on the **Hele-On Bus** (www.heleonbus.org, 808/961-8744, $1 per ride, $1 each for luggage, large backpacks, bikes).

FROM NORTH KOHALA TO SOUTH KOHALA

The North Kohala to South Kohala route bus essentially is a commuter route for those who work at the resorts. It only runs once daily Monday–Saturday, leaving from Kapa'au at 6:30 A.M., making stops south of Highway 270 (such as in Hawi and Kawaihae) and then on Highway 19 at all the resorts, ending at 7:40 A.M. at the Hilton Waikoloa Village. The bus returns north from the Hilton Waikoloa Village at 4:15 P.M., arriving in Kapa'au at 5:35 P.M.

FROM KOHALA TO KONA AND KEAUHOU VIA WAIMEA

A second option gets you farther south to Kona and east to Waimea, but unfortunately only runs Monday–Friday. The bus leaves from Kapa'au at 6:45 A.M. and travels south on Highway 270 to the junction of Highway 19, where it goes east to Waimea, arriving at the Parker Ranch Shopping Center at 7:45 A.M. From the Parker Ranch Shopping Center it is possible to connect on a different bus to the Hamakua Coast and Hilo. Otherwise, if you stay on the bus the route continues south on the upper road to Kona, stopping eventually on Ali'i Drive and ending at the Keauhou Shopping Center at 9:50 A.M. The bus makes the return trip leaving from the Keauhou Shopping Center at 1:35 P.M., arriving in Waimea at 3:25 P.M., and ending in Kapa'au at 4:55 P.M.

If you are trying to get straight to Kona or Keauhou and it's a Saturday (because this bus doesn't run any other day), it is better to take the direct bus that leaves Kapa'au at 9:15 A.M., arriving in Keauhou at 11:45 A.M. and returning at 2:30 P.M., arriving in Kapa'au at 4:35 P.M.

KA'U

While Ka'u often serves simply as the stretch that gets visitors between Kona and Volcanoes National Park, hidden away off the main highway are magnificent secluded beaches of all colors (from green to black to white sand) and sizes. Some of these beaches require a greater sense of adventure than others, and with that some of these journeys require more than just the average rental car (an all-wheel-drive or four-wheel-drive will serve you well here).

Formed from the massive slopes of Mauna Loa, the Ka'u district presents some of the most ecologically diverse land in the islands. The bulk of it stretches 50 miles from north to south and almost 30 miles from east to west, housing the longest undeveloped (or underdeveloped, depending on one's perspective) coastline in the state. Ka'u also holds the esteemed distinction of being "the southernmost place" in the United States, and many establishments in the area are happy to remind you of this fact and provide you with excellent picture opportunities.

At the bottom of Ka'u is **Ka Lae** (South Point), the southernmost tip of Hawaii and the southernmost point in the United States. It lies at a latitude 500 miles farther south than Miami and 1,000 miles below Los Angeles. Ka Lae was probably the first landfall made by the Polynesian explorers on the islands, and the entire area, particularly the more watered coastal spots, seems to have been heavily populated by early immigrants. A variety of archaeological remains support this belief.

In modern times, Ka'u was sugar country, and the vestiges of this era can still be seen in places like Pahala town, where one can rent out

HIGHLIGHTS

LOOK FOR ◖ TO FIND RECOMMENDED SIGHTS, ACTIVITIES, DINING, AND LODGING.

◖ **Manuka Bay:** Getting to Manuka Bay is a four-wheel-drive adventure – and it's worth it. The secluded white-sand beach is reminiscent of Mexico, and you can occupy your entire day by searching for ancient petroglyphs or foraging for salt (page 100).

◖ **Green Sand Beach (Papakolea):** A semiprecious stone called olivine gives the soft sand here its distinctive green tinge (page 101).

◖ **Punalu'u Black Sand Beach:** You're almost guaranteed to see turtles basking in the sun at this popular, easily accessed beach (page 103).

◖ **South Point Road and Ka Lae (South Point):** Drive down scenic South Point Road to Ka Lae, the southernmost place in the United States, for one of the most thrilling activities possible on the Big Island – a 50-foot jump into the ocean (page 105).

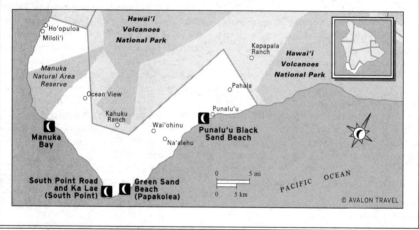

the entire seven-bedroom Plantation House, where the sugar plantation manager once lived. Nowadays, Ka'u is better known for its macadamia nut and coffee farms. In fact, some locals argue that Ka'u coffee is much better than its Kona counterpart. Nightlife in Ka'u is somewhat lacking, but it doesn't matter much because you will be exhausted from the long walk (or bumpy drive) to the secret beach or from jumping off of South Point. Regardless, it's worth packing it in early in order to get an early start at the Saturday swap meet in Ocean View (it doesn't get more local than this) or a walk through the private lava tubes of Kula Kai Caverns.

In Ka'u the sleepy former plantation towns don't even know how quaint they are, and at beach parks you can count on finding a secluded spot to pitch a tent. While Ka'u's main towns, **Ocean View, Na'alehu,** and **Pahala** are little more than pit stops, the real charms of the region, tucked away down secondary roads are hardly given a look by most unknowing visitors. If you take the time and get off the beaten track, you'll discover deserted beaches, turtles basking on the shore, a Tibetan Buddhist temple, and an electricity farm sprouting windmill generators. The upper slopes and broad pasturelands are the domain of hunters, hikers, and *paniolo,* who still ride the range on sure-footed horses. The majority of Ka'u's pleasures are accessible by standard rental car, but many secluded coastal spots can be reached only by

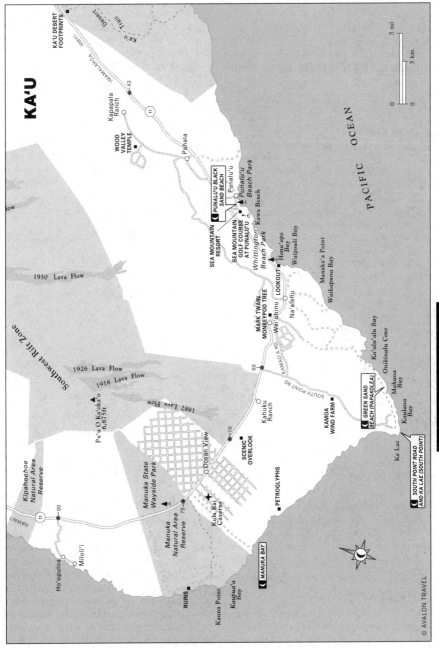

KA'U

KA'U DESERT FOOTPRINTS

Ka'u Desert

Ka'u Trail

MAMALAHOA HWY.

43

11

Kapapala Ranch

WOOD VALLEY TEMPLE

Pahala

1950 Lava Flow

PUNALU'U BLACK SAND BEACH

Punalu'u

Punalu'u Beach Park

SEA MOUNTAIN RESORT

SEA MOUNTAIN GOLF COURSE AT PUNALU'U

Whittington Beach Park

Kawa Beach

PACIFIC OCEAN

Hono'apo Bay

Waipouli Bay

Manaka'a Point

Waikapuna Bay

Southwest Rift Zone

1926 Lava Flow

1916 Lava Flow

1887 Lava Flow

Pu'u O Ka'oka'o 6,875ft

MARK TWAIN MONKEYPOD TREE

Wai'ohinu

LOOKOUT

Na'alehu

69

KAMOA RD.

SOUTH POINT RD.

Ka'alu'alu Bay

Onikinikia Cove

Mahana Bay

GREEN SAND BEACH (PAPAKOLEA)

Kaulana Bay

Ka Lae

SOUTH POINT ROAD AND KA LAE (SOUTH POINT)

Kahuku Ranch

76

SCENIC OVERLOOK

KAMOA WIND FARM

Kipahoehoe Natural Area Reserve

HAWAI'I

89

11

Ho'opuloa

Miloli'i

Manuka State Wayside Park

Ocean View

Manuka Natural Area Reserve

79

Kula Kai Caverns

PETROGLYPHS

MANUKA BAY

RUINS

Kauna Point

Kaupua'a Bay

PACIFIC OCEAN

5 mi

5 km

0

0

© AVALON TRAVEL

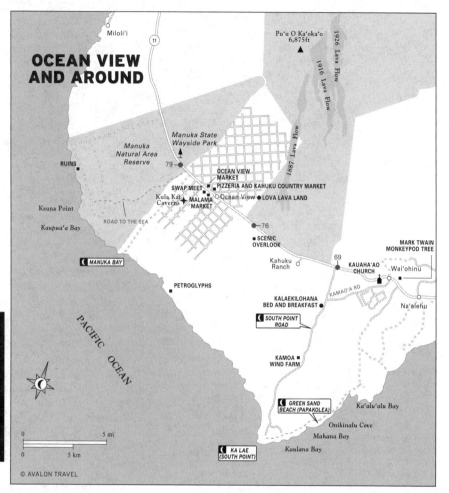

OCEAN VIEW AND AROUND

Miloli'i

11

Pu'u O Ka'oka'o
6,875ft

1926 Lava Flow

1916 Lava Flow

1887 Lava Flow

Manuka State
Wayside Park

Manuka
Natural Area
Reserve   79

RUINS

OCEAN VIEW
MARKET

SWAP MEET   PIZZERIA AND KAHUKU COUNTRY MARKET
Kula Kai   MALAMA   Ocean View   LOVA LAVA LAND
Caverns   MARKET

Kauna Point

Kaupua'a Bay   ROAD TO THE SEA

76

MANUKA BAY

SCENIC
OVERLOOK

MARK TWAIN
MONKEYPOD TREE

Kahuku
Ranch   69   KAUAHA'AO
CHURCH   Wai'ohinu

PETROGLYPHS

KALAEKILOHANA
BED AND BREAKFAST   KAMAO'A RD
Na'alehu

SOUTH POINT
ROAD

PACIFIC OCEAN

KAMOA
WIND FARM

GREEN SAND
BEACH (PAPAKOLEA)   Ka'alu'alu Bay

Onikinalu Cove

Mahana Bay

Kaulana Bay

0   5 mi

0   5 km

KA LAE
(SOUTH POINT)

© AVALON TRAVEL

KA'U

four-wheel-drive. Those willing to abandon their cars and hike the sparsely populated coast or interior of Ka'u are rewarded with areas unchanged and untouched for generations. Time in Ka'u moves slowly, and *aloha* still forms the basis of day-to-day life.

ORIENTATION

All the towns of Ka'u and main sights lie along Highway 11 or a few smaller byways that lead you from the highway into the backcountry.

Ocean View and Around

Driving south from the town of Captain Cook on the Kona side, after miles of uninterrupted winding road (not the easiest for those inclined to carsickness) Ocean View is the first town you'll pass—a sight for sore eyes for those who need to use the restroom, get a drink, or fill up on gas. Ocean View, with its cheap property for sale, is where many families move to build their retirement homes or the homes they would never be able to afford on the Kona side.

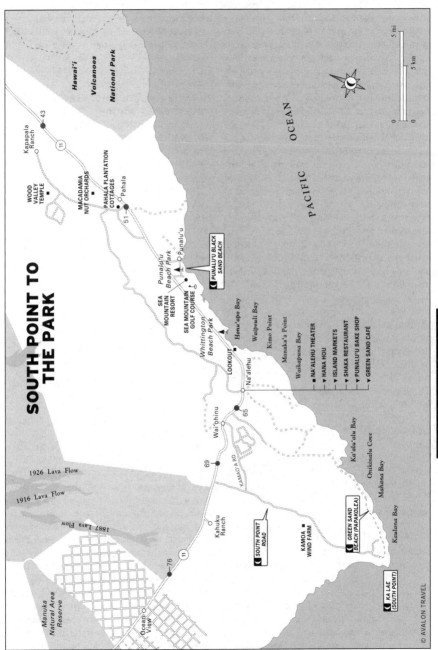

SOUTH POINT TO THE PARK

Hawai'i Volcanoes National Park

Kapapala Ranch

(11)

43

WOOD VALLEY TEMPLE

MACADAMIA NUT ORCHARDS

PAHALA PLANTATION COTTAGES

Pahala

51

Punalu'u

PUNALU'U BLACK SAND BEACH

Punalu'u Beach Park

SEA MOUNTAIN RESORT

SEA MOUNTAIN GOLF COURSE

Whittington Beach Park

Honu'apo Bay

Waiouli Bay

Kimo Point

Manaka'a Point

LOOKOUT

Nā'ālehu

Waikapuna Bay

■ NĀ'ĀLEHU THEATER
▼ HANA HOU
▼ ISLAND MARKETS
▼ SHAKA RESTAURANT
▼ PUNALU'U BAKE SHOP
▼ GREEN SAND CAFÉ

PACIFIC OCEAN

Wai'ōhinu

65

69

KAMAOA RD

Ka'alu'alu Bay

Omikinalu Cove

Mahana Bay

1926 Lava Flow

1916 Lava Flow

Kahuku Ranch

SOUTH POINT ROAD

KAMOA ■ WIND FARM

GREEN SAND BEACH (PAPAKOLEA)

Kaulana Bay

KĀ LAE (SOUTH POINT)

1887 Lava Flow

Manuka Natural Area Reserve

(11)

76

Ocean View

© AVALON TRAVEL

0   5 mi

0   5 km

Before you get to Ocean View, you have a sense of what the area is like when you stop at the highway scenic lookout spot near mile marker 75 and view the strong black lava flows that fill the horizon. Ocean View is often referred to as the largest subdivision in the state. In fact, it is a conglomeration of five subdivisions that is several miles wide and that pushes up the mountain about six miles and down toward the ocean another three. The highest lots are at about 5,000 feet. This unincorporated town of self-sufficient individuals who don't want to be bothered by anyone has been carved out of rough volcanic rubble with an overlay of trees and bush.

Services are located in two small shopping centers that flank the highway. Above the highway is Ocean View Town Center, and below the highway is Pohue Plaza. Besides a visit to the Kula Kai Caverns, there frankly is little to do in Ocean View itself if you are a visitor, but as there are few lights and little air pollution, this is one of the greatest locations for stargazing in the islands without going up to the top of the mountain. Note: Ocean View has some of the highest asthma rates on the island because it's downwind from the vog (volcanic smog) of Hawai'i Volcanoes National Park. Those with respiratory issues may want to pass by this area quickly.

South Point to Na'alehu

Looking at a map of the Big Island, South Point is exactly what you think it is—the very south landmass of the island and actually (technically) the United States of America. If you don't have time to visit the point itself (in Hawaiian it is known Ka Lae—The Point), you can catch the view as you approach the area from the west side of the island. Look for the massive windmills (many of them defunct) dotting the land and you'll know that you've seen South Point.

Cashing in on its proximity to South Point, the closest town, Na'alehu, is best known as the place that has all the "southernmost" restaurants, bars, and bakeries. It is a mecca of southernism, and in addition to that fun fact it

has some of the better culinary delights in the area. Check out the overhanging monkeypod trees forming a magnificent living tunnel in front of some of the former plantation managers' homes as you pass through on Highway 11.

Highway 11 South of Hawai'i Volcanoes National Park

As you climb north up the coast you'll pass through the small former community of Punalu'u. Punalu'u was an important port during the sugar boom of the 1880s and even had a railroad. Notice the tall coconut palms in the vicinity and the fishpond behind the beach, both unusual for Ka'u. Punalu'u means "diving spring," so named because freshwater springs can be found on the floor of the bay—making for some cold ocean water. Native divers once paddled out to sea, then dove with calabashes that they filled with freshwater from the underwater springs. This was the main source of drinking water for the region.

The string of flat-topped hills in the background is the remains of volcano cones that became dormant about 100,000 years ago. In sharp contrast with them is **Lo'ihi Seamount,** 20 miles offshore and about 3,000 feet below the surface of the sea. This very active submarine volcano is steadily building and should reach the surface in just a few tens of thousands of years. Opportunists suggest investing in real estate there now.

Some 22 miles southwest of Hawai'i Volcanoes National Park is Pahala, clearly marked off Highway 11. The Hawai'i Belt Road flashes past this town, but if you drive into it, you'll find one of the best-preserved examples of a classic sugar town in the islands. Not long ago, the hillsides around Pahala were blanketed by fields of cane and dotted with camps of plantation workers. It was once gospel that sugar would be king in these parts forever, but the huge mill is gone, and the background whir of a modern macadamia nut–processing plant now breaks the stillness. Change is afoot in Ka'u, just like everywhere in Hawaii. Sugar land has been sold, mostly in big chunks. Some may develop their land into ranches or

YOUR BEST DAY IN KA'U

- Start with an early morning lava tube tour with **Kula Kai Caverns.**

- Head to **Ka Lae** (South Point) and jump off the cliff.

- After you recover, travel farther down South Point Road for a not-too-bad hike or a bumpy ride to the **Green Sand Beach** to swim and to view, as the name implies, a beach with green sand.

- Or if you want to just relax, head straight to the **Punalu'u Black Sand Beach,** where you are guaranteed to see some turtles.

- Stop in at **Hana Hou** (the southernmost restaurant in the United States) for lunch (you can get it to go if you're heading to the beach) or dinner, and don't forget the award-winning

pie. If it's a Friday night you might be able to catch some live local music while you eat.

RAINY DAY ALTERNATIVE

The Ka'u district is one of the driest on the Island, so keep your fingers crossed that you don't witness one of their few wet days. If you happen to be around during a short downpour, not all is lost. Although they aren't always available for last-minute reservations, try booking a lava tube tour with **Kula Kai Caverns.** Nudging your way through these private lava tubes is a great way to stay dry while still having the opportunity to do some exploring. A second option is to drive to Wood Valley (via the highway along a scenic route) with the **Wood Valley Temple** as your destination. Wood Valley is already lush and green, and a little rain will only make it seem more extraordinary.

residential areas, while smaller plots are being turned into farms. At least 40 farms now produce Ka'u coffee in hillside plantations above Pahala; while not as well known as Kona coffee, it's gaining a reputation for itself.

PLANNING YOUR TIME

Although one could easily spend two or three days in this region, realistically, most visitors spend at most a day in this area as they travel back and forth from Kona and Hawai'i Volcanoes National Park. The best way to experience Ka'u is as a mini road trip—starting either on the west or east side of the district and stopping at successive places of interest dotted along Highway 11.

Ka'u often is the hottest part of the island, thus sights and beaches such as driving down South Point Road, walking to the Green Sand Beach, and exploring the Kahuku section of Hawai'i Volcanoes National Park are best experienced early in the morning while the day is still cool. The best midday adventures are those that involve cooling off. The easiest beach to access is the shaded Punalu'u Black Sand Beach,

and just because it is easy to get to doesn't make it any less attractive. In fact, this beach often becomes very crowded with locals picnicking and camping as well as visitors flocking to get a look at the many turtles that make Punalu'u their home (I can't guarantee much in life, but I can pretty much promise you'll see a turtle here).

If some alone time is what you're needing, those eager to use their shiny new four-wheel-drive cars can head to secluded beaches to bathe via the very rough Road to the Sea or Manuka Bay Road. If hot-weather off-roading doesn't suit you, but you're still keen for something out of the ordinary, make a reservation with Kula Kai Caverns to spelunk yourself (with a guide) through one of the most complex lava tube systems in the world.

For those on the culinary tour of the island, Ka'u houses the essential stops of the Hana Hou restaurant and Punalu'u Bake Shop, both in Na'alehu. These establishments know their desserts—macadamia nut pie, sweet breads, and *malasadas*—and will be welcome treats regardless of if you're heading to the national park or back to Kona.

KA'U

Beaches

OCEAN VIEW AND AROUND
◖ Manuka Bay

If you're tired of the busloads of tourists at other beaches, this is the spot for you. Without a doubt, you will think you are lost as you traverse the lava rocks on your way to the beach at Manuka Bay (Hwy. 11 near mile marker 83). The white-sand beach is secluded (reminiscent more of Mexico beaches than ones in Hawaii), and you can occupy your entire day by searching for the ancient petroglyphs on the north side of the bay or foraging for salt (collect some in a zipper-lock bag, take it home, and let it dry—you have your own Hawaiian sea salt). Watch out for the bees (don't bring honey or just remember your epi pen). On a recent visit they were swarming in abundance.

A four-wheel-drive is a must for this adventure, and in many ways this beach outing is as much about off-roading as it is about enjoying the beach. Near mile marker 83, turn right onto a dirt road on the *makai* side of the highway. A good marker to watch for when looking for this unmarked road is a sign about respecting the area that is sometimes located where the unmarked Manuka Bay road meets Highway 11. If you get to Manuka State Wayside Park, you've gone too far. Once on the road, always veer to the right if the road forks. The ride can be a difficult and long one, but it is well worth it.

Road to the Sea

Another excellent opportunity to go four-wheeling to a beach, the six-mile-long road called Road to the Sea (Hwy. 11 between mile markers 79 and 80) is very rough and not for the faint at heart (or for those who get carsick).

You'll need four-wheel-drive to get to Manuka Bay, but you're likely to have the place all to yourself.

© MARK WASSER

KA'U SCENIC DRIVE

The drive northeast on Highway 11 from Na'alehu to Hawai'i Volcanoes National Park is one of the prettiest drives on the Big Island for its splendid views of the coast and the rolling green hills (often filled with cows) on the *mauka* side of the road. As lovely as this drive is, if you've done it a bunch of times already or are just looking to spice things up, there is an alternative way to go on the upper road through the hills. This drive is slower than the highway route (the road is dirt but doesn't require a four-wheel-drive), but the views are spectacular and you'll feel like you have the entire island to yourself.

The drive can start from either direction – from the north in Pahala (about 22 miles south of Hawai'i Volcanoes National Park) or from the south in Na'alehu. It is somewhat easier to start in Na'alehu because the route is obvious from there. The drive starts on Ka'alaiki Road, directly to the left of the Punalu'u Bake Shop. Drive up the hill (passing a cemetery on your left) and continue up the hill veering right. Continue on this road for nearly 45 minutes, passing ranches, a large metal ball that is actually the southernmost FAA radar used for air traffic control, coffee plantations, and macadamia nut trees. The drive will end in the western part of Pahala town (you will sense that you've come to the end), and you can turn either left or right to get through the town and back to Highway 11. The easier way is to turn left and drive about 0.6 mile and then make a sharp right onto Pikake Street (which is likely unmarked here) and left onto Kamani Street, which leads back to Highway 11. Note: If you turn left (or north) onto Pikake Street (instead of turning right to get onto the highway), Pikake turns into Wood Valley Road and you can extend your drive and check out the Wood Valley Temple.

Turn *makai* onto the dirt road. Amazingly, as you will see, people live on this road and make the commute daily. The entire drive could take you almost 45 minutes for the short distance, but the journey is worth it to arrive at a secluded green- and black-sand beach where you can swim and snorkel (although do so carefully as the water depth drops off quickly).

Before you get to the end of the Road to the Sea where you'll find the secluded beach, on the right side of the road you will see a clear turnoff to another bad road. This road is a super four-wheel-drive road that requires a lot of clearance. If you can make it part of the way on the turnoff road, it's not too far to get out of the car and simply walk to the ocean (you'll see it). If you make it the full way, it will take you to Manuka Bay.

SOUTH POINT TO NA'ALEHU
◖ Green Sand Beach (Papakolea)
Ever wonder what happens when lava containing olivine, a green semiprecious stone, becomes weathered into sand-like particles? A visit to the Green Sand Beach (off of South Point Rd. from Hwy. 11 between mile markers 69 and 70) can answer this question for you. Don't expect to see something bright green—there is more of a green tinge to the sand. Getting to the beach is a process in itself, and some visitors like to make a day out of it (you can probably just make a half day out of it). You'll know you've arrived to the beach when you see an eroded cinder cone at the edge of the sea. Getting down to the beach takes some skill—go slow and use the path that has already been carved out. Watch your footing to ensure that you don't slip down. The sand here is soft (and greenish) and a nice place to relax, but it can get windy. Also, assess the water conditions before you get in as the waves here can get rough. If you're enjoying yourself so much that you don't want to leave, consider staying over. People do camp here, but it's unofficial and there is a chance of getting kicked out (although highly unlikely). There are no facilities around this area (even in the parking area), so prepare ahead of time.

To get to the beginning of the road/trail to the beach, take South Point Road to the end and then drive toward the left a few minutes on an obvious dirt road. You'll likely see other cars there. You'll know when to stop when you see other cars parked in a makeshift parking area near the ocean (but not directly next to it). From here you can drive to the beach or walk. Note: Locals really encourage visitors to walk, as driving is causing the land in this area to severely erode quickly.

From the "parking area," the road or trail to the Green Sand Beach starts near the boat ramp. If you're driving, the road here is a bit rougher than what you just drove on, so judge wisely if your car can handle it or not. From the parking area to the beach is an easy 45-minute walk (less than three miles)—just stay to the left. Bring lots of water, a hat, and some sunscreen given that the walk is completely in the sun and can get hot. The drive will still take you about 20 minutes (even though it's not that far), as it takes some skill to navigate over the rough terrain.

HIGHWAY 11 SOUTH OF HAWAI'I VOLCANOES NATIONAL PARK
Whittington Beach Park

Located three miles north of Na'alehu, Whittington Beach Park (Hwy. 11 near mile marker 60) makes for a great picnic stop or place to stretch your legs. The turnoff to the park is well marked from the main highway. On the north (or left) side of the parking lot are tide pools that are protected from the powerful ocean tide—an ideal area for snorkeling and swimming. It's also a great place to see turtles. On the right side (past the picnic tables) is a sugar plantation ruin—the remnants of an old dock. A rail line from the Ka'u cane lands terminated here for shipment of raw sugar to be processed elsewhere. You can walk out on the old dock and watch the waves. Camping here is possible (with a county permit), and the facilities, which include restrooms, drinking fountain, and a covered picnic area, are well-maintained, making this a good place to pitch a tent.

Kawa Beach is often deserted compared to the nearby crowded Punalu'u Black Sand Beach.

Kawa Beach

A black-sand beach much quieter (nearly secluded in fact) than its counterpart, Punalu'u, down the road, Kawa Beach (Hwy. 11 between mile markers 58 and 59) is Hawaiian Homeland territory, and therefore it's essential that you are friendly to those who reside on that land. There are no signs to alert you to the turnoff, just a bunch of Kanaka Maoli flags (*kanaka maoli* means "true people" in the Hawaiian language) and signs that say "take back Hawaii." The unmarked road is obvious, as others have journeyed on it before, and is not rental-car friendly. It will take you about 10 minutes to drive to the beach, and when you arrive you'll be happy you did. Locals use it for surfing (apparently it is known as an ancient surfing spot), but amateurs should be cautious of the waves here.

◖ Punalu'u Black Sand Beach

If you want to see some turtles lazily basking in the sun, I can almost guarantee that you will see one (and so will the busloads of tourists that you'll have to compete with to take a picture) at Punalu'u Black Sand Beach (Hwy. 11 between mile markers 56 and 57). It is the most easily accessible and nicest beach in the area, so it can get pretty busy on weekends. Park on either the right side of the beach near the picnic stands and bathroom area or on the left side closer to the beach itself (but farther from the bathrooms and shower). Closer to the left-side parking area (where there are drinks for sale on the weekends out of a shack) is a pond that is rumored to be privately maintained. It is completely out of place here and lovely for its peacefulness. Filled with lily pads and ducks, it's a wonder how it got there and how it could be side-by-side with palm trees and black sand. Camping is allowed here, and on holiday weekends local families take full advantage of it and it can get packed.

Recreation

KA'U

FISHING

The Ka'u coast with its impressive jagged coastline offers excellent conditions for shore fishing. If you are at South Point or Road to the Sea you'll likely see locals with their huge trucks and extremely long and flexible rods fishing for *ulua*, a general term for reef fish of several varieties that usually weigh between ten and a hundred pounds! You don't need a permit to fish in this area, but you'll need to respect the locals as fishing (and especially night fishing) can be a territorial endeavor, and your efforts in the same spot might not be welcomed. There aren't any rental places around here so you'll need to bring your own equipment.

HIKING

Ocean View and Around
MANUKA STATE WAYSIDE PARK

Once a privately owned botanical garden, the 13.4-acre Manuka State Wayside Park (Hwy. 11 near mile marker 81) perhaps is a must-see for plant enthusiasts who want to view the over 150 species of trees located here, but it's definitely not a necessary stop for those with limited time. There is signage to help you identify the flora you'll see over the two-mile loop around the park. The trail is easy and will only take you about 60–90 minutes to complete. There is a small lava pit to look at around the halfway point. Don't forget to lather on the mosquito spray before you go.

South Point to Na'alehu
KAHUKU SECTION OF HAWAI'I VOLCANOES NATIONAL PARK

The newly opened Kahuku section of Hawai'i Volcanoes National Park (Hwy. 11 between mile markers 70 and 71) was purchased in 2003 from the Kahuku Ranch (parts also are owned by the Nature Conservancy). What's so interesting about this 116,000-acre portion of the park is that it looks completely different than the main section of Hawai'i Volcanoes

National Park: There are lots of large old trees and many native species of Hawaii given that the area originally was preserved as ranch land and wasn't ravaged by lava. For now, the park is only open to the public on weekends 9 A.M.–3 P.M. (closed first Sat. of the month). A four-wheel-drive vehicle is needed to climb the five-mile main road from the highway to the start of the trail. There is no ranger station here, but at the bottom of the road (where it intersects with Hwy. 11) is an informational board with postings about the park and its offerings. Check the park website (www.nps.gov/havo) for monthly ranger-led hikes to explore rare plants in this old-growth forest, which is not open to the public. Reservations are required as the hike is limited to 15 people. If you aren't on a ranger-led tour, as of now, the only solo option is the public circular trail that passes by a pit crater. It takes about 45 minutes to an hour to loop and is a fairly easy walk although it requires proper hiking shoes (not just *slippahs*). There are no facilities here so plan ahead.

GOLF

There is only one golf course in this region of the island, and it might be because it's truly difficult to maintain a nice greenery when it's so dry out. Those who play the **Sea Mountain Golf Course** (Hwy. 11 between mile markers 56 and 57, 808/928-6222, daily 7 A.M.–2:30 P.M., $22.50–28.50) prefer it to nearby courses in Volcano and Hilo perhaps due to the combination of the course itself and the outstanding ocean views with nearby Punalu'u Beach (for a dip when you're finished with the round). Green fees are inexpensive (relatively speaking), with discounts given for tee times before 9 A.M. and after 1 P.M. weekdays. Bring your own snacks and drinks since, unfortunately, there is no snack bar in sight—just a now-defunct restaurant that back in the day had a great bar.

Sights

OCEAN VIEW AND AROUND
Kula Kai Caverns

Part of the Kanohina Lava Tube system—one of the most complex lava systems in the world—the Kula Kai Caverns (Hwy. 11 between mile markers 78 and 79, 808/929-9725, www.kulakaicaverns.com, $15–95) are more than 1,000 years old. There are other places on the island to view lava tubes (and many of these sites are free), but this tour is affordable and you won't regret going. The guide, Kat, has a background in Hawaiian history and is enthusiastic and extremely knowledgeable. She provides you with information not only about the formation of this particular tube, but about the geological formation of the greater area. There are several tours to pick from (all are private). The lighted tour is accessible to anyone who is able to walk. There are some uneven spots, but the paths are well lit and the guide moves you through

A SWAP MEET, HAWAII STYLE

If you are in Ocean View on a Saturday morning (6 A.M.-noon), check out the swap meet next door to the Malama Market (92-8701 Hawai'i Belt Rd./Hwy. 11, Pohue Plaza, *makai* side). Everyone in town comes to schmooze, to sift through the tables of used treasures from children's clothing to appliances (even fridges!) to paintings and jewelry, and to pick up produce from farmers (although pickings are slim). If you get hungry there is Thai food and burgers ready to eat. And no one is shy about having a burger and fries for breakfast. It's a great way to see local culture and pick up something great to eat. Come early because things really start winding down by 10 A.M.

slowly (you're in a wide-open space the entire time); it's about 45 minutes long (although longer if you ask a lot of questions—which Kat is happy to answer) and only $15 adults, $10 children)—although the price will likely be higher in 2012. Those who are not claustrophobic and want to spend more time underground should try the two-hour "crawl tour" ($50), which takes you on your hands and knees through some additional tunnels, or the three-hour "extended cave tour" ($95 adults, $65 children) to even more tunnels in the labyrinth. Advanced reservations are required and needed in order to gain entrance into the gated community where the tunnels are located.

SOUTH POINT TO NA'ALEHU
◖ South Point Road and Ka Lae (South Point)

Most people drive down South Point Road (off Hwy. 11 between mile markers 69 and 70) so that they can say they've been to the southernmost place in the United States and then to do one of the most thrilling (and free) activities possible on the Big Island—to jump off Ka Lae and enjoy the 50-foot fall into the ocean. On your way down South Point Road to Ka Lae, look at the Kamoa Wind Farm—where windmills go to die—and the mostly functioning Pakini Nui Wind Farm towering overhead. The intense power of the wind here is evident from the west-wind-blown trees (just wait to see what happens to your hair when you get out of the car). If you are not faint of heart, now is a good time to suit up (you'll have to do it in your car as there are no facilities of any kind here) and muster up enough strength to jump down. Please be sensible about the weather/water conditions— a day without waves is what you'll hope for. The good news is, strength is not needed for your way back up—there is a rope ladder available to get you back to the top. Unless you're pressed for time, don't be so quick to turn back just yet. From Ka Lae most visitors continue

KAU

© HAWAII'S BIG ISLAND VISITOR BUREAU (BIVB)

Constructed in the 1930s, the now-defunct Na'alehu Theater is a great artifact of the plantation days.

on to the **Green Sand Beach** just a few minutes east of the point.

The sign to South Point Road will be obvious off of Highway 11. Follow it south for 12 miles for some of the best photo opportunities on the Big Island. The drive down South Point is now paved and easy for any car, although it is narrow, so be aware of oncoming cars and pull off to the side if necessary. The road splits somewhat—stay to the right. Where the road ends you'll surely see many other cars parked and you should also park here.

Mark Twain Monkeypod Tree

All the guidebooks list the Mark Twain Monkeypod Tree (Hwy. 11 near mile marker 66) in Wai'ohinu as an attraction. I am going to be straight with you and tell you not to look for it—just stick your head out the window if you happen to see the very faded sign that indicates the location of the tree (which is still confusing because it's actually just a medium-size tree surrounded by a fence). The story goes that Mark Twain planted the original tree in 1866, but it was blown down during a hurricane in 1957. The tree that now stands grew from a shoot from the original tree trunk.

Na'alehu Theater

The Na'alehu Theater (Hwy. 11, corner of Na'alehu Spur Rd.) is a unique sight for those interested in plantation architecture or semi-urban decay. It is part of the same bunch of old theaters that were all constructed in the 1930s by a Japanese entrepreneur (the other two are the Kona Theater in Captain Cook and the Aloha Theatre in Kainaliu Town). At the height of the plantation days these theaters served as the center of entertainment and news for the communities they were housed in. Allegedly, at one time, each plantation community had its own theater. Nowadays, the graffiti on the exterior of the building says it all: "save me." The community hopes that it will eventually be restored and turned into a community theater, but until then, this modern ruin deserves some marveling (solely from the exterior).

HIGHWAY 11 SOUTH OF HAWAI'I VOLCANOES NATIONAL PARK
Pahala and Wood Valley

Just a few miles north of the Black Sand Beach you'll find the turnoff to Pahala town. There is little to do or see here; however, the town presents one of the best-preserved examples of a classic sugar town in the islands. Head into town on the main road from the highway and continue to the stop sign at Pikake Street. Turn right. Pikake takes you to the edge of town; continue straight up the road about five miles (gradual uphill past orchards, pastures, bridges) until you come to the forest. At the forest, follow the paved road left. You've arrived in Wood Valley—a hidden forest of eucalyptus trees in the back of town. Here you'll find the **Wood Valley Temple.** The temple is the first building on your right, marked by colorful prayer flags. Even if you aren't staying here (which is an option), park and walk up to the temple to see the gold Buddha. You'll feel like you're anywhere but Hawaii.

The retreat facility is called the Tara Temple and at one time housed a Japanese Shingon Mission in Pahala. When the Shingon sect moved to a new facility in Kona, this building was abandoned and given to Wood Valley Temple. A local contractor moved it to its present location in 1978, cranked it up one story, and built dormitories underneath. The grounds, hallowed and consecrated for decades, already held a Nichiren temple, the main temple here today, which was dismantled in 1919 at its original location and rebuilt on its present site to protect it from lowland flooding. The Dalai Lama came in 1980 to dedicate the temple and graced the temple once again in 1994 when he addressed an audience here of more than 3,500 people. Programs vary, but people genuinely interested in Buddhism come here for meditation and soul-searching as well as for peace, quiet, relaxation, and direction. Morning and evening services at 7 A.M. and 6 P.M. are led by the Tibetan monk in residence. Visitors are welcome, but enter the compound as quietly as possible and someone from the temple will likely shortly after come to assist you.

Entertainment and Events

ENTERTAINMENT

Nights tend to be quiet in Ka'u. If you're looking for live music, sporadically **Hana Hou** restaurant (95-1148 Na'alehu Spur Rd., Na'alehu, 808/929-9717) has live music with a prix fixe menu ($20) and is BYOB. There is no schedule, so call the restaurant in advance, as reservations usually are necessary for these events.

Although the hours posted indicate that **Shaka Restaurant** (Hwy. 11, Na'alehu, 808/929-7404, daily 10 A.M.–9 P.M., $10) closes at 9 P.M., on the weekends (or if there are people there) it tends to stay open later. Every so often you might also find live music or karaoke. It's on the west side of the center of Na'alehu.

EVENTS

Ka'u is trying really hard to bring more visitors to the region. With that, it seems like a new festival or event pops up monthly. A good place to check for listings is the blog for the *Ka'u Calendar* (http://kaunewsbriefs.blogspot.com), the local newspaper.

A new event worth attending is the two-day **Ka'u Coffee Festival** (www.kaucoffeefest.com), slated to take place annually during the month of May. This event is an effort to highlight the coffee from this region, which some argue is better than Kona coffee and finally deserves some recognition. The festival is set up county fair style, with coffee tastings, "best of" recipe competitions, farm tours, live music from local bands, coffee demonstrations, and a Miss Ka'u Coffee Pageant (it's a big deal—it's a qualifier for the state competition). Most events are free and a few (like the pageant) have a suggested donation ($5–15). Although the first year of the festival only saw a handful of local coffee growers, it's surely on its way to becoming an important festival in Hawaii.

Food

OCEAN VIEW

Overall, the food choices in Ocean View are not great—especially with the recent closing of a few choice restaurants. Most people head straight to the **Pizzeria** (425 Lotus Blossom Ln., Ocean View Town Center, 808/929-9677, Sun.–Thurs. 11 A.M.–7 P.M., Fri.–Sat. 11 A.M.–8 P.M., $15 for a small pizza). They only take local checks and cash, and make sure you bring enough of it because the pizzas (which are tasty) are a bit overpriced. But they can be when you're the only place open past 3 P.M. Salads and subs are also on the menu; they are nothing to write home about, but better priced than the pizzas. Vegetarian options are available and feel free to BYOB (a small grocery store a few doors down carries beer, liquor, and wine).

On the other side of town you'll find **El Pachuco** (in the Kau Outpost building a mile north of Ocean View, Wed.–Sun. 11 A.M.–6 P.M., $5), a recently opened Mexican restaurant. The chips and salsa are good, the tacos are just fine (you've had better), and the prices are cheap. The real draw here is the random assortment of art, like tikis and big bowls and items bought from Costco and then resold in the Kau Outpost. The art, on consignment from local artists, actually is a good deal here and fun to look at while you wait for your food.

Markets

The **Malama Market** (92-8701 Hawai'i Belt Rd./Hwy. 11, Pohue Plaza, *makai* side, 808/939-7560, daily 6:30 A.M.–8 P.M.) is part of the same chain of markets spread around the island. It has a good selection of fresh fruits and vegetables as well as some prepared food (including breakfast—but you *must* get there

STEAK LUNCH

Most days, beginning around 11 A.M. until they are sold out (probably around 5 P.M.), you'll see a table with a large banner stating Steak Lunch in the parking lot at the **Malama Market** (92-8701 Hawai'i Belt Rd./ Hwy. 11, Pohue Plaza, *makai* side) in Ocean View. The smell is what will bring you over (nothing beats out the smell of fresh barbecue in a parking lot), but your nose isn't fooling you. The appetizing smell is a pretty good indication of the actual taste. If that's not enough, the large portions of this local-style cuisine – beef, macaroni salad, and white rice (all for only $6, mind you) – will keep you satiated.

early for this—it sells out fast). They also sell wine and liquor. Pick up a bottle and enjoy it at one of the scenic overlooks (but not while you're driving) or later at a bed-and-breakfast. This market is a useful stop for its excellent bathroom, cash back (just buy a drink), and there is a Redbox here—one of those machines that allow you to rent a DVD for $1 a night. If you pick up a DVD you can return it later at several other locations around the island.

What the **Ocean View Market** (Hwy. 11, *mauka* side, diagonally across from Malama Market, 808/929-9843, daily 6 A.M.–9 P.M.) has going for it is that it's open an hour later than Malama Market. It offers a fairly good stock of groceries (including organic and gluten-free products) and sells beer and wine.

Kahuku Country Market (Ocean View Town Center, 808/929-9011, Mon.–Fri. 5 A.M.–8 P.M., Sat.–Sun. 6 A.M.–8 P.M.) serves coffee in the wee hours of the morning and also has a nice selection of local (gift-shop like) products as well as groceries. It's an older-looking, darker, and more cramped store than its grocery store counterparts in town.

SOUTH POINT TO NA'ALEHU

Your first stop into southern-dom is **Shaka Restaurant** (Hwy. 11, on the west side of the center of town, Na'alehu, 808/929-7404, daily 10 A.M.–9 P.M., $10). This southernmost bar in the United States (they highlight the bar since southernmost restaurant was already taken) is mediocre at best. The portions are large and well priced. The menu is mainly American and local food (grilled chicken, fries, fresh catch), and during the day the large TVs are blasting with sports games or CNN. Take a quick pit stop if you need to—you won't find another one for quite sometime after.

You'll easily find the **Punalu'u Bake Shop** (Hwy. 11 near Ka'alaiki Rd., central Na'alehu, 808/929-7343, www.bakeshophawaii.com, daily 9 A.M.–5 P.M., $3–7) from its smell and the large tourist buses parked in its lot. Peek into the kitchen (there are windows to the outside allowing you to be a voyeur) and then head into the bake shop (and gift shop) to pick up a treat. Offerings include *malasadas* (Portuguese doughnuts), coconut turnovers, and sweet bread that comes in flavors like taro or guava. A lunch menu is also available, with vegetarian options (actual vegetarian options, not just because they lack meat). The indoor seating tends to get overcrowded and loud, so instead try the picnic tables outside situated under the trees. This makes for a great pit stop (and the bake shop apparently agrees since they advertise their bathrooms along with their pastries).

Directly across the street from the Punalu'u Bake Shop (not on the main highway, but visible from it) is **Hana Hou** (95-1148 Na'alehu Spur Rd., 808/929-9717, Mon.–Wed. 8 A.M.–3 P.M., Thurs.–Sun. 8 A.M.–8 P.M., $12), your best choice for eating in the entire Ka'u district. The restaurant's decor has an eclectic and homey feel (not to mention that when you go to the bathroom in the back of the restaurant, around the koi ponds, you realize that this might be someone's house you are eating in). The burgers ($9) are delicious and served on homemade buns. I recommend the blue cheese burger. The specials are usually something local-style (like the catch of the day), and the homemade desserts are rotating but always something mouthwatering like macadamia nut cheesecake. Don't come hungry or

© BREE KESSLER

The Punaluʻu Bake Shop is an essential stop on the comparative *malasada* tour of the Big Island.

KAʻU

in a rush—the service is often very slow. Since BYOB is allowed here, to make the wait more bearable head across the parking lot to the market and grab a beverage. Every once in a while on the weekends there is also live music—a much needed social outlet in the area.

The family-run **Green Sand Café** is the new kid on the block (Hwy. 11, next to the 76 gas station on the east side of Naʻalehu, 808/929-8771, Mon.–Fri. 10 A.M.–4 P.M.), having opened in late 2010. It is a lunch place serving Italian-style cuisine with a local flair—such as Italian sausage served with macaroni salad, pastas with ahi fish, and truly delectable meatball subs. There is not much seating in the restaurant itself—an old couch (you'll feel like you're in your grandmother's living room) and one table is it. But the food is well seasoned and it seems as if consideration went into the menu. If there isn't space inside or if you are heading to a nearby beach, grab the food to go.

Markets

If you need supplies, make sure to stop at **Island Markets** (entrances off of Hwy. 11 and Naʻalehu Spur Rd. across the parking lot from Hana Hou restaurant, Mon.–Sat. 8 A.M.–7 P.M., Sun. 9 A.M.–6 P.M.), a good-size market with a surprising number of options, including beer, liquor, and wine. You won't find another market of this size for quite some distance if you're on your way to Volcanoes National Park (the next good-size market is in Keaʻau).

Information and Services

EMERGENCY SERVICES
Services are far and few between here. The only option in the area for emergencies is **Ka'u Hospital and Rural Health Clinic** (1 Kamani St., Pahala, 808/928-2050, www.kau.hhsc.org, 24 hours), a 21-bed critical care center. For less serious medical concerns, try the nurse-practitioner-run **Ocean View Family Health Clinic** (92-1471 Aloha Blvd., 808/929-9425, Mon. and Wed.–Fri. 7 A.M.–5 P.M.). There are no pharmacies in this area so make sure to pick up your prescriptions ahead of time.

BANKS
Again, the options are limited here. In Na'alehu there is the local **Ka'u Federal Credit Union** (95-5664 Mamalahoa Hwy./Hwy. 11, 808/929-7334, www.kaufcu.org). In Pahala, you'll find a branch of **Bank of Hawaii** (96-3163 Pikake St., 808/928-8356, www.boh.com), the only one for many many miles. Stand-alone ATMs that charge fees per use are available in nearly every grocery store or market in the area.

POST OFFICES
Post offices are easy to find in Ka'u. You'll pass by post offices in Ocean View (next to the Ocean View Market off of Hwy. 11 in the center of Ocean View), Na'alehu (directly off Hwy. 11 in the center of town), and in Pahala (96-3163 Pikake St.).

Getting There and Around

Since Ka'u is right smack in the middle of the east and west sides of the island, it's quite easy and relatively quick to travel to either side of the island from here.

EASTBOUND TRAVEL (HILO SIDE)
The **Hele-On Bus** (www.heleonbus.org, 808/961-8744, $1 per ride, $1 each for luggage, large backpacks, bikes) only makes one trip daily from Ocean View via Volcano to Hilo (the full route). It leaves Ocean View from the parking lot across from the Malama Market (92-8701 Hawai'i Belt Rd./Hwy. 11, Pohue Plaza, *makai* side) at 6:40 A.M., arriving in Hilo at 9:20 A.M. The bus then leaves Hilo at 2:20 P.M. and returns to the same spot in Ocean View at 5:15 P.M.

WESTBOUND TRAVEL (KONA SIDE)
It also is possible to travel west from Pahala to Ocean View to Kona (including the airport) and as far as the resorts in Kohala. The Hele-On bus from Kohala leaves daily at 7:15 A.M. and Monday–Saturday only at 2:30 P.M., passing by the Kona airport and arriving in Ocean View and Pahala about four hours later. The return trips from Pahala to Kohala are Monday–Saturday only at 8 A.M. and daily at 3:30 P.M. Check the Pahala to South Kohala bus schedule on the website for more information (www.heleonbus.org).

HAWAI'I VOLCANOES NATIONAL PARK AND VOLCANO VILLAGE

The indomitable power of Hawai'i Volcanoes National Park is apparent to all who come here. Mark Twain, enchanted by his sojourn through Volcanoes in the 1860s, quipped, "The smell of sulphur is strong, but not unpleasant to a sinner." Wherever you stop to gaze, realize that you are standing on a thin skin of cooled lava in an unstable earthquake zone atop one of the world's most active volcanoes.

Established in 1916 as the 13th U.S. national park, Hawai'i Volcanoes National Park now covers 333,000 acres. Based on its scientific and scenic value, the park was named an International Biosphere Reserve by UNESCO in 1980 and given World Heritage Site status in 1987 by the same organization, giving it greater national and international prestige. This is one of the top visitor attractions in the state.

With a multitude of ways to access the park (by foot, by car, by bike, and by helicopter), Hawai'i Volcanoes National Park truly does offer something for everyone. Even non-nature lovers are impressed by the environmental oddities offered there, such as the vastly different landscapes situated next to each other. Within moments one can pass through a tropical rainforest to what appears like a moon landscape. Even if this doesn't impress, it will be hard to tear yourself away from the lava flow or glow. It's surreal.

In conjunction with a visit to the park, you'll surely pass through Volcano Village, known for the cadre of artists and scientists that live there. With wineries, farmers markets, restaurants, and galleries, it can feel like the Sonoma of Hawaii and not just somewhere to pass through on the way to somewhere else.

HIGHLIGHTS

LOOK FOR [TO FIND RECOMMENDED SIGHTS, ACTIVITIES, DINING, AND LODGING.

[**Volcano Art Center Gallery:** One of the finest art galleries in the entire state, the art center boasts works from the best the islands have to offer (page 121).

[**Thomas A. Jaggar Museum:** This state-of-the-art museum offers a fantastic multimedia display of the amazing geology and volcanology of the area. At night you can watch the lava glow from the viewing area here (page 122).

[**Thurston Lava Tube:** Ferns and moss hang from the entrance of this remarkable natural tunnel, and if you stand just inside the entrance looking out, it's as if the very air is tinged with green (page 124).

[**Chain of Craters Road:** Every bend of this road offers a panoramic vista, and the grandeur and power of the forces that have been creating the earth from the beginning of time are right before your eyes (page 124).

[**Kilauea Iki Trail:** This trail takes you from the top of the crater and lush tropical rainforest of native vegetation and native birds to the bottom of the crater floor, which is devoid of vegetation but still breathes volcanic steam (page 131).

[**Hiking to Halape:** Your reward for the strenuous hike down to Halape is a white sugary beach and sheltered lagoon – it's by far one of the most remote and pristine beaches on the island (page 132).

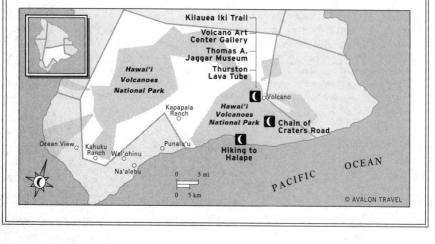

ORIENTATION
Hawai'i Volcanoes National Park

Practically speaking, you'll find the main entrance to the park off of Highway 11 near mile marker 28; however, the park itself extends far to the north and the south of the main entrance. The upper end of the park is the summit of stupendous Mauna Loa, the most massive mountain on earth. Mauna Loa Road branches off Highway 11 and ends at a foot trail for the hale and hearty who trek to the 13,679-foot summit. The park's heart is Kilauea Caldera, almost three miles across, 400 feet deep, and encircled by 11 miles of Crater Rim Drive. At the park visitors center you can give yourself a crash course in geology while picking up park maps, information, and backcountry camping permits. Nearby is Volcano House, Hawaii's oldest hotel, which has hosted a steady stream of adventurers, luminaries, royalty, and heads of state ever since it opened its doors in the 1860s. Just a short drive away is a pocket of indigenous

HAWAI'I VOLCANOES

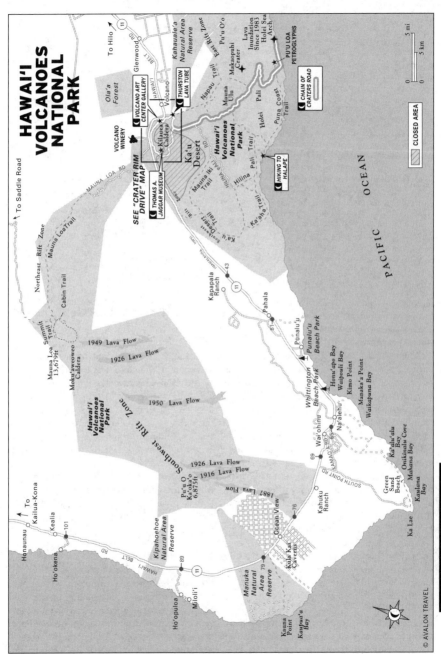

HAWAI'I
VOLCANOES
NATIONAL
PARK

To Saddle Road

To Hilo

To Kailua-Kona

PACIFIC OCEAN

© AVALON TRAVEL

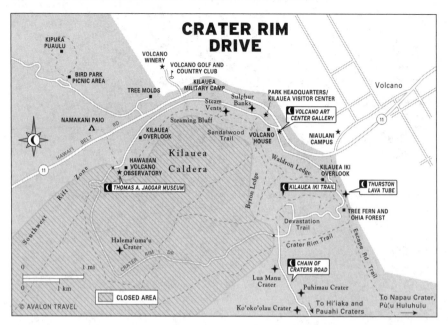

forest, providing the perfect setting for a bird sanctuary. In a separate detached section of the park is 'Ola'a Forest, a pristine wilderness area of unspoiled flora and fauna.

Crater Rim Drive circles Kilauea Caldera past steam vents, sulphur springs, and tortured fault lines that always seem on the verge of gaping wide and swallowing. On the way you can peer into the mouth of Halema'uma'u Crater, home of the fire goddess, Pele, and you'll pass Hawaiian Volcano Observatory (not open to public), which has been monitoring geologic activity since the turn of the 20th century. Adjacent to the observatory is the Thomas A. Jaggar Museum, an excellent facility where you can educate yourself on the past and present volcanology of the park. An easy walk is Devastation Trail, a paved path across a desolate cinder field where gray, lifeless trunks of a suffocated forest lean like old gravestones. Within minutes is Thurston Lava Tube, a magnificent natural tunnel overflowing with vibrant fern grottoes at the entrance and exit.

The southwestern section of the park is dominated by the Ka'u Desert, not a plain of sand but a semi-arid slope of lava flow, cinder, scrub bushes, and heat that's been defiled by the windblown debris and gases of Kilauea Volcano and fractured by the sinking coastline. It is a desolate region, an area crossed by a few trails that are a challenge even to the sturdy and experienced hiker. Most visitors, however, head down the Chain of Craters Road, down the *pali* to the coast, where the road ends abruptly at a hardened flow of lava and from where visitors can glean information about current volcanic activities from the small ranger station and try to glimpse the current volcanic activity in the distance.

Volcano Village

Driving north on Highway 11, you will pass by the park's entrance before reaching the main part of Volcano town (if you are driving from Hilo, you pass the town first). Although there are residential communities on both sides of the road, the *mauka* side (where you'll see a big green official sign stating lodging and

YOUR BEST DAY IN THE VOLCANO AREA

- Wake up early and walk the **Crater Rim Trail.**

- Stop at the **visitors center** to chat with a park ranger (before it gets crowded).

- Drive to the **Thurston Lava Tube** (go inside it), and if you're so inclined hike the **Kilauea Iki Trail.**

- Get back in the car and drive the **Chain of Craters Road,** stopping at a lookout to have your packed lunch.

- In the later afternoon, after a brief rest, stop by the **Volcano Winery** for a tasting (it closes at 5:30 P.M.).

- Have an early dinner in **Volcano Village.**

- Return to the park to watch the glow from the **Thomas A. Jaggar Museum.**

- If you're not too tired, go bowling at **Kilauea Military Camp** or visit the **Lava Lounge** for some karaoke with the locals.

© DANIEL HALLER/WWW.123RF.COM

cracks in the foggy Kilauea Iki crater

RAINY DAY ALTERNATIVE

I'll try to break it to you as gently as possible: It can rain at Hawai'i Volcanoes National Park. Sometimes it's a spritz and you can continue on with only getting slightly damp, and other times it can rain very hard (a tropical kind of rain) and outside activity is not really possible (or safe). There are a few inside places you can go while waiting for sunshine.

From facials to pedicures to traditional *lomilomi* massages, **Hale Ho'ola: Hawaiian Healing Arts Center and Spa** does it all and does it well at half the cost of spas on the Kona side. What makes this a truly great rainy day activity is that you can call last minute and owner Suzanne Woolley will try to accommodate you.

Art enthusiasts will love **2400 Fahrenheit Glass Blowing,** just a few minutes north of Hawai'i Volcanoes National Park. Even if glass blowing isn't taking place, this gallery makes for a worthy stop.

If the weather still hasn't cleared up, try the **Volcano Winery** for a tasting or drive to Hilo. Often the weather in Hilo can be drastically different than in Volcano (you can see the clouds moving as you drive north on Highway 11).

HAWAI'I VOLCANOES

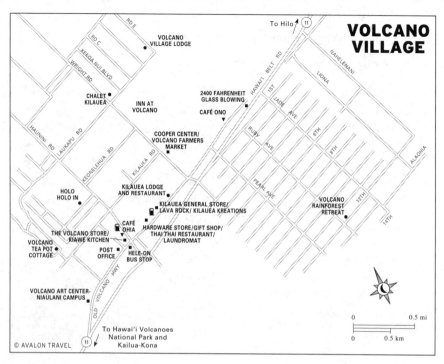

food) is where the center of Volcano town is. Nearly every restaurant and shop (the few that exist) is on the short Old Volcano Road—the inner road that parallels Highway 11 through town. The golf course area (referred to as such), where the Volcano Winery is also housed, is on Highway 11 between mile markers 30 and 31 just south of the park.

PLANNING YOUR TIME

It's best to decide ahead of time how much time you want to spend at the park and your medium for visiting (by car or by foot or by bike). Regardless of your plan, your first stop should be the visitors center to check with a park ranger about any new closures in the park, new safety advisories, or a special program going on that day (often there is a program taking place). Start early. The park looks entirely different in the early morning—the colors are different and it is much quieter before the busloads of tourists

start to arrive. Lastly, pack a lunch. The food options in the park are nearly nonexistent. Better to bring a great sandwich with you so that you don't have to return to town midday to get fed.

It is possible to see the park's "greatest hits" in one long day if you drive from sight to sight on Crater Rim and then Chain of Craters Road. You'll even have time to get out and walk around, have a leisurely dinner, and then come back to catch the glow or lava flow at night. There are a handful of fairly easy hikes that only take 2–3 hours. If you're planning on doing one or more of those hikes (such as Kilauea Iki), you might want to give yourself an extra day in the park. Two days at Hawai'i Volcanoes National Park will allow you to see all the major sights and accomplish at least two beginner- to medium-level hikes. For the serious hikers in the group, at least three days in the park will be necessary to get into the backcountry (and then maybe more importantly, to get back out).

KNOW BEFORE YOU GO

In this age of Internet, one can essentially be at the park without physically being there. If you're missing the lava glow when you get home or if you simply want to check out conditions before you head into the park (i.e., is it worth driving to the park at night), there are several useful websites you can use:

Checking Closures in the Park

- Trails: www.nps.gov/havo/closed_areas.htm

- Park hotline for lava flow/trail closures: 808/985-6000

Checking on the Lava Flow or Glow

- Lava status: http://volcano.wr.usgs.gov/ kilaueastatus.php (This is the flow that visitors see from the Puna viewing area or by boat in Puna.)

- Halema'uma'u Overlook Vent Webcam: http://volcanoes.usgs.gov/hvo/cams/ HMcam (This is the glow you'll see from the Thomas A. Jaggar Museum viewing area.)

Planning Your Visit

- www.nps.gov/havo/planyourvisit/hike.htm

Note: There is a free *Your Guide to Hawai'i Volcanoes National Park* app that iPhone users can download from iTunes. The app offers current information on volcano activities, road and trail closures, and a vast array of other park information.

Exploring Hawai'i Volcanoes National Park

Admission to Hawai'i Volcanoes National Park (www.nps.gov/havo) is $10 per vehicle (good for multiple entries over a seven-day period), $25 for a Hawaii Tri-park Annual Pass, $5 per individual (walkers and bikers), and free to those 62 and over with a Golden Age, Golden Eagle, or Golden Access passport. These "passports" are available at the park headquarters and are good at any national park in the United States. Note: There are several weekends throughout the year when the park is free—thanks to the Department of the Interior. Check the park's website to see if your visit coincides with one of these times.

THE VOLCANOES
Kilauea

Continuously active since 1983, Kilauea dominates the heart of Hawai'i Volcanoes National Park. Many of the park's sights are arranged one after another along **Crater Rim Drive,** which circles **Kilauea Caldera.** Most of these sights are the "drive-up" variety, but plenty of major and minor trails lead off here and there.

Expect to spend a full day atop Kilauea to take in all the sights, and never forget that you're on a rumbling volcano. Kilauea Caldera, at 4,000 feet, is about 10°F cooler than the coast. It's often overcast, and there can be showers. Wear walking shoes and bring a sweater or windbreaker. Binoculars, sunglasses, and a hat will also come in handy.

People with respiratory ailments, those with small children, and pregnant individuals should note that the fumes from the volcano can cause problems. That sour taste in your mouth is sulphur from the fumes. Stay away from directly inhaling from the sulphur vents and don't overdo it, and you should be fine.

Mauna Loa

It's a little discombobulating at times—you're sweating in the hot lava fields of the park and in the background you see the snowcapped Mauna Loa. The largest mass of mountain

HAWAI'I VOLCANOES

A MODERN HISTORY OF ERUPTIONS AT HAWAI'I VOLCANOES NATIONAL PARK

The first white man atop Kilauea was Rev. William Ellis, who scaled it in 1823. (Many Polynesians and Hawaiians scaled Kilauea before this date.) Until the 1920s, the floor of the caldera was exactly what people thought a volcano would be: a molten lake of lava. Then the forces of nature changed, and the fiery lava subsided and hardened over. Today, Kilauea is called the only "drive-in" volcano in the world, and in recent years it has been one of the most active, erupting almost continuously since 1983 at vents along its eastern fault. When it begins gushing, the result is not a nightmare scene of people scrambling away for their lives, but just the opposite; people flock *to* the volcano. Most thrill-seekers are in much greater danger of being run over by a tour bus hustling to see the fireworks than of being entombed in lava. The volcanic action, while soul-shakingly powerful and not really predictable, is almost totally safe.

The Hawaiian Volcano Observatory has been keeping watch since 1912, making Kilauea one of the best-understood volcanoes in the world. The vast volcanic field is creased by rift zones, or natural pressure valves. When the underground magma builds up, instead of *kaboom!* as in Mount St. Helens, it bubbles to the surface like a spring and gushes out as a river of lava. Naturally, anyone or anything in its path would be burned to a cinder, but scientists routinely walk within a few feet of the still-flowing lava to take samples and readings. In much the way canaries detected mine gas, longtime lava observers pay attention to their ears. When the skin on top begins to blister, they know they are too close. The lava establishes a course that it follows much like an impromptu mountain stream caused by heavy rains.

This does not mean that the lava flows are entirely benign, or that anyone should visit the area during an eruption without prior approval by the Park Service. When anything is happening, the local radio stations give up-to-the-minute news, and the Park Service provides a recorded message at 808/985-6000. In 1790 a puff of noxious gases was emitted from Kilauea and descended on the Ka'u Desert, asphyxiating a rival army of Kamehameha's that just happened to be in the area. Eighty people died in their tracks. In 1881, a flow of lava spilled toward undeveloped Hilo and engulfed an area within today's city limits. In 1942, a heavy flow came within 12 miles of the city. Still, this was child's play in comparison with the unbelievable flow of 1950. Luckily, this went down the western rift zone where only scattered homes were in its path. It took no lives as it disgorged well over 600 million cubic yards of magma that covered 35 square miles! The flow continued for 23 days and produced seven huge torrents of lava that sliced across the Belt Road in three different areas. At its peak, the lava front traveled six miles per hour and put out enough material to pave an eight-lane freeway twice around the world. In 1960, a flow swallowed the town of Kapoho on the east coast. In 1975, an earthquake caused a tsunami to hit the southeast coast, killing two campers and sinking a section of the coast by three feet.

The most recent – and very dramatic – series of eruptions, which spectacularly began on January 3, 1983, has continued virtually unabated ever since, producing more than one cubic kilometer of lava. Magma bubbled to the surface about two miles away from Pu'u O'o. The gigantic fissure fountained lava and formed Pu'u O'o Cinder Cone, at its largest some 800 feet high and almost 1,000 feet across. Over a 3.5-year period, there were 47 episodic eruptions from this vent. On July 20, 1986, a new fissure broke upon the surface at Kupa'ianaha, just outside the park in a nature reserve, and formed a lava lake about one acre in surface size and 180 feet deep. At the end of April 1987 all activity suddenly stopped and the lava drained from the lake and tube system, allowing scientists to accurately gauge the depth. About three weeks later, it started up again when lava poured back into the lake, went through the tube system, and flowed back down to the ocean.

More episodic eruptions followed; from that point the flow turned destructive and started

© HAWAII TOURISM JAPAN (HTJ)

On the Big Island you'll see two different kinds of lava: *pahoehoe* (smooth, seen here) and *'a'a* (rough).

taking homes. It flowed about seven miles to the coast through tubes and on the surface, wiping out Kapa'ahu, parts of Kalapana, and most of the Royal Gardens subdivision, with more than 180 homes incinerated. In May 1989 it moved into the national park proper, and on June 22, it swallowed the park visitors center at Waha'ula. Since 1992, lava has been flowing into the ocean within the park. Unexpectedly, in January 1997 the dramatic activity shifted two miles westward to the Napau Crater, where lava erupted in spouts of fire and flows, and Pu'u O'o ceased spewing. Since February 1997, the majority of activity moved back to Pu'u O'o Cinder Cone, where there has been a continual shift of vent locations on the west and southwestern flanks and constant renewed activity inside the crater, with lava reaching and entering the ocean at various points from 2002 until the present. Until 1997, remote Waha'ula Heiau was spared, but in August of that year lava inundated and buried the sacred spot.

Many of the homesteaders in the worst areas of the flow were rugged individualists and back-to-nature alternative types who lived in homes that generally had no electricity, running water, or telephones. The homes were wiped out. Some insurance companies with legitimate policyholders tried to wiggle out of paying premiums for lost homes, although the policies specifically stipulated loss by lava flow. The insurance companies griped that the 2,200°F lava never really touched some of the homes, and therefore they were exonerated from covering the losses. Their claims were resoundingly repudiated in the courts, and people were paid for their losses.

At its height, the output of lava was estimated at 650,000 cubic yards per day, which is equal to 55,000 truckloads of cement, enough to cover a football field 38 miles high. Since this activity started in 1983, it has averaged 300,000-600,000 cubic yards a day (that's over two billion cubic yards!), covered 45 square miles of land, added 570 acres of new land to the park and greater acreage to the areas outside the park, and buried about 13 miles of the Chain of Craters Road. For a history of the park's volcanic activity plus up-to-the-minute reports on current activity, see http://hvo.wr.usgs.gov, or check at the park visitors center. Related information is also available at www.soest.hawaii.edu/gg/hcv.

HAWAI'I VOLCANOES

to make up the Big Island at 13,680 feet, this magnificent mountain is a mere 116 feet shorter than its neighbor Mauna Kea, which is the tallest peak in the Pacific, and by some accounts, tallest in the world.

But still, Mauna Loa holds its own impressive statistics. It is the most massive mountain on earth, containing some 19,000 cubic miles of solid, iron-hard lava, and it's estimated that this titan weighs more than California's entire Sierra Nevada mountain range! In fact, Mauna Loa (Long Mountain), at 60 miles long and 30 miles wide, occupies the entire southern half of the Big Island. Unlike Mauna Kea, Mauna Loa has had some recent volcanic activity, spilling lava in 1949, 1950, 1975, and 1980. The top of this mountain is within the Hawai'i Volcanoes National Park boundary.

The summit of Mauna Loa, with its mighty **Moku'aweoweo Caldera,** is all within park boundaries. Mauna Loa's oval Moku'aweoweo Caldera is more than three miles long and 1.5 miles wide and has vertical walls towering 600 feet. At each end is a smaller round pit crater. From November to May, if there is snow, steam rises from the caldera. This mountaintop bastion is the least visited part of the park since this land is very remote and still largely inaccessible.

Plans for future use of this area include opening up several hundred miles of trails and Jeep tracks to hiking and perhaps other activities as well as creating additional campsites and cabins; these uses will undoubtedly take years to facilitate. For now, it is possible to drive or bike the 10-mile Mauna Loa Road to the trailhead at over 6,600 feet, hike nearly 20 miles to the summit, and stay overnight at some true backcountry cabins before you head back down (there is a shorter way back if you can get someone to pick you up near the Mauna Loa Observatory).

VISITORS CENTER AREA
Kilauea Visitor Center
As they say in the *Sound of Music,* "Let's start at the very beginning, the very best place to start," i.e., the park's Kilauea Visitor Center

(808/985-6000, daily 7:45 A.M.–5 P.M.) and headquarters. It's the first building you pass on the right after you enter through the gate. By midmorning it's jammed, so try to be an early bird. The center is well run by the National Park Service, which offers a free film about geology and volcanism, with tremendous highlights of past eruptions and plenty of detail on Hawaiian culture and natural history. It runs every hour on the hour starting at 9 A.M. Free ranger-led tours of the nearby area are also given on a regular basis, and their start times and meeting places are posted near the center's front doors. Also posted are After Dark in the Park educational interpretive program activities, held two or three times a month on Tuesdays at 7 P.M. If you are visiting with kids 5–12 years old then be sure to ask the rangers about the **Junior Ranger Program.** It's free and they'll give you a park-related activity book, pin, and patch for your kids.

The museum section of the visitors center looks like it was constructed at least 20 years ago before museums got technological updates, but it still offers relevant information about the geology of the area, with plenty of exhibits on flora and fauna. If you are interested in these topics, a quick stop here will greatly enrich your visit. A walk around the museum will only take about a half hour. If you're looking for more volcano-specific information, you'll find that at the Thomas A. Jaggar Museum a few minutes up the road.

The small gift shop in the visitors center has park posters, postcards, T-shirts, sweatshirts, and raincoats (which you often see people wearing) as well as lots of books and maps to help navigate you through the park and kid-friendly volcano-related toys, too.

In addition to all the fun stuff at the visitors center, there is serious business that takes place. For safety's sake, anyone hiking to the backcountry *must* register with the rangers at the visitors center, especially for sites that have occupancy limits. There is no charge for camping, and rangers can give you up-to-the-minute information on trails, backcountry shelters, and cabins. Trails routinely close due to lava flows, tremors, and rock slides. The rangers cannot help you if they don't know where you are, so it is imperative to let them know where you're going.

That said, many day trails leading into the caldera from the rim road are easy walks that need no special preparation. Before you head down the road, ask for a trail guide from the rangers at the visitors center, fill up your water bottle, and use the public bathroom (there are others in the park, though).

Volcano House

Across the road from the visitors center is Volcano House, which has been closed since 2010 in order to make it more earthquake proof. It is slated to reopen new and improved in late 2012, and even if your plans don't include an overnight stop here, go in for a look. A stop at the lounge provides refreshments and a tremendous view of the crater. Volcano House still has the feel of a country inn. This particular building dates from the 1940s, but the site has remained the same since a grass hut was perched on the rim of the crater by a sugar planter in 1846. He charged $1 a night for lodging (can you imagine?). A steady stream of notable visitors has come ever since: almost all of Hawaii's kings and queens dating from the middle of the 19th century, as well as royalty from Europe. Mark Twain was a guest, followed by Franklin Roosevelt. More recently, a contingent of astronauts lodged here and used the crater floor to prepare for walking on the moon. Originally privately owned, since 1986 the hotel has once again been under local management as a concessionaire to the National Park Service.

◖ Volcano Art Center Gallery

Across the parking lot at the visitors center is the Volcano Art Center Gallery (808/967-7565, daily 9 A.M.–5 P.M. except Christmas), which lives in the original 1877 Volcano House. A new show featuring one of the many superlative island artists is presented monthly, and there are always ongoing demonstrations and special events. Artworks on display are in a variety of media, including canvas, paper, wood, glass, metal, ceramic, fiber, and photographs. There is also a profusion of less expensive but distinctive items like posters, cards, and earthy basketry made from natural fibers collected locally. One of the functions of the art center is to provide interpretation for the national park. All of the 300 or so artists who exhibit here do works that in some way relate to Hawaii's environment and culture. Volcano Art Center is one of the finest art galleries in the entire state, boasting works from the best the islands have to offer. Definitely make this a stop.

As a community-oriented organization, the Volcano Art Center sponsors classes and workshops in arts, crafts, and yoga, the Kilauea Volcano Wilderness Runs, and a season of performing arts, which includes musical concerts, hula, dance performances, and stage plays. Some involve local performers, while others headline visiting artists. Performances, classes, and workshops take place at the Kilauea Theater at the military camp, at the hula platform within the park, or in Volcano at the Niaulani campus building. Tickets for performances are sold individually at local outlets or you can buy a season ticket. For current information and pricing, call the Volcano Art Center office (808/967-8222, www.volcanoartcenter.org) or check out its website for what's happening.

CRATER RIM DRIVE

The 11-mile road that circles the Kilauea Caldera and passes by nearly all the main sights in the park is Crater Rim Drive. Anyone who visited the park even four years ago remembers driving around the Caldera to experience a 360-degree view. The bad news is, for the past few years a part of the road has been closed due to elevated levels of sulphur dioxide gas related to the vent that opened within the Halema'uma'u Crater in March 2008. You can still drive on the road, but you can't complete the entire circle because of the closure. It's a bit confusing to some visitors because outdated guidebooks and websites (or poorly researched ones) don't mention this and visitors arrive expecting to complete the drive or guessing that the road must have just closed. I am here to tell you that it's been closed for years.

However, don't let this deter you. A large part of the road is still open, and even though you can't make a full circle now (instead you have to drive back the way you came), there are so many intriguing nooks and crannies to stop at along Crater Rim Drive that you'll have to force yourself to be picky if you intend to cover the park in one day.

Along this road you will travel from a tropical zone into desert, then through a volcanic zone before returning to lush rainforest. The change is often immediate and differences dramatic. Since you can't circle the caldera, the following sights are listed in two sections: those to the right of the visitors center and those to the left of the visitors center. The sights to the left of the visitors center can also be reached by turning left immediately after you pass through the entrance gate of the park.

To the Right of the Visitors Center
SULPHUR BANKS
You can easily walk to Sulphur Banks from the visitors center along a 10-minute paved trail. Your nose will tell you when you're close. Alternatively, walk the 0.6-mile trail from the Steam Vents parking lot (signs point you in the direction). A boardwalk fronts a major portion of this site. As you approach these fumaroles, the earth surrounding them turns a deep reddish-brown, covered over in yellowish-green sulphur. It's an amazing sight, especially in the morning when the entire area seems to look pink. The rising steam is caused by surface water leaking into the cracks, where it becomes heated and rises as vapor. Kilauea releases hundreds of tons of sulphur gases every day. This gaseous activity stunts the growth of vegetation. And when atmospheric conditions create a low ceiling, the gases sometimes cause the eyes and nose to water.

STEAM VENTS
Within a half mile you'll come to Steam Vents, which are also fumaroles, but without sulphur. In the parking lot there are some vents covered with grates, and if you walk just two minutes

from the parking lot toward the caldera on the gravel trail you'll see how the entire field steams. It is like being in a sauna or getting a wonderful free facial. There are no strong fumes to contend with here, just other tourists. If you walk back toward the caldera (away from the parking lot), you'll see a gravel trail that follows the caldera around. This is the **Crater Rim Trail,** and you can walk it from here to many of the sights, including the Thomas A. Jaggar Museum—an easy 20-minute walk (one-way) through the woods from here.

KILAUEA MILITARY CAMP
If you continue in the same direction on the road, you'll pass the Kilauea Military Camp. It's where military families come to vacation. Although it looks like it's not open to the public, many parts of it actually are open to non-military personnel, including the post office (if you want something stamped from Hawai'i Volcanoes National Park!), the Lava Lounge bar, the cafeteria, the bowling alley, and the Kilauea theater, used for community events.

KILAUEA OVERLOOK
Some distance beyond the Kilauea Military Camp is Kilauea Overlook, as good a spot as any to get a look into the caldera, and there are picnic tables near the parking lot. Here too is **Uwekahuna (Wailing Priest) Bluff,** where the *kahuna* made offerings of appeasement to the goddess Pele. A Hawaiian prayer commemorates their religious rites. Unless you're stopping for lunch or making your own (appropriate) offering, it's perhaps better to continue on to the observatory and museum, where you not only have the view outside but get a scientific explanation of what's happening around you.

◖ THOMAS A. JAGGAR MUSEUM
The **Hawaiian Volcano Observatory** (http://hvo.wr.usgs.gov) has been keeping tabs on the volcanic activity in the area since the turn of the 20th century. The actual observatory is filled with delicate seismic equipment and is closed to the public, but a lookout nearby gives you a spectacular view into the eye of

Halema'uma'u Crater (House of Ferns), Pele's home. From here, steam rises and, even more phenomenally spectacular, a lake of molten lava forms. The lava has been rising and falling over the last few years, and when it does rise, it puts on one of the best nighttime shows you'll ever see (the red glow can be seen from miles away). You can check the webcam (http://volcanoes.usgs.gov/hvo/cams/hmcam) located within the crater to see what it is doing and decide if it's worth heading back there at night to watch its performance.

This is a major stop for all passing tourists and tour buses. Information plaques in the immediate area tell of the history and volcanology of the park. One points out a spot from which to observe the perfect shield volcano form of Mauna Loa—most times too cloudy to see. Another reminds you that you're in the middle of the Pacific, an incredible detail you tend to forget when atop these mountains.

Next door to the observatory, the state-of-the-art Thomas A. Jaggar Museum (808/985-6049, daily 8:30 A.M.–8:30 P.M., admission free) offers a fantastic multimedia display of the amazing geology and volcanology of the area, complete with a miniseries of spectacular photos on movable walls, topographical maps, inspired paintings, and video presentations. The expert staff constantly upgrades the displays to keep the public informed on the newest eruptions. The 30–45 minutes it takes to explore the teaching museum will enhance your understanding of the volcanic area immeasurably. There is also a gift shop here, much like the one at the visitors center, which carries sweatshirts and raincoats that visitors are, at times, desperate to get their hands on. Drinking water and bathrooms are available here. *From the Jaggar Museum the rest of the Crater Rim Road is closed; thus, it's necessary to turn around and go back the way you came.*

To the Left of the Visitors Center
KILAUEA IKI OVERLOOK

The first parking lot you'll pass on the right is the gateway to **Kilauea Iki** (Little Kilauea). In 1959, lava spewed 1,900 feet into the air from a half-mile crack in the crater wall (there is an amazing picture showcasing this occurrence on

© MARK WASSER

Today, Kilauea Iki isn't as exciting to see as it was in 1959, but it's much safer to visit now, making it one of the most frequented trails in the park.

HAWAI'I VOLCANOES

a board in the parking lot). It was the highest fountain ever measured in Hawaii. Within a few weeks, 17 separate lava flow episodes occurred, creating a lake of lava. In the distance is the cinder cone, **Pu'u Pua'i** (Gushing Hill), where the lava flowed from its brownish-red base in 1959. The cone didn't exist before then. Present day, if you look down from the overlook into the crater floor you'll see something that resembles a desolate desert landscape that is still steaming in spots. Unbelievably, you can fairly easily walk across this on the Kilauea Iki trail. Surrounding the crater (up top) is a rainforest filled with native birds and plants.

◖ THURSTON LAVA TUBE

Just up the road from the overlook is the remarkable Thurston Lava Tube, otherwise called **Nahuku,** which resembles a Salvadar Dali painting. As you approach, the expected signboard gives you the lowdown on the geology and flora and fauna of the area. The paved trail starts as a steep incline, which quickly enters a fern forest. All about you are fern trees, vibrantly green, with native birds flitting here and there. As you approach the lava tube, it seems almost manmade, like a perfectly formed tunnel leading into a mine. Ferns and moss hang from the entrance, and if you stand just inside the entrance looking out, it's as if the very air is tinged with green. The tunnel is fairly large and shouldn't be a problem for those who suffer from mild claustrophobia. The walk through takes about 10 minutes, undulating through the narrow passage. At the other end, the fantasy world of ferns and moss reappears, and the trail leads back, past public restrooms, to the parking lot. Note: The entire tunnel is lit and paved; however, for some extra fun take with you a flashlight and visit the unlit portion that you'll find at the end of the lit tunnel. As you walk up the stairway to exit the tube, you'll see on your left an open gate that looks into the darkness: This small unlit section *is* open to the public at their own risk. If you're good on your feet and have a flashlight take a quick look in—it will only take you a few additional minutes.

◖ CHAIN OF CRATERS ROAD

The 36-mile round-trip Chain of Craters Road that once linked the park with Kalapana village on the coast in the Puna district was severed by an enormous lava flow in 1995 and can now only be driven to where the flow crosses the road beyond the Holei Sea Arch. It's pretty amazing when you get to the end of the road, though, where lava literally covers the pavement and you can see now-defunct street signs in the distance.

Remember that the volcanic activity in this area is unpredictable, and that the road can be closed at a moment's notice. As you head down the road, every bend—and they are uncountable—offers a panoramic vista. There are numerous pull-offs; plaques provide geological information about past eruptions and lava flows. The grandeur, power, and immensity of the forces that have been creating the earth from the beginning of time are right before your eyes. Although the road starts off in the *'ohi'a* forest, it opens to broader views and soon cuts diagonally across the *pali* to reach the littoral plain. Much of this section of the road was buried under lava flows from 1969 to 1974.

When the road almost reaches the coast, look for a roadside marker that indicates the Puna Coast Trail. Just across the road is the Pu'u Loa Petroglyph Field trailhead. The lower part of the road is spectacular. Here, blacker-than-black sea cliffs, covered by a thin layer of green, abruptly stop at the sea. The surf rolls in, sending up spumes of seawater. In the distance, steam billows into the air where the lava flows into the sea. At road's end you will find a barricade and an information hut staffed by park rangers throughout the afternoon and into the evening. Read the information and heed the warnings. The drive from atop the volcano to the end of the road takes about 45 minutes and drops 3,700 feet in elevation.

While hiking to the lava flow is not encouraged, park staff do not stop you from venturing out. They warn you of the dangers and the reality ahead. Many visitors do make the hike (the distance varies depending on where the lava is

Craters

As you head down Chain of Craters Road you immediately pass a number of the depressions for which the road is named. First on the right side is **Lua Manu Crater,** a deep depression now lined with green vegetation. Farther is **Puhimau Crater.** Walk the few steps to the viewing stand at the crater edge for a look. Many people come here to hear the echo of their voices as they talk or sing into this pit. Next comes **Ko'oko'olau Crater,** then **Hi'iaka Crater** and **Pauahi Crater.** Just beyond is a turnoff to the east, which follows a short section of the old road. This road ends at the lava flow, and from here a trail runs as far as **Napau Crater.**

The first mile or more of the Napau Trail takes you over lava from 1974, through forest *kipuka,* past lava tree molds, and up the treed slopes of **Pu'u Huluhulu.** A *kipuka* is a piece of land that is surrounded by lava but has not been inundated by it, leaving the original vegetation and land contour intact. From this cone you have a view down on Mauna Ulu, from which the 1969–1974 lava flow disgorged, and east toward **Pu'u O'o** and the currently active volcanic vents, some seven miles distant. Due to the current volcanic activity farther along the rift zone, you will need a permit to day hike beyond Pu'u Huluhulu; the trail itself may be closed depending upon where the volcanic activity is taking place. However, the trail does continue over the shoulder of **Makaopuhi Crater** to the primitive campsite at Napau Crater, passing more cones and pit craters, lava flows, and sections of rainforest.

Roadside Sights

For several miles, Chain of Craters Road traverses lava that was laid down about 40 years ago; remnants of the old road can still be seen in spots. There are long stretches of smooth *pahoehoe* lava interspersed with flows of the rough *'a'a.* Here and there, a bit of green pokes through a crack in the rock, bringing new life to this stark landscape. Everywhere you look, you can see the wild "action" of these lava flows, stopped in all their magnificent forms.

© MARK WASSER

The trail to the Napau Crater takes you over lava from 1974.

flowing), but there is no trail. The way is over new and rough lava that tears at the bottom of your shoes. Many hike during the day, but if you go in the evening when the spectacle is more apparent, a flashlight with several extra batteries is absolutely necessary. To hike there and back could take three to four hours. If you decide to hike, bring plenty of water. There is no shade or water along the way, and the wind often blows along this coast. Do not hike to or near the edge of the water, as sections of lava could break off without warning. Depending upon how the lava is flowing, it may or may not be worth the effort. When the lava is flowing, it is often possible to see the reddish glow at night from the end of the road, but you probably won't see much that's distinguishable unless you use high-power binoculars. When the lava is putting on a good show, there could be several hundred cars parked along the road, stretching back for over a mile, so expect a bit of a walk before you even get to the ranger station to start the hike over the lava. Note: For a much closer walk, park at the lava-viewing area near Kalapana in Puna.

At one vantage point on the way is **Kealakomo,** a picnic overlook where you have unobstructed views of the coast. Stop and enjoy the sight before proceeding. Several other lookouts and pull-offs have been created along the road to call attention to one sight or another. Soon the road heads over the edge of the *pali* and diagonally down to the flats, passing sections of the old road not covered by lava. Stop and look back and realize that most of the old road has been covered by dozens of feet of lava, the darkest of the dark.

The last section of road runs very close to the edge of the sea, where cliffs rise up from the pounding surf. Near the end of the road is the **Holei Sea Arch,** a spot where the wave action has undercut the rock to leave a bridge of stone. This is a small but a dramatic sight. Enjoy the scene, but don't lean too far out trying to get that perfect picture!

Pu'u Loa Petroglyphs

The walk out to Pu'u Loa Petroglyphs is delightful, highly educational, and takes less than one hour. As you walk along the trail (1.5 miles round-trip), note the *ahu,* traditional trail markers that are piles of stone shaped like little Christmas trees. Most of the lava field leading to the petroglyphs is undulating *pahoehoe* and looks like a frozen sea. You can climb bumps of lava, 8–10 feet high, to scout the immediate territory. Mountainside, the *pali* is quite visible and you can pick out the most recent lava flows—the blackest and least vegetated. As you approach the site, the lava changes dramatically and looks like long strands of braided rope.

The petroglyphs are in an area about the size of a soccer field. A wooden walkway encircles most of them and helps to ensure their protection. A common motif of the petroglyphs is a circle with a hole in the middle, like a doughnut; you'll also see designs of men with triangular heads. Some rocks are entirely covered with designs, while others have only a symbolic scratch or two. These carvings are impressive more for their sheer numbers than the multiplicity of design. If you stand on the walkway and trek off at the two o'clock position,

you'll see a small hill. Go over and down it, and you will discover even better petroglyphs, including a sailing canoe about two feet high. At the back end of the walkway a sign proclaims that Pu'u Loa meant Long Hill, which the Hawaiians turned into the metaphor "Long Life." For countless generations, fathers would come here to place pieces of their infants' umbilical cords into small holes as offerings to the gods to grant long life to their children. Concentric circles surrounded the holes that held the umbilical cords. The entire area, an obvious power spot, screams in utter silence, and the still-strong mana is easily felt.

The Big Island has the largest concentration of petroglyphs in the state, and this site holds its greatest number. One estimate puts the number at 28,000!

OTHER PARK ROADS AND AREAS
Hilina Pali Road

About two miles down the Chain of Craters Road, Hilina Pali Road shoots off to the southwest (to the left) over a narrow roughly paved road all the way to the end at Hilina Pali Lookout—about nine miles. Soon after you leave the Chain of Craters Road the vegetation turns drier and you enter the semi-arid Ka'u Desert. The road picks its way around and over old volcanic flows, and you can see the vegetation struggling to maintain a foothold. On the way you pass the **Mauna Iki trailhead,** Kulanaokuaiki Campground, and former Kipuka Nene Campground—closed to help the *nene* recover their threatened population. You should see geese here, but please leave them alone and definitely don't feed them.

The road ends right on the edge of the rift, with expansive views over the benched coastline, from the area of current volcanic flow all the way to South Point. From here, one trail heads down the hill to the coast while another pushes on along the top of the cliff and farther into the dry landscape. At the *pali* lookout is a pavilion and restrooms, but no drinking water. This is not a pleasure ride, as the road is rough, but it is passable. For most it probably isn't worth the time, but for those looking for isolation and a special vantage point, this could be it. If you drive just slightly past the turnoff for Hilina Pali Road, you'll arrive at **Devil's Throat,** a pit crater formed in 1912. It's not directly off the road, so you'll have to park your car at the small gravel area by the side of the road, cross the street, and walk back about 50 feet to catch a glimpse.

'Ola'a Forest

Off Highway 11 close to Volcano Village, turn on Wright Road (or County Road 148) heading toward Mauna Loa. On a clear morning you can see the mountain dead ahead. Continue for approximately three miles until you see a barbed-wire fence. The fence is distinctive because along it you'll see a profusion of *hapu'u* ferns that are in sharp contrast to the adjacent ranch property. The area is laced with cracks and lava tubes. Most are small ankle twisters, but others can open up under you like a glacial crevasse. Here is a true example of a quickly disappearing native forest. What's beautiful about an endemic forest is that virtually all species coexist wonderfully. The ground cover is a rich mulch of decomposing ferns and leaves, fragrant and amazingly soft.

Although open to the public, entrance to this area is *not* encouraged. There are no maintained trails, no well-recognized and marked trailheads, and no services whatsoever. It's a thick, dense forest that provides no easy visible clues to direction or location, and the park offers no maps of the forest to visitors. While some hunting trails lace the area, they are not user-friendly and it's very easy to get lost. If you get lost and if no one knows you're in there, it could be life-threatening. If you do venture in, bring a compass, a cell phone, plenty of water, warm clothing, and rain gear. Leave your name and telephone number with someone on the outside and set aside a time to contact that person. Also, be aware that you may be trampling native species or inadvertently introducing alien species. The Park Service is trying to bring the area back to its native Hawaiian rainforest condition through eradication of alien plants and elimination of feral pigs.

Mauna Loa Road

About 2.5 miles south of the park entrance on the Highway 11, Mauna Loa Road turns off to the north. This road will lead you to the Tree Molds and a bird sanctuary, as well as to the trailhead for the Mauna Loa summit trail. As an added incentive, a minute down this road leaves 99 percent of the tourists behind.

Tree Molds is an ordinary name for an extraordinary area. Turn right off Mauna Loa Road soon after leaving the Belt Road and follow the signs for five minutes. This road runs into the tree molds area and loops back onto itself. At the loop, a signboard explains what occurred here. In a moment, you realize that you're standing atop a lava flow, and that the scattered potholes were entombed tree trunks, most likely the remains of a once-giant koa forest. Unlike at Lava Tree State Monument, where the magma encased the tree and flowed away, the opposite action happened here. The lava stayed put while the tree trunk burned away, leaving the 15- to 18-foot-deep holes. While the "sights" of this site may not excite some visitors, realizing what happened here and how it happened is an eye-opener.

Kipuka Puaulu is a sanctuary for birds and nature lovers who want to leave the crowds behind, just under three miles from Highway 11 up Mauna Loa Road. The sanctuary is an island atop an island. A *kipuka* is a piece of land that is surrounded by lava but has not been inundated by it, leaving the original vegetation and land contour intact. A few hundred yards away, small scrub vegetation struggles, but in the sanctuary the trees form a towering canopy a hundred feet tall. The first sign takes you to an ideal picnic area called Bird Park, with cooking grills; the second, 100 yards beyond, takes you to Kipuka Puaulu Loop Trail. As you enter the trail, a bulletin board describes the birds and plants, some of the last remaining indigenous fauna and flora in Hawaii. Please follow all rules. The dirt trail is self-guided, and pamphlets describing the stations along the way may be dispensed from a box near the start of the path. The loop is only one mile long, but to really assimilate the area, especially if you plan to do any bird-watching, expect to spend an hour minimum. It doesn't take long to realize that you are privileged to see some of the world's rarest plants, such as a small, nondescript bush called *'a'ali'i*. In the branches of the towering *'ohi'a* trees you might see an *'elepaio* or an *'apapane,* two birds native to Hawaii. Common finches and Japanese white eyes are imported birds that are here to stay. There's an example of a lava tube, a huge koa tree, and an explanation of how ash from eruptions provided soil and nutrients for the forest. Blue morning glories have taken over entire hillsides. Once considered a pest and aggressively eradicated, they have recently been given a reprieve and are now considered good ground cover—perhaps even indigenous. When you do come across a native Hawaiian plant, it seems somehow older, almost prehistoric. If a precontact Hawaiian could come back today, he or she would recognize only a few plants and trees seen here in this preserve. As you leave, listen for the melodies coming from the treetops and hope the day never comes when no birds sing. To hear the birds at their best, come in early morning or late afternoon.

Mauna Loa Road continues westward and gains elevation for approximately 10 miles. It passes through thick forests of lichen-covered koa trees, cuts across **Kipuka Ki,** and traverses the narrow **Ke'amoku Flow.** At the end of the pavement, at 6,662 feet, you will find a parking area and lookout. If the weather is cooperating, you'll be able to see much of the mountainside; if not, your field of vision will be restricted. A trail leads from here to the summit of Mauna Loa. It takes two long and difficult days to hike. Under no circumstances should it be attempted by novice hikers or those unprepared for cold alpine conditions. At times, this road may be closed due to extreme fire conditions.

Ka'u Desert Footprints

An entry to the **Ka'u Desert Trail** starts about eight miles south of the park entrance along Highway 11, between mile markers 37 and 38. There isn't a parking lot here; just park your car on the side of the road on the gravel. There is

DON'T TAKE THE LAVA HOME!

Legend has it that taking lava rock from Hawaii will bring you bad luck. Pele, the goddess of fire, does not like when her rocks leave Hawaii. Every year the park receives lava rock returned to them by mail with notes of explanation handwritten by the recipients of bad luck. I am not saying either way whether or not I think this legend holds true, but I can say, it's best not to take the rock.

If you so happen to take something and want to send it back, you can send it to Hawai'i Volcanoes National Park. They have a pile of them. If you want your rock to return with a ceremony of forgiveness, with just a $15 donation you can send your rock to Rainbow Moon (Attn: Lava Rock Return, P.O. Box 699, Volcano, HI 96785). Your rock will be returned to its source wrapped in a ti leaf. In addition, Rainbow Moon will happily send you an email to confirm that your rock was returned appropriately.

usually one or two other cars there. You don't have to pay to walk on this trail since the trailhead isn't through the park entrance. It is just good old free fun.

It's a short 20-minute hike from this trailhead to the Ka'u Desert Footprints. The 1.6-mile round-trip trek across the small section of desert is fascinating, and the history of the footprints makes the experience more evocative—although, because of deterioration the footprints are fairly faint now and they are difficult to see. It might not be worth going unless you are dying to see these footprints or looking to stretch your legs.

The predominant foliage is *'ohi'a,* which contrasts with the bleak desert surroundings. You pass a wasteland of *'a'a* and *pahoehoe* lava flows to arrive at the footprints. A metal fence in a sturdy pavilion surrounds the prints, which look as though they're cast in cement.

Actually they're formed from pisolites: particles of ash stuck together with moisture, which formed mud that hardened like plaster. The story of these footprints is far more exciting than the prints themselves, which are eroded and not very visible.

In 1790, Kamehameha was waging war with Keoua over control of the Big Island. One of Keoua's warrior parties of approximately 80 people attempted to cross the desert while Kilauea was erupting. Toxic gases descended upon them, and the warriors and their families were enveloped and suffocated. They literally died in their tracks, but the preserved footprints, although romanticism would have it otherwise, were probably made by a party of people who came well after the eruption or perhaps at some time during a previous eruption. This unfortunate occurrence was regarded by the Hawaiians as a direct message from the gods proclaiming their support for Kamehameha.

Hiking and Biking

HIKING

There are over 150 miles of hiking trails within the park. One long trail heads up the flank of Mauna Loa to its top; a spiderweb of trails loops around and across Kilauea Caldera and into the adjoining craters; and from a point along the Chain of Craters Road, another trail heads east toward the source of the most recent volcanic activity. But by far the greatest number of trails, and those with the greatest total distance, are those that cut through the Ka'u Desert and along the barren and isolated coast. Many have shelters, and trails that require overnight stays provide cabins or primitive campsites.

Because of the possibility of an eruption or earthquake, it is *imperative* to check in at park headquarters, where you can pick up current trail information and excellent maps. In fact, a hiking permit is required for most trails outside the Crater Rim Drive area and that stretch along the coast beyond the end of Chain of Craters Drive. Pick up your free permit no more than one day in advance. Much of the park is hot and dry, so carry plenty of drinking water. Wear a hat, sunscreen, and sunglasses, but don't forget rain gear because it often rains in the green areas of the park. Stay on trails and stay away from steep edges, cracks, new lava flows, and any area where lava is flowing into the sea.

If you will be hiking along the trails in the Kilauea Caldera, the free park maps are sufficient to navigate your way. To aid with hikes elsewhere, it's best to purchase and use larger and more detailed topographical maps. One that is readily available and of high quality is the *Hawai'i Volcanoes National Park* map by Trails Illustrated, and it is available at the gift shop at the visitors center.

Self-Guided Easy Hikes

If you find yourself only having one day to venture through Hawai'i Volcanoes National Park, there are several short hikes that will offer you a glimpse of what it's like to live next to an active volcano.

VOLCANO ART CENTER'S NIAULANI CAMPUS TRAIL

Just outside the park in Volcano Village is a four-acre rare old-growth tropical rainforest growing in volcanic ash from the 18th century. Some of the trees at the Volcano Art Center (19-4074 Old Volcano Rd., Volcano, 808/967-8222) are at least 200 years old and more than 65 feet tall. The Niaulani Campus Trail, which is filled with placards explaining the area and art, is only a 0.7-mile-long loop and is flat. Bird lovers will delight in this opportunity to see native birds. The tour is easy to complete on your own, but a one-hour guided tour is available every Monday (including holidays) at 9:30 A.M. (free). If you get there early, you can participate in an hour-long **yoga** class on Monday

© MARK WASSER

Hiking around Hawai'i Volcanoes National Park is generally safe, but pay attention to the warning signs around the park.

at 7:30 A.M. ($10) or stop by to unwind on Tuesday at 5:30 P.M. after a day of hiking.

CRATER RIM TRAIL

Although a large part of Crater Rim Drive is currently closed due to the sulphur dioxide (vog) from Halema'uma'u, it is possible to hike along the Crater Rim Trail. If you park at the Thomas A. Jaggar Museum and hike along the Crater Rim toward the visitors center you will be offered unparalleled views of the vast Kilauea Caldera. Along the way you pass through desert-like conditions with sparse vegetation to lush native tropical forests. You will also encounter the **Steam Vents,** where the water heated from the volcanic heat rises up from cracks in the earth. The hike along the Crater Rim Trail to/from the Thomas A. Jaggar Museum to the visitors center is approximately 2.5 miles and can take anywhere from 45 minutes to an hour. Parts of it are shaded while other parts are in an open field. The trailhead for this Crater Rim hike is left of the museum

and parking lot and also across the street from the visitors center (next to Volcano House). Parts of the trail have been paved and provide a good place for road or mountain biking.

SULPHUR BANKS TRAIL

From the visitors center parking lot you can get a good glimpse of some interesting volcanic geology. The Sulphur Banks Trail is a short and easy hike that offers intriguing sights. Bright yellow mineral deposits of sulphur line the trail as volcanic gases spew from the earth. This trail may remind some people of the volcanic vents in Yellowstone, and it just reminds one of the geologic variety found here on the Big Island. Interpretive signs offer explanations of the volcanic activities so it's easy to understand what you're seeing. To get to this trail walk to the left of the visitors center past the Volcano Art Center. A paved trail will lead you through a grassy field with a *heiau* (temple) and down a hill. If you see signs warning you that you may encounter volcanic gases you're going the right

HAWAI'I VOLCANOES

way. It's 0.5 mile one way from the visitors center to the Sulphur Banks. If you want to make it into a longer hike, you can cross the road and connect to the Crater Rim trail by the Steam Vents and hike all the way to the Thomas A. Jaggar Museum.

EARTHQUAKE TRAIL
If from the visitors center you head left (behind the Volcano House facing the caldera) on Crater Rim Trail, you'll walk one mile round-trip toward **Waldron Ledge** on the Earthquake Trail, named so due to the damage this area received during the 1983 6.6 magnitude earthquake. Waldron Ledge is known to be one of the best views in the park, and the trail, which is paved and wheelchair- and stroller-accessible as well as bike-friendly, presents an easy walk.

DEVASTATION TRAIL
Farther up Crater Rim Drive, most visitors hike along the one-mile roundtrip Devastation Trail, which could aptly be renamed Regeneration Trail. The mile it covers is fascinating, one of the most-photographed areas in the park. It leads across a field devastated by a tremendous eruption from **Kilauea Iki.** The area was once an 'ohi'a forest that was denuded of limbs and leaves, then choked by black pumice and ash. The vegetation has regenerated since then, and the recuperative power of the flora is part of an ongoing study. Notice that many of the trees have sprouted aerial roots trailing down from the branches: This is total adaptation to the situation, as these roots don't normally appear. As you move farther along the trail, tufts of grass and bushes peek out of the pumice and then the surroundings become totally barren.

Self-Guided Moderate Hikes
If you're willing and able to complete more moderate hikes and want to experience the volcano with your own two feet, then attempt one or both of these hikes. Both hikes can easily be completed in one day (really less than a day).

◖ KILAUEA IKI TRAIL
The Kilauea Iki Trail takes you from the top of the crater and lush tropical rainforest of native vegetation and native birds (the most common you'll see is the red apapane) to the bottom of the crater floor, which is devoid of vegetation but still breathes volcanic steam. This is a moderate four-mile loop because you descend and ascend 400 feet to and from the crater floor. It takes on average three hours to complete. I've seen small children complete this hike as well as parents bringing strollers for children (the latter I do not recommend).

The trail for this hike is clearly marked. The parking lot for Kilauea Iki is the first one on the right on the Chain of Craters Road. It's usually packed. From the parking lot go right and follow the Kilauea Iki sign, which will keep you to the left. As you hike along the rim look to the left and down at the various railed off lookouts. Below you is where you'll be as you descend the trail into the crater floor (I'm serious). Essentially you are passing along the rim and then descending across the barren landscape and back up through the trees (and the parking lot).

Upon ascending the trail out of the crater floor you will pass by the **Thurston Lava Tube** parking lot. This is a worthy addition to the hike to see a lava tube, but it is also one of the most popular stops with tour buses so it can get very crowded. Note: Your car was not stolen; you are in the Thurston Lava Tube parking lot, not the lot you parked in. Keep walking through the parking lot to the next parking lot where you left your car.

The best time to do this hike is first thing in the morning for several reasons. It's cooler in the morning and more of a pleasant hike in the floor of the crater. When it's cooler it's also easier to spot all the steam vents, which are an active reminder that the crater could erupt again at any time. Finally, the birds are also much more active in the morning. Look for them along the crater rim as they search for insects to keep their bellies filled. Pick up a trail guide for this particular trail at the visitors center or download it from the park's website for further descriptions of the sights you'll pass on your way.

PU'U HULUHULU TRAIL

Another notable hike that can be completed in just two or three hours (depends how fast you walk) is the 2.5-mile roundtrip Pu'u Huluhulu Trail to **Mauna Ulu.** This hike is for those who like a bit of adventure, since the trail isn't marked very well. Follow the signs along the Chain of Craters Road. Turn left where the road splits (you can only go right or left) and there will be a sign for Mauna Ulu. Follow the road (and the signs) until it ends. The trailhead will be to the left of the parking lot. This moderate hike will take you to the summit of a steaming volcanic crater that can also provide you with 360-degree panoramic views of the park, and on a clear day, if you're lucky, you even see the ocean. The trail crosses lava flows from the 1970s so you will still see young plants sprouting out from cracks in the lava. Follow the trail to Pu'u Huluhulu (Hairy Hill), a crater that has an island of vegetation *(kipuka)* that didn't burn during the 1970s flows. It's a short hike to the top of the *pu'u* (hill), which

gives you a good view of Mauna Ulu, the big mountain right in front of you. You can't hike past Pu'u Huluhulu without a permit, but you can follow the old flows up toward the top of Mauna Ulu. There aren't official trail markers to the top but it's easy to pick your own way up the young lava and return the way you came back to the trail. From the top of Mauna Ulu you can peer into the crater, which is hundreds of feet deep, and imagine what it must have been like when lava was spewing from it up to 1,700 feet into the air. A trail guide is available at the visitors center or online on the park's website.

Self-Guided Advanced Hikes

For experienced hikers who want to do some overnight camping and hiking, the park has several options for backcountry wilderness trips.

(HIKING TO HALAPE

A large section of the park has trails that run along the coast and has several beaches that

The most popular backcountry hike at Hawai'i Volcanoes National Park takes you to pristine Halape.

offer premier camping. By far one of the most remote and pristine beaches on the island is **Halape.** Getting here is something you have to earn, though.

The absolute closest you can get is the **Hilina Pali Trailhead,** from where it is an eight-mile descent to the beach across very hot, dry, rugged terrain. The first two miles are straight down the *pali* (cliff) with multiple switchbacks to get you safely to the bottom. Halape is the sandiest beach along the coast, but there are also other beautiful places to access the ocean that aren't quite as sandy. One stunning option: After descending the switchbacks to the bottom of Hilina Pali, take the trail to the right toward Ka'aha. This is a nice bay that offers lots of room to explore all the way to the *pali* that extends to the ocean. Some nice tide pools here offer unique snorkeling and swimming. If you keep to the left, the trail will lead you to Halape after six extremely hot miles that include some more steep ascents and descents—but your reward is a white sugary beach and a sheltered lagoon that offer you sand and protection from the raw ocean that crashes just past the lagoon. This spot is popular, so you're likely see other campers, but you'll never see the crowd you would in the more accessible sections of the park. Bathroom facilities are available here. There is water available at the backcountry sites, but it must be treated before drinking since it is just from a cistern of collected rainwater. Before you go, make sure to ask a ranger if there is water available since at times there is a drought.

The park requires backcountry permits to camp in these sections. They are available for free at the visitors center. There is a limit to the number of people they allow at any given time, so plan accordingly and know to get your permits ahead of time before you begin your trek.

If you have the option for someone to pick you up (or if you think you can find or hitch a ride back to your car), the best route with the most variety is to hike down from Hilina Pali, spend a night or two at Halape, then enjoy a nice flat hike out by heading toward Keahou and Apua, both of which have shelter

and water. This route is technically longer distance wise, but it is not as steep as the route you came on.

HIKING TO MAUNA LOA'S SUMMIT

The most extreme hike of them all, Mauna Loa offers a unique experience to climb to the summit of the island's largest volcano. This trip will take you to high altitudes of almost 14,000 feet, so be prepared for altitude sickness (it can happen) and changes of weather. Winter conditions can occur any time of the year here. In 2011 it snowed here in May! Yes, it snows in Hawaii. There are cabins available to stay in along the way that are free but require a permit from the Kilauea Visitor Center; you can only get them the day before your hike. The Pu'u 'Ula'ula (Red Hill) cabin contains 8 bunks, and the Mauna Loa summit cabin has 12 bunks (actually, only 12 visitors are permitted per group). Visitors are allowed a three-night maximum stay per site. Pit toilets are available at the cabins as well as drinking water (although check with park rangers about the water level). Don't forget to treat the water. No water is available on the trails themselves.

There are two trail options for your hike: via the Mauna Loa Road trailhead (an hour drive from the Kilauea Visitor Center) or the Mauna Loa Observatory trailhead (a two-hour drive via Saddle Road), which is not in the park. The **Mauna Loa Road trail** ascends 6,600 feet over 18 miles (and not an easy 18 miles—it's mostly lava rock). Depending on your hiking speed, it will take 4–6 hours to hike the 7.5 miles from the trailhead to the Pu'u 'Ula'ula cabin. Then, it's 8–12 additional hours to hike the 11.5 miles from the Pu'u 'Ula'ula cabin to the Mauna Loa summit cabin.

The **Mauna Loa Observatory Trail** climbs 1,975 feet over 3.8 miles up the volcano's north slope until it reaches the rim of the Moku'aweoweo Caldera (the summit). From here, the Mauna Loa summit cabin is 2.1 miles. In all, it takes about 4–6 hours to hike from the Observatory trailhead to the Mauna Loa summit cabin. However, the hike back from the Mauna Loa summit cabin to the Mauna Loa Observatory trailhead is much quicker (you're going downhill)—only about three hours.

In summary, you have a few options for this hike. If you have friends on the ground (or means to hire a taxi), you can start from the Mauna Loa Road trailhead and finish at the Mauna Loa Observatory trailhead (for a quicker exit). But again, you'll need someone to pick you up or arrange to leave a car at the trailhead. Otherwise, most hikers choose to hike from the Mauna Loa Observatory to the Mauna Loa summit cabin and return to the observatory for a challenging but manageable hike. A great resource for this hike is available here: www.kinquest.com/misc/travel/trail-guide.php. The guide on this site provides a mile-by-mile description of what you'll see (both trail markers and geological marvels) while you hike.

Note: Mauna Loa is at a very high altitude, so it is *imperative* to wait at least 24 hours between scuba diving and ascending Mauna Loa in order to avoid getting the bends.

Guided Hikes

When picking a guided hike of the park, the most important factors to consider are: How many people will be on the tour? If the minimum isn't met, will the tour get canceled? How much hiking/walking will you actually be doing (will you mostly be driving and going on short walks)? Will the hiking be for beginners or more advanced walkers?

Ranger-led hikes are a great way to explore the park for free with certifiably experienced guides. The **Exploring the Summit hike** is offered daily at 10:30 A.M. and 1:30 P.M. This 45-minute walk over a paved trail meets in front of the Kilauea Visitor Center and takes guests around the rim while the ranger lectures on Hawaiian history and geology. Check the bulletin board outside the visitors center for daily postings of additional hikes. Often, there is at least one additional hike (on some specific topic) each day.

If you're one of the lucky few, you'll grab a spot on the highly desired ranger-led

Wednesday **Pua Po'o Lava Tube Tour.** The tour, which explores a lava tube that is otherwise not open to the public, must be reserved one week in advance (no sooner or later) by calling the visitors center (808/985-6000) at 7:45 A.M. (no earlier) the Wednesday before you want to attend. There are only 12 spots available and they go quickly! Really, some park employees haven't even made it on the tour yet. You can reserve spots for four people with each reservation, and children must be older than 10. If you do make it on the tour, it meets at 12:30 P.M. and lasts about five hours. You have to be in fairly good physical shape to attend as you descend a 15-foot ladder into a lava tube, scramble along it, and then walk over uneven surfaces. A truly one-of-a-kind experience.

Several private tour guides happily take groups around the park on hikes. Dr. Hugh Montgomery, the owner and president of **Hawaiian Walkways** (800/457-7759, www.hawaiianwalkways.com) receives excellent reviews for his Kilauea Volcano Discovery Tour ($119 children, $169 adults plus tax) as well as his private tours (by arrangement), which are actually a pretty good deal if your group has more than four people. Hugh is truly an expert on Hawaiian flora and fauna and offers a lot of personal attention to his small groups, making his tours a great choice for hikers at any level.

Volcano Discovery (808/640-4165, http://hawaii.volcanodiscovery.com, $150–250) is another tour company that persistently receives good feedback, especially for beginning hikers and/or families traveling with children. Tours are somewhat customizable, meaning participants can work with the guides to pick which hikes they'd like complete. There are some set tours that you can reserve if you're looking to join something already scheduled. The dates and prices for these tours are listed on the website. In general, a four-hour tour for 3–6 people will run you $150 per person and a six-hour tour for 3–6 people will set you back $175 per person, and so on up to a 12-hour tour. Tour guides are known as trained geologists and provide first-rate narration.

Similarly, Warren Costa, a.k.a. **Native Guide Hawaii** (808/982-7575, www.native-guidehawaii.com, $300 for one person or $150 parties of two or more, cash only!), will personally pick you up (and return you safely) after guiding you through the park on a hike that includes narration on Hawaiian culture, legends, and geology of the park. Warren is very much concerned with not only teaching about the environment about the park, but also raising awareness about how the environment relates to Hawaiian culture. Tours have a maximum of six guests, and children are welcome.

BIKING

Biking is permitted in the park on paved roads, paved sections of the Crater Rim Trail, and on some dirt trails. The park has created an excellent *Where to Bicycle* brochure available on the website: www.nps.gov/havo/planyour-visit/bike.htm.

The suggested bike rides include a moderate 11-mile loop to circle the rim, a moderate 18-mile round-trip ride on Hilina Pali Road, a challenging 40-mile roundtrip Summit to Sea ride following the Mauna Ulu eruption, and a challenging 27-mile round-trip ride up (climbing 2,600 feet!) and down Mauna Loa Road (the down part doesn't take so long). The guide includes several short offshoots from the Mauna Loa Road for those who want to do some mountain biking.

If you don't have a bike with you or are not an experienced rider, or you're simply looking for a different way to see the park, I highly recommend taking a guided bike tour of the park with **Bike Volcano** (808/934-9199, www.bikevolcano.com, children/van riders $95, adults $99 per person). What makes this a great way to see the park is that it takes some cars off the road (there are so many there!) and the ride is all downhill and truly easy for anyone (including youngsters and those of us who are out of shape). There are snacks at several stops on the four-hour tour. That said, experienced riders may be bored or frustrated by the slow pace. The ride stops at all the major sights along the Crater Rim, where the tour guide, who is not just a "bike dude" (as he says) but is trained in geology and Hawaiian culture, gives very informative talks about the park and Hawaii in general. In addition to this tour of the park, other options include a sunset ride to view the lava flow ($119–129) and the basic park tour with a winery visit/tasting as an add-on ($119–129). Bike Volcano offers several pickup points for riders (including from Hilo), or riders may meet at the Kilauea Visitor Center.

Another company that does a similar basic bike tour of the park, but picks up from both Hilo and the Kona side, is **Nui Pohaku** (808/937-0644, www.nuipohaku.com, $135–239). The bike tour guides between companies tend to know each other, so the actual tour and information given on the tour aren't that different. The main difference is that Nui Pohaku tends to use older bikes than the other companies (you might not notice the difference, though). In addition to the basic park ride, Nui Pohaku offers combo tours that include a nighttime guided hike to the lava flow in Puna (not by bike).

HAWAI'I VOLCANOES

Adventure Sports and Tours

BUS TOURS

If you have rented a car, there isn't much of a reason to take a tour bus around the park unless you really want to be able to ask questions of someone semi-knowledgeable while you're sightseeing. Otherwise (hopefully), this guide as well as the brochures available at the park visitors center should provide you with enough information for your journey.

Guided tour bus trips to the park tend to be best and most utilized by day trippers to the park—either those flying in from another island for the day or those traveling from the Kona side who don't want to worry about driving back to Kona late at night. These guided tours are also great for visitors who might need translation into languages besides English.

The most ubiquitous tour company of them all, **Roberts Hawaii** (866/898-2519, www.robertshawaii.com, $290) offers pickup from Hilo and then a full-day journey to the park with stops at the Mauna Loa Macadamia Nut Factory (in Hilo) and the major sights in the park. Roberts has been doing this tour for a very long time and has the schedule down pat. They know what they're doing, but you likely won't get much personal attention or willingness to alter their schedule at all (for instance if you want to stay longer at one of the sights).

A new player in town, **Kapoho Kine Adventures** (25 Waianuenue Ave., Hilo, 808/964-1000, www.kapohokine.com) is working hard to build its business and create exciting tours for its participants. They offer a range of incredibly full day tours to the park with possible pickup from the Kona side, traveling over the Saddle Road, then a second (or third) pickup from Hilo before heading to the park. In the later afternoon, if there is lava flowing, guests travel to Kaimu Beach in Puna for a gourmet dinner, possible farm tour, and to view the lava. The entire tour, from pickup to drop-off, is 16 hours long! The tour is $159 for children and $179 for adults (plus tax) with Kona pickup, less if you meet in Hilo or at the park. If a 16-hour tour (and very

early wake-up) sounds like no fun while you're on vacation, they also offer a shorter Evening Volcano Adventure tour (with later pickup) that visits solely the lava flow viewing area in Puna ($139 children, $159 adults plus tax).

The crème de la crème, for those leaving from the Kona side, is **Hawaii Forest and Trails** (808/331-8505 www.hawaii-forest.com, $149 children, $179 adults plus tax), with an eco-friendly ethic, extremely in-the-know tour guides, and flexibility with their small groups. This 12-hour roundtrip adventure (includes continental breakfast and lunch) is mainly a tour of the main park sights but makes stops along the Ka'u Coast (on the way to the park) for some sightseeing as well. Although you'll mostly stay on the bus during this tour, there are several less-than-a-mile walks—ideal for those who want to do some walking in the park.

A Twilight trip (no vampires) is also available and offers something a little different from the usual twilight excursion. Tour goers, leaving later in the afternoon, travel to the park via the Saddle Road, making stops at **Mauna Kea State Park** and near Hilo to explore the **Kaumana Cave** before arriving to the park around sunset to witness the lava flow from Puna or the glow from near the Thomas A. Jaggar Museum.

HELICOPTER TOURS

A very dramatic way to experience the awesome power of the volcano is to take a helicopter tour. The choppers are perfectly suited for the maneuverability necessary to get an intimate bird's-eye view. The pilots will fly you over the areas offering the most activity, often dipping low over lava pools, skimming still-glowing flows, and circling the towering steam clouds rising from where lava meets the sea. When activity is really happening, tours are jammed, and prices, like lava fountains, go sky-high. Remember, however, that these tours are increasingly resented by hikers and anyone else trying to have a quiet experience, and that new regulations might limit flights over the lava area.

Also, these tours are not without danger, as helicopters have crashed near lava flows during commercial sightseeing flights. Nonetheless, if you are interested, contact one of the helicopter companies located in Hilo or Kona. Alternatively, fixed-wing plane tour companies also offer flights over the volcano area from both Hilo and Kona.

Sunshine Helicopters (808/882-1233 or 800/622-3144, www.sunshinehelicopters.com), leaving from Hapuna on the Kona side, offers a two-hour Volcano Deluxe tour that circles the island ($510 per person with online discount or $485 for the early-bird tour).

Another large operation with a spotless safety record, **Blue Hawaiian Helicopters** (808/886-1768 in Waikoloa, 800/786-2583, www.bluehawaiian.com) operates tours from both the Kona and Hilo sides with two helicopter options—the A-Star and the Eco-star. The difference between the helicopters is that the Eco-star is "the first touring helicopter of the 21st century," meaning that its seats are more comfortable, it is quieter, and it has larger windows for a less obstructed view than the A-Star. Most importantly, it costs more. From the Kona side, there is a two-hour Big Island Spectacular ($396/$495), an all-encompassing trip that circumvents the island to witness all its highlights, including a quick flyover of the park. From the Hilo side, the one-hour Circle of Fire plus Waterfalls tour ($196/$241) will take you over the waterfalls near Hilo on your way to Hawai'i Volcanoes National Park.

BOAT TOURS

If you need still another way to catch a glimpse of the lava flow (there are so many), and you're not apt to get seasick, a boat ride is another possibility—with a strong caveat, if the lava happens to be flowing into the ocean at the time. Before you book your tour, check with the park (or on the website) to make sure that the lava is going in that direction since it doesn't always flow into the ocean. There are many stories about boat tour companies taking passengers aboard to see the lava flow that doesn't exist. At the time of writing, the lava was not flowing into the ocean.

The company with the best reputation, **Lava Ocean Adventures** (808/966-4200, www.lavaocean.com, $133 for adults, $107 for children under 12) provides a two-hour cruise along the Puna Coast en route to view the lava flowing into the ocean. On your way you'll see black-sand beaches and sea life galore (turtles and whales are a possibility December–May). Fishers can add an hour to the tour ($160/$140) and try their hand at catching *ono* and ahi. When the lava isn't always flowing, this company still takes riders out on the ocean and gives talks about the history and geology of the coast.

Other Recreation

GOLF

The oldest golf course on the island, dating back to the 1920s, the **Volcano Golf and Country Club** (Pi'i Mauna Dr., 808/967-7331, www.volcanogolfshop.com, $55 plus tax) may not be the best designed golf course in the world, but it has some pretty amazing views—Mauna Loa in the background and Hawai'i Volcanoes National Park right in front of you, and you are circled by pine and *'ohi'a* trees. The course can get crowded on a sunny day with visitors to the park taking an afternoon off to jet around the course and stopping for lunch at the country club (which is hardly a country club by any standards). Rental clubs are available at the pro shop.

SPA AND MASSAGE

From facials to pedicures to traditional *lomilomi* massages, **Hale Ho'ola: Hawaiian Healing Arts Center and Spa** (11-3913 7th St., 808/756-2421, www.halehoola.net, massages start at $75 an hour) does it all and does it well at half the cost of spas on the Kona

VOLCANO WINERY

On a clear day Mauna Loa dominates the landscape behind Volcano Winery (35 Pi'i Mauna Dr., 808/967-7772, www.volcanowinery.com) on the Big Island of Hawai'i. With the designation of "the southernmost winery in the United States," Volcano Winery is far from the traditional winery, as one can see from the lava tubes that cut deep into the property and one day may be transformed into cellars to age the Pinot Noir. Even with over 70,000 visitors a year and distribution throughout the Hawai-ian Islands and Alaska (their wines, when purchased at the tasting room, can be shipped to most states), essentially each bottle is individually crafted by a small group of employees tenderly using ancient-looking equipment to fill and cork them. The winery cannot guarantee that one bottle will taste exactly the same as the next as several of their selections are created from the mixture of grapes with local fruits, such as guava and jaboticaba, and flavors vary depending on their ripeness.

side. Suzanne Woolley, the owner and creator of the spa, starts each session allowing the client to sample scents and products (all made from local ingredients) so that she can truly tailor the experience to each individual. If you can't decide which treatment to try (she offers seven different types of massage), try one of the two-hour rejuvenation packages ($150), which are the best of what the spa has to offer. You can call last minute and Suzanne will try to accommodate you—she will even come to you at your hotel. Couples and groups of friends are also welcomed as additional therapists can be called in to assist.

Shopping

Volcano is known for two things (besides the obvious: volcanoes): the arts and the sciences. Art collectors/lovers will be pleased with the availability of reasonably priced art pieces in the area (science lovers might also like the art), ranging from sculptures to pottery to jewelry to photography. Many of the pieces use the surrounding environment as an inspiration. If you simply drive on Old Volcano Road in Volcano Village, you'll pass by a few different galleries. An Open sign will indicate that you should come in (sometimes they are closed to visitors).

Art enthusiasts will love **2400 Fahrenheit Glass Blowing** (Old Volcano Rd. off of Hwy. 11 between mile markers 23 and 24, 808/985-8667, www.2400F.com, Thurs.–Mon. 10 A.M.–4 P.M.). At times, you'll have the opportunity to see artists working on their pieces; otherwise you can walk around the gallery examining their lovely one-of-a-kind pieces inspired by the local environment. Even if glass blowing isn't taking place, this gallery makes for a worthy stop.

If you're curious about galleries outside Old Volcano Road, stop at the **Volcano Art Center–Niaulani Campus** (19-4074 Old Volcano Rd., Volcano, 808/967-8222) to inquire for listings of galleries of the area or suggestions of where to visit.

Otherwise, there really is not much shopping in the village except for a gift shop at the Thai Thai restaurant (tourist items like hats or sweatshirts) and **Kilauea Kreations** (on Old Volcano Rd. next to Lava Rock restaurant, 808/967-8090, www.kilaueakreations.com, Mon.–Fri. 9:30 A.M.–5:30 P.M., Sat.–Sun. 9 A.M.–5 P.M.), a cute shop that specializes in Hawaiian quilts, quilt patterns, and fabrics. They sometimes offer classes, so if

HAWAI'I VOLCANOES

BECOME A MEMBER OF THE VOLCANO ART CENTER

Even if you are only in Volcano for vacation, there are a few good reasons to become a member of the Volcano Art Center (volcano-artcenter.org), besides the good feeling that comes with donation to the arts. In addition to membership being tax deductible, it comes with discounts at the Volcano Art Center Gallery store (10 percent), price breaks on classes (like yoga, which is half off with the discount), reciprocity at other museums on the Mainland (really, if you show your membership card, even some museums in New York City will give you free entry), and invitations to gallery openings (if you are in Volcano when one being held, it is worth attending these events, which include an excellent food spread, free wine, and a chance to mingle with local volcano-ites). Seniors and students can join for as little as $25, and regular adults can join for $42. If you are buying a lot of art (or an expensive piece of art), it may be worth joining for the discount (and because the art center can use the money).

you're interested check the website or call for more information.

In the park, the delightful **Volcano Art Center Gallery** (808/967-7565, daily 9 A.M.–5 P.M. except Christmas) sells books, music, jewelry, and art in a variety of mediums.

There is some overlap between the Volcano Art Center Gallery and the **Kilauea Visitor Center** gift shop in terms of what books they sell, but if you're looking for a Hawai'i Volcanoes National Park raincoat, sweatshirt, or hat, then the visitors center is where you should go.

Entertainment and Events

ENTERTAINMENT

After a long day at the park, you might be too tired to do anything, but if you are looking to get out there are several opportunities for "nightlife" (lots of quotes are needed here) in Volcano.

The **Lava Lounge** at Kilauea Military Camp (in the park) can offer you not only cheap drinks but karaoke every Thursday night (it can get really rowdy), live music sometimes on the weekends, and big parties for holidays like Halloween and St. Patrick's Day. If want an activity to go along with your drinking the **Bowling Alley** across the street from the Lava Lounge has five old-school lanes and rents shoes. You don't have to drink while you bowl, and actually if you want alcohol you need to purchase it at the Lava Lounge and bring it to the bowling alley (it's allowed).

The **Volcano Art Center** (808/967-8222, volcanoartcenter.org) organizes monthly poetry slams (usually on a Friday night toward the end of the month), frequent music concerts (not just Hawaiian music), and demonstrations of Hawaiian culture such as hula. Check the website for additional information.

The **After Dark in the Park** program (Kilauea Visitor Center, Tues. 7 P.M., park entrance fee applies plus recommended $2 donation) presents talks by top experts in the fields of volcanology, geology, and Hawaiian culture. Check the schedule (www.nps.gov/havo/planyourvisit/events_adip.htm) for more information. Note: It's not always a lecture; sometimes there are slack-key guitarists or choral groups performing. In addition, some months additional programs are added on Wednesday nights. Check the bulletin board just outside the Kilauea Visitor Center for additional information of what's happening in the park.

HAWAI'I VOLCANOES

EVENTS

The **Volcano Art Center Rain Forest Runs** (808/967-8240, www.volcanoartcenter.org, $30–75 entry fee) event is an annual tradition in Volcano usually held in mid-August. For almost 25 years this run through the park was the largest trail run in the state of Hawaii. In 2010 it was decided that it wasn't appropriate to hold the race in the national park (for safety and probably also bureaucratic reasons) and it was moved to Volcano Village. Participants can choose from a 5K walk/run, 10K, or a half marathon. All three runs are out and back courses through the village at 4,000 feet elevation. Even though the run is no longer in the park, it still offers dramatic views of Mauna Loa in the distance and beautiful scenery.

Since 1986, around Thanksgiving each year the Volcano Village Hui artists have hosted the annual **Art Studio Tours** and sale (www.volcanovillageartistshui.com). Visitors can pick up a map at the Volcano Art Center—Niaulani Campus (19-4074 Old Volcano Rd., Volcano, 808/967-8222) that lists the participating sites. The village really comes alive as art walkers travel from gallery to gallery meeting with artists from several different mediums (fiber arts, pottery, glass art, block prints, etc.). Since the sale takes place at the artists' studios or homes the art for sale is often at bargain prices (for instance, you may see the same piece of art at the Volcano Art Center Gallery with a 30 percent markup).

Food

VOLCANO VILLAGE

I wish the dining experience in Volcano—with its captive audience of tourists who are starving after a long day touring the park—were so much better than it actually is. There are a few options, but they tend toward mediocre and overpriced, so keep your expectations low. If you're not too hungry, are in the area for a few days, or are simply in the mood for a drive, it might be worth heading to Hilo (only 40 minutes away) to seek better options. The options in Volcano are listed from south to north on Old Volcano Road. They are all within minutes (or less) of one another.

Often crowded, **Kiawe Kitchen** (19-4005 Huanani Rd.—but find it on Old Volcano Rd., 808/967-7711, breakfast Mon.–Fri. 7:30–10 A.M., lunch daily 11 A.M.–2:30 P.M., dinner daily 5:30–8:30 P.M., $25) offers above-average (if overpriced) food, but service is a consistent issue and they are often out of main dishes. It's a good place to get a starter and a cocktail (if you're not in a rush), or better yet, order one of the wood-fired thin-crust pizzas ($18) to go (call ahead, really) for the best possible experience with this restaurant.

In the back side of the same complex, the food is much more reasonably priced at **Café Ohia**

(corner of Old Volcano Rd. and Huanani Rd., daily 6 A.M.–7 P.M., $7). There never seem to be enough people working here for as crowded as it gets. But the crowds are here for a reason: homemade breads, pastries, and lunch specials. For $7 you have your choice of deli sandwich with Hawaiian-style sides (like macaroni salad). The portions are large. If you're not too hungry try the Portuguese bean soup. It's a non-vegetarian hearty stew that will warm you up during the sometimes chilly Volcano days. There is no indoor seating (just a room that you order in), so either take your sandwiches to go into the park or enjoy them outside on picnic tables. Since the wait can get long, the staff encourages patrons to head next door to the grocery store and grab a beer to enjoy outside.

The most romantic and rustic option in town is the long-standing **Kilauea Lodge** (19-3948 Old Volcano Rd., 808/967-7366, www.kilaealodge.com, daily 7:30 A.M.–2 P.M. and 5–9 P.M. lunch $11, dinner $30). The food is expensive, but the setting seems to match. The large fireplace (look for the book on the coffee table in front of it explaining its history) sets the mood for this truly lodge-like setting with game animals adorning the ceiling and featured on the menu. Vegetarian choices are limited here. The meat dishes are prepared well and come with satisfying sides like mashed potatoes, but overall, the meat dishes are better in the restaurants of Waimea. Foodies and those who like to drink might try their *li hing mui* (salted dried plum) rimmed cocktails, like *liliko'i* (passion fruit) margaritas. Eating isn't a requirement for drinking here. If you solely want drinks, you can simply walk in, cozy up on the couch in front of the fireplace (seating is very limited), and order away. Reservations are a must for dinner, and if you want to surprise your dinner guest, call ahead to ask for your name on the menu (they give shout-outs for birthdays and anniversaries).

Some locals say that (**Thai Thai** (19-4084 Old Volcano Rd., 808/967-7969, www.lavalodge.com/thaithairestaurant.htm, daily except Wed. noon–9 P.M., $11–28) is their favorite Thai food place on the island. (Mine is Sombat's Fresh Thai Cuisine in Hilo, but Thai Thai is a close runner-up.) The food is all spicy and authentic, with traditional dishes such as soups, rice noodles, and curries. Beer, wine, and plenty of gluten-free and vegetarian options are offered, and a children's menu is available. The restaurant is attached to a gift shop with tourist items (like trucker hats that say "Hawaii" on them) and toiletries. Call ahead; sometimes they don't follow their posted hours.

Farther down the road, **Lava Rock** (19-3972 Old Volcano Rd., 808/967-8526, Mon. 7:30 A.M.–5 P.M., Tues.–Sat. 7:30 A.M.–9 P.M., Sun. 7:30 A.M.–4:30 P.M., $12) serves burgers (made with local beef), sandwiches, local-style plate lunches, and Volcano-grown garden salads all at a reasonable price—such an anomaly for Volcano! The interior looks like a diner, with those leather booths that stick to you and waitresses who are simultaneously nice and assertive. Sit outside in the garden area if it's not raining. The food is on the high end of diner food—more of it is homemade than not. Even though there is the salad option, the bulk of items on the menu are fried and breaded. Not a haven for health-conscious eaters. Although locals don't really utilize this space as a coffee shop, it does have a variety of coffee drinks (with their own brew) and wireless Internet.

Right before the road comes to a dead end, you'll find Ira Ono's place (that's what the locals call it): **Café Ono** (19-3834 Old Volcano Rd., 808/967-7261, www.volcanogardenarts.com, gallery Tues.–Sun. 10 A.M.–4 P.M., café 11 A.M.–3 P.M., $11). It's the kind of place that you either love or hate. The menu lists only three or four mains, drinks, and one or two desserts each day—they are usually vegetarian, and some are even vegan and/or gluten free. But the food tastes like something you could have made but you probably would have seasoned better. The service is quick enough here (it's never that crowded). The setting is lovely, with a few tables in the back of the art gallery and more outdoors among the trees (and a goat).

Markets

The small **Volcano Store** (Old Volcano Rd., daily 5 A.M.–7 P.M.) is pretty much the equivalent of a bodega. From fresh *musubi* to chips, some frozen foods, books, local jams, wine, and some of the nicest flower bouquets around, it somehow has everything you might need in a small space, including an ATM inside. What it does not have is a great selection of food for camping (although it does have the standard instant rice). Prices are a little bit more expensive than the larger stores in Hilo or Kona.

Down the street, the **Kilauea General Store** (19-3872 Old Volcano Rd., 808/967-7555, Mon.–Sat. 7 A.M.–7:30 P.M., Sun. 7 A.M.–7 P.M.) has fewer goods than the Volcano Store, but still has wine, an ATM, and dry goods like bread and jam (actually, their jam is made in-house) as well as DVDs to rent. There is also an in-house sub shop ($6 for a make-your-own sub) open at lunchtime, but with fresh coffee on hand all day long.

The Sunday morning **Volcano Farmers Market** (19-4030 Wright Rd. at the Cooper Center, http://thecoopercenter.org/FarmersMarketVolcano.html, Sun. 6:30–10 A.M.) is attended by what seems like every single resident of Volcano Village. It serves as an important community event. It entails the usual farmers markets accoutrements like produce and plants, but it also has jams, chocolate brittle, and

HAWAI'I VOLCANOES

prepared foods. Come early for breakfast (really early!—most vendors are sold out by 8 A.M.) and stay to chitchat with the locals.

HAWAI'I VOLCANOES NATIONAL PARK AND SOUTH

Outside of Volcano Village there are a few noteworthy dining options. Just two miles south of the park, in the Volcano Golf Course subdivision, is the **Pele's Backyard** restaurant in the **Volcano Golf and Country Club** (Pi'i Mauna Dr., 808/967-8228, Mon.–Thurs. 10 A.M.–7 P.M., Fri. 8 A.M.–5 P.M., Sat. 8 A.M.–7 P.M., Sun. 8 A.M.–5 P.M., $10)—which is not really a country club in any shape or form. This unpretentious place happens to have the best mahimahi eggs Benedict ($11) this side of the island. Brunch is only served on the weekend, and sometimes they run out of the hollandaise sauce (so call ahead if you want to make sure they still have some). There are other options, like crepes and eggs. All good (not gourmet, though) and all reasonably priced (around $9). Lunch and dinner are also available but are just as mediocre as the bulk of Volcano's joints: local dishes like mahimahi,

chicken *katsu,* and *loco moco* as well as clubhouse food like burgers and chicken wings. Service is extremely friendly, but the kitchen can be slow if many people come in at the same time. Full bar available.

Inside the park there essentially are no eating options (at least not until Volcano House reopens) except at the Kilauea Military Camp (808/438-6707) eateries **Lava Lounge** (Mon.–Sat. 4 P.M. until no one is there, Sun. open at 2 P.M. in football season) and **Crater Rim Café** (Mon.–Fri. 6:30 A.M.–1 P.M., Sat.–Sun. 6:30–11 A.M., daily 5–8 P.M.). Both are entirely open to the public and the best way to mingle with park employees—especially at the Lava Lounge, where after a few drinks park employees are thrilled to speak with anyone who doesn't work at the park. The café serves breakfast, lunch, and dinner (à la carte and buffet options) and often has special events or themed meals for holidays. The Lava Lounge only offers a few options, entirely of the bar food variety, like chicken wings and garlic fries (actually, you order at the bar but someone at the bowling alley makes the food). But yes, they do have a full bar and lots of beer on draft.

Information and Services

EMERGENCY SERVICES

There are no hospitals or clinics located in Volcano or the park. The closest major hospital, in an emergency, is in Hilo (about 45 minutes away). For nonemergencies, the closest clinics are either in Ka'u (25 minutes to the south on Hwy. 11) or in Kea'au (20 minutes to the north on Hwy. 11).

Likewise, there are no pharmacies in Volcano Village. The closest pharmacy is the Longs Drugs in Kea'au. Standard over-the-counter medications like aspirin can be found at the Volcano Store in the village.

BANKS

There are no actual bank branches in Volcano. However, nondescript ATMs are available in both markets in Volcano Village (Volcano

Store and Kilauea General Store), and there's a machine that sometimes works in front of the Thai Thai restaurant.

POST OFFICE

Whereas health facilities are lacking, post offices are abundant: there are two. If you are desperate to get your postcard stamped "Volcano" then visit the post office in Volcano Village on Old Volcano Road (it's next to Volcano Store). Alternatively, if you want your postcard stamped "Hawai'i Volcanoes National Park" visit the post office at the Kilauea Military Camp inside the park.

LAUNDRY

If you have been in the backcountry for awhile, you might need to do laundry. Many of the accommodations in the area offer laundry either for free or for a fee; however, if this isn't an option for you there is a **laundry** (daily 8 A.M.–7 P.M.) in the back of the Ace Hardware store in Volcano Village on Old Volcano Road (behind the Thai Thai restaurant).

Getting There and Around

While it's not possible to travel inside the park on public transportation, you can get to and from the park on it with **Hele-On Bus** (www.heleonbus.org, 808/961-8744, $1 per ride, $1 each for luggage, large backpacks, bikes).

The bus travels thrice daily—twice in the morning and once in the evening—starting at the Kilauea Visitor Center, passing through Volcano Village, and then traveling north on Highway 11 to Hilo. The bus leaves from Hilo once in the morning and twice in the afternoon. The trip takes a little over an hour depending on how many people are getting on and off (sometimes it can be a lot).

It is possible from Hilo to make connections to the Kona side, Waimea, and the Hamakua Coast. Or, once a day the bus continues on to Ka'u, where it also is possible to make connections to the Kona side.

HAWAI'I VOLCANOES

PUNA

There is something magical about Puna. The trees towering over Highway 132 toward the Red Road create a canopy of greenery that sets the scene for a tropical fairy tale. The pace of life on the Big Island is slow, but somehow, it moves even slower in the southern Puna district, where free spirit types (who are sometimes referred to as Puna-tics, perhaps purposely meant to rhyme with lunatics) spend Sunday afternoon drumming at Kehena Beach, soaking in warm tide pools hidden in the forest, and practicing yoga at one of several retreat centers.

Formed from rivers of lava spilling from Mauna Loa and Kilauea again and again over the last million years or so, the Puna district continues to be the most volcanically active part of the island. The molten rivers stopped only when they hit the sea, where they fizzled and cooled, forming a chunk of semi-raw land that bulges into the Pacific—marking the state's easternmost point at **Cape Kumukahi.**

Highway 11 (the Hawai'i Belt Road) is a corridor cutting through the center of Puna, running uphill straight toward the town of Volcano. Cutting through well-established villages, this road passes some of the largest and best-known flower farms in the state, and on both sides of this highway are scattered residential subdivisions.

Pahoa, the major town in this region, was at one time the terminus of a rail line that took commodities and people to Hilo. This was timber country and later sugarcane land, but since the mills have closed, it's turned to producing

HIGHLIGHTS

LOOK FOR 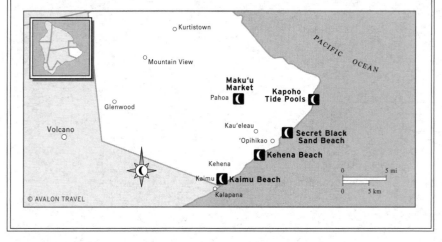 TO FIND RECOMMENDED
SIGHTS, ACTIVITIES, DINING, AND LODGING.

Kapoho Tide Pools: The landscape here is impressive, with tide pools surrounded by lava rocks and an ocean backdrop, but even better is the world under the water – it's a great spot for beginner snorkelers (page 151).

Secret Black Sand Beach: You can bask in the sun all day long at this deserted beach, and beyond it you'll find an even more secret black-sand beach (page 152).

Kehena Beach: Sundays are the day at Kehena Beach when lower Punans and like-minded visitors gather on Kehena Beach to drum and swim naked in the ocean. The vibe

here is friendly and you won't feel out of place if you are clothed (page 153).

Kaimu Beach: Here you can watch how a beach becomes a black-sand beach – from the waves hitting the black boulders and over time breaking them down into smaller pieces and, eventually, sand (page 153).

Maku'u Market: Part food truck fair, part farmers market, part antiques market, this is one of the best markets on the island, and unlike many other markets, you don't have to get here at the crack of dawn to be part of the action (page 160).

© AVALON TRAVEL

acres of anthuriums and papayas. Down the hill from town, **Lava Tree State Monument** was once a rainforest whose giant trees were covered with lava, like hot dogs dipped in batter. The encased wood burned, leaving a hollow stone skeleton. You can stroll through this lichen-green rock forest before you head farther east into the brilliant sunshine of the coast. Roads take you past a multitude of anthurium and papaya farms, oases of color in a desert of solid black lava.

Southward is a string of popular beaches that are truly off the beaten path. You can

camp, swim, surf, or just play in the water to your heart's delight, but realize that there are few places to stop for food, gas, or supplies. Also along the coast you can visit natural areas where the sea tortured the hot lava into caves, tubes, arches, and even a natural hot bath.

ORIENTATION
Highway 11 between Volcano and Hilo

The crossroads of the east side of the island, in the heart of Kea'au, the first town south of Hilo on Highway 11, is a strip mall at the

PUNA

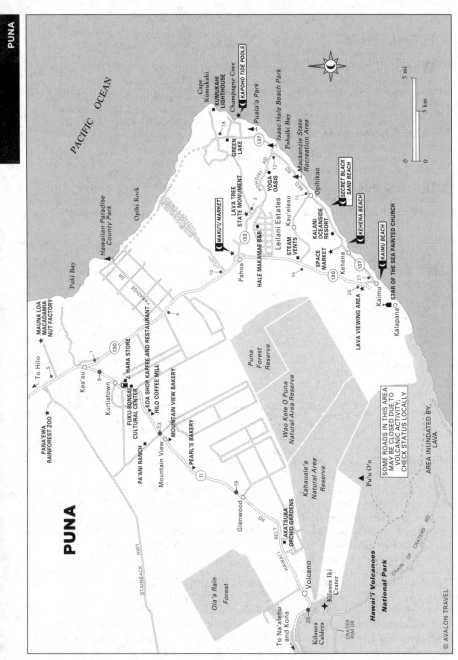

PUNA

Hawai'i Volcanoes National Park

SOME ROADS IN THIS AREA MAY BE CLOSED DUE TO VOLCANIC ACTIVITY; CHECK STATUS LOCALLY.

AREA INUNDATED BY LAVA

PACIFIC OCEAN

© AVALON TRAVEL

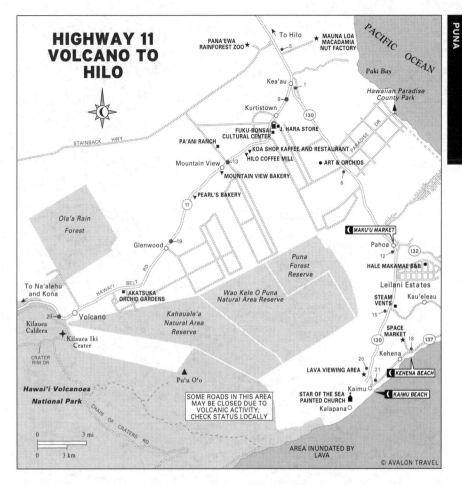

HIGHWAY 11
VOLCANO TO
HILO

PANA'EWA RAINFOREST ZOO ★
MAUNA LOA MACADAMIA NUT FACTORY ★
To Hilo
PACIFIC OCEAN
Paki Bay
Kea'au
Hawaiian Paradise County Park
Kurtistown
FUKU-BONSAI CULTURAL CENTER
J. HARA STORE
PA'ANI RANCH
KOA SHOP KAFFEE AND RESTAURANT
HILO COFFEE MILL
Mountain View
ART & ORCHIDS
MOUNTAIN VIEW BAKERY
PEARL'S BAKERY
STAINBACK HWY
Ola'a Rain Forest
MAKU'U MARKET
Glenwood
Pahoa
Puna Forest Reserve
HALE MAKAMAE B&B
Leilani Estates
To Na'alehu and Kona
HAWAI'I BELT RD
AKATSUKA ORCHID GARDENS
Wao Kele O Puna Natural Area Reserve
Kau'eleau
STEAM VENTS
Volcano
Kilauea Caldera
Kahaualeʻa Natural Area Reserve
SPACE MARKET
Kilauea Iki Crater
Kehena
CRATER RIM DR
LAVA VIEWING AREA
KEHENA BEACH
Hawai'i Volcanoes National Park
Pu'u O'o
Kaimu
KAIMU BEACH
CHAIN OF CRATERS RD
SOME ROADS IN THIS AREA MAY BE CLOSED DUE TO VOLCANIC ACTIVITY; CHECK STATUS LOCALLY
STAR OF THE SEA PAINTED CHURCH
Kalapana
0   3 mi
0   3 km
AREA INUNDATED BY LAVA
© AVALON TRAVEL

intersection where the road splits to travel on to Pahoa or north to Hilo or south toward Volcano. Before the sugar mill closed in 1984, this was a bustling town with great swaths of the surrounding land in cane. Kea'au and the numerous subdivisions that have mushroomed on both sides of the highway running to Pahoa and up to Volcano have become bedroom communities to Hilo. Highway 130 heads southeast from here to the steamy south coast, while Highway 11 heads southwest and passes through the mountain villages of Kurtistown,

Mountain View, Glenwood, and Volcano at approximately 10-mile intervals, then enters Hawai'i Volcanoes National Park. Highway 11 (the Hawai'i Belt Road), although only two lanes, is straight, well surfaced, and scrupulously maintained.

While you could just drive on through the area, there are some worthy attractions—especially worthy if it's raining everywhere on the island. For instance, you can make a reservation to travel through the Kazumura Cave in Glenwood, reputedly the longest lava tube

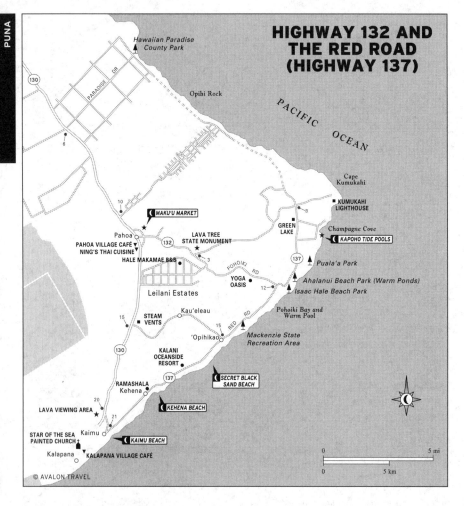

HIGHWAY 132 AND THE RED ROAD (HIGHWAY 137)

system in the world, or learn how to bonsai at the indoor Fuku-Bonsai Cultural Center.

Pahoa

Arriving in Pahoa town, you're entering into lower (or south) Puna district. Residents of upper Puna (places like Glenwood or Kurtistown) create this distinction to separate themselves from the poor (and unwarranted) reputation Pahoa holds of being a place where petty crime (like items stolen from cars) is rampant and fields are filled with marijuana plants. These assessments are only partially true (the second part is the more true one). Perhaps this reputation is only to keep outsiders away from sharing in the off-the-beaten track world Pahoa and its surroundings have to offer. I personally have been to Pahoa numerous times without any incident (and that is what most people will say). Pahoa isn't a necessary stop on a tour of south Puna, although the main street is lined with a few quaint shops. Be sure to stop in town on your way out for the day, as there are very few restaurants or grocery stores and no banks outside of town, and then be sure to come back in the evening for some of the best bar hopping the island has to offer.

Highway 132 and the Red Road (Highway 137)

The lush canopy of *albizzia* trees surrounds you on Highway 132 as you drive east. It really does feel like you are traveling through a tunnel. It might not look like what you think Hawaii should look like (it feels more like an enchanted forest than a tropical one), but you don't have to look too far to find mango fruits hanging off low branches or the ocean in the distance. Highway 137, a.k.a. The Red Road, a.k.a. Kapoho-Kalapana Road, meets Highway 132 at the "Four Corners" intersection and continues south and then west to Kaimu Beach, where the Kalapana lava flow of 1990 covered the road. As you will see, Highway 137 is nicknamed the Red Road because portions of it are actually red due to crushed red lava rock used to create the road. Most of it now is covered by black asphalt.

Most visitors to the Big Island (and actually many residents as well) never venture to this, the southeastern part of the island, as it can feel both physically and mentally out of the way. But again, this out-of-the-way-ness is what makes it such a gem. This area is the best and easiest way to have an adventure without trespassing. Some of the island's best snorkeling is within minutes of parking your car, and really you only need to stand in the water and stick your face in to see an abundance of underwater colors—more than you could imagine.

Southern Puna also borders Hawai'i Volcanoes National Park and the all-important viewing area where one can walk out—but not too far—to view the glowing reddish-orange stream of lava cut across the desolate landscape. To get a better sense of how the area looked before it was covered, stop at Kaimu Beach to witness the formation of one of the newest black-sand beaches on the island.

HEADING NORTH ON THE HAWAI'I BELT ROAD (HIGHWAY 11) FROM VOLCANO

As you coast down the hill from Volcano Village toward Hilo on Highway 11, you'll need to start peeling off your layers of clothes, as it can sometimes be 10-20 degrees warmer in this part of Puna (also known as upper Puna, which is very distinct from lower Puna, as you will see). Locals who live in these areas often commute either to Hilo or Volcano for work, as there are no real tourism sites here. But there are many resources – like large grocery stores and pharmacies – that aren't available for many miles afterward (e.g., if you are traveling south on Highway 11, you won't find another larger grocery store until you reach Ocean View over an hour away). So, stock up in Kea'au at Foodland or stretch your feet (or take a bathroom break) at the Akatsuka Orchid Gardens in Glenwood on the way to your next stop.

PLANNING YOUR TIME

For too long visitors with few days on the island have left Puna (especially lower Puna) untouched. This region is a must-see, especially for those who like to get away from tour buses. Ideally, your journey to Pahoa will be during the weekend when the markets, one of many highlights in the area, take place. Even if your visit is a weekday one, it's easy to spend a very full day hopping from beach to tide pool and then catching a quick bite to eat at the tasty Pahoa Village Café's happy hour (free pizza!) before heading to a nighttime walk (or cruise) to view the red hot lava moving slowly across the desolate landscape. Good news for those looking for some peace and quiet—there is no cell phone service in much of this area! Make sure to plan ahead for a day without a phone.

I recommend starting with Highway 132 and circulating south and then west on

PUNA

YOUR BEST DAY IN PUNA

- Start with early morning snorkeling at the **Kapoho tide pools.**

- Warm up at the **Ahalanui Beach Park** warm ponds.

- Take a stroll to a **secret black-sand beach** with tide pools.

- If it's Saturday, visit the **SPACE market** to see the quintessential "hippy" culture of Puna and try culinary treats like vegan pâté and raw pizza.

- If it's Sunday, visit the **Maku'u Market** – one of the best food and craft markets on the island.

- Or, stop at **Kalani Oceanside Retreat** for a vegetarian-friendly buffet lunch (warning – this is a nudity-friendly stop).

- If you're here on a Sunday, you can't miss the sounds of drumming from the road on top of **Kehena Beach** (again, this is a nudity-friendly stop and may not be family-friendly).

- Visit **Kaimu Beach** – the newest beach in the area – where you can catch a spectacular view of black landscape created from the Kalapana lava flow that covered the area in 1990.

- Take a quick break at **Uncle Robert's Kava Bar** before heading to the end of the road to try to catch a glimpse of the **lava flow at sunset** (call before you go to make sure there is a flow!).

- Finish your day at **Ning's Thai Cuisine** or the **Pahoa Village Café** for live music or karaoke.

RAINY DAY ALTERNATIVE

If you're stuck on Highway 11, stop at **Akatsuka Orchid Gardens** to check out the beautiful orchids in their indoor warehouse. If you haven't had your fill of flowers and plants, head to **Fuku-Bonsai Cultural Center** to make your own bonsai that you can bring home. It rarely will remain gloomy for an entire day in the southern part of Puna, but while you're waiting on the rain, check out the warm swimming hole at **Isaac Hale Beach Park** (it's shaded by trees that shield it from the rain) or head straight to **Kalani Oceanside Retreat,** where an attentive staff is able to set up last-minute massage appointments, or for $15 you can get a day pass to use the pool, hot tub, and sauna. Also, ask if there are any free 15-minute massage sessions offered that day. Just be aware that Kalani is "nude-friendly," meaning clothes are optional (but you can keep yours on).

Highway 137 (the route looks like a backward C) so that you can end your evening at the lava flow viewing area on Highway 130. Note: To stay on Highway 132, stay to the left when the road forks (if you go to the right you'll end up on Pahoa-Pohoiki Rd.).

If you stop at all the sights and beaches on the Red Road (Highway 137), it will take you the entire day (or longer if you decide to make longer stops for snorkeling and/or people-watching). Even if you don't stop anywhere on this road, the road itself makes for a great hour or so drive as it passes through coastal rainforest (there's very little of its kind in the world), and it hugs the ocean for the majority of the drive for some picturesque photos.

It's not really worth going out of your way to make stops on Highway 11 between Volcano and Hilo unless it is raining or you need a few minutes to stretch your feet.

Beaches

HIGHWAY 132 AND THE RED ROAD (HIGHWAY 137)
Champagne Pond

The crystal-clear Champagne Pond (off Kumukahi Lighthouse Rd.) is a naturally occurring warm pond heated by the volcano underneath. It's warm, but not hot. Bring your snorkeling equipment with you to witness the amazing life occurring under the water; however, you won't need snorkel gear to see the turtles that are lounging about.

To get there, at the junction of Highway 132 and Highway 137, called the "Four Corners" intersection, go east on Highway 132, which becomes a rental-car friendly dirt road, Kumukahi Lighthouse Road, and ends at the lighthouse. At the end of Kumukahi Lighthouse Road to your right there is a rough four-wheel-drive road to the public entrance of the ponds. The private entrance is through a nearby paved unnamed road to the Kapoho Beach Lots subdivision area, and you need a code to get through the gate—which you can get if you are renting a property there or know someone who lives there. If you don't have a four-wheel-drive car you can walk to the ponds. It will take you about 45 minutes over the rough road. Just walk keeping with the ocean on your left and it will be obvious when you've arrived to the ponds (they are next to an A-frame house).

◖ Kapoho Tide Pools

Some of the best snorkeling on the Big Island, the Kapoho tide pools (daily 7 A.M.–7 P.M., $3 suggested donation) are a great spot for beginners since the water is very shallow in some areas. Experts can swim farther out to experience greater depths. You'll be impressed by the landscape immediately. The tide pools surrounded by lava rocks with the ocean backdrop is a magnificent sight. But even better is the world under the water, filled with fish of various colors. Pay attention to where you put your things on the lava rock—when the

tide gets high your things will get wet. Also, you might want to bring a Band-Aid or two as it's quite common to get cut on the coral (I recommend that you wear water shoes even if you're not snorkeling). There are no facilities here (locals have been complaining of people making their own bathrooms in the trees in front of private properties), so go before you get here.

On Highway 137, 1.1 miles south from the Highway 132/Highway 137 intersection, turn left onto Kapoho Kai Road, which is marked and paved. Continue straight on the coconut-tree-lined road and turn left at Wai'opae Road where the road forms a T. Follow the signs to the State Marine Park.

Ahalanui Beach Park (Warm Ponds)

Although the official name of this beach park is Ahalanui Beach Park (Hwy. 137 between mile markers 10 and 11, daily 7 A.M.–7 P.M.), everyone just calls it "the warm ponds." The water is warm but not hot and very inviting if it's a cloudy day. Unlike the other hidden warm ponds in the area, this one is more official. You're not just climbing into a hole of water—there is cement surrounding it and stairs leading down into it. It gets quite crowded with families since the water here is not too deep and there is a lifeguard on duty. The right side of the pond is where the ocean water mixes with the pond. Do not enter into the water if you have an open cut as it could get infected. Some locals say they'd never go into the water. A longtime lifeguard in the area suggests that if you are worried about the cleanliness of the water, the best time to bathe is when the tide is moving (and the water isn't stagnant in the pond) during times of new and full moons. Check the local newspaper for tide schedules. The park has an area with picnic tables, showers (a good place to stop if you want to wash off from the Kapoho tide pools), and not-so-great portable toilets in the parking lot.

Isaac Hale Beach Park and Warm Pool

This park on Pohoiki Bay is newly renovated, and you can tell. On your left as you enter Isaac Hale Beach Park (off Hwy. 137, daily 7 A.M.–7 P.M.) you will see a field where the community holds festivals and sports activities. From Highway 137, turn *makai* at the Isaac Hale sign directly across from Pohoiki Road. The main road forms a T, and to the left there are really nice picnic areas with barbecues on the ocean side of the street (they are covered, which is nice in case of rain). On the *mauka* side of the street there is a new children's playground area. If you turn right at the T, park in the lot near the boat ramp. You'll see lots of people hanging around their big trucks drinking and eating. It's local hangout spot. Sometimes there are also food trucks here (burritos and pizza)—but not always. This is a good spot for body boarding and surfing, but people tend not to solely swim here. Just to the right of the boat ramp (in front of the private home with the No Trespassing—Kapu signs) is a very small *keiki* tide pool. If you continue walking on the dirt path into the forest (it's not marked, but obvious) between the tide pool and house, about 20 yards back on your right side you'll see a warm pond nestled behind the trees. Again, it's warm not hot. The park has facilities, such a shower near the boat ramp and bathrooms in the parking lot. Camping here is allowed with a county permit, but not recommended.

◖ Secret Black Sand Beach

Chances are that you'll be alone or only a few other people will be at the secret black-sand beach on Highway 137. If you set your odometer as you pass MacKenzie State Recreation Area, the secret black beach is exactly two miles west of the recreation area's entrance. You'll pass under a canopy of trees and the path to the beach is on the ocean or *makai* side of the road where the road curves and it looks like there is room for a car to park—if you're lucky there might be one parked there, which will alert you where to stop. The other marker to look for is two trees that look like they have

© BREE KESSLER

At the Secret Black Sand Beach, climb over the wall to the right and you'll happen upon this teacup-like tide pool formed out of the lava rock.

© MARK WASSER

Ever since Kaimu Beach was destroyed by the Kalapana lava flow, locals have been planting coconut trees on the beach so that one day Kaimu Beach can begin to resemble its former self.

fallen horizontally. Pass through the horizontal trees or go around them to the right—if you look closely you'll see that there is a trail worn from previous users. Head back through the forest toward the ocean and after two minutes you'll have arrived to the black-sand beach.

As you exit the forest onto the sand, you'll be pleasantly thrilled to have arrived on a deserted beach where you can bask in the sun all day long (you'll have to bask, as there is no shade here). But there is more! To the right it looks like there is a natural wall (and you can't see what's on the other side). Climb up it (it's not too hard and there is a clear path) and on the other side are small tide pools and an even more secret black-sand beach.

◖ Kehena Beach

Sundays are the day at Kehena Beach (Hwy. 137) when lower Punans and like-minded visitors gather to drum (you can hear it from the road), partake of *pakalolo* (marijuana), and swim naked in the ocean (there are kids here but it might not

be a kid-friendly stop). Other days, you might find only a few people lounging on the beach. The beach is sandy with lots of shaded areas, but the water is rough here, so take care, although it doesn't seem to deter anyone from swimming or body boarding. The vibe here is friendly and you won't feel out of place if you are clothed.

To get there, set your odometer at MacKenzie State Park; Kehena Beach is 5.4 miles west of there or 1.1 miles west of the King's Trail stop. Look on the *makai* side of the road for a parking area—essentially a place where there is a large area for cars to park facing the ocean. The entrance to the beach is to the left of there via a short dirt trail. The downhill trek can be tricky.

◖ Kaimu Beach

Legend (from the 1990s) goes that Kaimu Beach (Hwy. 137 where the road dead-ends) was the place to go. It was sandy and had beautiful coconut trees...until the Kalapana lava flow quickly covered it in the 1990s. From MacKenzie State Park it is 9 miles southwest or 5.6 miles from Kehena Beach. Park in the spots on the *makai* side of the road or in the lot on the *mauka* side (there are bathrooms there behind the restaurant) and follow the path to the left of the vendors out to the beach. The walk will take you about five minutes; it's not paved, but it's easy and straightforward.

As you start on the path, you'll see an information board that shows pictures of the beach before it was lava covered. As you can see, the beach used to extend to where you are standing. Look to your right as you walk out and you can see the entire area that was covered by lava—this used to be a subdivision! If you are there at night and the lava is flowing into the ocean, then you can also see the glow in the distance. As you continue to walk toward the ocean, you will also see small coconut trees growing. These

are gifts planted by locals over the last 20 years in an effort to rebuild the beach area. When you arrive at the beach, you will see a combination of fine-grain black sand and large black boulders. This beach is a great example of how a beach becomes a black-sand beach—from the waves hitting the black boulders and over time breaking them down into smaller pieces and, eventually, sand. It's not a great place to sit (most people just walk out and then go back) and you can't really go swimming here (the waves are rough and it's not recommended).

Note: The lava may have destroyed the area, but not cell phone service. If you are desperate to check your email or messages, head to Kaimu Beach. The open lava field has created a direct route from the nearby cell phone tower to you and your 3G service has been restored!

Recreation

WATER SPORTS

The Red Road offers some of the best snorkeling on the island. You'll have to tear yourself from the underwater world at the **Champagne Pond** or the **Kapoho tide pools.** For bodyboarding, surfing, and stand-up paddle-boarding, **Isaac Hale Beach Park** is your best bet—especially given how accessible it is. You can park your car and easily walk down the boat launch to get into the water within moments. And that is exactly what many islanders do, making these a very crowded spot on the weekend or in the summer. **Kehena Beach** is another spot where you'll find body boarders, but take care here because the waves can be very rough. Also, unlike at Isaac Hale Beach, at Kehena you must carry your things down a trail that requires watching your footwork. This can be a difficult task if you're carrying a board (or really anything) with you.

YOGA, MEDITATION, AND MASSAGE

Sometimes just being in lower Puna feels like one big meditative activity; however, there are

actual venues for yoga and meditation if you want to experience these activities with a group.

The most well-known spot is **Kalani Oceanside Retreat** (12-6860 Kalapana-Kapoho Beach Rd./Hwy. 137, Pahoa, 808/965-0468, www.kalani.com). One could arrange an entire vacation around the yoga, meditation, ecstatic dance, workshops (such as reiki attunement or working with herbs), and massage therapies offered here. Kalani offers accommodations, but you don't have to be staying here to take classes or even to eat here. The website offers an extensive listing of courses and events. Classes and workshops tend to be reasonably priced; however, if you're in the area for a while and short on cash, you can join a program to volunteer in exchange for classes. Note: Kalani is nudity friendly.

A second option that is a little bit more low-key (and less naked) is **Yoga Oasis** (Pohoiki Rd., Pahoa, 808/936-7710, www.yogaoasis. org). As at Kalani, accommodations are available, but you do not need to stay here to yoga here. Yoga classes are daily, and private partner yoga classes and advanced aerobic yoga classes are available upon request. In addition, various retreats occur throughout the year—from detox retreats to boot camps and even writing workshops. Check the website for additional information. Work exchange is available for those who live in the area.

For an all-inclusive experience, Rebecca Rogan with **Living Love Hawaii Retreats and Tours** (www.hawaiiretreatsandtours.com) can create a personalized retreat package for you (and your friends or lovers). Rebecca has an extensive background of teaching massage around the world. She is also trained as a yoga instructor. Although the retreats can be customized, they generally fall into the categories of losing weight, yoga, couples, or volcano tours. The best part is that you don't have to lift a finger. Rebecca sets your schedule, books your accommodations, and hires a personal chef (an amazing whole foods cook!). Retreats range from three days for $695, five days for $1,250 and seven days for $1,695 per person based on double occupancy. If you don't want to commit to a full retreat, you can book a five-hour Couples Massage Training Intensive ($275 per couple) where you learn how to massage your partner. It's a great activity for honeymooners or those looking to reconnect with a loved one.

Sights

HIGHWAY 11 BETWEEN VOLCANO AND HILO
Akatsuka Orchid Gardens
At Akatsuka Orchid Gardens (Hwy. 11 between mile markers 22 and 23, 808/967-8234, www.akatsukaorchid.com, daily 8:30 A.M.–5 P.M., free), an indoor warehouse filled with orchids, it's sometimes hard to find a parking spot, not because it's that crowded, but because the lot is filled with huge tour buses from the cruise ships. This isn't a must-see but it might make for a quick stop or a bathroom break and it's free. The flowers here make good souvenirs and are well priced (much better than you'll see at gift shops); many are prepackaged to take on the plane, and all of the flowers have already passed the agricultural check.

Kazumura Cave
The world's longest lava tube, the deepest cave in the United States, and the eighth longest cave in the world, the Kazumura Cave, was formed by lava carving out a tube many, years ago. A few tour companies will take you deep into the cave, but the best guide is **Harry Schick** (Hwy. 11 near mile marker 22, 808/967-7208, www.fortunecity.com/oasis/angkor/176, Mon.–Sat. 8 A.M.–6 P.M. by appointment, starting at $20 per person), who will explain in-depth lava tube geology. Three tours range 2–6 hours (with the shorter tours for beginners and the longer ones for experienced cavers). Children are welcome to come but must be over 11 years old. The walking isn't too challenging, but it's not always a flat surface, so the tour might not be ideal for someone who isn't the best walker or who is unable to climb the ladders that are used to get from room to room.

Pa'ani Ranch
The perfect stop for *keiki* (children), the Pa'ani Ranch (N. Kulani Rd. off of Hwy. 11 between mile markers 13 and 14, 808/968-7529, www.paaniranch.com, daily 8 A.M.–5 P.M.) houses a zipline course ($125) geared for children (adults should pick another one). The horseback riding ($69) and ATV rides ($69) might offer less impressive views than similar activities on the Kona side of the island, but the guides truly are focused on accommodating children and families (more than other tour operators). The Lil' Ranger program is for 2–8-year-olds ($69 per person for 1.5 hours—children under 5 must have an adult with them) and includes a wagon ride, pond pole fishing, hand-led pony ride, and petting zoo experience.

Fuku-Bonsai Cultural Center
Ever since you saw *Karate Kid* (the original

version with Ralph Macchio), haven't you wanted a bonsai tree? The road to the Fuku-Bonsai Cultural Center (Hwy. 11 between mile markers 9 and 10, 808/982-9880, www.fuku-bonsai.com, Mon.–Sat. 8 A.M.–4 P.M., free) is a bumpy one. Follow the signs from Highway 11—it's about a five-minute drive from there. If you have never seen a bonsai exhibit, this might be a worthy stop for you—and it's free! The handcrafting of each tree (and there are many of them scattered along the property) is unbelievable. Also, they offer a bonsai starter package for $25; it includes a 30-minute class, which can be done at the time of purchase without a reservation, to get you started as a bonsai master with your very own plant to keep. These plants are all approved to take back to the Mainland and shipping services also are offered.

HIGHWAY 132 AND THE RED ROAD (HIGHWAY 137)
Lava Tree State Monument

It's exactly like it sounds: a tree covered with lava. To see some for yourself swing by Lava Tree State Monument (Hwy. 132, open daylight hours, free). It's 2.7 miles southeast of Pahoa on the left side of the road after you pass the intersection of Pahoa-Pohoiki Road. This park makes for a nice quick stop (or a place for a picnic), but don't go out of your way to get here if you already stopped to see the lava trees in and around Hawai'i Volcanoes National Park. Under renovation in 2011, the facilities (including the bathrooms and picnic tables) and the path are all brand new. The trail, a loop, is only 0.7 mile and flat. It circumvents through the lava molds of 'ohi'a trees covered by a lava flow in 1790s.

Cape Kumukahi and Kumukahi Lighthouse

Kumukahi means "First Beginnings," and locals say that since it's the most eastern point in the chain of islands and the first place the air hits after it has traveled thousands of miles across the ocean that Cape Kumukahi has the cleanest in all of the state (and maybe even the northern hemisphere). Built in 1934 (although some histories say 1928 or even 1938),

© MARK WASSER

The newly restored Lava Tree State Monument is a fantastic way to witness what happens when lava covers a tree (many, many years ago) – a lava tree is born.

Kumukahi Lighthouse (off Hwy. 132) itself isn't what you think it is: It's not an East Coast–style lighthouse. It looks more like a utility tower. To get there, at the junction of Highway 132 and Highway 137, called the "Four Corners" intersection, go east on Highway 132, which becomes a rental-car friendly dirt road, Kumukahi Lighthouse Road, and ends at the lighthouse.

So while the lighthouse isn't that impressive, park your car at the end of the road and you can walk east from there (over uneven lava from the 1960 eruption that wiped out Kapoho) to the ocean. There is a somewhat non-obvious four-wheel drive road over the lava, and you can follow that path or make your own as you walk to the ocean. As you get closer to the edge, if you veer slightly right you'll see an *ahu* (Hawaiian version of a cairn marking a trail) and a tide pool with a lava roof (it's almost like a cave but open on both sides). Walk down a few lava rocks into the tide pool (careful not to slip). Note: Beware of large waves that can splash hard into the tide pool area.

Green Lake

Rumor has it that in the 1970s Jacques Cousteau came with a team of divers to find the bottom of Green Lake and couldn't. To get to Green Lake (Hwy. 137 just south of the Hwy. 132 intersection), look on the right side of the road between mile markers 8 and 9 for the obvious Green Lake sign on the fence. For entry call Smiley (808/965-5500 or 808/430-3071, $5 per person). Thus, some say that the lake was formed by a volcanic crater and is as deep as the ocean. You'll hear old-timers from the area say "I remember when anyone could go to Green Lake and camp and eat their fruit." Well, those days are over.

Along Highway 130 on the way toward Highway 137, off to the right is a hill covered with trees—that is Green Mountain and in the center of it is Green Lake—one of few natural lakes in all of Hawaii. The property is beautiful, and on the short hike to the lake you'll pass through some beautiful scenery (with lots of mosquitoes if it's been raining) like fruit trees and

huge monkeypod trees. However, the lake itself is now covered in algae that makes the water unwelcoming for swimming (these conditions could change). Green Lake is not a must-see if you only have one day in the area but is recommended if you're spending several days in the area.

MacKenzie State Recreation Area

You'll have a sense of eeriness as you enter MacKenzie State Recreation Area (on Hwy. 137 two miles west of Isaac Hale Beach Park, daily 7 A.M.–7 P.M.). Most tourists don't visit this park as there isn't beach access, and most Hawaiians use the park for solely fishing access, but they wouldn't be here after dark because they believe it's haunted. It is believed that ancestors are still roaming the King's Trail (the same trail that is more visible on the Kona side and circumvents the island), passing through the park late at night. That said, camping is allowed here with a permit, but it might not be a great place to camp unless you're on a ghost hunt.

The King's Trail

Part of the Ala Kahakai National Historic Trail, which is most visible throughout the Kona side, the King's Trail (Hwy. 137 before mile marker 18, 4.3 miles west from MacKenzie State Recreation Area) connects important historical and religious sites throughout the island and was later used in the late 1800s to herd cattle to port. This is one of very few places on the east side of the island where you can still see it and it hasn't been paved over or completely destroyed by lava.

To find the trail, look for a cleared area on the *makai* side of Highway 137 with lots of rocks. Walk about 10 feet from the road (over the rocks) and you'll see the stones in the shape of a path, remnants of the King's Trail.

Star of the Sea Painted Church

Originally located near Kalapana, Star of the Sea Painted Church (Hwy. 130 between mile markers 19 and 20, daily 9 A.M.–4 P.M.), dating from 1928, was moved to this location so that it wouldn't be destroyed by lava. Like an

WANT TO SEE SOME LAVA FLOW?

I mean, that's why you came to Hawai'i, right? I am sorry to say that you can't see it all the time. Months (even years) will go by when it's visible every night, and then (for instance, in March 2011, timed with the tsunami and a serious of small earthquakes that shook the Big Island) it disappears. So even if some assertive tour guide tells you that he or she will take you there, call the Kalapana lava viewing hotline (808/967-8862) first to see if there is actual lava flowing, or check online (http://volcanoes.usgs.gov/hvo/activity/kilauea status.php).

The **viewing area on Highway 130** (follow the signs and veer right when the road splits; it's right before it reaches Hwy. 137) opens mid-afternoon, but there is really no reason to get there before sunset since you can't see anything until it's dark. Aim for arriving around sunset (there is no better picture than lava with the sunset behind it). From the parking area to the viewing area, depending on conditions, is usually about a 15-minute walk – it used to be longer when they'd let you get closer to the flow. Bring a flashlight and some warm clothes, as it can get chilly at night.

© MARK WASSER

Lava rushes into the ocean near the Kalapana viewing area.

LAVA BY SEA

There are several ways to see the lava flow (if it is indeed flowing), and one of the ways is by boat. Arguably, it is not the most enjoyable way to see the lava – the water can be rough at night and it is not the most economical option. But it is a way to get close to it and take some great photos. Only a handful of companies organize these tours, and they all offer sunrise and sunset choices: **Lava Boat Tours** (808/934-7977, www.lavaboat.com, $165 per person), **Lava Ocean** (808/966-4200, www.lavaocean.com, $175 per person), and the small tour operator **Lava Roy's Ocean Adventure Tours** (808/883-1122, http://volcanooceanadventures.com, $150 per person). Confirm with the company which boat they plan to use. They tend to alternate between smaller Zodiacs and medium-size boats. Note: The companies will book you on a trip without making you aware that there is no lava to see! Please check with the lava-viewing hotline (808/967-8862) before you go.

© MARK WASSER

The only way to truly get up close and personal with this unbelievable phenomenon is by boat (but check first to make sure that the lava is flowing!).

inspired (but less talented) Michelangelo, a priest, Father Everest Gielen, painted the ceiling of the church, working mostly at night by oil lamp. Father Everest was transferred to Lana'i in 1941, and the work wasn't completed until 1964, when George Heidler, an artist from Atlanta, Georgia, came to Kalapana and decided to paint the unfinished altar section. The artwork itself can only be described as gaudy but sincere. The colors are wild blues, purples, and oranges. The ceiling is adorned with symbols, portraits of Christ, the angel Gabriel, and scenes from the Nativity. Behind the altar, a painted perspective gives the impression that you're looking down a long hallway at an altar that hangs suspended in air. The church is definitely worth a few minutes.

Steam Vents

Now in a sauna-like structure with seats to maximize the steaming experience, the steam vents (Hwy. 130 near mile marker 14, 808/965-2112, info@heavenlykingdom.net) have gone through several iterations (from a public scenic stop to an in-the-know spot in the back of this house). The steam vents now are probably in the best shape they've been in. The place is run by The Kingdom of Heaven, a religious organization. Thus, they do not charge for the experience but have a suggested donation of $20 per steam and $150 to stay the night in one of the bedrooms. Bathers are often unclothed. If you're merely interested in looking at the steam vents (but not going in) feel free to stop in. Ask the innkeeper to take you to the large hole (a gorge-like structure reminiscent of the critical scene in the movie *Garden State*) in the back (one of the largest on the Big Island). If you're lucky, you'll see an owl lurking about back there.

Shopping

In general, this area completely lacks any shopping whatsoever. Since Hilo is so close, most locals simply drive there (to Walmart or Ross Dress for Less) to pick up what they need. If you're looking to pick up a gift, your best bet is to stop by one of the weekend markets in the area, such as the SPACE market (Saturday) or Maku'u Market (Sunday), where you can find handmade soaps, clothing, and jewelry.

HIGHWAY 11 BETWEEN VOLCANO AND HILO

It will seem like an oasis to you—a small beacon of light on Highway 11 between Hilo and Volcano. The **J. Hara Store** (17-343 Volcano Rd./Hwy. 11 near mile marker 11, 808/966-5462, Mon.–Sat. 6 A.M.–8 P.M., Sun. 7 A.M.–7 P.M.) truly is a local institution. A relic of the pre-Walmart days, it is one of those stores that somehow pack everything into a small space. For instance, they have produce, hunting gear, liquor, and first aid items (really a must-have if you're going to sell hunting gear and liquor together).

In the same parking lot complex as J. Hara Store is a gas station (with relatively good prices for gas) owned by the **7-Eleven** (open 24 hours) located in back. Yes, they have Slurpees and all the usual sundries, but what is notable here is the Spam *musubi*, a local delicacy of rice and Spam (amazingly gluten-free) wrapped in nori (like a sushi roll). The 7-Eleven variety is available with egg on top of the Spam. These to-go sandwiches are delightful and cheap (just $1). Pick one up to bring with you for a day at the national park or just eat it right away (it's better served hot).

PAHOA

The main thoroughfare of Pahoa, Pahoa Village Road, is lined with a few small shops like the **Big Island Book Buyers** (Mon.–Sat. 10 A.M.–6 P.M., Sun. 11 A.M.–5 P.M.), a well-needed used book shop—the only one for quite some distance. But besides this shop, to be honest, I have never seen the majority of stores open as the hours seem to

be extremely variable. It's not worth stopping here to shop, but if you so happen to be in town catching a bite to eat, you might want to take a stroll and see what you can find.

◖ Maku'u Market

The Maku'u Market (Hwy. 130/Kea'au-Pahoa Rd. near mile marker 8, Sun. 8 A.M.–2 P.M.) is part food truck fair, part farmers market, part antiques market—one of the best markets on the island. Unlike at many other markets, you don't have to get here at the crack of dawn to be part of the action. In fact, many vendors start their mornings off at other nearby markets (like the one in Volcano) and then make their way here afterward. The prepared food selection here is tops: from Indian to Greek to local-style barbecue (Mister D BBQ truck is a staple and not to be missed). The produce selection is extensive and you'll find fruits here that are hard to find at other markets, such as the coveted mangosteen fruit. Bring the family as there is always some form of live entertainment under the picnic shelter. Also bring a raincoat or umbrella. Freak rainstorms are common here—but they offer a good opportunity to hang out under the covered shelter and make new friends and try new foods.

HIGHWAY 132 AND THE RED ROAD (HIGHWAY 137)
SPACE Market

Not outer space, rather it's the **Seaview Performing Arts Center for Education (SPACE) market** (12-247 W. Pohakupele Loop, Sat. 8 A.M.–noon). This market definitely reflects the laid-back off-the-grid culture of lower Puna, and likewise, it's one of the more interesting markets on the island. It's not too big—a straight walk through will only take you a few minutes, but if you stay and linger you'll be guaranteed some excellent people-watching time. Grab a raw wheat-free delight (I am serious) and some coconut turmeric tea (it is surprisingly delicious—both spicy and sweet) and head to the back covered picnic area. Produce is for sale as well as local crafts (think feather earrings and knitted bikinis).

To get there from Highway 137, turn *mauka*

into Seaview Estates (there is a sign). Mapuana is the main road in the neighborhood. Turn left on West Pohakupele Loop and follow signs to SPACE, which will be on your left.

Entertainment and Events

HIGHWAY 11 BETWEEN VOLCANO AND HILO

Hokulani's Steak House (808/966-5560, www.hokulanissteakhouse.food.officelive. com, Mon.–Fri. 10 A.M.–9:30 P.M., Sat.–Sun. 11 A.M.–9:30 P.M., happy hour daily 3–6 P.M., $12–26) always has a sign in front of it that states Live Music Tonight, and they mean it most nights. It's a classic American restaurant with big portions of steaks, burgers, and sandwiches. There is one vegetarian plate literally called "vegetarian plate." Locals like the happy hour for cheap drinks and eats.

PAHOA

If you're looking for your standard bar night-life, Pahoa town should be your first choice. The nightlife here resembles something like a college town filled with townie bars. You could bar hop or crawl (your choice) starting at **Kaleo's Bar and Grill** (15-2969 Pahoa Village Rd., 808/965-5600, http://kaleoshawaii.com, daily 11 A.M.–9 P.M.), where there is live music and creative cocktails, moving to **Black Rock Café** (15-2872 Pahoa Village Rd., 808/965-1177, daily 7 A.M.–9 P.M.) for cheap beer by the pitcher and a live cover band, and end your night at **Pahoa Village Café** (15-2471 Pahoa Village Rd., 808/965-7200, Sun.–Tues. 2–10 P.M., Wed. 2 P.M.–midnight, Thurs. 2 P.M.–1 A.M., Fri.–Sat. 2 P.M.–2 A.M., happy hour daily 3–6 P.M.), which stays open later than almost anywhere else on the Big Island, with karaoke, pool, and some more cheap beer.

If you're looking to learn more about the history of the area stop by the small **Pahoa Village Museum** (15-2931 Pahoa Village Rd., 808/430-1573, www.pahoavillagemuseum. net, Mon.–Thurs. 9 A.M.–6 P.M., Fri.–Sat. 10 A.M.–6 P.M.). Besides showcasing cultural

artifacts of the area, the space is also used as a coffee shop as well as a meeting place for events and workshops. The website isn't too useful, but check out their Facebook page for additional information on upcoming events.

HIGHWAY 132 AND THE RED ROAD (HIGHWAY 137)

Things tend to be very quiet (and dark) on Highways 132 and 137 at night. The main exception is at **Kalani Oceanside Retreat** (12-6860 Kalapana-Kapoho Beach Rd./Hwy. 137, 808/965-0468, www.kalani.com). Check the online calendar as it often hosts events from concerts to "ecstatic" dance or full moon parties to meditation or yoga sessions. All events are open to the public, but some require prior reservations.

A second option is **Uncle Robert's Kava Bar** (on Hwy. 137 where the road ends at Kaimu Beach). "You never know who is going to show up here," one local said concerning the recent sighting of a legendary musician who stopped by to play guitar. It's usually open by midafternoon, so grab a stool at this open-air bar to have some kava or *'awa*, as they say in Hawaiian. Don't try too much if you're a first timer because although it's supposed to relax you (it was used for several medicinal purposes by ancient Hawaiians), drinking lots of it has diuretic properties. As the night goes on, Uncle Robert's turns into a local hangout joint with music, at times, playing well into the night. The bar also serves as a somewhat unofficial lava flow information kiosk. You can come here to find out what's going on with the flow and to book a lava boat tour (if there is a flow). In the back of the bar, a small "exhibit" showcases photos of the area over the last 50 years including the lava flow of the 1990s that destroyed the area.

Food

HIGHWAY 11 BETWEEN VOLCANO AND HILO

The majority of people move quickly through this area on their way to eat either in Volcano or Hilo; however, I urge you to stop if you're on your way south. The food options here are much better than in Volcano, which is plagued by poor service and overpriced menus.

It's sort of like a New York deli, but Hawaii style. **Pearl's Bakery** (Hwy. 11 between mile markers 15 and 16, 808/756-1825, Tues.–Fri. 7 A.M.–4 P.M., Sat. 8 A.M.–3 P.M., $7) is completely unassuming (and you can easily drive by it if you're not looking for it), the ambiance inside is nonexistent, and thus this restaurant makes for a pleasant surprise of nicely crafted food in an area with a major lack of it. There are daily lunch specials, but I would opt for any of their fish dishes as they actually catch the fish themselves and then prep them for optimal taste (like their smoked ahi, which is absolutely mouthwatering). A sandwich alone will run you about $7 (but they are large portions), and you order sides separately. Their pastries are all house-made and the coffee is local.

The "stone cookies" at **Mountain View Bakery** (Old Volcano Rd. between mile markers 14 and 15, 808/968-6353, Mon.–Fri. 6:30 A.M.–1 P.M., Sat. 7:30 A.M.–1:30 P.M., cash only) are like a biscotti and tastier when dipped in a cup of coffee. I probably wouldn't go out of my way to stop here.

Most people think of Kona when they think of coffee on the Big Island, but there is in fact some mighty good coffee on the Hilo side. The **Hilo Coffee Mill** (17-995 Volcano Rd./Hwy. 11 between mile markers 12 and 13, 808/968-1333, www.hilocoffeemill.com, Mon.–Sat. 7 A.M.–4 P.M.) sells its own coffee and tea, and abbreviated tours and tastings (about 20 minutes long) are available on demand. Longer tours (about an hour long) are available with a comprehensive farm and facility tour (call ahead to reserve). On Saturday 8 A.M.–1 P.M. the Hilo Coffee Mill is the home of a farmers market (it also includes flea and craft items) that is mostly active early in the morning.

The breakfast special at **Koa Shop Kaffee and Restaurant** (17-4003 Ahuahu Pl., Hwy. 11 between mile markers 12 and 13, 808/968-1129, Tues.–Thurs. 7 A.M.–3 P.M., Fri.–Sat. 7 A.M.–9 P.M., Sun. 7 A.M.–7:30 P.M., $9) lists teriyaki beef, Spam, and Portuguese sausage—but instead of picking one, you actually get all of the meats (in small portions) served with rice, eggs, and miso soup. It's real local style and it's a good value for what you get although service can be slow at times. The Koa Shop Kaffee is in front of a koa wood workshop that is worth a quick browsing while you're waiting for your food or on your way out.

The crossroads of east Hawai'i, **Kea'au Shopping Center** (16-586 Old Volcano Rd., where Hwy. 11 meets Hwy. 130 toward Pahoa) presents a plethora of options. **Lemongrass Restaurant** (808/982-8558, Mon.–Sat. 10 A.M.–9 P.M.) is your standard Asian fast food restaurant in the mall. Locals like it because it's quick and cheap (it has a lunch special). Across the street (Kea'au-Pahoa Rd.) the small outdoor **Kea'au Market** (Tues.–Fri. 8 A.M.–5 P.M., Sat. 8 A.M.–3 P.M.) has some produce but mostly food stands of nearby restaurants such as **Bueno Burrito** (also located in Hilo) and a bakery with freshly made bread. If you're in the area and looking for a quick bite or want to pick up something to bring with you to a day at the beach in south Puna, it's definitely worth stopping here.

Markets

In addition to a slew of restaurants, Kea'au Shopping Center also is the location of the large chain supermarket **Foodland** (daily 6 A.M.–10 P.M.), which has an ATM inside as well as a Redbox for DVD rentals. If you're looking for gluten-free and vegan foods check out **Kea'au Natural Foods** (808/966-8877, Mon.–Fri. 8:30 A.M.–8 P.M., Sat. 8:30 A.M.–7 P.M., Sun.

9:30 A.M.–5 P.M.). It's the smallest of the island's natural food stores, but they have most of what you need. They carry their own brand of vitamins, which brings down the price, and have prepackaged small bags of bulk nuts and trail mixes.

PAHOA

All establishments are located on Main Government Road, also called Pahoa Village Road. Beware of the locations of restaurants on Google Maps as some establishments have noted that they are not placed correctly on the map.

One visitor said it best: "Why wouldn't you want to have beer with breakfast?" At **Black Rock Café** (15-2872 Pahoa Village Rd., 808/965-1177, daily 7 A.M.–9 P.M., $8) there is a restaurant area separate from the bar area, but the bar area is probably what you want for an opportunity to mingle with the locals. It's more than likely that you'll have a fun night out, especially the nights with live music (most weekends). The menu is more than standard bar fare—salads, chicken sandwiches, and burgers—but keep your expectations low so that you will be pleasantly surprised.

With so few local coffee shops on the Big Island (which is odd given the massive amount of coffee produced on the island!), **Sirus Coffee Connection** (15-2874 Pahoa Village Rd., 808/965-8555, Mon.–Thurs. 7 A.M.–6 P.M., Fri.–Sat. 7 A.M.–9 P.M., Sun. 7 A.M.–3 P.M.) is almost an anomaly. They have free wireless Internet, which is a big deal for locals who have a hard time getting Internet service at their off-the-grid joints. The atmosphere is not super cozy, but you could definitely spend a few hours with a book and a cup of coffee here. Breakfast and lunch sandwiches are available (there are vegetarian options), as are sweet treats. They also have gluten free bread.

This place has it all. The happy hour at **Pahoa Village Café** (15-2471 Pahoa Village Rd., 808/965-7200, Sun.–Tues. 2–10 P.M., Wed. 2 P.M.–midnight, Thurs. 2 P.M.–1 A.M., Fri.–Sat. 2 P.M.–2 A.M., happy hour daily 3–6 P.M., $10) is a real gem: free pizza (totally free!), free pool (although it can be hard to get a table), and cheap drinks. Most weekends as well as some Thursdays and Fridays there is

live music and the bar stays open very late—especially for Hawaii. For sports lovers, there are several large TVs that play games on the weekends. For vegetarians, there are excellent large salads made with local produce that you can customize with a variety of toppings.

The ambiance feels authentic at **Luquin's Mexican Restaurant** (15-2942 Pahoa Village Rd., 808/965-9990, www.luquinsmexicanrestaurant.com, daily 7 A.M.–9 P.M., happy hour 3–6 P.M., $10–20), with the vibe of a restaurant off the side of the road in Mexico, and the service can sometimes be very slow (maybe they are trying to be really authentic). It's not the best Mexican food you'll ever have, but the food is good enough and the potions are large. There's beer on draft (and there are usually pitcher specials) and gluten-free (corn tortilla) and vegetarian options (tofu enchiladas) on the menu. Wireless Internet is available (you'll appreciate this if you're coming from the southern part of Puna where Internet connection can be hard to find).

The Big Island has some of the best Thai food outside of Thailand itself, and **Ning's Thai Cuisine** (15-2955 Pahoa Village Rd., 808/965-7611, Mon.–Sat. noon–9 P.M., Sun. 5–9 P.M., $15) is one of the best on the island. The food is seasoned perfectly, and those who like their food spicy should try the hot option (it's Thai hot). Try the pineapple curry or the *massaman* curry and you won't be sorry (vegetarian options are abundant). The restaurant itself is quaint, but they do a good carryout business for those wanting to grab and go back to the beach or to a nearby bed-and-breakfast.

If you've ever been to a diner on the East Coast you've probably looked through the 12-page menu and then asked yourself, "How can they make so many different things?" The extensive menu at **Kaleo's Bar and Grill** (15-2969 Pahoa Village Rd., 808/965-5600, http://kaleoshawaii.com, daily 11 A.M.–9 P.M., $15–20) will leave you asking the same question; yet, somehow they are able to make Asian food, local food, burgers, fish, and Italian cuisine and it do it all well. The portions are huge (so much so that there is an $8 split charge since they realize that people could easily split one dish). The sandwiches and wraps are a very good value (you'll have leftovers). There are vegetarian options and also some to suit gluten-free diets. It is one of the more romantic restaurant settings in Pahoa town, and on the weekends there is often live music playing in the dining area. If you're looking for a less romantic dinner, grab a stool at the bar, where locals will surely engage you in conversation over a choice specialty cocktail stirred up by the friendly bartenders.

Markets

Part of the local supermarket chain, the **Malama Market** (15-2660 Pahoa Rd., 808/965-2105, 6 A.M.–10 P.M.) has everything you need in addition to a deli counter, fresh *poke*, and wine as well as liquor. There is also a Redbox inside (for your DVD needs) and an ATM. They also do cash back.

Another location of the local natural foods grocery store chain, **Island Naturals Market and Deli** (15-1403 Pahoa Village Rd., 808/965-8322, www.islandnaturals.com, Mon.–Sat. 7:30 A.M.–8 P.M., Sun. 9 A.M.–7 P.M.) has a coffee and smoothie bar as well as an excellent hot bar (they charge per pound) with many gluten-free and vegan options. Beer and wine (non-organic and organic varieties) are available and on sale for 20 percent off every Friday.

HIGHWAY 132 AND THE RED ROAD (HIGHWAY 137)

How far would you go for an organic, mostly local, very vegetarian friendly meal? Some islanders drive over an hour to be able to taste the all-you-can-eat buffets at **Kalani Oceanside Retreat** (12-6860 Kalapana-Kapoho Beach Rd./Hwy. 137, 808/965-0468, www.kalani.com, breakfast daily 7:30–8:30 A.M., $13; lunch daily noon–1 P.M., $15; dinner 6–7:30 P.M., $24, *kama'aina* discounts available). The options range from fish to chicken to tofu and tempeh—there are raw food options and gluten-free ones too. You only have about an hour to eat, and trust me, you will feel very full when it's over. But don't get too full; for an additional $5 you can stay around at Kalani to use the pool and hot tubs (nude friendly) and maybe even join a yoga class or an ecstatic dance event that suits you.

Kalapana Village Café (12-5037 Pahoa Kalapana Rd. where Hwy. 137 ends at Kaimu Beach, 808/965-0121, Mon.–Fri. 7 A.M.–7 P.M., Sat.–Sun. 8 A.M.–9 P.M., $8, *kama'aina* discounts available) looks like a hole-in-the-wall (although it has lovely outdoor seating), but you'll be thrilled to stop there for refreshments after a long day snorkeling and hot ponding. You'll be even more thrilled when you take the first bite of your food and realize that the food actually is first-rate here. There are vegetarian salads made from local produce, hamburgers, and large portions of french fries and onion rings. Or just pick up an ice cream cone from the café or from the small convenience store next door, **Kaimu Korner** (daily 8 A.M.–9 P.M.), on your way out to view Kaimu Beach.

Information and Services

EMERGENCY SERVICES

If you need serious medical care, your best bet is to drive (or be driven) to the main hospital in Hilo (it's not too far). For minor emergencies visit the **Kea'au Family Health Center** (16-192 Pilimua St., 808/930-0400, Mon.–Wed. and Fri. 7 A.M.–7 P.M., Thurs. 9:30 A.M.–7 P.M.) or the **Pahoa Family Health Center** (15-2866 Pahoa Village Rd., Bldg. C, Ste. A, 808/965-9711, Mon.–Wed. and Fri. 7 A.M.–7 P.M., Thurs. 9:30 A.M.–7 P.M.).

For your pharmacy needs your only options in this area are two branches of Longs Drugs. One is in the Kea'au Shopping Center: **Longs Drugs** (808/982-8600, Mon.–Fri. 9 A.M.–7 P.M., closed for lunch at variable times, Sat. 9 A.M.–1 P.M.). A second location is in Pahoa (15-1454 Kahakai Blvd.,

808/965-3144, Mon.–Fri. 8 A.M.–8 P.M., Sat.–Sun. 8 A.M.–5 P.M.). Longs actually is owned by CVS, which helps if you need to transfer a prescription from the Mainland.

BANKS
Highway 11 between Volcano and Hilo
There is an **HFS Federal Credit Union** (16-589 Old Volcano Rd., 808/930-1400) next to the Kea'au Shopping Center.

Pahoa
First Hawaiian Bank and **Bank of Hawaii** both have branches and ATMs on Pahoa Village Road in the heart of town. There also are **First Hawaiian Bank** ATMs located at the Malama Market and 7-Eleven (in town).

POST OFFICES
Nearly every town has its own post office. You'll pass by three driving north on Highway 11 from Volcano to Kea'au. The Kurtistown Post Office (17-345 Volcano Road) is extra special since it has a dedicated Netflix box. The Kea'au Post Office (16-578 Old Volcano Rd.) is a bit larger (but without the Netflix box). The Pahoa Village Post Office (15-2859 Pahoa Village Rd.) gets a bad rap for service and the clientele, but it's your only option as there isn't another post office in the southern Puna region.

Getting There and Around

TO PAHOA BY CAR
To get to Pahoa stay on Highway 130 heading south from Hilo or Kea'au. Turn right before the complex with the Longs Drugs (this road isn't marked but turns into Main Government/Pahoa Village Road). Be careful at this intersection as many accidents occur here because it is heavily used and there is no traffic light. Continue on Main Government/Pahoa Village Road as it curves to the left. After a mile, you will begin to drive through the main part of town. If you miss the right turn from Highway 130, continue on the highway for 1.5 miles and turn right on Kapoho Road. You are now entering the town from the south side (which is closer to where the restaurants are located).

PUBLIC TRANSPORTATION
The Hele-On bus route from the Glenwood area to Hilo is the same as the Ka'u (Volcano) route and is not very well serviced. On the other hand, the Hilo–Pahoa route has numerous buses (nearly hourly) and you can travel as far as Pohoiki (near Isaac Hale Beach Park). Remember, if you want to travel from Pahoa to Volcano or Kona, for instance, you will need to transfer buses in Hilo.

The **Hele-On Bus** (www.heleonbus.org, $1 per ride, $1 each for luggage, large backpacks, bikes) follows the Pahoa–Hilo route schedule, stopping in Pahoa at 6:10 A.M., 8:15 A.M., and then almost hourly (check the schedule) to 8:30 P.M. on its way to Hilo. The ride to Hilo takes about 70 minutes and makes all intermediate stops on the way. There are three buses (8:30 A.M., 1:15 P.M., 6:20 P.M.) from Pahoa town south to the Red Road area (south Puna with beaches) and back north on Highway 130 toward Pahoa. The entire route takes about an hour.

HILO AND AROUND

Hilo has the potential to be the new Brooklyn or the new Portland or maybe even an Ann Arbor or Berkeley. It has dive bars, walkable streets, historical buildings, cheap rents, two universities, and, most importantly, it's an underrated foodie mecca—all elements that could quickly lead to gentrification. But alas, Hilo has resisted change and happily retains itself as a relic of old Hawaii.

At around 40,000 people, Hilo has the second-largest population in the state after Honolulu. It is the county seat, has a bustling commercial harbor, and has a long tradition in agriculture and industry. Hilo is a classic tropical town, the kind described in books like Gabriel García Márquez's *Love in the Time of Cholera*. Many of the downtown buildings date back to the early 1900s, when the plantation industry was booming and

the railroad took workers and managers from the country to the big city of Hilo. Sidewalks in older sections of town are covered with awnings because of the rains, which adds a turn-of-the-20th-century gentility. You can walk the central area comfortably in an afternoon, but the town does sprawl some due to the modern phenomena of large shopping malls and residential subdivisions in the outlying areas.

Hilo really is both spiritually and physically the yin to the yang of Kailua-Kona. There, everything runs fast to a new and modern tune. In Hilo the old beat, the old music, and that feeling of a tropical place where rhythms are slow and sensual still exist. Hilo nights are alive with sounds of the tropics (also known as coqui frogs) and the heady smells of fruits and flowering trees wafting on the breeze. Hilo

HIGHLIGHTS

 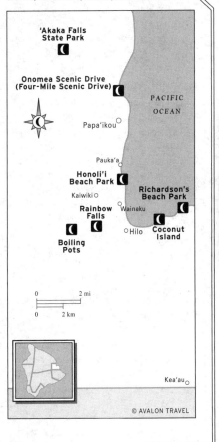
Richardson's Beach Park: Head to this black-sand beach near downtown Hilo for terrific snorkeling, swimming, or just snoozing in the shade (page 175).

Honoli'i Beach Park: This beach is known as one of the finest surfing spots on this side of the island, and even if you're not a surfer, it's worth coming here to watch the local talent hit the big waves (page 175).

Coconut Island: A favorite picnic spot for decades, Coconut Island offers the best panorama of the city, bay, and Mauna Kea beyond (page 182).

Rainbow Falls and Boiling Pots: The 80-foot Rainbow Falls is true to its name, its mists throwing flocks of rainbows into the air. At the potholed riverbed of Boiling Pots, river water cascades from one bubbling whirlpool tub into the next (page 185).

Onomea Scenic Drive (Four-Mile Scenic Drive): Start down this meandering lane into jungle that covers the road like a living green tunnel. Along the short four-mile route are sections of an ancient coastal trail, the site of a former fishing village, and the Hawaii Tropical Botanical Garden – not to mention one fine view after another (page 186).

'Akaka Falls State Park: Everybody's idea of a pristine Hawaiian valley is viewable at 'Akaka Falls, one of the most easily accessible forays into the island's beautiful interior (page 187).

HILO AND AROUND

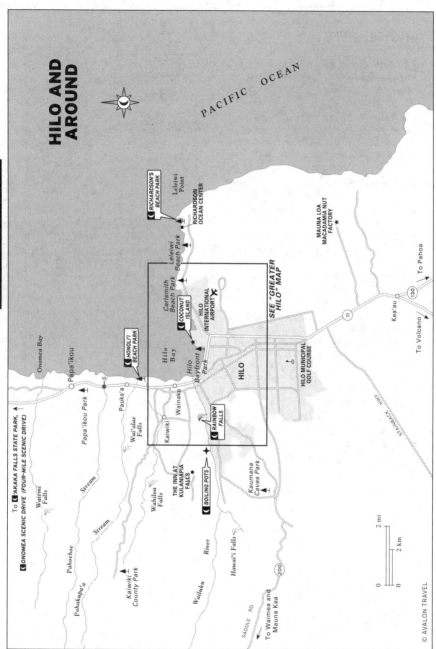

HILO AND AROUND

PACIFIC OCEAN

Onomea Bay

Papa'ikou

Papa'ikou Park

Pauka'a

Wai'alae Falls

Kaiwiki

Wainaku

Hilo Bay

HONOLI'I BEACH PARK

Carlsmith Beach Park

COCONUT ISLAND

Leleiwi Beach Park

RICHARDSON'S BEACH PARK

Leleiwi Point

RICHARDSON OCEAN CENTER

Hilo Bayfront Park

HILO INTERNATIONAL AIRPORT

HILO

HILO MUNICIPAL GOLF COURSE

SEE "GREATER HILO" MAP

RAINBOW FALLS

THE INN AT KULANIAPI'A FALLS

BOILING POTS

Kaumana Caves Park

Wahiloa Falls

Kaiwiki County Park

Pahoehoe

Pohakupa'a

Waimi Falls

Stream

Stream

Wailuku River

Hawai'i Falls

SADDLE RD

To Waimea and Mauna Kea

200

To MAKAKA FALLS STATE PARK,

ONOMEA SCENIC DRIVE (FOUR-MILE SCENIC DRIVE)

To Volcano

Kea'au

STAINBACK HWY

11

30

To Pahoa

MAUNA LOA MACADAMIA NUT FACTORY

0   2 mi

0   2 km

© AVALON TRAVEL

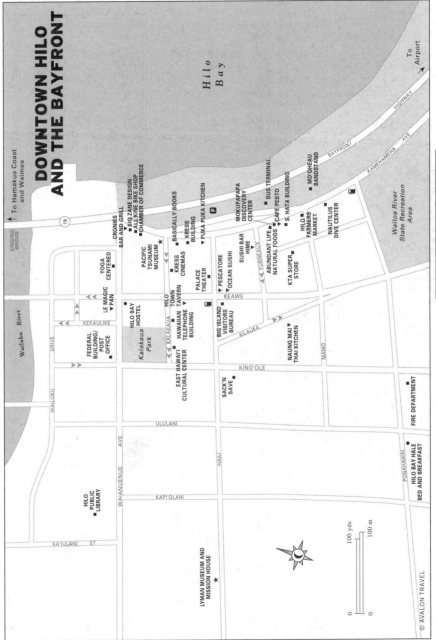

DOWNTOWN HILO AND THE BAYFRONT

To Hamakua Coast and Waimea

SINGING BRIDGE

19

Wailuku River

Wailuku River

Hilo Bay

To Airport

HIGHWAY

BAYFRONT

KAMEHAMEHA AVE

Wailoa River State Recreation Area

CRONIES BAR AND GRILL
SIG ZANE DESIGN
ALII KINE BIKE SHOP
CHAMBER OF COMMERCE

BASICALLY BOOKS
KRESS BUILDING
PUKA PUKA KITCHEN

MOKUPAPAPA DISCOVERY CENTER
BUS TERMINAL
CAFE PESTO
S. HATA BUILDING
MOʻOHEAU BANDSTAND

HILO FARMERS MARKET
NAUTILUS DIVE CENTER

PACIFIC TSUNAMI MUSEUM

KRESS CINEMAS

PALACE THEATER

PESCATORE
OCEAN SUSHI
SUSHI BAR HIME

FURNEAUX

ABUNDANT LIFE NATURAL FOODS
KTA SUPER STORE

YOGA CENTERED

LE MAGIC PAN

KEKAULIKE

KALAKAUA

HILO TOWN TAVERN

HILO BAY HOSTEL
Kalakaua Park

HAWAIIAN TELEPHONE BUILDING

KEAWE

KILAUEA

BIG ISLAND VISITORS BUREAU

NAUNG MAI THAI KITCHEN

MAMO

FEDERAL BUILDING/ POST OFFICE

DRIVE

WAILUKU

EAST HAWAIʻI CULTURAL CENTER

SACK'N SAVE

KINOʻOLE

FIRE DEPARTMENT

ULULANI

HAILI

WAIANUENUE AVE

KAPIʻOLANI

HILO PUBLIC LIBRARY

POHAKULANI

HILO BAY HALE BED AND BREAKFAST

KAʻIULANI   ST

LYMAN MUSEUM AND MISSION HOUSE

100 yds
100 m
0
0

© AVALON TRAVEL

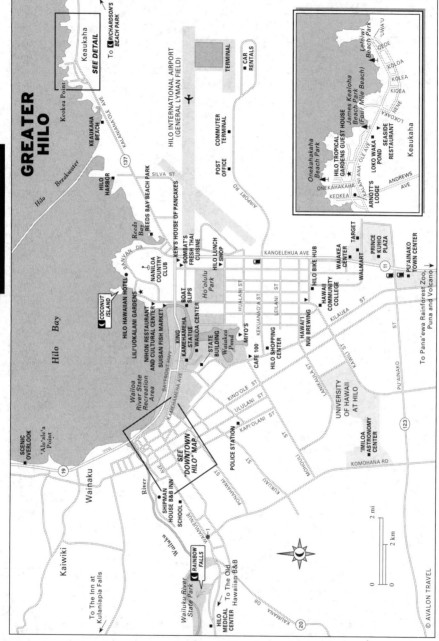

GREATER HILO

Keaukaha *SEE DETAIL*

To RICHARDSON'S BEACH PARK

Keokea Point

KEAUKAHA BEACH

KALANIANAOLE AVE

HILO HARBOR

(137)

SILVA ST

REEDS BAY BEACH PARK

Reeds Bay

Hilo Breakwater

Hilo Bay

COCONUT ISLAND

BANYAN DR

NANILOA COUNTRY CLUB

HILO HAWAIIAN HOTEL

LILI'UOKALANI GARDENS

NIHON RESTAURANT AND CULTURAL CENTER

SUISAN FISH MARKET

KING KAMEHAMEHA STATUE

WAILOA CENTER

STATE BUILDING

Wailoa Pond

Wailoa River State Recreation Area

BAYFRONT HWY

KAMEHAMEHA AVE

SCENIC OVERLOOK

'Ale'ale'a Point

(19)

Waihaku

River

Kaiwiki

To The Inn at Kulaniapia Falls

Wailuku

SHIPMAN HOUSE B&B INN

SCHOOL

WAIANUENUE AVE

PUNAHOA ST

RAINBOW FALLS

To The Old Hawaiian B&B

Wailuku River State Park

HILO MEDICAL CENTER

KAUMANA DR

(20)

KEOKEA AVE

HILO INTERNATIONAL AIRPORT (GENERAL LYMAN FIELD)

TERMINAL

CAR RENTALS

COMMUTER TERMINAL

POST OFFICE

AIRPORT RD

KEN'S HOUSE OF PANCAKES

SOMBAT'S FRESH THAI CUISINE

HILO LUNCH SHOP

Ho'olulu Park

KANOELEHUA AVE

HUALANI ST

LEILANI ST

KEKUANAO'O ST

MIYO'S

CAFE 100

HILO SHOPPING CENTER

KILAUEA ST

HAWAI'I NUI BREWING

HILO BIKE HUB

WAIAKEA CENTER

TARGET

WALMART

PRINCE KUHIO PLAZA

PU'AINAKO TOWN CENTER

(11)

HAWAI'I COMMUNITY COLLEGE

KAWILI ST

PU'AINAKO ST

To Pana'ewa Rainforest Zoo, Puna and Volcano

KINO'OLE ST

ULULANI ST

KAPIOLANI ST

POLICE STATION

PONAHAWAI ST

KUKUAU ST

LANIKAULA ST

MOHOULI ST

UNIVERSITY OF HAWAI'I AT HILO

'IMILOA ASTRONOMY CENTER

KOMOHANA RD

(123)

SEE "DOWNTOWN HILO" MAP

2 mi

2 km

0

0

© AVALON TRAVEL

[Inset: Keaukaha detail]

Leleiwi Beach Park

'UNA'U

O'O'E

KOLOA

KOLEA

KIOEA

NENE

James Kealoha Beach Park (Four Mile Beach)

HILO TROPICAL GARDENS GUEST HOUSE

LOKO WAKA POND

SEASIDE RESTAURANT

Keaukaha

Onekahakaha Beach Park

KALANIANA'OLE AVE

KEOKEA

ONEKAHAKAHA

ARNOTT'S LODGE

ANDREWS AVE

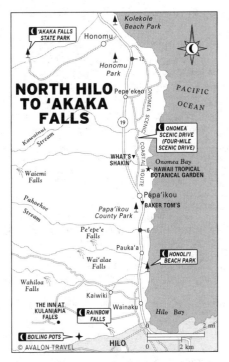

NORTH HILO TO 'AKAKA FALLS

wind you through a rainforest that smells overwhelmingly like papayas.

Back on the highway moving west, you'll arrive in Honomu (Silent Bay). During its heyday, Honomu was a bustling center of the sugar industry, boasting saloons, a hotel/bordello, and a church or two for repentance. It was even known as "Little Chicago." Now Honomu mainly serves as a stop as you head elsewhere, but you should definitely take the time to linger. Honomu is 10 miles north of Hilo and about a half mile or so inland on Highway 220, which leads to 'Akaka Falls. On entering, you'll find a string of false-front buildings doing a great but unofficial rendition of a living history museum. The town has recently awoken from a long nap and is now bustling—if that's possible in a two-block town—with a gaggle of art galleries, craft shops, and small cafés. It takes only minutes to walk the main street, but those minutes can give you a glimpse of history that will take you back 100 years.

ORIENTATION
Downtown Hilo and the Bayfront

You'll know you are nearing downtown when you start seeing parking spaces that require parallel parking (the quintessential feature of any downtown). The central downtown area is made up of Kamehameha Avenue (also called Bayfront), Kilauea Avenue (which turns into Keawe Street), and Kinoole Streets—parallel streets running north to south bounded on the east by Mamo Street and on the west by Waianuenue Avenue before one has to cross over a bridge to another section of Hilo.

This area is much denser than any other part of town and easily walkable. Within this area you'll find the bus station, Hilo Farmers Market, cafés, restaurants, grocery stores, and tourist shops. While this isn't where you would come to jump in the water (don't be misled by the name Bayfront), this area is where you'll see cruise ship passengers walking around (with the ship in the distance towering over the town) picking up souvenirs. Also, for those who love historical buildings, there is an excellent self-guided walking tour of these streets. Please

days epitomize tropical weather, with predictable afternoon showers during the winter and spring months. In spite of, and because of, the rain, Hilo is gorgeous. Hilo's weather makes it a natural greenhouse; botanical gardens and flower farms surround Hilo like a giant lei. Black-sand beaches are close by waiting for you to come cool off. To counterpoint this tropical explosion, Mauna Kea's winter snows backdrop the town. Hilo is one of the oldest permanently settled towns in Hawaii, and the largest on the windward coast of the island. Don't make the mistake of underestimating Hilo, or of counting it out because of its rainy reputation.

Leaving Hilo, it takes only moments to leave the urban behind and you're back in the tropics with no Target in sight (well, until you get to Kona). 'Akaka Falls is less than a half hour from downtown Hilo, but there is a lot to see on the way right off the highway, including an incredible four-mile scenic drive that will

YOUR BEST DAY IN HILO

- Wake up early and come to **Honoli'i Beach Park** to surf or to watch the surfers.

- Afterward, stop at the **Hilo Lunch Shop** to taste a piece (or pieces) of a local culinary tradition.

- If it's a Wednesday or Saturday, head to the **Hilo Farmers Market** to see the wide range of fruits that grow on the island.

- Take a **walking tour of downtown Hilo** to see the architecture of early-20th-century Hawaii.

- Stop in the **Pacific Tsunami Museum** or the **Lyman Museum.**

- In the afternoon, relax at one of the many black-sand beaches just 10 minutes from downtown, such as **Richardson's Bench Park.**

- Have dinner at one of Hilo's undervalued foodie joints **(Puka Puka Kitchen, Sushi Bar Himi,** or **Sombat's Fresh Thai Cuisine).**

- For a low-key night, catch an art film or a performance at the **Palace Theater** or an old blockbuster you missed at **Kress Cinemas** budget theater.

- For a high-energy night (with no need to dress up), meander over to **Kim's Karaoke Lounge** for drinks, pupu, and of course karaoke.

- Late (late) at night go where the locals go to end the evening: **Ken's House of Pancakes.**

RAINY DAY ALTERNATIVE

Hilo is a great place to spend a rainy day, given the large number of museums and movie theaters. Here are a few other ideas, and they are free (or almost free) and kid-friendly.

If you want to feel like you're outside even when you're not, the **Kapoho Kine Adventures** office has a small climbing wall inside – and it's free!

Hawaiiana Live at the Palace Theater (Wed. only) showcases Hawaiian history and culture through storytelling, music, film, and hula. If you haven't gone to a *lu'au*, this is a great way to see some traditional Hawaiian culture.

Right on the bayfront, it's easy to totally miss the **Mokupapapa Discovery Center for Hawaii's Coral Reefs.** This small museum is great for spending a few minutes perusing its information about reefs and fish of the Northwestern Hawaiian Islands.

note: For the purpose of this guide, I have also included in this section spots that are within walking distance (or under a five-minute drive) from this centralized downtown area.

Greater Hilo

Thanks to our old friend "urban sprawl," Hilo begins almost right after the Kea'au Shopping Center on Highway 11. Hilo has greatly expanded from its original roots by transforming its farmlands (and native Hawaiians settlements) into the area on Highway 11 that now houses the Hilo International Airport, Walmart, and the Prince Kuhio Mall. However, in addition to these features, which make Hilo look like any other American suburb, where

Highway 11 meets the ocean (the highway either ends or begins here depending on how you look at it) the greater Hilo area is where you'll find the town's secret jewels: its beaches. Travel east on Kalaniana'ole Avenue, where beaches are situated one after another, easily recognizable from the road by their official county park signs. Although these beaches are easily accessible, you'll be entering into a coastal wonderland that couldn't feel farther from the suburban enclave just up the road.

North Hilo to 'Akaka Falls

Pass over the "Singing Bridge" leaving downtown Hilo and soon after you're in the North Hilo district traveling on Highway 19 toward the Hamakua Coast. This route, one of the prettiest on the island with its ocean views, passes by several old plantation towns that are still residential communities (we could even call them Hilo bedroom or commuter communities) that do not offer anything of interest to tourists. Just seven miles out of Hilo, you'll pass the sign for Four-Mile Scenic Drive. You should turn onto it immediately; it's the old route that parallels the highway. Back on the highway as you drive north, you'll arrive at the town of Honomu, the gateway to 'Akaka Falls. From here it's still necessary to climb *mauka* on Highway 220 (about 20 minutes) until you reach the entrance to this must-see sight.

PLANNING YOUR TIME

While many visitors to the Big Island stay only on the Kona side, those who know the island well and appreciate its diversity split their time between the Kona and Hilo sides. Hilo, being the largest city and main hub on the east side, is the logical place to use as a base. The city is bite-size, but you'll need a rental car to visit most of the sights around town. Hilo itself has plenty to keep a traveler busy for a number of days. First, spend time exploring the natural beauty of the city and close-by botanical gardens, its bay and beaches, and the pretty waterfalls only a few minutes from downtown. Both Rainbow Falls and the potholed riverbed of Boiling Pots are very photogenic, and perhaps best when there's plenty of rain to make them perform at their best. Take an hour or two to walk under the giant banyan trees that canopy Banyan Drive, stroll through the relaxing Lili'uokalani Gardens, and walk the bridge to Coconut Island for a perfect view of the bay and waterfront with snowcapped Mauna Kea as a backdrop. While you are out that way, continue on down Kalaniana'ole Avenue for a morning or afternoon in the water at one of the small beaches along the Keaukaha strip.

Hilo is an old town. Reserve a morning or afternoon for a walking tour of town, viewing its well-kept historical buildings, and then spend a few hours at both the Pacific Tsunami Museum, where you will learn about the brutal waters that destroyed much of Hilo's bayfront, and the Lyman Museum and Mission House, where the life of early missionaries to Hawaii comes alive. A bit out of town is the Pana'ewa Rainforest Zoo, also good for a couple of hours to view tropical animals in a natural environment, and the opportunity to see some of the thick and luxuriant forest cover that surrounds the city. For exploration from Hilo, it's an hour's drive down to the steamy Puna Coast, about the same up to the stark lava lands of Hawai'i Volcanoes National Park or along the wet and wonderful Hamakua Coast to time-lost Waipi'o Valley, but a bit longer for a trek to the top of the Mauna Kea to see the astronomical observatories and experience a sunset from the heights.

Beaches

If you define a beach as a long expanse of white sand covered by a thousand sunbathers and their beach umbrellas, then Hilo doesn't have any. If a beach, to you, can be a smaller, more intimate affair where a good number of tourists and families can spend the day on pockets of sand between fingers of black lava, then Hilo has a few. Hilo's beaches are small and rocky—perfect for keeping crowds away. The best beaches all lie to the east of the city along Kalaniana'ole Avenue, an area known as the Keaukaha Strip, which runs six miles from downtown Hilo to its dead end at Leleiwi Point. Not all beaches are clearly marked, but even those are easily identified by the cars parked along the road.

DOWNTOWN HILO AND THE BAYFRONT
Hilo Bayfront Park

A thousand yards of gray-black sand that narrows considerably as it runs west from the

Wailoa River toward downtown, at one time Hilo Bayfront Park (along Kamehameha Ave.) went all the way to the Wailuku River and was renowned throughout the islands for its beauty, but commercialism of the waterfront ruined it. By 1960, so much sewage and industrial waste had been pumped into the bay that it was considered a public menace, and then the great tsunami came. Reclamation projects created the Wailoa River State Recreation Area at the east end, and shorefront land became a buffer zone against future inundation. Few swimmers come to the beach because the water is cloudy and chilly, but the sharks don't seem to mind! The bay is a perfect spot for canoe races, and many local teams come here to train. Notice the judging towers and canoe sheds of local outrigger canoe clubs. Toward the west end, near the mouth of the Wailuku River, surfers catch long rides during the winter months, entertaining spectators. There is public parking along the eastern half near the canoe clubs or at the Wailoa river mouth where the fishing boats dock.

GREATER HILO

Although these beaches are outside of the downtown area, they are really only a few minutes from downtown, and all the beaches are within minutes of one another. With only one exception, all the beaches are either black-sand beaches or have no sand and just a grassy area fronting the beach.

Reeds Bay Beach Park

Technically part of Hilo Bay, Reeds Bay Beach Park (at the end of Banyan Dr.) is a largely undeveloped area on the east side of the Waiakea Peninsula. The water here is notoriously cold because of a constantly flowing freshwater spring, hence the name Ice Pond, at its innermost end. Mostly it's frequented by fishers and locals having a good time on weekends and holidays, and some sailors park their private boats here. Restrooms, water, and shower facilities are available, and after renovations in late 2011 this area will have all new facilities as well as picnic tables.

Keaukaha Beach and Carlsmith Beach Park

Keaukaha Beach at Carlsmith Beach Park, located on Puhi Bay, is the first in a series of beaches as you head east on Kalaniana'ole Avenue. Look for Baker Avenue and pull off to the left into a rough parking area. This is a favorite spot with local people, who swim at Cold Water Pond, a spring-fed inlet at the head of the bay. A sewage treatment plant fronts the western side of Puhi Bay. Much nicer areas for swimming and snorkeling await you just up Kalaniana'ole Avenue, but this beach does have a restroom, shower, pavilion, and weekend lifeguard.

Onekahakaha Beach Park

Farther up the road, Onekahakaha Beach Park has it all: safe swimming, small white-sand beach, lifeguards, and amenities. Turn left onto Onekahakaha Road and park in the lot of Hilo's favorite family beach. Swim in the large, sandy-bottomed pool protected by a manmade breakwater. Outside the breakwater the currents can be fierce, and drownings have been recorded. Good thing there is a lifeguard on duty during the weekends. Walk east along the shore to find an undeveloped area of the park with many small tidal pools. Beware of sea urchins.

James Kealoha Beach Park (Four Mile Beach)

James Kealoha Beach Park, also known locally as Four Mile Beach, is next; people swim, snorkel, and fish here, and during winter months it's a favorite surfing spot. Stay to the left side of the beach since it's more protected than the right side, which can get rough with strong currents during times of high surf.

Just offshore is an island known as Scout Island because local Boy Scouts often camp there. This entire area was known for its fishponds, and inland, just across Kalaniana'ole Avenue, is the 60-acre Loko Waka Pond. This site of ancient Hawaiian aquaculture is now a commercial operation that raises mullet, trout, catfish, perch, tilapia, and others (you'll find the Seaside Restaurant nearby). There is a restroom here but no other amenities.

Leleiwi Beach Park

A favorite local spot for scuba divers due to its plentiful sea life, Leleiwi Beach Park lies along a lovely residential area carved into the rugged coastline. This park, unlike the majority of them, has a full-time lifeguard, and it is a good thing they have one since the shore here is open to the ocean, and currents may be strong.

€ Richardson's Beach Park

Adjacent is Richardson Ocean Park, known locally as Richardson's Beach Park. A seawall skirts the shore, and a tiny cove with a black-sand beach is the first in a series. This is a terrific area for snorkeling, with plenty of marine life, including *honu* (green sea turtles). Walk east to a natural lava breakwater. Behind it are pools filled and flushed by the surging tide. The water breaks over the top of the lava and rushes into the pools, making natural whirlpool tubs. This is one of the most picturesque swimming areas on the island and is often crowded with families since it offers a lot of shade and a full-time lifeguard on duty. Full amenities are available.

NORTH HILO TO 'AKAKA FALLS
€ Honoli'i Beach Park

Traveling north a few miles out of Hilo brings you to Honoli'i Beach Park (Hwy. 19 between mile markers 4 and 5). Turn right onto Nahala Street, then left onto Kahoa, and follow it around until you see cars parked along the road. The water is down a steep series of steps, and while the black-sand beach is not much appreciated for swimming, it is known as one of the finest surfing spots on this side of the island. If you're not a seasoned surfer, no worries, there is a "kiddie" area as well as two lifeguards if any issues should arise. I highly recommend just coming for a quick viewing session to see the local talent try their hand at big waves. Restroom facilities and showers are available.

Kolekole Beach Park

Kolekole Beach Park (Hwy. 19 near mile marker 14) is very popular with local people, who use its pavilions for all manner of special occasions, usually on weekends. A pebble beach fronts a treacherous ocean. The entire valley was inundated with more than 30 feet of water during the great 1946 tsunami. The stream running through Kolekole comes from 'Akaka Falls, four miles inland. Take care while wading across it—the current can be very strong and push swimmers out to sea. Local kids tend to take advantage of the ocean's pull to try their hand at body-boarding. Amenities include portable bathrooms, grills, electricity, picnic tables, pavilions, and a camping area (county permit required); no drinking water is available.

To get to Kolekole Beach Park, look for the tall bridge (100 feet high) a few minutes north of Honomu, where a sign points to a small road that snakes its way down the valley to the beach park below. Slow down and keep a sharp eye out, as the turnoff is right at the south end of the bridge and easy to miss.

Water Sports

Although all water sports are possible in Hilo, it's more difficult to rent equipment on this side of the island (versus the Kona side), probably because fewer tourists come to Hilo to engage in water sports.

CANOEING AND KAYAKING

The Hilo Bay is home to many outrigger canoe clubs. In fact, it's a pretty big club sport on this side of the island. If you glance out onto the Hilo Bay almost any day you'll see numerous canoes and kayaks rowing by. Most canoes on the bay are owned by clubs and they do not rent out their canoes. It may be possible to find a canoe rental if you hang out near the launch area on Bayfront and ask around. Finding a kayak is easier at **Aquatic Perceptions** (111 Banyan Dr., 808/935-9997), which rents kayaks ($15–35 for a single, $20–45 for a tandem) out by the hour or by the day.

DIVING AND SNORKELING

Nearly all the beach parks on on Kalaniana'ole Avenue offer worthy snorkeling and diving, but the best spots are at Leleiwi Beach Park and Richardson's Beach Park. Problem is, everyone knows those are the best spots and they can become crowded (like the type of crowded when you get kicked in the face by another snorkeler). However, if you swim out just a little bit you'll leave the crowds (mostly children) behind and it will just be you and the turtles.

For rentals or instruction **Nautilus Dive Center** (382 Kamehameha Ave., 808/935-6939, www.nautilusdivehilo.com, Mon. 9 A.M.–noon,

Tues.–Sat. 9 A.M.–5 P.M.) is the place to go. They offer introductory diving courses ($85 per person), three- to five-day scuba certification ($480 per person), and more advanced courses. Rentals are $35 per day and discounts are available for longer rental periods. If you're looking for guide, they do that too. For $85 (a bargain rate compared to the Kona side) you can arrange a charter tour that includes a two-tank dive. Nautilus also rents snorkel gear, but if you think you might snorkel for several days it's cheaper to buy your own gear at someplace like Walmart.

SURFING AND STAND-UP PADDLE-BOARDING

There are some top surfing and stand-up paddle-boarding destinations on this side of the island. The most popular is Honoli'i Beach Park (just outside of town), where surfers and boarders don't have to worry about getting in the way of swimmers. Hilo Bay also lacks swimmers, but the water is usually cold and murky. North of Hilo in Hakalau it is possible to surf near the bridge, where waves can reach up to 16 feet. At the beach parks on Kalaniana'ole Avenue, such as Richardson's, it's also possible to surf if the weather is right, but these beaches all are prime stand-up paddle-boarding haunts when the water is calmish.

The hardest part of your surfing/boarding attempt might not be getting up, it might be finding a board if you just want to rent one. Your best bet for renting is **Orchidland Surfboards** (262 Kamehameha Ave., 808/935-1533, www.orchidlandsurf.com).

Hiking and Biking

HIKING

Hilo really is an urban area, so although urban hikes are possible, not so much in Hilo. One nice trail is the **Onomea Bay Hike** (on Onomea Scenic Dr., 1.75 miles from the Hilo-side Hwy. 19 turnoff). To get here look for the trailhead on the *makai* side of the road and drive slowly past it looking for the curve in the road (on the *mauka* side) where you can park a car. Parking here is a problem as only a few cars can fit (you can also try to park on the other side of the road). The route, which actually is an old donkey trail, is less than a mile and requires that you go and return the

same way. Round-trip, the trail will take you only about 30 minutes, with the ascent back up taking up the majority of time. At the end of the route to your right is Hawaii Tropical Botanical Garden (but no sneaking in—they have it guarded from below as well). To your left are the remains of an arch and lava tube caves (explore at your own risk—or better yet, maybe don't explore at all). This is definitely a hike for a sunny day (you can take a dip in the river at the bottom if you're hot), and you might want to reconsider if it's rainy, as the trail can get slippery. Slap some mosquito spray on before you go as it can get buggy.

WHAT HAPPENS ON THE ISLAND STAYS ON THE ISLAND

What happens on the island stays on the island. Although this phrase now is most known for its reference to mischievous acts, in Hawaii, locals know that it means that whatever material goods arrive to the islands – cars, furniture, books – tend to stay on the islands. It's not so easy to move heavy or big items across the ocean, and this trend is more than apparent in the myriad of excellent thrift shops located throughout the islands. So, when you live on an island, you must constantly consider where things go when they get left behind and where you might be able to find a discarded treasure.

Hawaiian garbage is actually shipped to the Mainland since there is no place to leave it here. This past year, the state ran into a quandary when the shipping of 20,000 tons of garbage became delayed and began to send a foul odor throughout O'ahu. Some environmental activists argue that the best way to reduce our waste – our environmental imprint – is not only to recycle (recycling expends a lot of energy and you need space for a recycling plant and ways to ship items there) but, more importantly, to reuse. Thus, on Hawaii, this reusing principle is even more salient given the difficulties of getting rid of waste coupled with

the available resources, like used goods left behind by people (sadly) leaving Hawaii.

On the Big Island, Bill Jackson has created a creative and economical way to reuse. At his **All Kine Bike Shop** (144 Kamehameha Ave., Hilo, 808/345-3417, www.bicyclehawaii.com, Mon.-Fri. 10 A.M.-5 P.M., Sat. 9 A.M.-5 P.M.) on the Hilo bayfront, he buys used bikes and salvages some from dumps and then rebuilds them into "new" custom-made bikes. Jackson explains that bikes are the perfect item to recycle "because they are simple." The parts are essentially interchangeable since they all have frames and wheels and are easy to repair.

The shop's storage area is overflowing with over 200 bikes and thousands of parts in crates waiting to be stripped down and remade into wholly new machines. "If someone needs something, I probably have it," Jackson happily says as a man walks in and asks if he carries parts for BMX bikes. His clientele are mainly "people who love to ride and people who have to ride." With gas prices rising, Jackson foresees that his sales will go up as people try to save money on gas by biking. "Biking itself isn't unique to Hawaii," Jackson explains, "but Hawaii by bike is something unique."

BIKING

Hilo is a bike town, but not in the same way as Kona. You won't see a lot of fancy road bikes and riders decked out in skintight clothing. You're more likely to see a college-age student riding a fixed gear bike or someone in a poncho commuting on a hybrid bike from Puna to Hilo.

If you are looking for a tune-up or parts while on your trip (or to buy a new bike), the **Hilo Bike Hub** (318 E. Kawili St., 808/961-4452, www.hilobikehub.com, Mon.–Fri.

9 A.M.–5:30 P.M., Sat. 9 A.M.–5 P.M.) is by far the best bike shop for these items. Alternatively, if you want to rent a bike or get an inexpensive used bike for a trip around the island, then your better bet is the **All Kine Bike Shop** (144 Kamehameha Ave., Bayfront, 808/345-3417, www.bicyclehawaii.com, Mon.–Fri. 10 A.M.–5 P.M., Sat. 9 A.M.–5 P.M.). In fact, if you call ahead from the Mainland, they will ensure that they have a bike ready for you to rent or to purchase.

Other Recreation

GOLF

Hilo is not known for great golf; the rain and dearth of money and luxury resorts keep the best courses elsewhere. Yet even here you can swing your irons. The only county-maintained golf course on the island is high above downtown Hilo: **Hilo Municipal Golf Course** (340 Haihai St., 808/959-7711, $20–25) is a 6,325-yard, par-71 undulating course with mostly parallel fairways. Prices are much cheaper than on the Kona side of the island, and there are reduced rates for state and island residents. Cart rental is separate, and rental clubs are available. This is definitely a local course but it does provide some challenge. Call ahead for tee times.

HELICOPTER TOURS

Helicopter tours leaving from Hilo travel exclusively to Hawai'i Volcanoes National Park and sometimes over the Hamakua Coast en route to the volcano.

Blue Hawaiian Helicopters (808/886-1768 in Waikoloa, 800/786-2583, www.bluehawaiian.com) operates tours from both the Kona and Hilo sides with two helicopter options—the A-Star and the Eco-star. The difference between the helicopters is that the Eco-star is "the first touring helicopter of the 21st century," meaning that its seats are more comfortable, it is quieter, and it has larger windows for a less obstructed view than the A-Star. Most importantly, it costs more. From the Hilo side,

the one-hour Circle of Fire plus Waterfalls tour ($196/$241) will take you over the waterfalls near Hilo on your way to Hawai'i Volcanoes National Park.

YOGA AND MASSAGE
Yoga, Meditation, and Retreats

Hilo-ites are all about their yoga and there are two excellent centers to choose from.

Balancing Monkey (65 Mohouli St., 808/936-9590, www.balancingmonkey.com, $10, $5 community class) isn't actually just a yoga center. They also offer meditation courses and "rock your chakra" in addition to hatha yoga, courses with ropes, and pre-natal yoga. Their online booking system makes it easy to pre-register and pay for classes, although it's probably only necessary to pre-book their larger events and not their daily yoga classes.

Located right in downtown Hilo, **Yoga Centered** (37 Waianuenue Ave., 808/934-7233, www.yogacentered.com, $14 drop-in) holds workshops and events, and houses a tiny clothing shop. Their Ashtanga and flow courses are offered nearly daily in addition to pilates classes.

If you are in need of some more serious Zen work, sign yourself up for a **Personal Tao** retreat with Casey Kochmer (808/935-6346, www.personaltao.com). Casey started the "awakening dragon" school of Taoism based on modern sensibilities. Although his specialty is one-on-one work with individuals having marital problems or experiencing midlife crisis, Casey's heart-based practice is useful for anyone struggling. In the spirit of Taoism, each retreat with Casey is a bit different depending on the needs of the individual. Likewise, price is negotiated with each individual based on what they can pay, and discounted rates are available for larger groups.

Massage and Acupuncture

It can happen. You get off your 10-hour flight from the Mainland and your ears are ringing (or is that from your first time snorkeling?) and your neck is stiff. If you're willing to try anything, try the **Hilo Natural Health Clinic** (152 Puueo St., 808/933-4325, http://hilonaturalhealth.com) to get you back in shape. Catherine Wingate, the acupuncturist, is an expert and can almost always get in a last-minute appointment. Not to mention that it's very easy to book one through the online appointment system. Cat can even make you a tincture if that's what she thinks you need to heal you.

Located downstairs in the same building is the **Hilo Massage Clinic** (www.hilomassageclinic.com, one-hour massage $55). You should see Megan Neal here. Megan splits her time between Hilo and the Four Seasons Resort on the Kona side: This means that you are essentially getting a Four Seasons massage for a third the price. In general, it is much cheaper to get a massage in Hilo than on the Kona side. So if Megan is booked, try out one of the many small massage shops located in the downtown area. They are all licensed by the state and are legitimate operations.

Sights

Before the shift of tourism to the drier Kona side of the island, Hilo was the Big Island's major visitor destination. This old town and steamy tropical port still holds many attractions for those willing to look, from missionary homes to forest waterfalls, and landscaped tropical gardens to diminutive beaches with great snorkeling options.

DOWNTOWN HILO AND THE BAYFRONT
Lyman Museum and Mission House

A few short blocks above downtown Hilo, the Lyman Museum and Mission House (276 Haili St., 808/935-5021, www.lymanmuseum.org, Mon.–Sat. 10 A.M.–4:30 P.M., $10 adults, $8 seniors, $3 children, $21 family, $5 students) showcases the oldest wood building on the Big Island, originally built in 1839 for David and Sarah Lyman, some of the first Christian missionaries on the island. The museum is a Smithsonian affiliate and has a bit of everything, from fine art to mineral and gem collections to exhibits on habitats of Hawaii.

The first-floor Earth Heritage Gallery holds a mineral and rock collection that's rated one of the best in the entire country, and by far the best in Polynesia. The museum also holds a substantial collection of archival documents and images relating to Hawaii's history.

Next door is the Lyman Mission House, which opened as a museum in 1931. The furniture is authentic "Sandwich Isles" circa 1850. Some of the most interesting exhibits are of small personal items like a music box that still plays and a collection of New England autumn leaves that Mrs. Lyman had sent over to show her children what that season was like. Upstairs are bedrooms that were occupied by the Lyman children. Mrs. Lyman kept a diary and faithfully recorded eruptions, earthquakes, and tsunamis. Scientists still refer to it for some of the earliest recorded data on these natural disturbances. The master bedroom has a large bed with pineapples carved into the bedposts, crafted by a ship's carpenter who lived with the family for about eight months. The bedroom mirror is an original, in which many Hawaiians received their first surprised look

Stroll through the cafés, shops, and the famous farmers market in historic downtown Hilo.

at themselves. Guided tours of the Lyman Mission House are included with museum admission and are given twice a day (11 A.M. and 2 P.M.) by experienced and knowledgeable docents who relate many intriguing stories about the house and its occupants.

Pacific Tsunami Museum

Hilo suffered a devastating tsunami in 1946 and another in 1960. Both times, most of the waterfront area of the city was destroyed, but the 1930 Bishop National Bank building survived, owing to its structural integrity. Appropriately, the Pacific Tsunami Museum (130 Kamehameha Ave., 808/935-0926, www.tsunami.org, Mon.–Sat. 9 A.M.–4:15 P.M., $8 adults, $7 seniors, and $4 students) is now housed in this fine art deco structure and dedicated to those who lost their lives in the devastating waves that raked the city. The museum has numerous permanent displays, an audiovisual room, computer linkups to scientific sites, and periodic temporary exhibitions. While there is general scientific information, perhaps

the most moving displays of this museum are the photographs of the last two terrible tsunamis that struck the city and the stories told by the survivors of those events. Stop in for a look. It's worth the time.

Mokupapapa Discovery Center for Hawaii's Coral Reefs

A small museum right on the bayfront, the Mokupapapa Discovery Center for Hawaii's Coral Reefs (280 Kamehameha Ave., Suite 109, 808/933-8195, www.papahanuaumokuakea.gov, Tues.–Sat. 9 A.M.–4 P.M., free) has a few interactive features and is filled with information about reefs and fish of the Northwestern Hawaiian Islands.

Downtown Walking Tour

A walking tour of downtown Hilo will only take you an hour or two (unless you really meander). This tour is a must for architecture lovers, but others might want to just pick and choose sights or refer back to this section as they walk by something that catches their interest.

Start your tour of Hilo by picking up a pamphlet/map entitled *Walking Tour of Historic Downtown*, free at the Hawaii Visitors Bureau office (250 Keawe St., 800/648-2441) and many restaurants, hotels, and shops. This self-guiding pamphlet takes you down the main streets and back lanes, where you discover the unique architecture of Hilo's glory days.

On the median strip between the Bayfront Highway and Kamehameha Avenue is a bandstand and the main city bus terminal. The **Mo'oheau Bandstand** is all that's left of the dozens of structures that lined the ocean side of Kamehameha Avenue before the 1946 tsunami. Miraculously, this structure survived. The bandstand is sometimes used by the Hawai'i County Band for concerts and for other community events. A **tourist information kiosk** near the bandstand and bus stop has brochures and maps to dispense about the city.

The majority of the vintage buildings have been restored, and the architecture varies from the early-20th-century Kress (1932), S. Hata Building (1912), and First Trust Building (1908) to the Zen Buddhist Taishoji Soto Mission and Central Christian Church. Older are the Lyman House (1839) and the nearby New England–style Haili Congregational Church (1859; congregation founded in 1824). A remarkable building is the **Old Police Station** (1932) opposite Kalakaua Park (141 Kalakaua St.). On the National and State Registers of Historic Places and Buildings, this old colonial structure is now the home of the East Hawaii Cultural Center. Next door to the old police station is the **Hawaiian Telephone Building** by C. W. Dickey, a well-known practitioner of the Hawaiian Regional Style. Notice the hipped roof, a typical feature of this style, and the colorful tiles.

Set aside for public use by King Kalakaua himself, **Kalakaua Park** is a grassy area overseen by a huge banyan tree, a midtown oasis. A seated statue of King David Kalakaua, the Merrie Monarch, takes center stage. Across Waianuenue Avenue is the solid and stately **Federal Building** with its offices and downtown post office. This stone structure dates from 1917.

A short walk up Waianuenue Avenue brings you to the **Hilo Public Library.** Sitting at the entrance are two large stones. The larger is called the **Naha Stone,** known for its ability to detect any offspring of the ruling Naha clan. The test was simple: Place a baby on the stone, and if the infant remained silent, he or she was Naha; if the baby cried, he or she wasn't. It is believed that this 7,000-pound monolith was brought from Kaua'i by canoe and placed near Pinao Temple in the immediate vicinity of what is now Wailuku Drive and Keawe Street. Kamehameha the Great supposedly fulfilled a prophecy of "moving a mountain" by budging this stone. The smaller stone is thought to be an entrance pillar of the Pinao Temple. Just behind the library is the Wailuku River. Pick any of its bridges for a panoramic view down to the sea. Often, local fishers try their luck from the Wailuku's grassy banks. The massive, overgrown boulder sitting near the river's mouth is known as **Maui's Canoe.** During the tsunami of 1946, the railroad bridge that crossed the river at bay's edge was torn from its base like a weak Tinker Toy construction. The metal bridge that crosses the river today is known as the Singing Bridge because the mesh that creates the roadway hums or "sings" as rubber tires spin across it.

Around Banyan Drive

If your Hilo hotel isn't situated along Banyan Drive, go there. This bucolic horseshoe-shaped road skirts the edge of Waiakea Peninsula, which sticks out into Hilo Bay. Lining the drive is an almost uninterrupted series of banyan trees forming a giant canopy. Skirting its edge are the Lili'uokalani Gardens, a concentration of hotels, and Reed's Bay.

This peninsula was once a populated residential area, an offshoot of central Hilo. Like much of the city, it was destroyed during the tsunami of 1960. Park your car at one end and take a stroll through this park-like atmosphere. Or arrive early and join other Hilo residents for a morning jog around the loop.

The four dozen banyans that line this boulevard (the first planted in 1933, the last in 1972) were planted by notable Americans and foreigners, including Babe Ruth, President Franklin D. Roosevelt, King George V, Hawaiian volcanologist Dr. Thomas Jaggar, Hawaiian princess Kawananakoa, pilot Amelia Earhart, Cecil B. DeMille, and then-senator Richard Nixon. A placard in front of most trees gives particulars. Time has taken its toll here, however, and as grand as this drive once was, it is now a bit overgrown and unkempt in spots, with much of the area needing a little sprucing up.

LILI'UOKALANI GARDENS

The Lili'uokalani Gardens are formal Japanese-style gardens located along the west end of Banyan Drive. Meditatively quiet, they offer a beautiful view of the bay. Along the footpaths are pagodas, torii gates, stone lanterns, and half-moon bridges spanning a series of ponds and streams. Along one side sits a formal Japanese tea house, where women come to be instructed in the art of the tea ceremony. Few people visit this 30-acre garden, and if it

weren't for the striking fingers of black lava and the coconut trees, you could easily be in Japan.

COCONUT ISLAND

Coconut Island (Moku Ola) is reached by footbridge from a spit of land just outside Lili'uokalani Gardens. It was at one time a *pu'uhonua* (place of refuge) opposite a human sacrificial *heiau* on the peninsula side. Coconut Island has restrooms, a pavilion, and picnic tables shaded by tall coconut trees and ironwoods. It's been a favorite picnic spot for decades; kids often come to jump into the water from stone abutments here, and older folks come for a leisurely dip in the cool water. The only decent place to swim in Hilo Bay, it also offers the best panorama of the city, bay, and Mauna Kea beyond.

Wailoa River State Recreation Area

To the east of downtown is **Waiakea Pond**, a brackish lagoon where people often fish, although that might not be such a great idea

Local families spend the afternoon picnicking, sunbathing, and swimming at Coconut Island.

© MARK WASSER

given the rumored levels of pollution. The Wailoa River State Recreation Area, which encompasses the lagoon, is a 132-acre preserve set along both sides of this spring-fed pond. City residents use this big broad area for picnics, pleasure walks, informal get-togethers, fishing, and launching boats. On the eastern side are picnic pavilions and barbecue grills. Arching footbridges cross the river connecting the halves.

Stop at the **Wailoa Center** on the western side for tourist information and cultural displays (Mon.–Tues. and Thurs.–Fri. 8:30 A.M.–4:30 P.M., Wed. noon–4:30 P.M.). The walls in the upstairs gallery of this 10-sided building are used to display works of local artists and cultural/historic exhibits, changed on a regular basis. On the lower level hang astonishing pictures of the 1946 and 1960 tsunamis that washed through the city. The Wailoa Center sits in a broad swath of greenery, an open, idyllic park-like area that used to be a cramped bustling neighborhood known as Shinmachi. It, like much of the city, was almost totally destroyed during the tsunami of 1960. Nearby stands the **Tsunami Memorial** to the residents of this neighborhood who lost their lives in that natural disaster.

Also close by is the county **Vietnam War Memorial,** dedicated to those who died fighting that war, and a **statue of King Kamehameha,** a new version of that which graces the town of Kapa'au at the northern tip of the island.

East of Waiakea Pond and across Manono Street you'll see **Ho'olulu Park,** with the Civic Center Auditorium and numerous athletic stadiums. This is the town's center for organized athletic events, large cultural festivals, the yearly Merrie Monarch dance festival, and the annual county fair.

GREATER HILO
Mauna Loa Macadamia Nut Factory

Mauna Loa Macadamia Nut Factory (16-701 Macadamia Road, 808/966-8618, www.maunaloa.com, Mon.–Sat. 8:30 A.M.–5 P.M.) is several miles south of Hilo off Highway

11, nearly to Kea'au. Head down Macadamia Road for about three miles, through the 2,500-acre plantation, until you come to the visitors center. Inside is an informative free video explaining the development and processing of macadamia nuts in Hawaii. Walkways outside the windows of the processing center and chocolate shop let you view the process of turning these delicious nuts into tantalizing gift items, but this is best viewed from August through January when most of the processing is done. Then return to the snack shop for macadamia nut goodies like ice cream and cookies, and to the gift shop for samples and an intriguing assortment of packaged macadamia nut items (which are cheaper at nearby grocery stores). While you're here, step out back and take a self-guided tour of the small garden, where many introduced trees and plants are identified.

Pana'ewa Rainforest Zoo

Not many travelers can visit a zoo in such a unique setting, where the animals virtually live in paradise. The 150 animals at the 12-acre zoo are endemic and introduced species that would naturally live in such an environment. While small and local, the zoo is a delight and the only natural tropical rainforest zoo in the United States of America. The road to the Pana'ewa Rainforest Zoo (800 Stainback Hwy., 808/959-9233, www.hilozoo.com, daily 9 A.M.–4 P.M., closed Christmas and New Year's Day) is a trip in itself, getting you back into the country. On a typical weekday, you'll have the place much to yourself. The zoo, operated by the county Department of Parks and Recreation, does feedings every Saturday around 1:30 P.M., and the tiger is fed every day at 3:35 P.M., so you may want to be around for these events. Admission is free, although donations to the nonprofit Friends of the Pana'ewa Zoo, which runs the gift shop at the entrance, are appreciated.

Here you have the feeling that the animals are not "fenced in" so much as you are "fenced out." The collection of about 75 species includes ordinary and exotic animals from around the world. You'll see pygmy hippos from Africa, a rare white Bengal tiger named Namaste, a miniature horse and steer, Asian forest tortoises, water buffalo, monkeys, and a wide assortment of birds like pheasants and peacocks. The zoo hosts many endangered animals indigenous to Hawaii, like the *nene,* Laysan duck, Hawaiian coot, *pueo,* Hawaiian gallinule, and even a feral pig in his own stone mini-condo. There are some great iguanas and mongooses, lemurs, and an aviary section with exotic birds like yellow-fronted parrots and blue and gold macaws. The zoo makes a perfect side trip for families and will certainly delight the little ones.

To get to the zoo from Hilo, take Highway 11 (Hawai'i Belt Road) south toward Volcano. About 2.5 miles past Prince Kuhio Shopping Plaza look for the Zoo sign on a lava rock wall, just after the sign Kulani 19. Turn right on Mamaki.

'Imiloa Astronomy Center

Located on the upper campus of University of Hawai'i at Hilo, the 'Imiloa Astronomy Center (600 Imiloa Pl., 808/969-9700, www.imiloahawaii.org, Tues.–Sun. 9 A.M.–5 P.M., adults $17.50, children 4–12 $9.50, senior, military, and *kama'aina* discounts available) opened in 2006 dedicated to the integration of science and indigenous culture. The word *'imiloa* means "exploring new knowledge," and the center educates visitors by separating its exhibits into "origins" and "explorations." Although in another place, the combination of studying astronomy and voyages may not make as much sense, here in Hawaii the two matters are very much linked given that the ancient Polynesians used the stars to wayfind from Polynesia to Hawaii and back.

In addition to the exhibits, a planetarium hosts daily kids' programs (from *Sesame Street* to "Our Place in Space") as well as Friday night laser light shows, such as Led Zeppelin (a classic!). Special events and workshops frequently occur at the center. Check the website for more information and for the Hawaiian word of the

The 80-foot Rainbow Falls gets its name from the bands of color that are produced from the mist of the water.

© HAWAII TOURISM AUTHORITY (HTA) / KIRK LEE AEDER

day. Say it at the register and get a $2 discount for each individual who speaks the word.

◖ Rainbow Falls and Boiling Pots

A few miles out of town as you head west on Waianuenue Avenue, two natural spectacles within Wailuku River State Park are definitely worth a look. A short way past Hilo High School a sign directs you to **Rainbow Falls,** a most spectacular yet easily visited natural wonder. You'll look down on a circular pool in the river below that's almost 100 feet in diameter; cascading into it is a lovely waterfall. The 80-foot falls deserve their name because as they hit the water below, their mists throw flocks of rainbows into the air. Underneath the falls is a huge cavern, held by legend to be the abode of Hina, mother of the god Maui. Most people are content to look from the vantage point near the parking lot, but if you walk to the left, you can take a stone stairway to a private viewing area directly over the falls (be careful; it can be slippery!). Here the river, strewn with volcanic boulders, pours over the edge. Follow the path for a minute or so along the bank to a gigantic banyan tree and a different vantage point. The falls may be best seen in the morning when the sunlight streams in from the front.

Follow Waianuenue Avenue for two more miles past Hilo Medical Center to the heights above town. A sign to turn right onto Peʻepeʻe Falls Street points to **Boiling Pots.** Few people visit here. Follow the path from the parking lot past the toilets to an overlook. Indented into the riverbed below is a series of irregularly shaped depressions that look as though a peg-legged giant left his peg prints in the hot lava. Seven or eight resemble naturally bubbling whirlpool tubs as river water cascades from one into the next. This phenomenon is best after a heavy rain. Turn your head upriver to see **Peʻepeʻe,** a gorgeous, five-spouted waterfall. Although signs warn you not to descend to the river—it's risky during heavy rains—locals hike down to the river rocks below to sunbathe and swim in pools that do not have rushing water. Again, be very careful as it can get slippery; flash floods can and have occurred here.

Kaumana Cave

In 1881, Mauna Loa's tremendous eruption discharged a huge flow of lava. The river of lava crusted over, forming a tube through which molten lava continued to flow. Once the eruption ceased, the lava inside siphoned out, leaving the tube now called Kaumana Cave (Rte. 200). Follow a steep staircase down into a gray hole (actually a skylight of this cave) draped with green ferns and brightened by wildflowers. Smell the scent of the tropical vegetation. You can walk only a few yards into the cave before you'll need a strong flashlight and sturdy shoes. It's a thrill to turn around and look at the entrance, where blazing sunlight shoots through the ferns and wildflowers.

To get to Kaumana Cave from downtown Hilo, turn left on Waianuenue Avenue. Just past mile marker 1 stay to the left onto Kaumana Drive (Saddle Road). Kaumana Cave is on the right just past mile marker 4.

A SINGING BRIDGE AND A FANTASTIC MONKEYPOD TREE

I know that it sounds like something out of *Alice in Wonderland,* and maybe it is, but you won't know until you check it out, now will you? As you drive north out of Hilo on Kamehameha Avenue (which turns into Highway 19), you'll drive over the Wailuku Bridge, also known as the "Singing Bridge," so named for the noise it makes when you pass over it. Perhaps it's not an actual singing, but it's definitely a low hum produced from the combination of the steel grate material that makes up the bridge and the sound of the ocean below it. Soon after crossing the bridge, look to the left for one of the most beautiful trees you'll ever see, towering over graves at Alae Cemetery. This huge monkeypod tree appears to be protecting the graves below it, and it's breathtaking.

NORTH HILO TO 'AKAKA FALLS

◖ Onomea Scenic Drive (Four-Mile Scenic Drive)

Highway 19 heading from Hilo to Honoka'a has magnificent inland and coastal views one after another. Most people find the Onomea Scenic Drive when coming north from Hilo. Only five minutes from the city, you'll come to Papa'ikou town. Just past mile marker 7 and across the road from the Papa'ikou School, a road posted as the scenic drive dips down toward the coast. Take it. (If you are coming from the Kona side you'll see a sign between mile markers 10 and 11). Almost immediately, signs warn you to slow your speed because of the narrow winding road and one-lane bridges, letting you know what kind of area you're coming into. Start down this meandering lane past some very modest homes and into the jungle that covers the road like a living green tunnel. Prepare for tiny bridges crossing tiny valleys. Stop, and you can almost hear the jungle growing. Along this short four-mile route are sections of an ancient coastal trail and the site of a former fishing village. Drive defensively, but take a look as you pass one fine view after another. This road runs past the Hawaii Tropical Botanical Garden and a couple of places for quick eats before heading up to higher ground to rejoin Highway 19 at Pepe'ekeo.

If you're coming from Hilo, just a few minutes (or 1.5 miles) along the Onomea Scenic Drive is the **Hawaii Tropical Botanical Garden** (27-717 Old Mamalahoa Hwy., 808/964-5233, www.hawaiigarden.com, daily 9 A.M.–5 P.M., last entry 4 P.M., adults $15, children 6–16 $16). Remember that the entrance fee not only allows you to walk through the best-tamed tropical rainforest on the Big Island but helps preserve this wonderful area in perpetuity. Tours are offered Saturday at noon for an additional $5 per adult.

The gardens were established in 1978 when Dan and Pauline Lutkenhouse purchased the 25-acre valley and have been open for viewing since 1984. Mr. Lutkenhouse, a retired San

© MARK WASSER

At 442 feet, 'Akaka Falls is the tallest single-tier waterfall in the state.

Francisco businessman, personally performed the work that transformed it into one of the most exotic spots in all of Hawaii. The locality was amazingly beautiful but inaccessible because it was so rugged. Through personal investment and six painstaking years of toil aided by only two helpers, he hand-cleared the land, built trails and bridges, developed an irrigation system, acquired more than 2,000 different species of trees and plants, and established one mile of scenic trails and a water lily lake stocked with *koi* and tropical fish. Onomea was a favorite spot with the Hawaiians, who came to fish and camp for the night.

These inviting gardens, a "living museum" as they call it, will attract lovers of plants and flowers, and those looking to take really great photographs. The loop through the garden is about a mile long, and the self-guided tour, if done thoroughly, will take you about 90 minutes. As you walk, listen for the songs of the native birds that love this ancient spot. The walk is not difficult, but there are steps down to the gardens that are not wheelchair accessible. Golf carts ($5) are available to help those who need it down the boardwalk, and then non-motorized wheelchairs are allowed in the garden itself.

◀ 'Akaka Falls State Park

Everybody's idea of a pristine Hawaiian valley is viewable at 'Akaka Falls State Park (on Hwy. 220, gate open 7 A.M.–7 P.M., $5 per car or $1 per pedestrian, no charge for Hawaii residents), one of the most easily accessible forays into Hawai'i's beautiful interior. Take the Honomu turnoff from Highway 19 onto Highway 220 to get here. From the parking lot, walk counterclockwise along a paved "circle route" that takes you 0.4 mile in about a half hour. The footpath does require some physical exertion.

Along the way, you're surrounded by heliconia, ti, ginger, orchids, azaleas, ferns, and bamboo groves as you cross bubbling streams on wooden footbridges. Many varieties of plants that would be in window pots anywhere else are giants here, almost trees. An overlook provides views of **Kahuna Falls** spilling into a lush green valley below. The trail becomes an enchanted tunnel through hanging orchids and bougainvillea. In a few moments you arrive at **'Akaka Falls.** The mountain cooperates with the perfect setting, forming a semicircle from which the falls tumble 442 feet in one sheer drop, the tallest single-tier waterfall in the state. After heavy rains, expect a mad torrent of power; during dry periods marvel at liquid-silver threads forming mist and rainbows.

HILO AND AROUND

Shopping

DOWNTOWN HILO AND THE BAYFRONT

The bayfront area is most definitely set up to encourage shopping. Unfortunately, it doesn't always inspire shops to stay open late or to stay open at all. Don't be surprised if by 5 P.M. downtown Hilo feels like a ghost town. Likewise, while there are a few stores that have kept their doors open for over 20 years, many more close every year. So don't be surprised if your favorite store is nowhere to be found.

In general, the majority of shops on the bayfront cater to cruise ship passengers. It's difficult to distinguish from one shop to another and the same Hawaiiana tchotchke (made in China) that they offer. Nevertheless, one store that stands apart is **Basically Books** (160 Kamehameha Ave., 808/961-0144, www.basicallybooks.com, Mon.–Sat. 9 A.M.–5 P.M., 11 A.M.–4 P.M.). This isn't where you get recently published bestsellers; instead, it has a good selection of Hawaiiana, out-of-print books, and an unbeatable selection of maps and charts. You can get anywhere you want to go with these nautical charts, road maps, and topographical maps, including sectionals

for serious hikers. The store also features a very good selection of travel books, flags from countries throughout the world, as well as children's books and toys with Hawaii themes. The owners also publish books about Hawaii under their Petroglyph Press name.

Another longstanding store, **Sig Zane Design** (122 Kamehameha Ave., 808/935-7077, www.sigzane.com, Mon.–Fri. 9:30 A.M.–5 P.M., Sat. 9 A.M.–4 P.M.), sells distinctive island wearables in Hawaiian/tropical designs. This store is the real deal. Sig Zane designs the fabrics, and Sig's wife, Nalani, who helps in the shop, is a *kumu hula* who learned the intricate dance steps from her mother, Edith Kanakaole, a legendary dancer who has been memorialized with a local tennis stadium that bears her name. You can get shirts, dresses, and pareu, as well as affordable T-shirts, *hapi* coats, and even futon covers. The shelves also hold leather bags, greeting cards, and accessories.

GREATER HILO

The majority of shopping for everyday living happens within the same four corners off of Highway 11. More importantly, this area serves as a main wayfinding point for giving directions to all other points around town (including the airport, which is nearby).

In what is colloquially called "the Walmart shopping area," you can find (wait for it) **Walmart** (325 E. Makaala St., 808/961-9115, daily 5 A.M.–1 A.M.). Open nearly 24 hours, this store is constantly busy. It has everything you could ever imagine—including food. Until the summer of 2011, Walmart was the only one-stop-shop in town until **Target** (391 E. Makaala St., 808/920-8605, Mon.–Sat. 8 A.M.–10 P.M., Sun. 8 A.M.–9 P.M.) blessed the east side of the island with its presence.

In the same complex as Walmart you'll also find Hilo's second favorite store, **Ross Dress for Less** (307 E. Makaala St., 808/961-5102, Mon.–Sat. 8:30 A.M.–10 P.M., Sun. 9 A.M.–9:30 P.M.) as well as an **Office Max,** several restaurants, **Walgreens,** and the **Down to Earth** grocery store.

Across the road the **Prince Kuhio Plaza** (111 E. Puainako St., 808/959-3555, www.princekuhioplaza.com, Mon.–Thurs. 10 A.M.–8 P.M., Fri.–Sat. 10 A.M.–9 P.M., Sun. 10 A.M.–6 P.M.) is the closest thing the Big Island has to a Mainland-looking indoor mall. It's filled with mall stores like Radio Shack, Spencer's Gifts, Macy's, and Sears. And yes, there is a food court filled with your standard pretzel shop, hot dogs on a stick, and a Maui Taco. Since no mall would be complete without a cineplex, you'll find a Hollywood theater affiliate here too.

NORTH HILO TO 'AKAKA FALLS

The 'Akaka Falls road passes through the town of Honomu. In addition to the multitude of sarong shops dotting the main street (it's like the sarong capital of the world here), the non-sarong shops along the main street are worth a stop.

Glass from the Past (28-1672-A Old Mamalahoa Hwy., 808/963-6449) has been in Honomu for 25 years, and its merchandise has been in the area for nearly a hundred years. As the store's name indicates, it carries antique glass. What's so interesting about this glass is that it is from the different area plantations—all of which had their own soda works and dairy. Each piece of class tells a story about Hawai'i's past. Even if you're not going to make a purchase, stop in and *talk story* (as it were) with the shop owner, who scrounges the area to find his products. It's like a modern-day archaeological dig.

A few doors down, **Mr. Ed's Homemade Jams and Bakery** (808/963-5000, Mon.–Sat. 6 A.M.–6 P.M., Sun. 9 A.M.–4 P.M.) stocks every imaginable type of jam ($7) made from local ingredients like jaboticaba, jackfruit, starfruit, and purple sweet potato. The baked goods get bad reviews, but come in and taste one of the hundreds of jams (maybe not hundreds, but it seems like it). Low-sugar as well as no-sugar options are available and they ship jars to the Mainland if you don't want to check your luggage (jam counts as a liquid—it's confusing, I know).

Entertainment and Events

ENTERTAINMENT
Bars

People in Hilo tend not to stay out late. Maybe it's because we like to get up early and surf or maybe it's because (as many of the University of Hawai'i at Hilo students have complained) bars open and then quickly shut down due to noise complaints from neighbors. So for the most part, bars have stopped opening around town.

Nevertheless, driving around Hilo you'll surely see a lot of intriguing bars. Many of them are geared toward specific groups of locals. So there is one that serves Japanese clientele, and one that serves a Korean clientele, and one for Filipino clientele, etc. If you're not from the island or with a local, you might feel a little out of place at some of these establishments, but that doesn't mean you shouldn't check them out.

HAWAI'I NUI BREWING

Hilo has its own microbrewery, Hawai'i Nui Brewing (275 E. Kawili St., 808/934-8211, www.hawaiinuibrewing.com, Mon.-Sat. 8:30 A.M.-5:30 P.M.). A small operation – about 1,200 barrels a year – and in business since 1996, this microbrewery (formerly known as the Mehana Brewery) crafts five varieties of light beer with no preservatives, brewed especially for the tropical climate. Stop at the small tasting room/logo shop for a sample or gift any day except Sunday. If it's not too busy, someone may show you around. Note: If you're looking to order a keg for a holiday weekend don't forget to order early! There are few places in Hilo where one can get a keg, so the brewery tends to run out early.

A bar definitely worth experiencing is **Kim's Karaoke Lounge** (760 Piilani St., 808/935-7552, open late), the favorite bar of nearly every Hilo resident. Why is it so loved? After the purchase of two cheap drinks, the waitresses start bringing unlimited pupu (appetizers) and there is a lot of drunken karaoke. While I did receive more attentive service when I was there with a more "local" crowd, don't let this anecdotal evidence deter you from coming if you don't look local (just put on your *slippahs* and maybe they won't notice). Kim's is probably the furthest thing from a tourist bar.

Another place with pupu included with alcohol purchase is **Bamboo Garden** (718 Kinoole St., 808/935-8952). Less popular than Kim's, this place doesn't always have a crowd. This would be the place to come if you're not looking for a scene and want to ease yourself into the world of Hilo bars.

Hilo Burger Joint (776 Kilauea, 808/935-8880, http://hiloburgerjoint.com, daily 11 A.M.-11 P.M., happy hour daily 4-6 P.M., $11) is your quintessential college town bar (but the one that the graduate students and not the undergrads populate). The 20 varieties of Big Island beef burgers include the "Peter Kim"—Chee Burger (Korean style with cheese), the Nacho Burger, the Curry Burger, and the Greek Burger—you'll find something you'll like. Burgers can also be served on lettuce or rice (*loco moco* style). Vegetarian and non-beef burgers are also available. In addition to the burgers, the Hilo Burger Joint also has a full bar with lots of beers on draft. If you sit at a table (and not the bar), service can be slow at times since it's usually the bartender who has to wait on you. But if you're not in a huge rush you might enjoy the live music (usually something mellow) on the weekends.

That sports bar you've been searching for to watch your team on the big-ish screen is **Cronies Bar and Grill** (11 Waianuenue Ave., 808/935-5158, www.cronieshawaii.com, Mon.–Thurs. 11 A.M.–9 P.M., Fri. 11 A.M.–10 P.M., Sat. 11 A.M.–9 P.M., Sun. 11 A.M.–8 P.M., $15), although it would be better if it actually opened early enough to watch East Coast games. That issue aside, on the weekends, this restaurant/bar decorated with sports paraphernalia gets jammed with sports lovers rooting for their favorite teams, while simultaneously trying to advertise itself as a fine dining establishment. It's hard to be both. If you're not there to watch a game or to grab a quick drink at the bar, then I'd definitely eat my meal somewhere else in town. Cronies is tempting though for its prime location (right on Bayfront) and familiar menu of burgers ($10), Big Kahuna T-bone steak ($30), pork ribs ($18 half rack), wings ($9), and salads with a homemade papaya seed dressing. A children's menu is available.

The new kid on the block, the **Hilo Town Tavern** (168 Keawe St., 808/935-2171, Mon.–Fri. 2 P.M.–2 A.M., Sat. 10 A.M.–2 A.M., Sun. 10 A.M.–midnight, happy hour Mon.–Fri. 4–6 P.M., pizzas $8) has switched management (and with that cooks) at least three times since it opened in early 2011. Regardless, it fills a much-needed hole in downtown Hilo, where it seems like everything else closes down by

HILO AND AROU

5 P.M. Like most people, you might find yourself meandering inside after hearing live music as you walk by. The bands are all local and the music styles vary, but for no cover, why not come for a listen and a drink? The back part of the bar (which is kind of separate, or seems like it's in a side building) has a pool table and more chairs.

Movies and Live Performances

You'd think that given the fact that the island only has movie theaters in Hilo and Kona (and a small one in Honoka'a) that they would get packed. Well, not so much. The only place you have to worry about arriving early is the downtown **Kress Cinemas** (174 Kamehameha Ave., 808/935-6777), and this is mostly because tickets are only $1.50 on weekdays and 1.75 on weekends and the small theaters get packed. Even with the poor seating options, you can't beat the price for month-old blockbusters. But beware; as someone once said, "taking your kids to Kress is cheaper than a babysitter," and that's exactly what many families do.

Just around the corner, the renovated **Palace Theater** (38 Haili St., 808/934-7777, www.hilopalace.com) shows art films, is the venue of the yearly Hawaii International Film Festival, and hosts periodic live performances. Here you have stadium seating (the legroom is scarce), a proscenium stage, and wonderful old murals. If you're into art deco buildings and old cinemas, make this a stop. Movies are generally shown Friday–Tuesday at 7:30 P.M.; movie tickets are $7 adult and $6 seniors and students. Other performances may be at different times and ticket prices vary.

Hawaiiana Live at the Palace Theater (808/934-7010, Wed. 11–11:45 A.M., $5 adult, free for kids under 12) showcases Hawaiian history and culture through storytelling, music, film, and hula. You'll wish that it wasn't only on Wednesdays and only 45 minutes long. It's not much different than the *lu'au* you might have already attended at the resorts, but if you haven't gone, it's a great way to see some of traditional Hawaiian culture.

THE BEST OF THE ARTS IN HILO

East Hawaii Cultural Center (141 Kalakaua St., 808/961-5711, www.ehcc.org, 10 A.M.-4 P.M. Mon.-Sat.) is a nonprofit organization that supports local arts and hosts varying festivals, performances, and workshops throughout the year, here and at other locations on the island. It also hosts Shakespeare in the Park performances by a local repertory group that stages, directs, designs, and enacts Shakespearean plays under the large banyan tree in Kalakaua Park during the month of July. If you're in Hilo at this time, it shouldn't be missed.

Monthly juried and non-juried art exhibits are shown on the main floor gallery; a venue for various performing artists is upstairs. The bulletin board is always filled with announcements of happenings in the local art scene. Stop in as there is always something of interest on the walls, and because this organization is worthy of support. The Big Island Dance Council, Hawaii Concert Society, Hilo Community Players, and Bunka No Izumi are all member groups.

For some real stadium seating (you know, seats that go back and lots of legroom) your only option is the Hollywood chain **Prince Kuhio Theater** (111 E. Puainako St., 808/961-3456) at the Prince Kuhio Plaza. This cinema is your typical big movie theater showing blockbuster films, IMAX, and those live telecast events. Tickets are $9.50 adult, $6.50 senior, and $6.25 for children.

EVENTS
Hilo to Volcano 50K Ultra Marathon Relay

Start your new year off right with the Hilo to Volcano 50K Ultra Marathon Relay each January. Or you could just eat *malasadas* like the rest of us. Starting at Coconut Island in Hilo and ending at the Cooper Center in Volcano, each relay team is made up of three

HILO AND AROUND

© MARK WASSER

The annual Merrie Monarch Festival celebrates hula and Hawaiian culture.

runners. There is no official website for this run, but you can get information at www.big-islandroadrunners.org.

Merrie Monarch Festival

Beginning in 1964, the annual Merrie Monarch Festival (www.merriemonarch.com), which usually starts right after Easter, is the talk of the town (and sometimes even the entire state). Tickets for the three-day hula competition start selling at the end of December. This is one of those events that it's worth planning your trip around, either because you really want to attend the event (there are some free parts that don't require tickets) or because you should plan on avoiding Hilo at this time when rooms are all booked up and traffic is terrible. But if you're willing to join the crowds, you will be in for a grand treat and exposure to the world's best hula dancers. The weeklong festival includes a craft fair, demonstrations, performances, and a parade. In general, the Merrie Monarch Festival is an excellent entrée into Hawaiian culture and tradition as well as a way to see performances from hula dancers outside of Hawaii.

May Day Lei Day

May Day Lei Day is always the first Sunday in May. Writer Grace Tower Warren initiated this holiday after Don Blanding, a writer and poet, wrote an article in 1928 recommending that a holiday be created around the Hawaiian custom of making and wearing leis. Usually, festivities involving lei-making demonstrations take place in Kalakaua Park in downtown Hilo to commemorate this holiday.

Big Island Hawaiian Music Festival

In mid-July, the University of Hawai'i at Hilo Performing Arts Center and the East Hawaii Cultural Center (www.ehcc.org) host the Big Island Hawaiian Music Festival ($5–10). This two-day event showcases the talent of local musicians. The price is right for the event, so considering attending even if you aren't familiar with the music.

Hawaii County Fair

In September with the beginning of the school year comes the Hawaii County Fair held at the Hilo Civic Fairgrounds. It's a lot like any other county fair: booths with local community groups, local bands playing cover songs, fried foods that you wouldn't eat in any other circumstances, rides, and a petting zoo. If you're around and looking for something fun to do for an hour or two, come out and support the Hilo Jaycees, who sponsor the event. It's also a great way to get a sense of life in Hilo.

Aloha Festival Hoolaulea

The biggest party of the year is the Aloha Festival Hoolaulea in late September. This annual festival closes down the streets on Bayfront and brings out what seems like nearly the entire town for a good time. With two different stages of musicians playing simultaneously at opposite ends of the street, it's quite a sight (and very loud). Parking can get be difficult and traffic even worse due to the street closures, so plan ahead. For more information, call 808/935-5461.

Hilo Wayfinding Festival

If you love old-looking boats and sailing, then you'll love the annual Hilo Wayfinding Festival held at the 'Imiloa Astronomy Center (www.imiloahawaii.org) each October. This free festival celebrates "the feats of Pacific navigators" with lectures, a small film festival, workshops, and demonstrations on wayfinding

and the *Hokulea* voyaging canoe in the Pacific. It's not necessary to stay for all the events, so if you are intrigued check the online schedule of events and simply pop in for a bit.

Black and White Night

Another one of Hilo's biggest parties of the year, Black and White Night takes to the street each November. In a town where things shut down by 5 P.M. it can feel like a breath of fresh air to be able to stroll around downtown until 9 P.M. checking out sales, free samples (food and goods), and art work. Also, everyone dresses up in black and white and people really do it up since there is a cash prize for the best outfit. If you're not tired after wandering the streets, join the after-party at a local bar. Visit www.downtownhilo.com for more information on the night's events.

Paradise Roller Girls' Thanksgiving Game

It's like *Whip It,* but in Hawaii. Paradise Roller Girls (www.paradiserollergirls.com) are the hottest thing to hit the island since Spam. Their bouts (as they are called), especially the Thanksgiving game between the Puna team and the Volcano team, are rockin'. The entire civic auditorium fills with fans cheering for their favorite players (by screaming expletives). Check the website for the exact date of the game (usually the Saturday of Thanksgiving weekend) and for other event listings.

Food

DOWNTOWN HILO AND THE BAYFRONT

Establishments are listed from east to west on each respective street beginning farther from the bay and ending on Bayfront (also known as Kamehameha Avenue).

Saimin, a noodle soup that developed during Hawaii's plantation days, is just one of many dishes served at **Nori's Saimin**

and Snacks (688 Kinoole St., 808/935-9133, Mon. 10:30 A.M.–3 P.M., Tues.–Sat. 10:30 A.M.–3 P.M. and 4 P.M.–midnight, Sun. 10:30 A.M.–10 P.M., $7). Even though this Korean-style noodle house is featured in a Hawaiian Airlines ad, it doesn't get a lot of tourists. The daily specials greatly range from fried chicken to pigs' feet soup to meatloaf, making it a little difficult to get a handle on

SHAVE ICE

It's not a misspelling – it is "shave" (not "shaved") ice. And it's deeply embedded into Hawaiian culinary culture. I am not talking about a snow cone or the Puerto Rican *piraquas* that fill the streets of the Bronx on summer nights. This is something completely different: They are made by finely shaving a block of ice. The result is ice that is smooth (like butter) instead of crushed, which helps better absorb the flavored syrup poured on top. Oh, and the flavors! Try Hawaiian-inspired essences like guava, *liliko'i*, and *li hing mui*. Locals all have their favorite shave ice place, but with 18 different flavors, **Wilson's by the Bay** (224 Kamehameha Ave., Hilo, 808/969-9191, $3) on the bayfront is a standard crowd pleaser.

homemade smoked salmon bagels (Hilo really is a bagel desert) and quiches. Weekdays are stocked full of deals. The early-bird special 8–10 A.M. gets you coffee and a bagel sandwich for $6, and during the afternoon happy hour 2:30–4:30 P.M. many of the desserts and beverages are heavily discounted. Vegetarian and wheat-free options are available, along with wireless Internet. However, use the restroom before you go—they don't have one on the premises.

Yes, Starbucks is nearly across the street from **Just Cruisin' Coffee** (835 Kilauea Ave., 808/934-7444, daily 5:30 A.M.–8 P.M., $6), and yes, they both have wireless Internet, drive-thru windows, and outdoor seating. But where Just Cruisin' Coffee excels is with their delectable chicken macadamia nut salad with pesto sandwich ($7.25), hot breakfast sandwiches ($5), cold brewed coffee, smoothies, and coffee milk shakes.

Named after a famous all-Japanese fighting battalion, the **Cafe 100** (969 Kilauea Ave., 808/935-8683, http://cafe100.com, Mon.–Thurs. 6:30 A.M.–8:30 P.M., Fri. 6:30 A.M.–9 P.M., Sat. 6:30 A.M.–7:30 P.M., $5) is a Hilo institution. The Miyashiro family has been serving food at its indoor-outdoor restaurant here since the late 1950s. Although the *loco moco*, a cholesterol atom bomb containing a hamburger and egg atop rice smothered in gravy, was invented at Hilo's Lincoln Grill, the Cafe 100, serving it since 1961, has actually patented this belly-buster and turned it into an art form. Offerings include the regular *loco moco*, teriyaki *loco*, Spam *loco*, hot dog *loco*, *oyako loco*, and, for the health conscious, the mahimahi *loco*. So, if your waistline, the surgeon general, and your arteries permit, this is *the* place to have one. With few exceptions, they cost $7 or less. Breakfast choices include everything from bacon and eggs to coffee and doughnuts, while lunches feature beef stew, salmon mixed plate, and fried chicken, or an assortment of sandwiches from teriyaki beef to good old BLT. Make your selection and sit at one of the picnic tables under the veranda to watch the people of Hilo go by.

Nori's culinary identity. But what is for certain is that the portions are large and inexpensive and there is Hello Kitty paraphernalia surrounding the Formica booths. If you want to taste a bunch of local dishes in one sitting, try the Big Plate with ahi tempura, fried noodles, kalbi ribs, teri beef, chicken sticks, *musubi*, and macaroni salad ($15). I have seen a good eater attempt to eat this himself and he needed some help. It is a legitimately big plate. Be sure to order one of their self-designated "famous" chocolate *mochi* cookies and cakes. I am skeptical of their fame, but you can't go wrong with a chocolate-*mochi* mix.

A bit of a gourmet anomaly in Hilo, **Short N Sweet Bakery and Café** (374 Kinoole St., 808/935-4446, www.shortnsweet.biz, Mon.–Fri. 8 A.M.–4:30 P.M., Sat.–Sun. 8 A.M.–3 P.M., $9) earned itself the designation of "America's most beautiful cakes" by *Brides* magazine in 2010. This is a well-deserved honor. Don't be mistaken, though; Short N Sweet is more than a bakery. Their lunch menu of panini and salads is a welcome break from local cuisine, and their Sunday brunch menu is gaining in popularity thanks to those who stumble upon their

The "Best Thai Food" of the Big Island showdown continues at **Naung Mai Thai Kitchen** (86 Kilauea Ave., 808/934-7540, www.hilothai.com, daily 11 A.M.–9 P.M., $12), where the great lunch specials, pineapple curry, and vegan tapioca pudding give the other "best" Thai restaurants a run for their money. (This is where I would go if Sombat's Fresh Thai Cuisine was closed or out of the lunch special.) The space is intimate.

Next door to Naung Mai is the newly opened **Pho Viet** (80 Kilauea Ave., 808/935-1080, Mon.–Sat. 11 A.M.–9 P.M., $8), serving the traditional Vietnamese soup called *pho* (pronounced "fuh"): beef noodle or chicken noodle soup served with sprouts and lime on the side. At the time of writing the restaurant ambiance resembled that of a cafeteria with white walls and fluorescent lighting, but decoration concerns aside, the *pho* is *pho*-nomenal. Vegetarian options are available and the soups are gluten-free-friendly.

Nearby, **Ocean Sushi** (250 Keawe St., 808/961-6625, Mon.–Sat. 10:30 A.M.–2 P.M. and 5–9 P.M., rolls start at $2, mains $10) is a favorite of University of Hawai'i at Hilo students who recognize that this is one of those places where you can eat well for not too much money. Walk by this place on a Friday night (or many nights) and it will be packed. The sushi is all right, not the best in town, but there is some stark competition. It feels like a sushi factory (and kind of looks like one too), but that means you get your sushi cheaply and fairly quickly without much service.

At the end of Keawe Street in a beautiful historical building you'll find **Le Magic Pan** (64 Keawe St., 808/935-7777, daily 11 A.M.–2 P.M. and 5–9 P.M., $10–15), and it's worth stopping by. Both dessert crepes (Nutella and bananas) and savory crepes (like shrimp with pesto) are available. The newest additions to the menu are gluten-free options (crepes made with chickpea or buckwheat flour) and vegan options. The meals are surprisingly filling, and with live music (most nights) filling the air of this stylish long-standing building, Le Magic Pan makes for a good date night option.

Front and center on Bayfront, with a black-and-white checkerboard floor, linen on the tables, an open-air kitchen, a high ceiling with ceiling fans, and the calming effect of ferns and flowers, is **Cafe Pesto** (308 Kamehameha Ave., 808/969-6640, www.cafepesto.com, Sun.–Thurs. 11 A.M.–9 P.M., Fri.–Sat. 11 A.M.–10 P.M., reservations recommended, lunch $14, dinner $20), in the historic S. Hata Building. One of Hilo's fine established restaurants, it offers affordable gourmet food in an open, airy, and unpretentious setting that looks out across the avenue to the bay. Pizzas from the *'ohi'a* wood–fired oven can be anything from a simple cheese pie for $8.50 to a large Greek or chili-grilled shrimp pizza for $18; you can also create your own. Lunchtime features sandwiches, calzones, and pasta. For dinner, try an appetizer like Asian Pacific crab cakes or sesame-crusted Hamakua goat cheese. Heartier appetites will be satisfied with the main dinner choices, mostly $15–28, which might be mango-glazed chicken, island seafood risotto, or a combination beef tenderloin and tiger prawns with garlic mashed potatoes. Follow this with a warm coconut tart or *liliko'i* cheesecake. Cafe Pesto also has a brass-railed bar where you can order caffe latte or a fine glass of wine to top off your meal. A kids' menu is available.

It has it all: well priced food with flavors your palate may not be familiar with in a cute (very local) setting. It's imperative to get to **◖ Puka Puka Kitchen** (270 Kamehameha Ave., 808/933-2121, lunch Mon.–Sat. 11 A.M.–2:30 P.M. and dinner Fri.–Sat. 5:30–8:30 P.M., $12) early, otherwise the best dishes are gone. However, if you get there late (after 2 P.M.) the bento boxes are half price and quite a deal. The food is Middle Eastern meets Indian food meets Hawaii with Japanese writing on the menu. The sautéed lamb plate is delicious, with tender pieces of meat (locally sourced) served with a green salad and rice. Order the house garlic rice (you have a choice) to create the perfect plate of flavors. Other choices (for when the lamb sells out) are the ahi (fish) plate, curry dishes, and the pita sandwiches—all good hearty options. I would not get the barbecued chicken or the falafel as they do their other plates better. There are several vegetarian options on the menu and they accommodate special diets.

Even with only 10 seats in the restaurant, one rarely has to wait a few minutes to try the freshest and best-styled sushi in town at gem-in-the-wall **◖ Sushi Bar Himi** (14 Furneaux Ln., 808/961-6356, daily 11:30 A.M.–2:30 P.M. and 5–8 P.M.). The menu, which also adorns the wall on colorful scraps of paper, is a mixture of the usual with the unimaginable. It includes maki rolls in pink soy wrappers, mushrooms stuffed with crab and smothered with warm hollandaise sauce, and daily specials with creative names highlighting local fish like mahimahi and topped with a dash of tahini sauce. If you are short on time, don't worry. Each plate arrives within minutes after ordering but always appears as if extra care was taken to plate it perfectly, giving Bar Himi's food a one-of-a-kind taste.

For a town with a university, there are very few places in Hilo where you can go to sit, use wireless Internet, and get a good coffee or noncoffee drink. **Surf Break Café** (13 Haili St., 808/934-8844, daily 6 A.M.–3 P.M., $7 meals) is the place. The walls are painted brightly and it always feels cool inside even when it's a scorcher outside. It's easy to spend a few hours here working away at one of the funky tables while sipping on a coffee or smoothie and eating a panini or bagel. But don't come here for the food—it's just nice to have the option if you're planning on spending a few hours here. A kids' menu is available.

Kava is one of those local specialties that tourists who are keen on experiencing all Hawaii has to offer should try, and **Bayfront Coffee, Kava, and Tea Co.** (116 Kamehameha Ave., 808/935-1155, http://bayfrontkava.com, Mon.–Thurs. 9 A.M.–10 P.M., Fri.–Sat. 10 A.M.– 10 P.M., $5) is the place to do it. However, besides offering kava, the "coffee" or "tea" or "café" part of the name is a bit misleading. To be clear, they do have coffee and tea, but nothing fancy—essentially you can order a cup of coffee (maybe an espresso) and a tea. There are only a few tables inside and a couple of seats outside (these are nice for people-watching). Sit at the bar and order a kava shell ($5) and don't be afraid to ask how to drink it and what's the importance of kava in Hawaiian tradition. Café workers are very excited to introduce non-drinkers to 'awa (the Hawaiian word for kava). You should be warned, though: Kava doesn't taste very good; it's an acquired taste, and until you acquire it, it tastes much like dirt. In addition to drinks, there is a limited menu of bagels ($3) and sandwiches ($6). On the weekend the café gets buzzing with live music and a regular crowd of onlookers.

GREATER HILO

If you're aching for the huevos rancheros (scrambled eggs with onion and tomato) from your last vacation to Oaxaca, drive quickly to **◖ Emma's** (Shipman Industrial Park, 16-203 Wiliama Pl., Kea'au, 808/966-6300, Mon.–Fri. 8 A.M.–2 P.M., $7). The flavors are spot on at this hidden gem situated in a hole in the wall. Upgrade to the "plate" portion, which includes rice and beans, but don't forget to save room for the homemade churros—essentially elongated doughnuts. There are daily lunch specials, and most locals talk endlessly about Friday's fish tacos. And did I mention the corn tortillas? They are made right here in Hilo (sold at grocery stores) and you're likely to see the *abuelita* (the grandmother) sitting in the dining room shucking corn during your visit. Most dishes can be made vegetarian (substituting meat for tofu), and corn tortillas can easily be substituted for gluten-free eaters.

The menu at the **Hilo Bay Café** (315 Makaala St., Hilo, 808/935-4939, www.hilobaycafe.com, Mon.–Sat. 11 A.M.–9:30 P.M., Sun. 5–9:30 P.M., lunch $15, dinner $22) seems like it was written by a food writer. It has dishes such as: vegetarian flax sweet potato burger ($10) and roasted free-range chicken breast stuffed with cilantro-cumin mascarpone ($19). The names of the dishes certainly make it hard to pick just one. The menu changes with the season and the meat, fish, and produce are

TWO LADIES KITCHEN

Mochi isn't so novel anymore. Well, at least not to the shoppers of Trader Joe's or Whole Foods who are familiar with the *mochi* ice cream stocked in their freezers. Please, give it another try. Two Ladies Kitchen (274 Kilauea Ave., 808/961-4766, Wed.-Sat. 10 A.M.-5 P.M.) brings *mochi* to a whole different level (out of this world). Their homemade *mochi* carefully crafted from sweet rice flour in the background of their small storefront is soft and light, and each piece looks like a work of art. Their secret recipe (although I know it and won't share it) is a family recipe, and the back room still maintains a family atmosphere with their dedicated staff.

Mochi here isn't filled with ice cream; rather, their number one seller is the strawberry-filled *mochi*. You can sense the sheer excitement when the sign comes up that reads "we still have strawberry *mochi* today." The strawberries are real, which leads to a second sign that reads "you can't bring them to the Mainland," due to the agricultural inspection. You'll wish you could, though.

In addition to the strawberry varieties, there are peanut-butter-filled *mochi*, *liliko'i*, peach, plum, brownie – the list goes on. Since each *mochi* is handcrafted, they do take time, so I recommend calling ahead with your order ($6.80 for eight assorted pieces), especially if you just want a few strawberry ones ($2.65 each and well worth it). The box stuffed with *mochi* comes wrapped like a present, and you'll feel like you're opening one when you peek inside.

Two Ladies also sells *manju*, which are harder and more cookie-like and made with wheat flour. Note: Since the *mochi* are made from sweet rice flour they are hypothetically gluten-free (although not made in a dedicated kitchen). Ask to make sure your purchase is entirely made from rice flour because some of the flavors, like the brownie *mochi*, are made with wheat flour as well.

---

from local farmers (for the most part). The food here tastes good and they make excellent cocktails that are classics with a Hawaii twist (like raspberry grapefruit margarita). Service is attentive. A children's menu is available.

A one-stop shop for local flavors, the **(Hilo Lunch Shop** (421 Kalanikoa St., Hilo, 808/935-8273, Tues.-Sat. 5:30 A.M.-1 P.M., $3) is a must for those who love to try new foods integral to local culture. The friendly staff is happy to explain each dish even when the customer line is long (and it's often long). The restaurant is set up in *okazuya* style (a Japanese word that translates as side dish store). There is a long buffet and as you walk down it you point to what you want and a nice server boxes it for you. Most items are around $1 per piece or under and the selections include nori chicken (a must try!), tempura, cone sushi, fishcakes, and salads. You can mix and match as you like and still not pay over $10 for a lot of food. There is limited seating inside but most

people take their food to go. Come early! They often are sold out before noon.

Another restaurant that reflects Hilo's Japanese Hawaiian culinary tradition, this is the restaurant to go to for a romantic evening: **Miyo's** (400 Hualani St., Hilo, 808/935-2273, Mon.–Sat. 11 A.M.–2 P.M. and 5:30 A.M.–8:30 P.M., reservations recommended, $13) is set up like a Japanese tea house and overlooks a pond. The overall atmosphere makes eaters feel like they are no longer in Hawaii. The menu is short: combination plates of sashimi or tempura served with chicken or beef. Miso butterfish is always on the menu (one of the best dishes) and there is always a fish special. The restaurant is BYOB and has live music on weekends.

With no exaggeration, **(Sombat's Fresh Thai Cuisine** (88 Kanoelehua, Hilo, 808/969-9336, www.sombats.com, Mon.–Fri. 10:30 A.M.–1:30 P.M. and 5–8:30 P.M., Sat. 5–8:30 P.M., lunch $7, dinner $14) is probably some of the best Thai food you'll ever have outside of Thailand. Sombat, the owner and chef, grows the herbs in her garden in order to get her dishes flavored just right. Eaters can often see her in the restaurant (you'll recognize her because there is a beauty queen picture of her hanging on the wall in the dining area), chatting with guests and checking to make sure everything is up to par. The lunch special (starting at $7) is an outstanding deal with portions almost large enough to feed two people. Usually you choose between a curry and a noodle dish (or both for $8). Come early, as the special often sells out by 12:30 P.M. and then only the à la carte options are available. Similarly, the dinner menu prices are reasonable and huge portions. Try the coco soup with ahi ($14). It's good anytime, but an excellent remedy if you're under the weather or tired of heavy foods. The soup is large enough that it can feed two or more people. The restaurant is BYOB. Note: Spice levels in Hawaii are different than those on the Mainland. Hot in Hawaii is very, very hot on the Mainland. So you might want to order a level down.

Pancakes are only about one-tenth of the massive menu at (**Ken's House of Pancakes** (1730 Kamehameha Ave., Hilo, 808/935-8711, www.kenshouseofpancakes.com, 24 hours), an institution in Hilo, so don't let the pancake part throw you off. Year after year Ken's wins awards for "Best Diner on the Island," and the accolade is well deserved. There are so many good things about Ken's it's hard to know where to start. To begin with, it's one of few places in Hawai'i that is open 24 hours. Next, it looks like an old diner and the waitresses are made to wear "uniforms." Check the menu for nightly specials: Sunday is all-you-can-eat spaghetti night. Breakfast is available anytime, but you'll be torn between a three-egg omelet with Portuguese sausage or the short ribs. Or, go big and order the Sumo Loco: six scoops of rice, five ounces of Spam, gravy, and three eggs. If that seems like overdoing it then turn to page 10 or 15 (I don't know if that's the actual page number) and order off the kids' menu (it's allowed) or from the "lighter stuff," which includes the same items from the regular menu (mahimahi, teriyaki chicken) but

in smaller portions served with a starch or cottage cheese. Save room, if you are capable, for the homemade pies.

Perhaps the most traditional Japanese restaurant in Hilo, **Nihon Restaurant and Cultural Center** (123 Lihiwai St., Hilo, 808/969-1133, www.nihonrestaurant.com, Mon.–Sat. 11 A.M.–1:30 P.M. and 5–8 P.M., lunch $17, dinner $24) feels like a study abroad experience (if you're not from Japan) with a spectacular view of Hilo Bay. If you're not Japanese, it's very possible that you might be the only non-Japanese person in the restaurant. But that's half of the fun of eating here. The menu is larger than that of Miyos, but offers similar combos. The "Hatamoto" (businessperson's lunch, $17) or dinner combo ($24) includes two entrées, such as *katsu* or teriyaki chicken. Sushi platters are priced as a package dinner ($24 for 22 pieces) or can be ordered à la carte. Overall, the food is a bit pricey considering that it tastes a bit bland. You'll be paying for the outdoor scene (the indoor scene looks like a mess hall) and the experience.

With a pond-side view as opposed to an actual ocean view the name of **Seaside Restaurant** (1790 Kalaniana'ole Ave., Hilo, 808/935-8825, www.seasiderestaurant.com, Tues.–Thurs. and Sun. 4:30–8:30 P.M., Fri.–Sat. 4:30–9 P.M., reservations recommended, appetizers $10, mains $25) can be misleading. The dinner mains are typical of the upscale restaurants in town, including choices like macadamia-nut-crusted mahi and grilled teriyaki chicken. But although you are getting the same dish as at, let's say, Ken's House of Pancakes, here you'll pay at least $20 and a share charge if you decide to go that route. Appetizers are too small to substitute for a main. The service here is good, the tablecloths white, and there is a large wine list with suggested pairings on the menu. Vegetarian options and a children's menu are available.

NORTH HILO TO 'AKAKA FALLS

The options in this area are beyond few and far between so plan accordingly.

The debate is ongoing on the Big Island regarding who has the best *malasadas* (Portuguese doughnuts). Some argue that it is **Baker Tom's** (27-2111 Mamalahoa Hwy./Hwy. 19 between mile markers 6 and 7, Papaʻikou, 808/964-8444, open early until sold out). Baker Tom (yes, he's real) makes the *malasadas* with the help of a few others. The recipe is a combination of six different recipes—allegedly, some Food Network show is on to them and they will be featured on the channel soon. In addition to the *malasadas,* there are a few savory options, such as hamburgers and breakfast sandwiches, available.

Halfway through the Onomea Scenic Drive you'll come across the glorious oasis of ❰ **What's Shakin'** (27-999 Old Mamaloahoa Hwy., Pepeʻekeo, 808/964-3080, daily 10 A.M.–5 P.M., smoothies $7, lunch $10). It might sound like a lot, $7 for a smoothie—but I can almost guarantee that it will be the best smoothie you'll ever have and they are filling enough to split between two people. The fruit is all grown on the farm that houses this stand, and you can taste the freshness in every sip (also, they use frozen bananas instead of ice for blending so that the flavor doesn't get diluted). The food, usually a daily special as well as their standard menu of nachos, salmon burgers, and burritos, is equally delicious with huge portions and several vegetarian options. Note: If you are coming from the Kona direction, you'll pass a different smoothie stand as you turn right onto the scenic drive—What's Shakin' is just two minutes up the road from there.

MARKETS

For groceries and general food supplies try **KTA Super Store** downtown (321 Keawe Ave., Hilo, 808/935-3751) or in the Puʻainako Town Center (off of Hwy. 11, 808/959-9111); **Safeway** (111 E. Puʻainako, 808/959-3502); or **Sack 'n Save** at Puʻainako Town Center (808/959-5831) or downtown (250 Kinoole, 808/935-3113).

Since 1977, **Abundant Life Natural Foods** (292 Kamehameha Ave., 808/935-7411, www.abundantlifenaturalfoods.com, Mon.–Tues. and Thurs.–Fri. 8:30 A.M.–7 P.M., Wed. and Sat. 7 A.M.–7 P.M., Sun. 10 A.M.–5 P.M.) has

been doing business in downtown Hilo. The store's shelves are stocked with an excellent selection of fresh fruits and veggies, bulk foods, cosmetics, vitamins, and herbs, and the bookshelves cosmically vibrate with a selection of tomes on metaphysics and new-age literature. The store's kitchen puts out daily specials of smoothies, soup, salads, sandwiches, and *bento,* most for under $6.

In Hilo Shopping Center, at **Island Naturals Market and Deli** (1221 Kilauea Ave., 808/935-5533, www.islandnaturals.com, Mon.–Sat. 7 A.M.–8 P.M., Sun. 9 A.M.–7 P.M.) fresh fruit and produce line the shelves, as do packaged, refrigerated, frozen, and bulk natural foods, plus personal care items, supplements, vitamins, and minerals. The deli has ready-to-order foods, a hot bar, and pre-made items. You'll get wholesome healthy foods here at this full-service shop, with a good vibe from people who care about what they sell. Stop by on Fridays for 20 percent off beer and wine.

Non-meat-eaters will delight in the all-vegetarian **Down to Earth** (303 Makaala St., Waiakea Center, 808/935-5515, www.downtoearth.org, Mon.–Fri. 7:30 A.M.–9 P.M., Sat.–Sun. 8 A.M.–8 P.M.). They offer goods similar to Abundant Life and Island Naturals (the prices are similar too). Likewise, they also have a lunch and dinner per pound buffet and pre-packaged salads, desserts, and pizzas.

Fish Market

Suisan Fish Market (93 Lihiwai St., 808/935-9349, Mon.–Fri. 8 A.M.–5 P.M., Sat. 8 A.M.–4 P.M.) is as close to the harbor as you can get for fresh fish, and they have as good a selection as anyone in town. A window counter to the side of the building is open early for avid anglers who come to try their luck along the water near the harbor and in the adjacent park.

Farmers Market

On Wednesday and Saturday mornings, stop by the corner of Kamehameha Avenue and Mamo Street for the **Hilo Farmers Market,** perhaps the best farmers market on the island. This is a lively affair, great for local color, where you can get healthy locally grown produce and bouquets of colorful flowers at bargain prices; however, it is not all locally grown so be sure to ask where it comes from if that is important to you. Across the street at The Market Place and also a few steps up the road under the big tents are more vendors selling flowers, arts and crafts, and other gift items.

Information and Services

EMERGENCY SERVICES
Hilo Medical Center (1190 Waianuenue Ave., 808/974-4700, www.hmc.hhsc.org) has both outpatient services and a 24-hour emergency room. Just up the street is a **Kaiser Permanente** clinic (1292 Waianuenue Ave., 808/934-4000). Alternatively, try **Hilo Urgent Care Center** (45 Mohouli, 808/969-3051, www.hilourgentcare.com, Mon.–Fri. 8:30 A.M.–9 P.M., Sat.–Sun. 9:30 A.M.–4 P.M.).

For pharmacies, try **Shiigi Drug** (333 Kilauea Ave., 808/935-0001), **Longs Drugs** (555 Kilauea Ave., 808/935-3357), and the **KTA Super Store** pharmacy (50 E. Puʻainako, 808/959-8700).

BANKS
All the state's big banks have branches in Hilo. Try **Bank of Hawaii** (120 Pauahi St., 808/935-9701), **First Hawaiian Bank** (1205 Kilauea Ave., 808/969-2211), or **American Savings Bank** (100 Pauahi St., 808/935-0084).

POST OFFICE
The **Hilo Main Post Office** (1299 Kekuanaoa) is an efficiently run, modern post office, clearly marked on the access road to the airport. It is extremely convenient for mailings prior to departure. A downtown postal station (154 Waianuenue Ave., 808/933-3014) is in the federal building across from Kalakaua Park.

Getting There and Around

BY PLANE
The **Hilo International Airport** (code ITO) is right in town—so much so, that you can see the Hawaiian Airlines logo overhead on the planes that are about to land (it's like the beginning montage of *Hawaii Five-0*). The airport is currently only an international airport in theory. Most international flights have to connect through one of the other Hawaii airports (like Honolulu or Kona or Maui) before arriving to Hilo.

After many years of no direct flights to the Mainland, in June 2011, United Airlines began direct service between Hilo and Los Angeles and San Francisco. These flights are only a few times a week.

Otherwise, the airport is mostly used by interisland flights serviced by either **Hawaiian Airlines** (www.hawaiianair.com)

or **Go!Mokulele** (www.iflygo.com). To get to the other islands, it is often necessary to travel through Honolulu. Hawaiian Airlines offers one direct flight to Maui daily.

Note: The Hilo airport is tiny! Unlike the Kona airport, though, it is indoors. Sometimes the security line can get long, so it is necessary to arrive early enough before your flight; however, interisland flights generally board at the time it shows they are supposed to leave. Just keep that in mind if you're planning on heading to the airport a few hours early. You might be waiting around for a while. If you are coming to the airport to pick someone up, it's free to park in the lot if you are there less than 20 minutes.

BY BUS
Travel to Regions Outside of Hilo
Hilo's **Mooheau Bus Terminal** (between

Kamehameha Ave. and Bayfront Hwy.) is the only proper bus terminal on the island—it's so official that there is actually a **tourist information kiosk** located inside.

From the bus terminal it is possible to get anywhere on the island by utilizing the **Hele-On Bus** (www.heleonbus.org, 808/961-8744, $1 per ride, $1 each for luggage, large backpacks, bikes). Buses make almost hourly trips to Waimea via the Hamakua Coast as well as to Puna. For Volcano, Ka'u, Kona, and Kohala, a little bit more planning is necessary as there are only 3–4 daily direct buses to these regions. Check the website for exact times.

Note: Please remember that in Hawaii the noted times for the bus pickups are approximations (or mere suggestions). Since buses make on-demand stops they sometimes arrive 10 minutes early and sometimes 20 minutes late. If you really need to get somewhere by a certain time, best to arrive on the road early to hail down the bus, and don't get too nervous if it doesn't show up on time.

Travel Within Hilo

There are four separate intra-Hilo routes; however, some of these routes overlap. All the buses pass through the downtown terminal, and by selecting the correct route (please check the website or ask at the terminal) it is possible to travel to the in-town beaches, shopping areas (like Walmart), and the University of Hawai'i at Hilo. During peak times you can catch a bus nearly every 20 minutes or so. By the evening it's more like every 40 minutes or every hour. If you're not going too far, it usually is quicker to walk to your destination than wait for the bus.

BY TAXI

There are nearly two dozen taxi companies in town. For service 24 hours a day try **Ace One Taxi** (808/935-8303) and **Hot Lava Taxi** (808/557-0879). Hot Lava Taxi services the Hilo airport, along with **Percy's Taxi** (808/969-7060) and **Bobby Taxi** (808/937-6008). You can get most anywhere in town or to/from the airport for under $13. If you're interested in a shared ride taxi, you must purchase pre-paid vouchers. Call 808/961-8744 for additional information on where to purchase the coupon books. For shared rides, it's one coupon per person for traveling 1–4 miles and two coupons per person for traveling 4.1–9 miles. Farther afield, you might expect about $50 to Pahoa, $75 to Volcano, and $100 to Honoka'a.

HAMAKUA COAST, WAIMEA, AND THE SADDLE ROAD

When residents of the Big Island talk about the Big Island, they separate the island into two regions: "Hilo side" and "Kona side"—entirely leaving Hamakua and Waimea off the map. In an effort to increase visitors to the region, there is a movement afoot to start thinking about the Big Island in north (Hamakua and Waimea) and south (Ka'u) terms. Whatever way you divvy up the island, you'll be surprised by how, yet again, this northern slice of the island appears and feels so drastically different from other regions of the island.

The **Hamakua** stretch of the island has recently been named the "Hilo-Hamakua Heritage Coast" in an effort to draw attention to its historical and cultural significance, and that is what visitors should focus on, since there is not much beach to be had on this coast, as rough cliffs create difficult access to the ocean. Along the 50-mile stretch of Highway 19 from Hilo to Honoka'a, the Big Island grew its sugarcane for 100 years or more. Water was needed for sugar—a ton to produce a pound—and this coast has plenty. Present day, Hamakua is becoming known for its fertile growing land that is ideal for kava, mushrooms, vanilla, and macadamia nuts. Restaurants around the region source their ingredients from Hamakua, so be sure to indulge in some culinary delights on your drive around the coast.

With a population of around 2,200, **Honoka'a** (Rolling Bay) is the major town on the Hamakua Coast. In the past, it was a center for cattle, sugar, and macadamia nut industries. Now it's mainly a tourist town. The main street, Mamane Street, is filled with old

HIGHLIGHTS

LOOK FOR ◖ TO FIND RECOMMENDED SIGHTS, ACTIVITIES, DINING, AND LODGING.

◖ **Waimanu Valley:** The hike down to Waipi'o and over the *pali* to Waimanu Valley, half the size of Waipi'o but wilder and more verdant, is considered by many one of the top three treks in Hawaii (page 211).

◖ **Hakalau Bay:** Photographers and history buffs will be eager to visit the plantation-era ruins of Hakalau Mill, destroyed in the tsunami of 1946 (page 219).

◖ **Waipi'o Valley:** Once a burial ground of Hawaiian royalty where *kahuna* came to commune with spirits, this verdant valley is post-card perfect—locals know it as one of the best (if not the very best) views on all of the Big Island (page 221).

◖ **Mauna Kea Observatory Complex:** View the heavens from the top of Mauna Kea, where astronomers have come to expect an average of 325 crystal-clear nights per year, perfect for observation (page 226).

◖ **Dining in Waimea:** Home to the Hawaii Regional Cuisine movement, Waimea offers inspired dining in the heart of cowboy country (page 233).

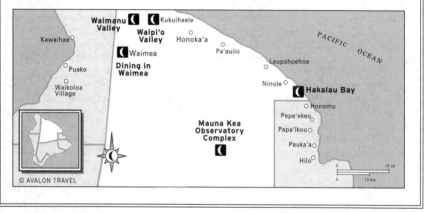

© AVALON TRAVEL

false-front wooden buildings built in the 1920s and 1930s by Chinese and Japanese workers who left the sugar plantations to go into business for themselves. From Honoka'a, Highway 19 slips down the long Hamakua Coast to Hilo and Highway 240 heads north for nine miles to the edge of Waipi'o Valley, which you should not miss.

Waipi'o Valley (Curving Water) is the kind of place that is hard to believe unless you see it for yourself. It's vibrantly green, always watered by Waipi'o Stream and lesser streams that spout as waterfalls from the *pali* at the rear and to the side of the valley. The green is offset by a wide band of black-sand beach. From the overlook at the top of Waipi'o, you can make out the overgrown outlines of garden terraces, taro patches, and fishponds in what was Hawaii's largest cultivated valley.

Waimea, also known as Kamuela, is technically in the South Kohala district, but because of its inland topography of high mountain pasture on the broad slope of Mauna Kea, it is vastly different than the long Kohala coastal district. It also has a unique culture inspired by the range-riding *paniolo* (cowboys) of the expansive Parker Ranch. But a visit here isn't one-dimensional. In town are homey accommodations, inspired country dining, and varied shopping opportunities. The town supports arts and crafts in fine galleries and has the island's premier performance venue. There's an

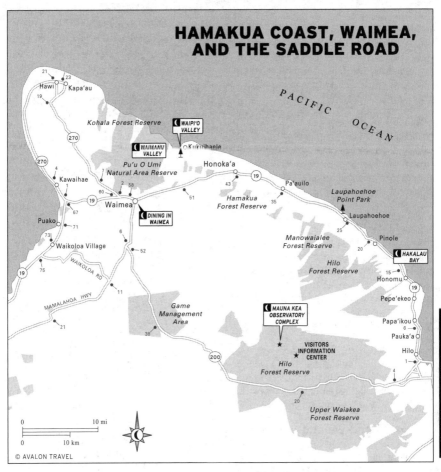

HAMAKUA COAST, WAIMEA, AND THE SADDLE ROAD

PACIFIC OCEAN

Hawi
Kapa'au
Kohala Forest Reserve
WAIPI'O VALLEY
WAIMANU VALLEY
Kukuihaele
Pu'u O Umi Natural Area Reserve
Honoka'a
Pa'auilo
Laupahoehoe Point Park
Kawaihae
Waimea
Hamakua Forest Reserve
Laupahoehoe
DINING IN WAIMEA
Puako
Manowaialee Forest Reserve
Pinole
Waikoloa Village
WAIKOLOA RD
Hilo Forest Reserve
HAKALAU BAY
Honomu
MAMALAHOA HWY
Pepe'ekeo
Game Management Area
MAUNA KEA OBSERVATORY COMPLEX
Papa'ikou
Pauka'a
VISITORS INFORMATION CENTER
Hilo
Hilo Forest Reserve
Upper Waiakea Forest Reserve

0   10 mi
0   10 km
© AVALON TRAVEL

HAMAKUA COAST

abundance of fresh air and wide-open spaces, the latter not so easily found in the islands.

There is old lava along both sides of the road as you approach the broad tableland of the **Saddle Road.** Much of the lava here is from the mid-1800s, but some is from a more recent 1935 flow. Everyone with a sense of adventure loves this bold cut across the Big Island through a broad high valley separating the two great mountains, **Mauna Loa** and **Mauna Kea.** Heading up to the observatories at the top of Mauna Kea, the tallest peak in the Pacific,

affords some truly stellar stargazing, while massive Mauna Loa offers one of the most extreme hikes on the island.

Note: This chapter is organized as if you are driving east to west on Highway 19 from Hilo along the Hamakua Coast toward Waimea. If you are coming from the Kona side, follow this chapter in reverse.

ORIENTATION
Hamakua Coast
Officially, the Hamakua Coast begins soon

after the four-mile Onomea Scenic Drive out of Hilo and curls around to Waimea, but in reality the entire coastline should be named an official scenic drive. Even people who hate driving love this drive. This is the kind of road that asks for a convertible with a great soundtrack playing from the stereo.

The Hamakua Coast is a good application of appreciating the journey and not necessarily the end point. The entire drive, without stopping, takes only 45 minutes. But you can extend your drive by taking one of the many side roads that jettison off the main highway. Unfortunately, the majority of these roads end up paralleling the highway (it's actually the old highway) and don't go very far—mainly through the old housing areas from the plantation days.

If you are inclined to make stops along the way, there are several scenic points that allow you to soak in the magnificent ocean views down below. If you're looking for some longer excursions close to the road, stop at the Laupahoehoe Train Museum to peruse artifacts showcasing the history of the region or visit some actual plantation artifacts at Hakalau Bay. If you really want to get out of the car and into the trees, hike one of the short trails of Kalopa Native Forest State Park, which is filled with native trees and birds, or try ziplining through the canopy of the World Botanical Gardens in Hakalau.

Honoka'a and Waipi'o Valley

Located on Highway 19 just 45 minutes west of Hilo and 20 minutes north of Waimea, Honoka'a is sort of a Hawaiian-style bedroom community. Follow the green sign pointing *makai* (and downhill) from Highway 19 to Mamane Street, the main street passing through the center of town that leads toward Highway 240 and Waipi'o Valley and the meeting points for the majority of organized Waipi'o trips. Mamane Street has a number of shops specializing in locally produced handicrafts, local-style restaurants, clothing and gift shops, and general merchandise stores next to antiques shops. The town also holds a small health center, a post office, two banks, a movie theater, public library, and a nine-hole golf course.

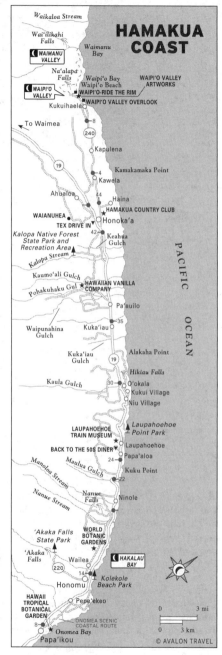

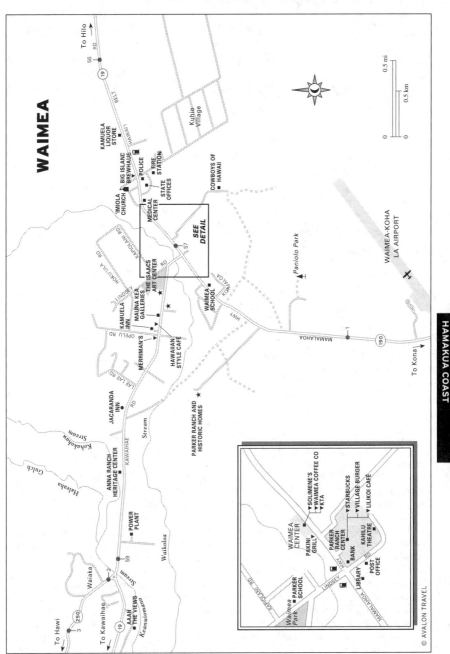

WAIMEA

To Hilo

To Hawi

To Kawaihae

To Kona

KAMUELA LIQUOR STORE
BIG ISLAND BREWHAUS
'IMIOLA CHURCH
POLICE
FIRE STATION
STATE OFFICES
MEDICAL CENTER
COWBOYS OF HAWAII
SEE DETAIL
THE ISAACS ART CENTER
MAUNA KEA GALLERIES
KAMUELA INN
MERRIMAN'S
HAWAIIAN STYLE CAFÉ
WAIMEA SCHOOL
Paniolo Park
WAIMEA-KOHA LA AIRPORT
JACARANDA INN
ANNA RANCH HERITAGE CENTER
POWER PLANT
AAAH THE VIEWS
PARKER RANCH AND HISTORIC HOMES

BELT RD
HAWAI'I BELT
KAMUELA RD
HOKU'ULA RD
LINDSEY
OPELU RD
LAE LAE RD
KAWAIHAE RD
MAMALAHOA HWY
KOHALA
MAMALAHOA

Kohāko'ohau Stream
Waikoloa Stream
Haleaha Gulch
Waiaka
Keanuioma'o
Waikoloa

Kūhiō Village

0   0.5 mi
0   0.5 km

WAIMEA CENTER
SOLIMENE'S
WAIMEA COFFEE CO
PAKINI GRILLY
STARBUCKS
VILLAGE BURGER
KTA
PARKER RANCH CENTER
LILIKOI CAFÉ
KAHILU THEATRE
PARKER SCHOOL
BANK
LIBRARY
POST OFFICE
Waimea Park

KAPI'OLANI RD
LINDSEY
MAMALAHOA

© AVALON TRAVEL

HAMAKUA COAST

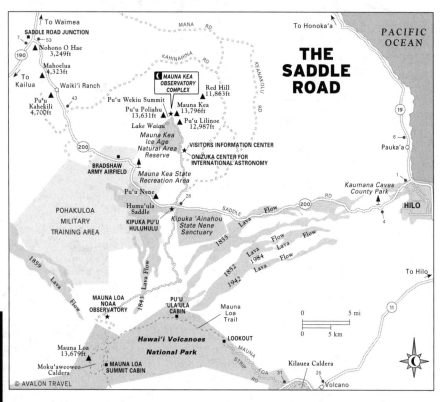

Highway 240 ends a minute outside of Kukuihaele at an overlook, and 900 feet below is Waipi'o (Curving Water), the island's largest and most southerly valley of the many that carve into the Kohala Mountains. A sacred land for ancient Hawaiians, the valley is a mile across and six miles from the ocean to its back end.

You can spend an hour in the sleepy Honoka'a town checking out the quaint handicraft boutiques and then stop back again at the end of the day after a visit to Waipi'o Valley to watch a game at Hamakua Sports Bar—the only sports bar (as they advertise) on the Hamakua Coast. And believe me, you'll be ready to relax after traveling by four-wheel-drive, horse, all-terrain vehicle, or your own two legs down the nearly vertical road to Waipi'o Valley.

Waimea

Parker Ranch, founded early in the 19th century by John Palmer Parker, dominates the heart and soul of the region. Waimea revolves around ranch life and livestock, with herds of rodeos and "Wild West shows" scheduled throughout the year.

Waimea is also known as **Kamuela,** the Hawaiianized version of Samuel, after one of John Parker's grandsons. Kamuela is used as the post office address, so as not to confuse this town of Waimea with towns of the same name on the islands of O'ahu and Kaua'i. (If you try to Google any address in Waimea, it will likely send you to O'ahu, so remember to use "Kamuela" in the search.)

In the last 30 years, Waimea has experienced real and substantial growth. In 1980 it had no traffic lights and was home to about 2,000 people. Now the population has grown more than threefold, there are three lights along the main highway, and there are occasional traffic jams. Waimea is modernizing and gentrifying, and its cowboy backwoods character is rapidly changing.

The town, at elevation 2,670 feet, is split almost directly down the center—the east side is the wet side, and the west is the dry side. Generally houses on the east side are easy to find and reasonable to rent, while houses on the dry side are expensive and usually unavailable. You can literally walk from verdant green fields and tall trees to semi-arid landscape in a matter of minutes. This imaginary line also demarcates the local social order: upper-class ranch managers (dry), and working-class *paniolo* (wet).

Waimea is at the crossroads of nearly all the island's roads: Highway 19 from Hilo (via the Hamakua Coast) and Highway 190 from Kailua-Kona. Highway 19 continues west through town, reaching the coast at Kawaihae, where it turns south and cuts along the Kohala Coast, passing by all the resorts on the way to Kailua-Kona. The upper road, Highway 190, connects Waimea to Kailua-Kona and the route looks much more like Marlboro Country than the land of *aloha,* with grazing cattle amid fields of cactus. On Highway 190 seven miles south of Waimea you'll find the turnoff to the Saddle Road (Highway 200), the road leading up to the Mauna Kea Observatory. This is the only road that travels through the middle of the island, and it's currently in the process of being paved and expanded.

Mauna Kea and the Saddle Road

Slicing across the midriff of the island in a gentle arch from Hilo to the Mamalahoa Highway near Waimea is Highway 200, the Saddle Road. Access to both Mauna Loa and Mauna Kea is possible from the Saddle Road.

Along this stretch of some 55 miles you pass rolling pastureland, broad swaths of lava flows, arid desert-like fields that look a bit like Nevada, a *nene* sanctuary, trailheads for several hiking trails, mist-shrouded rainforests, an explorable cave, and spur roads leading to the tops of Mauna Kea and Mauna Loa. Here as well is the largest military training reserve in the state, with its live firing range, and the Bradshaw Army Airfield. What you won't see is much traffic or many people. It's a great adventure for anyone traveling between Hilo and Kona. Keep your eyes peeled for convoys of tanks and armored personnel carriers as they sometimes sally forth from the Pohakuloa Training Area, and also watch out for those who make this a high speed shortcut from one side of the island to the other.

The Saddle Road was constructed in 1942 and left as gravel until about 30 years ago. While the road up both sides is at a good incline, the saddle itself is reasonably flat and at about 6,000–6,500 feet. Car-rental companies cringe when you mention the Saddle Road. Most still do not allow their cars on this road even though it is reasonably well paved through most of its length. Check your rental agreement, as it'll be very specific on this point. They're terrified you'll rattle your cars to death. For the most part, these fears are groundless, as there are only short sections that are rough, due mostly to military use, and with little or no solid shoulder. The road is very curvy, though, with several one-lane bridges and sections that do not have good sight lines. Plus, it is known to have a higher accident rate than other two-lane roads on the island. Drive defensively at a reasonable speed and do not pass.

The Hilo side is wider, has better shoulders, and has seen more repair than the Kona side. Department of Transportation plans call for widening and new pavement, adequate shoulders, better drainage, and some rerouting over the next several years. However, one cannot escape the fact that this road *is* isolated, and there are no facilities whatsoever along its length. If you do have trouble, you'll need to go a long way for assistance, but if you bypass it, you'll miss some of the best scenery on the Big Island. On the Kona side, the Saddle Road turnoff is about six miles south of Waimea along Highway 190, about halfway between Waimea and Waikoloa Road. From Hilo, follow Waianuenue Avenue inland. Saddle Road, Highway 200, also signed

YOUR BEST DAY IN THE HAMAKUA COAST, WAIMEA, AND THE SADDLE ROAD

- Wake up early to catch the **view of Mauna Kea** from Waimea before the clouds come rolling in.

- Get breakfast at **Hawaiian Style Café** in Waimea.

- Head to Waipi'o Valley to join a group tour or venture down into the valley on your own.

- In the afternoon take a drive east on Highway 19, stopping at **Hakalau Bay** to see some plantation ruins.

- Either head back the way you came or travel through Hilo and back over the Saddle Road, grabbing food (and drinks, if desired) for a picnic. Aim to arrive at the **Onizuka Center for International Astronomy** visitors information center on **Mauna Kea** just at sunset.

- Settle in for some **stargazing** that will astound you.

RAINY DAY ALTERNATIVE

At some point during the day, rain (or a mist) is expected in Waimea — so don't let that throw you off. If it's really raining hard, you have a few options. The good news is, from Waimea you can see if it's raining down below in Kohala. If it's not, travel down the hill the 20 minutes to soak up the sun.

If you want to stay in Waimea, visit the **Anna Ranch Heritage Center.** You can spend at least an hour or two touring on your own or with a guide. If you pay for the tour, for a few extra dollars you can get an "enhanced tour" that includes arts and crafts (like making your own leather bracelet). The activities aren't just for kids (well, they don't have to be).

If you're on the Hamakua Coast, visit the **Laupahoehoe Train Museum** (in Laupahoehoe), a small museum packed full with history and artifacts of the region.

Or, also on the coast, make a last-minute reservation with the **Hawaiian Vanilla Company** for a tour and tasting.

---

as Kaumana Drive, splits left after about a mile and is clearly marked. Passing Kaumana Caves Park, the road steadily gains elevation as you pass into and then out of a layer of clouds. Expect fog or rain.

About 28 miles out of Hilo and 25 miles up from the Kona side, a clearly marked spur road to the north, officially called the John A. Burns Way, but most often referred to as the Mauna Kea Access Road, leads to the summit of Mauna Kea. You can expect wind, rain, fog, hail, snow, and altitude sickness. Intrigued? Proceed—it's not as bad as it sounds. In fact, the road, while steep, is well paved for the first six miles, and from there the road is graded gravel, banked, and usually well maintained but sometimes like a washboard, with the upper four miles paved so that dust is kept to a minimum to protect the sensitive "eyes" of the telescopes. A

four-wheel-drive vehicle is required beyond the visitors center, and if there's snow, the road may not be passable at all. (For current road conditions, call 808/935-6268.)

The Mauna Loa Observatory Road, a one-lane paved road with long stretches of potholes and rough patches, turns south off the Saddle Road between mile markers 27 and 28 and leads about 17 miles in a big zig and zag and gentle incline up to the Mauna Loa NOAA Atmospheric Observatory.

PLANNING YOUR TIME

If you came to Hawaii not to sit on the beach (or not *just* to sit on the beach), but instead, to do a lot of sightseeing where it's not too hot, this region is ideal for you. Regardless of if you're starting your trip from the east or west side of the island, you'll want to plan around being in **Waipi'o Valley** during the morning when the weather is better and when the majority of organized trips are set to leave. Unless you're going to do an overnight hiking trip through the valley, you really only need a day (or a few hours) to see the valley and trek down it in whatever capacity.

Since the Hamakua Coast drive, without stops, actually is only 45 minutes, it can easily be completed in an afternoon even if you make several stops along the way. If you plan ahead, you can book reservations for a tasting at the **Hawaiian Vanilla Company** and/or trapezing through the **World Botanical Gardens** with **Zip Isle**. No planning is required to stop at any of the scenic overlooks of parks along the highway.

It's unfortunate that there isn't more to see in Waimea because there is so much good food to eat there you'll want to stay all day (if not longer)! I recommend visiting Waimea as a way to cool off from the hot afternoons of the Kohala Coast (only 20 minutes away) or to pick up provisions on your way to Mauna Kea (close to an hour away). For instance, in the late afternoon stroll through the stores at **Parker Square** or schedule a private tour with arts and crafts projects for the kids at **Anna Ranch Heritage Center** before heading to dinner (where to eat, so many choices . . .).

Regardless of how much time you want to spend at the top of **Mauna Kea,** it's important to account for how much time it will take to get there. First there is traveling on the Saddle Road (which can be a carsickness nightmare for some) to the observatory access road, which depending on weather can take about an hour from Waimea. Then, the drive up to the visitors center takes an additional half hour and an additional 40 minutes (more or less) to the summit after you've spent time at the visitors center to acclimate to the altitude. If you're driving in the dark, these travel times can be much longer.

The point is, a trip to Mauna Kea is hardly a quick jaunt and especially is not quick if you're traveling on a group tour. Those planning on traveling to the summit to catch the sunset (an unbelievable sight) should leave a few hours ahead of time and even earlier if you might hike around the area first (I recommend packing a picnic dinner to take with you). Generally, after sunset, most visitors to Mauna Kea reconvene at the visitors center for an hour (or two) of star and planet gazing. Don't expect to head down before 8 P.M.—it will be hard to walk away from the most awe-inspiring sky you might ever see.

Beaches

It seems as if this region should be a prime beach spot, but it isn't. Although the Hamakua district has some of the most spectacular ocean views of the entire Big Island, there is little access to the water from the soaring cliffs (if you're not afraid of heights look down—it's a pretty far drop). Waimea is completely landlocked (so no beaches there); however, it feels like the beach is so close because you can see it from town!

HONOKA'A AND WAIPI'O VALLEY
Waipi'o Beach
Stretching over a mile, Waipi'o Beach (access via Waipi'o Valley Rd.) is the longest

black-sand beach on the island. A tall and somewhat tangled stand of trees and bushes fronts this beach, capping the dune. If you hiked the one-hour vertical road to get here you'll likely want to jump in immediately, but be careful: The surf here can be very dangerous, and there are many riptides. If there is strong wave action, swimming is not advised. It is, however, a good place for surfing and fishing. There are two sections of the beach, and in order to get to the long expanse of beach across the mouth of the stream, you have to wade across it. It's best to try closer to where it enters the ocean as there are fewer slippery boulders there. To compound matters, waves sometimes wash water up the mouth of the

GULCHES AND TRAFFIC DELAYS

Driving the extremely scenic Highway 19 through the Hamakua Gulch, you'll see several signs for "gulches." A gulch is a deep ravine formed by erosion, sometimes with a stream running through it, and is usually larger than a gully. These gulches are also newly notable because they are the sites of huge traffic delays (and headaches) in the area. The county recently received funds to better secure the cliffs from the problem of rocks coming loose from them and falling onto cars (small rocks, not big ones – mostly they cause dings on cars). For the next few years, as construction crews work their way down the coast to place netting onto the cliffs, traffic is reduced to one lane Monday-Friday 10 A.M.-3 P.M. Plan for some extra time if you are in a rush.

stream. Be advised, and if possible go at low tide. Note there are no changing areas here. Portable bathrooms (not the cleanest) are located behind the beach near the parking area.

To get to the beach, you have to get down the gripping Waipiʻo Valley Road first. Regardless of if you walk or drive down, when you get to the bottom turn at the first right (instead of continuing straight into the valley and into private property). You'll find the next portion of your walk or drive (which is flat, shady, and short!) to be muddy and filled with potholes. This road takes you directly to the beach. If you drove, park your car in the area under the trees, where there will likely be other cars. If you walked, it's often possible to hitch a ride back up with someone driving from the beach.

Hiking

This region is hike central, and there are so many different kinds of hikes (from very difficult to beginner) with every type of scenery imaginable. Other guidebooks (or other companies) may reveal off-the-beaten path hikes that encompass trespassing through private land. I am here to encourage you not to trespass in this area. Local residents feel very serious about not having hikers wander through their backyards on the way to find a hidden view. There are plenty of on-the-beaten track and underutilized legal hikes in this area for you to challenge yourself with for days.

KALOPA NATIVE FOREST STATE PARK AND RECREATION AREA

This spacious natural area is five miles southeast of Honokaʻa, 12 miles north of Laupahoehoe, three miles inland on a well-marked secondary road, and 2,000 feet in elevation. Little used by tourists (or residents), Kalopa Native Forest State Park and Recreation Area (Kalopa Rd., off Hwy. 19 between mile markers 39 and 40, gate open daily 7 A.M.–8 P.M.) is a great place to get away from the coast and up into the hills. Hiking potentially is terrific throughout the park and adjoining forest reserve on a series of nature trails—but the trails are not marked clearly and are difficult to follow. Most of the forest here is endemic, with few alien species. Some of what you will see are ʻohiʻa, koa, the hapuʻu tree fern, and kopiko and pilo, both species of the coffee tree family. Near the entrance and camping area is a young arboretum of Hawaiian and Polynesian plants. Beyond the arboretum is a 0.75-mile nature loop trail through an ʻohiʻa forest, and a three-mile loop trail takes you along the gulch trail and back to camp via an old road. Next to the area where you park your car there is a board with pamphlets outlining the trails. Unfortunately, the actual trails bear no resemblance to the map; however, someone with some time and know-how might have a great time exploring. Birdlife here may not be as varied as high up the mountainside, but still you can catch sight of *'elepaio, auku'u* (a night heron), the white-eye, cardinal, and the Hawaiian hoary bat. The park is best used for day-use picnicking, tent camping, and large furnished cabins (state permit required) that can house up to eight people. For reservations, contact the state park office (75 Aupuni St. #204, Hilo, HI 96721, 808/974-6200).

To get to Kalopa Native Forest State Park, turn *mauka* on Kalopa Road and follow the signs up to the park—it will take about 15 minutes. There is more than one way from the highway to the park, so don't worry if you end up turning *mauka* on a different road.

◖ WAIMANU VALLEY

The hike down to Waipi'o and over the *pali* to Waimanu Valley is considered by many one of the top three treks in Hawaii. You must be fully prepared for camping and in excellent condition to attempt this hike. Also, water from the streams and falls is not good for drinking due to irrigation and cattle grazing topside; hikers should bring purification tablets or boil or filter it to be safe. To get to Waimanu Valley, a switchback trail, locally called the Z trail but otherwise known as the **Muliwai Trail,** leads up the 1,200-foot *pali,* starting about 100 yards inland from the west end of Waipi'o Beach. Although not long, this is by far the most difficult section of the trail. Waimanu was bought by the State of Hawaii some years ago, and it is responsible for trail maintenance.

The trail ahead is decent, although it can be muddy, but you go in and out of more than a dozen gulches before reaching Waimanu. In the third gulch, which is quite deep, a narrow cascading waterfall tumbles into a small pool right at trailside, just right for a quick dip or to dangle your feet. Another small pool is found in the fifth gulch. After the ninth gulch is a trail shelter. Finally, below is Waimanu Valley,

HAMAKUA COAST

© MARK WASSER

The Waimanu Valley hike isn't accessible to everyone, given its difficulty, but you can't expect that the island would give away those unbelievable views without a little bit of work.

half the size of Waipiʻo but more verdant, and even wilder because it has been uninhabited for a longer time. Cross Waimanu Stream in the shallows where it meets the sea. The trail then continues along the beach and back into the valley about 1.5 miles, along the base of the far side, to Waiʻilikahi Falls, some 300 feet high. For drinking water (remember to treat it), walk along the west side of the *pali* until you find a likely waterfall. The Muliwai Trail to the Waimanu Valley floor is about 15 miles round-trip from the trailhead at the bottom of the *pali* in Waipiʻo Valley, or 18 miles round-trip from Waipiʻo Lookout.

Regardless of how long it takes you to complete this hike, it's quite the badge of honor. Some have been known to finish it in 24 hours (including an overnight stay) and others take a few leisurely days at normal hiking speed. To stay overnight in Waimanu Valley you must have a camping permit available through the Division of Forestry and Wildlife (http://camping.ehawaii.gov); permits are for up to six people ($12 residents, $18 non-Hawaii residents). Note: Before you go, check the news release section of the Division of Forestry and Wildlife website (http://hawaii.gov/dlnr) to make sure that the trail is not closed due to hazardous conditions such as rain and/or mud.

MAUNA KEA

Hiking on Mauna Kea means high altitude hiking. Although the height of the mountain (13,796 feet) is not necessarily a problem, the elevation gain in a short hour or two of getting to the top is. It takes time for the body to acclimatize, and when you drive up from the ocean you rob yourself of the chance to acclimatize easily. What you may expect to experience normally are slight dizziness, a shortness of breath due to reduced oxygen levels, and reduced ability to think clearly and react quickly. Some people are more prone to elevation problems, so if you experience more severe symptoms, get to a lower elevation immediately! These symptoms include prolonged or severe headache, loss of appetite, cramped muscles, prolonged malaise or weakness, dizziness,

reduced muscle control and balance, and heart palpitations. Use your head, know your limits, and don't push yourself. Carry plenty of water (more than you would at a lower elevation) and food. Wear a brimmed hat, sunglasses, sunscreen, and lip balm, a long-sleeved shirt and long pants, and sturdy hiking boots or shoes. Carry a jacket, sweater, and gloves, as it can be very cold and windy at and near the top. Don't alter the natural environment and stay on established trails.

There are a few good trails on the mountain. About six miles above the Onizuka Center for International Astronomy Visitors Information Center, a dirt track heads off the access road to the west and downhill to a parking lot. From the parking area, it's about one mile farther west, over the saddle between two small cones, to Lake Waiau and its placid waters. This should take less than 30 minutes. On the way, you cross the Mauna Kea Humuʻula Trail, which starts at the third parking lot near the T intersection above and heads down the mountain to the visitors center. Taking the Humuʻula Trail to Lake Waiau should also take about 30 minutes. Continuing on down the Humuʻula Trail a couple of miles brings you past an ancient adze quarry site. Perhaps the most convenient hike is that to the true summit of the mountain. Start from the roadway across from the University of Hawaiʻi's 2.2-meter telescope, cross over the guardrail, and follow the rough path down into the saddle and steeply up the hill, a distance of less than half a mile.

THE SADDLE ROAD

Besides having the access road to Mauna Kea, the Saddle Road is a great place to explore by foot—especially on your way to Mauna Kea or on your way to/from the Hilo side and the Kona side.

Puʻu Oʻo Trail

Just after mile marker 24 on the way up from Hilo is the trailhead for Puʻu Oʻo Trail. From the small parking lot along the road, this trail heads to the south about four miles where it meets Powerline Road, a rough four-wheel-drive track, and returns to the Saddle Road. This area is good for bird-watching, and you might have a chance to see the very rare *'akiapola'au* or *'apapane,* and even wild turkeys. This area is frequently shrouded in clouds or fog, and it could very well rain on you. You may want to walk only partway in and return on the same trail, rather than making the circle.

Kipuka Pu'u Huluhulu

Bird-watchers or nature enthusiasts should turn into the Kipuka Pu'u Huluhulu parking lot across the road from the Mauna Kea Access Road turnoff. A *kipuka* is an area that has been surrounded by a lava flow, but never inundated, that preserves an older and established ecosystem. The most recent lava around Pu'u Huluhulu is from 1935. At the parking lot you'll find a hunters' check-in station. From there, a hiking trail leads into this fenced, 38-acre nature preserve. One loop trail runs through the trees around the summit of the hill, and there is a trail that runs down the east side of the hill to a smaller loop and the

two exits on Mauna Loa Observatory Road, on its eastern edge. Pu'u Huluhulu means Shaggy Hill, and this diminutive hill (about 200 feet high) is covered in a wide variety of trees and bushes, which include *mamane, naio, 'iliahi* (sandalwood), koa, and *'ohi'a.* Some of the birds most often seen are the greenish-yellow *'amakihi,* the red *'i'iwi* and *'apapane,* and the dull brown and smoky-gray *'oma'o.* In addition, you may be lucky enough to spot a rare *'io,* Hawaiian hawk, or the more numerous *pueo,* a short-eared owl. The entire loop will take you 45 minutes or less, so even if you are not particularly drawn to the birds or the trees, this is a good place to get out of the car, stretch your legs, and get acclimatized to the elevation before you head up to Mauna Kea.

MAUNA LOA

The Saddle Road is the other choice, besides near Hawai'i Volcanoes National Park, for accessing Mauna Loa and its trails. The **Mauna Loa Observatory Road** turns south off the Saddle Road and zigs and zags up to the **Mauna Loa**

© MARK WASSER

The Mauna Loa hike is one of the most technically difficult in the state.

NOAA Atmospheric Observatory at 11,140 feet, which you can see high on the hillside above as you progress along this road. According to the signboard below this small complex, measurements are gathered here for carbon dioxide, carbon monoxide, methane, CFCs, ozone, solar radiation, atmospheric dust, stratospheric aerosols, and temperatures, among other items. Even a two-wheel-drive vehicle could handle this road without problems, but driving it would abrogate your rental car contract. Use a four-wheel-drive rental vehicle that is approved for this road. Although it could be done faster, give yourself an hour to take in the surroundings, check out the distant sights, and reach the end of the road. Use your vehicle lights, particularly if there are low clouds, and straddle the reflective white line that runs down the center of this single-lane road all the way up to the observatory, pulling over only to let vehicles from the other direction get by. The atmospheric observatory is not open to the public, but you can park in a small parking lot below it at the end of the pavement.

About two miles in from the turnoff is a rock formation at the side of the road that, at a certain angle, looks remarkably like Charles deGaulle, former president of France—and you don't have to use your imagination much at all. As you continue, you get a fine, distant look at the observatories on top of Mauna Kea across the saddle, Pu'u Huluhulu below at the turnoff, and the military reservation beyond to the west. About four miles in, at a turn in the road, there is a gravel road that heads over the horizon to the west, an abandoned attempt at a highway shortcut to Kailua-Kona. About eight miles up, at a point where there are a number of telephone and television transmitter towers, the road makes a big zag and heads almost in a straight-line shot, following power poles to the observatory. Notice the different colors of lava that the road crosses and the amount of vegetation on each type. The older brown lava has some grasses and small bushes growing from it, while the newer black lava is almost totally barren. There are large areas of red lava as well, and some of that has been used as road base and paving material. You will see several collapsed lava tubes near the road as you make your way up. Still farther on, areas of ropy *pahoehoe* lava stick up through newer *'a'a* lava. Around mile 15, new pavement has been laid so your ride gets smoother even as the road goes through a series of roller coaster waves as you approach the end of the road. Beyond the end of the pavement, an extremely rough Jeep track continues—best used as a hiking trail. This track zigzags up the mountainside, eventually ending near the crater rim after about seven miles. The **Mauna Loa Observatory Trail** leaves the gravel Jeep track several hundred yards beyond the end of the pavement and heads almost straight up the mountainside, crossing the Jeep trail several times. The Observatory Trail climbs 1,975 feet over 3.8 miles up the volcano's north slope until it reaches the rim of the Moku'aweoweo Caldera (the summit). From this point, the Mauna Loa summit cabin is 2.1 miles. It takes about 4–6 hours all together to hike from the Observatory trailhead to the Mauna Loa summit cabin. The hike back from the Mauna Loa summit cabin to the Mauna Loa Observatory trailhead is only about three hours, since you're going downhill.

A very helpful resource for this hike can be found at www.kinquest.com/misc/travel/trailguide.php. This site provides a guide with a mile-by-mile description of what you'll see (both trail markers and geological marvels) while you hike.

The Mauna Loa summit cabin is available to stay in for free but requires a permit from the Kilauea Visitor Center in Hawai'i Volcanoes National Park; you can only get them the day before your hike. The Mauna Loa summit cabin has 12 bunks (actually, only 12 visitors are permitted per group). Visitors are allowed a three-night maximum stay. Pit toilets are available at the cabin as well as drinking water (although check with park rangers about the water level). Don't forget to treat the water. There's no water available on the trail.

Note: Mauna Loa is at a very high altitude, so it is *imperative* to wait at least 24 hours between scuba diving and ascending Mauna Loa in order to avoid getting the bends.

Touring Waipi'o Valley

Seeing Waipiʻo Valley is truly one of the highlights of the Big Island. Don't spend a lot of time thinking about going to see it—just go—and instead, spend a few minutes deciding which method of visiting Waipiʻo meets your (and your companions') needs, depending on how much time you have, how much money, your physical prowess, and your desire to learn about Hawaiian history and nature. The other important factor to consider is whether or not you want to actually go into the valley or simply go around the rim from above. The majority of organized tours meet at stores in Kukuihaele, a small town just a few miles east of Waipiʻo. As you drive west on Highway 240 from Honokaʻa, when the road forks go toward the right (the sign will point to the right for Kukuihaele). Follow the road and you will see the tour storefronts on the *makai* side of the road.

BY ATV (ALL-TERRAIN VEHICLE)

As you can probably guess, **Ride the Rim** (check in at Waipiʻo Valley Artworks, 48-5416 Kukuihaele Rd., Kukuihaele, 808/775-1450, www.ridetherim.com, morning and afternoon tours, $160 per person) offers a three-hour tour around the rim (not the valley) through eucalyptus trees, stopping to swim at a secluded waterfall. Riders must be over 16 years old and weigh between 100 and 350 pounds; however, those who can't (or don't want to) drive can ride in an open-air buggy driven by a tour guide. This is a good way for families to tour together even if not everyone wants to get down and dirty with an ATV.

Similarly, **Waipiʻo On Horseback** (Hwy. 240 at mile marker 7, *mauka* side, 808/775-9888 www.waipioonhorseback.com, daily 9:30 A.M., 1:30 P.M., and 4:30 P.M. during summer, $100 plus tax, discount if booked with horseback riding) takes you (or the ATV takes you) on a 2.5-hour trip through a working ranch and beside the old Hamakua Ditch

(the irrigation system built over 100 years ago during plantation days). There are views of the valley, but you're not actually in the valley itself. Reservations must be made 24 hours in advance.

BY WAGON

Perhaps the most unexpected way to experience the valley is by mule-drawn wagon. This narrated cultural and historical tour organized by **Waipiʻo Valley Wagon Tours** (meet at Last Chance Store, Kukuihaele, 808/775-9518, www.waipiovalleywagontours.com, three tours Mon.–Sat., adults $55, senior $50, children 4–12 $25) allows you to get down into the valley without exhausting yourself. The tour is only 1.5 hours and that is a bit short given the amount of time it takes to actually get down into the valley. It's a good option for people short on time (or attention spans) or families who want to travel together.

BY FOOT

It is possible to walk into the valley on your own. More complicated, however, is to walk the rim, as it is essentially private property and tour companies lease rights to pass through it. Most people only take the journey into the valley as a means to the end—the end being the beach at the end of the road. To begin the vertical trek down (seriously, vertical) into the valley park your car in the lot at the end of Highway 240 or, inevitably, on the street (the lot gets filled fast). The road walkers take down to the bottom and onward to the beach is the same paved road the cars use (meaning: be careful of the cars; many drivers are not too savvy with four-wheel driving). Bring *plenty* of water and sunscreen for the walk—and a snack (I recommend picking up *malasadas* at Tex's in Honokaʻa before you go—you'll thank me for this tip). You'll be sweaty and thirsty by the time you get to the bottom. And don't underestimate the downhill part of the journey—for many it's actually more challenging

HAMAKUA COAST

than the uphill part since it's quite hard on the knees. Give yourself about 45 minutes to get down and an hour (or so) to get back to the top (or there is no shame in doing as many before you have done and hitching a ride back up). There are no public restrooms in the valley and just the portable potties at the beach, so use the nicer facilities (restrooms and drinking fountains) at the Waipi'o Overlook before you head down.

BY HORSEBACK

Waipi'o Ridge Stables (check in at Waipi'o Valley Artworks, 48-5416 Kukuihaele Rd., Kukuihaele, 808/775-1007, www.waipioridgestables.com, morning and afternoon 2.5-hour ride $85, five-hour morning ride $165) can accommodate beginners, but it may be nerve-wracking since no training is provided. The horses essentially are on auto-pilot, so there isn't much for you to do but enjoy the views. The important thing to note is that the ride is not through the valley, but through a eucalyptus forest to a great lookout spot. The ride is still nice and relaxing, but it doesn't offer the nonstop outstanding views that a ride through the valley might have. Also, while the wranglers are incredibly friendly and want to make you feel comfortable, they offer minimum background information about the area while you ride.

But if touring the valley is what you want, then your best option is **Na'alapa Stables** (check in at Waipi'o Valley Artworks, 48-5416 Kukuihaele Rd., www.naalapastables.com, Mon.–Sat. 9 A.M. and 12:30 P.M., $68–89). Known for their quality service and excellent guides who share stories of Hawaiian history and culture, this tour books up quickly, so make sure to plan ahead. Riders meet at Waipi'o Valley Artworks and then are transported down into the valley in the ranch's four-wheel vehicle. The road down to the valley is very steep, so this trip might not be for the faint of heart. The entire tour is 2.5 hours, but actual horse time is not that long given the amount of time it takes to travel up and down into the valley.

Similarly, **Waipi'o On Horseback** (Hwy. 240 at mile marker 7, *mauka* side, 808/775-9888, www.waipioonhorseback.com, daily 9:30 A.M. and 1:30 P.M., $85 plus tax, discount if booked with ATV tour) is another valley trip that will get you there and near to the waterfalls (if they are actually flowing—sometimes they aren't when there is a drought), The ride through the valley is similar to those of other companies, but the guides do not seem as knowledgeable or as engaged with riders as guides at other companies.

BY FOUR-WHEEL-DRIVE OR SHUTTLE

The road leading down to Waipi'o is outrageously steep and narrow, averaging a 25 percent gradient! If you attempt it in a regular car, it'll eat you up and spit out your bones. More than 20 fatalities have occurred since people started driving it, and it has only been paved since the early 1970s (they leave the old car wreckages by the side of the road as a warning to newbies). You'll definitely need four-wheel-drive to make it; vehicles headed downhill yield to those coming up.

That said, it is understandable that not everyone can walk down to the valley on their own or has time or funds to join a tour. But residents of the area have asked me to nicely request that you do not drive down unless it is completely and utterly necessary. Residents have been organizing the last few years to cut off the tourist traffic to the valley as the cars not only create a preventable traffic mess on the road but also inflict environmental havoc on the landscape.

If you do want to be shuttled down to the bottom, the **Waipi'o Valley Shuttle** (808/775-7121, www.waipiovalleytour.com, $45 adults, $20 children under 11, reservations recommended) makes a 90-minute descent and tour of Waipi'o Valley in air-conditioned, four-wheel-drive vans that leave from Waipi'o Valley Artworks in Kukuihaele, at 9 A.M., 11 A.M., 1 P.M., and 3 P.M. Monday–Saturday. Along the way, you'll be regaled by legends and stories and shown the most prominent sights in the valley by drivers who live in the area. This is the easiest way into the valley, and the guys know what they're doing as they've been at it since 1970. Sometimes drivers of this shuttle will give hikers a ride down to the valley floor or up the road to the overlook parking lot for a few bucks, if there's room in the vehicle.

Other Recreation

HORSEBACK RIDING

All the available outfitters more or less have the same restrictions for riders: usually no children under 7 (the exact age might vary), and riders above 250 pounds must notify the tour operator prior to the ride of their exact weight. It is also important to be honest with the tour operator about the your ability level, since some operators do not allow beginners on certain tours and others do not want advanced level riders (if the horses already are trained in a specific manner they don't want that training modified by an advanced rider).

Views of the Kona and Kohala Coasts are abundant on **Paniolo Adventures** (mile 13.2 Kohala Mountain Rd./Rte. 250, 808/889-5354, www.panioloadventures.com, tours range $69–159 depending on length). Paniolo Adventures has a good reputation for being professional, knowing what they are doing, and enjoying their work. With six different rides ranging from picnic adventures to sunset trots, you'll likely find a ride that suits your skill level and your schedule.

If you're aching to see the actual Parker Ranch this is your chance. **Cowboys of Hawaii** (check in at blacksmith shop at Pukalani Road Stables behind Parker Ranch Shopping Center, 808/885-5006, www.cowboysofhawaii.com, daily morning and afternoon rides available, $79). The two-hour ride will take you through parts of ranch, where you'll learn more about the history of the Parker dynasty and how the ranch still functions today. Beginners to advanced riders are welcome.

Dehana Ranch (47-4841 Old Mamalahoa Hwy./Hwy. 19, 808/885-0057, www.dahanaranch.com, daily, $70–130) offers a menu of choices (from 1.5-hour to 2.5-hour rides) and is excellent at meeting the needs of riders. Most rides are through the ranch with lovely faraway views of Waipi'o and Mauna Kea. If you are looking for a longer (or larger) cowboy experience, they offer a weekend package ($1,195 plus tax) that includes a one-bedroom cottage at their ranch, riding lessons, and participating in a cattle drive!

ZIPLINING

Zipline rides, also known as canopy tours, are booming on the Big Island, with each company competing with the next for the best course. Not all the courses are "certified" or have insurance, and accidents, although rare, have occurred with those who are not. Inquire about the company's credentials before you go.

The only course that is certified in this area is **Zip Isle** (Hwy. 19 at mile marker 16, *mauka* side, Hakalau, 808/963-5427, www.zipisle. com, daily 9 A.M.–5:30 P.M., $147, *kama'aina* discounts available), located in the World Botanical Gardens, the state's largest botanical garden. If you have gone ziplining in Costa Rica, this course isn't for you. The thrills are minimal (and you don't zip over the waterfall as the brochure implies!), but the staff is friendly and knowledgeable, making this an ideal course for first-timers and children (minimum weight requirement of 70 pounds although they are lenient on this). Also, the course was constructed in partnership with certified engineers in order to guarantee the utmost safety for zipliners. There are six tours daily and it's a good idea to reserve a week in advance.

GOLF

Golfing on the Big Island can be an adventure in itself due to the hilly and rocky terrain.

PANIOLO: HAWAIIAN COWBOYS

In 1793 on a visit to the Big Island, Captain George Vancouver gave cattle as a gift to King Kamehameha I, the first on the island. In 1830 King Kamehameha III invited three *vaqueros* from Mexico to Hawaii to teach locals cowboy skills. The story goes that when the Hawaiians asked the new visitors who they were, the Mexican cowboys responded *"Español"* (Spanish). The Hawaiians then pronounced the word *español* as *paniolo* and thus were born Hawaiian cowboys known as *paniolo.*

To learn more about the unique history of cowboys in Hawaii visit the **Paniolo Heritage Center** (at Pukalani Stables on Pukalani Rd., Waimea, behind Parker Ranch Shopping Center, 808/854-1541, Tues. and Thurs. 10 A.M.-2 P.M., $5 suggested donation). It's run by the **Paniolo Preservation Society** (www.paniolopreservation.org).

© MARK WASSER

Try your hand at being a *paniolo* (Hawaiian cowboy) with one of many horseback riding tours around Waimea or into Waipi'o Valley.

For instance, carts aren't even allowed on the 15-acre course at the **Hamakua Country Club** (Hwy. 19 between mile markers 42 and 43, 808/775-7244, $15–20) because of how steep it is (the course is small and you play the nine holes twice). Designed in the 1920s by Frank Anderson, the course works on the honor system, with a box for dropping off payment next to the course. The course is usually only open to nonmembers during the weekdays, but call ahead to check.

The Scottish links style course at the **Waimea Country Club** (Hwy. 19 between mile markers 51 and 52, 808/885-3517, www.waimeagolf.com, daily first tee time 7:45 A.M., last tee time 2:45 P.M., $25–60) is a great alternative to the Kona and Kohala Coast courses due to the lower fees here and

A VANILLA CULINARY ADVENTURE

Not many people think about where vanilla comes from, but if you are someone who does or someone who enjoys tea time, the **Hawaiian Vanilla Company** (43-2007 Paauilo Mauka Rd., 808/776-1771, www.hawaiianvanilla.com, gift shop Mon.-Sat. 10 A.M.–5 P.M.) is for you. Visitors can pick between a short vanilla presentation and tasting (10:30 A.M. for 45 minutes, $25 per person), tours of the vanillery and farm (1-2 P.M., $25 per person), or for the full experience (and better deal) a tour and tasting with a vanilla-inspired lunch (2 hours, $39 for adults, $15 for children 4-12). Your best bet is to skip the lunch and opt for the tea (Mon.-Fri. 3 P.M., $25 plus tax), which includes some sweet vanilla-infused treats and teas. It makes for a nice pairing after a day of horseback riding or walking through Waipi'o Valley. To get to Hawaiian Vanilla Company from Highway 19, between mile markers 36 and 37 turn *mauka* onto Pōhakea Road and follow it for three miles. Bear right onto Paauilo Mauka Road. Reservations are required for lunch.

the cool temperatures with lush greenery carved from rangeland located at over 2,000 feet in elevation. If you're in the mood for some additional exercise take the walk (instead of cart) option and save nearly half the price for the round of golf. A snack bar with light snacks and drinks is open daily 7:30 A.M.–5 P.M.

MASSAGE

If you're staying in the area, try **Kate Butler Tanimoto** (808/895-1375, www. waimeamassage.com, $65 for 60 minutes). She works from home and offers several different types of massages (from deep muscle to Thai) and body treatments, including a unique infrared sauna ($12 for 15 minutes) to get you back in shape quickly. Her easy online booking system also allows you to confirm your appointment quickly. If you want someone to come directly to your room, many bed-and-breakfast properties are able to recommend their favorite massage therapists to guests and arrange for them to do an in-room treatment.

Sights

HAMAKUA COAST
C Hakalau Bay

There are residents of the Big Island who have never been to see the abandoned plantation remnants in Hakalau Bay, a short detour off the highway. To get here from Highway 19, between mile markers 15 and 16 turn *makai* near the footbridge and follow the street around under the bridge and down toward the ocean and the park. Local kids come here to swim in the stream under the highway bridge (look up and you'll see that this bridge was once a train track and was turned upside down to be used as a road). Even if you're not interested in swimming in the murky water that flows into the ocean (there is no beach; you park your car and jump in), photographers and history buffs will be eager to visit the ruins of Hakalau Mill, destroyed in the tsunami of 1946, which are scattered around the parking lot.

World Botanical Gardens

Touted as the state's largest botanical garden with over 5,000 different species, the World Botanical Gardens (Hwy. 19 at mile marker 16, *mauka* side, 808/963-5427, www.wbgi.com, daily 9 A.M.–5:30 P.M., self-guided tours adults $13, teens $6, children 5–12 $3, guided

HAMAKUA COAST

© BREE KESSLER

The ruins at Hakalau Bay provide great insight into the decline of the plantation culture on the Big Island.

tours adults $33, teens $23, children $13) is really the backdrop of the Zip Isle zipline that makes use of the botanical gardens (and views of the ocean). The entry fee to the gardens is included with the price of the zipline, and during the zip course itself you'll end up walking around a large portion of the gardens. When you are doing zipping, you can walk down to the river on a short (buggy) trail or drive up to catch a glimpse of their waterfall (the zipline does not go over the waterfall as the brochures lead you to believe). If you are planning to just come for the botanical gardens portion (no zipline), your better bet might be to visit the Hawaii Tropical Botanical Garden in Onomea Bay down the road.

Laupahoehoe Train Museum
Although small in size, the Laupahoehoe Train Museum (36-2377 Mamalahoa Hwy./ Hwy. 19 near mile marker 25, 808/962-6300, www.thetrainmuseum.com, Mon.–Fri. 9 A.M.–4:30 P.M., Sat.–Sun. 10 A.M.–2 P.M.,

adults $4, seniors $3, children $2, families $16) is big on the history of the Hamakua region. Interwoven with the history of the coastal train route, a 34-mile stretch with 21 stops that was destroyed in 1946 by a tsunami, the museum offers abundant archival photos detailing what life on the Big Island looked like in the early 1900s. Next to the museum is a reconstructed train car and tracks that kids (and adults) seem to enjoy. It is visible from the road (most tourists just drive by wondering what it is). You only need about a half hour here, but it's worth stopping in if you have the time (a stop here is also nicely paired with lunch or dessert at the Back to the 50s Diner next door).

Laupahoehoe Point Park
This wave-lashed peninsula is a popular place for weekend family outings. A plaque at water's edge commemorates the tragic loss of 20 schoolchildren and their teacher, who were taken by the great tsunami of 1946.

Laupahoehoe Point is a popular park for picnics and family get-togethers.

Afterward, the village was moved to the high ground overlooking the point. Laupahoehoe Point Park (Laupahoehoe Point Rd. off of Hwy. 19 between mile markers 27 and 28) now occupies the low peninsula; it has nice shaded picnic tables, showers, electricity, and a county camping area. The park can get busy on the weekends with local families cooking out and bringing their ukuleles around to play some tunes. The sea is too rough to swim in, except perhaps by the boat launch ramp, but many anglers come here, along with some daring surfers. The road down to the park is narrow and winding and runs past several rebuilt homes and a restored Jodo Mission. It will take about 10 minutes to drive down to the park from the highway.

HONOKA'A AND WAIPI'O VALLEY
◀ Waipi'o Valley

Waipi'o, which means curved or arched waters, is known to Hawaiians as the Sacred Valley of the Kings. Locals know it as one of the best (if not the very best) views on all of the Big Island—the valley really is postcard perfect, with a river running through deep green hills.

The valley itself has been inhabited by Hawaiians for over 1,200 years and is the site of many ancient temples and burial sites. Traditionally, the valley also held importance as a fertile ground for growing taro that is made into poi, a staple of the Hawaiian diet. Today, Waipi'o Valley (where Hwy. 240 ends) is home to waterfalls (the two most recognizable ones are Hi'ilawe and Hakalaoa), ancient fishponds close to the front of the valley (near where the Z trail to Waimanu Valley is visible), and, closer to the shore, sand dunes intermixed with old burial grounds.

You can travel down into the valley in nearly every imaginable way: by horse, by ATV, by foot, by car, etc. It really depends on how much time you have to spend there, how much money you want to spend, and

WAIPI'O THEN AND NOW

When Captain Cook came to Hawaii, 4,000 natives lived in Waipi'o; a century later only 600 remained. At the turn of the 20th century many Chinese and Japanese moved to Waipi'o and began raising rice and taro. People moved in and out of the valley by horse and mule, and there were schools, stores, a post office, churches, and a strong community spirit. Waipi'o was painstakingly tended. The undergrowth was kept trimmed and you could see clearly from the back of the valley all the way to the sea. World War II arrived, and many people were lured away from the remoteness of the valley by a changing lifestyle and a desire for modernity. The tsunami in 1946 swept away most of the homes, and the majority of the 200 people who lived there then pulled up stakes and moved away. For 25 years the valley lay virtually abandoned. The Peace Corps considered it a perfect place to build a compound in which to train volunteers headed for Southeast Asia. This too was later abandoned. Then in the late 1960s and early 1970s a few "back to nature" hippies started trickling in. Most only played Tarzan and Jane for a while and moved on,

especially after Waipi'o served them a "reality sandwich" in the form of the flood of 1979.

Waipi'o is still very unpredictable. In a three-week period from late March to early April of 1989, 47 inches of rain drenched the valley. Roads were turned to quagmires, houses washed away, and more people left. Part of the problem is the imported trees in Waipi'o. Until the 1940s, the valley was a manicured garden, but now it's very heavily forested. All of the trees you will see are new; the oldest are mangroves and coconuts. The trees are both a boon and a blight. They give shade and fruit, but when there are floods, they fall into the river, creating logjams that increase the flooding dramatically. Waipi'o takes care of itself best when humans do not interfere. Taro farmers, too, have had problems because the irrigation system for their crops was washed away in the last flood.

Nowadays, many of the old people have died or moved topside (above the valley) with relatives. Those who live in the valley learned to accept life in Waipi'o and genuinely love the valley, while others come only to exploit its

---

your physical ability. For those who just want to catch a glimpse and a photo of the valley's glory from above without much effort, in front of the parking area there is a lovely scenic overlook with restroom facilities that is easily accessible to anyone, including those who are wheelchair-bound.

Every foodstuff known to the Hawaiians once flourished here; even Waipi'o pigs were said to be bigger than pigs anywhere else. In times of famine, the produce from Waipi'o could sustain the populace of the entire island. On the valley floor and alongside the streams you'll still find avocados, bananas, coconuts, passion fruit, mountain apples, guavas, breadfruit, tapioca, lemons, limes, coffee, grapefruit, and pumpkins. The old fishponds and streams are alive with prawns, wild pigs roam the interior, as do wild horses, and there are abundant fish in the sea. Carrying on the traditions of

farmers of old, some farmers in the valley still raise taro, and this has once again become one of the largest taro-producing regions on the island and one of the principal production centers in the state.

WAIMEA
Parker Ranch and Historic Homes

Due to the downturn in the economy, the ubiquitous Parker Ranch organization has reorganized, leading to changes for visitors wanting a glimpse of Parker Ranch life. The ranch's **historic homes** (67-1435 Mamalahoa Hwy./ Hawai'i Belt Rd., 808/885-7311, www.parkerranch.com), dating from the 19th century, are no longer open to the public on a regular basis, but the surrounding gardens are still open for visitors to walk around. At least one of the homes is expected to be open for tours beauty. Fortunately, the latter underestimate the raw power of Waipi'o. Developers have eyed the area for years as a magnificent spot in which to build a luxury resort. But even they are wise enough to realize that nature rules Waipi'o, not humankind. For now the valley is secure. A few gutsy families with a real commitment have stayed on and continue to revitalize Waipi'o. The valley now supports perhaps 40 residents. More people live topside but come down to Waipi'o to tend their gardens.

In the summer of 1992, the Bishop Museum requested an environmental impact survey on Waipi'o Valley because the frequency of visitors to the valley had increased tremendously. Old-time residents were complaining not only about the overuse of the valley but about the loss of their quiet and secluded lifestyle. Some tour operators cooperated fully and did their best to help in the preservation and reasonable use of one of Hawaii's grandest valleys; others did not. Because of the impact study, commercial tours are not allowed to go to the beach area on the far side of the stream, which is now open to foot traffic only.

A type of socio-ethnic battle has evolved in the valley. Long-term residents, mostly but not exclusively of Hawaiian descent, have largely withdrawn the spirit of *aloha* from the visitors to their wonderful valley. Their dissatisfaction is not wholly without basis, as some who have come to the valley have been quite disrespectful, trespassing on private property, threatening to sue landowners for injuries caused by themselves, or finding themselves stuck in a river that no one in their right mind would try to cross in a vehicle. Many wonderful, open, and loving people still live in the valley, but don't be too surprised to get the "stink face" treatment from others. Be respectful and stay on public property. If the sign says Kapu (which means "forbidden") or Keep Out, believe it. It is everyone's right to walk along the beach, the switchback that goes to Waimanu, and generally waterways. These are traditional free lands in Hawaii open to all people, and they remain so. It's really up to you. With proper behavior from visitors, Waipi'o's mood can change, and *aloha* will return.

in the future; call ahead or check the website to see if tours have become available.

If you are really eager to see part of the ranch, you can visit parts of it via a two-hour horseback riding tour organized through **Cowboys of Hawaii** (808/887-1046 or 808/885-5006, www.cowboysofhawaii. com, Mon.–Sat., twice a day, 8:15 A.M. and 12:15 P.M., $79).

The Isaacs Art Center

One of the preeminent galleries on the island is The Isaacs Art Center (65-1268 Kawaihae Rd., 808/885-5864, www.isaacsartcenter. org, Tues.–Sat. 10 A.M.–5 P.M.). This art store/museum, part of Hawai'i Preparatory Academy, is worth a stop in. In the next two years they will be expanding into two distinct spaces, but for now the museum and the store are intermixed, and the pieces dating from

19th- and 20th-century Hawaii and Asia are some of the finest (and priciest) on the island. Even if you don't have the means to afford fine art, the center's staff is happy to talk about each piece and give you a little lesson on Hawaiian art.

Anna Ranch Heritage Center

Dedicated to Anna Leialoha Lindsey Perry-Fiske (yes, all of that), the "first lady of ranching" in Hawaii, the living history museum at Anna Ranch Heritage Center (65-1480 Kawaihae Rd., Hwy. 19 near mile marker 58, 808/885-4426, www.annaranch. org, Tues.–Sat. 10 A.M.–4 P.M., guided tours 10 A.M. and 1 P.M. by appointment $10–20, self-guided garden tour free) is a great entrée into what Hawaiian ranch life was like in the early 20th century. The property consists of the original house, a restored blacksmith area, and placards explaining the surrounding views of Waimea. Anna's house is nicely staged with lots of original artifacts to look at (none are behind glass), including parts of Anna's extensive hat and clothing collections. Fashion lovers will truly appreciate the collection. If you walk around the house yourself, you might only need about 30 minutes. The guided tour, on the other hand, can run nearly two hours. If you don't think you'll make it to one of the scheduled tours, call ahead to schedule a tour at a convenient time. Also, if you call ahead it is possible to schedule an enhanced tour that includes activities for the kids: a lesson in lassoing, leather crafting (bracelets or keychains), and a blacksmith demonstration.

MAUNA KEA
Onizuka Center for International Astronomy Visitors Information Center

The entire mountaintop complex, plus almost all of the land area above 12,000 feet, is managed by the University of Hawai'i. Visitors are welcome to tour the observatory complex and stop by the visitors information center at the Onizuka Center for International Astronomy (808/961-2180, www.ifa.hawaii.edu/info/vis, daily 9 A.M.–10 P.M.) at the 9,300-foot level. Named in honor of astronaut Ellison Onizuka, born and raised on the Big Island, who died in the *Challenger* space shuttle tragedy in 1986, this center is a must-stop for stargazers. Inside are displays of astronomical and cultural subjects, informational handouts, computer links to the observatories on the hill above, and evening videos and slide shows, as well as a small bookstore and gift shop. At times, 11- and 16-inch telescopes are set up outside during the day to view the sun and sunspots; every evening they are there to view the stars and other celestial objects. The visitors center is about one hour from Hilo and Waimea and about two hours from Kailua-Kona. A stop here will allow visitors a chance to acclimate to the thin, high-mountain air—another must. A stay of one hour here is recommended before you

head up to the 13,796-foot summit. The visitors center provides the last public restrooms before the summit and is a good place to stock up on water, also unavailable higher up.

Free stargazing is offered nightly 6–10 P.M., and there's a summit tour every Saturday and Sunday (weather permitting) at 1 P.M. These programs are free of charge. For either activity, dress warmly. Evening temperatures will be 40–50°F in summer and might be below freezing in winter, and winds of 20 miles per hour are not atypical. For the summit tour, you must provide your own four-wheel-drive transportation from the visitors center to the summit.

Going Up the Mountain

If you plan on continuing up to the summit, you must provide your own transportation and it must be a four-wheel-drive vehicle. People with cardiopulmonary or respiratory problems or with physical infirmities or weakness and women who are pregnant are discouraged from attempting the trip. In addition, those who have been scuba diving should not attempt a trip to the top until at least 24 hours have elapsed. As the observatories are used primarily at night, it is requested that visitors to the top come during daylight hours and leave by a half hour after sunset to minimize the use of headlights and reduce the dust from the road, both factors that might disrupt optimum viewing. It's suggested that on your way down you use flashing warning lights that let you see a good distance ahead of you while keeping bright white lights unused. However, as one security person has stated, safety is their primary concern for drivers, so if you feel you must use your headlights to get yourself down without an accident, by all means do so. Some rental companies have changed their rules regarding taking cars up to the summit and it is not allowed. Others have not wavered. Cars can have a difficult time handling the climb up (I personally have had two older cars not make it to the top), so decide for yourself if it is worth making the trip on your own. Note: It is possible to hitch a ride from the visitors center to the summit with a nice passerby, but plan ahead to make sure that you also

MAUNA KEA: FROM SILVERSWORD TO SNOW

As you climb Mauna Kea (White Mountain), you pass through the clouds to a barren world devoid of vegetation. The earth is a red, rolling series of volcanic cones. You get an incredible vista of Mauna Loa peeking through the clouds and what seems like the entire island lying at your feet. In the distance the lights of Maui flicker.

Off to your right is **Pu'u Kahinahina,** a small hill whose name means Hill of the Silversword. It's one of the few places on the Big Island where you'll see this very rare plant. The mountaintop was at one time federal land, and funds were made available to eradicate feral goats, one of the worst destroyers of the silversword and many other native Hawaiian plants.

Lake Waiau (Swirling Water) lies at 13,020 feet, making it the third-highest lake in the United States. For some reason, ladybugs love this area. This lake is less than two acres in size and quite shallow. Oddly, in an area that has very little precipitation and very dry air, this lake never dries up or drains away, as it apparently is fed by a bed of melting permafrost below the surface.

Here and there around the summit are small caves, remnants of ancient quarries where Hawaiians came to dig a special kind of fired rock that is the hardest in all Hawaii. They hauled roughed-out tools down to the lowlands, where they refined them into excellent implements that became coveted trade items. These adze quarries, Lake Waiau, and a large triangular section of the glaciated southern slope of the mountain have been designated **Mauna Kea Ice Age Natural Area Reserve.**

A natural phenomenon is the strange thermal properties manifested by the cinder cones that dot the top of the mountain. Only 10 feet or so under their surface is permafrost that dates back 10,000 years to the Pleistocene epoch. If you drill into the cones for 10–20 feet and put a pipe in, during daylight hours air will be sucked into the pipe. At night, warm air

© MARK WASSER

The summit of Mauna Kea was once covered in 500 feet of ice.

comes out of the pipe with sufficient force to keep a hat levitating.

Mauna Kea was the only spot in the tropical Pacific thought to be glaciated until recent investigation provided evidence that suggests that Haleakala on Maui was also capped by a glacier when it was higher and much older. The entire summit of Mauna Kea was covered in 500 feet of ice. Toward the summit, you may notice piles of rock – these are terminal moraines of these ancient glaciers – or other flat surfaces that are grooved as if scratched by huge fingernails. The snows atop Mauna Kea are unpredictable. Some years it is merely a dusting, while in other years, such as 1982, there was enough snow to ski from late November to late July.

have a ride back! It would be a long cold walk down in the dark.

Alternatively, make arrangements for a **guided tour** to the top. These tours usually run seven to eight hours and run $175–200 per person. Tour operators supply the vehicle, guide, food, (very good) snacks, and plenty of warm clothing for your trip. They also supply telescopes for your private viewing of the stars near the visitors center after seeing the sunset from the top. From the Kona side, try **Mauna Kea Summit Adventures** (808/322-2366 or 888/322-2366, www.maunakea.com) or **Hawaii Forest and Trail** (808/331-5805 or 800/464-1993, www.hawaii-forest.com). In Hilo, contact **Arnott's Hiking Adventures** (808/969-7097, www.arnottslodge.com, discounts available for hotel guests). Take extra layers of warm clothing and your camera.

MAUNA KEA OBSERVATORY COMPLEX

Atop the mountain is a mushroom grove of astronomical observatories, as incongruously striking as a futuristic earth colony on a remote planet of a distant galaxy. The crystal-clear air and lack of dust and light pollution make the Mauna Kea Observatory site *the* best in the world. At close to 14,000 feet, it is above 40 percent of the earth's atmosphere and 98 percent of its water vapor. Temperatures generally hover around 40–50°F during the day, and there's only 9–11 inches of precipitation annually, mostly in the form of snow. The astronomers have come to expect an average of 325 crystal-clear nights per year, perfect for observation. The state of Hawaii leases plots at the top of the mountain, upon which various institutions from all over the world have constructed telescopes. Those institutions in turn give the University of Hawai'i up to 15 percent of their viewing time. The university sells the excess viewing time, which supports the entire astronomy program and makes a little money on the side. Those who work at the top must come down every four days because the thin air makes them forgetful and susceptible to making calculation errors. Scientists from around the world book months in advance for a squint through one of these phenomenal telescopes, and institutions from several countries maintain permanent outposts there.

The second telescope that you see on your left is the United Kingdom's **James Clerk Maxwell Telescope** (JCMT), a radio telescope with a primary reflecting surface more than 15 meters in diameter. This unit was operational in 1987. It was dedicated by Britain's Prince Philip, who rode all the way to the summit in a Rolls Royce. The 3.6-meter **Canada-France-Hawaii Telescope** (CFHT), finished in 1979 for $33 million, was the first to spot Halley's Comet in 1983.

A newer eye to the heavens atop Mauna Kea is the double **W. M. Keck Observatory.** Keck I was operational in 1992 and Keck II in 1996. The Keck Foundation, a philanthropic organization from Los Angeles, funded the telescopes to the tune of over $140 million; they are among the world's most high-tech, powerful, and expensive. Operated by the California Association for Research in Astronomy (CARA), a joint project of the University of California and Cal Tech, the telescopes have an aperture of 400 inches and employ entirely new and unique types of technology. The primary reflectors are fashioned from a mosaic of 36 hexagonal mirrors, each only three inches thick and six feet in diameter. These "small" mirrors have been very carefully joined together to form one incredibly huge, actively controlled light reflector surface. Each of the mirror segments is capable of being individually positioned to an accuracy of a millionth of an inch; each is computer-controlled to bring the heavenly objects into perfect focus. These titanic eyeballs have already spotted both the most distant known galaxy and the most distant known object in the universe, 12 and 13 billion light years from earth, respectively. The light received from these objects today was emitted not long after the "Big Bang" that created the universe theoretically occurred. In a very real sense, scientists are looking back toward the beginning of time!

In addition to these are the following: The

NASA Infrared Telescope Facility (IRTF), online since 1979, does only infrared viewing with its three-meter mirror. Also with only infrared capabilities, the **United Kingdom Infrared Telescope** (UKIRT), in operation since 1979 as well, searches the sky with its 3.8-meter lens. Directly below it is the **University of Hawai'i 0.6-meter Telescope.** Built in 1968, it was the first on the mountaintop and has the smallest reflective mirror. Completed in 1970, the **University of Hawai'i 2.2-meter Telescope** was a huge improvement over its predecessor but is now the second smallest telescope at the top. The **Caltech Submillimeter Observatory** (CSO) has been looking into the sky since 1987 with its 10.4-meter radio telescope. **Subaru** (Japan National Large Telescope) is a monolithic 8.3-meter mirror capable of both optical and infrared viewing. It is the most recently completed telescope on the mountain, fully operational since 2000. The **Gemini Northern 8.1-meter Telescope,** also with both optical and infrared viewing, is run by a consortium from the United States, United Kingdom, Canada, Chile, Argentina, and Brazil. Its southern twin is located on a mountaintop in Chile, and together they have been viewing the heavens since 1999. Situated to the side and below the rest is the **Submillimeter Array,** a series of eight six-meter-wide antennae. About two miles distant from the top is the **Very Long Baseline Array,** a 25-meter-wide, centimeter wavelength radio dish that is one in a series of similar antennae that dot the 5,000-mile stretch between Hawaii and the Virgin Islands.

Currently, while the state is considering expansion of the complex to include additional telescopes and support facilities, a number of groups, including The Hawaiian-Environmental Alliance, are calling upon the state to proceed in a culturally and environmentally friendly manner or to not proceed at all. This is a highly contested issue on the island.

VISITING THE TELESCOPES
At present, only the **Subaru Telescope** (www.naoj.org) allows visitors on organized tours, and you *must* reserve at least one week ahead

of time. These free, 40-minute tours are given at 10:30 A.M., 11:30 A.M., and 1:30 P.M. only on weekdays that they are offered. Tours are run in English and Japanese, with the first and last tours of the day usually in English. The tour schedule is posted two months in advance on the telescope website. Transportation to the telescope is the visitor's responsibility. This tour is a brief introduction to the telescope itself and the work being performed. There is no opportunity to actually view anything through the telescope. All safety precautions pertaining to visiting the summit also apply to visiting this telescope for the tour.

While the Keck telescopes do not offer tours, the visitors gallery at the telescope base is open weekdays 10 A.M.–4:30 P.M. for a 12-minute video, information about the work being done, and a "partial view of the Keck I telescope and dome." Two public restrooms are also available to visitors. For those who cannot visit the summit, the same information and video are available in the lobby at the Keck headquarters in Waimea.

ALONG THE SADDLE ROAD
Pohakuloa
The broad, relatively flat saddle between Mauna Kea and Mauna Loa is an area known as Pohakuloa (Long Stone). At an elevation of roughly 6,500 feet, this plain alternates between lava flow, grassland, and semi-arid desert pockmarked with cinder cones. About seven miles west of the Mauna Kea Access Road, at a sharp bend in the road, you'll find a cluster of cabins that belong to the Mauna Kea State Recreation Area. This is a decent place to stop for a picnic and potty break. No camping is allowed, but housekeeping cabins that sleep up to six can be rented (permits are required). Nearby is a game management area, so expect hunting and shooting of wild pigs, sheep, and birds in season. A few minutes west is the Pohakuloa Training Area, where maneuvers and bomb practice can sometimes disturb the peace in this high mountain area. If the military is on maneuvers while you're passing through, be very attentive to vehicles on or crossing the road.

Shopping

HONOKA'A AND WAIPI'O VALLEY

Honoka'a isn't a shopping destination, but the town is so cute that you'll probably want to get out and walk around to make the most of it. It looks like there are quite a few shops on the main street, Mamane Street; however, many of them seem to never be open. What shops tend to be left standing are congregated on the eastern and *makai* side of Mamane Street. There are a few antiques and collectible stores that include Hawaiiana items like old aloha shorts, airline posters from the 1960s, and glass bottles from the old plantation bottle works. Also, a few souvenir shops have Hawaiian prints, quilts, and local cooking books. Hopefully in the future businesses will take advantage of this prime real estate to open up some new shops in the area.

WAIMEA

There are three main shopping areas in Waimea, each a little bit different from the next. The Parker Ranch Center and Waimea Center essentially are strip malls, although the Parker Ranch Center is the more upscale of the two. Parker Square also houses shops in an open air setting, but in a more historical-looking building with several galleries worth browsing through.

Parker Ranch Center

The long-established Parker Ranch Center (67-1185 Mamalahoa Hwy./Hwy. 19, www.parkerranchcenterads.com) was totally rebuilt in 2002, completely changing the face of the center of town. With more of a country look, the mall now has more store space than it originally held and many new upscale vendors. Anchoring the center is the Foodland grocery store with a Starbucks next door. There is a food court in the center of the complex and many fast-food joints. The **Parker Ranch Store** (808/885-5669), in its prominent spot up front, focuses on its country cowboy heritage; the shop sells boots, cowboy hats, shirts, skirts, and buckles and bows, and many handcrafted items are made on the premises. Filling in some of the shops surrounding the Parker Ranch Store are midrange clothing stores selling items like jeans and surf wear. Note: If you need to get a few extra layers of clothing before heading up to Mauna Kea (it's cold up there!) this shopping area is a good place to stop to grab a sweatshirt and/or socks with cowboys on them.

Waimea Center

Across the street from the Parker Ranch Center and behind McDonald's is the Waimea Center. Most Waimea Center stores are open 9 A.M.–5 P.M. weekdays and 10 A.M.–5 P.M. Saturday. Among its shops you will find a **KTA Super Store,** with everything from groceries to pharmaceuticals; a number of eateries, including **Solimene's** with coffees, teas, and Italian fare; as well as a few lower end gift shops (with cards and other knickknacks).

Parker Square

Located along Hwy. 19, heading west from town center, Parker Square has a collection of fine boutiques and shops, as well as the Waimea Coffee Company shop. Here, like an old trunk filled with family heirlooms, the **Gallery of Great Things** (808/885-7706, www.galleryofgreatthingshawaii.com) really is loaded with great things. Inside you'll find novelty items like a carousel horse, silk dresses, straw hats, koa paddles, Japanese woodblock prints, and less expensive items like shell earrings and koa hair sticks. The Gallery of Great Things represents about 200 local artists on a revolving basis, and the owner, Maria Brick, travels throughout the Pacific and Asia collecting art, some contemporary, some primitive. With its museum-quality items, the Gallery of Great Things is definitely worth a careful browse.

Also in the complex is the **Waimea General Store** (808/885-4479, Mon.–Sat.

9 A.M.–5:30 P.M., Sun. 10 A.M.–4 P.M.), which sells mostly high-end sundries with plenty of stationery, kitchen items, children's games, stuffed toys, books on Hawaiiana, and gadgets—overall, lots of neat and nifty gifts. At the end of the complex is the similarly themed **Bentley's Home and Garden Collection** (808/885-5565), stacked filled with kitchenware, Hawaii-themed cookbooks, and locally made soaps.

Entertainment and Events

ENTERTAINMENT

This region, luckily, attracts musicians, dancers, and performers (and some fairly big names) to its venues big and small. In Honoka'a, the **Honoka'a People's Theater** (43 Mamane St., 808/775-0000, http://honokaapeople.com) doubles as an art movie theater (tickets $6 adults, $4 seniors, $3 children) and a live music venue. Built in the 1930s by the Tanimoto family (who built several of the other historical theaters on the Big Island), it was and remains the largest theater on the island, with seating capacity of 525 people. In its heyday, it must have been a sight, as plantation workers would pack the building to watch the newest Hollywood films. With the closing of the plantation industry, the theater went into disrepair and closed for a few years. When the theater reopened in the late 1990s, it once again truly became a centerpiece of the community—used by community groups in need of space. Check the schedule online for event listings. There is not always something going on, but often there are one or two movies showing during the week (usually at 7 P.M.), and a few times a month there are live performances with local musicians as well as semi-popular Mainland groups traveling through the area.

Also in Honoka'a, even if it sounds counterintuitive, check out the **Hamakua Sports Bar** (45-3490 Mamane St., 808/775-1444) on Friday and/or Saturday night at 7 P.M. for live music. They also have karaoke and open mic events at varying times during the week.

For some live music and dancing to

RICHARD SMART: FROM PARKER RANCH TO BROADWAY AND BACK

Richard Smart, born in 1913, was the only child of Henry Gaillard Smart and Thelma Parker. Not long after Richard's birth, both parents passed away, leaving him as the sole heir of the Parker Ranch fortune. While growing up Richard developed a love for the theater, drama, and music and as a young man left Hawai'i and headed for the bright lights of New York City. A naturally gifted singer, dancer and actor, Smart performed for 30 years on Broadway as well as in name cabarets and clubs in the United States and abroad. He was a headliner at the Coconut Grove in Los Angeles, the Monte Carlo in New York, and the Lido in Paris and starred opposite top actresses of the era, such as Eve Arden, Carol Channing, and others. At the same time he was successfully pursuing his stage career, Smart kept in touch with the Parker Ranch. Smart eventually returned and took on the many responsibilities of ranch operations, but the stage never left his blood. Though officially theatrically retired, he performed in productions in Honolulu and the U.S. Mainland, commuting from the Big Island. Sometime in the 1970s and with the financial wherewithal to make it possible, Smart decided to build a theater in his hometown.

accompany dinner, the **Back to the 50s Diner** (Hwy. 19, *mauka* side, Laupahoehoe, 808/962-0808) has cowboy and swing music (yes, cowboy and swing, not a typo) on Friday and Saturday nights. It gets jam-packed with locals looking for a night out, so get there early to save your spot.

In Waimea, theatergoers will be impressed by the newish (from 1981) structure built by Richard Smart, heir to the Parker ranch, that now houses his private collection of Broadway memorabilia. The **Kahilu Theatre** (67-1186 Lindsey Rd., Parker Ranch Shopping Center, www.kahilutheatre.org, 808/885-6868) attracts first-rate local and Mainland performers, like the Martha Graham dance company, internationally known jazz musicians, and master ukulele players. Best of all, tickets are very reasonably priced and at times even free (for the community events). In addition to the usual season schedule, the theater also hosts community performances, such as the Hawaii youth symphony and sometimes the **Waimea Community Theater** (65-1224 Lindsey Rd., Parker School Theater, 808/885-5818, www. waimeacommunitytheatre.org), which has been performing plays and musicals on the Big Island since 1964.

For some less formal entertainment your best bet in Waimea is the **Big Island Brewhaus** (Hwy. 19 between mile markers 56 and 57 at intersection of Kamamiu St., 808/887-1717, http://bigislandbrewhaus.com) at their Tuesday and Thursday open mic nights or Friday night for live music—usually a local rock band. The crowd is usually on the younger side and the venue is very small, so expect to feel a little claustrophobic (or perhaps invigorated by the beats and beer).

For a more mature crowd in a larger space, the **Pakini Grill** (65-1144 Mamalahoa Hwy./ Hwy. 19, 808/885-3333) on Thursday, Friday, and Saturday nights has local bands playing anything from slack key to bluegrass. This is more of a *paniolo* crowd, but they are welcoming here and you won't feel out of place here if you are from out of town.

EVENTS

Held throughout Waimea town at various venues, the **Waimea Cherry Blossom Festival** (808/961-8706, first Saturday in February) celebrates the Japanese tradition of viewing the blooming of the historic cherry trees on Church Row. Although the festival is centered around the cherry trees, there are additional events, such as a live entertainment, a craft fair, sake tastings, and demonstrations of bonsai, origami, tea ceremony, and *mochi* pounding.

Also in February is the **Laupahoehoe Music Festival** (Laupahoehoe Point Beach Park off of Hwy. 19 near mile marker 27, http://laupahoehoemusicfestival.com, $10–15), a fundraising event for local projects and scholarships for college-bound students. Featuring Hawaiian music and hula entertainers, the park makes for a beautiful setting for this all day festival, and local families come in droves for the event. The scene can feel intimidating if you're not local, but if you're new to the area or visiting this festival is a great introduction to Hawaiian culture.

Hawaiians on horseback can be very fascinating, and for watching this phenomenon come to the **Honoka'a Western Week** (Honoka'a town, http://westernweek.com, end of May). Events include a *paniolo* parade, block party, a "saloon girl" competition, and live music. Events are mainly geared for families and are all free.

What's more American on the 4th of July than a rodeo? The **Parker Ranch Annual Independence Weekend Rodeo and Horse Races** (Rodeo Arena, Parker Ranch offices on Hwy. 190, www.parkerranch.com, $5, children under 10 free) is a prime entrée into the Big Island's *paniolo* culture and a great way to spend the 4th of July. With the 50th anniversary of the festival coming in 2012 expect something over the top; however, you can expect kids' activities like roping practice and pony rides as well as what you'd expect from a rodeo: roping, ranch mugging (not what you think it is—but you have to go there to see it), and horse races.

Food

HAMAKUA COAST

The food choices on the coast are (very) far and few between. It's a wonder that some restaurateur hasn't taken advantage of its location, but I digress.... The only real choice (literally) is the **Back to the 50s Diner** (Hwy. 19, *mauka* side, Laupahoehoe, 808/962-0808, Wed.–Thurs. 8 A.M.–7 P.M., Fri. 8 A.M.–8 P.M., Sun. 8 A.M.–3 P.M., $12). I know it will be hard to believe—because the restaurant's name is kind of cheesy and passersby always exclaim "how could that place be good?"—but the diner is really awesome for both its food quality and its kitsch. It really feels like the 1950s in there. You'd think it had been there since the '50s, but truth be told, it's just reconstructed in that way as sort of a community effort of individuals donating their personal paraphernalia from the era. On Friday and Saturday nights there is live music, which is not what you're thinking (Motown) but cowboy and swing (surprise!). The menu is extensive and reasonably priced with burgers and local favorites (chicken and pork prepared Hawaiian style). Vegetarian and gluten-free options are possible. Try their salad or anything they offer with Hamakua mushrooms. Even if you hate mushrooms (especially if you do), these local shrooms will change your mind. You'll be thinking about them for days later.

HONOKA'A AND WAIPI'O VALLEY

Warning: Do not have your heart set on eating somewhere specific in Honoka'a. Although hours are posted for restaurants, they frequently change (or just blatantly don't follow the posted hours). Waimea is only about 15 minutes away and offers many top-notch dining options, so it might be worth the extra few minutes in the car rather than eating in Honoka'a.

A Big Island institution, and rightfully so, it's hard to not want to stop daily at **⟨ Tex Drive In** (Hwy. 19 at the corner of Pakalana St., 808/775-0598, daily 6 A.M.–8 P.M.). The long-established Hamakua restaurant is known for its fresh *malasadas*: sugared Portuguese pastries (like doughnuts but without a hole) filled with passion fruit cream, or chocolate, or strawberry (the choices are endless). Best of all, you can watch the production process showcased behind plate glass windows inside. It's such a treat and only $1. But try to get there before 7 P.M. or they'll probably be sold out. Every month, 15,000 of these tasty treats are sold—sometimes many more. Tex has a fast-food look, a drive-up window, walk-up counter, and inside and outside tables, but the cavernous dining room in the back is still there and the food is still as filling and reasonable as ever. Besides the *malasadas* (if there could be anything else you could think of), they serve *"ono kine"* local food, specializing in *kalua* pork, teriyaki chicken and beef, hamburgers, and fresh fish. Prices are very

Kalua pork can be found at such restaurants as Tex Drive In.

© STACEY SHINTANI/FLICKR.COM

HAMAKUA COAST

reasonable, with most dinners around $9 and sandwiches less.

In Honoka'a town, you'll find **Cafe Il Mondo** (Mamane St. at the corner of Lehua St., 808/775-7711, www.cafeilmondo.com, Mon.–Sat. 11 A.M.–8 P.M., $12 small pizzas and calzones, cash only), an Italian pizzeria and coffee bar that's the best Honoka'a has to offer. But that doesn't say much. This is a cheery place with Italian music on the sound system and Hawaiian prints on the walls. Here you feel the spirit of Italy. While handmade pizzas with toppings, mostly $12–13, are the main focus, you can also get tasty calzones, pasta dishes, sandwiches, and salads for under $10, as well as ice cream and gourmet coffee. Medium and large pizzas aren't served in-house and are only available to go. When having dinner, it's okay to bring your own bottle of wine.

"Made with real butter and cream" is their motto, and it sure tastes like it. Peek in for a quick to-go treat at the **Hamakua Fudge Shop** (45-3611 Mamane St. #105, 808/775-1430, www.hamakuafudge.com, Mon.–Sat. 10:30 A.M.–4 P.M.) to bring with you on your Waipi'o adventure, or stay in for some ice cream in their small attached café. There are over 25 flavors, all made in-house, so certainly you will find something to your taste.

As the only sports bar in the Hamakua region, the **Hamakua Sports Bar** (45-3490 Mamane St., 808/775-1444, Sun.–Thurs. 3–10 P.M., Fri.–Sat. 3 P.M.–midnight) does have that novelty factor going for it (and lack of competition), on top of the fact that it looks like an old cowboy bar. I think what makes it a sports bar is that there is a large TV in it that usually plays sporting events. As of now, the owners serve up the standard cheap beers on draft as well as some from the Kona Brewing Company, but they hope one day soon to serve their own homebrew. Don't come here super hungry, they only have bar appetizers available (mostly the fried varieties). Note: Remember that sporting events are on much earlier in Hawaii because of the time difference. If there is a big game on, the bar is likely to open earlier to accommodate viewers!

HAWAII REGIONAL FOOD VS. LOCAL FOODS

Before eating local foods became trendy there was Hawaii Regional Cuisine. Surprisingly, even with the amazing amount and variety of produce that is grown on the islands (for display at farmers markets), Hawaii still imports lots of food from the Mainland and abroad. So in the early 1990s, a group of chefs across the Hawaiian Islands created Hawaii Regional Cuisine as a way to showcase what could be done with local island ingredients. Actually, it's sort of confusing because in Hawaii the term "local food" tends to refer to local-style foods (like macaroni salad or Spam *musubi*) and not to where the food came from. Instead, Hawaii Regional Cuisine is the term that denotes dishes created from products sourced from nearby farms – like Big Island beef or Hamakua mushrooms. On the Big Island you can experience this cuisine from one of the movement's founders, Peter Merriman, at his Merriman's restaurants in Waimea and Kohala.

Markets

On Mamane Street as you drive west to Waipi'o Valley you'll pass the **Malama Market** (Mamane St. at the corner of Lehua St., 808/775-0631, daily 6:30 A.M.–8 P.M.), a branch of the small local grocery chain. Although it's not a huge market, it has everything you need including prepared foods, a deli, and nice produce. You'll also find an ATM inside and a Redbox for DVD rentals (all the Malama Markets have them so you can easily return DVDs between them).

On Mamane Street, on the *mauka* side of the road, is **J.J.'s Country Market** (45-3745 Mamane St., 808/775-7744, Mon.–Wed. 7 A.M.–6 P.M., Thurs. 7 A.M.–7 P.M., Fri.–Sat. 7 A.M.–8 P.M., Sun. 8:30 A.M.–7 P.M.) doesn't have much in it, but it does have the best grass-fed local beef at outstanding prices. The meet is prepackaged in the freezer in every cut imaginable. It is here that I saw the biggest steak of my life. If you're barbecuing later on be sure to pick up a steak or the short ribs (they are phenomenal).

WAIMEA

It's almost guaranteed that eating in Waimea will lead you to exclaim, "that was the best steak of my life!" (except if you are a vegetarian). The beef doesn't get more local than this and has the reputation of being grass fed with ocean views (the cows look so happy). Waimea also is home to several longstanding upscale restaurants. Entries are listed from north to south and then east to west on Highway 19.

You'd think there would be more barbecue in Waimea given its country feel, but **Huli Sue's** (64-957 Mamalaho Hwy./Hwy. 19 across from mile marker 56, 808/885-6286, www.hulisues.com, Mon.–Sat. 11:30 A.M.–8 P.M., $10–29) is the only game in town. The restaurant is charming with its picnic tables, serving ware, and furniture resembling something from a down-home barbecue joint of North Carolina. The restaurant is the sister of an Italian restaurant at the Mauna Lani Clubhouse in Kohala—this is worth mention because it helps explain why the restaurant's atmosphere and menu are minimalist but the prices better reflect those of a resort eatery. If you're dining with a friend or loved one, try the sampler plate ($24), which is more than enough for two people and comes with brisket, local ribeye, pork, and chicken. The platter comes with sides like slaw, fries, corn pudding, and bok choy (a little Asian fare mixed in—classic Hawaii style!). There are also burgers, hot dogs, and fish tacos on the menu, but I'd stick to the barbecue options. Overall, it's not the best barbecue you'll ever have, but you can pretty much guarantee that the beef came from down the road (a bonus for locavores), and the various sauces have good flavor.

Nearly across the street is the restaurant formally known as Tako Taco (many listings still call it that), now called **Big Island Brewhaus** (Hwy. 19 between mile markers 56 and 57 at intersection of Kamamiu St., 808/887-1717, http://bigislandbrewhaus.com, Mon.–Sat. 11 A.M.–8:30 P.M., Sun. noon–8:30 P.M., $10). It's not only the newest brewery on the island (one of three), but also the highest brewery in Hawaii at 2,812 feet (funny story—when they first opened they printed the wrong elevation on their brewery's stickers and then added a few feet to make it higher). The restaurant is decorated from the point of view of someone who wanted it to look straight out of Mexico—it's sort of Mexican kitsch meets Hawaii. The food isn't so *authentico* Mexican, but it's priced right and overall hits the spot. There are the standard dishes like burritos, tortilla soup (which is excellent), enchiladas, and tacos. Vegans and gluten-free eaters rejoice with the substantial options available. What isn't so splendid here is the service. In fact, at times it's so terrible it can be downright frustrating. Arguably, now that they have their homebrews on tap, it makes the wait more bearable—but oftentimes it doesn't make any sense why you have to wait 45 minutes for a taco. Don't come hungry or in a rush. Tuesdays and Thursdays are open mic night and Friday there is live music (sometimes with a Latin spin).

At **Pakini Grill** (65-1144 Mamalahoa Hwy./Hwy. 19, 808/885-3333, Mon., Tues., Thurs. 11 A.M.–10 P.M., Wed., Fri., Sat. 11 A.M.–midnight, Sun. 11 A.M.–9 P.M., drinks happy hour daily 3–6 P.M., food happy hour Sun., Wed., Fri. 3–6 P.M., $10–20), a local-style restaurant (e.g., *loco moco*, short ribs, *poke* platter), it isn't the best food you'll ever have but it's one of the best values around and the service is quick. Besides the fact that it is one of few restaurants open on a Sunday afternoon in the area, the 50 percent appetizer happy hour offers excellent choices, such as smoked pork ($4 happy hour price) and *tinono* ($4 happy hour price), a marinated pork seasoned to perfection. Even though these are appetizers the portions are as large as a standard main meal. That means you can have a full meal and a beer on draft for about $7 during happy hour—what a deal!

Not as good of a deal other times, though. On Thursday, Friday, and Saturday there is live entertainment (ranging from slack-key guitar to bluegrass), and Sunday this is the place to watch sporting events at the bar. A kids' menu is available.

The cool temperatures in Waimea afford lots of coffee shops in the area. For a local coffee shop, you'll find **Solimene's** (65-1158 Mamalahoa Hwy./Hwy. 19, 808/887-1313, Mon.–Sat. 11 A.M.–3 P.M. and 5–9 P.M., Sun. 7 A.M.–noon, $15). A café and restaurant duo, Solimene's is another unassuming restaurant located in a strip mall. The café serves excellent coffee and tea in dozens of varieties, and the Italian restaurant next door offers 20 different combinations of pizzas (like goat cheese fig), pastas, fresh salads with mozzarella, vegetarian options, and daily specials. Sunday mornings are a jam-packed treat with made-to-order omelets and waffles topped off with a mimosa and bloody mary station.

There is some hard competition in the area, yet **Lilikoi Café** (67-1185 Mamalahoa Hwy./Hwy. 19, Parker Ranch Shopping Center, 808/887-1400, Mon.–Sat. 7:30 A.M.–4 P.M., breakfast $7, lunch $9) still fares well. The atmosphere along with the menu is simple: sandwiches, fresh salads that come as a combo with a choice of deli meat, and crepes for vegetarians. The breakfast choices of granola, burritos, and crepes are ideal for those looking to eat a wholesome and nourishing meal that doesn't include Spam, as many breakfast options do on the island.

Also in the Parker Ranch Shopping Center is literally one of the best burgers you will ever have (and so agrees *USA Today*, in its list of 50 burgers you must have before you die). **Village Burger** (67-1185 Mamalahoa Hwy./19, Parker Ranch Center Food Court, 808/885-7319, www.villageburgerwaimea.com, Mon.–Sat. 10 A.M.–8 P.M., Sun. 10:30 A.M.–6 P.M., $8–12) is a true farm-to-table establishment with nearly every ingredient sourced from a nearby farm. The veal burger (a common special) is spectacular (and can be served on a beautiful bed of lettuce for those who don't want the bun). The taro burger is an excellent vegan option—it's not just one of the standard non-meat burgers; it's really a well-thought-out conglomeration of garden vegetables. As expected, to go with an amazing burger are well-seasoned hand-cut fries. Try the *mamake* ice tea: a blend of a local leaf (with medicinal properties), mint, and tarragon. The only unfortunate part of the entire experience is that the restaurant is located in the food court with no ambiance and little seating. So grab it go and take it with you to Mauna Kea, although truth be told, you'll probably finish your burger off by the time you walk from the restaurant to your car.

Still in the Parker Ranch Shopping Center is one of the few **Starbucks** locations (67-1185 Mamalahoa Hwy./Hwy. 19, Parker Ranch Center, Sat.–Thurs. 4:30 A.M.–9 P.M., Fri.–Sun. 4:30 A.M.–10 P.M.) on the island. It's just like every other Starbucks that you've ever been to, but more special when there isn't one on every corner.

On weekends be prepared to wait as visitors line up around the corner patiently (and eagerly) anticipating the scrumptious breakfast at ◀ **Hawaiian Style Café** (65-1290 Kawaihae Rd./Hwy. 19 between mile markers 57 and 58, 808/885-4295, Mon.–Sat. 7 A.M.–1:30 P.M., Sun. 7 A.M.–noon, breakfast $8, plate lunch $9–17). It's not healthy food, it's comfort food served by a friendly staff. Be prepared to make new friends as the semicommunal counter area invokes conversation with fellow eaters. Try the *kalua* hash with eggs ($8). It provides a huge portion (there is a split fee, but right there on the menu the owners recommend simply ordering a side for $3.50 to avoid the fee), and it's the kind of food that's so good that you just keep eating it, even though you're full. Other local favorites are on the menu, like several varieties of *loco moco* (Spam with rice and gravy)—try the Internet Loco Moco with Spam and more Spam (just like your email inbox!).

Another alternative to Starbucks, **Waimea Coffee Company** (65-1279 Kawaihae Rd./Hwy. 19, 808/885-8915, www.waimeacoffee

company.com, Mon.–Fri. 6:30 A.M.–5:30 P.M., Sat. 8 A.M.–4 P.M., Sun. 9 A.M.–3 P.M., lunch $8) has a college town coffee shop atmosphere. This is definitely the kind of place where you can bring a book, grab a (good) coffee, bagels and lox, or soup and sandwich while sitting outside enjoying the brisk Waimea air.

As one of the original homes of Hawaii Regional Cuisine, **Merriman's** (65-1227 Opelo Rd., 808/885-6822, http://merriman-shawaii.com, Mon.–Fri. 11:30 A.M.–1:30 P.M., daily 5:30–9 P.M., reservation recommended, lunch $11–15, dinner $25–38) has a lot of street cred—and that's without adding the fact that its owner, Peter Merriman, is a James Beard Finalist (which means a lot in certain circles). In theory, it's fairly amazing that Merriman's started doing local foods decades before it was trendy, but in practice the restaurant is perhaps a bit overrated now that everyone is going local. That said, the dining experience is superb, with well-trained waitstaff and white linen tablecloths. It's a good place to go if you are looking for fine dining. The menu changes (remember, it's local and seasonal) but offers the usual Hawaiian dishes of mahimahi or ahi, spicy soups, and local vegetables. Perhaps go for lunch instead of dinner. The lunch menu is similar to the dinner menu and much more reasonable in terms of cost.

Markets

Besides the fact that there are few wine (or liquor) stores on the island, **Kamuela Liquor Store** (64-1010 Mamalahoa Hwy./Hwy. 19, 808/885-4674, Mon.–Sat. 8:30 A.M.–7 P.M., Sun. 9 A.M.–5 P.M., wine tasting Fri. 3–6 P.M.) deserves recognition because the building looks like it's from the old West (and it opens up around breakfast time for those in desperate need of a morning cocktail). They stock high-end wines (many on sale) as well as liquors and beer (including gluten-free varieties!). Stop by on Friday afternoon for the wine tasting.

Up there with fantastic Big Island farmers markets, the **Waimea Homestead Farmers Market** (Hwy. 19 near mile marker 55,

HULI HULI CHICKEN AND CASCARON

Huli huli chicken, Hawaiian-style rotisserie chicken (*huli* is the Hawaiian word for "turn"), is not to be missed. Marinated in Asian-inspired sauces and spices such as ginger, sesame, and soy sauce, *huli huli* chicken can be spotted about a mile away, not just from the wonderful smell drifting down the street, but from the smoke billowing up from the grill. The best *huli huli* chicken is usually found roadside, and one of the best stands is in the parking lot across the street from Big Island Brewhaus (on Hwy. 19 at the intersection of Kamamaiu, Saturdays only). You can pick a whole or half chicken – but I'd go for the whole one, which only costs $10 dollars and can feed 4-6 people. If you're on your way to camp out at one of the parks on the coast or going up to Mauna Kea for some stargazing it's a great to-go meal. If that weren't enough, at the same stand you'll want to grab a *cascaron* ($1), a Filipino doughnut made of rice flour. Two or three are served piping hot on a stick – the grease-stained bag that it comes in says it all.

Sat. 7 A.M.–noon) is one not to be missed. Nearly 20 years old, this market offers everything from prepared foods to local goat cheese to flowers and produce. I recommend coming hungry.

If you happen to be in Waimea on Wednesday then stop by the **Midweek Farmer's Market at Anna Ranch** (65-1480 Kawaihae Rd., Wed. 12:30–5 P.M.) for produce and crafts. Although it's fairly small now, expect this farmers market to get bigger quickly as there is a lot of excitement about what it has to offer.

There are no concerns about going hungry in Waimea, as the center area is a mecca of grocery stores, including the local chain, **KTA** (Waimea Shopping Center, daily

6 A.M.–11 P.M.), the Mainland chain **Foodland** (67-1185 Mamalahoa Hwy./Hwy. 19 in the Parker Ranch Center, daily 5 A.M.–11 P.M.), and the small **Natural Foods and Deli** (67-1185 Mamalahoa Hwy./Hwy. 19, Parker Ranch Center, Mon.–Sat. 9 A.M.–7 P.M., Sun. 9 A.M.–5 P.M.). Locals have their preference for

where to shop (KTA for shopping at a local business and Foodland if you want discounted liquor), but all grocery stores pretty much offer the same items, including organic foods, although the Natural Foods and Deli store has a larger bulk section of nuts, organic flours, and other specialty products.

Information and Services

EMERGENCY SERVICES

In Waimea, the **North Hawaii Community Hospital** (67-1125 Mamalahoa Hwy./Hwy. 19, 808/885-4444, www.nhch.com, 24 hours) is a full-service center well-equipped for emergencies, and it is known for a great birthing center. In Honoka'a, the **Hamakua Health Center** (45-549 Plumeria St., 808/775-7204, www.hamakua-health.org, Mon.–Fri. 8 A.M.–7 P.M., Sat. 9 A.M.–1 P.M.) is a quality health clinic with a welcoming staff that can handle non-emergencies if you call ahead.

BANKS

There are no actual bank branches on the Hamakua Coast—only in the bigger towns such as Honoka'a and Waimea. In Honoka'a,

both Bank of Hawaii and First Hawaiian Bank have offices on Mamane Street, the main street in town. In Waimea's Parker Ranch Center there are branches of Bank of Hawaii, First Hawaiian, and Hawaii First Federal Credit Union.

POST OFFICES

On the Hamakua Coast, there is a post office in nearly every town off the highway. In Honoka'a the post office is just downhill of the main intersection in town along Lehua Street. In Waimea, the post office is in the Parker Ranch Center, at the main intersection in town. The U.S. Postal Service designates Waimea as Kamuela, so as not to confuse it with the Waimeas on O'ahu and Kaua'i.

Getting There and Around

All roads lead through Waimea—or at least many of them do since it's a bus hub for the **Hele-On Bus** (www.heleonbus.org, 808/961-8744, $1 per ride, $1 each for luggage, large backpacks, bikes) traveling between the east and west sides of the island.

THE HAMAKUA COAST: HILO TO HONOKA'A

This new route has eight daily trips, with five additional buses during weekdays, and makes all intermediate stops between Hilo and Honoka'a, taking about an hour. In Hilo you can get the bus at the Mooheau

Bus Terminal on Bayfront (and twice daily it makes additional stops throughout Hilo). In Honoka'a, buses begin pickup at Blane's Drive-in on Mamane Street, the main street in town.

WAIMEA TO HILO VIA THE HAMAKUA COAST

With seven daily trips and three additional weekday buses, it couldn't be any easier to travel the two hours (sometimes less) between Waimea and Hilo. Buses pick up/drop off passengers at the back of the Parker Ranch Center and make all intermediate stops on the Hamakua Coast ending at the Mooheau Bus Terminal on Bayfront (and twice daily it makes additional stops throughout Hilo).

HILO TO KONA VIA WAIMEA AND THE HAMAKUA COAST

The buses traveling from Kona to Hilo make two daily morning stops and one afternoon stop at the back parking lot of the Parker Ranch Center. Those traveling on to Hilo take the Hamakua Coast route, making all intermediate stops and arriving about two hours later (sometimes less) to Hilo. Buses traveling to Kona take the lower road, passing by all the Kohala resorts and traveling as far as Captain Cook and Honaunau in the afternoon. The entire route takes about two hours.

INTRA-WAIMEA SHUTTLE

Not a super-useful service for tourists, but ideal for residents, the **Waimea Shuttle** makes hourly trips 6:30 A.M.–4:30 P.M. around Waimea from the west side to east side of Highway 19. When the bus was free, locals utilized this service for quick shopping trips, but it likely won't be too crowded now that you must pay $1 just to go a few minutes. For more information, check www.heleonbus.org.

ACCOMMODATIONS

Choosing Accommodations

HOTELS, BED-AND-BREAKFASTS, AND VACATION RENTALS

Here are some helpful suggestions for how to pick the best accommodations for you:

1. **Decide if you want to stay at a hotel, bed-and-breakfast, or rental property.** There are some Big Island hotels where you can pay to get first-class attention (such as at The Fairmont Orchid and Four Seasons Resort), but generally hotels are more impersonal and not as attentive to your needs as a bed-and-breakfast. That said, bed-and-breakfasts are often not private even if the room has a private entrance. There is usually lots of interaction with other guests and the hosts. So if you want to be anonymous, opt for a hotel or rental property. Remember to check which "extras" are included at your hotel. Many hotels charge for wireless Internet (most B&Bs and rental properties do not), and the breakfast included at your bed-and-breakfast does have a lot of value these days. Essentially, you are saving about $30–40 by including breakfast for two with your room (breakfast at the hotels does not come cheap!).

2. **There might be a good compromise place.** There are new "boutique hotels" springing up on the Big Island. For the most part,

© MATT KRANE

they consider themselves bed-and-breakfasts (since they include breakfast), but since they are in most cases managed by staff (and not the owners) and include amenities (like handmade soaps), they have the feel of a boutique hotel. Hawaii Island Retreat at Ahu Pohaku Hoʻomaluhia (North Kohala), Hawaiian Oasis Bed and Breakfast (Kona), Kalaekilohana Bed and Breakfast (Kaʻu), and Waianuhea (Hamakua Coast) are some examples.

3. **If you're interested in staying at a bed-and-breakfast, call!** Although it seems counterintuitive in the world of technology, having a brief conversation with the bed-and-breakfast owner/innkeeper will give you a good sense of if the place is a good fit for you. In fact, most owners share that they can tell almost instantly after speaking with someone if their place is right for a visitor. Also, you might want to ask at the end of the conversation if there are any discounts available. With the economy being down, many owners are looking to fill rooms and may be willing to make a deal. Lastly, don't forget to ask about pets! Some B&Bs have dogs, cats, and even birds around their homes. Find out in case you're allergic or simply don't like pets.

4. **Check for online specials.** Nearly all the hotels and even bed-and-breakfasts offer "specials" online either for low seasons or for additional freebies (like tours or breakfast or car rentals). Don't be afraid to call an establishment and ask if it can offer you a deal or offer you a previous deal if you just missed one.

5. **A great website to utilize for vacation rentals on the island is www.vrbo.com.** The island's best properties are listed here and there are reviews from previous guests posted on the site.

A Note on Extra Fees and High-Season Prices

The prices listed here are the rates for accommodations during the low and medium/average seasons. If you are booking for the high season (major holidays such as Christmas and Thanksgiving as well as school holiday times), prices can increase 30 percent above the rates posted here.

In addition, advertised rates often do not include tax. There is the Hawaii General Excise Tax (4.166 percent) and the Hawaii Hotel Room Tax (9.25 percent). On top of that, many of the larger hotels and resorts charge a "resort fee" ($10–25). With this fee sometimes you get free parking and other times you get...absolutely nothing. So just be warned to ask about these additional charges ahead of time (although they come up if you're booking online), and don't be surprised if your hotel seems to cost $70 more than you think it should. Note: Some bed-and-breakfasts include the tax in the price of the room. Usually their websites will indicate if the rate is inclusive of tax or not.

CAMPING

The Big Island has the best camping in the state, with more facilities and less competition for campsites than on the other islands. Nearly three dozen parks fringe the coastline and sit deep in the interior; almost half offer camping. The ones with campgrounds are state-, county-, or nationally operated, ranging from remote walk-in sites to housekeeping cabins. All require camping permits—inexpensive for the county and state parks, free for the national parks. Camping permits can be obtained by walk-in application to the appropriate office or by writing ahead. Although there is usually no problem obtaining campsites, it's best to book ahead of time using the online reservation system. There are different online sites for county, state, and national parks so note which kind of park you'll be staying at and use the appropriate site.

In general, most campgrounds have pavilions, fireplaces, toilets (sometimes pits), and running water, but usually no individual electrical hookups. Pavilions often have electric lights, but sometimes campers appropriate the bulbs, so it's wise to carry your own. Drinking water is available, but at times brackish water

ACCOMMODATIONS

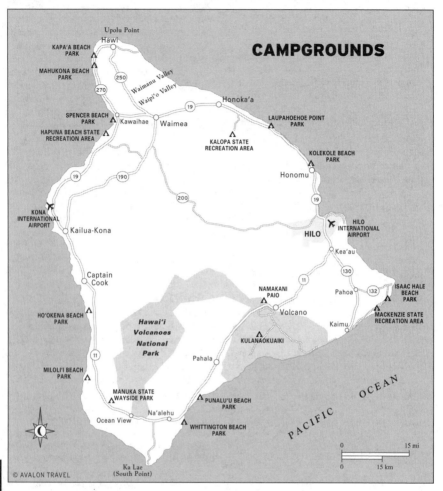

CAMPGROUNDS

is used for flushing toilets and for showers, so read all signs regarding water. Backcountry shelters have catchment water that needs purification, but never hike without an adequate supply of your own since water might not be available at times of draught. Cooking fires are allowed in established fire pits, but no wood is provided. Charcoal is a good idea, or bottled fuel for those hiking. When camping in the mountains, be prepared for cold and rainy weather.

County Parks

Permits are required for overnight tent and RV camping at county parks. County parks that allow camping are Isaac Hale in Puna, Kolekole north of Hilo, Laupahoehoe Point in Hamakua, Kapa'a and Mahukona in North Kohala, Spencer Beach in South Kohala, Ho'okena and Miloli'i in South Kona, and Punalu'u and Whittington in Ka'u. Camping is limited to one week at any one site June–August and to two weeks at any one site for the rest of the year. The permit-issuing office is the Department of Parks and Recreation, County of Hawai'i (101 Pauahi St., Ste. 6, Hilo, HI 96720, 808/961-8311, www.hawaiicounty. gov/parks-and-recreation, 7:45 A.M.–4:30 P.M. Mon.–Fri.). However, a much easier way to obtain permits is through the online system: www.ehawaii.gov/Hawaii_County/camping/exe/campre.cgi. Fees are $5 adults per day (plus $1 online transaction fee); children 13–17, $2 per day (plus $0.25 online transaction fee); under 12, $1 per day. Pavilions for exclusive use are $25 per day with kitchen, $10 without.

State Parks

Day use of state parks is free, with no permit required, but you will need a permit for tent camping and for cabins. Five consecutive nights is the limit for either camping or cabins at any one site. If you want a permit, at least one week's notice is required regardless of availability. State park permits are issued no more than one year in advance. The easiest way to obtain a permit is through http://camping.ehawaii.gov.

Camping is permitted at Kalopa Native Forest State Park and Recreation Area, MacKenzie State Recreation Area, and Manuka State Wayside Park for a $12 resident, $18 nonresident fee per campsite per night for up to six people. Eight-person forest cabins are located at Kalopa State Recreation Area and cost $60 for residents, $90 for nonresidents. Four-person A-frame cabins are at Hapuna Beach State Recreation Area ($30 residents, $50 nonresidents). Located along the Saddle Road near Pohakuloa Training Area, Mauna Kea State Recreation Area is open for overnight use of the housekeeping cabins, which range $50–80 for up to six people per night, up to five nights. For details about Ainapo Cabin in the Kapapala Forest Reserve and camping in Waimanu Valley, see the website.

National Parks

For overnight backcountry camping in Hawai'i Volcanoes National Park, permits are required but available free through the park visitors center. Your stay is limited to seven days per campground per year. There are a half dozen walk-in primitive campsites and two trail cabins in the park; you can't reserve them and should expect to share them with other hikers. Applications for camping and hiking are taken only one day in advance. No open fires are permitted. At primitive campsites along the coast, there are three-sided, open shelters that offer a partial covering against the elements. Camping is also available at both Namakani Paio and Kulanaokuaiki drive-in campgrounds, but there are no shower facilities. There is no charge for tent camping at these two campsites, and no reservations are required. For information on camping and hiking in the park, stop by the Kilauea Visitor Center or write the park headquarters (P.O. Box 52, Hawai'i Volcanoes National Park, HI 96718, 808/985-6000, daily 7:45 A.M.–5 P.M.).

There are A-frame cabins at Namakani Paio Campground and arrangements are made through Volcano House (808/967-7321 or 800/325-3535, www.volcanohousehotel.com) on a first-come, first-served basis. Volcano House and the cabins are expected to reopen in 2012. A cooking pavilion has fireplaces, but wood and drinking water are not provided. Each of the 10 small cabins sleeps up to four people. When they were open they cost $40 single or double, and $8 each for a third or fourth person (the price may change with the renovations). Linens, soap, towels, and a blanket are provided, but you would be wise to bring an extra sleeping bag, as it can get cold. Each cabin contains one double bed and two single bunk beds and an electric light, but no electrical outlets. There is a picnic table and barbecue grill for each cabin, but you'll need to bring your own charcoal and cooking utensils. Check in at Volcano House after 3 P.M. and check out by noon.

Kona

The majority of Kona's accommodations lie along the six miles of Ali'i Drive from Kailua-Kona to Keauhou. Most hotels/condos fall in the moderate to expensive range. A few inexpensive hotels are scattered here and there along Ali'i Drive. If you're looking to branch out from Ali'i Drive, the town of Holualoa is an excellent alternative located only 20 minutes away from Kailua on the mountain above.

HOSTELS
Under $50

The least expensive place to stay in the area is **Pineapple Park** (81-6363 Mamalahoa Hwy., Kealakekua 808/323-2224 or 877/800-3800, www.pineapple-park.com, $25–85). This clean and commodious hostel accommodation is in a converted plantation-era house along the main highway. Running $25 a bed, the dorm rooms are located in the converted walk-out basement, which also has a TV lounge and free wireless Internet access. A private room runs $65 for shared bath and $85 with private bath. Discounts are available for longer stays. All guests share baths, have use of laundry facilities and a large kitchen, and can rent kayaks and snorkel gear on-site for minimal fees. If you don't have a car, you'll need to be a real whiz on the bus to get around since the hostel isn't that close to town (although it's right off the highway). Guests are friendly with one another (inspired by the hostel—not hostile—atmosphere), but rumor has it that management can be rude.

BED-AND-BREAKFASTS AND INNS
$100-150

Mango Sunset (73-4261 Mamalahoa Hwy./Hwy. 190, Kailua-Kona, 808/325-0909, www.mangosunset.com, $100–120) is definitely not for everyone and would be a better deal if it were about $30 less per room. Right off the bat, they want you to know this is a working coffee farm. It is just up the road—well, far up the road—from the airport (so it's convenient for an early-morning or late-night flight) and has excellent views of Kona below. It's a good place to come if you are truly interested in coffee and want an extensive history about it from the owner and grower, Hans (he used to be in academics and approaches coffee with the same sort of research ethic). It is not a good place to stay if you are looking for luxury and large rooms. The rooms are very simple (all but one have private bathrooms) and without TV (there is a shared one in a small common area). The rooms are wheelchair-accessible. Laundry is available for $5 a load and wireless Internet is free. Hot breakfast, which utilizes mainly ingredients from the farm, includes large portions and they accommodate food allergies with ample notice. Mango Sunset has the feel of a hostel to it, but it would be a good experience for someone who wants to see and stay on a working coffee farm. The falls are paper thin, so it's not a great place for someone who is a light sleeper.

Navigating the nearly vertical road up to **Lilikoi Inn** (75-5339C, Mamalahoa Hwy., Holualoa, 808/333-5539, www.lilikoiinn.com, $110–135) quickly alerts you that you're not arriving to a run-of-the-mill place. The house is surrounded by lush greenery (papaya and banana trees as well as some coffee), and the views from the lanai are spectacular. You can see nearly all of Kailua as well as the ocean below, and that's exactly what you'll see while eating your breakfast on the lanai at a large communal table. Shai and Trina, the owners and expats from the Bay Area, are friendly and talkative, and their B&B is the kind of place that feels less like a hotel and more like you're staying at your friend's house with a private entrance. The four rooms (two upstairs and two downstairs) are decorated nicely. The two upstairs rooms are smaller (less expensive), and the downstairs rooms with queen-size sleigh beds—the Green Papaya ($125) and Plumeria ($125) rooms—are separated by a lounge area in the middle and can be rented out as one large space to accommodate a family. There is a kitchen available for guest use and it's completely separate from the family kitchen, which is a certified industrial kitchen. And food is where the Lilikoi Inn excels, given that Shai is a trained chef who once owned a restaurant and catering business in the Bay Area. The breakfast reflects Shai's experience—meaning he can go beyond the standard B&B macadamia nut French toast dish and create something gourmet with local ingredients (many from their land). Portions are huge and Shai is happy to wrap up leftovers for guests to enjoy later. Additional amenities include cable television, DVD player, wireless Internet, and a hot tub that will make you feel like you're in the rainforest. They can accommodate food allergies. It's not a romantic place, but it has a great views and top-notch service. Clientele ranges from young couples to older ones, and they attract an international crowd since Shai and Trina speak several languages. It's a good deal for the area and for those who don't want to be right in town (it's about a 15-minute drive to Kailua and 25 minutes to the airport). Keep in mind that temperatures in Holualoa tend to be cooler than in Kailua, a welcome change if it's really hot near the ocean, but Holualoa also gets more rainfall than Kailua.

Areca Palms Estate Bed and Breakfast (Hwy. 11, Captain Cook, 808/323-2276, www.konabedandbreakfast.com, $115–145) was once considered one of the best on the island, but with lots of new competition (and newer homes) it seems like innkeepers Janice and Steve Glass are working very hard to earn back their title. Likewise, their operation is a bit old school: The clientele tends to be on the older side, and they have no online reservation or availability system. All reservations must be done by phone or email. The rooms are on the smaller side and decorated with Hawaiiana such as floral design quilts. The house is always perfumed by freshly cut flowers, and Hawaiian music plays in the background to set the mood. Cable and wireless Internet are available in each room. Set in a

broad manicured lawn surrounded by tropical flowers and areca palms, the outdoor hot tub deck is the premier spot on the property. Rates for the four rooms range $115–145, inclusive of the sumptuous breakfast feast; a two-night minimum stay is required. Areca Palms is a good deal. The price is definitely right for what it has to offer: smaller (but very clean) rooms, a huge breakfast, and a location near to Kealakekua Bay.

$150-250

Owners Kona Dave and Wendi once worked with rock stars, and now they want all their guests to feel like rock stars. In fact, before guests even get here, Wendi emails them a questionnaire so that she can begin preparing suggestions before arrival. The property at **Honu Kai** (74-1529 Hao Kuni St., Kailua-Kona, 808/329-8676, www.honukai.com, $160–195) isn't amazing, but their love and attention and utter dedication to ensuring that their guests are having the best (and most Zen-like) experience at their home and on the Big Island makes this property very attractive. Their guest rooms are pleasant with Hawaiian decor, large beds, and a small bathroom. One of the rooms has wheelchair accessibility. It's peaceful here. Amenities include free use of beach gear (chairs, towels, boogie boards, snorkel equipment), access to a private beach at the Mauna Lani in Kohala (they own another property there), laundry facilities, a cooking area available just for guests, cable television, and wireless Internet. They accommodate dietary needs. A two-night minimum is required and no children are allowed. Wendi and Kona Dave are definitely in the know (e.g., they can call ahead to restaurants and get a table reserved for you even when one might not be available). The location is in a residential neighborhood just 10 minutes north of Ali'i Drive and 20 minutes from the airport—ideal for those who want to be close to the action but not right in it.

A perfect place for honeymooners and large families alike, ◖ **Hawaiian Oasis Bed and Breakfast** (74-4958 Kiwi St., Kailua-Kona,

ACCOMMODATIONS

KONA ACCOMMODATIONS

Name (Location)	Type	Price	Features	Why Go Here	Best Fit For
Areca Palms Estate B&B (Captain Cook)	B&B	$115-145	immaculate rooms	near Kealakekua Bay	first-timers to Hawai'i, an older crowd
Aston Kona by the Sea (Kailua-Kona)	condo	$180-300	kitchen, washer/dryer, pool and hot tub, barbecue, cable TV	close to downtown Kailua, one-bedroom units all have sofa beds	families, older couples
Casa de Emdeko (Kailua-Kona)	condo	$100-135	two pools, barbecue area, beach equipment	inexpensive, residents like to mingle	older couples, younger families
Courtyard King Kamehameha's Kona Beach Hotel (Kailua-Kona)	hotel	$140	pool, *lu'au*, small beach	clean chain hotel, close to downtown bars and restaurants	families, late arrivals/ early departures from airport, festival-goers
Dragonfly Ranch (Captain Cook)	B&B	$100-250	unique "tropical fantasy" decor, wholesome breakfast	close to snorkeling and dolphin swimming	new age free thinkers
Four Seasons Resort, Hualalai at Historic Ka'upulehu (north of Kona airport)	resort	$220-600	multiple pools, spa, day-care service	Four Seasons quality service, truly exclusive	luxury lovers, families
Hale Kona Kai (Kailua-Kona)	condo	$150-195	cable TV, small kitchen, sofa bed, lanai, pool, barbecue area, two parking lots	walkable to downtown Kailua, wireless Internet at the pool	older couples, young families
✔ Hawaiian Oasis B&B (Kailua-Kona)	B&B	$195-305	pool, tennis courts, beautiful outdoor kitchen for guests	close to downtown action, definitely makes you feel like you're on vacation	couples, large families who can rent out the entire house

Name (Location)	Type	Price	Features	Why Go Here	Best Fit For
◪ Holualoa Inn (Holualoa)	B&B	$295-405	pool, kitchen for guests only, chef-prepared breakfast	more like a boutique hotel than B&B, great views, excellent service, quiet area	honeymooners, luxury lovers
Holua Resort at Mauna Loa Village (Keauhou)	condo	$150-250	cable TV, kitchen, pool and hot tub, activities desk	uncrowded pool, easy parking, helpful staff	couples, young families
Honu Kai (Kailua-Kona)	B&B	$160-195	laundry and shared cooking facilities for guests	top-notch concierge service, lots of free extras like beach gear, close to downtown action	first-timers to Hawai'i, older couples
Hotel Manago (Captain Cook)	hotel	$36-78	good restaurant, near to bus route	you'll feel like you're abroad or in 1960s Hawaii	budget travelers, those who want to stay between Kona and South Point or Hawai'i Volcanoes National Park
Kona Bali Kai (Kailua-Kona)	condo	$100-300	indoor pool, tasty poke restaurant	frequent upgrades to a larger room, you can hear the ocean at night	budget-minded and younger party crews who want to fit a lot of people into one place
Kona Seaside Hotel (Kailua-Kona)	hotel	$69-125	pool	close to downtown area, great place to stay for late arrivals/early flights	budget travelers who don't mind noise
Lilikoi Inn (Holualoa)	B&B	$110-135	top-notch breakfast and huge portions	cooler temperatures, great view of Kailua below	couples, families, those who enjoy interacting with the B&B host

(continued on next page)

ACCOMMODATIONS

KONA ACCOMMODATIONS (continued)

Name (Location)	Type	Price	Features	Why Go Here	Best Fit For
◖ Luana Inn (Captain Cook)	B&B	$155-205	pool, delicious breakfast	one of the best views around, super-sweet hosts	couples of all ages, those who want to be close to Kealakekua Bay
Mango Sunset (close to Kona airport)	B&B	$100-120	includes a free coffee tour	you've dreamt of sleeping at a working coffee farm	young foodies and history buffs
Outrigger Keauhou Beach Resort (Keauhou)	resort	$170-450	pool, tennis courts, activities desk, fitness center, near to beach	one of the few true resorts in Kona, good deals especially during low season	families, those who want easy access to a mall
Pineapple Park (Captain Cook)	hostel	$25-85	kayak rental, free wireless Internet	you yearn for the hostel scene of your college trip to Europe	budget travelers
◖ Sheraton Keauhou Bay Resort and Spa (Keauhou)	resort	$125-450	pool with water slide, tennis courts, full spa, business center	watching manta rays from the bar	families
Silver Oaks Ranch (close to Kona airport)	vacation rental	$125-200	kitchen, TV, washer/dryer, farm animals	privacy of a vacation rental with attentive service of a hotel	families, older couples

808/937-6453, www.hawaiianoasis.com, $195–305 per room or $1,000 for entire house) has Hawaii-meets-India decor that makes it feel dreamy and exotic—especially the Aloha Room ($305) and the Waterfall Suite ($260). This is the kind of house—with the view—that you wish you owned. It has it all: poolside outdoor kitchen, hot tub, and tennis courts. Unlike at many other bed-and-breakfasts, guests have the entire house to themselves, as it is solely a guest residence. In fact, oftentimes the house is rented as a single unit for large families or parties (they do a lot of weddings here). Amenities include free laundry, common TV, and wireless Internet in every room. The bottom rooms are wheelchair accessible. When the house isn't rented as an entire estate, hot breakfast is included and is served in huge portions on the balcony. Currently, the host of the property is Jenifer, who has years of experience as a concierge to the stars at the big resorts in Kohala. In addition to the great stories she has to tell about her prior work, she is eager to assist guests in booking excursions and recommending restaurants (some of which she has managed). The property is beautiful and the rooms are the kind of space you want to be in while on vacation. Rumor is that the property is for sale, so make sure Jenifer is your host before you book!

The view of Kealakekua Bay from the **C Luana Inn** (82-5856 Napo'opo'o Rd., Captain Cook, 808/328-2612, www.luanainn.com, $155–205) is priceless, but it's available at an extremely reasonable price. Unlike many other B&B hosts, Ken and Erin (with their two adorable children) have fully dedicated their time to this business—so much so, that they have made their own booklet of restaurant reviews (it's extremely informative). The rooms overlooking the pool/hot tub (the rooms with the view) are identically furnished to look like an IKEA showroom and include a kitchenette with sink, microwave, mini-fridge, and coffeemaker. Wireless Internet and TVs with DVD players are also available. The rooms are large with king-size beds; however, the bathrooms are shower only with no tub. The whole foods breakfast (large and nutritious) is served in the adjoining main house (again, with the view), and communal hangout space is in the downstairs section of the house. Located on the back of this large property is the Ohana Cottage, which houses a full kitchen and room for four—but no ocean view. A $30 short-stay fee is charged for stays under three nights. Luana Inn is a new property and I expect that as soon as they have a solid clientele base they will raise their rates. The location is fantastic, only a few minutes' drive down to the bay for snorkeling and kayaking or to Pu'uhonua O Honaunau National Historical Park for some sightseeing. The room decor isn't anything special, but they are comfortable and you'll be distracted by the view from your screen door. You definitely get your money's worth with the breakfast—especially those who appreciate food on the healthier side. Also, they offer one of the best gluten-free breakfast options on the island.

Dragonfly Ranch (near Pu'uhonua O Honaunau, Captain Cook, 808/328-2159 or 800/487-2159, www.dragonflyranch.com, $100–250) is really not for everyone. Maybe that's why owner Barbara Moore has posted on her website a piece called "A Marriott We Are Not." The Dragonfly offers "tropical fantasy lodging" set among thick vegetation on the way down to Pu'uhonua O Honaunau. Rainbow streamers and a Buddha in a butterfly banner greet you as you turn in the drive. Rooms are intriguing and range from the Honeymoon Suite (featuring a king-size bed in a screened outdoor room), the airy Lomi Lomi suite, and the more private Writer's Studio to the smaller Dragonfly and Dolphin rooms. All rooms include a small refrigerator and basic cooking apparatus, indoor bathroom, private outdoor shower, cable TV, stereo, and small library. There is a three-night minimum, with discounts for longer stays, and breakfast, which is a dream come true for those who love chia seeds or gluten-free bread, is included. Those who don't love organic yogurt with flax will need to have a second breakfast afterward. This is an open, airy place, where the outside and inside boundaries begin to blur. The hosts are very friendly and inviting, indeed, but definitely have an alternative, counterculture, new age leaning. Occasionally, alternative healing arts and wellness workshops are given. Free-spirited adventurers will feel comfortable here; others may not. The Dragonfly would be more attractive with a lower price point, although the $100 a night room is reasonable. Barbara, at times, is open to bargaining, so if the price is what is keeping you from booking (and not the granola breakfast), then it might be possible to arrange a deal.

Over $250

It's the perfect place for a honeymoon or those looking to rekindle romance. More a boutique hotel than a bed-and-breakfast, ❰ **Holualoa Inn** (76-5932 Mamalahoa Hwy., Holualoa, 808/324-1121, www.holualoainn. com, $295–405) was the retirement home of Thurston Twigg-Smith, CEO of the *Honolulu Advertiser* and member of an old *kama'aina* family. Twigg-Smith built the original home in 1978, but, tragically, it burned to the ground.

Undaunted, he rebuilt, exactly duplicating the original. After living here a few years Twigg-Smith decided it was too quiet and peaceful and went back to live in Honolulu. In 1987 it was converted into a bed-and-breakfast. The home is a marvel of taste and charm—light, airy, and open. Top to bottom, it is the natural burnished red of cedar and eucalyptus. Here the Hawaiian tradition of removing your shoes upon entering a home is made a pleasure with cool, smooth eucalyptus floors. The front lanai is pure relaxation, and stained glass puncturing the walls here and there creates swirls of rainbow light. A pool table holds king's court in the commodious games room, as doors open to a casual yet elegant sitting room where breakfast is served. A back staircase leads to a gazebo, floored with tile and brazenly open to the elements, while the back lanai is encircled by a roof made of copper. From here, Kailua-Kona glows with the imaginative mistiness of an Impressionist painting, and, closer by, 50 acres are dotted with coffee trees and cattle raised by the family. Just below is the inn's swimming

The Holualoa Inn is a top pick for honeymooners.

pool, tiled in blue with a torch ginger motif, and off to the side is the hot tub. The six island-theme rooms, each with private bathroom and superb views of the coast, all differ in size and decor. The Coffee Cherry Room ($310–350) has a private (what appears to be heart shaped) hot tub just outside the room. Other rooms offer private sitting areas and even a sofa bed that can accommodate a third person (for an additional charge, of course). The downstairs has a communal sitting area with kitchen area available for guest use. The laundry machine is available at no charge. There is a two-night minimum and discounts for stays longer than seven days. Breakfast is included. No preteen children, please. Some years back, Twigg-Smith was offered $7 million for the home. Much to our benefit, he declined. This is a gem. You'll feel like you've really "gotten away" at the Holualoa Inn. Unlike the traditional B&B, this place has a staff including a professional chef, who has worked at some of the best restaurants on the island. This means that you don't feel like you're inconveniencing anyone if you make a request. If you can afford to stay here, I highly recommend that you do so and book it quickly. This place can fill up fast!

HOTELS AND RESORTS

A Kona Coast institution and a happening spot (for those who could afford it) since it opened its doors in 1965, the Kona Village Resort bore the brunt of the March 2011 tsunami, which nearly destroyed the resort's entire compound. Located on Kahuwai Bay, a picture-perfect cove of black and white sand dotted with coconut palms, the village's accommodations were 125 distinctive *hale*, individual renditions of thatch-roofed huts found throughout Polynesia and Hawaii. Since the tsunami, the resort (to the dismay of its faithful cadre of fans) has been closed for repairs with rumors back and forth of its rebuilding or its possible closing. The latest rumor on this side of the island tends to be that it will reopen in late 2013. Contact the resort (808/325-5555 or 800/367-5290, www.konavillage.com) for the latest information.

$50-100

Kona Seaside Hotel (75-5646 Palani Rd., Kailua-Kona, 808/329-2455 or 800/560-5558, http://seasidehotelshawaii.com, $69–125) is the hotel to stay in if you don't want to spend a lot of money, will only be in your room to sleep, and would like to be close to the action on Ali'i Drive. The rooms are on the smaller side and the decor is old (think Hawaii in the early 1980s), but rooms stay cool with excellent air-conditioning and ceiling fans. Cable TV is available, but no wireless Internet. Spend some time on the sundeck, which looks out to the ocean across the street, and take a dip in the pool (but not at night—the pool closes at dusk). Prices range from $95 standard to $125 for a deluxe room with an ocean view. There are AAA and *kama'aina* discounts that bring the rate down to as low as $69 a night. Some rates also come with a free or discounted breakfast (book online for those deals!). There is an extra charge for parking per night, but guests can park at a nearby public lot for free.

If you're looking for a budget place to stay, book a room at the **Hotel Manago** (Hwy. 11 between mile markers 109 and 110, Captain Cook, 808/323-2642, www.managohotel.com, $33–75 single, $36–78 double, each additional person $3). A family-run hotel since 1917 (the same family!), this hotel isn't trying to be anything but what it is—a family-run historic hotel offering basic services. In fact, how you know it's an "old school" hotel is that they have a smoking section. Rates increase by floor (so lower floors are cheaper than higher floors). The rooms are small and can be musty. Rooms with private bathrooms or communal baths are available, and discounts are offered for weekly stays. The hotel's restaurant (closed Monday) is a favorite of locals for its combo lunches of huge portions. It's a simple place with a local feel—the kind of place you'd expect to find while traveling abroad. It's right on the main highway about 45 minutes from the Kona airport, so it's ideal for someone traveling to/from Hawai'i Volcanoes National Park and the airport. It's one of few truly locally owned and operated hotels and a great way to support local business on the Big Island.

$100-150

By the end of 2011 when renovations are complete, the **Courtyard King Kamehameha's Kona Beach Hotel** (75-5660 Palani Rd., Kailua-Kona, 808/329-2911, www.konabeachhotel.com, average price $140), despite the addition of "Courtyard" to its name, will still hold the same reputation that it has had for decades. The March 2011 tsunami hit this hotel fairly hard, causing immense damage to the lobby area, *lu'au* grounds, and restaurant. Nevertheless, the hotel never closed (not even for a night!) since none of the damage hit the actual rooms. Even before the tsunami hit, the King Kam (as it's called) had received a major revamping to bring its outdated rooms into the 21st century. The 452-room hotel is ideally located next to all the action of Ali'i Drive and it's the place you'll want to stay during many of the large festivals in the area (like the Kona Brewers Festival or Kona Coffee Cultural Festival), many of which take place at the hotel. The King Kam also offers one of the best *lu'au* on the island. You don't need to be a guest to attend the *lu'au*, but if you are staying over, it's easier to crawl back to your room after the open bar and massive buffet. Wireless Internet is available (sometimes at a cost), and parking is extra (although there is a public free lot close by). For the best deal look at their website for specials. Standard rooms range $185–250 for an oceanfront view; however, the online specials can bring the price down to $140 a night (and less for *kama'aina*) or include parking and breakfast with the room rate. This hotel is definitely not a resort, but a hotel set right in the middle of things, meaning it can get loud outside. There is a nice oceanfront pool, but the ocean access, which is essentially Kailua pier, is not that nice. The kids like the beach here because it is shallow and there is a small sandy area. It's best to stay here if you are doing something in town (like a festival) or need somewhere to stay close to the airport.

$150-250

The **Outrigger Keauhou Beach Resort** (78-6740 Ali'i Dr., Kailua-Kona, 808/322-3441 or 800/688-7444, www.keauhoubeachresort-hawaii.com, $170–450) is built on a historic site that includes the remains of three *heiau*, a reconstruction of King Kamehameha III's summer cottage, two freshwater springs, and several fishponds. Kahalu'u Bay Beach Park is adjacent with its white-sand beach and famous surf break, and the entire area is known for fantastic tide pools. This famous Kona hotel underwent an extensive renovation in 1999 and the result is a wonderful feeling of old-fashioned Hawaii. Rates range from $170 for a garden view up to $215 for deluxe oceanfront room, with suites at $400; rates are lower during value season, and many special discounts (like free breakfast buffet) are available all year. Check the Specials and Packages tab on the website. Each of the 309 rooms has air-conditioning, TV, phone, private lanai, and small refrigerator. For food, the hotel has the open-air Kama'aina Terrace restaurant, open for breakfast and dinner; the Kalanikai Bar and Grill near the water serves wraps, sandwiches, and other light fare for lunch; and the Verandah Lounge offers drinks throughout the day and free music every evening. The resort also has a swimming pool, activities desk, and a fitness center. As at many of the resorts on the Kona side, there are daily activities and presentations in Hawaiian dance, music, arts and crafts, as well as a torch lighting ceremony. A free cultural tour is offered daily that takes you around to the historical sites on the hotel grounds. For the tennis player, Island Slice Tennis is on the property. If you're looking for a proper resort on the south side of Kona, this is your best bet, as the Sheraton (just down the road) is more of a hotel than a resort. It's not worth paying full price for rooms at this property, but definitely book it if they are offering a special.

Sitting on the black lava seashore south of Keauhou Bay, the 521-room █ **Sheraton Keauhou Bay Resort and Spa** (78-128 Ehukai St., Kailua-Kona, 808/930-4900 or 888/488-3535, www.sheratonkeauhou.com, $125–450) has risen like a phoenix from the old Kona Surf Hotel, greatly transforming the bones of the hotel and opening up the property to the water. The grounds have been extensively landscaped to add color and some formality to this otherwise black and forbidding coastline. The resort has three separate multistory buildings that face the water and one that looks inland for mountain views. These buildings surround a large courtyard swimming pool with a long and twisting water slide. Comfortable, with good views, all rooms and public areas have been totally redone and all amenities are new, but don't appear as new as some of the resorts on the Kohala Coast. Amenities includes the Keiki Club children's program, a business center, fitness center, tennis courts, basketball court, the full-service Ho'ola Spa, a large convention center, and a *lu'au* and Polynesian show that's held on the lawn twice a week. As a destination resort, the Sheraton prepares food and drink at the finedining Restaurant Kai, the poolside and very casual Manta Ray Bar and Grill, the more stylish Crystal Blue Lounge, and the ground-level Cafe Hahalua. The Kona Coast is known for manta rays, and the resort shines a light on the water each evening hoping to attract the rays as they come to feed on fish. Manta ray viewing is best May–October, even though these sea creatures live along the coast all year long.

The Sheraton is a real winner, the only fivestar hotel in the Keauhou-Kailua strip, and it intends to lure visitors looking for luxury at a less-than-luxury price. The prices here are extremely reasonable, which attracts a lot of local families and those on a budget. The pool area is gorgeous. There are two pools—one overlooks the ocean—but there isn't access to the beach directly from the hotel. There are a lot of kids here so the pool area tends to be loud with lots of little ones running around. The manta ray viewing from the bar is excellent and a must-see. The location is near the Keauhou shopping area, including a grocery store and movie theater, and it's about a 15-minute drive in one direction to Kailua and in the other direction to Captain Cook.

Over $250
The **Four Seasons Resort, Hualalai at**

Historic Ka'upulehu (100 Ka'upulehu Dr., 888/340-5662, www.fourseasons.com/hualalai, $220–600), opened in late 1996 but recently had a second opening, if you will, after closing briefly after the March 2011 tsunami to repair their torn up landscape. This 243-room AAA Five-Diamond resort is split into 36 low-rise bungalows in four crescent groups that front a half-mile beach. Located in among old lava flows from the Hualalai volcano, 32 of these units have ocean views, while four are located along the 18th green of the accompanying golf course. Authentic Hawaiian art pieces from the late 1700s to the present are displayed throughout the hotel. There is no skimping on space, furnishings, or amenities in any of the rooms or suites. The bathrooms are large as well, and each room looks out onto a private garden, lanai, or patio. If the room is feeling cramped, no worries, you can send the kids (5–12) to the hotel's supervised day care service. For teens (and their parents), Hale Kula is the activity center for indoor games. Hualalai Tennis Club is open for resort guests only. Located adjacent to the tennis courts is the Sports Club and Spa, a full-service facility that offers a variety of instructional classes, a 25-meter lap pool, exercise machines, massage and spa therapies, and sand volleyball and half-court basketball courts. For the duffer, the private Hualalai Golf Club offers 18 holes of challenging play along the ocean for resort guests. Be sure to check out the Cultural Center with its 1,200-gallon reef aquarium just downstairs from the lobby, where you can learn about the surrounding waters, the Ka'upulehu area, and the life and lifestyle of ancient Hawaiians. In addition to the natural lagoons, the resort has both freshwater and saltwater swimming pools set just back from the beach. A water sports kiosk on the beach can fix you up with needed gear or water activities. An exceptional place, this destination resort tends to be a bit more expensive than others of its kind in the area. Rooms run $220–350 per night in the off-season, suites are $600–900 per night. To help keep all the guests fed and happy, the resort has three on-site restaurants and two bars. Four Seasons is known worldwide for luxury and they deliver it here. It is a bit closer to Kailua-Kona and the airport than the other resorts in the area (nice if you want to go out to dinner at night).

CONDOS AND VACATION RENTALS
$100-150

A Castle Resorts and Hotels property, **Kona Bali Kai** (76-6246 Ali'i Dr., Kailua-Kona, 808/329-9381 or 800/367-5004, www.castleresorts.com, $100–300) is a very decent, comfortable place with an indoor swimming pool, activities desk, concierge, and *poke* shop on property. The 154 condos—split between three-floor buildings on the *mauka* and *makai* sides of Ali'i Drive—include studio, one-bedroom, two-bedroom, and three-bedroom units that all contain fully equipped kitchens and cable TV. The *makai* building has an elevator; however, not all rooms are large enough for wheelchairs to navigate. All apartments are individually owned so the decor differs, but most have muted colors and an old tropical feel. Rates run $100–300 depending on the unit size and its view (ocean, partial ocean, or mountain). There are often online specials available, and when booking you have a good chance of getting "upgraded" for no additional charge (e.g., booking a studio and receiving a one-bedroom or magically being given an oceanfront view—although you won't find out until check-in). This place is a sweet deal if you don't mind that it's kind of run-down. If you're traveling with a large group of friends, this is a great place to crash with a bunch of people and still be very close to the action (although one would have to drive or taxi back from the bars of Ali'i Drive).

Not all the condos at **Casa de Emdeko** (75-6082 Ali'i Dr., Kailua-Kona, www.casadeemdeko.org) are up to the Moon Handbook standards—they are individually owned by people off-island, and the quality of the condos in this complex really varies. That said, you can rent worry-free the one-bedroom condos numbered 125 ($135 double, $10 each additional guest) and 327 (starting at $100 a night). If you are interested in the other condos in the complex, I recommend asking for photos or ensuring that they are updated. Rooms have king-size beds, but there are also pull-out sofa beds in the living area. The condos are all stocked with all the beach equipment you'll need. The complex has two pools. Also on the grounds is a sandy beach area and barbecue area where guests tend to mingle. It's best to book directly from the owners, who have numbers and emails listed on the website. Some condos require a three-night minimum stay (10 nights during Ironman and the Christmas season). This place is unbelievably cheap for the area close to downtown Kailua. The only risk is that since the condos in the complex differ so greatly, you can't be sure what you're getting. Do some additional research about the unit before you rent to ensure that the owner hasn't changed and that the unit is still up-to-date. At these prices, it's worth doing the research.

$150-250

Owned and managed by Aston, the one- and two-bedroom suites at **Aston Kona by the Sea** (75-6106 Ali'i Dr., Kailua-Kona, 808/327-2300, www.astonhotels.com, $180–300) have all the amenities one would desire in a home away from home: kitchen, washer/dryer, swimming pool/hot tub, barbecue area, cable TV, wireless Internet in the lobby, and activities desk. A range of rooms are available, and of course you pay extra for the ocean view. You'll also pay extra with an "amenity fee" for Internet, DVD rentals, and in-room coffee. The freebie, however, is that even the one-bedrooms come with pull-out sofa, so they are big enough to sleep up to four people. Some of the rooms are a bit outdated, so take a peek before you commit by requesting an updated room, asking for photos ahead of time, or by asking to see a few rooms before you unpack. It's a good budget option and close enough to downtown Kailua to get there quickly, but not close enough to be able to walk there. The condo staff offers good service that slightly makes up for dirty room complaints, but they can't always fix room issues. Because of their reasonable rates, you must book early. These condos sell out fast during high season.

Sometimes the best vacations are the ones where you can access wireless Internet from the pool. If this is your dream vacation (sometimes it is mine), then check out the one-bedroom condos at **Hale Kona Kai** (75-5870 Kahakai Rd., Kailua-Kona, 800/421-3696, www.halekonakai-hkk.com, $150–195). Almost all are oceanfront, and all come with a small kitchen, cable TV, sofa beds, and lanai—some with better ocean views than others. Shared extras include a nicely sized pool (right on the ocean) and a barbecue area. They are also really proud of their two (not just one) parking lots. Like many other vacation condo rentals, each unit is individually owned, so the decor and datedness of furniture (as well as TVs and kitchen appliances) tends to vary. Look at the pictures of the units on the website before you decide which one to rent. Many condos require a three-night minimum. The location sets you close to the downtown area—even close enough to walk for those who don't mind a bit of a stroll. The price is definitely right for a rental in the area, but if you think you'll spend a lot of time in the room, I'd rent elsewhere.

Sometimes the best way to experience the ocean is from way above it. If this sounds about right to you, come stay at **Silver Oaks Ranch** (808/325-2000, www.silveroaksranch. com, $125–200). Although this property is not in the standard tourist area of Kona, it's really only 10 minutes from downtown and quite close to the airport. There are two types of rentals here: the Ranch House Cottages ($200), with a large bedroom, kitchen, TV, washer/dryer, and wireless Internet, and the Garden Cottage ($125), which has the same amenities except it only has a kitchenette. While this rental sounds pretty standard, it is the hosts—and the added touches that they bring—that set it apart. For instance, they offer you a laptop computer for the wireless (if you forgot to bring all your devices), stock the fridge, provide beach equipment, and offer you advice about things to do in the area. This is a farm, so there are also tons of animals around. A five-night minimum stay is required. This place is the best of both worlds—the privacy of a vacation rental with the concierge service of a hotel. Also, it's close to the hustle and bustle of Kona, but just far enough away to get some space from the touristy area.

At the **Holua Resort at Mauna Loa Village** (78-7190 Kaleiopapa St., Keauhou, 808/324-1550, www.shellhospitality.com, $150–250), each condo cluster (made up of about eight units) has its own small pool and hot tub, so the pool is never too crowded and you can always get a lounge chair. One- and two-bedroom condos are available, with a pull-out sleeper sofa, kitchen, large cable TV, and carpet that is new and (very) brightly colored. The parking is covered, there is lots of it, and it's near to the unit. There is a very helpful staff and activities desk that can help you book activities and set you up with tennis lessons and tee times. Keauhou shopping is nearby for quick trips to the grocery store and to see a movie. Holua Resort is best suited for couples and families. Many of the guests are involved with Shell hospitality's time share program, but you don't have to be to stay here. Note: Sometimes the web search for availability doesn't work well; if you're getting no availability, then I suggest you call them directly to check.

CAMPING

You will see the sign for **Ho'okena Beach Park** (Hwy. 11 near mile marker 101) on the ocean side of the road. It offers pavilions, restrooms, and picnic tables, but no potable water. For drinking water, a tap is attached to the telephone pole near the beginning of your descent down the spur road. Camping is allowed with a county permit that can be obtained online or starting at 9 A.M. at the beach from the attendant. Even as remote as this is, this is one place where you'll get your permit checked in the evening—be sure to have one. Note: The area is popular with locals and can get crowded and rowdy at night, so it might not be the best place if you're camping with kids or looking for a very peaceful evening.

Likewise, the **Miloli'i Beach Park** (Hwy. 11 near mile marker 55) is a favorite with local people on the weekends; camping is allowed by permit. Tents are pitched in and around the parking lot, just under the ironwoods at road's end. There are flush toilets, a basketball court, and a brackish pond in which to rinse.

Kohala

I want to expand your thinking of what it means to stay in Kohala. It doesn't have to mean staying at a large chain resort—although it can mean that, if that's what you want. Here is where you'll find the big hotels, the ones with a few hundred rooms and lots of staff. However, Kohala also is where you'll find updated vacation rentals (a great deal for large families staying together) and a few new players: boutique-like rentals and retreat centers. So when you think of Kohala don't just think about the Waikoloa and Mauna Launi resort areas; also consider looking at places near Hawi on the northwest tip of the island. No matter where you stay in Kohala, this district is how you imagined your Hawaii vacation: first-rate beaches near first-rate restaurants.

HOTELS AND RESORTS
$150-250

On a perfect spot fronting the palm-fringed 'Anaeho'omalu Bay (A Bay), **Waikoloa Beach Marriott Resort and Spa** (69-275 Waikoloa Beach Dr., Waikoloa, 808/886-6789, www.marriotthawaii.com, $150–350) looks out over ponds that once stocked fish for passing *ali'i*. The hotel lobby is a spacious open-air affair that lets the trade winds blow through across its cool sandstone floor. Six floors of rooms extend out in wings on both sides, flanking the landscaped courtyard with swimming pool and water slide. Greeting you as you enter the lobby is a marvelous old koa outrigger canoe set in front of a three-part mural by renowned Hawaiian artist Herb Kane of a royal canoe and Western frigate meeting off the Kona Coast. All 555 hotel rooms and suites are tastefully decorated in light soothing colors, with king-size beds, rattan furnishings, custom quilts, and island prints of a mid-20th century art deco style. Each room has air-conditioning, color TV, high-speed Internet access (with a fee), *yakuta* robes, in-room safe, small refrigerator, marble vanities, and a private lanai. Rooms are reasonably priced with online discounts (dropping the price to $159 at low season); however, it seems like most of the guests are there to use their Marriott points. Hotel services and amenities include an activities desk for all on-site and off-property excursions and several retail shops and boutiques. You can take part in daily Hawaiian cultural programs, use the business center, or have your kids properly cared for at the Waikoloa Keiki Club children's program. Enjoy the garden swimming pool/hot tubs, spa and fitness center, six Plexi-pave tennis courts, and a grand beach with plenty of water activities. The hotel is just a few minutes' stroll past the royal fishponds to the beach or to the remains of a nearby ancient but now restored *heiau*. For a self-guided walk through the historical, cultural, and natural points of note from the hotel property down to the beach, pick up a copy of *A Walking Tour of Our Hawaiian Treasures* at the guest service desk in the lobby of the hotel. It's a Marriott and the rooms reflect the brand, meaning they are nice but small and all the same. The service at the hotel is probably the worst of all the resorts in the area. There are not enough people working at the front desk and it can be hard to get their attention. The pool area is wonderful (lots of chairs to sit on and the hot tubs are great at night) and you're seconds from a great beach that offers all kinds of water activities (with a booth set up right there for paddle board, snorkeling, and surfing rentals). The shopping area is just a three-minute walk away—giving you easy access to restaurants and the grocery store if you don't want to eat at the overpriced restaurants at the hotel. This is a good hotel to stay at if you have Marriott points or get a good deal. Otherwise, I'd try another nearby chain resort for better service.

At the **Hilton Waikoloa Village** (425 Waikoloa Beach Dr., Waikoloa, 808/886-1234 or 800/445-8667, www.hiltonwaikoloavillage. com, $200–315), the idea was to create a reality so beautiful and naturally harmonious that anyone who came here would be guaranteed a glimpse of paradise. The three main towers, each enclosing a miniature botanical garden, are spread over the grounds almost a mile apart and are linked by pink flagstone walkways, canals navigated by hotel launches, and a quiet, space-age tram. The museum promenade displays choice artwork from Hawaii, Oceania, and Asia—pick up a brochure from the sundries shops at the hotel explaining this $7 million collection or choose one of the twice-weekly art tours—and here and there around the property are brilliant artistic flourishes. The beach fronting the property offers excellent snorkeling, while two gigantic pools and a series of lagoons are perfect for water activities and sunbathing. You can swim in a private lagoon accompanied by reef fish, help feed the dolphins, dine at any one of the nine first-rate restaurants, take in the extravagant dinner show of the twice-weekly Legends of the Pacific *lu'au,* relax to a soothing massage after a game of tennis at the Kohala Sports Club and Spa, leave your kids for the day in the experienced hands of the Camp Menehune staff, participate in a plethora of other daily activities, or just let your cares slip away as you lounge in perfect tranquility.

This resort is definitely a distinctive undertaking, a step apart from any other resort complex in the state. Yet with all the grandeur, beauty, and expansiveness, somehow it seems a bit overblown and incongruous with its surroundings. Forget intimacy—you don't come here to get away, you come here to participate. With 1,240 rooms (it's like three hotels in one) on a 62-acre property, it's so big that entering the lobby can be like walking into Grand Central Station, and navigating

certain walkways, particularly at dinnertime, is like pushing through throngs at a fair. For all that, the Hilton still offers plenty for everyone, gives you unlimited options for a great vacation, treats families well, and does that at a fair and very competitive price, making a stay at this resort the best bet for many visitors who desire to experience this wonderful Kohala Coast. The Hilton offers a variety of room options. Check out the website for discounts, packages, and special offers, most of which include free breakfast or free *lu'au* or golfing discounts.

The Hilton is a bit of a zoo, with kids everywhere (great for kids, not great for adults who want quiet), boats, and a train going around. There is a popular *lu'au* here, offering traditional dancing (both the show and food are mediocre). Those who come here like that they don't have to leave the resort. The rooms are a bit outdated (they look circa 1980s), but larger than the Marriott's rooms. Cable TV is available, but in-room wireless Internet and parking have an additional fee. If this is the only way you can get to Hawaii (by using your Hilton points or a great discount through their website), then take it. But if you're seeking something with a greater sense of *aloha,* then look elsewhere.

Over $250

Jeanne Sunderland had a vision about this place, and when she happened to come upon it one day (in real life) she knew she had to purchase the land for ◖ **Hawaii Island Retreat at Ahu Pohaku Ho'omaluhia** (250 Maluhia Rd., Kapa'au, 808/889-6336, www. hawaiiislandretreat.com, $195–500). The 50-acre property is fantastic. The nine-bedroom house, built to Jeanne's specifications, looks like a mansion in the Mediterranean. The center courtyard is open with beautiful landscaping, and all rooms ($425–500) have private balconies that overlook either the ocean, valley, or garden. There is a shared library and TV room for guests and wireless Internet available throughout the house. The downstairs has meeting rooms (perfect for a reunion or

KOHALA ACCOMMODATIONS

Name (Location)	Type	Price	Features	Why Go Here	Best Fit For
◪ Aston Shores at Waikoloa (Waikoloa Beach)	condo	$175–300	full kitchen, cable TV, washer/dryer, pool, private lanai, some beach gear	on nicer end of spectrum of nearby condos, spacious, you don't just feel like you're staying in someone's rented condo	families, long-term vacationers
The Fairmont Orchid (Mauna Lani Hotel area)	hotel	$225–500	pool, hot tub, beach, water sport rentals, *lu'au*, fitness center, golf course, tennis courts, well-respected spa	exemplifies class, has one of the best *lu'au* on the island	honeymooners, families, luxury lovers
Hale Ho'okipa (Kapa'au)	vacation rental	$145	kitchen, washer/dryer, cable TV, beach gear	a place to stay if you don't want to feel like a tourist, near some of the island's best restaurants	families (even extended)
Hapuna Beach Prince Hotel (South Kohala)	resort	$300–650	golf, beach and pool, spa, fitness center	lots and lots of golf	golfers, those who want to be near Waimea but still stay close to beach
◪ Hawaii Island Retreat at Ahu Pohaku Ho'omaluhia (near Hawi)	inn	$195–500	shared lounge with DVD library, ocean views, infinity pool, spa, yoga and meditation room	luxury boutique hotel, serves almost entirely local/organic food, personalized spa experience	honeymooners, solace seekers, weddings or reunions
Hilton Waikoloa Village (Waikoloa Beach)	resort	$200–315	cable TV, pools with water slide, penguins and dolphins, several restaurants, *lu'au*	a true mega resort (the kind of place you can park yourself for a week and never leave)	families, resort seekers

Name (Location)	Type	Price	Features	Why Go Here	Best Fit For
◼ Mauna Kea Beach Hotel (Kohala near Waimea junction)	hotel	$325–950	pool, hot tub, beach access, cable TV, restaurant, tennis court, golf course	classy joint with both beach and pool access, easy access to walking trails and golfing	honeymooners, couples
◼ Mauna Lani Bay Hotel and Bungalows (Mauna Lani Hotel area)	hotel	$350–1,500	pool, hot tub, beach, excellent restaurant, cultural events, nearby golf	access to swimmable beach, pool, and nearby shopping with more restaurants	honeymooners, romantics, luxury lovers
Mauna Lani Terrace (Mauna Lani Hotel area)	condo	$350–575	pool, hot tub, kitchen, washer/dryer, golf and beach access very near	inexpensive way to access nearby beach and golf courses	golfers, older couples, long-term vacationers
Outrigger Fairway Villas	condo (Waikoloa Beach)	$190–285	tennis courts, pool, kitchen, private lanai, some beach gear	inexpensive way to stay in an often expensive area, close to shopping and beaches	families, long-term vacationers
◼ Puakea Ranch (near Hawi)	vacation rental	$235–650	cable TV, private pool, state-of-the-art kitchen, complimentary garden produce and fresh eggs, horseback riding, children's play room	beautifully decorated house you'll wish you owned, evokes complete relaxation	couples, families
Waikoloa Beach Marriott Resort and Spa (Waikoloa Beach)	resort	$150–350	cable TV, restaurants, beachfront, pool with water slide, hot tub, *lu'au*	easy access to a great beach, water activities, and nearby shopping	families, those with lots of Marriott points

wedding) and a dining area. Breakfast usually is included with the room rate and changes daily based on what is available from the well-tended garden and orchards. Dinner is available upon request and worth requesting given the new wood-burning oven that they are experimenting with.

In addition to the main house, there is a second option called "Hawaiian Hales," which are really yurts, located down the hill from the house. Each *hale* has accommodation for two (queen-size bed or twin beds) and private toilet. The shower is nearby in the spa locker room, which is equivalent to what you'd find at a five-star hotel. Jeanne was the founder of the Spa Without Walls at the former Ritz Carlton at Mauna Lani (now The Fairmont Orchid) and is well known in the community as a healing arts therapist including traditional Hawaiian massage. Hawaii Island Retreat is probably the closest thing the Big Island has to a boutique hotel. It's as Jeanne describes—"elegant earth-friendly living." There's a two-night minimum stay with a $50 charge for additional persons occupying a room. Large discounts are given for stays of three nights or more, or opt for an all-inclusive package that includes three meals a day and spa treatments. You'll most definitely feel like you're on vacation at Hawaii Island Retreat. The property is great for exploring (through the gardens and cliffs) or for staying in one place and reading, doing yoga (there's a room for this purpose), relaxing at the modern pool (there is no good beach access here for swimming), or experiencing one of many spa treatments from well-trained staff. For those who want five-star service without having to go to a large resort, this is probably the best option on the island. An added bonus is that Hawaii Island Retreat is quite close to the numerous dining options in Hawi.

The **[** **Mauna Kea Beach Hotel** (62-100 Mauna Kea Beach Dr., Kohala Coast, 808/882-7222 or 800/882-6060, www.maunakeabeachhotel.com, $325–950) has set the standard of excellence along Kohala's coast ever since former Hawaii governor William Quinn interested Laurance Rockefeller in the lucrative possibilities of building a luxury hideaway for the rich and famous. Beautiful coastal land was leased from the Parker Ranch, and it opened in 1965. The Mauna Kea was the only one of its kind for a few years, until others saw the possibilities and more luxury hotels were built along this coast. Over the years, the Mauna Kea aged a bit and suffered stiff competition from newer resorts nearby. After an extensive one-year restoration, the Mauna Kea reopened with youthful enthusiasm in December 1995 and shines again as the princess it always was. Class is always class, and the landmark Mauna Kea again receives very high accolades as a fine resort hotel.

The Mauna Kea fronts the beautiful Kauna'oa Beach, one of the best on the island. Million-dollar condos also grace the resort grounds, and hotel guests tend to come back year after year. The hotel itself is an eight-story terraced complex of simple, clean-cut design. The grounds and lobbies showcase more than 1,000 museum-quality art pieces from throughout the Pacific (pick up a brochure from the front desk and take a self-guided tour), and more than a half million plants add greenery and beauty to the surroundings. The award-winning Mauna Kea Golf Course surrounds the grounds, and on a bluff overlooking the water, the 11 courts of the tennis center (plus an additional two by the golf clubhouse) vie for use. Swimmers can use the beach or the round courtyard swimming pool, set just off the small fitness center, and horseback riding is available at the Parker Ranch up in Waimea. A host of daily activities are scheduled, including a twice-weekly stargazing program.

The 310 beautifully appointed rooms, starting at $325, feature an extra-large lanai and specially made wicker furniture. From there, rates rise to $575–675 for beachfront units, and $550–650 for deluxe ocean-view rooms. Numerous packages are available that include breakfast, car rental, and tee times. The rooms are, like the rest of the hotel, the epitome of understated elegance. A television-free resort at its inception, the hotel now has TVs in the rooms as part of the restoration; however, they are beautifully hidden behind a moveable screen on the wall. The Mauna Kea has four restaurants and several lounges, but a resort shuttle operates between here and the Hapuna Beach Prince Hotel, where Mauna Kea guests have signing privileges. It's the resort that has it all. It has a beach with good access for swimming and water sports, a small pool, nearby trails that take you to a secret beach, modern rooms that make you feel as if you're on a secluded beach in Thailand, but with all the amenities for when you want to be connected (TV and wireless Internet). The downside is that the restaurant choices are just mediocre and expensive. You'll likely want to drive somewhere to eat. The good news is that Waimea is only 15–20 minutes away and there are excellent eating options there.

Fronting Hapuna Beach, the aptly named **Hapuna Beach Prince Hotel** (62-100 Kaunaʻoa Dr., Kohala Coast, 808/880-1111, www.hapunabeachprincehotel.com, $300–650) is about one mile down the coast from its sister resort, the Mauna Kea Beach Hotel. These two hotels are separate entities but function as one resort. Long and lean, this AAA Four-Diamond Prince hotel steps down the hillside toward the beach in eight levels. A formal portico fronts the main entryway, through which you have a splendid view of palm trees and the ocean. Lines are simple and decoration subtle. An attempt has been made to simplify and let surrounding nature become part of the whole. As at the Mauna Kea, visitors are not overwhelmed with sensory overload. A free periodic shuttle connects the Hapuna Beach to the Mauna Kea, and all services available at one are open to guests of the other.

Bedrooms are spacious, allowing for king-size beds, and the bathrooms have marble floors. Each of the 350 large and well-appointed rooms has an entertainment center, comfy chairs, and a lanai. Although rooms are air-conditioned, they all have louvered doors, allowing you to keep out the sun while letting breezes flow through. Rates for the 350 guest rooms start at $300 and go up to $650 a night; suites run $1,200. In addition, there is an 8,000-square-foot estate on the property that rents for $7,000 a night. Four restaurants serve a variety of food for all meals during the day, and the lounges stay open for evening drinks.

Recreation options include the links-style Hapuna Golf Course and the hotel's physical fitness center. While the spa/fitness center has weights, its main focus is on dance and yoga with various massage therapies and body treatments also available. Set in the garden below the lobby, the swimming pool is great recreation during the day and reflects the stars at night. Speaking of the stars, four nights a week, the hotel hosts a stargazing program for hotel guests (reservations required, $25), and numerous other activities are scheduled through the week. A few shops whet the appetite of those needing sundries or resort wear. At the Prince Keiki Club at the Hapuna children 5–12 years old can fill their time with fun activities and educational projects. If you love your golf, stay here. Otherwise, stay at the Mauna Kea—it has a nicer beach and a more Zen feel to it than the Hapuna Prince.

As soon as you turn off Highway 19, the entrance road, trimmed in purple bougainvillea, sets the mood for **◖ Mauna Lani Bay Hotel and Bungalows** (68-1400 Mauna Lani Dr., Kohala Coast, 808/885-6622 or 800/367-2323, www.maunalani.com, $350–1500), a 350-room hotel that opened in 1983. A short stroll beyond the central courtyard leads you past the swimming pool and through a virtual botanical garden to a white-sand beach perfect for island relaxation. From here, any number of water sports activities can be arranged. Nearby are convoluted lagoons, and away from the shore you find the Sports and Fitness Club with tennis courts, a lap pool, and weights, the full-service Mauna Lani Spa, and exclusive shops. Jogging and walking trails run throughout and a cave complex and petroglyph field lies right in the middle of the resort complex. Surrounding the hotel is the marvelous Francis Iʻi Brown Golf Course, whose artistically laid-out fairways, greens, and sand traps make it a modern landscape sculpture.

Rooms at the AAA Five-Diamond

award-winning Mauna Lani Bay Hotel run $350 (with AAA discount, $400 without discount) for mountain view to $900 for corner oceanfront, suites $1,000–1,500. Rooms are oversized; the majority come with an ocean view, and each includes a private lanai, cable TV, in-room safe, and all the comforts of home. The very exclusive 4,000-square-foot, two-bedroom bungalows rent for an average of $4,000 a night, but each comes complete with a personal chef, butler, and swimming pool. In addition, one-, two-, and three-bedroom home-like villas go for $650–2,115, three-night minimum required. Weekly rates are available on the villas and bungalows, and there are always many different specials and packages. Guest privileges include complimentary use of snorkeling equipment, Hawaiian cultural classes and activities, hula lessons, complimentary morning coffee, and resort and historical tours. Five restaurants and lounges cater to the culinary needs of resort guests, from quick and casual to classic island fare. The hotel offers the Kids' Club of Mauna Lani for children ages 5–12. While you play, the kids are shepherded through games and activities. One of the favorite evening activities at the hotel, Twilight at Kalahuipua'a, takes place once a month at the Eva Parker Woods cottage. For this free event, Hawaiian musicians, dancers, and storytellers gather to share their cultural talents with community and resort guests. Ask the concierge for particulars and for information about the numerous daily activities.

You feel like you're in good hands here from the minute you walk in and receive a lei, hand towel, and refreshing beverage. This is old Hawaii without trying hard to be old Hawaii. The standard rooms are average size, but the grounds are perfection with a nice pool as well as a swimming beach. It's also a great area to explore, with the historical sights just a few minutes walk away as well as some additional excellent beaches just down the road (some are walkable). For an added bonus, the on-site restaurant, **The Canoe House** offers five-star cuisine and service with excellent sunset views. It's a great place for honeymooners and loving couples of any age.

In a tortured field of coal-black lava made more dramatic by pockets of jade-green lawn rises ivory-white **The Fairmont Orchid** (1 N. Kaniku Dr., Kohala Coast, 808/885-2000 or 800/845-9905, www.fairmont.com/orchid, $225–500). A rolling drive lined with *haku* lei of flowering shrubs entwined with stately palms leads to the open-air porte cochere. Nature, powerful yet soothing, surrounds the hotel in a magnificent free-form pool and trimmed tropical gardens of ferns and flowers. Walls are graced with Hawaiian quilts and excellent artwork on view everywhere; every set of stairs boasts a velvety smooth koa banister carved with the pineapple motif, the Hawaiian symbol of hospitality. The Fairmont Orchid is elegant in a casual European sense, a place to relax in luxury and warm *aloha.*

Located in two six-story wings off the main reception hall, the 539 hotel rooms, each with private lanai and sensational view, are a mixture of kings, doubles, and suites. Done in neutral tones, the stylish and refined rooms feature handcrafted quilts, twice-daily room attendance, an entertainment center, fully stocked honor bar, in-room safe, and spacious marble bathrooms. Room rates begin at $225 for a garden view to $750 for a deluxe oceanfront room. One-bedroom executive suites run $950, and the two magnificent Presidential Suites are, well, very expensive. If you have some extra cash, I highly recommend splurging and staying on the Gold Floor (rooms start at $475), where you are offered complimentary breakfast, pupu, an honor bar, free valet parking, and a personal concierge. Rates run substantially higher during the Christmas and New Year's holiday. Some special packages are available.

In addition to several restaurants and lounges, the hotel offers first-rate guest services, amenities, and activities that include a small shopping mall with everything from sundries to designer boutiques; complimentary shuttle to and from Mauna Lani's famous championship golf courses; golf bag storage; 11 tennis courts (with seven lit for evening play); a fitness center; snorkel equipment; the full-service Spa Without Walls for massage, body treatments, and exercise; an enormous swimming pool, hot tubs, and sun deck; double-hulled canoe sailing; Hawaiian crafts; a property botanical tour; safe deposit boxes; on-property car rental; baby-sitting; the Keiki Aloha instructional day camp program for children 5–12, and much, much more. Note: They offer an "activity pass" that seems like a good deal (free rentals on water equipment for $75 a person per day), but it's not a great deal because there isn't enough equipment to go around so it's actually very difficult to get your hands or feet on anything. The Fairmont has even gone "green," being more environmentally sensitive throughout its facility and grounds. This is a class joint. It's romantic and pretty everywhere. Where other hotels are lacking with service, this hotel almost has too much service, with staff constantly monitoring what guests are doing (a turnoff to guests who like to be left alone). The pool area is lovely and large, but there is only a very small area for beach access. The *lu'au* at the hotel is one of the better ones in the area, but not traditional. It's like Lady Gaga designed it, and thus even if it's not standard, it's really fun to watch. In addition, the food is excellent—probably the best *lu'au* food around (also the most expensive). Overall, the Fairmont chain, per usual, exemplifies luxury and is worth the price you pay for it.

CONDOS AND VACATION RENTALS
$100-150

Surrounded by fruit trees (lemons, limes, avocados, mangos) that you can pick from, **Hale Ho'okipa** (in Kapa'au on the road to Keokea Beach Park, reserve through www.vrbo.com/87130, $145) has a large wraparound lanai with barbecue and great ocean/mountain views. This three-bedroom, 2.5-bath rental sleeps six and is tastefully decorated with island furniture. The property is an excellent space to relax in. Additionally, the kitchen is packed with everything you need to make gourmet meals, washer/dryer, and cable TV. Snorkel gear and beach gear/toys are available

in the garage. A three-night minimum is required and there's a $125 cleaning fee for stays of less than a week. This is a location where tourists often don't think to rent a house. It's a great place to spend a few days—not too far from the nearby beaches and the valley as well as a few minutes drive from nearby Hawi, with its galleries and exceptional restaurants.

$150-250

The attractive three story **Outrigger Fairway Villas** (69-200 Pohakulana Pl., Waikoloa, 808/886-0036 or 800/688-7444, www.outrigger.com, $190–285) is opposite the Kings' Shops. Deluxe two- and three-bedroom units have all top-of-the-line amenities as well as a private pool, exercise center, and guest service center. The two-bedroom with two-bath ($189 during low season) is very reasonably priced (considering the rates of the nearby resorts) and could likely fit 4–6 people as many of the units have convertible sofas. The units themselves are decorated with the standard Hawaii condo furniture (pictures of shells and pink couches). It's nice enough, but nothing special. The rates are good because they have a lot of units even when others are sold out. It's close to the Waikoloa action and walking distance to the beach.

While it looks very similar to a lot of the other condo areas around, **◖ Aston Shores at Waikoloa** (69-1035 Keana Pl., Waikoloa, 808/886-5001, www.astonhotels.com, $175–300) does indeed offer something a bit different. Guests choose from one- and two-bedroom suites or two-bedroom villas. The units, decorated in a much more modern fashion than many of the condos in the area, have well-stocked kitchens, washer/dryers, private lanai, cable TV and Internet, as well as daily maid service. The gated community also offers a swimming pool, hot tub, free tennis courts, fitness center, and outdoor barbecues. The two-bedroom deluxe suite (on average $200) is an excellent deal and is large enough to sleep 4–6 people utilizing the pull-out couch. These condos feel newer than many of the others in the area. Call ahead and request photos of the

ACCOMMODATIONS

unit to make sure that you are getting one that you like (as there is some variation in their decor and size). If you're a traveler who prefers to have a pool close by and to be able to cook some meals, this is the best choice for you.

Over $250

You'll want to stay here forever. There is nothing else, on the Big Island at least, like **Puakea Ranch** (Hwy. 270 near Hawi, http://puakearanch.com, $235–650). It's the Hamptons in Hawaii. The four guest bungalows originally date from the early 1900s and were the homes of plantation workers, cowboys, and their families working the surrounding 2,000 acres. Christie Cash, the owner, who came to the Big Island from the Los Angeles area, recently purchased the property (and the homes) and personally transformed each one into a space that looks like it could be in a magazine. Every single detail of the home is gorgeous, from the linens to the couches to four post beds to the state-of-the-art kitchen. My favorite (if I had to pick just one) is Yoshi's House ($525–630), a two-bedroom house with two bathrooms (one of which is a separate structure with an antique copper tub for two people—the nicest tub you'll ever see). The house sleeps six and has its own private pool. In addition, each house has wireless Internet and phone available since there is no cell phone service here. The house is often used for events from weddings to dinner parties. Also, guests can help themselves to fresh eggs in the morning (yep, just go into the chicken coop) and fresh herbs and produce from the garden. The other houses on the property are equally as nice as Yoshi's, and prices tend to vary depending on the size of the house and the season. A three- to five-night minimum stay is required during high season, and a departure cleaning fee of $200 is applied to every room reservation. At the time of writing this property wasn't in any other guidebooks and was just featured in *Sunset Magazine*. This means that soon enough, it will most likely be very difficult to get a reservation here after word gets out. Be sure to book ahead, and if you have the funds (or family and friends who want to join in), consider a stay at Yoshi's House.

Located just behind the Mauna Lani Bay Hotel and Bungalows is the **Mauna Lani Terrace** (69-1399 Mauna Lani Dr., Kohala Coast, 800/822-4252, www.southkohala.com, $350–575). The complex is spread out across a small pond and offers one- and two-bedroom condos (superior and deluxe) with rates varying depending on size and length of stay (discounts for stays over a week long). All units have a kitchen, washer/dryer, twice weekly maid service, cable and wireless Internet, as well as a lanai overlooking the pond and further out the ocean. There is a pool on-site, a hot tub, and a fitness center. The condos in this complex are managed by different entities, many by South Kohala Management, which receives mixed reviews on their service and quickness in fixing problems with the condo. The condos themselves are average (there are better and there are worse) but have the advantage of having access to the beach at the Mauna Lani resort and some of the amenities in the area (such as a parking pass to the beach club down the road). Stay here if you're looking to get out of the hustle and bustle of the Waikoloa area, but definitely check online reviews for the particular unit that you are renting as they all differ.

CAMPING

If you are looking for the *Lost* experience on the Big Island, **Pololu Valley** (trail starts where Hwy. 270 ends) is it and it's free. Park your car in the lot at the end of the highway (there will be many other cars there catching the spectacular views of the coastline), grab your bathing suit, tent, and some food and water, and hike the one-mile trail to the beach (about 30 minutes down and 45 minutes up). Locals swear that you don't need a permit to stay here. It's not patrolled at night, but no safety issues have ever been reported. Pitch your tent on top of one of the small green hills (many already have fire pits left from previous campers) and it's likely that you will have the place to yourself. There are no facilities, so make sure to bring enough food and water for your visit. Enjoy a nighttime dip in the ocean, but take care because the tide can be rough.

Kapa'a Beach Park (Hwy. 270 near mile marker 16) is five minutes father north. It's primarily for day use and fishing, but it has a pavilion, some barbecue grills, and a restroom—but, again, no potable water. Camping is allowed with a county permit.

Mahukona Beach Park (Hwy. 270 near mile marker 14) offers picnic facilities, including a large but somewhat run-down pavilion and tables, but no drinking water. There are also cold-water showers and restrooms, and electricity is available in the pavilion. Both tent and trailer camping are allowed with a county permit near the parking lot. When you enter, go to the left for the camping area (the snorkeling area is on the right)

At **Hapuna Beach State Recreation Area** (Hwy. 19 near mile marker 69), camping is available in six A-frame screened shelters that rent for $30 resident, $50 nonresident per night and accommodate up to four. Provided are sleeping platforms (you bring your own bedding), electrical outlets, cold-water showers, and toilets in separate comfort stations, plus a shared range and refrigerator in a central pavilion.

🄲 **Spencer Beach Park** (Hwy. 19 near Kawaihae junction) is one of the best camping spots the island has to offer. It provides pavilions, restrooms, cold-water showers, electricity, picnic facilities, and even tennis courts. Day use is free, but tent and trailer camping are by county permit only. Permit or no permit, arrive early as camping spots go quickly, especially on the weekend. This is a great spot for families as the scene is calm and quiet. It's also a great place for solo campers as there is a real camaraderie here among campers.

Ka'u

Ka'u is home to most of the "different" or, let's call them "adventurous," accommodations on the island. The majority of folks who stay here do so for a night on the way to/from Kona and Hawai'i Volcanoes National Park. It can be harder to stay here for longer since there is only a day or two worth of activities to do in Ka'u itself. Given the interesting variety of accommodations in this area, I urge you to consider a stay here—especially since you'll be getting a great deal because rates here are inexpensive compared to the surrounding areas.

HOSTELS
Under $50
Some of us have always dreamt of that road trip we never took in a Volkswagen camper van. You can live half that dream at **Lova Lava Land Eco-Resort** (Hawaiian Ocean View Estates, Ocean View, www.lovalavaland.com, $40 campers, $60 yurt). It's a surreal experience to sleep in a camper van on a lot of lava. Its novelty makes it worth it even if the Volkswagens don't actually run anymore

(their interiors are in great shape, though). Otherwise, the price seems a little steep for a camper and outdoor kitchen with rudimentary bathroom—especially given there is an additional $20 charge for laundry if you don't have your own linens. Nevertheless, check the website to see if they're having a deal. A recent special had the price as low as $15 a night. One of the weirder places to stay on the island, this budget option is a fun experience (for a night at least) for urban dwellers who want to semi-camp. You must book ahead of time to make sure that the property manager is on-site when you arrive and that you receive detailed directions for how to arrive at the property. If you want to save some money, bring your own linens with you.

BED-AND-BREAKFASTS AND INNS
Under $50
As you approach the Tibetan prayer flags hanging outside the **Wood Valley Temple** (Pahala, 808/928-8539, www.nechung.org,

KA'U ACCOMMODATIONS

Name (Location)	Type	Price	Features	Why Go Here	Best Fit For
◩ Kalaekilohana B&B (South Point)	B&B	$249	wine and social hour locally sourced breakfast	one-of-a-kind hosts who are incredibly knowledgeable about the area, beautiful home	honeymooners, couples
Lova Lava Land Eco-Resort (Ocean View)	campers/yurt	$40-60	kitchen	you've always dreamt of spending a night in a VW camper	budget travelers eco-conscious travelers
◩ Pahala Plantation Cottages (Pahala)	vacation rental	$95-200	quiet, a taste of life in the real Hawai'i	old plantation homes that will make you feel like you are in Georgia	budget travelers who like to get off the beaten path, large groups
Sea Mountain at Punalu'u (near Pahala)	vacation rental	$150-220	pool, next to golf course, near Black Sand Beach	Kona-style vacation rentals but on east side of island, great ocean views	families
Wood Valley Temple (Pahala)	inn	$65-85	meditation and yoga available	lovely setting, feels like a retreat, close to Black Sand Beach	Buddhist and budget-conscious free thinkers

ACCOMMODATIONS

You need not be Buddhist to stay at the Wood Valley Temple.

$65–85) you'll feel like you just stepped into Asia. You need not be Buddhist to stay here, but the main reason why someone would stay here is to participate with the temple. The house with the 15 rooms (a mix of singles and doubles) is next to the parking area among the trees. The temperatures here are noticeably cooler than the rest of the area. Guests share a large communal kitchen, bathrooms, and areas for meditation and yoga. Meals are not provided. All require a three-night minimum stay or a $25 surcharge for only one night. Weekly discounts and group rates are available. Definitely call or write to make reservations and get directions. The Wood Valley Property is a beautiful out-of-the-way retreat center. Those who stay here often do so for a long time and negotiate discounts and work exchanges with the temple.

$150-250

Everyone in this area knows the place as the big yellow house on the way to South Point. It's the kind of place that tourists drive by and wonder "who lives there?" Well, you could live (for a few nights at least) at the **⟨ Kalaekilohana Bed and Breakfast** (94-2152 South Point Rd., Na'alehu, 808/939-8052, www.kau-hawaii.com, $249). Everything about Kalaekilohana is inviting, from the innkeepers to the huge porch looking out onto the road to the calming rooms. The innkeepers, Kenny and Kilohana, built the bed-and-breakfast by hand ("it's just a box on top of a box," they shared with me) and really thought about every detail of it and how the environment could be shaped to create the best experiences for guests. The four rooms, all on the second floor (not wheelchair-accessible), have the same exact layout: nicely furnished with just the right furniture that looks brand new and clean. The rooms are without TV (but have wireless Internet), lending to the restful atmosphere of Kalaekilohana. Although it's a bed-and-breakfast, Kalaekilohana is more like a boutique hotel or resort given the kind of attention given to the guests. There is a nightly wine hour (followed by chatting on the porch), dinner and tours can be arranged upon request, and Kilohana, a master artist, offers lei making, feather, and weaving classes to guests for

© ANNE FARAHI

© OLIVIER KONING

Kalaekilohana Bed and Breakfast is located just minutes away from South Point and the Green Sand Beach.

$45 for three hours. In addition, locavores will delight in the delectable breakfast made from their garden produce and that of nearby farmers—and the leftovers are composted! Also, they can accommodate food allergies. For a deal, book Kalaekilohana with **Wainuahea Bed and Breakfast** on the Hamakua Coast as part of the "north-south" package deal being offered to get tourists to think of the island in north-south terms instead of the traditional "Kona-Hilo" (east-west) ones. This is one of the top five bed-and-breakfast spots on the island. It is a place that is a destination in itself, so it's worth spending a night or two here just to experience the hospitality of Kenny and Kilohana, who have made their own audio tour of the area that they give out to guests!

CONDOS AND VACATION RENTALS
$100-150

When the sugar mill closed, many people left Pahala and the surrounding area. The town slumped but never disappeared. It has hung on and has slowly managed to infuse life back into itself. Recently, travelers have started to discover what a peaceful area of the island this is and what a fine example Pahala is of a former plantation community. To cater to the traveling public and to provide accommodations for those visiting the volcano, **(Pahala Plantation Cottages** (Pahala, 808/928-9811, www.pahala-hawaii.com, $95–750) offers a number of vacation rental accommodations in town, including the renovated seven-bedroom, four-bath plantation manager's house, which rents for $750 a night or $4,950 a week; it can sleep 14 or so people. The house, which looks like it could be outside Atlanta, Georgia, once really did function as the home of the plantation manager. It has a huge dining room, living room, sitting room, and library, a fully functional kitchen, broad wraparound lanai, a large yard with banyan trees, and wireless Internet. It's perfect for functions, group events, meetings, reunions, seminars, and weddings. A cook can be arranged upon request. The house is filled with relics (old records, books, pictures) and tattered furniture—but it all somehow fits the feel of the house.

Other nearby renovated and spacious one- to four-bedroom plantation cottages, with their original wooden floors and high ceilings, period pieces, and antiques, run $95–225 a night and are sizable enough for a family. As each has a full kitchen, no meals are provided, and some amenities include laundry facilities, cable television, VCRs, and computer access. The renovation of these plantation homes has been the work of Julie Neal and friends, who are very well connected in the area (in fact, Julie runs the local paper and blog in town).

$150-250

Sea Mountain at Punalu'u (Hwy. 11 between mile markers 56 and 57, Pahala, 808/928-6200, www.villaresorts.com/smount.htm, $150–220) is a time-share condominium that also rents available units to the general public on a nightly basis when available. Options include studio, one-bedroom, and two-bedroom units at $150–250, depending on the time of year. Because it's not in a tourist location, Sea Mountain can offer secluded accommodations for reasonable prices. Your condo unit will be a low-rise, Polynesian-inspired bungalow with a steep shake roof. The standard units, all tastefully furnished, offer TVs, full kitchens, full baths, ceiling fans, and a lanai. The resort itself has a small swimming pool and spa pool, laundry facilities, four unlit tennis courts, and a golf course. Although the units vary, all are furnished in an island theme, typically with rattan couches and easy chairs. The feeling throughout the well-tended resort is a

friendly, home-away-from-home atmosphere. Outside your door are the resort's fairways and greens, backdropped by the spectacular coast. The condos are nice, similar to many of the older ones on the Kona side but at a much better price. The pool area is small and well attended by guests, who interact with one another and barbecue together at night. If you're a golfer, the location next to the course is ideal. That said, you're not near anything. Hawai'i Volcanoes National Park is about a 25-minute drive to the north.

CAMPING

Three miles north of Na'alehu is **Whittington Beach Park** (Hwy. 11 near mile marker 60), with full amenities and camping with county permit, but no drinking water. This park is fairly quiet during the day except for locals and tourists who stop by to picnic (it's so quiet because it's not a good place to swim). If you're looking for some solitude this is a perfect camping spot as you'll likely be the only one around.

Punalu'u Beach Park (Hwy. 11 near mile marker 56) is a county park with full amenities and is famous for its black-sand beach and turtles. Here you'll find a pavilion, bathrooms, showers, drinking water, telephone, and open camping area (permit required). During the day there are plenty of tourists around, but at night the beach park empties, and you virtually have it to yourself unless there is a family reunion going. If this is the case, head to the left side of the beach (away from the pavilions) to camp and you'll find some peace and quiet.

Hawai'i Volcanoes National Park and Volcano Village

There are a great number of accommodations in and around Volcano Village. While most are near the heart of the village, several are located in the fern forests south of the highway and a few are located around the golf course about two miles west of town. Most are bed-and-breakfasts, some are vacation homes where you take care of your own meals, and there is one hostel. These places run from budget and homey to luxurious and elegant, but most are moderate in price and amenities. Some of these establishments also act as agents for other rental homes in the area, so your choices are many. Note: The weather in Volcano is substantially colder than the rest of the island. Don't look for rooms with air-conditioning; instead make sure they have warm blankets. In addition, please check if bed-and-breakfasts actually serve hot breakfast. It is very difficult for establishments in Volcano to become certified kitchens (it has to do with the fact there is no county water here), so the majority of B&Bs don't really serve breakfast but simply provide muffins.

HOSTELS
Under $50
Your only option for staying somewhere inexpensive and not camping is **Holo Holo In** (19-4036 Kalani Honua Rd., Volcano, 808/967-7950 www.volcanohostel.com, private rooms $56–71, dorms $22). The most important thing to know about this hostel is that due to their cleaning schedule, there is daily lockout 11 A.M.–4:30 P.M. This means that you can't access the place at all during this time. This might not be ideal for someone who likes to stop back in during the day and take a break, but perhaps it's not a problem for those who plan on hiking all day and really just need somewhere to crash with a hot shower and free wireless Internet throughout. Nevertheless, the daily lockout is also a plus because it means that the owners are committed to maintaining cleanliness at Holo Holo. Dorm beds are available ($22), as are private rooms with bath

($71) or with shared bathroom ($56). Other communal spaces include a comfortable lounge area with books, computer, television, and couches as well as a shared kitchen and laundry facilities (a bonus after camping for a few days!). This is excellent inexpensive lodging for the area if you want to go low-budget but not camp. The majority of guests are hikers (of all ages), lending a nice sense of camaraderie. The "In" is located in Volcano Village close to the park, and it's possible to walk from here to the park if you don't have a car (a 30-minute walk). This is a great place to stay the night before heading out or coming back from a big backcountry trip.

BED-AND-BREAKFASTS AND INNS
Over $250
You'll feel like you're in the middle of a secluded rainforest while staying at **C Volcano Village Lodge** (19-4183 Road E, Volcano, 808/985-9500 http://emmaspencerliving.com/volcano-village-lodge, $215–315). This is one of the places that isn't someone's home, but a purposeful luxury getaway. The five rooms are spread out across the property. All are romantically decorated with large beds, sitting areas, and views of the trees surrounding you. When you arrive you'll find a bottle of wine waiting for you as well as supplies to make your own breakfast (store-bought items like yogurt, cereal, and some boiled eggs). Wireless Internet is available and there is a TV (no cable) in each room. They have a library stacked with DVDs and books in the common area. A hot tub is also available. The staff at the lodge can arrange an in-room couples massage and it seems that many take them up on the offer. There's a two-night minimum for stays. Village Lodge has great management and staff very willing to make sure their guests have a memorable stay. The rooms are great for short stays—there is something ethereal about them. But for longer stays you'll want to opt for somewhere with a full kitchen.

HAWAI'I VOLCANOES NATIONAL PARK AND VOLCANO VILLAGE ACCOMMODATIONS

Name (Location)	Type	Price	Features	Why Go Here	Best Fit For
Chalet Kilauea Inn at Volcano (Volcano Village)	hotel	$125–400	hot tub, shared lounge, cable TV	rainforest atmosphere with all the amenities you could want	couples
Holo Holo In	hostel (Volcano Village)	$22–56	hot showers	the only super cheap lodging in this area	budget travelers, those who just need a night to stay before camping
◼ Kilauea Lodge (Volcano Village)	hotel	$170–185	cable TV, excellent restaurant on-site, breakfast included, hot tub	perfect place to warm up on the cold Volcano nights, easy access location	couples, those who want full-service accommodations
Tutu's Place (Volcano Village)	vacation rental	$200	fireplace, full kitchen, cable TV	mix of vacation and hotel stay (associated with Kilauea Lodge)	families, couples
Volcano House (inside Hawai'i Volcanoes National Park)	hotel	$100–230	restaurant on-site, easy access to the national park	you can see the volcano glow from your room	everyone who loves volcanoes
Volcano Places (Volcano Village)	vacation rental	$110–205	cable TV, kitchen	cabin-in-the-woods feel, friendly management	couples
◼ Volcano Rainforest Retreat (Volcano Village)	vacation rental	$110–260	full kitchen, Japanese-style *ofuro* tubs	well-managed cozy rentals that offer a rainforest setting	families, couples, laid-back honeymooners
◼ Volcano Teapot Cottage (Volcano Village)	vacation rental	$195	antique gas fireplace, hot tub, TV, stocked kitchen	it's like staying in a fairy tale	couples
◼ Volcano Village Lodge (Volcano Village)	inn	$215–315	hot tub in secluded rainforest setting, shared library, TV with DVD player	embodies romance, good service	honeymooners

ACCOMMODATIONS

HOTELS AND RESORTS
$150-250

◖ **Kilauea Lodge** (19-3948 Old Volcano Rd., Volcano, 808/967-7366, www.kilauealodge. com, $170–185), owned and operated by Lorna and Albert Jeyte, is the premier restaurant and lodge atop Volcano, as well as one of the very best on the island. The solid stone and timber structure was built in 1938 as a YMCA camp and functioned as such until 1962, when it became a "mom and pop operation." It faded into the ferns until Lorna and Albert revitalized it in 1987, opening in 1988. The lodge is a classic, with a vaulted, open-beamed ceiling. A warm and cozy "international fireplace" dating from the days of the YMCA camp is embedded with stones and plaques from all over the world. Assorted rooms, ranging $170–185 and including a complete breakfast for all guests in the restaurant, are located in three adjacent buildings on the property, and there is a hot tub for guests in the rear garden. The brooding rooms of Hale Maluna, the original guesthouse section, were transformed into bright, cozy, and romantic suites. Each room has a bathroom with vaulted 18-foot ceilings and a skylight, a working fireplace, queen-size or twin beds, and swivel rocking chair. A separate one-bedroom cottage, set in the ferns to the side, features a gas fireplace (central heat, too), a queen-size bed, private bath, and small living room with queen-size pull-out sofa. All rooms in this building are spacious, with vaulted ceilings and tastefully furnished with wicker furniture, white curtains, and fluffy quilts to keep off the evening chill. Many are hung with original artwork by Gwendolyn O'Connor. One downstairs room is wheelchair-accessible. Each room has wireless Internet and cable TV. It's the kind of place you expect to be staying at when at a national park (although it's not located in the park itself). The main lodge building is the essence of rustic (think dead animals hanging around), with a fireplace that you will crave on the cold Volcano nights. Since this is one of few restaurants in the area, it's also a place where you'll feel constantly in the action as both visitors and locals come here in the evenings to eat and lounge around.

Peeking from the *hapu'u* fern forest in a manicured glen is **Chalet Kilauea Inn at Volcano** (19-4178 Wright Rd., Volcano, 808/967-7786 or 800/937-7786, www.volcano-hawaii.com, $125–400). Downstairs there's an outdoor lounge area, and a black-and-white checkerboard dining room where wrought-iron tables sit before a huge picture window. A three-course candlelight breakfast is served here every morning (for $6–12 to the chagrin of the clientele). Enter the second level of the main house to find a guest living room where you can while away the hours playing chess, listening to a large collection of CDs, or gazing from the wraparound windows at a treetop view of the surrounding forest, ferns, and impeccable grounds. Beyond the koi pond in the garden, a freestanding gazebo houses an eight-person hot tub available 24 hours a day. The main house, called The Inn at Volcano, is known for elegance and luxury. It holds four suites and two theme rooms, including the Jade Room, Out of Africa Room, Continental Lace Suite, and the Treehouse Suite. An adjacent "cabin" is the Hapu'u Suite. It has a fireplace in the cozy living room, but perhaps its best feature is the master bathroom, which looks out onto the back garden. The best room at the inn is the Treehouse Suite, which is two floors with a huge bed and tub for two. The other rooms at the inn are smaller and noise seems to travel easily between them. Rooms all have wireless Internet and cable TV (and some even have cable TV in the bathroom).

The Chalet Kilauea collection is trying to rebrand itself. The Inn at Volcano, even though advertised as a boutique hotel, is closer to a vacation rental. The staff aren't really around (except for breakfast and cleaning times). And that's fine, if you know that's what you're getting.

Chalet Kilauea also has many other accommodations in Volcano Village. **Lokahi Lodge** has four rooms that run $125–185, or rent the entire property for a group of up to 14 people. For those on a tighter budget, the **Volcano Hale** rents rooms for $65–90 and still has plenty of common space. The entire house can be rented and can sleep 13. In addition, several vacation homes dotted here and there about town in the secluded privacy of the forest are available for $375–775. Whatever your price range and whatever your needs, Chalet Kilauea will have something for you, and breakfast is an option at most accommodations.

Have you ever dreamed of sleeping with a goddess? Well, you can cuddle up with Pele by staying at **Volcano House** (inside Hawai'i Volcanoes National Park, www.volcanohouse-hotel.com, $100–230). *Note: This property is currently closed but scheduled to reopen in late 2012.* If your plans don't include an overnight stop, go in for a look. Sometimes this is impossible, because not only do tour buses from the Big Island disgorge here, but tour groups are flown in from Honolulu as well. A stop at the lounge provides refreshments and a tremendous view of the crater. Volcano House still has the feel of a country inn. This particular building dates from the 1940s, but the site has remained the same since a grass hut was perched on the rim of the crater by a sugar planter in 1846. He charged $1 a night for lodging. A steady stream of notable visitors has come ever since: almost all of Hawaii's kings and queens dating from the middle of the 19th century, as well as royalty from Europe. Mark Twain was a guest, followed by Franklin Roosevelt. Most recently, a contingent of astronauts lodged here and used the crater floor to prepare for walking on the moon. In 1866 a larger grass hut replaced the first, and in 1877 a wooden hotel was built. It is now the Volcano Art Center and has been moved just across the road. In 1885, an expansion added 14 rooms and the dining room, and 35 more rooms were constructed in the mid-1920s. An accident caused the hotel to burn down in 1940, but it was rebuilt the next year as the main building that stands today. Currently the hotel is managed by the National Park Service.

In 2010 the hotel closed for renovations to ensure that it was secure in case of an earthquake. The renovations have taken almost a year longer than planned, but it is expected that when the hotel reopens it will be even better than it was before, with some much needed updates to its decor and general facilities. It wasn't the nicest place to stay in Volcano, but it was well worth it for the view. You could see the glow of the crater from the window—how cool is that! When it does reopen, the anticipated upgrades to the restaurant and rooms will surely put this hotel in high demand.

CONDOS AND VACATION RENTALS
$150-250

Just up the road from the Kilauea Lodge (but managed by it) is a cute little two-bedroom cottage, **Tutu's Place** (808/967-7366, www.kilauealodge.com, $200). Built in 1929 by Uncle Billy of hotel chain fame for "Tutu" (Grandma), it was bought several decades later by the Warner family. Mr. Warner was a minister and was involved in Hawaiian politics. His wife, Ruth Warner, lived in the cottage for 30 years until it was bought in 1995 by Lorna Larson-Jeyte, the owner of the Kilauea Lodge, who used to visit as a child. Although it's been completely refurbished, people in the know say that the cottage is still imbued with the spirit of Ruth Warner. This two-bedroom house, done in a theme of rattan and koa, has a fireplace in the living room, a full kitchen, and a wonderful little bathroom. For a small place, it has a surprisingly roomy feel. Wireless Internet and cable TV are available. Rate is based on double occupancy and it is $20 for each additional person. Full breakfast at the lodge is included with room rate. It's a mix of a vacation rental and hotel stay. Great for someone who wants the added convenience of a breakfast at the lodge and the availability of the staff at the lodge for assistance.

Embraced within the arms of ferns, *'ohi'a,* and bamboo are the three cottages of **◖ Volcano Rainforest Retreat** (11-3832 12th St., Volcano, 808/985-8696, www.volcanoretreat.com, $110–260), a luxury accommodation for discriminating guests wanting privacy for their stay in the rainforest. Constructed in an open style of cedar and redwood, these handcrafted buildings are warm and welcoming, rich in color and detail, and have plenty of windows that look out onto the encircling forest. Hale Kipa (Guest Cottage, $185–200) has a cozy living room with full kitchen and sleeping loft, perfect for a couple or small family. The six-sided Hale Hoʻano (Sanctuary House, $110–140), the smallest and with the most obvious Japanese influence, has the benefit of an outdoor *ofuro* tub and shower, and is conducive to meditation and spiritual enrichment. The octagonal Hale Nahele (Forest House, $155–170) is one large room with an attached full bath, efficiency kitchen and sitting area, and covered lanai—just right for a cozy couple. Each has a small heater for those rare chilly nights. Rates are discounted for three nights or longer, and some of the rooms have a $20 charge for stays of just one night. The newest addition is the cedar-shingle Bamboo Guest House at $245–260 a night. This exquisite one-bedroom vacation rental has a full kitchen and dining area, sitting room under clerestory windows, and a relaxing bath with outdoor *ofuro* tub. All units are stocked with breakfast foods to have at your leisure and have wireless Internet. This vacation rental is well managed and well designed. Like all the other so-called "bed-and-breakfasts" in the area, it offers store-bought muffins and bagels. The rooms are close to town and the park, and overall it's a perfect place to spend your time while exploring the park. The word "sanctuary" gets thrown around a lot when talking about this place, and that praise indeed is deserved. An excellent choice for honeymooners.

For a one-stop vacation rental shop check out **Volcano Places** (808/967-7990, www.volcanoplaces.com, $110–205). The properties range from studios to two bedrooms and have a very "cabin in the woods" feel to them. There is nothing luxurious here, just comfortable places to stay like you were going for a visit to a family member's home (and they cleaned up real good before you got there). There are four rentals available. The top-rated Nohea ($205–240) is a one-bedroom cottage with high ceilings that can fit three adults (but really it is for a couple). The cottage has a nicely sized kitchen, living area, wireless Internet, and cable TV. It

backs up to a state forest that you can sit and enjoy from your private lanai. The best way to describe this place is that it is warm. Just the place you want to return to after a long day at the park. For all rentals, discounts are given for stays longer than three days. Rates are for double occupancy plus $15 per guest for each additional guest. Kathryn, the owner, receives rave reviews for her friendliness and spotless accommodations. There are no hidden surprises when you stay here. The website pictures are true to form. The rentals are all close to town and close to the park and you'll be well tended to if you stay at one of Kathryn's volcano places.

This place gets booked so quickly that by the time you finish reading this sentence it's probably already booked for the dates that you want. That's how good ◀ **Volcano Teapot Cottage** (19-4041 Kilauea Rd., Volcano, 808/967-7112, www.volcanoteapot.com, $195) is. Why so much in demand, you must be wondering? The service is great and the place is really charming. Bill and Antoinette Bullough pay attention to details and pay attention to their guests. Originally built in the early 1900s by a Hilo businessman, the cottage is two bedrooms and one bath filled with antiques and a gas fireplace. Even though the cottage is two bedrooms, the owners really only like two people in it (you'll have to negotiate for a third). Mixed with the historical elements of the house are wireless Internet, a TV with DVD player, and a hot tub situated in the lush landscape behind the house. A two-night minimum stay is required. Breakfast items are stocked daily in the kitchen. It's fun here because it's like a fairy tale and something different. It's cozy but has all the modern amenities that you'd want, including easy access to the park. Sheer perfection.

CAMPING

The main campground in Volcanoes, **Namakani Paio,** clearly marked off Highway 11, is situated in a stately eucalyptus grove. There is no charge for tent camping and no reservations are required. It's first-come, first-served. There are cooking grills by each campsite, but no wood or drinking water is provided. While there are toilets, there are no shower facilities for those camping and hiking within the park, so make sure you're with people who like you a whole bunch. On-site there are 10 small **cabins** available through Volcano House. They are currently undergoing renovations and are slated to open sometime during 2012. When they do open, each cabin will contain one double bed and two single bunk beds. A picnic table and barbecue grill are outside, but you must provide your own charcoal and cooking utensils. There is a half-mile hiking trail from the campground entrance to the Thomas A. Jaggar Museum.

There are also camping spaces and restrooms at **Kulanaokuaiki,** halfway down Hilina Pali Road. As at Namakani Paio, these are on a first-come, first-served basis. No reservations are required and no fee is charged. As it sits in the middle of this arid desert, it's hot, dry, and has little shade. No drinking water is provided.

For backcountry overnight camping, apply at the Kilauea Visitor Center (7:45 A.M.–4:45 P.M.) for a free permit no earlier than the day before you plan to hike. Camping is permitted only in established sites and at trail shelters. No open fires are permitted. Carry all the drinking water you will need, and carry out all that you take in.

Puna

This is where to come to get away from it all—well, at least from cell phones (reception here essentially is nonexistent). This area sees fewer tourists than other areas of the island, meaning that room rates are substantially lower. There are no big resorts, only bed-and-breakfasts and retreat centers. Everything is very close to the ocean although nothing is right on the ocean on this coast. Visitors to this area tend to stay a few nights and spend their time relaxing, doing yoga, and snorkeling in some of the best spots on the island. With several nearby restaurants, it's a wonder why more people don't stay in this area.

BED-AND-BREAKFASTS AND INNS
$100-150

《 Art and Orchids (16-1504 39th Ave., Keaʻau, 808/982-8197, www.artandorchids.com, $95–130) at first glance does not seem to have the best location—in the in-between community of Orchidland not that close to any main attractions. However, it is actually the perfect base to explore Hawaiʻi Volcanoes National Park, Hilo, and the south Puna area as this establishment is in the middle of all three. The residence is an unexpected delight. The owners, Markie and Jerry, are artists themselves (and so much more), and the rooms are adorned

with works of local artists, mosaics designed by Markie, and of course orchids. Due to the artsy nature of the place, they tend to attract guests who are looking to *talk story* about art and nature (many tend to be from the San Francisco Bay Area) and aren't too bothered by the immense number of potholes on the road to their house. Cell phone service is patchy here, but there is wireless Internet, dish TV, as well as a hot tub and a beautiful (underused by guests) pool with an artificial waterfall. Families are welcome and the garden room ($130 for double occupancy), which is huge, can sleep up to four (there is a bed and futon) and is wheelchair accessible, although the bathroom is not ADA approved. Guests in the two upstairs rooms ($95 and $110 for double occupancy) have a shared living room space (not part of the family's residence) with kitchen, library, and small gift shop of art. Breakfast is served as a buffet on the upstairs lanai, and they are able to accommodate food allergies. Some guests are thrown off by the bad road to Art and Orchids. Well, that's residential Hawaiʻi for you. Art and Orchids is probably one of the most undervalued bed-and-breakfast spots on the island. The rooms are well lit (Jerry is a talented electrician) and the artistic details all over the house are fantastic. This is a great place to come with kids

ACCOMMODATIONS

PUNA ACCOMMODATIONS

Name (Location)	Type	Price	Features	Why Go Here	Best Fit For
◪ Art and Orchids (Kea'au)	B&B	$95-130	pool, hot tub, dish TV	rooms decorated wonderfully with mosaics, location central to several regions of the island	artsy types, families
Dolphin Bay House (Paradise Park near Pahoa)	vacation rental	$140-150	cable TV, residential neighborhood	splendid ocean view, near to jogging path	families who are familiar with the island
Hale Makamae B&B (Leilani Estates near Pahoa)	B&B	$100-155	apartment-style rooms with small kitchens, hearty breakfast	hosts you'll want to talk story with for a long time	families, budget travelers
◪ Kalani Oceanside Retreat (Red Road area)	hotel	$40-275	pool, hot tub, nudity welcome, best vegetarian-friendly buffet, yoga, activities galore	an all-encompassing life-altering experience	yoga lovers, nudists, trance dance lovers, vegetarians
◪ Ramashala (Red Road area)	hotel/condo	$50-200	hot tub, furniture you wish you owned, state-of-the-art kitchen in some rentals	ocean sounds, drumming from Kehena Beach	young couples, budget travelers, drummers, those who really want to get away from it all
Yoga Oasis (Pahoa)	inn	$45-185	yoga classes, workshops, eco-adventures	cabins in the jungle and "jungalow" tent camping, easy access to south Puna beaches, personal attention of a smaller yoga retreat	yoga lovers, budget-minded free-thinkers

because Markie and Jerry will babysit for an additional fee. For older kids they have great arts and crafts activities to keep them occupied. Perhaps this isn't the best place for a first timer to the island who doesn't know their way around or wants to stay right in the heart of things, but regulars to the island should consider this place as a great base to explore from.

Located in the Leilani Estates subdivision, **Hale Makamae Bed and Breakfast** (13-3315 Makamae St., 808/965-9090, www.bnb-aloha. com, $100–155) can feel a bit like a homestay. Although the guest rooms are separated from the main residence and each room has a private entrance, you still feel as though you are part of their lives because noise travels and there is a lot of interaction with the owners' family (who are lovely and full of great stories). The owners are incredibly friendly and knowledgeable and want to share their experiences and recommendations with guests. The property has wireless Internet but lacks some of the amenities of other bed-and-breakfast establishments (like a hot tub or pool), and cell phones tend not to get service in this area. Two apartment-style rooms, a one-bedroom ($135) and a two-bedroom ($155), are renovated and a good deal, especially the two-bedroom apartment, the only room with a TV, which is ideal for a family. The one-bedroom apartment could be accessible to someone in a wheelchair (there are no stairs). I would skip the studio room option ($100). The breakfast is hearty (fruit, pancakes, and coffee) and they accommodate food allergies. Petra and John have been serving guests for a long time (at hostels around the world) and really love interacting with guests. You'll feel welcomed here and have great conversation, but it's not a place that is superbly relaxing.

The embracing arms of the Puna rainforest surround you as you make your way down the driveway to the quiet and secluded retreat center **Yoga Oasis** (Pohoiki Rd., Pahoa, 808/965-8460 or 800/274-4446, www.yogaoasis.org, $45–185). Set on 26 acres of forest, with plenty of fruit and nut trees and numerous stands of bamboo, this yoga center and alternative accommodation offers yoga retreats, cooking workshops, and eco-adventure tours. While you can come for the accommodations only, the optional morning yoga classes are a treat. The seclusion is perfect for those who just want a little time to themselves, but the location offers easy access to coastal Puna sights and restaurants in Pahoa, and it is close enough to both Hilo and Hawai'i Volcanoes National Park for easy day trips. Private rooms with shared bath in the main building and the very basic cedar cabin run $75 single or $100 double. Tucked into the jungle are the secluded Coconut and Pine cabins with their private bathrooms and showers. These are $125 single or $145 double a night, with a two-night minimum. Tent camping in the meadow (in what they call a "jungalow"), with bathroom and shower use in the main building, is also an option at $45 for one person or $65 for a couple. Room rates include the morning yoga class (8–10 A.M.), and a vegetarian brunch is available for an extra cost. Healthy, homemade vegetarian dinners run $15–20, while massage, cooking classes, eco-tours, and other activities are added features at additional cost. Yoga workshops and classes are held in the screened and vaulted, spring-floor exercise room on the upper level of the main building. Yoga Oasis is a solar-powered facility and there are no televisions or phones in the rooms, but phone lines at the main building are available for telephone and there is free wireless Internet in the rooms. You'll really get a sense of Puna if you stay here (the flow of the Puna life). Compared to Kalani (the most similar accommodation in the area), Yoga Oasis is a much smaller venture—which means there are fewer classes and workshops offered, but more personal attention. If you do book at Yoga Oasis, heed their warning and come during daylight hours as this place is nearly impossible to find at night (take it from a local who spent two hours driving in circles trying to find it).

HOTELS AND RESORTS
$150-250
C **Kalani Oceanside Retreat** (Hwy. 137, Pahoa, 808/965-7828 or 800/800-6886, www.kalani.com, $40–275) is a nonprofit,

international conference and holistic retreat center, a haven where people come when they truly want to step aside for a time. The entrance is a few miles east of Kaimu on Route 137 between mile markers 17 and 18, on the mountain side of the road. Look for a large Visitors Welcome sign and proceed uphill until you see the office and sundries shop. Depending upon the yearly schedule, activities include massage, hula, meditation, yoga, lei-making, *lau hala*-weaving, and hikes, for men, women, couples, and families, gay or straight. The grounds have a botanical atmosphere, with a rain-fed swimming pool (clothing optional), a *watsu* pool, hot tub, whirlpool tub, assembly studios, classrooms, cottages, and cedar lodges with kitchen facilities. Kalani is not an oceanfront property, and only some rooms have an ocean view over the trees. Nightly rates range from $90 a night for a lodge room with a shared bathroom to $275 for an ocean-view cottage. The middle-range rooms are loft spaces or cottages with private bathrooms. You can also camp for $40 a night. Discounts are usually available when accommodation is booked with workshops or with one of the all-inclusive packages, which include meals. A blown conch shell calls you to breakfast at 8 A.M., lunch at noon, and dinner at 6 P.M. (nonguests welcome). The meals cost $11, $12, and $22 respectively, with a meal ticket pre-purchased at the office. Food is served from the buffet line in the open-air dining hall, and fruits and vegetables from the property are used when possible. The generator (and hence the lights) goes off at 11 P.M., but candles are provided for night owls. Kalani is not for everyone, but if you are looking for unpretentious peace and quiet, healthful food, and inner development, this is one place you may find it. If you're not comfortable with nudity, don't come here. That doesn't mean you have to be nude, it just means you must be comfortable with those around you being nude. This place is like camp for adults. Meals are communal and there is a lot of interacting at the pool/hot tub and classes. A great place for travelers looking to spend quality time with like-minded individuals on a similar life path.

CONDOS AND VACATION RENTALS
$100-150

A three-bedroom, two-bath home located in Hawaiian Paradise Park subdivision, **Dolphin Bay House** (Puna, www.vacationrentalpeople. com, reference number 10136, $140–150) is right on the ocean with whales, dolphins, and turtles in sight from the lanai. The house itself isn't the nicest, although it has cable and wireless Internet, but the location makes up for it. It is clean and adequate. The decor is outdated and more like your family's summer vacation home. Yet, perhaps it is worth it to wake up and see the ocean a few steps away, although there is no easy swimming access here. The area does have fine walking/jogging paths through the neighborhood and along the coastline. This neighborhood is very residential and 20 minutes from dining and shopping in Pahoa, 45 minutes from Hilo and Volcano. Stay here if you've got roots on the island or are familiar with the area and how to get around.

It feels like you're on vacation when staying at **C Ramashala** (12-7208 Kalapana-Kapoho Rd./Hwy. 137, 808/965-0068, www. ramashala.com, $50–200). The beautiful tapestries, Indian-looking furniture, and stainless steel appliance kitchen create a tranquil (and romantic) setting. There are six rooms to choose from, but the best one is the Mandala Suite ($150), with king bed, double bed futon, sundeck, and private bath. For a budget option, book one of the rooms with single beds and shared bath ($50–60). There is a hot tub available for guests, and the ocean at Kehena Beach is only 200 yards away (so close in fact that you can hear the drumming from the beach in your room). Yoga classes are available on-site a few mornings a week but not included with the price. This place is so nicely decorated that a rumor got started that it was owned by the Hilton family (it's not true). The Mandala Suite with a full kitchen is huge and is the kind of place that you're happy to come back to at the end of the day. The bad news is that there is a bad wireless Internet connection here, no cell phone service, and no TV, so it's not the right place for someone who wants to stay connected.

CAMPING

You can't miss **Isaac Hale Beach Park** (junction of Rte. 137 and Pohoiki Rd.) on Pohoiki Bay. Amenities include a pavilion, restrooms, and a picnic area; potable water is not available. Camping is permitted with a county permit. Just down the road is **MacKenzie State Recreation Area** (along Rte. 137, two miles south of Pohoiki). Picnic facilities are available, but there is no drinking water. A state permit is required for overnight camping. Locals adamantly are against camping at these spots under the belief that they are haunted (they are located on the old King's Trail). Thus, both spots tend to be vacant at night, contributing to the haunting feeling. If you're keen on camping in Puna, either camp at Isaac Hale or pitch at tent at one of the retreat centers that charge a minimal fee for camping.

Hilo and Around

Lots of visitors come to Hilo for the day but don't want to stay here. "Too much rain!" they say. Well, depends when you come and what time of day it is. Don't come November–March in the afternoon and you'll be fine; however, due to global climate change, the season has been more erratic, with some years completely dry and other years very wet. Regardless, Hilo doesn't have the large resorts like the Kona side has; instead, it has many historical (or dedicated) bed-and-breakfasts with eager innkeepers. All of this for less than you'd pay in the Kona side. There is no reason not to make Hilo your base to explore the island. It is only 45 minutes to Volcano from here, the beginning of the driving on the Hamakua Coast, 45 minutes to Puna, and about an hour to Mauna Kea. And yes, it does have beaches, too. They aren't as large and white-sanded as on the Kona side, but they offer good access for swimming, snorkeling, and surfing. So, if you're looking for a strictly beach vacation (and one right outside your front steps), this might not be the best area to stay in; however, if you know you'll do a lot of exploring, Hilo could be an excellent choice as a base (not to mention you're right next to an airport!).

HOSTELS
Under $50

For budget travelers, **Arnott's Lodge** (98 Apapane Rd., 808/969-7097, www.arnottslodge.com, $25–130) and **Hilo Bay Hostel** (101 Waianuenue Ave., 808/933-2771, www.hawaiihostel.net, $70 private, $25 dorm) are good options in Hilo. Hilo Bay Hostel is downtown, while Arnott's Lodge is out near the beaches east of town. Arnott's recently did away with their dorm-style bunk-bed rooms and now only have a few $25 open-air bunks and six two-person lockable rooms for $30 (single) or $50 (double) with shared bath. A room with private bath that can sleep three is $70, and a two-bedroom suite for up to five people is $130. Aside from lodgings, Arnott's has tenting space ($10 per person) on the lawn and runs wonderful and inexpensive touring excursions. Free wireless Internet is available throughout. Note: No check-in is available after 10 P.M. Hilo Bay Hostel's building is huge and historical (originally a hotel built in 1912) and is similar to a hostel you'd find in Quito or Bogota. There is a shared kitchen (with lots of people around cooking) and free wireless Internet available. It's very close to the bus station and downtown shops. One could possibly get around from here without a car. Stay at one of these places if you're traveling solo—otherwise, it's not that much more expensive for two people to stay at some of the nearby bed-and-breakfasts when splitting the cost. Another reason to stay at one of these places is if you're into the hostel scene and want to meet up with like-minded travelers.

The best of the hostels category is **Hilo Tropical Gardens Guest House** (1477

HILO AREA ACCOMMODATIONS

Name (Location)	Type	Price	Features	Why Go Here	Best Fit For
Arnott's Lodge (Hilo near beach parks)	hostel	$25-130	close to the beach, shared kitchen	organizes outings and adventures	those who want to be reminded of their days backpacking around South America
☑ Hilo Bay Hale (downtown Hilo)	B&B	$119-159	cable TV, stunning bathroom, private lanai	the urban experience of Hawai'i	hip young couples and singles, queer-friendly
Hilo Bay Hostel (downtown Hilo)	hostel	$25-70	historic building, shared kitchen	room types from dorm to private rooms, close to bus station	those who love sharing, solo travelers
Hilo Hawaiian Hotel (Hilo near beach parks)	hotel	$105-300	pool, restaurant, close to beaches and Coconut Island	the only real choice for a standard hotel in Hilo	conference attendees, short-term guest
☑ Hilo Tropical Gardens Guest House (Hilo near beach parks)	hostel	$25-65	steps away from the beach, barbecue area, communal kitchen, convenience store	best of the area's backpacker options, nice camping facilities	older backpacker types looking for privacy but also somewhere to hang out
☑ The Inn at Kulaniapia Falls (greater Hilo)	B&B	$139-225	dish TV, hot tub, massage, waterfall, made-to-order breakfast	more like a boutique hotel than B&B, a waterfall in your backyard	those who want to be close to the city but feel like they are far away, honeymooners
The Old Hawaiian B&B (near downtown Hilo)	B&B	$80-110	fridge and microwave, shared lanai, huge delicious breakfast	best value B&B	budget-minded singles and couples
Orchid Tree B&B (very close to downtown Hilo)	B&B	$149 plus	pool, hot tub, cable TV, shared lanai	best place to stay if you want a pool near the ocean	surfers, families, couples of all ages
☑ Shipman House B&B Inn (very close to downtown Hilo)	B&B	$219-249	historic home full of Hawaiian history, very quiet, outstanding breakfast	one of the most well-known families and houses in Hawai'i	couples, history buffs

Kalaniana'ole Ave., 808/217-2650, www.hilo-gardens.com, camping $15, dorms $25, private $55–65 double). The guest house is a stone's throw from all the beaches of Kalaniana'ole Avenue (the main beach drag of Hilo). The general atmosphere at the guest house is relaxed with lots of backpacker-like folk hanging around playing games and watching TV. Features include a barbecue area, a communal kitchen, and a convenience store in the front of the building (owned by the same family). More importantly, the **Hilo Tropical Café** ice cream shop (home of the homemade Hilo ice cream), also owned by the same family as the guest house, is in front. Between the three true hostel options in the area, this is the best one because of what you get for your money (and that it's closer to the beach). The coolest part of the extensive guest house property is the backyard, which is an amazing tropical garden. This is the area where there are sites set up for camping. If you have a tent with you and want a bit more infrastructure and privacy than what is offered at the county and state parks, I'd camp here. It's peaceful and quiet and has a nearby bathroom, shower, wireless Internet, and TV!

BED-AND-BREAKFASTS AND INNS
$50-100

Overlooking the Wailuku River near the Boiling Pots, **The Old Hawaiian Bed and Breakfast** (1492 Wailuku Dr., Hilo, 808/961-2816, www.thebigislandvacation.com, $80–110) is one of the best values Hawai'i has to offer—especially for low-budget travelers. Stewart and Lory have transformed the back of their house into a three-bedroom bed-and-breakfast, allowing guests to have private entryways to their rooms. The rooms, all with private baths, overlook the large manicured lawn and the river (although you can't really see the river from the room). Rooms are without TV but do have wireless Internet and share a covered lanai with microwave and refrigerator for guest use. Rate for the larger rooms (one of the rooms is smaller) is $110 per night per couple with $10 per night for an extra person.

One-night stays have an additional $15 charge. Children 12 and over are welcome. Lory is a master chef. The breakfast here is so good and huge and she can cook amazing gluten-free pastries as well. For a couple, the breakfast itself would run you about $30 if you were to order it at a local café. Overall, this place is just a fantastic deal. It's near to town and easy to find. If you are traveling with a friend or lover, I'd skip the hostel or other low-budget places and come straight here.

$100-150

It's a slice of Brooklyn in Hilo. Matthew and Danny, the innkeeper and owner of ◖ **Hilo Bay Hale** (301 Ponahawai St., 808/745-5049, www.hilobayhale.com, $119–159), have transformed this traditional plantation-style house into a hipster's Hawaiian dream. The furniture has been carefully selected to create the ambiance of Hawaii in the 1950s. What's so amazing is that nothing looks old or worn here; rather, the rooms are perfectly decorated with just the right amount of reappropriated antiques and artifacts. The house has four rooms, but my favorite is The James Michener (an homage to the famous author, $119–139), with a nonfunctioning record player, queen-size bed, private lanai overlooking a koi pond, and blue tiled bathroom (it's gorgeous) with an amazing tub. The breakfast, served on a lanai off the kitchen, offers large portions of quiches, cereal, yogurt, and bacon. With notice, they can try to accommodate dietary restrictions. Hilo Bay Hale is really one of few "urban" choices for accommodations. And it's so hip. Located just a few minutes' walk up the hill from the farmers market and the downtown shops, this is where you'd want to live if you lived in Hilo. Not to mention that Matthew and Danny are super interesting and enjoyable. Hilo Bay Hale is another place that should be on the radar of budget travelers.

$150-250

◖ **Shipman House Bed and Breakfast Inn** (131 Ka'iulani St., 808/934-8002, www.hilo-hawaii.com, $219–249) is the grandest

© BARBARA ANDERSON

The Victorian-era Shipman House Bed and Breakfast Inn is on both the State and National Registers of Historic Places.

B&B in all Hawaii. This Victorian house is one of the few such grand houses in Hawaii and was once the home of the Shipman family, one of the most prominent Big Island landowners, and now presided over by a Shipman descendant. The main house offers three guest rooms with antique beds, private baths, and stately views through enormous windows. Other guests will lodge in the Cottage, a separate building on the grounds, originally built for the express purpose of accommodating visitors. The Cottage contains two spacious bedrooms, each with queen-size bed, window seats, and private bath. Both rooms have private entrances, ceiling fans, and a small refrigerator. This is strictly a no-smoking establishment and a "no TV zone," and children are not encouraged, as there are so many antiques in the house and a steep ravine outside. Room rates are $219–249 single or double; $25 per extra person, add $25 for a single-night stay. The library is open to guests, along with use of the 1912 Steinway piano whose keys were once tickled by Lili'uokalani, and you can look

around the house on your own in those areas where the doors are open. One evening a week, a hula class is held on the lanai and guests can participate. Breakfast, served 7:45–9 A.M. (earlier upon request, and special diets are accommodated), is an expanded continental with homemade cereals, assorted local fruits (there are 20 varieties of fruit trees on the property), fruit juices, Kona coffee, yogurt, fruit bread, muffins, popovers, or cinnamon rolls.

The Shipman House is on both the State and National Registers of Historic Places. Barbara, the host, is a descendant of the Shipman dynasty and, man, does she have stories to tell. The house is in town, but in a section that was once reserved for the wealthier families (walk around the street—the home designs are really interesting and different than in other parts of Hilo). This is a place where guests are encouraged to interact with one another and the hosts so it's not the best place for privacy. Also, it's very quiet and you can somewhat hear what's happening in other rooms—not enough to interrupt sleep, though. History buffs should stay here and revel in the outstanding antiques that fill the house. Barbara is happy to *talk story* about recipes, hula (she has been practicing for a long time), and all things Hawaii. She is extremely knowledgeable. The rooms are large and white and make you feel like you're staying at your fancy grandmother's house. Definitely a special experience.

Located just minutes from the Honoli'i surfing beach is a small neighborhood scattered with vacation rentals and bed-and-breakfasts because of its proximity to the great ocean views. Within the many choices in the neighborhood, **Orchid Tree Bed and Breakfast** (6 Makakai Pl., 808/961-9678, www.orchidtree.net, $149 plus tax) has an outstanding reputation for consistently offering good service. Steve, the owner and innkeeper of Orchid Tree, is a laid-back surfing guy who wants his guests to relax and have a great time. That's not a hard task here. The house looks small from the front, but the backside has a small swimming pool (very hard to find at B&Bs on the Hilo side), covered hot tub (just asking for a hot tub party), and a great outdoor lanai for guests to use. The Hula Suite is a converted section of the main house that sleeps four ($149 for double occupancy and $15 a night for additional guests). The room is large but awkward since it's obvious that it was converted into a suite from the living room. The second room (also $149 for double occupancy), in a detached space to the left of the house, is a perfect suite for couples. It's light and airy and decorated tastefully. In addition to a huge bed there is a couch, making this room a great place to hang out during the day. Both rooms have cable TV and wireless Internet. Breakfast is served on the lanai (or private balcony of the second room) and includes a funky arrangement of fruits (the design is funky, not the taste) and usually waffles or pancakes. They cannot accommodate food allergies. Orchid Tree is close to town and a really chill place. The best part is how you can hear the ocean from your room (even though it's a street over from the ocean), and if you're a surfer, you're minutes from the best surfing beach this side of the island. Breakfast is fine, but nothing to write home about. But if you're looking for a B&B with a pool, definitely book here.

You'll be surprised that you're anywhere near Hilo when you arrive at **C The Inn at Kulaniapia Falls** (1 Kulaniapia Dr., Hilo, 866/935-6789, www.waterfall.net, $139–225). Just a 10-minute drive from town (and that's because the road can be hard to navigate), this inn is more like a boutique hotel spread out across three properties with the backdrop of a waterfall. Yes, they own a waterfall (lucky). The inn is a great way to be near to Hilo but really feel away from it all. The owners traveled to the Far East to purchase items to furnish the house and the result is a Japanese-style aesthetic—but only partially. Rooms are small with large flat-screen TVs hanging from the wall (almost too large for the room). Cable TV and wireless Internet are available. In addition to the rooms in the two main houses, each of which has its own respective breakfast area for guests with its own staff to prepare the breakfast, there is also a private pagoda ($225 double occupancy) that can sleep up to six people ($25 for each additional guest). Breakfast is not offered but the fridge in the pagoda is stocked for guests to make their own food. This place has a waterfall—'nough said. You do have to sign a waiver to go swimming in the waterfall/pond, but it's a must-do. Try to get a room that faces the waterfall as the rushing water noise is just as soothing as your noise machine (otherwise, rooms face the front of the house away from the waterfall). The bad is that the rooms are clean and hotel-like, but not beautiful or peaceful, and it's a bit of a schlep to get to town—especially at night when the road isn't well lit. But still, even with the negatives, it's a good place to stay for a night or two in order to have easy access to Hilo and its surroundings while still staying in a tropical paradise.

HOTELS AND RESORTS
$150-250

The **Hilo Hawaiian Hotel** (71 Banyan Dr., 808/935-9361 or 800/367-5004, www.castleresorts.com, $105–300) occupies the most beautiful grounds of any hotel in Hilo. From the vantage of the hotel's colonnaded veranda, you overlook formal gardens, Coconut Island, and Hilo Bay. Designed as a huge arc, the hotel's architecture blends well with its surroundings and expresses the theme set by the bay, that of a long, sweeping crescent. While neat, clean, well maintained, and with all necessary amenities, the hotel still has somewhat of a 1970s feel. If you want flash and glamour, try one of the new resorts on the Kona side. However, for down-home quality with a touch of class in Hilo, you can't do better than the Hilo Hawaiian. Prices at this property run $115–210 for a standard room, $155–300 for an ocean-view room, and $200–405 for suites and kitchenettes; substantial online discounts are available, especially during low season. All rooms have air-conditioning, phone, and cable TV, plus there's a swimming pool on the property. Guest services include a gift shop, launderette, free parking, and a front-desk safety deposit box. There are restaurants on the property for guests' convenience, but you'd do better to walk the five minutes to Ken's House of Pancakes for a better meal. This really is a classic Hawaii hotel. If you want a nice place where you don't have to interact with anyone else, this is your best choice in Hilo. Also, they have a pool, which can be very extremely nice on Hilo's humid days. Check online for specials or call the hotel to negotiate. If there isn't an event going on, it seems like prices can be discounted.

CAMPING

At **Kolekole Beach Park** (Hwy. 19 near mile marker 14), amenities include restrooms, grills, electricity, picnic tables, pavilions, and a camping area (county permit required); no drinking water is available. It's a nice spot given that it's not right off the road, but under the road (far under the highway bridge) and right next to the ocean. The area can get flooded (or just be muddy) and be buggy so be cautious. Also, it's a popular spot for locals to gather during the weekend; however, most do not stay over.

Hamakua Coast, Waimea, and the Saddle Road

You want views, I'll give you some views. The accommodations on the Hamakua Coast and Waimea offer some of the best scenes around: You get your ocean and your mountain (sometimes snowcapped) at the same time. It's utter perfection. The best places to stay in this area tend to be the bed-and-breakfasts—each offering something unique. Due to the difference in the extra amenities, rates tend to vary, but are lower than what one would find in Kona or Kohala nearby. If staying on the Hamakua Coast, you'll have to drive a bit to get some dinner. If you're in Waimea, you'll be minutes away from the island's best cuisine (not to mention Starbucks).

BED-AND-BREAKFASTS AND INNS
$150-250

Quite literally the most spectacular view on the island can be found by simply stepping out of your room at ◖ **Waipi'o Rim** (48-5561 Honoka'a-Waipi'o Rd., Waipi'o Valley, 808/775-1727, www.waipiorim.com, $200). This new B&B, owned by Nancy and Steve Roberson, overlooks Waipi'o Valley and all its splendor. There is only one room available, in a building separate from the Robersons' main house; it has awkwardly placed furniture including a queen bed, eating area, couch, and a TV that is placed on top of an armoire (so you really have to stretch to see it). Wireless Internet is available as is cable TV and access to the Robersons' Netflix account (really—their instant queue). But the room becomes secondary given the backdrop of Waipi'o and the overall experience at Waipi'o Rim. Nancy and Steve are incredibly nice and interesting and are passionate about the area. Also, since you are their only guests you get a lot of attention including welcome wine and pupu as

HAMAKUA COAST, WAIMEA, AND THE SADDLE ROAD ACCOMMODATIONS

Name (Location)	Type	Price	Features	Why Go Here	Best Fit For
Aaah the Views (Waimea dry side)	B&B	$115-195	TV, filling breakfast	one of the best sunset views, good base for exploring most of the island	budget travelers, solo travelers
Hotel Honoka'a Club (downtown Honoka'a)	hotel	$20-130	clean and friendly, continental breakfast	the only hotel located in Honoka'a proper	economy tourists, those who want to get an early start at Waipi'o
Kamuela Inn (central Waimea)	hotel	$59-185	TV, continental breakfast	they'll have a room when everyone else is booked	budget travelers
The Jacaranda Inn (Waimea dry side)	inn	$120-200	fireplaces in or around rooms	good location close to Kohala Coast and Waimea restaurants	couples
☑ Waianuhea (near Honoka'a)	B&B	$210-400	hot tub, TV, extensive DVD library, chef-made breakfast, wine and pupu hour	really a boutique hotel with first-class staff and lots of free extras	honeymooners, couples who desire luxury
☑ Waipi'o Rim (Waipi'o Valley)	B&B	$200	wine and pupu upon arrival, Netflix	best view of anywhere on the island, friendly and knowledgeable hosts, great way to see and explore the valley	honeymooners, couples

© HEIDI MADSEN

The view of Waipi'o Valley from your room's balcony at Waipi'o Rim is priceless − on average, two couples get engaged here weekly.

well as a scrumptious breakfast made from local produce. Guests with food allergies will be extremely pleased by the offerings and Nancy's cooking. The rate is $200 per night, double occupancy, and after four consecutive nights, your fifth night is free. It can be hard to get a reservation here since they only have one room, so book early. It's a special experience here: to be able to wake up to Waipi'o Valley and watch the sunset from your private deck is really a once-in-a-lifetime event. The breakfast is top 10 on the island and for me that outweighs the awkwardness of the room setup. The biggest downside is that it's a little out of the way. It's about 15 minutes or so to Honoka'a, 30 minutes to Waimea, and about an hour to Hilo. It's a great place to stay for a night or two but doesn't make for a good base to explore the island. Note: Ask Steve about the trails surrounding the house. These are the same trails that the horseback riding and ATV trips use for their tours—but if you stay at Waipi'o Rim, you can just walk them on your own with Steve's directions.

Aaah the Views (66-1773 Alaneo St.,

808/885-3455, www.aaahtheviews.com, $115–195)—really, the views. The views (I'll say it again) are really worth a stay at this bed-and-breakfast. There are all the usual amenities (TV/DVD and wireless Internet), but no hot tub or swimming pool (although their property borders a river for the adventurous types). The rooms are a good value, on the smaller size but priced well. Opt for one of the rooms with views of Mauna Kea (the Dream Room or Stream Room, which has a shared bath), or if you're traveling with a family you can rent the two upper rooms (Stream Room and Sunset Room as a suite—the Treetop Suite). In fact, the Treetop Suite was initially built for budget travelers, and each room has a small loft with a bed in it (it is rented as a double and extra guests are $20 each). Hypothetically, 3–4 people could fit in each room and a large family really could utilize the entire suite for themselves. Although the owners will allow shorter than two-night stays, you will be charged extra for just the one night. Breakfast is served early (at 7:30 A.M.) and is filling but just okay. The rooms themselves are clean, but average. But you'll be so distracted by the view out of the large windows or balcony that you won't care about the size or the decor of the room. The property's location is excellent, just a few minutes west of the center of Waimea and only 10–15 minutes drive to the Kohala Coast. It makes a great base to explore a large part of the island.

Built in 1897 as the Parker Ranch manager's house, this plantation estate has gone through several metamorphoses and has now turned into **The Jacaranda Inn** (65-1444 Kawaihae Rd., 808/885-8813, www.jacarandainn.com, $120–200 for rooms, $250–450 for the cottage). This estate, with its raspberry-colored roof, dominates a broad lawn. A white ranch fence and bougainvillea hedge separate it from the road. Set amidst towering trees, the main house retains the original Hawai'i Victorian flavor, with rich koa wood and numerous antiques. Enter the huge living room with its imposing fireplace, and from there you can move to the dining rooms, library, billiard room, bar, or terrace. Separate oversized suites have also been constructed to the rear as guest rooms. They are all decorated according to different themes and colors, and while each shows individual character and style, they all have a similar romantic feel. The eight guest rooms, with pretty flower names like White Lily, Iris, Orchid, and Passion Flower, rent for $120–200. In addition, a three-bedroom, three-bath cottage that can sleep up to six goes for $250–450 a night (depending on the number of guests) with a three-night minimum. When you drive past this inn from the road, you'll want to stay here—its exterior is welcoming, and it sits perched over a view of the valley. However, in recent years the quality of the inn has drastically gone downhill. The rooms still retain their beauty but are in need of a revamping and some cleaning. In addition, breakfast is no longer included in the price of accommodation. It's definitely romantic here, but you might be frustrated that no one has taken the time to turn it back into the gem that it could be.

Over $250

The staff is so attentive at ◖ **Waianuhea** (near Honoka'a, 808/775-1118, www.waianuhea.com, $210–400) that it might be hard to stay anywhere else afterward. It's not the easiest place to get to (their directions are good, it's just a windy dirt road), but make sure you arrive by their late afternoon wine and pupu hour. Although a gourmet (mainly organic and local) breakfast prepared by an exceptional chef is included in the price of accommodation, Waianuhea is really a boutique hotel, converted from a couples retreat center. There are a lot of open spaces where guests can interact (or just spend time alone). Kaulana Akea ($400) is the full suite located out of the main section of the house. It has a bedroom with a king bed and a living room with a queen sleeper sofa, making it ideal for a family or several adults traveling together. The suite also comes with gas-burning stove. If this weren't romantic enough, there is a private patio area fenced by lava rock, featuring a two-person spa. In the house there is the Malamalama Suite ($310), with a sleigh bed, sofa sleeper, and large bathroom with tub. The in-house lower priced rooms ($210) are on the smaller size, but again, there is so much open space in the house and outdoors (including a hot tub), that you won't feel claustrophobic.

What I like here is that they've thought of everything—and perhaps that's easy to do when there is paid staff. There is a huge DVD library, lots of magazines to borrow, goat milk soaps in the bathrooms (made by the chef, actually), cell phones in each room in case your cell phone doesn't get service, and a three- or five-course dinner to order served over candlelight. It's a great choice for honeymooners or those who want something plush and intimate. The only down side is that the road is a bit of a pain. It takes about 10 minutes or so to get back to the main road, and the closest town is Honoka'a. Waimea is only another 20 minutes away. This is a good place to stay for two nights (maybe three), but given that it doesn't have easy access to everywhere, it would be better to split your stay between here and another

© DOMINIC ARIZONIA BONUCCELLI

With a top-rated chef, a wine and cheese hour, and a DVD library that rivals a small Netflix, Waianuhea sets the bar for bed-and-breakfasts in the area.

place—like Kalaekilohana Bed and Breakfast in Ka'u, with whom they offer a package for "north-south" island vacationing.

HOTELS AND RESORTS
$50-100

Centrally located along Route 240 in downtown Honoka'a is **Hotel Honoka'a Club** (45-3480 Mamane St., Honoka'a, 808/775-0678, www.hotelhonokaa.com, $20–130). Built in 1908 as the plantation manager's club, it's still infused with the grace and charm of the old days. What it lacks in elegance it makes up for in cleanliness and friendliness. The hotel, mostly used by local people, is old and well used but clean and comfortable, and it's the only hotel right in town. From the back rooms, you get a view over the tin roofs of residential Honoka'a and the ocean. Rooms run $120–130 for a two-room suite; $95.50–$105.50 for an ocean-view room with TV, private bath, and queen-size bed; and $65–80 for an economy room with a private bath. Rates include a simple continental breakfast and wireless Internet

in every room. Hostel rooms, located in the basement, all with shared bath and kitchen facilities, are separated into three private rooms that are available for $20–30. It's not a fancy place, but there is something about it that makes it sweet and likable. A good budget option if you want to stay near Waipi'o Valley in order to get your hike on early or if you prefer to stay at small locally run places.

The **Kamuela Inn** (65-1300 Kawaihae Rd., Waimea, 808/885-4243 or 800/555-8968, www.hawaii-bnb.com/kamuela.html, $59–185) is where you stay when you haven't booked a room and are desperate to find something nearby and inexpensive. The rooms smell moldy, which is partially the fault of being on the cusp of Waimea's wet side and partly the fault of what seems to be a lackadaisical staff. The basic motel rooms are small, with twin or double beds with wicker headboards, private bathrooms, and color TV, but no air-conditioning (although it's not needed). About one-third of the units have kitchens. The deluxe Penthouse is upstairs in the old wing and breaks into two joinable units that can accommodate up to five guests. The "newer" wing has larger rooms with hardwood floors and king-size or twin beds, and it features deluxe Executive Suites with full kitchens. The breakfast that is complimentary with the room is muffins and bread from Costco. If you stay here, head to Hawaiian Style Café down the road for the best breakfast ever. Stay here if you're on a tight budget or really can't find anywhere else to stay.

CAMPING

Laupahoehoe Point Park (Hwy. 19 near mile marker 27) occupies the low peninsula; it has picnic tables, showers, electricity, and a county camping area. The area sees a lot of day use from local families. It's a beautiful setting here and the facilities are cleaner than at many other county parks. This site is one of the better camping options on the island.

◖ **Kalopa Native Forest State Park and Recreation Area** provides an excellent opportunity to explore some of the lush gulches of the Hamakua Coast, as well as day-use picnicking, tent camping, and furnished cabins (state permit required) that can house up to eight people. Camping and cabin use is limited to five consecutive days per party. The bunk-style cabins, each with a bathroom and shower, rent for $60 resident, $90 nonresident for 1–8 campers. A great place for a group get-together. Linens and blankets are provided, and you may cook in the recreation hall. Do reserve ahead of time as these cabins get booked quickly! The

camping area is in a separate grassy area that is well protected and quiet—one of the best camping sites on the island due to its cleanliness and green surroundings (no beach, though). For reservations, go to the state permit website (http://camping.ehawaii.gov).

To stay overnight in ◖ **Waimanu Valley** you must have a camping permit ($12 resident, $18 nonresident) available through the state camp permit site (http://camping.ehawaii.gov). Each of the nine designated campsites along the beach has a fireplace, and there are three composting outhouses in the valley for use by campers. Carry out what you carry in! Note: Check with the Division of Forestry and Wildlife before you go (808/974-4221, http://hawaii.gov/dlnr/dofaw) to check on trail conditions (or ask the attendant at the booth at the Waipi'o Valley Lookout). At times the trail is closed for maintenance or unsafe conditions.

About seven miles west of the Mauna Kea Road, at a sharp bend in the road, you'll find a cluster of cabins that belong to the **Mauna Kea State Recreation Area.** No camping is allowed, but housekeeping cabins that sleep up to six can be rented for $45 a night for 1–4 people and $5 per person for the fifth and sixth. Bedding is provided, and there is electricity, but you must bring your own cooking utensils and water. Permits are required for these cabins. For additional information and reservations, contact the state park office (75 Aupuni St. #204, Hilo, HI 96721, 808/974-6200, http://camping.ehawaii.gov).

BACKGROUND

The Land

GEOGRAPHY

The Big Island, Hawai'i, is the southernmost and easternmost of the Hawaiian Islands—it is also the largest. This island dwarfs all the others in the Hawaiian chain at 4,028 square miles and growing. It accounts for about 63 percent of the state's total landmass; the other islands could fit within it two times over. With 266 miles of coastline, the island stretches about 95 miles from north to south and 80 miles from east to west. Cape Kumukahi is the easternmost point in the state, and Ka Lae (South Point) is the southernmost point in the country.

Science and the *Kumulipo* oral history differ sharply on the age of the Big Island. Scientists say that Hawai'i is the youngest of the islands, being a little over one million years old; the chanters claim that it was the first "island-child" of Wakea and Papa. It is, irrefutably, closest to the "hot spot" on the Pacific floor, evidenced by Kilauea's frequent eruptions. The geology, geography, and location of the Hawaiian Islands, and their ongoing drifting and building in the middle of the Pacific, make them among the most fascinating pieces of real estate on earth.

Separating the Big Island from Maui to the northwest is the 'Alenuihaha Channel, which at about 30 miles wide and over 6,800 feet deep is the state's second widest and second deepest channel.

© BREE KESSLER

The Mountains

The tremendous volcanic peak of **Mauna Kea** (White Mountain), located in north-central Hawai'i, has been extinct for over 3,500 years. Its seasonal snowcap earns Mauna Kea its name and reputation as a good skiing and snowboarding area in winter. Over 18,000 feet of mountain below sea level rise straight up from the ocean floor—making Mauna Kea over 31,000 feet tall, almost 3,000 feet taller than Mount Everest; some consider it the tallest mountain in the world. At 13,796 feet above sea level, it is without doubt the tallest peak in the Pacific. Near its top, at 13,020 feet, is **Lake Waiau,** the highest lake in the state and third-highest in the country. Mauna Kea was obviously a sacred mountain to the Hawaiians, and its white dome was a welcome beacon to seafarers. On its slope is the largest adze quarry in Polynesia, from which high-quality basalt was taken to be fashioned into prized tools. The atmosphere atop the mountain, which sits mid-Pacific far from pollutants, is the most rarefied and cleanest on earth. The clarity makes Mauna Kea a natural for astronomical observatories. The complex of telescopes on its summit is internationally staffed and provides data to scientists around the world.

The **Kohala Mountains** to the northwest are the oldest and rise only to 5,480 feet at Kaunu o Kaleiho'ohie peak. This section looks more like the other Hawaiian Islands, with deep gorges and valleys along the coast and a forested interior. As you head east toward Waimea from Kawaihae on Highway 19, for every few miles you travel you pick up about 10 inches of rainfall per year. This becomes obvious as you begin to pass little streams and rivulets running from the mountains.

Mount Hualalai, at 8,271 feet, is the backdrop to Kailua-Kona. It's home to many of the Big Island's endangered birds and supports many of the region's newest housing developments. Just a few years ago, Mount Hualalai was thought to be extinct, since the last time it erupted was in 1801. It is now known that within the last 1,000 years, the mountain has erupted about every two or three centuries. In 1929 it suffered an earthquake swarm, which means that a large movement of lava inside the mountain caused tremors. United States Geological Survey (USGS) scientists now consider Mount Hualalai only dormant and very likely to erupt at some point in the future. When it does, a tremendous amount of lava is expected to pour rapidly down its steep sides. From the side of this mountain grows the cone Pu'u Wa'awa'a. At 3,967 feet, it's only slightly shorter than the very active Kilauea on the far side of Mauna Loa. Obsidian is found here, and this is one of the few places in Hawaii where this substance has been quarried in large quantities.

Even though **Mauna Loa** (Long Mountain) measures a respectable 13,679 feet, its height isn't its claim to fame. This active volcano, 60 miles long by 30 wide, comprises 19,000 cubic miles of lava, making it the densest and most massive mountain on earth. In 1950, a tremendous lava flow belched from Mauna Loa's summit, reaching an astonishing rate of 6,750,000 cubic yards per hour. Seven lava rivers flowed for 23 days, emitting over 600 million cubic yards of lava that covered 35 square miles. There were no injuries, but the villages of Ka'apuna and Honokua were partially destroyed, along with the Magoo Ranch. Its last eruption, in 1984, was small by comparison yet created fountaining inside the summit crater and a "curtain of fire" along its eastern rift.

The lowest of the island's major peaks, **Kilauea** rises only to 4,078 feet. Its pragmatic name means "The Spewing," and it's the world's most active volcano. In the last hundred years, it has erupted on the average once every 11 months. The Hawaiians believed that the goddess Pele inhabited every volcano in the Hawaiian chain, and that her home is now Halema'uma'u crater in Kilauea Caldera. Kilauea is the most scientifically watched volcano in the world, with a permanent observatory built right into the crater rim. When it erupts, the flows are so predictable that observers run toward the mountain, not away from it!

The flows, however, can burst from fissures far from the center of the crater in areas that don't seem "active." This occurs mainly in the Puna district. In 1959, Kilauea Iki crater came to life after 91 years, and although the flow wasn't as massive as others, it did send blazing fountains of lava 1,900 feet into the air. Kilauea has been continuously active since 1983, with eruptions occurring at least once a month and expected to continue. Most activity has been from a vent below Pu'u O'o crater. You might be lucky enough to see this phenomenon while visiting.

Volcanoes as Island Builders

The Hawaiians worshiped Madame Pele, the fire goddess whose name translates equally well as Volcano, Fire Pit, or Eruption of Lava. When she was angry, she complained by spitting fire, which cooled and formed land. Volcanologists say that the islands are huge mounds of cooled basaltic lava surrounded by billions of polyp skeletons that have formed coral reefs. The Hawaiian Islands are shield volcanoes that erupt gently and form an elongated dome much like a turtle shell. The Big Island is a perfect example of this. Once above sea level, its tremendous weight sealed the fissure below. Eventually the giant tube that carried lava to the surface sunk in on itself and formed a caldera, as evidenced atop Kilauea. More eruptions occur periodically, and they cover the already existing island like frosting on a titanic cake. Wind and water took over and relentlessly sculpted the raw lava into deep crevices and cuts that became valleys. The most dramatic of these scars occur as the numerous gulches and valleys on the northeast side of the Big Island. Because of less rain and runoff, the west side is smoother, more uniform, and much less etched.

Lava

Lava flows in two distinct types, for which the Hawaiian names have become universal geological terms: **'a'a** and **pahoehoe**. They're easily distinguishable in appearance, but chemically they're the same. 'A'a is extremely rough and spiny and will quickly tear up your shoes if you do much hiking over it. Also, if you have the misfortune to fall down, you'll immediately know why they call it 'a'a. Pahoehoe, a billowy, rope-like lava resembling burned pancake batter, can mold into fantastic shapes. Examples of both types of lava are frequently encountered on various hikes throughout the Big Island. Other lava oddities you may spot are peridots (green, gem-like stones called Pele's diamonds); clear, feldspar-like, white cotton candy called Pele's hair; and gray lichens known as Hawaiian snow covering the older flows.

As it is relatively young, the Big Island has had less time than the other islands in the chain to be broken down by the forces of wind and rain. Yet, even here, there are areas, particularly in the north on the slopes of the Kohala Mountains, where a thick layer of soil sustains lush grasses and vegetation.

Tsunamis

Tsunami is the Japanese word for tidal wave. It ranks up there with the worst of them in sparking horror in human beings. But if you were to count up all the people in Hawaii who have been swept away by tidal waves in the last 50 years, the toll wouldn't come close to those killed on bicycles in only a few Mainland cities in just five years. A Hawaiian tsunami is actually a seismic sea wave generated by an earthquake or underwater landslide that could easily have originated thousands of miles away in South America or Alaska. Some waves have been clocked at speeds up to 500 mph. The safest place during a tsunami, besides high ground well away from beach areas, is out on the open ocean, where even an enormous wave is perceived only as a large swell. A tidal wave is only dangerous when it is opposed by land. The Big Island has been struck with the two worst tidal waves in Hawaii's modern history. A giant wave smashed the islands on April 1, 1946, and swept away 159 people and over 1,300 homes. Hilo sustained most of these losses, but Waipi'o Valley was washed clean, devastating the community there, and the schoolyard at Laupahoehoe Point was awash in water, dragging 20 schoolchildren and a teacher to their deaths. On May 23, 1960, Hilo again took the brunt of a wave that rumbled through its business district, killing 61 people. As a result of a major earthquake in Japan, on March 11, 2011, Hawaii again experienced a tsunami. Although, luckily, no lives were lost due to the tsunami, there was substantial damage to homes and several of the resorts on the Kona side. The tsunami wave also caused significant change to the shape of the some of the beaches in the Kona area as the sand was washed away. As of late 2011 the Big Island was still working to restore the beaches to their original form and restore damage to affected buildings.

Earthquakes

These rumblings are also a concern in Hawaii and offer a double threat because they can generate tsunamis. If you ever feel a tremor and are close to a beach, get as far away as fast as possible. The Big Island, because of its active volcanoes, experiences hundreds of technical earthquakes, although 99 percent can only be felt by very delicate equipment. In the last two decades, the Big Island has experienced about one earthquake a year in the range of 5.0–6.0 on the Richter scale, which account for about 60 percent of all quakes of that magnitude in the state. The last major quake on the Big Island occurred in late November 1975, reaching 7.2 on the Richter scale and causing many millions of dollars' worth of damage in the island's southern regions. The only loss of life occurred when a beach collapsed and two people from a large camping party drowned. Like the other islands, the Big Island has an elaborate warning system against natural disasters. You will notice loudspeakers high atop poles along many beaches and coastal areas; these warn of tsunamis, hurricanes, and earthquakes. The loudspeakers are tested at 11 A.M. on the first working day of each month. All island telephone books contain a civil defense warning and procedures section with which

you should acquaint yourself—note the maps showing which areas traditionally have been inundated by tsunamis, and what procedures to follow in case an emergency occurs.

Beaches and Ponds

The Big Island takes the rap for having poor beaches—this isn't true! They are certainly few and far between, but many of them are spectacular. Hawai'i is big and young, so distances are greater than on other islands, and the wave action hasn't had enough time to grind much new lava and coral into sand. The Kona and South Kohala Coast beaches, along with a few nooks and crannies around Hilo, are gorgeous. Each of the large valleys along the rugged North Kohala Coast—Waipi'o, Waimanu, and Pololu—has a long beach of gray sand. Harder to get to, these beaches have a greater reward because of their isolation. The beaches of Puna and Ka'u are of incredible black sand, a few only years old, and the southern tip of the island has a hidden green-sand beach or two enjoyed only by those intrepid enough to get to them.

Just north of the Kona International Airport is Makalawena, a beautiful white-sand beach. Inland is its associated wetland pond, one of the most important on the Big Island. Other coastal ponds on the Kona side are located in Kaloko-Honokohau National Historical Park, just north of the Honokohau Harbor, at Kiholo Bay, and at the Kona Village, Waikoloa, and Mauna Lani resorts. On the Hilo side, the most well known, perhaps, are the ponds in Lili'uokalani Gardens in Hilo and at Kapoho in Puna.

Land Ownership

The County of Hawai'i comprises over 2.5 million acres. Of this total, the state controls about 800,000 acres, mostly forest preserves and undeveloped land; the federal government has large acreage in the Hawai'i Volcanoes National Park, Pohakuloa Training Area, and Hakalau Forest National Wildlife Refuge. Large landowners control most of the rest except for about 116,000 acres of Hawaiian

Homelands. The major large landowners are the Bishop Estate, Parker Ranch, and the Samuel Damon Estate.

CLIMATE

The average temperature around the island varies between 72 and 78°F. Summers raise the temperature to the mid-80s and winters cool off to the low 70s. Both Kona and Hilo maintain a year-round average of about 74°F, and the South Kohala Coast is a few degrees warmer. As usual, it's cooler in the higher elevations, and Waimea sees most days in the mid-60s to low 70s, while Volcano maintains a relatively steady 60°F. Atop Mauna Kea, the temperature rarely climbs above 50°F or dips below 30°F, while the summit of Mauna Loa is about 10 degrees warmer. The lowest recorded temperature on the Big Island (and for the state) was 1°F at the Mauna Kea summit in January 1970, while the highest ever recorded was in April 1931 at Pahala in Ka'u—a scorching (for Hawaii) 100°F.

Altitude drops temperatures about three degrees for every 1,000 feet; if you intend to visit the mountain peaks of Mauna Loa and Mauna Kea (both over 13,000 feet), expect the temperature to be at least 30 degrees cooler than at sea level. On occasion, snows atop Mauna Kea last well into June, with nighttime temperatures at or below freezing.

The Big Island is indeed big—and tall. With its arid desert regions, tropical rainforests, temperate upland areas, and frigid alpine slopes, the island has 11 of 13 climatic zones.

The winter months (December through February) tend to have more rain, but in the last few years that has been unpredictable. Generally speaking, the Kona side (the island's west side) tends to have less rain than the Hilo side (or east side) of the island.

Kona Winds

Kona means leeward in Hawaiian, and when the trades stop blowing, these southerly winds often take over. To anyone from Hawaii, "Kona wind" is a euphemism for bad weather, for it brings in hot, sticky air. Luckily, Kona winds are most common October–April, when they appear roughly half the time. The temperatures drop slightly during the winter so these hot winds are tolerable, and even useful for moderating the thermometer. In the summer they are awful, but luckily—again—they hardly ever blow during this season.

A Kona storm is another matter. These subtropical low-pressure storms develop west of the Hawaiian Islands, and as they move east they draw winds up from the south. Usually only in winter, they can cause considerable damage to crops and real estate. There is no real pattern to Kona storms—some years they come every few weeks while in other years they don't appear at all.

Flora and Fauna

Anyone who loves a mystery will be intrigued by the speculation about how plants and animals first came to Hawaii. Most people's idea of an island paradise includes swaying palms, dense mysterious jungles ablaze with wildflowers, and luscious fruits just waiting to be plucked. In fact, for millions of years the Hawaiian chain consisted of raw and barren islands where no plants grew and no birds sang. Why? Because they are geological orphans that spontaneously popped up in the middle of the Pacific Ocean. The islands, more than 2,000 miles from any continental landfall, were therefore isolated from the normal ecological spread of plants and animals. Even the most tenacious travelers of the flora and fauna kingdoms would be sorely tried in crossing the mighty Pacific. Those that made it by pure chance found a totally foreign ecosystem. They had to adapt or perish. The survivors evolved quickly, and many plants and birds became so specialized that they were limited not only to specific islands in the chain but to habitats that frequently consisted of a single isolated valley. It was as if after traveling so far, and finding a niche, they never budged again. Luckily, the soil of Hawaii was virgin and rich, the competition from other plants or animals was nonexistent, and the climate was sufficiently varied and nearly perfect for most growing things.

The evolution of plants and animals on the isolated islands was astonishingly rapid. A tremendous change in environment, coupled with a limited gene pool, accelerated natural selection. For example, many plants lost their protective thorns and spines because there were no grazing animals or birds to destroy them. Before settlement, Hawaii had no fruits, vegetables, coconut palms, edible land animals, conifers, mangroves, or banyans. The early Polynesians brought 27 varieties of plants that they needed for food and other purposes. About 90 percent of plants on the Hawaiian Islands today were introduced after Captain Cook first set foot here. Tropical flowers, wild and vibrant as we know them today, were relatively few. In a land where thousands of orchids now brighten every corner, there were only four native varieties, the least in any of the 50 states. Today, the indigenous plants and animals have the highest rate of extinction anywhere on earth. By the beginning of the 20th century, native plants growing below 1,500 feet in elevation were almost completely extinct or totally replaced by introduced species. The land and its living things have been greatly transformed by humans and their agriculture. This inexorable process began when Hawaii was the domain of its original Polynesian settlers, then greatly accelerated when the land was inundated by Western peoples.

The indigenous plants and birds of the Big Island have suffered the same fate as those of the other Hawaiian Islands; they're among the most endangered species on earth and disappearing at an alarming rate. There are some sanctuaries on the Big Island where native species still live, but they must be vigorously protected. Do your bit to save them; enjoy but do not disturb.

FLORA
Introduced Plants

Hawaii's indigenous and endemic plants, flowers, and trees are both fascinating and

© BREE KESSLER

Breadfruit, known as *ulu* in Hawaiian, can be easily foraged around the Big Island.

beautiful, but, unfortunately, like everything else that was native, they are quickly disappearing. The majority of flora considered exotic by visitors was introduced either by the original Polynesians or by later white settlers. The Polynesians who colonized Hawaii brought foodstuffs, including coconuts, bananas, taro, breadfruit, sweet potatoes, yams, and sugarcane. They also carried along gourds to use as containers, 'awa (kava) to make a basic intoxicant, and the ti plant to use for offerings or to string into hula skirts. Non-Hawaiian settlers over the years have brought mangoes, papayas, passion fruit, pineapples, and the other tropical fruits and vegetables associated with the islands. Also, most of the flowers, including protea, plumeria, anthuriums, orchids, heliconia, ginger, and most hibiscus, have come from every continent on earth. Tropical America, Asia, Java, India, and China have contributed their most beautiful and delicate blooms. Hawaii is blessed with national and state parks, gardens, undisturbed rainforests, private reserves, and commercial nurseries that offer an exhaustive botanical survey of the island. The following is a sampling of the common native and introduced flora that add dazzling color and exotic tastes to the landscape.

Native Trees

Koa and 'ohi'a are two indigenous trees still seen on the Big Island. Both have been greatly reduced by the foraging of introduced cattle and goats, and through logging and forest fires. The **koa,** a form of acacia, is Hawaii's finest native tree. It can grow to over 70 feet high and has a strong, straight trunk that can measure more than 10 feet in circumference. Koa is a very quick-growing legume that fixes nitrogen in the soil. It is believed that the tree originated in Africa, where it was very damp. It then migrated to Australia, where it was very dry, which caused the elimination of leaves, so all that was left were bare stems that could survive in the desert climate. When koa came to the Pacific islands, instead of reverting to the true leaf, its leaf stem just broadened into sickle-shaped, leaflike foliage that produces an

inconspicuous, pale-yellow flower. When the tree is young or damaged it will revert to the original feathery, fernlike leaf that evolved in Africa millions of years ago. The koa does best in well-drained soil in deep forest areas, but scruffy specimens will grow on poorer soil. The Hawaiians used koa as the main log for their dugout canoes, and elaborate ceremonies were performed when a log was cut and dragged to a canoe shed. Koa wood was also preferred for paddles, spears, and even surfboards. Today it is still considered an excellent furniture wood. Although fine specimens can be found in the reserve of Hawai'i Volcanoes National Park, loggers elsewhere are harvesting the last of the big trees.

The **'ohi'a** is a survivor and therefore the most abundant of all the native Hawaiian trees. Coming in a variety of shapes and sizes, it grows as miniature trees in wet bogs or as 100-foot giants on cool, dark slopes at higher elevations. This tree is often the first life in new lava flows. The 'ohi'a produces a tuftlike flower—usually red, but occasionally orange, yellow, or white, the latter being very rare and elusive—that resembles a natural pompon. The flower was considered sacred to Pele; it was said that she would cause a rainstorm if 'ohi'a blossoms were picked without the proper prayers. The flowers were fashioned into lei that resembled feather boas. The strong, hard wood was used to make canoes, poi bowls, and especially temple images. 'Ohi'a logs were also used as railroad ties and shipped to the Mainland from Pahoa. It's believed that the golden spike linking rail lines between the U.S. East and West Coasts was driven into a Puna 'ohi'a log when the two railroads came together in Ogden, Utah.

Tropical Rainforests

When it comes to pure and diverse natural beauty, the United States is one of the finest pieces of real estate on earth. As if purple mountains' majesty and fruited plains weren't enough, it even received a tiny, living emerald of tropical rainforest. A tropical rainforest is where the earth takes a breath and exhales pure sweet oxygen through its vibrant green canopy.

Located in the territories of Puerto Rico and the Virgin Islands and in the state of Hawaii, the rainforests of the United States make up only one-half of 1 percent of the world's total, and they must be preserved. The U.S. Congress passed two bills in 1986 designed to protect the unique biological diversity of its tropical areas, but their destruction has continued unabated. The lowland rainforests of Hawaii, populated mostly by native 'ohi'a, are being razed. Landowners slash, burn, and bulldoze them to create more land for cattle and agriculture and, most distressingly, for wood chips to generate electricity! Introduced wild boars gouge the forest floor, exposing sensitive roots and leaving tiny, fetid ponds where mosquito larvae thrive. Feral goats roam the forests like hoofed locusts and strip all vegetation within reach. Rainforests on the higher and steeper slopes of mountains have a better chance, as they are harder for humans to reach. One unusual feature of Hawaii's rainforests is that they are "upside down." Most plant and animal species live on the forest floor, rather than in the canopy as in other forests.

Almost half of the birds classified in the United States as endangered live in Hawaii, and almost all of these make their homes in the rainforests. We can only lament the passing of the rainforests that have already fallen to ignorance, but if this ill-fated destruction continues on a global level, we will be lamenting our own passing. We must nurture the rainforests that remain, and, with simple enlightenment, let them be.

FAUNA
Birds

One of the great tragedies of natural history is the continuing demise of Hawaiian birdlife. Perhaps only 15 original species of birds remain of the more than 70 native families that thrived before the coming of humans. Since the arrival of Captain Cook in 1778, 23 species have become extinct, with 31 more in danger. And what's not known is how many species were wiped out before white explorers arrived. Experts believe that the Hawaiians annihilated

about 40 species, including seven species of geese, a rare one-legged owl, ibises, lovebirds, sea eagles, and honeycreepers—all gone before Captain Cook arrived. Hawaii's endangered birds account for 40 percent of the birds officially listed as endangered or threatened by the U.S. Fish and Wildlife Service. In the last 200 years, more than four times as many birds have become extinct in Hawaii as in all of North America. These figures unfortunately suggest that a full 40 percent of Hawaii's endemic birds no longer exist. Almost all of O'ahu's native birds are gone, and few indigenous Hawaiian birds can be found on any island below the 3,000-foot level.

Native birds have been reduced in number because of multiple factors. The original Polynesians helped wipe out many species. They altered large areas for farming and used fire to destroy patches of pristine forests. Also, bird feathers were highly prized for making lei, for featherwork in capes and helmets, and for the large *kahili* fans that indicated rank among the *ali'i*. Introduced exotic birds and the new diseases they carried are another major reason for reduction of native bird numbers, along with predation by the mongoose and rat—especially upon ground-nesting birds. Bird malaria and bird pox were also devastating to the native species. Mosquitoes, unknown in Hawaii until a ship named the *Wellington* introduced them at Lahaina in 1826 through larvae carried in its water barrels, infected most native birds, causing a rapid reduction in birdlife. Feral pigs rooting deep in the rainforests knock over ferns and small trees, creating fetid pools in which mosquito larvae thrive. However, the most damaging factor by far is the assault upon native forests by agriculture and land developers. The vast majority of Hawaiian birds evolved into specialists. They lived in only one small area and ate a very limited number of plants or insects, which once removed or altered soon killed the birds.

You'll spot birds all over the Big Island, from the coastal areas to the high mountain slopes. Some are found on other islands as well, but the indigenous ones listed here are found only or mainly on the Big Island. Every bird listed is either threatened or endangered.

HAWAII'S OWN

The **nene,** or Hawaiian goose, deserves special mention because it is Hawaii's state bird and is making a comeback from the edge of extinction. The *nene* is found only on the slopes of Mauna Loa, Hualalai, and Mauna Kea on the Big Island; in Haleakala Crater on Maui; and at a few spots on Moloka'i and Kaua'i. It was extinct on Maui until a few birds were returned there in 1957, but some experts maintain that the *nene* lived naturally only on the Big Island. *Nene* are raised at the Wildfowl Trust in Slimbridge, England, which placed the first birds at Haleakala; and at the Hawaiian Fish and Game Station at Pohakuloa, along the Saddle Road on Hawai'i. By the 1940s, fewer than 50 birds lived in the wild. Now approximately 125 birds live on Haleakala and 500 on the Big Island. Although the birds can be raised successfully in captivity, their life in the wild is still in question.

The *nene* is believed to be a descendant of the Canada goose, which it resembles. Geese are migratory birds that form strong kinship ties, mating for life. It's speculated that a migrating goose became disabled and, along with its loyal mate, remained in Hawaii. The *nene* is smaller than its Canadian cousin, has lost a great deal of webbing in its feet, and is perfectly at home away from water, often foraging and nesting on rugged and bleak lava flows, although it also lives in coastal regions and on grassy mountainsides.

Good places to view *nene* are in Hawai'i Volcanoes National Park at Kipuka Nene Campground, the summit caldera, Devastation Trail, and Volcano Golf and Country Club, at dawn and dusk. The birds gather at the golf course because they love to feed on grasses. The places to view them on the Kona side are Pu'ulani, a housing development north of Kailua-Kona; or Kaloko Mauka, another housing development on the slopes of Mount Hualalai. At the top of the road up Mount Hualalai is a trail, also a good place to see the

© STEFFEN FOERSTER/WWW.123RF.COM

The *nene,* or Hawaiian goose, is highly endangered – take care not to hit one while driving near Hawai'i Volcanoes National Park, where they like to hang out.

nene. Unfortunately, as the housing developments proliferate and the residents invariably acquire dogs and cats, the *nene* will disappear. The *nene* is a perfect symbol of Hawaii: Let it be, and it will live.

The **Hawaiian crow,** or *alala,* is reduced to fewer than 12 birds living on the slopes of Hualalai and Mauna Loa above the 3,000-foot level. It looks like the common raven but has a more melodious voice and, sometimes, dull brown wing feathers. The *alala* breeds in early spring, and the greenish-blue, black-flecked eggs hatch from April to June. It is extremely nervous while nesting, and any disturbance will cause it to abandon its young.

The **Hawaiian hawk** *('io)* primarily lives on the slopes of Mauna Loa and Mauna Kea below 9,000 feet. It travels from there to other parts of the island and can often be seen kiting in the skies over Hawai'i Volcanoes National Park, upland from Kailua-Kona, and in remote spots like Waimanu Valley. This noble bird, the royalty of the skies, symbolized the *ali'i* (Hawaiian royalty). The *'io* population was once dwindling, and many scientists feared that the bird was headed for extinction. The hawk exists only on the Big Island for reasons that are not entirely clear. The good news is that the *'io* is making a dramatic comeback, also for reasons still unclear. Speculation is that it may be gaining resistance to some diseases, including malaria, or that it may have learned how to prey on the introduced rats, or even that it may be adapting to life in macadamia nut groves and other alternative habitats.

The *'akiapola'au,* a honeycreeper, is a five-inch yellow bird hardly bigger than its name. It lives mainly on the eastern slopes in *'ohi'a* and koa forests above 3,500 feet. It has a long, curved upper beak for probing and a smaller lower beak that it uses woodpecker-fashion. The *'akiapola'au* opens its mouth wide, strikes the wood with its lower beak, and then uses the upper beak to scrape out any larvae or insects. Listen for the distinctive rapping sound to spot this melodious singer. The *'akiapola'au* can be seen at the Hakalau Forest National Wildlife Refuge and along the Pu'u O'o Trail in Hawai'i Volcanoes National Park. It's estimated that only about 1,000 of these birds, one of the rarest of the island's rare winged creatures, are left.

Two other endangered birds of the Big Island are the **koloa maoli,** a duck that resembles the mallard, and the slate gray or white **'alae ke'oke'o** coot.

Other Hawaiian Animals

Hawaii had only two indigenous mammals, the monk seal or *'ilio holu i ka uaua* (found mostly in the Northwestern Hawaiian Islands) and the hoary bat (found primarily on the Big Island); both are threatened and endangered. The rest of the Big Island's mammals are transplants. But like anything else that has been in the islands long enough, including people, they take on characteristics that make them "local." There are no native amphibians, reptiles, ants, termites, or cockroaches. These have all been imported.

Among the transplants are the Indian mongoose and coqui tree frogs. The squirrel-like mongooses were brought to the Hawaiian Islands in 1883 to kill the rats eating up the sugarcane crops. And then it was learned that mongooses and rats have different sleeping schedules. Now they are an invasive species that is a menace to many of the native species. You'll see them often as road kill. The coqui tree frog, a small light-brown to dark-colored frog native to Puerto Rico, is another invasive species—a loud one. Their noise levels have been measured at up to 80–90 decibels, comparable to the noise produced by a lawnmower. Many areas have tried to eradicate them, but they are still present in droves on the island. They are particularly bad in Hilo, where you can hear them "singing" all night long (it actually sounds like they are singing "coqui, coqui").

Marine Life

The **humpback whale,** known in Hawaii as *kohola,* migrates to Hawaiian waters yearly, arriving in late December and departing by mid-May. While whales can be seen anywhere around the Big Island, some of the best places to view them are along the South Kona Coast, especially at Keauhou, Kealakekua Bay, and Ka Lae (South Point), with many sightings off the Puna Coast around Isaac Hale Beach Park, and from the luxury resorts of the South Kohala area.

Hawai'i Volcanoes National Park stretches from the top of Mauna Kea all the way down to the sea. It is here, around Apua Point, that three of the last known nesting sites of the very endangered **hawksbill turtle** *(honu'ea)* are found. This creature has been ravished in the Pacific, where it is ruthlessly hunted for its shell, which is made into women's jewelry, especially combs. It is illegal to bring items made from turtle shell into the United States, but the hunt goes on.

While they can be seen more often, **green sea turtles** *(honu)* are also endangered. Periodically, they haul themselves up on a beach to rest and warm up. This is normal and they are okay, even when their mottled green shell begins to turn a bit dusky white. Leave them alone in or out of the water; don't disturb or get too close to them. They'll return to the water when they are good and ready.

Although magnificent game fish live in various South Sea and Hawaiian waters, catching them is easiest in the clear, smooth waters off the Kona Coast. The billfish—swordfish, sailfish, marlin, and *a'u*—share two distinctive common features: a long, spear-like or swordlike snout and a prominent dorsal fin. The three main species of billfish caught here are the blue, striped, and black marlin. Of these three, the **blue marlin** is the leading game fish in Kona waters. The blue has tipped the scales at well over 1,000 pounds, but the average fish weighs in at 300–400 pounds. When alive, this fish is a striking cobalt blue, but death brings a color change to slate blue. It feeds on skipjack tuna; throughout the summer, fishing boats look for schools of tuna as a tip-off to blues in the area. The **black marlin** is the largest and most coveted catch for blue-water anglers. This solitary fish is infrequently found in the banks off Kona. Granddaddies can weigh 1,800 pounds, but the average is a mere 200. The **striped marlin** is the most common commercial billfish, a highly prized food served in finer restaurants and often sliced into sashimi. Its coloration is a remarkable royal blue. It leaps spectacularly when caught, giving it a great reputation as a fighter. The striped marlin is smaller than the other marlins, so a 100-pounder is a very good catch.

History

The Big Island plays a significant role in Hawaii's history. A long list of "firsts" occurred here. Historians generally believe (backed up by the oral tradition) that the Big Island was the first in the Hawaiian chain to be settled by the Polynesians. Hawaii is geographically the closest island to Polynesia; Mauna Loa and especially Mauna Kea, with its white summit, present easily spotted landmarks. Psychologically, the Polynesian wayfarers would have been very attracted to Hawai'i as a lost homeland. Compared to Tahiti and most other South Sea islands (except Fiji), it's huge. It *looked* like the promised land. Some may wonder why the Polynesians chose to live atop an obviously active volcano and not bypass it for a more congenial island. The volcanism of the Big Island is comparatively gentle; the lava flows follow predictable routes and rarely turn killer. The animistic Hawaiians would have been drawn to live where the godly forces of nature were so apparent. The mana (power) would be exceptionally strong, and therefore the *ali'i* would be great. Human sacrifice was introduced to Hawaii at Waha'ula Heiau in the Puna district in the 13th century, and from there *luakini* (human-sacrifice temples) spread throughout the islands.

THE ROAD FROM TAHITI
The Great Navigators

No one knows exactly when the first Polynesians arrived in Hawaii, but the great "deliberate migrations" from the southern islands seem to have taken place A.D. 500–800, though anthropologists keep pushing the date backward in time as new evidence becomes available. Even before that, however, it's reasonable to assume that the first people to set foot on Hawaiian soil were probably fishermen, or perhaps defeated warriors whose canoes were blown hopelessly northward into unfamiliar waters. They arrived by a combination of extraordinary good luck and an uncanny ability to sail and navigate without instruments (to wayfind), using the sun by day and the moon and rising stars by night. They could feel the water and determine direction by swells, tides, and currents. The movements of fish and cloud formations were also utilized to give direction. Since their arrival was probably an accident, they were unprepared to settle on the fertile but uncultivated lands, having no stock animals, plant cuttings, or women. Forced to return southward, many undoubtedly lost their lives at sea, but a few wild-eyed stragglers must have made it home to tell tales of a paradise to the north where land was plentiful and the sea bounteous. This is affirmed by ancient navigational chants from Tahiti, Moorea, and Bora Bora, which passing from father to son revealed how to follow the stars to the "heavenly homeland in the north." Possibly a few migrations followed, but it's known that for centuries there was no real reason for a mass exodus, so the chants alone remained and eventually became shadowy legend.

Where They Came From

It's generally agreed that the first planned migrations were from the violent cannibal islands that Spanish explorers called the Marquesas, 11 islands in extreme eastern Polynesia. The islands themselves are harsh and inhospitable, breeding a toughness into these people that enabled them to withstand the hardships of long, unsure ocean voyages and years of resettlement. Marquesans were a fiercely independent people whose chiefs could rise from the ranks because of bravery or intelligence. They must have also been a savage-looking lot. Both men and women tattooed themselves in complex blue patterns from head to foot. The warriors carried massive, intricately designed ironwood war clubs and wore carved

whale teeth in slits in their earlobes that eventually stretched to the shoulders. They shaved the sides of their heads with sharks' teeth, tied their hair in two topknots that looked like horns, and rubbed their heavily muscled and tattooed bodies with scented coconut oils. Their cults worshiped mummified ancestors; the bodies of warriors of defeated neighboring tribes were consumed. They were masters at building great double-hulled canoes launched from huge canoe sheds. Two hulls were fastened together to form a catamaran, and a hut in the center provided shelter in bad weather. The average voyaging canoe was 60–80 feet long and could comfortably hold an extended family of about 30 people. These small family bands carried all the staples they would need in the new lands.

For five centuries the Marquesans settled and lived peacefully on the new land, as if Hawaii's *aloha* spirit overcame most of their fierceness. The tribes coexisted in relative harmony, especially since there was no competition for land. Cannibalism died out. There was much coming and going between Hawaii and Polynesia as new people came to settle for hundreds of years. Then, it appears that in the 12th century a deliberate exodus of war-like Tahitians arrived and subjugated the settled islanders. They came to conquer. This incursion had a terrific significance on the Hawaiian religious and social system. Oral tradition relates that a Tahitian priest, Pa'ao, found the mana of the Hawaiian chiefs to be low, signifying that their gods were weak. Pa'ao built a *heiau* at Waha'ula on the Big Island, then introduced the war-like god Ku and the rigid *kapu* system through which the new rulers became dominant. Voyages between Tahiti and Hawaii continued for about 100 years, and Tahitian customs, legends, and language became the Hawaiian way of life. Then suddenly, for no recorded or apparent reason, the voyages discontinued and Hawaii returned to total isolation.

THE REST OF THE WORLD DISCOVERS HAWAII (AGAIN)

The late 18th century was an extraordinary time in Hawaiian history. Monumental changes seemed to happen all at once. First,

Captain James Cook, a Yorkshire farm boy fulfilling his destiny as the all-time greatest Pacific explorer, found Hawaii for the rest of the world. For better or worse, it could no longer be an isolated Polynesian homeland. For the first time in Hawaiian history, a charismatic leader, Kamehameha, emerged, and after a long civil war he united all the islands into one centralized kingdom. The death of Captain Cook in Hawaii marked the beginning of a long series of tragic misunderstandings between whites and natives. When Kamehameha died in 1819, the old religious system of *kapu* came to an end, leaving the Hawaiians in a spiritual vortex. Many takers arrived to fill the void: missionaries after souls, whalers after their prey and a good time, traders and planters after profits and a home. The islands were opened and devoured like ripe fruit. Powerful nations, including Russia, Great Britain, France, and the United States, yearned to bring this strategic Pacific jewel under their own influence.

Captain Cook Sights Hawaii

In 1776 Captain James Cook set sail for the Pacific from Plymouth, England, on his third and final expedition into this still largely unexplored region of the world. On a fruitless quest for the fabled Northwest Passage across the North American continent, he sailed down the coast of Africa, rounded the Cape of Good Hope, crossed the Indian Ocean, and traveled past New Zealand, Tasmania, and the Friendly Islands (where the "friendly" natives hatched an unsuccessful plot to murder him). On January 18, 1778, Captain Cook's 100-foot flagship, HMS *Resolution,* and its 90-foot companion, HMS *Discovery,* sighted O'ahu. Two days later, they sighted Kaua'i and went ashore at the village of Waimea. Though anxious to get on with his mission, Cook decided to make a quick sortie to investigate this new land and reprovision his ships. He did, however, take time to remark in his diary about the close resemblance of these newfound people to others he had encountered as far south as New Zealand and marveled at their widespread habitation across the Pacific.

Almost a year later, when winter weather forced Cook to return from the coast of Alaska, his discovery began to take on far-reaching significance. Cook had named Hawaii the Sandwich Islands, in honor of one of his patrons, John Montague, the Earl of Sandwich. On this return voyage, he spotted Maui on November 26, 1778. After eight weeks of seeking a suitable harbor, the ships bypassed it, but not before the coastline was duly drawn by Lieutenant William Bligh, one of Cook's finest and most trusted officers. (Bligh would find his own drama almost 10 years later as commander of the infamous HMS *Bounty.*) The *Discovery* and *Resolution* finally found safe anchorage at Kealakekua Bay on the Kona Coast of the Big Island. It is very lucky for history that on board was Mr. Anderson, ship's chronicler, who left a handwritten record of the strange and tragic events that followed. Even more important were the drawings of John Webber, ship's artist, who rendered invaluable impressions in superb drawings and etchings. Other noteworthy men aboard were George Vancouver, who would lead the first British return to Hawaii after Cook's death and introduce many fruits, vegetables, cattle, sheep, and goats; and James Burney, who would become a long-standing leading authority on the Pacific.

By all accounts Cook was a humane and just captain, greatly admired by his men. Unlike many supremacists of that time, he was known to have a respectful attitude toward any people he discovered, treating them as equals and recognizing the significance of their cultures. Not known as a violent man, he would use his superior weapons against natives only in an absolute case of self-defense. His hardened crew had been at sea facing untold hardship for almost three years; returning to Hawaii was truly like reentering paradise.

A strange series of coincidences sailed with Cook into Kealakekua Bay on January 16, 1779. It was *makahiki* time, a period of rejoicing and festivity dedicated to the fertility god of the earth, Lono. Normal *kapu* days were suspended and willing partners freely enjoyed each other sexually, as well as dancing, feasting, and the islands' version of Olympic games. It was long held in Hawaiian legend that the great god Lono would return to earth. Lono's image was a small wooden figure perched on a tall, mast-like crossbeam; hanging from the crossbeam were long, white sheets of tapa. Who else could Cook be but Lono, and what else could his ships with their masts and white sails be but his sacred floating *heiau*? This explained the Hawaiians' previous fascination with his ships, but to add to the remarkable coincidence, Kealakekua Harbor happened to be considered Lono's private sacred harbor. Natives from throughout the land prostrated themselves and paid homage to the returning god. Cook was taken ashore and brought to Lono's sacred temple, where he was afforded the highest respect. The ships badly needed fresh supplies so the Hawaiians readily gave all they had, stretching their own provisions to the limit. To the sailors' delight, this included full measures of the *aloha* spirit.

The Fatal Misunderstanding

After an uproarious welcome and generous hospitality for over a month, it became obvious that the newcomers were beginning to overstay their welcome. During the interim a seaman named William Watman died, convincing the Hawaiians that the *haole* were indeed mortals, not gods. Incidents of petty theft began to increase dramatically. The lesser chiefs indicated it was time to leave by "rubbing the Englishmen's bellies." Inadvertently many *kapu* were broken by the Englishmen, and once-friendly relations became strained. Finally, the ships sailed away on February 4, 1779.

After plying terrible seas for only a week, *Resolution*'s foremast was badly damaged. Cook sailed back into Kealakekua Bay, dragging the mast ashore on February 13. The natives, now totally hostile, hurled rocks at the sailors. Orders were given to load muskets with ball; firearms had previously only been loaded with shot and a light charge. Confrontations increased when some Hawaiians stole a small boat and Cook's men set after them, capturing the fleeing canoe, which held an *ali'i* named Palea. The English treated him roughly; to the Hawaiians' horror, they even smacked him on the head with a paddle. The Hawaiians then furiously attacked the mariners, who abandoned the small boat.

Next the Hawaiians stole a small cutter from the *Discovery* that had been moored to a buoy and partially sunk to protect it from the sun. For the first time, Captain Cook became furious. He ordered Captain Clerk of the *Discovery* to sail to the southeast end of the bay and stop any canoe trying to leave Kealakekua. Cook then made a fatal error in judgment. He decided to take nine armed mariners ashore in an attempt to convince the venerable King Kalani'opu'u to accompany him back aboard ship, where he would hold him for ransom in exchange for the cutter. The old king agreed, but his wife prevailed upon him not to trust the *haole*. Kalani'opu'u sat down on the beach to think while the tension steadily grew.

Meanwhile, a group of sailors fired upon a canoe trying to leave the bay, and a lesser chief, No'okemai, was killed. The crowd around Cook and his men reached an estimated 20,000, and warriors outraged by the killing of the chief armed themselves with clubs and protective straw-mat armor. One bold warrior advanced on Cook and struck him with his *pahoa* (dagger). In retaliation, Cook drew a tiny pistol lightly loaded with shot and fired at the warrior. His bullets spent themselves on the straw armor and fell harmlessly to the ground. The Hawaiians went wild. Lieutenant Molesworth Phillips, in charge of the nine sailors, began a withering fire; Cook himself slew two natives.

Overpowered by sheer numbers, the sailors headed for boats standing offshore, while Lieutenant Phillips lay wounded. It is believed that Captain Cook, the greatest seaman ever to enter the Pacific, stood helplessly in knee-deep water instead of making for the boats because he could not swim! Hopelessly surrounded, he was knocked on the head, then countless warriors passed a knife around and hacked and mutilated his lifeless body. A sad Lieutenant King lamented in his diary, "Thus fell our great and excellent commander."

Captain Clerk, now in charge, settled his men and prevailed upon the Hawaiians to return Cook's body. On the morning of February 16 a grisly piece of charred meat was brought aboard: The Hawaiians, according to their custom, had afforded Cook the highest honor by baking his body in an underground oven to remove the flesh from the bones. On February 17 a group of Hawaiians in a canoe taunted the mariners by brandishing Cook's hat. The English, strained to the limit and thinking that Cook was being desecrated, finally broke. They leveled their cannons and muskets on shore and shot anything that moved. It is believed that Kamehameha the Great was wounded in this flurry, along with four *ali'i*, and 25 *maka'ainana* (commoners) were also killed. Finally, on February 21, 1779, the bones of Captain James Cook's hands, skull, arms, and legs were returned and tearfully buried at sea. A common seaman, one Mr. Zimmerman, summed up the feelings of all who sailed under Cook when he wrote, "He was our leading star." The English sailed the next morning after dropping off their Hawaiian girlfriends who were still aboard.

THE UNIFICATION OF HAWAII

Hawaii was already in a state of political turmoil and civil war when Cook arrived. In the 1780s the islands were roughly divided into three kingdoms. War ravaged the land until a remarkable chief, Kamehameha, rose and subjugated all the islands under one rule. Kamehameha initiated a dynasty that would last for about 100 years, until the independent monarchy of Hawaii forever ceased to be.

To add a zing to this brewing political stew, Westerners and their technology were beginning to come in ever-increasing numbers. Hawaii under Kamehameha was ready to enter its "golden age." The social order was medieval, with the *ali'i* as knights owing their military allegiance to the king, and the serf-like *maka'ainana* paying tribute and working the lands. The priesthood of *kahuna* filled the posts of advisors, sorcerers, navigators, doctors, and historians. This was Polynesian Hawaii at

its apex. But like the uniquely Hawaiian silversword plant, the old culture blossomed and, as soon as it did, began to wither. Ever since, all that was purely Hawaiian has been supplanted by the relentless foreign influences that began bearing down upon it.

Young Kamehameha

The greatest native son of Hawaii, Kamehameha was born under mysterious circumstances in the Kohala district on the Big Island, probably in 1753. He was royal born to Keoua Kupuapaikalaninui, the chief of Kohala, and Kekuiapoiwa, a chieftess from Kona. Accounts vary, but one claims that before his birth, a *kahuna* prophesied that this child would grow to be a "killer of chiefs." Because of this, the local chiefs conspired to murder the infant. When Kekuiapoiwa's time came, she secretly went to the royal birthing stones near Mo'okini Heiau and delivered Kamehameha. She entrusted her baby to a manservant and instructed him to hide the child. He headed for the rugged and remote coast around Kapa'au. Here Kamehameha was raised in the mountains, mostly by men. Always alone, he earned the nickname "The Lonely One."

Kamehameha was a man noticed by everyone; there was no doubt he was a force to be reckoned with. He had met Captain Cook when the *Discovery* unsuccessfully tried to land at Hana on Maui. While aboard, he made a lasting impression, distinguishing himself from the multitude of natives swarming the ships by his royal bearing. Lieutenant James King, in a diary entry, remarked that Kamehameha was a fierce-looking man, almost ugly, but that he was obviously intelligent, observant, and very good-natured. Kamehameha received his early military training from his uncle Kalani'opu'u, the great king of Hawaii and Hana who fought fierce battles against Alapa'i, the usurper who stole his hereditary lands. After regaining Hawaii, Kalani'opu'u returned to his Hana district and turned his attention to conquering all of Maui. During this period young Kamehameha distinguished himself as a ferocious warrior and earned the nickname of "the hard-shelled crab."

Increasing Contact

By the time Kamehameha had won the Big Island, Hawaii was becoming a regular stopover for numerous ships seeking the lucrative sandalwood trade with China. In February 1791, Captain George Vancouver, still seeking the Northwest Passage, returned to Kealakekua, where he was greeted by a throng of 30,000.

The captain at once recognized Kamehameha, who was wearing a Chinese dressing gown that he had received in tribute from another chief who in turn had received it from the hands of Cook himself. The diary of a crew member, Thomas Manby, relates that Kamehameha, missing his front teeth, was more fierce-looking than ever as he approached the ship in an elegant double-hulled canoe propelled by 46 rowers. The king invited all to a great feast prepared for them on the beach. Kamehameha's appetite matched his tremendous size. It was noted that he ate two sizable fish, a king-sized bowl of poi, a small pig, and an entire baked dog. Kamehameha personally entertained the English by putting on a mock battle in which he deftly avoided spears by rolling, tumbling, and catching them in midair, all the while hurling his own spear a great distance. The English reciprocated by firing cannon bursts into the air, creating an impromptu fireworks display. Kamehameha requested from Vancouver a full table setting, with which he was provided, but his request for firearms was prudently denied.

Captain Vancouver became Kamehameha's trusted advisor and told him about the white man's form of worship. He even interceded for Kamehameha with his headstrong queen, Ka'ahumanu, and coaxed her from her hiding place under a rock when she sought refuge at Pu'uhonua O Honaunau. The captain gave gifts of beef cattle, fowl, and breeding stock of sheep and goats. The ship's naturalist, Archibald Menzies, was the first *haole* to climb Mauna Kea; he also introduced a large assortment of fruits and vegetables. The Hawaiians were cheerful and outgoing, and they showed remorse when they indicated that the remainder of Cook's bones had been buried at a temple close to Kealakekua. During the next two decades of Kamehameha's rule, the French, Russians, English, and Americans discovered the great whaling waters off Hawaii. Their increasing visits shook and finally tumbled the ancient religion and social order of *kapu*.

Kamehameha's Rule

Kamehameha was as gentle in victory as he was ferocious in battle. Under his rule, which lasted until his death on May 8, 1819, Hawaii enjoyed a peace unlike any the warring islands had ever known. The king moved his royal court to Lahaina, where in 1803 he built the Brick Palace, the first permanent building of Hawaii. The benevolent tyrant also enacted the "Law of the Splintered Paddle." This law, which protected the weak from the exploitation of the strong, had its origins in an incident of many years before.

In Kapa'au, the statue of King Kamehameha, who founded the Kingdom of Hawaii, is draped with lei.

A brave defender of a small overwhelmed village had broken a paddle over Kamehameha's head and taught the chief—literally in one stroke—about the nobility of the commoner.

However, just as Old Hawaii reached its golden age, its demise was at hand. The relentless waves of *haole* innocently yet determinedly battered the old ways into the ground. With the foreign ships came prosperity and fanciful new goods after which the *ali'i* lusted. The *maka'ainana* were worked mercilessly to provide sandalwood for the China trade. This was the first "boom" economy to hit the islands, but it set the standard of exploitation that would follow. Kamehameha built an observation tower in Lahaina to watch for ships, many of which were his own, returning laden with riches from the world at large.

In the last years of his life Kamehameha returned to his beloved Kona Coast, where he enjoyed the excellent fishing renowned to this day. He had taken Hawaii from the darkness of warfare into the light of peace. He died true to the religious and moral *kapu* of his youth, the only ones he had ever known, and with him died a unique way of life. Two loyal retainers buried his bones after the baked flesh had been ceremoniously stripped away. A secret burial cave was chosen so that no one could desecrate the remains of the great chief, thereby absorbing his mana. The tomb's whereabouts remain unknown, and disturbing the dead remains one of the strictest *kapu* to this day. The Lonely One's kingdom would pass to his son, Liholiho, but true power would be in the hands of his beloved and feisty wife, Ka'ahumanu. As Kamehameha's spirit drifted from this earth, two forces sailing around Cape Horn would forever change Hawaii: the missionaries and the whalers.

MISSIONARIES AND WHALERS

The year 1819 was of the utmost significance in Hawaiian history. It marked the death of Kamehameha, the overthrow of the ancient *kapu* system, the arrival of the first "whaler" in Lahaina, and the departure of Calvinist missionaries from New England determined to convert the heathen islands. Great changes began to rattle the old order to its foundations. With the *kapu* system and all of the ancient gods abandoned (except for the fire goddess of Kilauea, Pele), a great void was left in the souls of the Hawaiians. In the coming decades Hawaii, also coveted by Russia, France, and England, was finally consumed by America. The islands had the first American school, printing press, and newspaper *(The Polynesian)* west of the Mississippi. Lahaina, in its heyday, became the world's greatest whaling port, accommodating over 500 ships of all types during its peak years. Sailors snatched brief pleasure in every port and jumped ship at every opportunity, especially in an easy berth like Lahaina. In exchange for *aloha,* they gave drunkenness and insidious death by disease—common conditions such as colds, flu, venereal disease, and sometimes smallpox and cholera devastated the Hawaiians, who had no natural immunities to these foreign ailments.

Into this vortex sailed the brig *Thaddeus* on April 4, 1820. Coming ashore at Kailua-Kona, the Reverends Bingham and Thurston were granted a one-year trial missionary period by King Liholiho. They established themselves on the Big Island and O'ahu and from there began the transformation of Hawaii. The missionaries were people of God, but also practical-minded Yankees. They brought education, enterprise, and most importantly, unlike the transient seafarers, a commitment to stay and build. By 1824, the new faith had such a foothold that Chieftess Keopuolani climbed to the fire pit atop Kilauea and defied Pele. Keopuolani ate forbidden *'ohelo* berries and cried out, "Jehovah is my God." Over the next decades the governing of Hawaii slipped away from the Big Island and moved to the new port cities of Lahaina on Maui and, later, Honolulu.

The year 1824 also marked the death of Keopuolani, who was given a Christian burial. She had set the standard by accepting Christianity, and a number of the *ali'i* had followed the queen's lead. Liholiho had sailed off to England, where he and his wife contracted measles and died.

During these years, Ka'ahumanu allied herself with Reverend Richards, pastor of the first mission in the islands, and together they wrote Hawaii's first code of laws based upon the Ten Commandments. Foremost was the condemnation of murder, theft, brawling, and the desecration of the Sabbath by work or play. The early missionaries had the best of intentions, but like all zealots they were blinded by the single-mindedness that was also their greatest ally. They weren't surgically selective in their destruction of native beliefs. *Anything* native was felt to be inferior, and they set about wiping out all traces of the old ways. In their rampage they reduced the Hawaiian culture to ashes, plucking self-will and determination from the hearts of a once-proud people. More so than the whalers, they terminated the Hawaiian way of life.

PLANTATION DAYS

It's hard to say just where the sugar industry began in Hawaii. The Koloa Sugar Plantation on the southern coast of Kaua'i successfully refined sugar in 1835. Others tried, and one success was at Hana, Maui, in 1849. A whaler named George Wilfong hauled four blubber pots ashore and set them up on a rocky hill in the middle of 60 acres he had planted in sugar. A team of oxen turned "crushing rollers" and the cane juice flowed down an open trough into the pots, under which an attending native kept a roaring fire burning. Wilfong's methods of refining were crude but the resulting high-quality sugar turned a neat profit in Lahaina. The main problem was labor. The Hawaiians, who made excellent whalers, were basically indentured workers. They became extremely disillusioned with their contracts, which could last up to 10 years. Most of their wages were eaten up by manufactured commodities sold at the company store, and it didn't take long for them to realize that they were little more than slaves. At every opportunity they either left the area or just refused to work.

Imported Labor

The Masters and Servants Act of 1850, which allowed importation of laborers under the contract system, ostensibly guaranteed an endless supply of cheap labor for the plantations. Chinese laborers were imported but were too enterprising to remain in the fields for a meager $3 per month. They left as soon as opportunity permitted and went into business as small merchants and retailers. In the meantime, Wilfong had sold out, releasing most of the Hawaiians previously held under contract, and his plantation fell into disuse. In 1860 two Danish brothers, August and Oscar Unna, bought land at Hana to raise sugar. They solved the labor problem by importing Japanese laborers, who were extremely hardworking and easily managed. The workday lasted 10 hours, six days a week, for a salary of $20 per month plus housing and medical care. Plantation life was very structured, with stringent rules governing even bedtimes and lights out. A worker was fined for being late or for smoking on the job. The workers had great difficulty functioning under these circumstances, and improvements in benefits and housing were slowly gained.

Changing Society

The sugar plantation system changed life in Hawaii physically, spiritually, politically, and economically. Now boatloads of workers came not only from Japan but from Portugal, Germany, and even Russia. The white-skinned workers were most often the field foremen *(luna)*. With the immigrants came new religions, new animals and plants, unique cuisines, and a plantation language known as pidgin, or better yet, *da' kine*. Many Asians and, to a lesser extent, the other groups—including the white plantation owners—intermarried with Hawaiians. A new class of people properly termed "cosmopolitan" but more familiarly and aptly known as "locals" was emerging. These were the people of multiple race backgrounds who couldn't exactly say *what* they were but it was clear to all just *who* they were. The plantation owners became the new "chiefs" of Hawaii who could carve up the land and dispense favors. The Hawaiian monarchy was soon eliminated.

THE LONG (AND CONTESTED) ROAD TO STATEHOOD
The Revolution

When Queen Lili'uokalani took office in 1891, the native population was at a low of 40,000, and she felt that the United States had too much influence over her homeland. She was known to personally favor the English over the Americans. She attempted to replace the liberal constitution of 1887 (adopted by her pro-American brother) with an autocratic mandate in which she would have had much more political and economic control of the islands. When the McKinley Tariff of 1890 brought a decline in sugar profits, she made no attempt to improve the situation. Thus, the planters saw her as a political obstacle to their economic growth; most of Hawaii's American planters and merchants were in favor of a rebellion. She would have to go! A central spokesperson and firebrand was Lorrin Thurston, a Honolulu publisher who, with a central core of about 30 men, challenged the Hawaiian monarchy. Although Lili'uokalani rallied some support and had a small military potential in her personal guard, the coup was ridiculously easy—it took only one casualty. Captain John Good shot a Hawaiian policeman in the arm and that did it. Naturally, the conspirators could not have succeeded without some solid assurances from a secret contingent in the U.S. Congress as well as outgoing president Benjamin Harrison, who favored Hawaii's annexation. Marines from the *Boston* went ashore to "protect American lives," and on January 17, 1893, the Hawaiian monarchy came to an end.

The provisional government was headed by Sanford B. Dole, who became president of the Hawaiian Republic. Lili'uokalani surrendered not to the conspirators but to U.S. ambassador John Stevens. She believed that the U.S. government, which had assured her of Hawaiian independence, would be outraged by the overthrow and would come to her aid. Incoming president Grover Cleveland *was* outraged, and Hawaii wasn't immediately annexed as expected. When queried about what she would do with the conspirators if she were reinstated, Lili'uokalani said that they would be hung as traitors. The racist press of the times, which portrayed the Hawaiians as half-civilized, bloodthirsty heathens, publicized this widely. Since the conspirators were the leading citizens of the land, the queen's words proved untimely. In January 1895 a small, ill-fated counterrevolution headed by Lili'uokalani failed, and she was placed under house arrest in 'Iolani Palace. Officials of the republic insisted she use her married name (Mrs. John Dominis) to sign the documents forcing her to abdicate her throne. She was also forced to swear allegiance to the new republic. Lili'uokalani went on to write *Hawaii's Story* and the lyric ballad "Aloha O'e." She never forgave the conspirators and remained "queen" to the Hawaiians until her death in 1917.

Annexation

The overwhelming majority of Hawaiians opposed annexation and desired to restore the monarchy. But they were prevented from voting by the new republic because they couldn't meet the imposed property and income qualifications—a transparent ruse by the planters to control the election. Most *haole* were racist and believed that the "common people" could not be entrusted with the vote because they were childish and incapable of ruling themselves. The fact that the Hawaiians had existed quite well for 1,000 years before white people even reached Hawaii was never considered. The Philippine theater of the Spanish-American War also prompted annexation. One of the strongest proponents was Alfred Mahon, a brilliant naval strategist who, with support from Theodore Roosevelt, argued that the U.S. military must have Hawaii in order to be a viable force in the Pacific. In addition, Japan, victorious in its recent war with China, protested the American intention to annex, and in so doing prompted even moderates to support annexation for fear that the Japanese themselves coveted the prize. On July 7, 1898, President McKinley signed the annexation agreement, and this "tropical fruit" was finally put into America's basket.

ENTER THE 20TH CENTURY

Hawaii entered the 20th century totally transformed from what it had been. The old Hawaiian language, religion, culture, and leadership were all but gone; Western dress, values, education, and recreation were the norm. Native Hawaiians were now unseen citizens who lived in dwindling numbers in remote areas. The plantations, new centers of social order, had a strong Asian flavor; more than 75 percent of their workforce was Asian. There was a small white middle class, an all-powerful white elite, and a single political party ruled by that elite. Education, however, was always highly prized, and by the turn of the 20th century all racial groups were encouraged to attend school. By 1900, almost 90 percent of Hawaiians were literate (far above the national norm), and schooling was mandatory for all children ages six to 15. Intermarriage was accepted, and there was a mixing of the races like nowhere else on earth.

The military became increasingly important to Hawaii. It brought in money and jobs, dominating the island economy. The Japanese attack on Pearl Harbor, which began U.S. involvement in World War II, bound Hawaii to America forever. Once the islands had been baptized by blood, the average Mainlander felt that Hawaii was American soil. A movement among Hawaiians to become part of the Union began to grow. They wanted a real voice in Washington, not merely a voteless delegate as provided under their territory status. Hawaii became the 50th state in 1959, and the jumbo-jet revolution of the 1960s made it easily accessible to growing numbers of tourists from all over the world.

Pearl Harbor Attack

On the morning of December 7, 1941, the Japanese carrier *Akagi,* flying the battle flag of the famed Admiral Togo of the Russo-Japanese War, received and broadcast over its PA system island music from Honolulu station KGMB. Deep in the bowels of the ship a radioman listened for a much different message, coming thousands of miles from the Japanese mainland. When the ironically poetic message "east wind rain" was received, the attack was launched. At the end of the day, 2,325 U.S. servicemen and 57 civilians were dead; 188 planes were destroyed; 18 major warships were sunk or heavily damaged; and the United States was in the war. Japanese casualties were ludicrously light. The ignited conflict would rage for four years until Japan, through the bombings at Nagasaki and Hiroshima, was vaporized into total submission. At the end of hostilities, Hawaii would never again be considered separate from America.

Statehood

A number of economic and political reasons explain why the ruling elite of Hawaii desired statehood, but, put simply, the vast majority of people who lived there, especially after World War II, considered themselves Americans. The first serious mention of making "The Sandwich Islands" a state was in the 1850s under President Franklin Pierce, but it wasn't taken seriously until the monarchy was overthrown in the 1890s. For the next 50 years statehood proposals were made repeatedly to Congress, but there was stiff opposition, especially from the southern states. With Hawaii a territory, an import quota system beneficial to Mainland producers could be enacted on produce, especially sugar. Also, there was prejudice against creating a state in a place where the majority of the populace was not white.

During World War II, Hawaii was placed under martial law, but no serious attempt to intern the Japanese population was made, as in California. There were simply too many Japanese, and many went on to gain the respect of the American people with their outstanding fighting record during the war. Hawaii's own 100th Battalion became the famous 442nd Regimental Combat Team, which gained notoriety by saving the Lost Texas Battalion during the Battle of the Bulge and went on to be *the* most decorated battalion in all of World War II. When these GIs returned home, no one was going to tell them that they were not loyal Americans. Many of these AJAs (Americans of Japanese Ancestry) took advantage of the GI Bill and received higher educations. They were from the common people, not the elite, and they rallied grassroots support for statehood. When the vote finally occurred, approximately 132,900 voted in favor of statehood, with only 7,800 votes against. Congress passed the Hawaii State Bill on March 12, 1959, and on August 21, 1959, President Eisenhower announced that Hawaii was officially the 50th state.

In November 1993, President Bill Clinton signed United States Public Law 103-150, the "Apology Resolution," to acknowledge the 100th anniversary of the January 17, 1893, overthrow of the Kingdom of Hawaii, and to offer an apology to Native Hawaiians on behalf of the United States for the overthrow.

Government and Economy

GOVERNMENT

The major difference between the government of the state of Hawaii and those of other states is that it's "streamlined," and in theory more efficient. There are only two levels of government: the state and the county. With no town or city governments to deal with, considerable bureaucracy is eliminated. Hawaii, in anticipation of becoming a state, drafted a constitution in 1950 and was ready to go when statehood came. Politics and government are taken seriously in the Aloha State, which consistently turns in the best national voting record per capita. For example, in the first state elections, 173,000 of 180,000 registered voters voted—a whopping 94 percent of the electorate. In the election to ratify statehood, hardly a ballot went uncast, with 95 percent of the voters opting for statehood. The bill carried in every island of Hawaii except Ni'ihau, where most of the people (total population 250 or so) were of relatively pure Hawaiian blood. When Hawaii became a state, Honolulu became its capital. Since statehood, the legislative and executive branches of state government have been dominated by the Democratic Party. Elected in 2010, the current governor is Neil Abercrombie (D). Hawaii is represented in the U.S. Congress by two senators, currently Daniel K. Inouye (D) and Daniel K. Akaka (D), and two representatives, currently Colleen Hanabusa (D) and Mazie Hirono (D).

County of Hawai'i

The current mayor of the County of Hawai'i is a democrat, William P. Kenoi (known as Billy). The mayor is assisted by an elected county council consisting of nine members, one from each council district around the island. Hilo is the county seat.

Of the 25 state senatorial districts, the County of Hawai'i is represented by three. The First District takes in the whole northern section of the island: the Hamakua Coast, Mauna Kea, North and South Kohala, and part of North Kona. The Second District is mainly Hilo and its outlying area. The Third District comprises Puna, Ka'u, South Kona, and most of North Kona. The County of Hawai'i has 6 of 51 seats in the State House of Representatives. For information on the county see www.hawaiicounty.gov.

ECONOMY

Hawaii's mid-Pacific location makes it perfect for two prime sources of income: tourism and the military. Tourists come in anticipation of endless golden days on soothing beaches, while the military is provided with the strategic position of an unsinkable battleship. Each economic sector nets Hawaii billions of dollars annually, money that should keep flowing smoothly and even increase in the foreseeable future. Tourism alone reaps over $11 billion. These revenues remain mostly aloof from the normal ups and downs of the Mainland U.S. economy. Also contributing to the state revenue are, in descending proportions: manufacturing, construction, and agriculture (mainly sugar and pineapples). As long as the sun shines and the balance of global power requires a military presence, the economic stability of Hawaii is guaranteed.

Agriculture

The Big Island's economy is the state's most agriculturally based. Over 5,000 farmhands, horticultural workers, and *paniolo* (cowboys) work the land to produce about one-third of the state's vegetables and melons, over 75 percent of the total fruit production, 95 percent of the papayas, 75 percent of the bananas, 95 percent of the avocados, and 50 percent of the guavas. Much of the state's taro is also produced on the Big Island, principally in the Waipi'o Valley and along the Hamakua Coast, and ginger production has become a major economic factor with more than six million pounds grown annually. The Big Island also produces some 50 million pounds of macadamia nuts yearly, about 90 percent of the total amount grown in the state. While that's a respectable number, it's less than half the world's total. The Big Island used to have the only commercial coffee plantations in the country, but now coffee is grown on all the major Hawaiian islands. Due to the increased interest in gourmet Kona coffee, the coffee industry's share in the economy of the island is increasing, and the Big Island grows about three million pounds of coffee every year. More than 350 horticultural farms produce the largest number of orchids and anthuriums in the state, leaving the Big Island awash in color and fragrance. Other exotic flowers and foliage are also a growing concern. In the hills, entrepreneurs raise *pakalolo* (marijuana), which has become the state's most productive although illicit cash crop.

Hawai'i used to be the state's largest sugar grower, with over 150,000 acres in cane. These commercial fields produced four million tons of refined sugar, 40 percent of the state's output. The majority of sugar land was along the Hamakua Coast, long known for its abundant water supply. At one time, the cane was even transported to the mills by water flumes. Other large pockets of cane fields were found on the southern part of the island in Ka'u and Puna, as well as at the northern tip in North Kohala. With the closing of the last mill in 1996, sugar is no longer grown commercially on the island. Still, small entrepreneurial farms grow it on greatly reduced acreage. The big cane trucks have ceased to roll, and the few remaining smokestacks stand in silent testimony to a bygone era.

The upland Kona district is a splendid area for raising coffee; it gives the beans a beautiful tan. Lying in Mauna Loa's rain shadow, the district gets dewy mornings followed by sunshine and an afternoon cloud shadow. Kona coffee has long been accepted as gourmet quality and is sold in the better restaurants throughout Hawaii and in fine coffee shops around the world. It's a dark, full-bodied coffee with a rich aroma. Approximately 600 small farms produce nearly $15 million a year in coffee revenue. Few, however, make it a full-time business. The production of Kona coffee makes up only about one-tenth of 1 percent of the coffee grown around the world. The rare bean is often blended with other varietals. When sold unblended it is quite expensive. With its similar climactic conditions, the district of Ka'u has also begun to grow coffee, albeit in much smaller quantities. While not yet well known, Ka'u coffee has gained a loyal following.

Hawai'i's cattle ranches produce over five million pounds of beef per year, 50 percent of the state's total. More than 450 independent ranches are located on the island, with total acreage of over 650,000 acres, but they are dwarfed both in size and production by the massive Parker Ranch, which alone has 175,000 acres and is about half the size of O'ahu. While beef is the largest player in the livestock market, pork, dairy products, eggs, poultry, sheep, goats, bees, and honey also are components, and together constitute perhaps half of the island's livestock revenues.

Military

On average, about 60 military personnel are stationed on the Big Island at any one time, with about the same number of dependents. Most of these people are attached to the enormous Pohakuloa Training Area in the center of the island; a lesser number are at a few minor installations around Hilo, Kailua, and at Kilauea Volcano.

People and Culture

POPULATION

Nowhere else on earth can you find such a kaleidoscopic mixture of people as in Hawaii. Every major (socially constructed) race is accounted for, and over 50 ethnic groups are represented throughout the islands, making Hawaii the most racially integrated state in the country. Its population of 1.2 million includes some 80,000 permanently stationed military personnel and their dependents. Until the year 2000, when California's white population fell below 50 percent, Hawaii was the only U.S. state where white individuals were not the majority. About 56 percent of Hawaiian residents were born there, 26 percent were born on the U.S. Mainland, and 18 percent are foreign-born.

The population has grown steadily in recent times, but fluctuated wildly in the past. In 1876, it reached its lowest ebb, with only 55,000 permanent residents. This was the era of large sugar plantations; their constant demand for labor was the primary cause for importing various peoples from around the world and led to Hawaii's racial mix. World War II saw the population swell from 400,000 to 900,000. Most of the 500,000 military personnel left at war's end, but many returned to settle after getting a taste of island living. There is no ethnic majority on the Big Island; population numbers include 32 percent Caucasian, 28 percent mixed, 27 percent Asian, 11 percent Hawaiian, and 2 percent other.

LANGUAGE

Hawaii is part of America and people speak English there, but that's not the whole story. If you turn on the TV to catch the evening news, you'll hear "Walter Cronkite" English, unless of course you happen to tune in to a Japanese-language broadcast designed for tourists from that country. You can easily pick up a Chinese-language newspaper or groove to the music on a Filipino radio station, but let's not confuse the issue. All your needs and requests at airports, car-rental agencies, restaurants, hotels, or wherever you happen to travel will be completely understood, as well as answered, in English. However, when you happen to overhear islanders speaking, what they're saying will sound somewhat familiar but you won't be able to pick up all the words, and the beat and melody of the language will be noticeably different.

Hawaii—like New England, the Deep South, and the Midwest—has its own unmistakable linguistic regionalism. All the ethnic peoples who make up Hawaii have enriched the English spoken there with words, expressions, and subtle shades of meaning that are commonly used and understood throughout the islands. The greatest influence on English has come from the Hawaiian language itself, and words such as "aloha," "hula," "lu'au," and "lei" are familiarly used and understood by most Americans.

Other migrant peoples, especially the Chinese, Japanese, and Portuguese, influenced the local dialect to such an extent that the simplified plantation lingo they spoke has become known as "pidgin." A fun and enriching part of the "island experience" is picking up a few words of Hawaiian and pidgin. English is the official language of the state, business, education, and perhaps even the mind, but pidgin is the language of the people, the emotions, and life, while Hawaiian (also an official language of the state, but used "only as provided by law") remains the language of the heart and the soul.

Pidgin

The dictionary definition of pidgin is a simplified language with a rudimentary grammar used as a means of communication between people speaking different languages. Hawaiian pidgin is a little more complicated than that. It had its roots during the plantation days of the 19th century when white owners and *luna* (foremen) had to communicate with recently arrived Chinese, Japanese, and Portuguese laborers. It evolved as a simple language of the here and now, primarily concerned with the necessary functions of working, eating, and sleeping. It has an economical noun-verb-object structure (although not necessarily in that order).

Hawaiian words make up most of pidgin's non-English vocabulary. It includes a good smattering of Chinese, Japanese, and Samoan; the distinctive rising inflection is provided by the melodious Mediterranean lilt of the Portuguese. Pidgin is not a stagnant language. It's kept alive by hip new words introduced by cool people and especially by slang words introduced by teenagers. It's a colorful English, and is as regionally unique as the speech of Cajuns in rural Louisiana bayous. Hawaiians of all socio-ethnic backgrounds can at least understand pidgin. Most islanders are proud of it, while some consider it a low-class jargon. The Hawaiian House of Representatives has given pidgin an official sanction, and most people feel that it adds a real local style and should be preserved.

Pidgin is first learned at school, where all students, regardless of background, are exposed to it. The pidgin spoken by young people today is "fo' real" different from that of their parents. It's no longer only plantation talk but has moved to the streets and picked up some sophistication. At one time there was an academic movement to exterminate it, but that idea died away with the same thinking that insisted on making left-handed people write with their right hand. It is strange, however, that pidgin has become the unofficial language of Hawaii's grassroots movement, when it actually began as a white owners' language that was used to supplant Hawaiian and all the languages brought to the islands.

Although hip young *haole* use pidgin all the time, it has gained the connotation of being the language of the nonwhite locals and is part of the "us against them" way of thinking. All local people, *haole* or not, do consider pidgin their own island language and don't really like it when it's used by *malihini* (newcomers). If you're in the islands long enough, you don't have to bother learning pidgin; it'll learn you. There's a book sold all over the islands called *Pidgin to da Max,* written by a *haole* from Nebraska named Doug Simonson. You might not be able to understand what's being said by locals speaking pidgin (that's usually the idea), but you should be able to *feel* what's being meant.

Hawaiian

The Hawaiian language sways like a palm tree in a gentle wind. Its words are as melodious as a love song. Linguists say that you can learn a lot about people through their language; when you hear Hawaiian you think of gentleness and love, and it's hard to imagine the ferocious side so evident in Hawaii's past. With its many Polynesian root words easily traced to Indonesian and Malay, Hawaiian is obviously from this same stock. The Hawaiian spoken today is very different from old Hawaiian. Its greatest metamorphosis occurred when the missionaries began to write it down in the 1820s, but in the last couple of decades there has been a movement to reestablish the Hawaiian language. Not only are courses in it offered at the University of Hawai'i, but there is a successful elementary immersion school program in the state, some books are being printed in it, and more and more musicians are performing it. Many scholars have put forth translations of Hawaiian, but there are endless, volatile disagreements in the academic sector about the real meanings of Hawaiian words. Hawaiian is no longer spoken as a language except on Ni'ihau, and the closest tourists will come to it is in place-names, street names, and words that have become part of common usage, such as aloha (a greeting) and mahalo (thank you).

Thanks to the missionaries, the Hawaiian language is rendered phonetically using only 12 letters. They are the five vowels (a, e, i, o, and u), sounded as they are in Italian, and seven consonants (h, k, l, m, n, p, w), sounded exactly as they are in English. Sometimes "w" is pronounced as "v," but this only occurs in the middle of a word and always follows a vowel. A consonant is always followed by a vowel, forming two-letter syllables, but vowels are often found in pairs or even triplets. A slight oddity about Hawaiian is the glottal stop called 'okina. This is an abrupt break in sound in the middle of a word, such as "uh-oh" in English, and is denoted with a reversed apostrophe (').

PRONUNCIATION KEY

For those unfamiliar with the sounds of Italian or other Romance languages, the vowels are sounded as follows:

A—in stressed syllables, pronounced as in "ah" (that feels good!). For example, Haleakala is pronounced "hah-lay-AH-kah-LAH."

E—short "e" is "eh," as in "pen" or "dent" (thus *hale* is "HAH-leh"). Long "e" sounds like "ay" as in "sway" or "day." For example, the Hawaiian goose *(nene)* is a "nay-nay," not a "knee-knee."

I—pronounced "ee" as in "see" or "we" (thus *pali* is pronounced "PAH-lee").

O—pronounced as in "no" or "oh," such as "KOH-uh" (koa) or "OH-noh" (ono).

U—pronounced "oo" as in "do" or "stew"; for example, "KAH-poo" *(kapu)* or "POO-nah" (Puna).

Diphthongs

There are also eight vowel pairs known as "diphthongs" (ae, ai, ao, au, ei, eu, oi, and ou). These are the sounds made by gliding from one vowel to another within a syllable. The stress is placed on the first vowel. In English, examples would be s**oi**l and b**ai**l. Common examples in Hawaiian are lei and *heiau*.

Stress

The best way to learn which syllables are stressed in Hawaiian is by listening closely. It becomes obvious after a while. There are also some vowel sounds that are held longer than others; These can occur at the beginning of a word, such as the first "a" in '*aina,* or in the middle of a word, like the first "a" in lanai. Again, it's a matter of tuning your ear and paying attention.

When written, these stressed vowels, called *kahako,* occur with a macron, or short line, over them. Stressed vowels with marks are not written as such in this guide. No one is going to give you a hard time if you mispronounce a word. It's good, however, to pay close attention to the pronunciation of street names and place-names because many Hawaiian words sound alike and a misplaced vowel here or there could be the difference between getting where you want to go and getting lost.

ARTS AND CRAFTS

Since everything in old Hawaii had to be fashioned by hand, almost every object was either a genuine work of art or the product of a highly refined craft. With the "civilizing" of the natives, most of the "old ways" disappeared, including the old arts and crafts. Most authentic Hawaiian art by master crafters exists only in museums, but with the resurgence of Hawaiian roots, many old arts are being revitalized, and their legacy lives on in a few artists who have become proficient in them.

Canoes

The most respected artisans in old Hawaii were the canoe makers. With little more than a stone adze and a pump drill, they built canoes that could carry 200 people and last for generations—sleek, well proportioned, and infinitely seaworthy. The main hull was usually a gigantic koa log, and the gunwale planks were minutely drilled and sewn to the sides with sennit rope. Apprenticeships lasted for years, and a young man knew that he had graduated when one day he was nonchalantly asked to sit down and eat with the master builders. Small family-sized canoes with outriggers were used for fishing and perhaps carried a spear rack; large oceangoing double-hulled canoes were used for migration and warfare. On these, the giant logs had been adzed to about two inches thick. A mainsail woven from pandanus was mounted on a central platform, and the boat was steered by two long paddles. The hull was dyed with plant juices and charcoal, and the entire village helped launch the canoe in a ceremony called "drinking the sea."

Carving and Woodworking

Wood was a primary material used by Hawaiian craftsmen. They almost exclusively used koa because of its density, strength, and natural luster. It was turned into canoes, woodware, calabashes, and furniture used by the *ali'i*. Temple idols were another major product of woodcarving. Various stone artifacts were also turned out, including poi pounders, mirrors, fish sinkers, and small idols.

While the carving and fashioning of old traditional items has by and large disappeared, lathe-turning of wooden bowls and the creation of wooden furniture from native woods is alive and strong. Old Hawaiians used koa almost exclusively because of its density, strength, and natural luster, but koa is becoming increasingly scarce. Costly *milo* and monkeypod, as well as a host of other native woods, are also excellent for turnings and household items and have largely replaced koa. These modern wooden objects are available at numerous shops and galleries. Countless inexpensive carved items are sold at variety stores, such as tikis, hula dancers, or salad servers, but most of these are imported from Asia or the Philippines.

Weaving

Hawaiians became the best basket makers and mat weavers in all of Polynesia. *Ulana* (woven mats) were made from *lau hala* (pandanus leaves). Once the leaves were split, the spine was removed and the leaves stored in large rolls. When needed they were soaked, pounded, and then fashioned into various floor coverings and sleeping mats. Intricate geometrical patterns were woven in, and the edges were rolled and well fashioned. Coconut palms were not used to make mats in old Hawaii, but a wide variety of basketry was made from the aerial root *'ie'ie*. The shapes varied according to use. Some baskets were tall and narrow, some were cones, others were flat like trays, while many were woven around gourds and calabashes.

The tradition of weaving has survived in Hawaii but is not strong. Older experienced weavers are dying, and few younger ones are showing interest in continuing the craft. The

© MARK WASSER

Hats are woven from *lau hala*, the leaves of the pandanus tree.

time-tested material of *lau hala* is still the best, although much is now made from coconut fronds. *Lau hala* is traditional Hawaiian weaving from the leaves *(lau)* of the pandanus *(hala)* tree. These leaves vary greatly in length, with the largest over six feet, and they have a thorny spine that must be removed before they can be worked. The color ranges from light tan to dark brown. The leaves are cut into strips one-eighth-inch to one-inch wide and are then employed in weaving. Any variety of items can be made or at least covered in *lau hala*. It makes great purses, mats, baskets, and table mats. You can still purchase items from bags to a woven hat, and all share the desirable qualities of strength, lightness, and ventilation.

Woven into a hat, *lau hala* is absolutely superb but should not be confused with a palm-frond hat. A *lau hala* hat is amazingly supple and even when squashed will pop back into shape. A good one is expensive and with proper care will last for years. All *lau hala* should be given a light application of mineral oil on a monthly basis, especially if it's exposed to the sun. For flat items, iron over a damp cloth and keep purses and baskets stuffed with paper when not in use. Palm fronds also are widely used in weaving. They, too, are a great natural raw material, but not as good as *lau hala*. Almost any woven item, such as a beach bag woven from palm, makes a good authentic yet inexpensive gift or souvenir.

Featherwork

This highly refined art was practiced only on the islands of Tahiti, New Zealand, and Hawaii, but the fashioning of feather helmets and idols was unique to Hawaii. Favorite colors were red and yellow, which came only in a very limited supply from a small number of birds, such as the *'o'o*, *'i'iwi*, *mamo*, and *'apapane*. Professional bird hunters in old Hawaii paid their taxes to *ali'i* in prized feathers. The feathers were fastened to a woven net of *olona* cord and made into helmets, idols, and beautiful flowing capes and cloaks. These resplendent garments were made and worn only by men, especially during battle, when a fine cloak

became a great trophy of war. Featherwork was also employed in the making of *kahili* fans and lei, which were highly prized by the noble *ali'i* women.

Lei-Making

Any flower or blossom can be strung into a lei, but the most common are orchids or the lovely smelling plumeria. Lei, like babies, are all beautiful, but special lei are highly prized by those who know what to look for. Of the different stringing styles, the most common is *kui*—stringing the flower through the middle or side. Most "airport-quality" lei are of this type. The *humuhumu* style, reserved for making flat lei, is made by sewing flowers and ferns to a ti, banana, or sometimes hala leaf. A *humuhumu* lei makes an excellent hatband. *Wili* is the winding together of greenery, ferns, and flowers into short, bouquet-type lengths. The most traditional form is *hili,* which requires no stringing at all but involves braiding fragrant ferns and leaves such as *maile*. If flowers are interwoven, the *hili* becomes the *haku* style, the most difficult and most beautiful type of lei.

Every major island is symbolized by its own lei made from a distinctive flower, shell, or fern. Each island has its own official color as well, though it doesn't necessarily correspond to the color of the island's lei. The island of Hawai'i's lei is made from the red (or rare creamy white or orange) *'ohi'a lehua* blossom. The lehua tree grows from sea level to 9,000 feet and produces an abundance of tufted flowers.

Tapa Cloth

Tapa, cloth made from tree bark, was common throughout Polynesia and was a woman's art. A few trees such as the *wauke* and *mamaki* produced the best cloth, but a variety of other types of bark could be utilized. First the raw bark was pounded into a felt-like pulp and beaten together to form strips (the beaters had distinctive patterns that helped make the cloth supple). The cloths were decorated by stamping (a form of block printing) and dyed with natural colors from plants and sea animals in shades of gray, purple, pink, and red. They were even painted with natural brushes made from pandanus fruit, with an overall gray color made from charcoal. The tapa cloth was sewn together to make bed coverings, and fragrant flowers and herbs were either sewn or pounded in to produce a permanent fragrance. Tapa cloth is still available today, but the Hawaiian methods have been lost, and most comes from other areas of Polynesia.

Aloha Wear

Wild Hawaiian shirts or bright *mu'umu'u,* especially when worn on the Mainland, have the magical effect of making wearers feel like they're in Hawaii, while at the same time eliciting spontaneous smiles from passersby. Maybe it's the colors, or perhaps it's just the "vibe" that signifies "party time" or "hang loose," but nothing says Hawaii like alohawear. There are more than a dozen fabric houses in Hawaii turning out distinctive patterns, and many dozens of factories creating their own personalized designs. These factories often have attached retail outlets, but in any case you can find hundreds of shops selling aloha wear. Aloha shirts were the brilliant idea of a Chinese merchant in Honolulu, who used to hand-tailor them and sell them to the tourists who arrived by ship in the glory days before World War II. They were an instant success. *Mu'umu'u* or "Mother Hubbards" were the idea of missionaries, who were appalled by Hawaiian women running about au naturel and insisted on covering their new Christian converts from head to foot. Now the roles are reversed, and it's Mainlanders who come to Hawaii and immediately strip down to as little clothing as possible.

At one time aloha wear was exclusively made of cotton or from manmade, natural fiber–based rayon, and these materials are still the best for any tropical clothing. Beware, however: Polyester has slowly crept into the market! No material could possibly be worse for the island climate, so when buying your aloha wear make sure to check the label for material content. On the bright side, silk also is used and makes a good material but is a bit heavy for some. *Mu'umu'u* now come in various styles and can be worn for the entire spectrum of social occasions in Hawaii. Aloha shirts are basically cut the same as always, but the patterns have undergone changes; apart from the original flowers and ferns, modern shirts might depict an island scene in the manner of a silk-screen painting. A basic good-quality *mu'umu'u* or aloha shirt is guaranteed to be worth its price in good times and happy smiles. The connoisseur might want to purchase *The Hawaiian Shirt, Its Art and History,* by R. Thomas Steele. It's illustrated with more than 150 shirts that are now considered works of art by collectors the world over.

Scrimshaw

The art of etching and carving on bone and ivory has become an island tradition handed down from the times of the great whaling ships. Examples of this Danish sailors' art date all the way back to the 15th century, but, like jazz, it was really popularized and raised to an art form by Americans—whalers on decade-long voyages from "back east" plying vast oceans in search of great whales. Frederick Merek, who sailed aboard the whaling ship *Susan,* was the best of the breed; however, most sailors only carved on the teeth of great whales to pass the time and have something to trade for whiskey, women, and song in remote ports of call. When sailors, most of whom were illiterate, sent scrimshaw back to family and friends, it was considered more like a postcard than artwork. After the late 1800s, scrimshaw faded from popular view and became a lost art form until it was revived, mostly in Lahaina, during the 1960s. Today, scrimshaw can be found throughout Hawaii, but the center remains the old whaling capital of Lahaina, Maui. Scrimshaw is used in everything from belt buckles to delicate earrings and even coffee-table centerpieces. Prices go from a few dollars up to thousands and scrimshaw can be found in limited quantities in some galleries and fine art shops around the island.

Quilts

Along with the gospel and the will to educate,

the early missionaries brought skills and machines to sew. Many taught the Hawaiians how to quilt together small pieces of material into designs for the bed. Quilting styles and patterns varied over the years and generally shifted from designs familiar to New Englanders to those more pleasing to Hawaiian eyes, and a number of standard patterns include leaves, fruits, and flowers of the islands. Most Hawaiian-design quilts seen for sale in the islands today are now made in the Philippines under the direction of Hawaiian designers. Because of labor costs, they are far less expensive than any quilt that is actually made in Hawaii.

Paintings

One thing is for sure: Like the rest of the Hawaiian Islands, Hawai'i draws painters. Multitudes of painters. Captivated by the island's beauty, color, natural features, and living things, these artists interpret what they see and sense in a dizzying display from realism to expressionism. From immense *pali* cliffs to the tiniest flower petals, and humble workers' homes to the faces of the island people, they are all portrayed. Color, movement, feeling are captured, and the essence of Hawai'i is the result. Galleries and shops around the island display local artists' work, but there is a concentration of galleries in Holualoa above Kailua-Kona. Well-known artists charge a handsome fee for their work, but you can find some exceptional work for affordable prices hidden here and there among the rest.

Jewelry

Jewelry is always an appreciated gift, especially if it's distinctive, and Hawaii has some of the most original. The sea provides the basic raw materials of pink, gold, and black corals that are as beautiful and fascinating as gemstones. Harvesting coral is very dangerous work. The Lahaina beds off Maui have one of the best black coral lodes in the islands, but unlike reef coral, these trees grow at depths bordering the outer limits of a scuba diver's capabilities. Only the best can dive 180 feet after the black coral, and about one diver per year dies in pursuit of it. Conservationists have placed great pressure on the harvesters of these deep corals, and the state of Hawaii has placed strict limits and guidelines on the firms and divers involved.

Puka shells (with small, naturally occurring holes) and *'opihi* shells are also made into jewelry. Many times these items are very inexpensive, yet they are authentic and are great purchases for the price.

HULA

The hula is more than an ethnic dance; it is the soul of Hawaii expressed in motion. It began as a form of worship during religious ceremonies and was only danced by highly trained men. It gradually evolved into a form of entertainment, but in no regard was it sexual. The hula was the opera, theater, and lecture hall of the islands all rolled into one. It was history portrayed in the performing arts. In the beginning an androgynous deity named Laka descended to earth and taught men how to dance the hula. In time the male aspect of Laka departed for the heavens, but the female aspect remained. The female Laka set up her own special hula *heiau* at Ha'ena on the Na Pali Coast of Kaua'i, where it still exists. As time went on, women were allowed to learn the hula. Scholars surmise that men became too busy wresting a living from the land to maintain the art form.

Men did retain a type of hula for themselves called *lua*. This was a form of martial art employed in hand-to-hand combat that evolved into a ritualized warfare dance called *hula ku'i*. During the 19th century, the hula almost vanished because the missionaries considered it vile and heathen. King Kalakaua is generally regarded as having saved it during the 1800s, when he formed his own troupe and encouraged the dancers to learn the old hula. Many of the original dances were forgotten, but some were retained and are performed to this day. Although professional dancers were highly trained, everyone took part in the hula. *Ali'i,* commoners, young, and old all danced.

Hula is art in swaying motion, and the true form is studied rigorously and taken very seriously. Today, hula *halau* (schools) are active on every island, teaching hula and keeping the old ways and culture alive. (Ancient hula is called *hula kahiko,* and modern renditions are known as *hula auana.*) Performers still spend years perfecting their techniques. They show off their accomplishments during the fierce competition of the Merrie Monarch Festival in Hilo every April. The winning *halau* is praised and recognized throughout the islands.

Hawaiian hula was never performed in grass skirts; tapa or ti-leaf skirts were worn. Grass skirts came to Hawaii from the Gilbert Islands, and if you see grass and cellophane skirts in a "hula revue," it's not traditional. Almost every major resort offering entertainment or a *lu'au* also offers a revue. Most times, young island beauties accompanied by proficient local musicians put on a floor show for the tourists. It'll be fun, but it won't be traditional.

A hula dancer has to learn how to control every part of her/his body, including facial expressions, which help to set the mood. The hands are extremely important and provide instant background scenery. For example, if the hands are thrust outward in an aggressive manner, this can mean a battle; if they sway gently overhead, they refer to the gods or to creation; they can easily become rain, clouds, sun, sea, or moon. Watch the hands to get the gist of the story, but as one wise guy said, "You watch the parts you like, and I'll watch the parts I like!" The motion of swaying hips can denote a long walk, a canoe ride, or sexual intercourse. Foot motion can portray a battle, a walk, or any kind of conveyance. The overall effect is multidirectional synchronized movement. The correct chanting of the *mele* is an integral part of the performance. These story chants, accompanied by musical instruments, make the hula very much like opera; it is especially similar in the way the tale unfolds.

ISLAND MUSIC

The missionaries usually take a beating when it's recounted how much Hawaiian culture they destroyed while "civilizing" the natives. However, they seem to have done one thing right. They introduced the Hawaiians to the diatonic musical scale and immediately opened a door for latent and superbly harmonious talent. Before the missionaries, the Hawaiians knew little about melody. Though sonorous, their *mele* were repetitive chants in which the emphasis was placed on historical accuracy and not on "making music." The Hawaiians, in short, didn't *sing.* But within a few years of the missionaries' arrival, they were belting out good old Christian hymns, and one of their favorite pastimes became group and individual singing.

Early in the 1800s, Spanish *vaqueros* from California were imported to teach the Hawaiians how to be cowboys. With them came guitars and moody ballads. The Hawaiian *paniolo* (cowboys) quickly learned how to punch cows and croon away the long lonely nights on the range. Immigrants who came along a little later in the 19th century, especially from Portugal, helped create a Hawaiian-style music. Their biggest influence was a small, four-stringed instrument called a *braga* or *cavaquinho.* One owned by Augusto Dias was the prototype of a homegrown Hawaiian instrument that became known as the ukulele. "Jumping flea," the translation of ukulele, is an appropriate name devised by the Hawaiians when they saw how nimble the fingers were as they "jumped" over the strings.

King Kalakaua (The Merrie Monarch) and Queen Lili'uokalani were both patrons of the arts who furthered the Hawaiian musical identity at the turn of the 20th century. Kalakaua revived the hula and was also a gifted lyricist and balladeer. He wrote the words to "Hawaii Pono'i," which became the anthem of the nation of Hawaii and later the state anthem. Lili'uokalani wrote the hauntingly beautiful "Aloha O'e," which is often pointed to as the "spirit of Hawaii" in music. Detractors say that its melody is extremely close to that of the old Christian hymn, "Rock Beside the Sea," but the lyrics are so beautiful and perfectly fitted that this doesn't matter.

Just prior to Kalakaua's reign, a Prussian bandmaster, Captain Henri Berger, was invited to head the fledgling Royal Hawaiian Band, which he turned into a very respectable orchestra lauded by many visitors to the islands. Berger was open-minded and learned to love Hawaiian music. He collaborated with Kalakaua and other island musicians to incorporate their music into a Western format. He headed the band for 43 years, until 1915, and was instrumental in making music a serious pursuit of talented Hawaiians.

Making Hawaiian Music

Hawaiian music has a unique twang, a special feeling that says the same thing to everyone who hears it: "Relax, sit back in the moonlight, watch the swaying palms as the surf sings a lullaby." This special sound is epitomized by the bouncy ukulele, the falsettos of Hawaiian crooners, and the smooth ring of the "steel" or "Hawaiian" guitar. The steel guitar is a variation originated by Joseph Kekuku in the 1890s. Stories abound of how Joseph Kekuku devised this instrument; the most popular versions say that Joe dropped his comb or pocketknife on his guitar strings and liked what he heard. Driven by the faint rhythm of an inner sound, he went to the machine shop at the Kamehameha Schools and turned out a steel bar for sliding over the strings. To complete the sound he changed the catgut strings to steel and raised them so they wouldn't hit the frets. Voilà!—Hawaiian music as the world knows it today.

The first melodious strains of **slack-key guitar** *(ki ho'alu)* can be traced back to the time of Kamehameha III and the *vaqueros* from California. The Spanish had their way of tuning the guitar, and they played difficult and aggressive music that did not sit well with Hawaiians, who were much more gentle and casual in their manners.

Hawaiians soon became adept at making their own music. At first, one person played the melody, but it lacked fullness. There was no body to the sound. So, as one *paniolo* fooled with the melody, another soon learned to play bass, which added depth. But, players were often alone, and by experimenting they learned that they could get the right hand going with the melody, and at the same time play the bass

note with the thumb to improve the sound. Singers also learned that they could "open tune" the guitar to match their rich voices.

Hawaiians believed knowledge was sacred, and what is sacred should be treated with utmost respect—which meant keeping it secret, except from sincere apprentices. Guitar playing became a personal art form whose secrets were closely guarded, handed down only to family members, and only to those who showed ability and determination. When old-time slack-key guitar players were done strumming, they loosened all the strings so no one could figure out how they had had their guitars tuned. If they were playing, and some interested folks came by who weren't part of the family, the Hawaiians stopped what they were doing, put their guitars down, and put their feet across the strings to wait for the folks to go away. As time went on, more and more Hawaiians began to play slack-key, and a common repertoire emerged.

Accomplished musicians could easily figure out the simple songs, once they had figured out how the family had tuned the guitar. One of the most popular tunings was the "open G." Old Hawaiian folks called it the "taro patch tune." Different songs came out, and if you were in the family and were interested in the guitar, your elders took the time to sit down and teach you. The way they taught was straightforward—and a test of your sincerity at the same time. The old master would start to play. He just wanted you to listen and get a feel for the music—nothing more than that. You brought your guitar and *listened*. When you felt it, you played it, and the knowledge was transferred. Today, only a handful of slack-key guitar players know how to play the classic tunes classically. The best-known and perhaps greatest slack-key player was Gabby Pahinui, with The Sons of Hawaii. He has passed away but left many recordings behind. Another slack-key master was Raymond Kane. None of his students were from his own family, and most were *haole* musicians trying to preserve the classical method of playing.

Hawaiian music received its biggest boost from a remarkable radio program known as

Hawaii Calls. This program sent out its music from the Banyan Court of Waikiki's Moana Hotel from 1935 until 1975. At its peak in the mid-1950s, it was syndicated on over 700 radio stations throughout the world. In fact, Japanese pilots heading for Pearl Harbor tuned in island music as a signal beam. Some internationally famous classic tunes came out of the 1940s and 1950s. Jack Pitman composed "Beyond the Reef" in 1948; more than 300 artists have recorded it and it has sold well over 12 million records. Other million-sellers include: "Sweet Leilani," "Lovely Hula Hands," "The Cross-Eyed Mayor of Kaunakakai," and "The Hawaiian Wedding Song."

By the 1960s, Hawaiian music began to die. Just too corny and light for those turbulent years, it belonged to the older generation and the good times that followed World War II. One man was instrumental in keeping Hawaiian music alive during this period. Don Ho, with his "Tiny Bubbles," became the token Hawaiian musician of the 1960s and early 1970s. He persevered long enough to become a legend in his own time, and his Polynesian Extravaganza at the Hilton Hawaiian Village packed visitors in until the early 1990s. Al Harrington, "The South Pacific Man," until his retirement had another Honolulu "big revue" that drew large crowds. Of this type of entertainment, perhaps the most Hawaiian was Danny Kaleikini, the Ambassador of Aloha, who entertained his audience with dances, Hawaiian anecdotes, and tunes on the traditional Hawaiian nose flute.

The Beat Goes On

Beginning in the mid-'70s, islanders began to assert their cultural identity. One of the unifying factors was the coming of age of "Hawaiian" music. It graduated from the "little grass shack" novelty tune and began to include sophisticated jazz, rock, and contemporary rhythms. Accomplished musicians whose roots were in traditional island music began to highlight their tunes with this distinctive sound. The best embellish their arrangements with ukuleles, steel guitars, and traditional percussion and melodic instruments. Some excellent modern recording artists have become island institutions. The local people say that you know the Hawaiian harmonies are good if they give you "chicken skin."

Each year special music awards, **Na Hoku Hanohano,** or Hoku for short, are given to distinguished island musicians. The following are some of the Hoku winners considered by their contemporaries to be among the best in Hawaii: Barney Isaacs and George Kuo, Na Leo Pilimihana, Robi Kahakalau, Kealii Reichel, Darren Benitez, Sonny Kamahele, Ledward Kaapana, Hapa, Israel Kamakawiwioʻole, Amy Hanaialiʻi, and Pure Heart. Though most do not perform on the Big Island, if they're playing, don't miss them. Some, unfortunately, are no longer among the living, but their recorded music can still be appreciated.

Past Hoku winners who have become renowned performers include the Brothers Cazimero, who are blessed with beautiful harmonic voices; Krush, highly regarded for their contemporary sounds; The Peter Moon Band, fantastic performers with a strong traditional sound; Henry Kapono, formerly of Kapono and Cecilio; and The Beamer Brothers. Others include Loyal Garner, Del Beazley, Bryan Kessler & Me No Hoa Aloha, George Kahumoku Jr., Olomana, Genoa Keawe, and Irmagard Aluli.

Those with access to the Internet can check out the Hawaiian music scene at one of the following: Hawaiian Music Island (www.mele.com) or Nahenahenet (http://nahenahe.net). While these are not the only Hawaiian music websites, they are a good place to start. For listening to Hawaiian music on the Web, try Kauaʻi Community Radio (http://kkcr.org) or Hawaii Public Radio (www.hawaiipublicradio.org).

FOOD

Hawaiian cuisine consists of several genres: "plantation foods," "local foods," and "Hawaii Regional Cuisine." But before we get to all that, there's the food of the multitude of immigrants (Polynesian, Korean, Japanese, Filipino, Portuguese, Chinese, Thai, Mainlanders, and

EATING VEGETARIAN AND VEGAN ON THE BIG ISLAND

Good news: It's easy to be a vegetarian or vegan on the Big Island, and I don't just mean it's easy to order a salad. First, the abundance of coconuts means coconut milk instead of cow milk is readily available, and coconut oil is used for cooking. So all you vegans, if you want to order a smoothie, don't be afraid to ask for coconut milk instead of regular milk. Chances are they'll have it. Also, many desserts (especially those bought at the farmers markets) are made from coconut milk, such as tapioca pudding and *haupia* (coconut pudding), which is a traditional Hawaiian dessert (also gluten free!).

For vegetarian and vegan groceries and prepared food, head to the **Island Naturals Market and Deli** (www.islandnaturals.com). The market, which has four locations on the Big Island, has a hot bar and refrigerated section with copious amounts of veg and vegan prepared foods. If you would prefer to shop somewhere that's entirely meat free, in Hilo try **Down to Earth,** where meatless Mondays are every day. This is where you go when you are desperate for tofurky or a seitan burger. And if you're in south Puna, try the lunch or dinner buffet at **Kalani Oceanside Retreat.** Although it's not entirely vegetarian, abundant vegetarian options (as well as local, organic, and gluten free) are available here. Not to mention some beautiful salad.

the new Mexican population) who populate the islands. So, for instance, when you order food at a Thai restaurant here, the food is as it would be if ordered in the home country. If you've never had Samoan food, here is a good place to try it (you'll often find it at festivals). Or go to a *lu'au* and try foods from across Polynesia (each country has its own typical foods, so I won't generalize here). Much of it is plant based (like taro or breadfruit) and coconut based (read: excellent desserts).

"Plantation foods" are a kind of "local foods" (local-style hybrid foods) and are a direct result of a combination of the dietary habits of the laborers working the fields and what foods were available during this era and easy to bring to work (prepared foods that could be left out all day). Even though the plantation days are gone, the resulting cuisine remains a staple of the Hawaiian diet: Spam *musubi,* plate lunches (a meat with macaroni salad and/or potato salad and/or rice), and the most important of them all—the *loco moco* (two scoops of rice, meat, a fried egg, and gravy).

Developing as a movement against "local foods" (which are confusingly not really made from local products), the **Hawaii Regional Cuisine** (HRC) movement began in the 1990s. It's a precursor to the modern-day locavore movement. The chefs most associated with this movement are: Peter Merriman, Alan Wong, Sam Choy, and Roy Yamaguchi. Out of the nonprofit organization they created (called Hawaii Regional Cuisine), in 1994 they published a cookbook by Janice Wald Henderson, *The New Cuisine of Hawaii.* The most important thing to know about HRC is that it is dedicated to preserving the traditions of Hawaiian foods, while utilizing what the islands have to offer. And luckily, the islands have a lot to offer, from fish to Big Island beef to an abundance of seasonal produce (papayas, mangos, passion fruit, avocados, nearly 50 kinds of bananas, and so much more).

For an excellent food history of Hawaii, check out Rachel Laudan's *The Food of Paradise.* This book is a rich narrative that dissects the main local foods and offers recipes too.

FESTIVALS AND EVENTS

In addition to all the American national holidays, Hawaii celebrates its own festivals, pageants, and a multitude of specialized exhibits. They occur throughout the year—some particular to only one island or locality, others (such as Aloha Festivals and Lei Day) celebrated on all the islands. At festival time, everyone is welcome. Many happenings are annual events, while others are onetime affairs. Check local newspapers and the free island magazines for exact dates. Island-specific calendar and event information is also available on the Web (www.konaweb.com/calendar).

One event held islandwide is the **Hawai'i Performing Arts Festival** (www.hawaii-performingartsfestival.org, $25 per event). Mainland-style performing arts events are uncommon on the Big Island, so this nearly three-week-long festival, held in June or July, marks one of few opportunities to see a variety of chamber music, opera, and musical theater. If the events are too expensive or if you are a student of music, you might want to join one of the free informal brown-bag afternoon events where you can hear a short concert or a speaker discuss a musical topic.

In December, look for arts and crafts festivals around the Big Island, where handicrafts are on sale for the holiday season.

ESSENTIALS

Getting There

With the number of visitors each year approaching seven million—and another several hundred thousand just passing through—the state of Hawaii is one of the easiest places in the world to get to by plane. About half a dozen large North American airlines (plus additional charter airlines) fly to and from the islands. About twice that number of foreign carriers, mostly from Asia and Oceania, also touch down there on a daily or weekly basis. Hawaii is a hotly contested air market. Competition among carriers is fierce, and this makes for some sweet deals and a wide choice of fares for the money-wise traveler. It also makes for pricing chaos. Airlines usually adjust their flight schedules about every three months to account for seasonal differences in travel and route changes.

There are two categories of airlines you can take to Hawaii: **domestic,** meaning American-owned, and **foreign**-owned. An American law, penned at the turn of the 20th century to protect American shipping, says that *only* an American carrier can transport you between two American cities. In the airline industry, this law is still very much in effect. It means, for example, that if you want a round-trip flight between San Francisco and Honolulu, you *must* fly on a domestic carrier. If, however, you are flying from San Francisco to Tokyo,

© BREE KESSLER

you are at liberty to fly a foreign airline, and you may even have a stopover in Hawaii, but you must continue to Tokyo or some other foreign city and cannot fly back to San Francisco on the foreign airline. Travel agents know this, but if you're planning your own trip, be aware of this fact.

If you fly to Hawaii from another country, you are free to use either an American or foreign carrier.

FLIGHTS TO THE BIG ISLAND

Most direct Mainland–Big Island flights land at the **Kona International Airport** (airport code KOA) on the west side of the island; however, as of June 2011 United Airlines now offers direct service from Los Angeles and San Francisco to the **Hilo International Airport** (airport code ITO) on the east side of the island. If you don't have a direct flight, most domestic and foreign carriers fly you to Honolulu and have arrangements with Hawaiian Airlines for getting you to the Big Island. This involves a plane change, but your baggage can be booked straight through.

VISAS

Entering Hawaii is like entering anywhere else in the United States. Foreign nationals must have a current passport, and most must have a proper visa, an ongoing or return air ticket, and sufficient funds for the proposed stay in Hawaii. Be sure to check in your country of origin to determine whether you need a visa for U.S. entry. A visa application can be made at any U.S. embassy or consular office outside the United States. Canadians do not need a visa but must have a passport.

AGRICULTURAL INSPECTION

Everyone visiting Hawaii must fill out a "Plant and Animals Declaration Form" and present it to the appropriate official upon arrival in the state (sometimes it doesn't get collected, though). Anyone carrying any of the listed items must have these items inspected by an agricultural inspection agent at the airport. These items include but are not limited to fruits, vegetables, plants, seeds, and soil, as well as live insects, seafood, snakes, and amphibians. For more information on what is prohibited, contact the Hawaii Department of Agriculture, Kona International Airport (808/326-1077, www.hawaiiag.org/hdoa).

Remember that before you leave Hawaii for the Mainland, all of your bags are again subject to an agricultural inspection, a usually painless procedure taking only a minute or two. To facilitate your departure, leave all bags unlocked until after inspection. There are no restrictions on beach sand from below the high water line, coconuts, cooked foods, dried flower arrangements, fresh flower lei, pineapples, certified pest-free plants and cuttings, or seashells. However, papayas must be treated before departure. Some restricted items are berries, fresh gardenias, jade vines, live insects and snails, cotton, plants in soil, soil itself, and sugarcane. For any questions pertaining to plants that you want to take to the Mainland, call the U.S. Department of Agriculture, Plant Protection and Quarantine office (808/933-6930 in Hilo, 808/326-1252 in Kona). Foreign countries may have different agricultural inspection requirements for flights from Hawaii (or other points in the United States) to those countries. Be sure to check with the proper foreign authorities for specifics.

PETS AND QUARANTINE

Hawaii has a very rigid pet quarantine policy designed to keep rabies and other Mainland diseases from reaching the state. All domestic pets are subject to a **120-day quarantine** (a 30-day quarantine or a newer 5-day-or-less quarantine is allowed by meeting certain pre-arrival and post-arrival requirements—inquire), and this includes substantial fees for boarding. Unless you are contemplating a move to Hawaii, it is not feasible to take pets. For complete information, contact the Department of Agriculture, Animal Quarantine Division in Honolulu (99-951 Halawa Valley St., 'Aiea, HI 96701, 808/483-7151, http://hawaii.gov/hdoa/ai/aqs/info).

Getting Around

BY AIR

Getting to and from the Big Island via the other islands is easy and convenient, although expensive. The only effective way for most visitors to travel between the Hawaiian Islands is by air. Luckily, Hawaii has excellent air transportation that boasts one of the industry's safest flight records. Items restricted on flights from the Mainland and from overseas are also restricted on flights within the state. Baggage allowances are the same as anywhere, except that due to space constraints, carry-on luggage on the smaller prop planes may be limited in number and size. The longest direct interisland flight in the state, 214 miles, is between Honolulu and Hilo and takes about 45 minutes. If you want to fly from the Big Island to Kaua'i, Lanai, or Moloka'i, you must connect through Honolulu. For Maui, Hawaiian Airlines does offer one daily direct flight between Hilo and Kahului (on Maui) and two daily direct flights between Kona and Kahului. In general, **Hawaiian Airlines** (www.hawaiianair.com) and **Go!Mokulele** (www.iflygo.com), the new interisland carrier, have competitive prices, with interisland flights at about $100–150 each way.

BY SEA

There are no public ferries between the Big Island and the other islands in the Hawaiian chain (but Maui is so close!). Private ship lines such as Royal Caribbean, Carnival, Celebrity, and Norwegian Cruise Line do offer cruises of the islands, making stops at both the Hilo and Kailua-Kona ports. Check with these companies as their ports of call do vary. Some of these boats leave from Los Angeles and others from Vancouver, sailing all the way to Hawaii. Others leave from Honolulu and make a quick jaunt around the Hawaiian Islands.

BY LAND

The most common way to get around Hawaii is by rental car. The abundance of agencies keeps prices competitive. Hawaii also has

WHY DO SOME PLACES HAVE TWO NAMES?

The two-name system on the Big Island (such as Kailua-Kona or Waimea-Kamuela) has nothing to do with colonialism – although that would make for an interesting story. It is simply to avoid confusion with the post office. There is already a Kailua on the island of O'ahu, so the name of the Big Island town is actually Kailua and it is in the Kona district (which encompasses several other towns). In Waimea's case, Kamuela is used to distinguish the Big Island's Waimea from places of the same name on O'ahu and Kaua'i.

limited public bus service, expensive taxis, and reasonable bicycle, motorcycle, and moped rentals. Hitchhiking, while illegal on the Big Island, is still used by some to get around.

Highway Overview

Getting around the Big Island is fairly easy. There is one main highway called the Hawai'i Belt Road (also called Mamalahoa Highway) that circles the island, one cross-island highway called the Saddle Road, and a few other highways and secondary roadways. The Hawai'i Belt Road is known by different numbers in various sections around the island, and this may lead to some confusion. Connecting Kailua-Kona and Hilo around the south end, the number is Highway 11. Major roads that lead off of it are Napo'opo'o Road, which runs down to Kealakekua Bay; Ke Ala O Keawe Road to Pu'uhonua O Honaunau National Historical Park; South Point Road, which drops down to the southernmost tip of the island; Chain of Craters Road, which leads through Hawai'i Volcanoes National Park to the lava-covered littoral Puna Coast;

and Keaʻau-Pahoa Road (Highway 130) from Keaʻau to the hinterland of Puna. In Puna, Kapoho-Pahoa Road (Highway 132) and Kapoho-Kalapana Beach Road (Highway 137) make a circle with Highway 130 from Pahoa, down along the shore, and back again.

Going north from Kailua-Kona, the Hawaiʻi Belt Road (Highway 190), which starts off for the first few miles as Palani Road, cuts across the upper slopes of the volcanoes to Waimea. Slicing through coffee country, as part of the Belt Road, is Highway 180. From Honalo, Highway 11 heads down toward Kailua, first as Kuakini Highway, which itself makes a tangent into town, and then continues as Queen Kaʻahumanu Highway. Heading north from Kailua, Queen Kaʻahumanu Highway becomes Highway 19. In Kawaihae, it turns uphill to Waimea, becoming Kawaihae Road. In Waimea, Highways 19 and 190 merge, and Highway 19 becomes the designation as the Hawaiʻi Belt Road continues along and down the Hamakua Coast back to Hilo. Connecting Highway 19 and Highway 190 through the town of Waikoloa is Waikoloa Road. In Honokaʻa, Highway 240 leaves the Belt Road and runs north to the edge of Waipiʻo Valley. North Kohala is cut by two roads: Akoni Pule Highway (Highway 270) runs along the coast up and around the tip as far as the Pololu Valley. Connecting this road and the town of Waimea is the Kohala Mountain Road (Highway 250). Off-limits to most rental cars, the Saddle Road (Highway 200) rises to about 6,500 feet between the tall peaks of Mauna Loa and Mauna Kea, making a shortcut between Hilo and Waimea or the Kohala Coast. From along the Saddle Road, four-wheel-drive roads lead up to the observatories atop Mauna Kea and nearly to the top of Mauna Loa.

Rental Cars

Rental-car options in Hawaii are as numerous as anywhere in the United States, from a subcompact to a full-size luxury land yacht. The most numerous seem to be compact cars and midsize sedans, but convertibles and four-wheel-drive jeeps are very popular (and a sure

giveaway that a tourist is driving that car), and some vans and SUVs are also available. Nearly all have automatic transmissions and air-conditioning. Generally, you must be 21 years old; a few agencies will rent to 18-year-olds, while some require you to be 25 for certain vehicles. Those ages 21–24 will usually be charged an extra fee, which may be significant.

If you're traveling during the peak seasons of Christmas, Easter, or summer, absolutely reserve your car in advance. If you're going off-peak, you stand a very good chance of getting the car you want at a price you like once you land in the islands. You can get some sweet deals. To be on the safe side, and for your own peace of mind, it's generally best to book ahead. Another way to try to get a deal is to rent at the off-airport locations in Hilo and Kona.

All major car-rental companies in Hawaii use flat-rate pricing, which provides a fixed daily rate and unlimited mileage. Most car companies, local and national, offer special rates and deals, like AAA discounts. These deals are common, but don't expect rental companies to let you know about them. Make sure to inquire. The basic rates aren't your only charges, however. On top of the actual rental fee, you must pay an airport access fee, airport concession fee, state tax, and a road tax surcharge—in total, an additional 25–30 percent.

Most car companies charge you a fee if you rent the car in Hilo and drop it off in Kona, and vice versa. Agencies prohibit their vehicles from being used on the Saddle Road and are prejudiced against the spur road leading to South Point. The road to the top of Mauna Kea is a four-wheel-drive-only road. Heed the signs, not so much for going up, but for needed braking power coming down. No way whatsoever should you attempt to drive down to Waipiʻo Valley in a regular car! The grade is unbelievably steep, and only a four-wheel-drive can make it. Put simply, you have a good chance of being killed if you try it in a car.

Hele-On Bus

The County of Hawaiʻi maintains the Mass Transit Agency, known throughout the island as the Hele-On Bus. For information, schedules, and fares contact the Mass Transit Agency (www.heleonbus.org).

The main bus terminal is in downtown Hilo at Moʻoheau Park, just at the corner of Kamehameha Avenue and Mamo Street. The Hele-On Bus system now has a mostly modern fleet of large buses that are clean and comfortable. The Hele-On operates daily routes all around the island. There are a number of intra-Hilo routes with additional intercity routes to points around the periphery of the island, but these all operate on a very limited schedule, sometimes only once a day. Check the website for schedules and maps. If you're in a hurry then definitely forget about taking the bus, but if you want to meet the people of Hawaii, there's no better way. The bus can be a frustrating experience for those used to proper timetables and bus stops. While there are a few actual bus stops (noted on the website), most people simply hail the bus down on the side of the road. You have to be somewhat aggressive to get the driver's attention. Note: Large items like surfboards and boogie boards aren't allowed on board, but bicycles can be put on the front of the bus. As of July 2011, the county has reinstituted a $1 fare for all bus routes on the island (it was free for a while!). There are 10-ticket books and monthly passes available if you plan to take the bus a lot or stick around for a while.

Taxis

Both the Hilo and Kona airports always have taxis waiting for fares. Fares are regulated. From Hilo's airport to downtown costs about $15, to the Banyan Drive hotels about $10. From the Kona airport to hotels and condos along Aliʻi Drive in Kailua fares run $25–40, north to Waikoloa Beach Resort they run about $50, and fares are approximately $70 as far north as the Mauna Kea Beach Hotel. Obviously, a taxi is no way to get around if you're trying to save money. Most taxi companies, both in Kona and Hilo, also run sightseeing services for fixed prices.

An alternative in the Kona area is **Speedi-Shuttle** (808/329-5433 or 877/521-2085, www.

A NOTE ABOUT DIRECTIONS: *MAUKA* AND *MAKAI*

Many of the directions listed in this guide include Hawaiian terms that are used by locals when giving directions. **Mauka** indicates towards the mountains or inland. Therefore, if a place such as a restaurant is on the *mauka* side of the road, then it is on the inland or mountain side. If a place is **makai,** that means that it is on the ocean side.

speedishuttle.com). Operating daily 7 A.M.–10 P.M., SpeediShuttle runs multi-seat vans, so its prices are cheaper per person the more people you have riding. It also would be appropriate if you have lots of luggage. SpeediShuttle has a courtesy phone at the airport for your convenience as well as an iPhone-friendly mobile reservation system. Reservations a day ahead are not necessary but may be helpful to get a ride at the time you want.

Biking

It's not for everyone, but it's also not not for everyone. One doesn't need to be a super-experienced biker or an Ironman in order to ride around the island. Pedaling around the Big Island can be both fascinating and draining. If you circle the island, it's nearly 300 miles around on its shortest route. Most pick an area and bike there. Generally, roads are flat or of gradual gradient, making for some relatively easy riding. The major exceptions are the roads from Kailua to Holualoa, Kawaihae to Waimea, from Waimea up over the mountain to Hawi, the Saddle Road, and the road up to the summit of Mauna Kea. Generally, roads are well paved, but the shoulders on secondary highways and back roads are often narrow and sometimes in poor shape. Be especially careful on Mamalahoa Highway from Palani Junction south through Holualoa to Honalo and from there south to Honaunau, as there is plenty of traffic and the road is narrow and windy.

You might be better off bringing your own bike, but there are a handful of bike-rental shops around the island. Road bikes are great for touring and for a workout along the Kona highways and from Hilo to Volcano. Otherwise, you're better off with a cruiser for pedaling around town or along the beach or a mountain bike that can handle the sometimes poor back-road conditions as well as limited off-road biking possibilities.

If you are coming to the island for a short trip and you want to go it by bike, I suggest starting in Kona and moving south in order to avoid some very big hills (you don't want to travel uphill from Hilo to Volcano). It's possible to ride the entire island in two days; however, four to seven makes for a much nicer experience. For more information about riding the Big Island, a great resource is the **Hilo Bike Hub** (318 E. Kawili St., 808/961-4452, www.hilobikehub.com, Mon.–Fri. 9 A.M.–5:30 P.M., Sat. 9 A.M.–5 P.M.). Many of their staff have done this trip (or even written about this trip) and can offer you tips and suggestions. For mountain biking and trail information on all the major islands, pick up a copy of *Mountain Biking the Hawaiian Islands,* by John Alford (Ohana Publishing, Honolulu, 877/682-7433, www.bikehawaii.com).

Biking is also a great way to commute on the island. Park employees who live in Volcano often commute to work, and the same goes for individuals who live and work in Hilo. Another popular commute is between Puna and Hilo, where the road is mainly flat. If you get tired on the way or if you don't want to ride round-trip, the Hele-On Bus has a bike rack on the front of it. So no problem with securing your bike and riding yourself home on public transportation. Note: The most difficult part with bike riding in Hawaii is that there is not always somewhere to lock your bike as bike racks can be far and few between. Sometimes you have to get creative with locking your bike, so be prepared with extra locks.

GETTING YOUR BIKE TO THE BIG ISLAND

Transporting your bike to Hawai'i from one of the neighbor islands is no problem, but can be very expensive. All of the interisland carriers will fly it for you for about $35 one-way on the same flight as you take—just check it in as baggage. Bikes must be packed in a box or hard case, supplied by the owner. Handlebars must be turned sideways and the pedals removed or turned in. Bikes go on a space-available basis only—usually not a problem, except, perhaps, during bicycle competitions. In addition, a release of liability for damage may have to be signed before the airline will accept the bike. If you plan ahead, you can send your bike the previous day by air freight, but that is more expensive.

Getting your bike to Hawaii from the Mainland will depend upon which airline you take. Most will accept bicycles as baggage with the approximate additional charge of $100 each way since it is deemed an oversized object.

Recreation

SCUBA DIVING

If you think that Hawaii is beautiful above the sea, wait until you explore below. Warm tropical waters that average 75–80°F year-round and coral growth make it a fascinating haven for reef fish and aquatic plantlife. You'll discover that Hawaiian waters are remarkably clear, with excellent visibility. Fish in every fathomable color parade by. Lavender clusters of coral, red and gold coral trees, and over 1,500 different types of shells carpet the ocean floor. In some spots the fish are so accustomed to humans that they'll nibble at your fingers. In other spots, lurking moray eels add the special zest of danger. Sharks and barracudas pose less danger than scraping your knee on the coral or being driven against the rocks by a heavy swell. There are enormous but harmless sea bass and a profusion of sea turtles. All this awaits you below the surface of Hawaii's waters.

The Big Island has particularly generous underwater vistas open to anyone donning a mask and fins. Those in the know consider the deep diving along the steep drop-offs of Hawai'i's geologically young coastline some of the best in the state. The ocean surrounding the Big Island has not had a chance to turn the relatively new lava to sand, which makes the visibility absolutely perfect, even to depths of 150 feet or more. There's also 60–70 miles of coral belt around the Big Island, which adds up to a magnificent diving experience. Only advanced divers should attempt deep-water dives, but beginners and snorkelers will have many visual thrills inside the protected bays and coves. While most people head to the west (Kona) side, there is very good diving on the east side as well, particularly near Hilo. As always, weather conditions will dictate how the water and underwater conditions will be, so always inquire about sites and conditions with one of the dive shops before you head for the water.

If you're a scuba diver you'll have to show your certification card before local shops will rent you gear, fill your tanks, or take you on a charter dive. Plenty of outstanding scuba instructors will give you lessons toward certification, and they're especially reasonable because of the stiff competition. Prices vary, but you can take a three- to five-day semiprivate certification course including all equipment for about $350–500. Divers unaccustomed to Hawaiian waters should not dive alone regardless of their experience. Most opt for dive tours to special dive grounds guaranteed to please. These vary also, but an accompanied single-tank dive where no boat is involved goes for about $60; expect to spend about $100 for a two-tank boat dive. Most introductory dives will be about $130. Special charter dives, night dives, and photography dives are also offered. Basic equipment costs $25–35 for the day, and most times you'll only need the top of a wet suit.

SNORKELING

Snorkeling is simple and can be enjoyable to anyone who can swim. In about 15 minutes you can be taught the fundamentals of snorkeling—you really don't need formal instructions. Other snorkelers or dive-shop attendants can tell you enough to get you started. Because you can breathe without lifting your head, you get great propulsion from the fins and hardly ever need to use your arms. You can go for much greater distances and spend longer periods in the water than if you were swimming. Experienced snorkelers make an art of this sport, and you, too, can see and do amazing things with a mask, snorkel, and flippers. Don't, however, get a false sense of invincibility and exceed your limitations.

Some hotels and condos have snorkel equipment for guests, but if it isn't free, it will almost always cost more than if you rent it from a snorkel or dive shop. These shops rent snorkel gear at competitive rates; depending upon the quality of gear, snorkel gear rental runs about $3–9 a day. Sporting goods stores and department stores like Kmart and Walmart also have this equipment for sale; a basic set might run as little as $20.

Miles of coral reef ring the island, and it's mostly close to shore so you don't have to swim too far out to see coral communities. These are some of the most popular snorkeling sites:

- **Kona:** Kekaha Kai State Park, Pawai Bay, White Sands Beach (a.k.a. Disappearing Sands Beach), Kahalu'u Beach Park, Kealakekua Bay by the Captain Cook monument (often said to be the best on the island), and at Pu'uhonua O Honaunau in Honaunau Bay.

- **Kohala:** 'Anaeho'omalu Beach, Hapuna Beach, Mauna Kea Beach, Puako coastal area, Spencer Beach Park, and Mahukona Beach Park.

- **Puna:** Kapoho tide pools and Isaac Hale Beach Park.

- **Hilo:** Leleiwi Beach Park and Richardson's Beach Park.

Before you put your mask on, however, ask at a snorkel shop about which locations are best for the season and water conditions. Inquire about types of fish and other sea creatures you might expect to see, water clarity, entry points, surf conditions, water current, and parking.

KAYAKING

Ocean kayaking has gained much popularity in Hawaii in the last several years. The state has no white-water kayaking, and there are no rivers on the Big Island appropriate for river kayaking. Although the entire coastline would offer adventure for the expert kayaker, most people try sections of the west coast near Kealakekua Bay or Puako and east out of Hilo that offer excellent shoreline variation and great snorkeling. Generally speaking, water conditions on the Kona Coast are best in the winter and on the Hilo side are better in the summer.

Be sure to check with the kayak shops to get the latest information about sea conditions, and consider taking one of their organized tours. Tours go to exceptional places, and while they vary, the tours generally run about $75–100 for a half day.

Kayaks (the sit-upon kind) generally rent for about $25 single or $50 tandem for a day. Most shops want day-rental kayaks back by 5 P.M. Some shops rent carriers to haul the kayak. A few are located near a launch site, but many have shops away from the water, so you will have to strap the kayak to a rack and drive to where you want to set in the water.

FISHING

Hawaii has some of the most exciting and productive "blue waters" in all the world. Here you can find a sportfishing fleet made up of skippers and crews who are experienced professional anglers. You can also fish from jetties, piers, rocks, or the shore. If rod and reel don't strike your fancy, try the old-fashioned throw net, or take along a spear when you go snorkeling or scuba diving. There's nighttime torch fishing that requires special skills and equipment, and freshwater fishing in public areas. Streams and irrigation ditches yield introduced trout, bass, and catfish. While you're at it, you might want to try crabbing, or working low-tide areas after sundown hunting octopus, a tantalizing island delicacy.

Deep-Sea Fishing

Hawaii is positioned well for deep-sea fishing. Within eight miles there are waters to depths of 18,000 feet. Most game-fishing boats work the waters on the calmer Kona side of the island. Some skippers, carrying anglers who are accustomed to the sea, will also work the rougher windward coasts and island channels where the fish bite just as well. Trolling is the preferred method of deep-sea fishing; this is done usually in waters of 1,000–2,000 fathoms (a fathom is six feet). The skipper will either "area fish," which means running in a crisscross pattern over a known productive area, or "ledge fish," which involves trolling over submerged ledges where game fish are known to feed. The most advanced marine technology, available on many boats, sends sonar beeps searching for fish. On deck, the crew and anglers scan the horizon in the age-old Hawaiian tradition, searching for clusters of seabirds feeding on bait fish pursued to the surface by the huge and aggressive game fish. "Still fishing" or "bottom fishing" with hand-lines yields some tremendous fish.

The most thrilling game fish in Hawaiian waters is **marlin,** generically known as "billfish" or a'u to the locals. The king of them is the blue marlin, with record catches of well over 1,000 pounds, and these are called "granders." The mightiest caught in the waters off this island was a huge 1,649 pounds—caught in 1984. There are also striped marlin and sailfish, which often go over 200 pounds. The best times for marlin are during spring, summer, and fall. The fishing tapers off in January and picks up again by late February. "Blues" can be caught year-round, but, oddly enough, when they stop biting it seems as though the striped marlin pick up. Second to the marlin are **tuna.** Ahi (yellowfin tuna) are caught in Hawaiian waters at depths of 100–1,000 fathoms. They can weigh 300 pounds, but 25–100 pounds is common. There are also aku (skipjack tuna) and the delicious ono (wahoo), which average 20–40 pounds. **Mahimahi,** with its high prominent forehead and long dorsal fin, is another strong, fighting, deep-water game fish abundant in Hawaii. These delicious fish can weigh up to 70 pounds. No license is needed for recreational saltwater fishing.

Shore Fishing

Shore fishing and bait casting yield *papio,* a jack tuna. *Akule,* a scad (locally called *halalu*), is a smallish schooling fish that comes close to shore and is great to catch on light tackle. *Ulua* are shore fish and can be found in tide pools. They're excellent eating, average two to three pounds, and are taken at night or with spears. *'O'io* are bonefish that come close to shore to spawn. They're caught by bait casting and bottom fishing with cut bait. They're bony, but they're a favorite for fish cakes and *poke. Awa* is a schooling fish that loves brackish water. It can grow up to three feet long and is a good fighter; a favorite for throw-netters, it's even raised commercially in fishponds. Besides these there are plenty of goatfish, mullet, mackerel, snapper, sharks, and even salmon. No license is needed for recreational saltwater fishing.

Charters

By and large, the vast majority of charter fishing boats on the Big Island berth at the Honokohau Harbor just north of Kailua-Kona. A few boats also leave from Keauhou Bay and Kawaihae Harbor on the west side, and some use the river mouth in Hilo. Captains of these vessels invariably have been fishing these waters for years and know where to look for a catch. Rates vary, as do the length of outings (usually four, six, or eight hours) and number of passengers allowed on the boats. Although pricing varies, fishing excursions generally run in the vicinity of $150 for a half-day charter to $230 for a full-day shared charter, and $500 half-day to $1,000 full-day exclusive charter.

HIKING

Hiking on the Big Island is stupendous. There's something for everyone, from quick short walks at scenic points to exhausting treks to the summit of Mauna Loa. The largest number of trails, and the most outstanding according to many, are laced across Hawai'i

Volcanoes National Park. In the north you'll find Waipi'o, Waimanu, and Pololu Valleys. The Division of Forestry and Wildlife (19 E. Kawili St., Hilo, 808/974-4221, http://hawaii. gov/dlnr/dofaw) also maintains a number of trails in various locations around the island that cater to all levels of hikers. Check in the Hilo office for details and maps.

Don't leave your valuables in your tent, and always carry your money, papers, and camera with you. At the least, let someone know where you are going and when you plan to be back; supply an itinerary and your expected route, then stick to it.

There are many reasons to stay on designated trails—this not only preserves Hawaii's fragile environment, it also keeps you out of dangerous areas. Occasionally, trails will be closed for maintenance, so stay off those routes. Most trails are well maintained, but trailhead markers are sometimes missing. Look for mileage markers along many park and forest reserve trails to gauge your progress. They are usually metal stakes set about a foot off the ground, with numbers indicating the distance from a trailhead. The trails themselves can be muddy, and therefore treacherously slippery.

Many trails are used by hunters of wild boar, deer, or game birds. If you hike in hunting areas during hunting season, you should wear brightly colored or reflective clothing. Often, forest reserve trails have check-in stations at trailheads. Hikers and hunters must sign a logbook, especially if they intend to camp. The comments by previous hikers are worth reading for up-to-the-minute information on trail conditions.

Twilight is short in the islands, and night sets in rapidly. In June, sunrise is around 6 A.M. and sunset 7 P.M.; in December, these occur at 7 A.M. and 6 P.M. If you become lost, find an open spot and stay put; at night, stay as dry as you can. If you must continue, walk on ridges and avoid the gulches, which have more obstacles and make it harder for rescuers to spot you. Do not light a fire. Some forest areas can be very dry and fire could spread easily. Fog is only encountered at the 1,500- to 5,000-foot level, but be careful of disorientation.

© MARK WASSER

This looks like the moon, but it's actually the Big Island, specifically the hike to the Mauna Loa summit.

Generally, stay within your limits, be careful, and enjoy yourself.

GOLF

The Big Island has some of the most beautiful golf links in Hawaii. The Kohala-area courses taken together are considered by some to be the crown jewel of the state's golf options. Robert Trent Jones Sr. and Jr. have both built exceptional courses here. Dad built the Mauna Kea Beach Hotel course, while the kid built his at the Waikoloa Beach Resort. The Mauna Kea course bedevils many as the ultimate challenge. Other big-name golf course architects (and players), such as Jack Nicklaus, Arnold Palmer, and Tom Weiskopf, have added their talents here as well. Sometimes the Kohala golf courses are used for tournament play, like the Senior Skins Tournament at the Francis H. I'i Brown South Course. If the Kohala courses are too rich for your blood, there are a few in the Kailua area that are less expensive, or you can play a round in Hilo for about $25 and hit nine holes in Honoka'a for $20. How about golfing at Volcano Golf and Country Club, where, if you miss a short putt, you can blame it on an earthquake?

Most golf courses offer lessons. Many have driving ranges, some that are lighted. The majority have pro shops and clubhouses with a restaurant or snack shop. Most courses offer reduced *kama'aina* (resident) rates and discount rates for play that starts later in the day. Be sure to ask about these rates as they often afford substantial savings. Guests of resorts affiliated with a golf course also get reduced greens fees.

Deciding at the last minute to golf? Want a discount rate? Willing to golf where it may not necessarily be your first choice? Try **Stand-by Golf** (808/322-2665, www.hawaiistandby-golf.com), where you can arrange tee times for great savings. Call one day in advance or in the morning on the day you want to play.

Tips for Travelers

CONDUCT AND CUSTOMS

The best principle to go by is "do it with *aloha*." *Aloha*, a common greeting, also refers to the *aloha* spirit, a way of living and treating each other with love and respect. One translation is "joyfully sharing life." It refers to the attitude of friendly acceptance for which the Hawaiian Islands are so famous.

Everything (with one exception, and I'll get to it) moves slower on the Big Island than on the Mainland. Expect a quick trip to the grocery store to take double the time when the person ahead of you in line gets to talking story with the cashier. Likewise, posted hours for shops and restaurants are mere suggestions. Sometimes they don't open at all and sometimes they stay open later if people are around.

Where Big Islanders like to move fast is in their cars. There is nothing locals hate more than riding behind a slow-moving (tourist) car on a two-lane highway with nowhere to go. It is standard practice, if you're moving slower than everyone else (and it's fine if you are), to put your blinker on and move over as best as you can (even if there isn't a shoulder) and let everyone pass you. This is how you will retain a sense of *aloha* on the road.

Another road rule worth noting is that Big Islanders do slow down on one-lane roads to let other cars pass (and then usually you give the other driver a *shaka* sign, a hand wave where only the thumb and baby finger stick out). The rule is, the downhill person yields to the uphill person (it's harder to stop if you're climbing vertically). This is very useful information on your way up to Mauna Kea or down to Waipiʻo Valley.

ACCESSIBILITY FOR TRAVELERS WITH DISABILITIES

A person with a disability can have a wonderful time in Hawaii; all that's needed is a little pre-planning. The key for a smooth trip is to make as many arrangements ahead of time as possible. Tell the transportation companies and hotels you'll be dealing with the nature of your ability in advance so that they can make arrangements to accommodate you, if possible. Bring your medical records and notify medical establishments of your arrival if you'll be needing their services. Travel with a friend or make arrangements for an aide on arrival.

Bring your own wheelchair if possible and let airlines know if it is battery-powered; boarding interisland flights often requires steps. Airlines can board you early on special lifts, but they must know that you're coming. Many hotels and restaurants accommodate persons with disabilities, but always call ahead just to make sure, given that some of the smaller establishments (especially bed-and-breakfasts) have lots of stairs and no ramps.

Services

At Hilo International Airport, all passengers arrive or leave via a jetway on the second level, and there are escalators, stairs, and some elevators between levels. Baggage claim, bathrooms, and telephones are accessible. Parking is convenient in designated areas. The Kona International Airport is all one level. Boarding and deplaning by lift is possible for travelers with disabilities. There are no jetways. Bathrooms and telephones are accessible, and there is specially designated handicapped parking.

All rental-car agencies can install hand controls on their cars if given enough notice—usually 48–72 hours. Your own state parking placard will be honored here. Medical help, nurses, and companions can be arranged through the **Center for Independent Living** (808/935-3777 in Hilo or 808/323-2221 in Kona). Doctors are referred by **Hilo Medical Center** (808/974-4700) and the **Kona Community Hospital** (808/322-9311). Medical equipment rentals are available in Hilo from **Apria Healthcare** (808/969-1221), **Rainbow Medical Supply** (808/935-9393), and **Shiigi Drug** (808/935-0001); and in Kona from **Big Island Medical Equipment** (808/323-3313).

TRAVELING WITH CHILDREN

The Big Island is extremely child friendly, or *keiki* friendly (as children are called here). Many restaurants offer children's menus, resort hotels have activities geared for children (some offer day care), there are many beach areas with shallow wading water perfect for small children and lifeguards on duty, and the national parks all have Junior Ranger programs with special activity books for kids. Best of all, a lot of these kid-friendly activities are free, including the many playgrounds located throughout the island (not just in Hilo and Kona, but also Pahoa, Honoka'a, and Volcano). Note: Before you book any tours, check with the tour providers to see if there are restrictions involving children. For instance, many of the horseback riding and ziplining tours can't accommodate individuals (not just children) under a certain weight and height—but some can. Likewise, there are ATV tours that will allow children to ride with an adult, while others don't take any rider under 16 years old.

SENIOR TRAVELERS

Not a tour company per se, but an educational opportunity for seniors, **Road Scholar** (800/454-5768, www.roadscholar.org), developed by Elderhostel, offers short-term programs on five of the Hawaiian Islands. Different programs focus on history, culture, cuisine, and the environment in association with one of the colleges or universities in the islands. Most programs use hotels for accommodations.

GAY AND LESBIAN TRAVELERS

Same-sex marriage is legal in Hawaii, as of 2011. If you're looking to make contact with the LGBT community, the best place to go to is the Pahoa area, where the free spirit vibe tends to attract this crowd. A few bed-and-breakfast establishments particularly cater to these groups; look for them on **Purple Roofs**

(www.purpleroofs.com), a website dedicated to LGBT travel.

For additional LGBT resources on the Big Island or in Hawaii, check out the very comprehensive website of **Out in Hawaii** (www.outinhawaii.com).

OPPORTUNITIES FOR STUDY AND VOLUNTEERING

You don't need to leave the country to study abroad. The University of Hawai'i at Hilo (UHH, http://hilo.hawaii.edu) has exchange programs with many U.S. Mainland universities (the majority are on the West Coast) that allow students to study for a semester at UHH for a discounted price while able to transfer credit back to their home institutions. Check with your Mainland university and UHH to see if an exchange is possible. Another possibility is to apply directly for admission to UHH or Hawaii Community College (http://hawaii.hawaii.edu).

There are two really excellent ways to volunteer long term on the Big Island. First, through the **World Wide Opportunities on Organic Farms** (WWOOF, www.wwoof.org) organization. Their Hawaii-specific website (www.wwoofhawaii.org) links farmers to interested volunteers. Take care to do research about the farm and contact previous volunteers. Conditions and arrangements from farm to farm vary substantially. Some require 50 hours of work while others require only 20. Some offer free room and board (food from Costco or food from the farm) while others have workers pay for accommodations. Likewise, accommodations can range from a tent to a small shared cabin. Nonetheless, WWOOFing is a great opportunity to try your hand at farming and learn about the land in Hawaii.

A second opportunity is with **Hawai'i Volcanoes National Park.** Again, responsibilities and compensation vary from position to position, but generally, volunteers must commit to at least two months of full-time service (some positions last up to a year), and in exchange, volunteers are offered housing in the park and a daily stipend (between $20–25 per day). Contact the park directly (www.nps.gov/

BIG ISLAND, SMALL BUDGET

It's a misconception that you need a big budget for the Big Island. The *kama'aina* don't go to resorts for their meals and why should you? The tips below are "priceless" ideas for how to save on transportation, where to stay for less, eat for cheap, and days of free fun (the beach is always free!).

TIP 1: TRANSPORTATION

It is possible to get around the island solely by bus; however, since buses can be sparse, you really need to plan ahead to ensure the timing works for you. Also, buses don't usually travel through neighborhoods, so when planning your accommodations, check to see how far they are from the main road. A second consideration is that the bus stops at the terminal at the Kona airport, but not the Hilo airport (and it's quite a walk to the highway from the airport). However, the airport in Hilo is right near the downtown and a cab ride to your lodging should only run you about $15.

A second option, if you don't want to or can't rent a car, is to bring a bike, rent a bike, or call ahead and get a recycled bike made for you by **All Kine Bike Shop** in Hilo. If you're planning on riding your way around the island, you'll want to travel counterclockwise in order to avoid some big hills!

If you do get a car, it's important to know that gas prices really vary all over the island, with the highest prices in Kona and Kohala and the lowest in Hilo. Gas prices in general are much higher than on the Mainland, so get yourself a car that isn't a gas guzzler. The island actually isn't that big (relatively speaking), so even if you're driving around it, you won't have to fill up your tank that often. But when you do have to fill up, try to do so in Hilo or, if you have a membership, at Costco in Kona (where the price of gas tends to be nearly 10 cents cheaper per gallon than anywhere around).

TIP 2: LODGING

The obvious cheap way to stay on the Big Island is in your own tent at a county, state, or national park. There are only a few technically free spots to stay, such as **Polulu Valley** (you'll likely have the place to yourself); otherwise, other sites such as **Spencer Beach Park,** another excellent space to camp that's easy to access, require a permit that you can easily purchase through the respective agencies' websites. If pitching a tent isn't your thing, there are still plenty of options with roofs. There are some standard hostels in Hilo, Kona, and Volcano. There are also some options around the island that offer reasonable rates without having to stay in a dorm room: **Hotel Manago** (Kona), **The Old Hawaiian Bed and Breakfast** (Hilo), and **Hotel Honoka'a Club** (Hamakua Coast) are just a few options of where to stay inexpensively and have some privacy.

TIP 3: EATING

There ain't nothing cheaper than free. Food foraging on the Big Island is possible (meaning, grabbing fruit or vegetables off of trees or bushes in public spaces), but please do so responsibly. In **Hawai'i Volcanoes National Park,** the rule is that one quart of *'ohelo* berries per person may be taken each month and only for personal consumption. Check with the rangers at the visitor center for more information about food foraging in the park. For free food that involves less work, hit happy hour at **Pahoa Village Café** (Puna), where free pizza is often for the taking (you have to be quick; it disappears the moment they bring out a new pie).

The best deal on the Kona side of the island is on Friday and Saturday nights after 10 P.M. at

Sansei Seafood Restaurant and Sushi Bar (Kohala), when sushi and appetizers are 50 percent off and drink specials are available. There is also free karaoke. Likewise, **Pakini Grill** (Waimea) offers 50 percent off appetizers during their daily happy hour and the portions are huge!

In general, it's easier to find a culinary bargain in Hilo than on the Kona side. Pick up Japanese *okazuya* (side dishes) at the **Hilo Lunch Shop;** each item is less than a dollar and some are only 30 cents. You can easily feed yourself for less than a few bucks. But if you're looking for a good deal in Kailua-Kona, head straight to **Quinn's Almost By The Sea** for their short ribs. They are just as good and maybe even better than the best restaurants around town at a fraction of the price.

As any thrifty traveler knows, one of your best bets for saving money on food is the grocery store. But with **Island Naturals Market and Deli** (four locations on the island), you don't have to sacrifice quality (or local organic foods) to eat cheaply. Eat to your stomach's content at their hot bar daily after 7 P.M. (times may vary depending on the store) and your meal, which is priced per pound, is discounted. Fridays are the best day to stop by this grocery chain as beer and wine are 20 percent off!

Lastly, as the most important part of your day is breakfast, the most inexpensive way to start off your day is with a **Spam *musubi.*** This rice, Spam, and nori "roll" can be picked up for under $2 (try 7-Eleven for Spam and egg *musubi* – it's like a McDonald's breakfast sandwich Hawaii style).

TIP 4: ACTIVITIES

First order of business: Stop at one of the large chain stores and pick up your own **snorkel set** if you don't already have one. The cost of buying the snorkel set isn't that much more than you'd be charged for a day's rental, so if you plan on snorkeling for a few days, this purchase will save you about $50. And did you want to use that snorkel to night dive with the **manta rays** but don't want to spend $100 (more or less) on a trip? Well, save the snorkel gear you just purchased and head straight to the **Sheraton Keauhou Bay Resort and Spa,** where you can watch the manta rays from the bar at the hotel. I know it's not the same as being in the water with them, but you still get a pretty good look (they are attracted to plankton that are attracted to the lights of the hotel) and have the benefit of staying dry (and having a drink at the same time).

But saving money doesn't mean excusing yourself from all tours. All the national parks and historical sites on the island offer free tours of their parks. At **Hawai'i Volcanoes National Park** there is at least one free daily ranger-led tour of certain areas of the park. On Wednesdays there is a super-exclusive free lava tube tour (must be reserved a week in advance). There are monthly free tours of the **Kahuku** section of the park located in Ka'u. The same goes for **Mauna Kea.** Although the price for most tours to the summit is $200, there are various free tours offered at Mauna Kea.

Next, check the websites of **yoga** studios for their "community class" hours. These classes, although sometimes shorter than a full-price class, are usually only $5 (versus $10–15) and taught by the same teachers. Likewise, you don't need to have lots of cash to indulge in some self-care. Massages in Hilo are at least half the price of those offered at the resorts and hotels in Kona and Kohala, and the same goes for acupuncture.

havo) for additional information or check out www.volunteer.gov for more information. Also, positions are sometimes posted on www.idealist.org; search for Hawaii.

GREEN TOURISM

It's not easy being green—well, actually it is in Hawaii. The easiest way to lower your ecological footprint while on the Big Island is to eat locally. This task is not too difficult given the multitude of farmers markets throughout the island, the local produce available at mainstream supermarkets, and fruits that literally fall from the trees in front of you.

A second option is to go off the grid. Campsites are abundant through the island and they are located on prime oceanfront (or mountainside) real estate. There are also several hotels that are off the grid or utilize green technologies to reduce their imprint.

The biggest challenge to being green on the Big Island is transportation. The public transportation system isn't ideal and most people simply avoid it. If you're not in a rush, try it out. You'll be saving (a lot) of money on gas while reducing pollution. Otherwise, try to carpool when possible or even walk or bike ride to your destinations.

Lastly, it goes without saying, don't trash the island. Remember the "Leave No Trace" principle. Many of the other islands have already gotten rid of plastic bags in stores, and hopefully the Big Island will soon adopt this law. Plastic is a particularly large problem because of how it impacts our oceans and marine life (look up the "Great Pacific Garbage Patch" for more information on this issue). So if you're at a store, forgo the plastic bag and maybe even the plastic water bottle while you're at it.

WHAT TO TAKE

It's a snap to pack for a visit to the Big Island. Everything is on your side. The weather is moderate and uniform on the whole, and the style of dress is delightfully casual. The rule of thumb is to pack lightly—especially since the majority of bed-and-breakfasts and vacation rentals have laundry machines. If you forget something at

home, it won't be a disaster. You can buy everything you'll need in Hawaii (that's why they brought Target and Ross Dress for Less here).

A few points are worthy of note. While shorts and T-shirts or short-sleeve shirts and blouses might be your usual daily wear, jeans or other long pants and closed-toe shoes are best and sometimes required if you plan on taking a horseback ride or dusty ATV tour. Remember to bring a hat for the rain and sun; if you forget, inexpensive baseball caps and straw or woven hats are found easily throughout the island. Only a few classy restaurants in the finest hotels require men to wear a sport coat for dinner. If you don't have one, those hotels can supply you with one for the evening. For women, a dress of the "resort wear" variety will suffice for most any occasion. By and large, "resort casual" is as dressy as you'll need to be in Hawaii.

One occasion for which you'll have to consider dressing warmly is a visit to the mountaintop. If you intend to visit Mauna Kea, Mauna Loa, or view the lava flow/glow at night, it'll be downright chilly. In a pinch, a jogging suit with a hooded windbreaker/raincoat will do the trick, although you'll be more comfortable in warmer clothing like a wool sweater or thick jacket, cap, and gloves. If your hands get cold, put a pair of socks over them.

Tropical rain showers can happen at any time, so you might consider a fold-up umbrella. Nighttime winter temperatures may drop into the lower 60s or upper 50s, even on the coast, so be sure to have a light sweater and long pants along.

Dressing your feet is hardly a problem. For locals, rubber flip-flops, also called slippers (Locals brand is popular), are appropriate for every event. However, there are times when you might want to consider a shoe with more support, such as for crossing streams or wet trails. If you plan on heavy-duty hiking, you'll definitely want your hiking boots: The lightweight version is usually sufficient. Lava, especially 'a'a, is murderous on shoes (in fact, I have a separate pair of shoes just for walking on 'a'a). Most backcountry trails are rugged and muddy, and you'll need those good old lug soles for traction and laces for ankle support. If you plan moderate hikes, running shoes should do.

Two specialty items that you might consider bringing along are binoculars and snorkel gear. A pair of binoculars really enhances sightseeing—great for viewing birds and sweeping panoramas, and almost a necessity if you're going whale-watching. Flippers, mask, and snorkel can easily be bought or rented in Hawaii but don't weigh much or take up much space in your luggage. They'll save you a few dollars in rental fees and you'll have them when you want them.

Lastly, I suggest that you bring a reusable bag or two for grocery shopping. Currently, Kaua'i has banned plastic bags on the island and hopefully the Big Island will soon follow suit. If you don't have one to bring, or want to pick up a fantastic souvenir, I recommend getting a hot/cold bag available at any of the large grocery store chains (such as KTA or Foodland). These bags do indeed keep items hot or cold (as the name suggests), and they have fun island designs on them (like fish or Spam *musubi*). In fact, you might want to buy a few extra to bring home!

Health and Safety

STAYING HEALTHY

In a survey published some years ago by *Science Digest,* Hawaii was cited as the healthiest state in the United States in which to live. Indeed, Hawaiian citizens live longer than residents anywhere else in America: men to 76 years and women to 82. Lifestyle, heredity, and diet help with these figures, but Hawaii is still an oasis in the middle of the ocean, and germs just have a tougher time getting there. There are no cases of malaria, cholera, or yellow fever. Because of a strict quarantine law, rabies is also nonexistent. On the other hand, tooth decay—perhaps because of a wide use of sugar and the enzymes present in certain tropical fruits—is 30 percent above the national average. Also, obesity and related heart problems and hard drug use—especially "ice"—are prevalent among native Hawaiians. With the perfect weather, a multitude of fresh-air activities, soothing negative ionization from the sea, and a generally relaxed and carefree lifestyle, everyone feels better there. Hawaii is just what the doctor ordered: a beautiful, natural health spa. That's one of its main drawing cards. The food and tap water are perfectly safe, and the air quality is the best in the country.

Handling the Sun

Don't become a victim of your own exuberance. People can't wait to strip down and lie

VOLCANIC SMOG

That sulphur (egg-like) taste in your mouth is volcanic smog, also called "vog." Just like Los Angeles has smog alert days, Volcano can experience bad "vog" days. The vog can travel as far north as Hilo and as far south as South Point. Hypothetically, it doesn't harm your health except that it leaves a literal bad taste in your mouth. Some holistic practitioners argue that it causes headaches. In addition, recent studies have shown that there are higher asthma rates for children who live downwind of Hawai'i Volcanoes National Park (not from the vog, but from the small particles in the air). You should be fine taking it in for a day or three during your visit to the park.

on the sand like beached whales, but the tropical sun will burn you to a cinder if you're silly. The burning rays come through more easily in Hawaii because of the sun's angle, and you don't feel them as much because there's always a cool breeze. The worst part of the day is 11 A.M.–3 P.M. The Big Island lies between 19 and 20 degrees north latitude, not even close to the equator, but it's still over 1,000 miles south of sunny Southern California beaches. Be sure to apply plenty of sunscreen.

Don't forget about your head and eyes. Use your sunglasses and wear a brimmed hat. Some people lay a towel over their neck and shoulders when hiking and others will stick a scarf under their hat and let it drape down over their shoulders to provide some protection.

Whether out on the beach, hiking in the mountains, or just strolling around town, be very aware of dehydration. The sun and wind tend to sap your energy and your store of liquid.

Bugs

Everyone, in varying degrees, has an aversion to vermin and creepy crawlers. Hawaii isn't infested with a wide variety, but it does have its share. Mosquitoes were unknown in the islands until their larvae stowed away in the water barrels of the *Wellington* in 1826 and were introduced at Lahaina. They bred in the tropical climate and rapidly spread to all the islands. They are a particular nuisance in the rainforests. Be prepared and bring a natural repellent like citronella oil, available in most health stores on the islands, or a commercial product available in groceries and drugstores. Campers will be happy to have mosquito coils to burn at night as well. Note: You might notice that there aren't any mosquitoes in Volcano, Mauna Loa, or Mauna Kea. Mosquitoes hate altitude. So if you're sick of the mosquitoes just head up the hill and you'll be amazed how there are none to be found.

Cockroaches are very democratic insects. They hassle all strata of society equally. They breed well in Hawaii, and most hotels are at war with them, trying desperately to keep them from being spotted by guests. One comforting thought is that in Hawaii they aren't a sign of filth or dirty housekeeping. They love the climate like everyone else, and it's a real problem keeping them under control.

WATER SAFETY

Hawaii has one very sad claim to fame: More people drown here than anywhere else in the world. Moreover, there are dozens of victims yearly with broken necks and backs or with injuries from scuba and snorkeling accidents. These statistics shouldn't keep you out of the sea, because it is indeed beautiful—and benevolent in most cases—and a major reason to go to Hawaii. But if you're foolish, the sea will bounce you like a basketball and suck you away for good. The best remedy is to avoid situations you can't handle. Don't let anyone dare you into a situation that makes you uncomfortable. Ask lifeguards or beach attendants about conditions, and follow their advice. If local people refuse to go in, there's a good reason. Even experts get in trouble in Hawaiian waters. Some beaches are as gentle as lambs; others, especially on the north coasts during the winter months, are frothing giants.

While beachcombing, or especially when walking out on rocks, never turn your back to the sea. Be aware of undertows (the waves drawing back into the sea). They can knock you off your feet. Before entering the water, study it for rocks, breakers, and reefs. Look for ocean currents, especially those within reefs that can cause riptides when the water washes out a channel. Observe the water well before you enter. Note where others are swimming or snorkeling and go there. Don't swim alone if possible, and obey all warning signs. Come in *before* you get tired.

When the wind comes up, get out. Stay out of the water during periods of high surf. High surf often creates riptides that can pull you out to sea. Riptides are powerful currents, like rivers in the sea, that can drag you out. Mostly they peter out not too far from shore, and you can often see their choppy waters on the surface. If caught in a "rip," don't fight to swim directly against it. You'll lose and only exhaust yourself. Swim diagonally across it, while going along with it, and try to stay parallel to the shore until you are out of the strong pull.

When bodysurfing, never ride straight in; come to shore at a 45-degree angle. Remember, waves come in sets. Little ones can be followed by giants, so watch the action awhile instead of plunging right in. Standard procedure is to duck under a breaking wave. You can survive even thunderous oceans using this technique. Don't try to swim through a heavy froth, and never turn your back and let it smash you.

Stay off of coral. Standing on coral damages it, as does breaking it with your hands, and it might give you a nasty infection.

Leave the fish, turtles, and seals alone. Fish should never be encouraged to feed from humans. Green sea turtles and seals are endangered species, and stiff fines can be levied on those who knowingly disturb them. Have a great time looking, but give them space.

Hawaiians want to entertain you, and they want you to be safe. The county, for its part, doesn't put up ocean conditions signs at beaches just to waste money. They're there for your safety. Pay heed. The last rule is, "If in doubt, stay out."

Hazards

Sharks live in all the oceans of the world. Most mind their own business and stay away from shore. Hawaiian sharks are well fed—on fish—and don't usually bother with unsavory humans. If you encounter a shark, don't panic! Never thrash around because this will trigger its attack instinct. If it comes close, scream loudly.

Portuguese man-of-wars put out long, floating tentacles that sting if they touch you. It seems that many floating jellyfish are blown into shore by winds on the eighth, ninth, and 10th days after the full moon. Don't wash the sting off with freshwater, as this will only aggravate it. Hot saltwater will take away the sting, as will alcohol (the drinking or the rubbing kind), aftershave lotion, and meat tenderizer (MSG), which can be found in any supermarket or Chinese restaurant.

Coral can give you a nasty cut, and it's known for causing infections because it's a living organism. Wash the cut immediately and apply an antiseptic. Keep it clean and covered, and watch for infection.

Poisonous sea urchins, such as the lacquer-black *wana,* can be beautiful creatures. They are found in shallow tide pools and will hurt you if you step on them. Their spines will break off, enter your foot, and burn like blazes. There are cures. Vinegar and wine poured on the wound will stop the burning. If those are not available, the Hawaiian solution is urine.

It might seem ignominious to have someone pee on your foot, but it'll put the fire out. The spines will disintegrate in a few days, and there are generally no long-term effects.

Hawaiian reefs also have their share of moray eels. These creatures are ferocious in appearance but will never initiate an attack. You'll have to poke around in their holes while snorkeling or scuba diving to get them to attack. Sometimes this is inadvertent on the diver's part, so be careful where you stick your hand while underwater.

Leptospirosis is a disease caused by *freshwater*-borne bacteria deposited by the urine of infected animals that are present in streams, ponds, and muddy soil. From two to 20 days after the bacteria enter the body, there is a *sudden* onset of fever accompanied by chills, sweats, headache, and sometimes vomiting and diarrhea. Preventive measures include: staying out of freshwater sources where cattle and other animals wade and drink; not swimming in freshwater if you have an open cut; and not drinking stream water.

PREVENTING THEFT

From the minute you sit behind the wheel of your rental car, you'll be warned not to leave valuables unattended and to lock up your car tighter than a drum. Signs warning about theft at most major tourist attractions help to fuel your paranoia. Many hotel and condo rooms offer safes so you can lock your valuables away and relax while getting sunburned. The majority of theft in Hawaii is of the "sneak thief" variety. If you leave your hotel door unlocked, a camera sitting on the seat of your rental car, or valuables on your beach towel, you'll be inviting a very obliging thief to pad away with your stuff. You'll have to take precautions, like covering up your purse with a towel if you leave it in your car while at the beach, but they won't be anything like those employed in rougher areas of the world—just normal American precautions. Hawaii's reputation is much worse than the reality. Besides, Hawaiians are still among the friendliest, most giving, and understanding people on earth.

Information and Services

MONEY
Currency
U.S. currency is all the same size, with little variation in color; those unfamiliar with it should spend some time getting acquainted so they don't make costly mistakes. U.S. coins in use are: penny ($0.01), nickel ($0.05), dime ($0.10), quarter ($0.25), half dollar ($0.50), and $1; paper currency is $1, $2 (uncommon), $5, $10, $20, $50, and $100. Bills larger than $100 are not in common usage. Since 1996, new designs have been issued for the $100, $50, $20, $10, and $5 bills. Both the old and new bills are accepted as valid currency.

Banks
Full-service bank hours are generally Monday–Thursday 8:30 A.M.–4 P.M. and Friday until 6 P.M. Weekend hours are rare and weekday hours will be a bit longer at counters in grocery stores and other outlets. All main towns on Hawaii have one or more banks: Hilo, Kailua-Kona, Waimea, Kealakekua, Honoka'a, Pahoa, Waikoloa, and Hawi. Virtually all branch banks have automated teller machines (ATMs) for 24-hour service, and these can be found at some shopping centers and other venues around the island. ATMs work only when the Hawaiian bank you choose to use is on an affiliate network with your home bank. Of most value to travelers, banks sell and cash travelers checks, give cash advances on credit cards, and exchange and sell foreign currency (sometimes with a fee). Major banks on the Big Island are American Savings Bank, Bank of Hawaii, First Hawaiian Bank, and Central Pacific Bank.

COMMUNICATIONS AND MEDIA
Post Office
Normal business hours are Monday–Friday 8 A.M.–4:30 P.M.; very few branches are open on Saturday. However, some branches open as early as 7 A.M. and close before 3 P.M. Most are closed during lunchtime since they usually are only staffed by one person (everyone has to eat). The central post office on Hawaii is in Hilo, and there are 25 branch post offices in towns around the island.

Telephone
The telephone system on the main islands is modern and comparable to any system on the Mainland. Any phone call to a number on that island is a **local call;** it's **long distance** when dialing to another island. You can "direct dial" from Hawaii to the Mainland and more than 160 foreign countries. Undersea cables and satellite communications ensure top-quality phone service. Toll-free calls are preceded by 800, 888, 877, or 866; there is no charge to the calling party.

For directory assistance, dial: 411 (local), 1-555-1212 (interisland), area code/555-1212 (Mainland), or 800/555-1212 (toll-free). The **area code** for all the islands of Hawaii is 808.

Cell phone service and even 3G service is available in the majority of areas of the island, although sometimes service varies depending on what carrier you use. As of 2011, cell phone service (that also means your 3G) was not available south of Pahoa (specifically the Red Road area—but then it works again at Kaimu Beach), in Waipi'o Valley, on some parts of the Saddle Road, and in the Pololu Valley near Kapa'au. Plan ahead if you depend on your cell phone as a GPS device.

Newspapers
Major daily newspapers on the Big Island include *Hawaii Tribune-Herald* (www.hilo-hawaiitribune.com), a Hilo publication, and *West Hawaii Today* (www.westhawaiitoday.com), published in Kona. Both are owned by the same parent company.

The alternative newspaper *Big Island Weekly* (http://bigislandweekly.com) is published weekly on Wednesday and provides a great resource for special events going on around the island and ongoing classes. Also, even if you're not interested in the newspaper's content, I recommend skimming the ads, as oftentimes there are coupons for local restaurants.

Much like how during the plantation era each town had its own bottleworks, it seems like the new thing is that every town has its own weekly or monthly newspaper or newsletter. For instance, *Volcano Community Association Voice* and the *Ka'u Calendar* (www.kaucalendar.com) just to name a few. Again, local papers are a great way to find out what is happening in town.

Libraries

Libraries are located in towns and schools all over the island, with the main branch in Hilo (300 Waianuenue Ave., 808/933-8888). This location can provide information regarding all libraries. In Kailua-Kona, the library is in the center of town (75-140 Hualalai Rd., 808/327-4327). Check with each individual branch for times and services. Library cards are available free for Hawaii state residents and military personnel stationed in Hawaii, $25 for nonresidents (valid for five years), and $10 for three months for visitors. Free Internet access is available to library cardholders.

TOURIST INFORMATION
Hawaii Visitors Bureau

The Hawaii Visitors Bureau or HVB (www.gohawaii.com) is a top-notch organization providing help and information to all of Hawaii's visitors. Anyone contemplating a trip to Hawaii should visit a nearby office or check out its website for any specific information that might be required. The Hawaii Visitors Bureau's advice and excellent brochures on virtually every facet of living in, visiting, or simply enjoying Hawaii are free. The material offered is too voluminous to list, but for basics, request individual island brochures, maps, vacation planners (also on the web at www.hshawaii.com), and an all-island members directory of accommodations, restaurants, entertainment, and transportation. Allow 2–3 weeks for requests to be answered.

There are two Big Island HVB offices: **Big Island Hawaii Visitors Bureau, Hilo**

Branch (250 Keawe St., Hilo, 808/961-5797 or 800/648-2441, www.bigisland.org) and **Big Island Hawaii Visitors Bureau, Kona Branch** (250 Waikoloa Beach Dr., Suite B-15, Waikoloa, 808/886-1655).

Maps

Aside from the simple maps in the ubiquitous free tourist literature, the Big Island Visitors Bureau, Hawaiian Airlines, and other organizations put out folding pocket maps of the island that are available free at the airport and tourist brochure racks around the island. Various island and street maps are available at Basically Books (160 Kamehameha Ave., Hilo, 808/961-0144, www.basicallybooks.com) and Kona Stories (78-6831 Ali'i Dr., Keauhou, 808/324-0350, www.konastories.com). Perhaps the best and most detailed of these island maps is the University of Hawai'i Press reference map *Hawai'i, The Big Island*. This map can be found at gift and sundries shops around the island, and at bookshops. If you are looking for detail, the best street map atlas of the Big Island is a two-volume publication by Odyssey Publishing: *The Ready Mapbook of West Hawaii* and *The Ready Mapbook of East Hawaii*.

In addition, Basically Books carries USGS maps, and Kona Marine Supply (74-425 Kealakehe Pkwy. #9, Kailua-Kona, 808/329-1012) carries nautical charts. The Division of Forestry and Wildlife office in Hilo (19 E. Kawili St., 808/974-4221, http://hawaii.gov/dlnr/dofaw) has map and trail description handouts for trails in the Na Ala Hele state trail system, and the visitors center at Hawai'i Volcanoes National Park carries hiking trail maps for park trails.

LOCAL EMERGENCIES
Emergencies

For **police, fire, and ambulance** anywhere on the Big Island, dial **911**. For **nonemergency police** assistance and information, dial 808/935-3311.

In case of natural disaster such as hurricanes or tsunamis on the Big Island, call **Civil Defense** (808/935-0031). **Coast Guard**

Search and Rescue can be reached at 800/552-6458.

The **Sexual Assault Crisis Line** is 808/935-0677.

Weather, Marine, and Volcano Reports

For recorded information on **local island weather,** call 808/961-5582; for the **marine report,** call 808/935-9883; and for **volcano activity,** call 808/985-6000.

Consumer Protection

If you encounter problems finding accommodations or experience bad service or downright rip-offs, try the following: the Chamber of Commerce in Hilo (808/935-7178) or in the Kona/Kohala area (808/329-1758), the Office of Consumer Protection (808/933-0910), or the Better Business Bureau of Hawaii on O'ahu (877/222-6551).

WEIGHTS AND MEASURES

Hawaii, like all of the United States, employs the "English method" of measuring weights and distances. Basically, dry weights are in ounces and pounds; liquid measures are in ounces, quarts, and gallons; and distances are measured in inches, feet, yards, and miles. The metric system is known but is not in general use.

Electricity

The same electrical current is in use in Hawaii as on the U.S. Mainland and is uniform throughout the islands. The system functions on 110 volts, 60 cycles of alternating current (AC). Appliances from Japan will work, but there is some danger that they will burn out, while those requiring the normal European voltage of 220 will not work.

Time Zones

There is no daylight saving time in Hawaii. When daylight saving time is not observed on the Mainland, Hawaii is two hours behind the West Coast, four hours behind the Midwest, five hours behind the East Coast. While daylight saving is observed, Hawaii is an additional hour behind.

Hawaii, being just east of the International Date Line, is almost a full day behind most Asian and Oceanian cities. Hours behind these countries and cities are: Japan, 19 hours; Singapore, 18 hours; Sydney, 20 hours; New Zealand, 22 hours; Fiji, 22 hours.

RESOURCES

Glossary

PRONUNCIATION IN THE HAWAIIAN LANGUAGE

Five vowels (a, e, i, o, and u) and seven consonants (h, k, l, m, n, p, and w) are all there is to the Hawaiian alphabet. Hawaii had no written language before Western contact (except for petroglyph symbols), so if you're wondering why these letters, you can thank the European explorers and American missionaries for the Latinization of the Hawaiian language. Some basic rules:

- In the Hawaiian language, a consonant is always followed by a vowel. So yes, all Hawaiian words end in vowels.

- The letter "w" is sometimes pronounced as a "v," as in the traditional pronunciation of the word Hawai'i, which is "ha-VI-ee" instead of "ha-WHY-ee."

- The macron symbol over a vowel, called a kahako, means that the vowel sound is elongated.

- The backward apostrophe symbol, called an 'okina, means to make a phonetic glottal stop (to separate the word where the 'okina is placed). This is common in many Polynesian languages. For example, in the word Hawai'i there should be a glottal stop between the last two syllables.

- Vowels are pronounced as follows: "a" as "ah"; "e" as "eh"; "i" as "ee"; "o" as "oh"; and "u" as "oo."

HAWAIIAN

The following list gives you a taste of Hawaiian and provides a basic vocabulary of words in common usage that you are likely to hear. Becoming familiar with them is not a strict necessity, but they will definitely enhance your experience and make talking with local people more congenial. Many islanders spice their speech with certain words and you, too, can use them just as soon as you feel comfortable. You might even discover some Hawaiian words that are so perfectly expressive they'll become regular parts of your vocabulary. Some Hawaiian words have been absorbed into the English language and are found in English dictionaries. The definitions given below are not exhaustive, but are generally considered the most common.

'a'a rough clinker lava. 'A'a has become the correct geological term to describe this type of lava found anywhere in the world.

'ae yes

ahu traditional trail markers that are piles of stone shaped like little Christmas trees

ahupua'a pie-shaped land divisions running from mountain to sea that were governed by konohiki, local ali'i who owed their allegiance to a reigning chief

aikane friend; pal; buddy

'aina land; the binding spirit to all Hawaiians. Love of the land is paramount in traditional Hawaiian beliefs.

akamai smart; clever; wise

akua a god, or simply "divine"

ali'i a Hawaiian chief or noble

aloha the most common greeting in the islands; can mean both hello and good-bye, welcome and farewell, as well as love, affection, or best wishes

aloha spirit a way of living and treating each other with love and respect; joyfully sharing life

anuenue rainbow

'anu'u oracle tower

'a'ole no

'aumakua a personal or family god, often an ancestral spirit

auwe alas or ouch; a traditional wail of mourning

'awa also known as kava, a mildly intoxicating traditional drink made from the juice of chewed 'awa root, spat into a bowl, and used in religious ceremonies

halakahiki pineapple

halau school, as in hula school

hale house or building; often combined with other words to name a specific place, such as Haleakala (House of the Sun)

hana work; combined with pau means end of work or quitting time

hanai literally "to feed." A hanai is a permanent guest, or an adopted family member, usually an old person or a child. This is an enduring cultural phenomenon in Hawaii, in which a child from one family (perhaps that of a brother or sister, and quite often one's grandchild) is raised as one's own without formal adoption.

haole a word that at one time meant foreigner but now means a white person or Caucasian

hapa half, as in a mixed-blooded person being referred to as hapa haole

hapai pregnant; used by all ethnic groups when a keiki is on the way

haupia a coconut custard dessert often served at a lu'au

he'enalu surfing

heiau a platform made of skillfully fitted rocks, upon which temporary structures were built as temples and offerings were made to the gods

holomu an ankle-length dress that is much more fitted than a mu'umu'u, and which is often worn on formal occasions

hono bay, as in Honolulu (Sheltered Bay)

honu green sea turtle

ho'oilo traditional Hawaiian winter that begins in November

ho'olaule'a any happy event, but especially a family outing or picnic

ho'omalimali sweet talk; flattery

hui a group; meeting; society. Often used to refer to Chinese businesspeople or family members who pool their money to get businesses started.

hukilau traditional shoreline fish-gathering in which everyone lends a hand to huki (pull) the huge net. Anyone taking part shares in the lau (food). It is much more like a party than hard work, and if you're lucky you'll be able to take part in one.

hula a native Hawaiian dance in which the rhythm of the islands is captured by swaying hips and stories told by lyrically moving hands. A halau is a group or school of hula.

huli huli: barbecue, as in huli huli **chicken**

i'a fish in general; i'a maka is raw fish

imu underground oven filled with hot rocks and used for baking. The main cooking method featured at a lu'au, used to steam-bake pork and other succulent dishes.

ipo sweetheart; lover; girl- or boyfriend

kahili a tall pole topped with feathers, resembling a huge feather duster. It was used by an ali'i to announce his or her presence.

kahuna priest; sorcerer; doctor; skillful person. In old Hawaii kahuna had tremendous power, which could be used for both good and evil. The kahuna ana'ana was a feared individual who practiced "black magic" and could pray a person to death, while the kahuna lapa'au was a medical practitioner bringing aid and comfort to the people.

kai the sea; many businesses and hotels employ kai as part of their name

kalua means roasted underground in an imu; a favorite island food is kalua pork

kama'aina a child of the land; an old-timer; a longtime island resident of any ethnic background; a resident of Hawaii or native son or daughter. Hotels and airlines often offer discounts called "kama'aina rates" to anyone who can prove island residency.

kanaka man or commoner; later used to distinguish a Hawaiian from other races. Tone of voice can make it a derisive expression.

kane means man, but actually used to signify a relationship such as husband or boyfriend. Written on a lavatory door it means "men's room."

kapu forbidden; taboo; keep out; do not touch

kaukau slang word meaning food or chow, as in kaukau wagons, trucks that sell plate lunches and other morsels

kauwa a landless, untouchable caste once confined

to living on reservations. Members of this caste were often used as human sacrifices at heiau. Calling someone *kauwa* is still a grave insult.

kava see '*awa*

keiki child or children; used by all ethnic groups

kia akua carved temple image posts, a Polynesian art form

kiawe an algaroba tree from South America commonly found in Hawaii along the shore. It grows a nasty long thorn that can easily puncture a tire.

kipuka an area that has been surrounded by a lava flow, but never inundated, that preserves an older and established ecosystem

ko'ala any food that has been broiled or barbecued

kokua help, as in, "Your *kokua* is needed to keep Hawaii free from litter."

kolohe rascal

konane a traditional Hawaiian game, similar to checkers, played with pebbles on a large flat stone used as a board

Kona wind a muggy subtropical wind that blows from the south and hits the leeward side of the islands; usually brings sticky hot weather

ko'olau windward side of the island

kukui a candlenut tree whose pods are polished and then strung together to make a beautiful lei. Traditionally the oil-rich nuts were strung on the rib of a coconut leaf and used as a candle.

kuleana homesite; the old homestead; small farms. Especially used to describe the small spreads on Hawaiian Homelands on Moloka'i.

Kumulipo ancient Hawaiian genealogical chant that records the pantheon of gods, creation, and the beginning of humankind

kupuna a grandparent or old-timer; usually means someone who has gained wisdom

la the sun. Often combined with other words to be more descriptive, such as Lahaina (Merciless Sun) or Haleakala (House of the Sun).

lanai veranda or porch. You'll pay more for a hotel room if it has a lanai with an ocean view.

lani sky or the heavens

lau hala traditional Hawaiian weaving of mats, hats, etc., from the prepared fronds of the pandanus (screw pine)

lei a traditional garland of flowers or vines. Given at any auspicious occasion, but especially when arriving or leaving Hawaii.

lele the stone altar at a *heiau*

limu edible seaweed of various types. It's used to garnish many island dishes and is a favorite at *lu'au*.

lolo crazy, as in "*lolo buggah*" (stupid or crazy guy)

lomilomi traditional Hawaiian massage; also, raw salmon made into a vinegared salad with chopped onion and spices

lua the toilet; the bathroom

luakini a human-sacrifice temple. Introduced to Hawaii in the 13th century at Waha'ula Heiau on the Big Island.

lu'au a Hawaiian feast featuring poi, *imu*-baked pork, and other traditional foods. Good ones provide some of the best gastronomic delights in the world.

luna foreman or overseer in the plantation fields

mahalo thank you. *Mahalo nui* means "big thanks" or "thank you very much."

mahele division. The "Great Mahele" of 1848 changed Hawaii forever when the traditional common lands were broken up into privately owned plots.

mahimahi a favorite eating fish. Often called a dolphin, but a mahimahi is a true fish, not a cetacean.

mahu a homosexual; often used derisively like "fag" or "queer"

maile a fragrant vine used in traditional lei. It looks ordinary but smells delightful.

maka'ainana a commoner; a person "belonging" to the '*aina* (land), who supported the *ali'i* by fishing and farming and as a warrior

makai toward the sea; used by most islanders when giving directions

make dead; deceased

malama 'aina take care of the environment

malihini a newcomer; a tenderfoot; a recent arrival

malo the native Hawaiian loincloth. Never worn anymore except at festivals or pageants.

mana power from the spirit world; innate energy of all things animate or inanimate; the grace of god. Mana could be passed on from one person to another, or even stolen. Great care was taken to protect the *ali'i* from having their mana defiled. *Kahuna* were often employed in the regaining or transference of mana.

manini stingy; tight. Also a type of fish.

manuahi free; gratis; extra

mauka toward the mountains; used by most islanders when giving directions

mauna mountain. Often combined with other words to be more descriptive, such as Mauna Kea (White Mountain)

mele a song or chant in the Hawaiian oral tradition that records the history and genealogies of the *ali'i*

Menehune the legendary "little people" of Hawaii. Like leprechauns, they are said to shun humans and possess magical powers.

moa chicken; fowl

moana the ocean; the sea. Many places have *moana* as part of their name.

moe sleep

mo'olelo ancient tales kept alive by the oral tradition and recited only by day

mu'umu'u a "Mother Hubbard," an ankle-length dress with a high neckline introduced by the missionaries to cover the nakedness of the Hawaiians. It has become fashionable attire for almost any occasion in Hawaii.

nani beautiful

nui big; great; large; as in *mahalo nui* (thank you very much)

'ohana a family; the fundamental social division; extended family. Now often used to denote a social organization with grassroots overtones.

'okolehau literally "iron bottom"; a traditional booze made from ti root. *'Okole* means "rear end" and *hau* means "iron," which was descriptive of the huge blubber pots in which *'okolehau* was made. Also, if you drink too much it'll surely knock you on your *'okole*.

oli chant not done to a musical accompaniment

'ono delicious; delightful; the best. *Ono ono* means "extra or absolutely delicious." Also a type of fish.

'opihi a shellfish or limpet that clings to rocks and is gathered as one of the islands' favorite pupu

'opu belly; stomach

pahoehoe smooth, ropy lava that looks like burnt pancake batter. It is now the correct geological term used to describe this type of lava found anywhere in the world.

pakalolo "crazy smoke"; marijuana

pake a Chinese person. Can be derisive, depending on the tone in which it is used. It is a bastardization of the Chinese word meaning "uncle."

pali a cliff; precipice. Hawaii's geology makes them quite common. The most famous are the *pali* of O'ahu where a major battle was fought.

paniolo a Hawaiian cowboy; derived from the Spanish *español*. The first cowboys brought to Hawaii during the early 19th century were Mexicans from California.

papale hat

pa'u long split skirt often worn by women when horseback riding. In the 1800s, an island treat was watching *pa'u* riders in their beautiful dresses at Kapi'olani Park in Honolulu. The tradition is carried on today at many of Hawaii's rodeos.

pau finished; done; completed. Often combined into *pau hana*, which means end of work or quitting time.

pilau stink; bad smell; stench

pilikia trouble of any kind, big or small; bad times

poi a glutinous paste made from the pounded corm of taro, which ferments slightly and has a light sour taste. Purplish in color, it's a staple at *lu'au*, where it is called "one-, two-, or three-finger" poi, depending upon its thickness.

poke cubed raw fish (usually ahi tuna) sashimi marinated with sea salt, soy sauce, sesame oil, and seaweed

pono righteous or excellent

pua flower

puka a hole of any size. *Puka* is used by all island residents, whether talking about a pinhole in a rubber boat or a tunnel through a mountain. Also a shell.

punalua a traditional practice, before the missionaries arrived, of sharing mates. Western seamen took advantage of it, leading to the spread of contagious diseases and eventual rapid decline of the Hawaiian people.

pune'e bed; narrow couch. Used by all ethnic groups. To recline on a *pune'e* on a breezy lanai is a true island treat.

pupu an appetizer; a snack; hors d'oeuvres; can be anything from cheese and crackers to sushi. Oftentimes, bars or nightclubs offer them free.

pupule crazy; nuts; out of your mind

pu'u hill, as in Pu'u 'Ula'ula (Red Hill)

tapa a traditional paper cloth made from beaten bark. Intricate designs were stamped in using beaters, and natural dyes added color. The tradition was lost for many years but is now making a comeback. Also called *kapa*.

taro the staple of old Hawaii, brought by the first Polynesians. A plant with a distinctive broad leaf that produces a starchy root. According to the oral tradition, the life-giving properties of taro hold mystical significance for Hawaiians, since it was created by the gods at about the same time as humans.

ti a broad-leafed plant that was used for many purposes, from plates to hula skirts. Especially used to wrap religious offerings presented at the heiau.

tutu grandmother; granny; older woman. Used by all as a term of respect and endearment.

ukulele a small guitar-like instrument; *uku* means "flea" and *lele* means "jumping," so literally "jumping flea" – the way the Hawaiians perceived the quick finger movements used on the banjo-like Portuguese folk instrument called a *cavaquinho*. The ukulele quickly became synonymous with the islands.

ulu breadfruit

wahine young woman; female; girl; wife. Used by all ethnic groups. When written on a lavatory door it means "women's room."

wai freshwater; drinking water

wela hot. *Wela kahao* is a "hot time" or "making whoopee."

wiki quickly; fast; in a hurry. Often seen as *wiki wiki* (very fast), as in "Wiki Wiki Messenger Service."

Useful Phrases

a hui hou until we meet again
aloha ahiahi good evening
aloha au ia'oe I love you
aloha kakahiaka good morning
aloha nui loa much love; fondest regards
hau'oli la hanau happy birthday
hau'oli makahiki hou happy new year
komo mai please come in; enter; welcome
mele kalikimaka merry Christmas
'okole maluna bottoms up; cheers

PIDGIN

The following are a few commonly used words and expressions that should give you an idea of pidgin. It really can't be written properly, merely approximated, but for now, *"Study da' kine an' bimbye it be mo' bettah, brah! Okay? Lesgo."*

an' den and then? big deal; so what's next?

auntie respected elderly woman

bad ass very good

bimbye after a while; bye and bye. *"Bimbye, you learn pidgin."*

blalah brother, but actually only refers to a large, heavy-set, good-natured Hawaiian man

brah all the bros in Hawaii are brahs; brother; pal. Used to call someone's attention. One of the most common words even among people who are not acquainted. After a fill-up at a gas station, a person would say *"Tanks, brah."*

chicken skin goose bumps

cockaroach steal; rip off. If you really want to find out what *cockaroach* means, just leave your camera on your beach blanket when you take a little dip.

da' kine a catchall word of many meanings that epitomizes the essence of pidgin. *Da' kine* is a euphemism for pidgin and is substituted whenever the speaker is at a loss for a word or just wants to generalize. It can mean: you know? watchamacallit; of that type.

geev um give it to them; give them hell; go for it. Can be used as an encouragement. If a surfer is riding a great wave, the people on the beach might yell, *"Geev um, brah!"*

grinds food

hana ho again. Especially after a concert the audience shouts *"hana ho"* (one more!).

hele on let's get going

howzit? what's happening? how's it going? The most common greeting, used in place of the more formal "How do you do?"

huhu angry! *"You put the make on the wrong da' kine wahine, brah, and you in da' kine trouble if you get one big Hawaiian blalah plenty huhu."*

lesgo let's go! do it!

li'dis an' li'dat like this or that; a catch-all grouping especially if you want to avoid details; like, ya' know?

lolo buggah stupid or crazy guy (person). Words to a tropical island song go, "I want to find the *lolo* who stole my *pakalolo*."

mo' bettah better, real good! great idea. An island sentiment used to be, *"mo' bettah you come Hawaii."* Now it has subtly changed to, *"mo' bettah you visit Hawaii."*

ono number one! delicious; great; groovy. *"Hawaii is ono, brah!"*

pakalolo literally "crazy smoke"; marijuana

pakiki head stubborn; bull-headed

pau a Hawaiian word meaning finished; done; over and done with. *Pau hana* means end of work or quitting time. Once used by plantation workers, now used by everyone.

seestah sister, woman

shaka hand wave where only the thumb and baby finger stick out, meaning thank you, all right!

slippahs slippers, flip-flops, "Locals" (a brand name)

stink face or stink eye; basically frowning at someone; using facial expression to show displeasure. Hard looks. What you'll get if you give local people a hard time.

swell head burned up; angry

talk story spinning yarns; shooting the breeze; throwing the bull; a rap session. If you're lucky enough to be around to hear *kupuna* (elders) *talk story*, you can hear some fantastic tales in the tradition of old Hawaii.

tanks, brah thanks, thank you

to da max all the way

waddascoops what's the scoop? what's up? what's happening?

Suggested Reading

Many publishers print books on Hawaii. Following are a few that focus on Hawaiian topics. **University of Hawai'i Press** (www.uhpress.hawaii.edu) has the best overall general list of titles on Hawaii. The **Bishop Museum Press** (www.bishopmuseum.org/press) puts out many scholarly works on Hawaiiana, as does **Kamehameha Schools Press** (www.kamehamehapublishing.org). Also good, with more general-interest lists, are **Bess Press** (www.besspress.com) and **Petroglyph Press** (www.basicallybooks.com). In addition, a website specifically oriented toward books on Hawaii, Hawaiian music, and other things Hawaiian is **Hawaii Books** (www.hawaiibooks.com).

ASTRONOMY

Bryan, E. H. *Stars over Hawaii.* Hilo, HI: Petroglyph Press, 1977. An introduction to astronomy, with information about the constellations and charts featuring the stars filling the night sky in Hawaii, by month. An excellent primer.

Rhoads, Samuel. *The Sky Tonight—A Guided Tour of the Stars over Hawaii.* Honolulu: Bishop Museum, 1993. Four pages per month of star charts—one each for the horizon in every cardinal direction. Exceptional!

COOKING

Alexander, Agnes. *How to Use Hawaiian Fruit.* Hilo, HI: Petroglyph Press, 1984. A slim volume of recipes using delicious and different Hawaiian fruits.

Beeman, Judy, and Martin Beeman. *Joys of Hawaiian Cooking.* Hilo, HI: Petroglyph Press, 1977. A collection of favorite recipes from Big Island chefs.

Choy, Sam. *Cooking from the Heart with Sam Choy.* Honolulu: Mutual Publishing, 1995.

This beautiful, hand-bound cookbook contains many color photos by Douglas Peebles.

Fukuda, Sachi. *Pupus, An Island Tradition.* Honolulu: Bess Press, 1995.

Margah, Irish, and Elvira Monroe. *Hawaii, Cooking with Aloha.* San Carlos, CA: Wide World, 1984. Island recipes, as well as hints on decor.

Rizzuto, Shirley. *Fish Dishes of the Pacific—from the Fishwife.* Honolulu: Hawaii Fishing News, 1986. Features recipes using all the fish commonly caught in Hawaiian waters (husband Jim Rizzuto is the author of *Fishing, Hawaiian Style*).

CULTURE

Dudley, Michael Kioni. *Man, Gods, and Nature.* Honolulu: Na Kane O Ka Malo Press, 1990. An examination of the philosophical underpinnings of Hawaiian beliefs and their interconnected reality.

Hartwell, Jay. *Na Mamo: Hawaiian People Today.* Honolulu: Ai Pohaku Press, 1996. Profiles 12 people practicing Hawaiian traditions in the modern world.

Heyerdahl, Thor. *American Indians in the Pacific.* London: Allen and Unwin Ltd., 1952. Theoretical and anthropological accounts of the influence on Polynesia of the Indians along the Pacific coast of North and South America. Though no longer in print, this book is fascinating reading, presenting unsubstantiated yet intriguing theories.

Kamehameha Schools Press. *Life in Early Hawaii: The Ahupuaʻa.* 3rd ed. Honolulu: Kamehameha Schools Press, 1994. Written for schoolchildren to better understand the basic organization of old Hawaiian land use and its function, this slim volume is a good primer for people of any age who wish to understand this fundamental societal fixture.

Kirch, Patrick V. *Feathered Gods and Fishhooks: An Introduction to Hawaiian Archaeology and Prehistory.* Honolulu: University of Hawaiʻi Press, 1997. This scholarly, lavishly illustrated, yet very readable book gives new insight into the development of precontact Hawaiian civilization. It focuses on the sites and major settlements of old Hawaiʻi and chronicles the main cultural developments while weaving in the social climate that contributed to change. A very worthwhile read.

FAUNA

Boom, Robert. *Hawaiian Seashells.* Photos by Jerry Kringle. Honolulu: Waikiki Aquarium, 1972. A collection of 137 seashells found in Hawaiian waters, featuring many found nowhere else on earth. Broken into categories with accompanying text including common and scientific names, physical descriptions, and likely habitats. A must for shell collectors.

Carpenter, Blyth, and Russell Carpenter. *Fish Watching in Hawaii.* San Mateo, CA: Natural World Press, 1981. A color guide to many of the reef fish found in Hawaii and often spotted by snorkelers. If you're interested in the fish that you'll be looking at, this guide will be very helpful.

Fielding, Ann, and Ed Robinson. *An Underwater Guide to Hawaii.* Honolulu: University of Hawaiʻi Press, 1987. If you've ever had a desire to snorkel/scuba the living reef waters of Hawaii and to be familiar with what you're seeing, get this small but fact-packed book. The amazing array of marine life found throughout the archipelago is captured in glossy photos with accompanying informative text. Both the scientific and common names of specimens are given. This book will enrich your underwater experience and serve as an easily understood reference guide for many years.

Goodson, Gar. *The Many-Splendored Fishes of Hawaii.* Stanford, CA: Stanford University

Press, 1985. This small but thorough "fish-watchers" book includes entries on some deep-sea fish.

Hawaiian Audubon Society. *Hawaii's Birds.* 5th ed. Honolulu: Hawaii Audubon Society, 1997. Excellent bird book, giving description, range, voice, and habits of the over 100 species. Slim volume; good for carrying while hiking.

Hobson, Edmund, and E. H. Chave. *Hawaiian Reef Animals.* Honolulu: University of Hawai'i Press, 1987. Colorful photos and descriptions of the fish, invertebrates, turtles, and seals that call Hawaiian reefs their home.

Kay, Alison, and Olive Schoenberg-Dole. *Shells of Hawaii.* Honolulu: University of Hawai'i Press, 1991. Color photos and tips on where to look.

Mahaney, Casey. *Hawaiian Reef Fish, The Identification Book.* Planet Ocean Publishing, 1993. A spiral-bound reference work featuring many color photos and descriptions of common reef fish found in Hawaiian waters.

Nickerson, Roy. *Brother Whale, A Pacific Whalewatcher's Log.* San Francisco: Chronicle Books, 1977. Introduces the average person to the life of earth's greatest mammals. Provides historical accounts, photos, and tips on whale-watching. Well-written, descriptive, and the best "first time" book on whales.

Pratt, Douglas. *A Pocket Guide to Hawaii's Birds.* Honolulu: Mutual Publishing, 1996. A condensed version of Pratt's larger work with a focus on birds of the state.

Pratt, H. D., P. L. Bruner, and D. G. Berrett. *The Birds of Hawaii and the Tropical Pacific.* Princeton, NJ: Princeton University Press, 1987. Useful field guide for novice and expert bird-watchers, covering Hawaii as well as other Pacific Island groups.

Tomich, P. Quentin. *Mammals in Hawaii.* Honolulu: Bishop Museum Press, 1986. Quintessential scholarly text on all mammal species in Hawaii, with description of distribution and historical references. Lengthy bibliography.

Van Riper, Charles, and Sandra van Riper. *A Field Guide to the Mammals of Hawaii.* Honolulu: Oriental Publishing, 1982. A guide to the surprising number of mammals introduced into Hawaii. Full-color pages document description, uses, tendencies, and habitat. Small and thin, this book makes a worthwhile addition to any serious hiker's backpack.

FLORA

Kepler, Angela. *Hawaiian Heritage Plants.* Honolulu: University of Hawai'i Press, 1998. A treatise on 32 utilitarian plants used by the early Hawaiians.

Kepler, Angela. *Hawaii's Floral Splendor.* Honolulu: Mutual Publishing, 1997. A general reference to flowers of Hawaii.

Kepler, Angela. *Tropicals of Hawaii.* Honolulu: Mutual Publishing, 1989. This small-format book features many color photos of nonnative flowers.

Kuck, Lorraine, and Richard Togg. *Hawaiian Flowers and Flowering Trees.* Rutland, VT: Tuttle, 1960. A classic, though no longer in print, field guide to tropical and subtropical flora illustrated in watercolor. A "to the point" description of Hawaiian plants and flowers with a brief history of their places of origin and their introduction to Hawaii.

Merrill, Elmer. *Plant Life of the Pacific World.* Rutland, VT: Tuttle, 1983. This is the definitive book for anyone planning a botanical tour to the entire Pacific Basin. Originally published in the 1930s, it remains a tremendous work, worth tracking down through out-of-print book services.

Miyano, Leland. *A Pocket Guide to Hawaii's Flowers.* Honolulu: Mutual Publishing, 2001. A small guide to readily seen flowers in the state. Good for the backpack or back pocket.

Miyano, Leland. *Hawaii, A Floral Paradise.* Honolulu: Mutual Publishing, 1995. Photographed by Douglas Peebles, this large-format book is filled with informative text and beautiful color shots of tropical flowers commonly seen in Hawaii.

Sohmer, S. H., and R. Gustafson. *Plants and Flowers of Hawai'i.* Honolulu: University of Hawai'i Press, 1987. Sohmer and Gustafson cover the vegetation zones of Hawaii, from mountains to coast, introducing you to the wide and varied floral biology of the islands. They give a good introduction to the history and unique evolution of Hawaiian plantlife. Beautiful color plates are accompanied by clear and concise plant descriptions, with the scientific and common Hawaiian names listed.

Teho, Fortunato. *Plants of Hawaii—How to Grow Them.* Hilo, HI: Petroglyph Press, 1992. A small but useful book for those who want their backyards to bloom into tropical paradises.

Wagner, Warren L., Derral R. Herbst, and H. S. Sohner. *Manual of the Flowering Plants of Hawai'i.* Rev. edition, vol. 2. Honolulu: University of Hawai'i Press in association with Bishop Museum Press, 1999. Considered the bible for Hawaii's botanical world.

Valier, Kathy. *Ferns of Hawaii.* Honolulu: University of Hawai'i Press, 1995. One of the few books that treat the state's ferns as a single subject.

HEALTH

Gutmanis, June. *Kahuna La'au Lapa'au.* Rev. ed. Honolulu: Island Heritage, 2001. Text on Hawaiian herbal medicines: diseases, treatments, and medicinal plants, with illustrations.

McBride, L. R. *Practical Folk Medicine of Hawaii.* Hilo, HI: Petroglyph Press, 1975. An illustrated guide to Hawaii's medicinal plants as used by the *kahuna lapa'au* (medical healers). Includes a thorough section on ailments, diagnosis, and the proper folk remedy. Illustrated by the author, a renowned botanical researcher and former ranger at Hawai'i Volcanoes National Park.

Wilkerson, James A., M.D., ed. *Medicine for Mountaineering and Other Wilderness.* 4th ed. Seattle: The Mountaineers, 1992. Don't let the title fool you. Although the book focuses on specific health problems that may be encountered while mountaineering, it is the best first-aid and general health guide available today. Written by doctors for the layperson to use until help arrives, it is jam-packed with easily understandable techniques and procedures. For those planning extended hikes, it is a must.

HISTORY

Apple, Russell A. *Trails: From Steppingstones to Kerbstones.* Honolulu: Bishop Museum Press, 1965. This "Special Publication #53" is a special-interest archaeological survey focusing on trails, roadways, footpaths, and highways and how they were designed and maintained throughout the years. Many "royal highways" from precontact Hawaii are cited.

Ashdown, Inez MacPhee. *Kaho'olawe.* Honolulu: Topgallant Publishing, 1979. The tortured story of the lonely island of Kaho'olawe by one of the family who owned the island until it was turned into a military bombing target during World War II. It's also a first-person account of life on the island.

Barnes, Phil. *A Concise History of the Hawaiian Islands.* Hilo, HI; Petroglyph Press, 1999. An examination of the main currents of Hawaiian history and its major players, focusing on the important factors in shaping the social, economic, and political trends of the islands. An easy read.

Cameron, Roderick. *The Golden Haze.* New York: World Publishing, 1964. An account of Captain James Cook's voyages of discovery throughout the South Seas. Uses original diaries and journals for an "on the spot" reconstruction of this great seafaring adventure.

Cox, J. Halley, and Edward Stasack. *Hawaiian Petroglyphs.* Honolulu: Bishop Museum Press, 1970. The most thorough examination of petroglyph sites throughout the islands.

Daws, Gavan. *Shoal of Time, A History of the Hawaiian Islands.* Honolulu: University of Hawai'i Press, 1974. A highly readable history of Hawaii dating from its "discovery" by the Western world down to its acceptance as the 50th state. Good insight into the psychological makeup of influential characters who helped form Hawaii's past.

Dorrance, William H., and Francis S. Morgan. *Sugar Islands: The 165-Year Story of Sugar in Hawai'i.* Honolulu: Mutual Publishing, 2000. An overall sketch of the sugar industry in Hawaii from inception to decline, with data on many individual plantations and mills around the islands. Definitely a story from the industry's point of view.

Finney, Ben, and James D. Houston. *Surfing, A History of the Ancient Hawaiian Sport.* Los Angeles: Pomegranate, 1996. Features many early etchings and old photos of Hawaiian surfers practicing their native sport.

Fornander, Abraham. *An Account of the Polynesian Race; Its Origins and Migrations, and the Ancient History of the Hawaiian People to the Times of Kamehameha I.* Rutland, VT: C. E. Tuttle Co., 1969. This is a reprint of a three-volume opus originally published 1878–1885. It is still one of the best sources of information on Hawaiian myth and legend.

Free, David. *Vignettes of Old Hawaii.* Honolulu: Crossroads Press, 1994. A collection of short essays on a variety of subjects.

Fuchs, Lawrence. *Hawaii Pono.* Honolulu: Bess Press, 1961. A detailed, scholarly work presenting an overview of Hawaii's history, based upon ethnic and sociological interpretations. Encompasses most socio-ethnological groups from native Hawaiians to modern entrepreneurs. This book is a must for obtaining some social historical background.

Handy, E. S., and Elizabeth Handy. *Native Planters in Old Hawaii.* Honolulu: Bishop Museum Press, 1972. A superbly written, easily understood scholarly work on the intimate relationship of precontact Hawaiians and the *'aina* (land). Much more than its title implies, this book should be read by anyone seriously interested in Polynesian Hawaii.

Ii, John Papa. *Fragments of Hawaiian History.* Honolulu: Bishop Museum, 1959. Hawaii's history under Kamehameha I as told by a Hawaiian who actually experienced it.

Joesting, Edward. *Hawaii: An Uncommon History.* New York: W. W. Norton Co., 1978. A truly uncommon history told in a series of vignettes relating to the lives and personalities of the first Caucasians in Hawaii, Hawaiian nobility, sea captains, writers, and adventurers. Brings history to life. Absolutely excellent!

Kamakau, S. M. *Ruling Chiefs of Hawaii.* Rev. ed. Honolulu: Kamehameha Schools Press, 1992. A history of Hawaii from the legendary leader 'Umi to the mid-Kamehameha dynasty, from oral tales and from a Hawaiian perspective.

Kurisu, Yasushi. *Sugar Town, Hawaiian Plantation Days Remembered.* Honolulu: Watermark Publishing, 1995. Reminiscences of life growing up on sugar plantations on the

Hamakua Coast of the Big Island. Features many old photos.

Lili'uokalani. *Hawaii's Story by Hawaii's Queen*. 1898. Reprint, Honolulu: Mutual Publishing, 1990. Originally written in 1898, this moving personal account recounts Hawaii's inevitable move from monarchy to U.S. Territory by its last queen, Lili'uokalani. The facts can be found in other histories, but none provides the emotion or point of view expressed by Hawaii's deposed monarch. This is a must-read to get the whole picture.

McBride, Likeke. *Petroglyphs of Hawaii*. Hilo, HI: Petroglyph Press, 1997. A revised and updated guide to petroglyphs found in the Hawaiian Islands. A basic introduction to these old Hawaiian picture stories.

Nickerson, Roy. *Lahaina, Royal Capital of Hawaii*. Honolulu: Hawaiian Service, 1978. The story of Lahaina from whaling days to present, spiced with ample photographs.

Tabrah, Ruth M. *Ni'ihau: The Last Hawaiian Island*. Kailua, HI: Press Pacifica, 1987. Sympathetic history of the privately owned island of Ni'ihau.

Takaki, Ronald. *Pau Hana: Plantation Life and Labor in Hawaii*. Honolulu: University of Hawai'i Press, 1983. The story of immigrant labor and the sugar industry in Hawaii until the 1920s from the worker's perspective.

INTRODUCTORY

Carroll, Rick, and Marcie Carroll, eds. *Hawaii: True Stories of the Island Spirit*. San Francisco: Travelers' Tales, Inc., 1999. A collection of stories by a variety of authors that were chosen to elicit the essence of Hawaii and Hawaiian experiences. A great read.

Cohen, David, and Rick Smolan. *A Day in the Life of Hawaii*. New York: Workman, 1984. On December 2, 1983, 50 of the world's top photojournalists were invited to Hawaii to photograph the variety of daily life on the islands. The photos are excellently reproduced and accompanied by a minimum of text.

Day, A. G., and C. Stroven. *A Hawaiian Reader*. 1959. Reprint, Honolulu: Mutual Publishing, 1984. A poignant compilation of essays, diary entries, and fictitious writings that takes you from the death of Captain Cook through the "statehood services."

Department of Geography, University of Hawai'i at Hilo. *Atlas of Hawaii*. 3rd ed. Honolulu: University of Hawai'i Press, 1998. Much more than an atlas filled with reference maps, this also contains commentary on the natural environment, culture, and sociology; a gazetteer; and statistical tables. Actually a mini-encyclopedia on Hawaii.

Michener, James A. *Hawaii*. New York: Random House, 1959. Michener's fictionalized historical novel has done more to inform *and* misinform readers about Hawaii than any other book ever written. A great tale with plenty of local color and information, but read it for pleasure, not facts.

Piercy, LaRue. *Hawaii This and That*. Honolulu: Mutual Publishing, 1994. Illustrated by Scot Ebanez. A 60-page book filled with one-sentence facts and oddities about all manner of things Hawaiian. Informative, amazing, and fun to read.

Steele, R. Thomas: *The Hawaiian Shirt: Its Art and History*. New York: Abbeville Press, 1984.

LANGUAGE

Elbert, Samuel. *Spoken Hawaiian*. Honolulu: University of Hawai'i Press, 1970. Progressive conversational lessons.

Elbert, Samuel, and Mary Pukui. *Hawaiian Dictionary*. Honolulu: University of Hawai'i Press, 1986. The best dictionary available on the Hawaiian language. The *Pocket Hawaiian Dictionary* is a less expensive, condensed version of this dictionary, and adequate for most travelers with a general interest in the language.

Pukui, Mary Kawena, Samuel Elbert, and Esther T. Mookini. *Place Names of Hawaii.* Honolulu: University of Hawai'i Press, 1974. A comprehensive listing of Hawaiian and foreign place-names in the state, giving pronunciation, spelling, meaning, and location.

Schutz, Albert J. *All About Hawaiian.* Honolulu: University of Hawai'i Press, 1995. A brief primer on Hawaiian pronunciation, grammar, and vocabulary. A solid introduction.

MYTHOLOGY AND LEGENDS

Beckwith, Martha. *Hawaiian Mythology.* 1940. Reprint, Honolulu: University of Hawai'i Press, 1976. Since its original printing in 1940, this work has remained the definitive text on Hawaiian mythology. Beckwith compiled this book from many sources, giving exhaustive cross-references to genealogies and legends expressed in the oral tradition. If you are going to read one book on Hawaii's folklore, this should be it.

Beckwith, Martha. *The Kumulipo.* 1951. Reprint, Honolulu: University of Hawai'i Press, 1972. Translation of the Hawaiian creation chant.

Colum, Padraic. *Legends of Hawaii.* New Haven: Yale University Press, 1937. Selected legends of old Hawaii, reinterpreted but closely based upon the originals.

Elbert, S. H., ed. *Hawaiian Antiquities and Folklore.* Honolulu: University of Hawai'i Press, 1959. Illustrated by Jean Charlot. A selection of the main legends from Abraham Fornander's great work, *An Account of the Polynesian Race.*

Kalakaua, David. *The Legends and Myths of Hawaii.* Edited by R.M. Daggett, with a foreword by Glen Grant. Honolulu: Mutual Publishing, 1990. In this book originally published in 1888, Hawaii's own King Kalakaua draws upon his scholarly and formidable knowledge of the classic oral tradition to bring alive ancient tales from precontact Hawaii. A powerful yet somewhat Victorian voice from Hawaii's past speaks clearly and boldly, especially about the intimate role of pre-Christian religion in the lives of the Hawaiian people.

Melville, Leinanai. *Children of the Rainbow.* Wheaton, IL: Theosophical Publishing, 1969. A book on higher spiritual consciousness attuned to nature, which was the basic belief of pre-Christian Hawaii. The appendix contains illustrations of mystical symbols used by the *kahuna.* An enlightening book in many ways.

Pukui, Mary Kawena, and Caroline Curtis. *Hawaii Island Legends.* Honolulu: The Kamehameha Schools Press, 1996. Hawaiian tales and legends for pre-teens.

Pukui, Mary Kawena, and Caroline Curtis. *Tales of the Menehune.* Honolulu: The Kamehameha Schools Press, 1960. Compilation of legends relating to Hawaii's "little people."

Pukui, Mary Kawena, and Caroline Curtis. *The Waters of Kane and other Hawaiian Legends* Honolulu: The Kamehameha Schools Press, 1994. Tales and legends for the pre-teen.

Thrum, Thomas. *Hawaiian Folk Tales.* 1907. Reprint, Chicago: McClurg and Co., 1950. A collection of Hawaiian tales from the oral tradition as told to the author from various sources.

Westervelt, W. D. *Hawaiian Legends of Volcanoes.* 1916. Reprint, Boston: Ellis Press, 1991. A small book concerning the volcanic legends of Hawaii and how they related to the fledgling field of volcanism in the early 1900s. The vintage photos alone are worth a look.

NATURAL SCIENCE AND GEOGRAPHY

Carlquist, Sherwin. *Hawaii: A Natural History.* National Tropical Botanical Garden, 1984. Definitive account of Hawaii's natural history.

Clark, John. *Beaches of the Big Island.* Honolulu: University of Hawai'i Press, 1997. Definitive guide to beaches, including many off the beaten path. Features maps and black-and-white photos. Also *Beaches of O'ahu, Beaches of Kaua'i and Ni'ihau,* and *Beaches of Maui County.*

Hazlett, Richard, and Donald Hyndman. *Roadside Geology of Hawai'i.* Missoula, MT: Mountain Press Publishing, 1996. Begins with a general discussion of the geology of the Hawaiian Islands, followed by a road guide to the individual islands offering descriptions of easily seen features. A great book to have in the car as you tour the islands.

Hubbard, Douglass, and Gordon Macdonald. *Volcanoes of the National Parks of Hawaii.* 1982. Reprint, Volcanoes, HI: Hawaii Natural History Association, 1989. The volcanology of Hawaii, documenting the major lava flows and their geological effect on the state.

Kay, E. Alison, comp. *A Natural History of the Hawaiian Islands.* Honolulu: University of Hawai'i Press, 1994. A selection of concise articles by experts in the fields of volcanism, oceanography, meteorology, and biology. An excellent reference source.

Macdonald, Gorden, Agatin Abbott, and Frank Peterson. *Volcanoes in the Sea.* Honolulu: University of Hawai'i Press, 1983. The best reference to Hawaiian geology. Well explained for easy understanding. Illustrated.

Ziegler, Alan C., *Hawaiian Natural History, Ecology, and Evolution.* Honolulu: University of Hawai'i Press. An overview of Hawaiian natural history with treatment of ecology and evolution in that process.

POLITICAL SCIENCE

Bell, Roger. *Last Among Equals: Hawaiian Statehood and American Politics.* Honolulu: University of Hawai'i Press, 1984. Documents Hawaii's long and rocky road to statehood, tracing political partisanship, racism, and social change.

SPORTS AND RECREATION

Alford, John D. *Mountain Biking the Hawaiian Islands.* 2nd ed. Honolulu: Ohana Publishing, 2010. Good off-road biking guide to the main Hawaiian Islands.

Ambrose, Greg. *Surfer's Guide to Hawai'i.* Honolulu: Bess Press, 1991. Island-by-island guide to surfing spots.

Ball, Stuart. *The Hiker's Guide to the Hawaiian Islands.* Honolulu: University of Hawai'i Press, 2000. This excellent guide includes 44 hikes on each of the four main islands.

Cagala, George. *Hawaii: A Camping Guide.* Boston: Hunter Publishing, 1994. Useful.

Chisholm, Craig. *Hawaiian Hiking Trails.* Lake Oswego, OR: Fernglen Press, 1989.

Cisco, Dan. *Hawaii Sports.* Honolulu: University of Hawai'i Press, 1999. A compendium of popular and little-known sporting events and figures, with facts, tidbits, and statistical information. Go here first for a general overview.

Lueras, Leonard. *Surfing, the Ultimate Pleasure.* Honolulu: Emphasis International, 1984. One of the most brilliant books ever written on surfing.

McMahon, Richard. *Camping Hawaii: A Complete Guide.* Honolulu: University of Hawai'i Press, 1997. This book has all you need to know about camping in Hawaii, with descriptions of different campsites.

Morey, Kathy. *Hawaii Trails*. Berkeley, CA: Wilderness Press, 1997. Morey's books are specialized, detailed hiker's guides to Hawaii's outdoors. Complete with useful maps, historical references, official procedures, and plants and animals encountered along the way. If you're focused on hiking, these are the best to take along. *Maui Trails, Oahu Trails,* and *Kauai Trails* are also available.

Rosenberg, Steve. *Diving Hawaii*. Locust Valley, NY: Aqua Quest, 1990. Describes diving locations on the major islands as well as the marine life divers are likely to see. Includes many color photos.

Smith, Robert. *Hawaii's Best Hiking Trails*. Kula, HI: Hawaiian Outdoor Adventures, 1991. Other guides by this author include *Hiking Oahu, Hiking Maui, Hiking Hawaii,* and *Hiking Kauai*.

Sutherland, Audrey. *Paddling Hawaii*. Rev. ed. Honolulu: University of Hawai'i Press, 1998. All you need to know about sea kayaking in Hawaiian waters.

Wallin, Doug. *Diving & Snorkeling Guide to the Hawaiian Islands,* 2nd ed. Pisces Books, 1991. A guide offering brief descriptions of diving locations on the four major islands.

Internet Resources

GOVERNMENT
www.hawaiicounty.gov
The official website of the County of Hawai'i. Includes, among other items, a county data book, information about parks and camping, and island bus schedules.

www.hawaii.gov
Official website for the state of Hawai'i. Includes information for visitors, on government organizations, on living in the state, business and employment, education, and many other helpful topics.

TOURIST INFORMATION
www.instanthawaii.com
This site has wide-ranging information about the Big Island and topics pertaining to the state in general. Good for an introduction before you travel.

www.gohawaii.com
This official site of the Hawaii Visitors and Convention Bureau, the state-run tourism organization, has information about all the major Hawaiian islands: transportation, accommodations, eating, activities, shopping, Hawaiian products, an events calendar, a travel planner, as well as information about meetings, conventions, and the organization itself.

www.bigisland.org
The official site of the Big Island Visitors Bureau, a branch of the Hawaii Visitors Bureau, has much the same information as www.gohawaii.com but specific to the island of Hawai'i. A very useful resource.

www.bestplaceshawaii.com
Produced and maintained by H&S Publishing, this first-rate commercial site has general and specific information about all major Hawaiian islands, a vacation planner, and suggestions for things to do and places to see. For a nongovernmental site, this is a great place to start a search for tourist information about the state or any of its major islands. One of dozens of sites on the Internet with a focus on Hawaii tourism-related information.

www.konaweb.com
This site offers a multiplicity of tourist information for those wishing to visit or move to the island, information on island living, and an events calendar.

www.alternative-hawaii.com
Alternative source for eco-friendly general information and links to specific businesses, with some cultural, historical, and events information.

www.hawaiiecotourism.org
Official Hawaii Ecotourism Association website. Lists goals, members, and activities and provides links to member organizations and related ecotourism groups.

www.stayhawaii.com
Website for the Hawaii Island Bed and Breakfast Association, Inc., the only islandwide B&B member organization. Lists a majority of the island's registered B&Bs. Some registered B&Bs are not members of this organization.

CHAMBERS OF COMMERCE
www.gohilo.com
Hawaii Island Chamber of Commerce site. Strong on business and economic issues, particularly relating to the eastern side of the island. Much additional general information.

www.kona-kohala.com
Chamber of Commerce website for west Hawai'i.

CULTURAL EVENTS
http://calendar.gohawaii.com
For events of all sorts happening throughout the state, visit the calendar of events listing on the Hawaii Visitors Bureau website. Information can be accessed by island, date, or type.

www.hawaii.gov/sfca
This site of the State Foundation of Culture and the Arts features a calendar of arts and cultural events, activities, and programs held throughout the state. Information is available by island and type.

INTERISLAND AIRLINES
www.hawaiianair.com
http://iflygo.com
These websites for Hawaiian Airlines and Go!Mokulele list virtually all regularly scheduled commercial air links throughout the state.

MUSIC
www.mele.com
Check out the Hawaiian music scene at Hawaiian

Music Island, one of the largest music websites, which focuses on Hawaiian music, books and videos related to Hawaiian music and culture, concert schedules, Hawaiian music awards, and links to music companies and musicians.

www.nahenahe.net
For general interest music industry information try this site.

BOOKS ON HAWAII
www.uhpress.hawaii.edu
www.bishopmuseum.org/press/
  press.html
www.kamehamehapublishing.org
www.besspress.com
www.petroglyphpress.com
The University of Hawai'i Press website has the best overall list of titles for books published on Hawaiian themes and topics. Other publishers to check for substantial lists of books on Hawaiiana are the Bishop Museum Press, Kamehameha Schools Press, Bess Press, and Petroglyph Press.

NEWSPAPERS
www.westhawaiitoday.com
www.hilohawaiitribune.com
Web presence for the newspapers *West Hawaii Today,* published in Kona, and *Hawaii Tribune-Herald,* published in Hilo. Good for local and statewide news. Both have the same parent company.

www.starbulletin.com
www.honoluluadvertiser.com
Websites for Hawaii's two main English-language dailies, the *Honolulu Star Bulletin* and the *Honolulu Advertiser,* both published in Honolulu. Both have a concentration of news coverage about O'ahu but also cover major news from the neighbor islands.

MUSEUMS
www.hawaiimuseums.org
This site is dedicated to the promotion of museums and cultural attractions in the state of Hawaii with links to member sites on each of the islands. A member organization.

www.bishopmuseum.org

Site of the premier ethnological and cultural museum dedicated to Hawaiian people, their culture, and cultural artifacts.

NATIONAL PARKS
www.nps.gov/havo

This official site of Hawai'i Volcanoes National Park is a wealth of general information about the park.

www.nps.gov/puho
www.nps.gov/puhe

Pu'uhonua O Honaunau, a restored Hawaiian temple of refuge, and Pu'ukohola Heiau, a restored Hawaiian temple, are both national historical sites administered by the National Park Service.

ASTRONOMICAL OBSERVATORIES
www.ifa.hawaii.edu

For information about the astronomical observatories and individual telescope installations on the top of Mauna Kea on the Big Island as well as the Onizuka Center for International Astronomy on the mountain's flank, log onto this University of Hawai'i Institute for Astronomy website and follow the links from there.

VOLCANO INFORMATION
http://hvo.wr.usgs.gov

For a history of the Kilauea Volcano volcanic activity, plus up-to-the-minute reports on current activity, see this Hawaiian Volcano Observatory website.

www.soest.hawaii.edu/gg/hcv

Volcanic information is also available at the Hawaii Center for Volcanology.

NATIVE HAWAIIAN AFFAIRS
www.freehawaii.org
www.pixi.com/~kingdom

These are two of the many independent native Hawaiian rights organizations that are pushing for various degrees of sovereignty or independence for native Hawaiian people.

www.oha.org

Official site for the state-mandated organization that deals with native Hawaii-related affairs.

Index

List of Maps

Acknowledgments

FROM THE AUTHOR

Thank you to the public relations people and small business owners of the Big Island who made this book possible. I would especially like to thank the innkeepers of the island's many wonderful bed-and-breakfasts, who were incredibly generous not only with their breakfast offerings and accommodations but also with making time to *talk story*. A million thank yous to Mark Wasser, the brilliant photographer, who provided the majority of photos for this book. His knowledge and passion for the Big Island clearly is evident in his work. If you are interested in purchasing any of his prints please check out his website at http://wasser-photography.com. Thank you to my (life) partner, Adam, who assisted me on many of my outings (especially the ones that caused motion sickness), helped me try food when I couldn't possibly eat anymore, and led me on hikes while explaining them to me in words I understand (i.e., as an urbanite stuck in the wilderness). Lastly, thank you to the 'Aina. We've had some hard times together, but I am stronger for it. *A hui hou.*

FROM THE PUBLISHER

The first edition of *Moon Big Island of Hawai'i* was published in 1990. Its original author was J.D. Bisignani (1947–1997), whose *Japan Handbook* (1983) was one of Moon's founding publications. The next five editions of *Moon Big Island of Hawai'i* were revised by Joe and by Robert Nilsen (also the author of *Moon South Korea*), who took over as sole author after Joe's death in 1997. Joe and Bob brought the same spirit of adventure to their Hawaii coverage as they did to Moon's pioneering coverage of Asia. We wish them both aloha.

Color Photo Credits

www.moon.com

DESTINATIONS | ACTIVITIES | BLOGS | MAPS | BOOKS

MOON.COM is ready to help plan your next trip! Filled with fresh trip ideas and strategies, author interviews, informative travel blogs, a detailed map library, and descriptions of all the Moon guidebooks, Moon.com is all you need to get out and explore the world—or even places in your own backyard. While at Moon.com, sign up for our monthly e-newsletter for updates on new releases, travel tips, and expert advice from our on-the-go Moon authors. As always, when you travel with Moon, expect an experience that is uncommon and truly unique.

KEEP UP WITH MOON ON FACEBOOK AND TWITTER
JOIN THE MOON PHOTO GROUP ON FLICKR

MAP SYMBOLS

▭▭▭	Expressway	◖	Highlight	✕	Airfield	⚑	Golf Course
▭▭▭	Primary Road	○	City/Town	✈	Airport	P	Parking Area
▭▭▭	Secondary Road	◉	State Capital	▲	Mountain	▱	Archaeological Site
- - - -	Unpaved Road	⊛	National Capital	✚	Unique Natural Feature	▯	Church
- - - - -	Trail	★	Point of Interest			▯	Gas Station
⋯⋯⋯	Ferry	•	Accommodation	⚑	Waterfall	▱	Glacier
▭▭▭	Railroad	▼	Restaurant/Bar	⚑	Park	▱	Mangrove
▭▭▭	Pedestrian Walkway	▪	Other Location	▣	Trailhead	▱	Reef
▭▭▭	Stairs	▲	Campground	⛷	Skiing Area	▱	Swamp

CONVERSION TABLES

°C = (°F - 32) / 1.8
°F = (°C x 1.8) + 32
1 inch = 2.54 centimeters (cm)
1 foot = 0.304 meters (m)
1 yard = 0.914 meters
1 mile = 1.6093 kilometers (km)
1 km = 0.6214 miles
1 fathom = 1.8288 m
1 chain = 20.1168 m
1 furlong = 201.168 m
1 acre = 0.4047 hectares
1 sq km = 100 hectares
1 sq mile = 2.59 square km
1 ounce = 28.35 grams
1 pound = 0.4536 kilograms
1 short ton = 0.90718 metric ton
1 short ton = 2,000 pounds
1 long ton = 1.016 metric tons
1 long ton = 2,240 pounds
1 metric ton = 1,000 kilograms
1 quart = 0.94635 liters
1 US gallon = 3.7854 liters
1 Imperial gallon = 4.5459 liters
1 nautical mile = 1.852 km

°FAHRENHEIT | °CELSIUS

230 — 110
220 —
210 — 100 WATER BOILS
200 —
190 — 90
180 —
170 — 80
160 —
150 — 70
140 —
130 — 60
120 —
110 — 50
100 —
90 — 40
80 —
70 — 30
60 —
50 — 20
40 —
30 — 10
20 — 0 WATER FREEZES
10 —
0 — -10
-10 —
-20 — -20
-30 — -30
-40 — -40

INCH 0 1 2 3 4

CM 0 1 2 3 4 5 6 7 8 9 10

MOON BIG ISLAND OF HAWAI'I

Avalon Travel
a member of the Perseus Books Group
1700 Fourth Street
Berkeley, CA 94710, USA
www.moon.com

Editor and Series Manager: Kathryn Ettinger
Copy Editor: Deana Shields
Graphics and Production Coordinator: Tabitha Lahr
Cover Designer: Tabitha Lahr
Map Editor: Mike Morgenfeld
Cartographers: Chris Henrick, Andrea Butkovic
Indexer: Deana Shields

ISBN-13: 978-1-61238-109-1
ISSN: 1531-4138

Printing History
1st Edition – 1990
7th Edition – August 2012
5 4 3 2

Text © 2012 by Bree Kessler and Avalon Travel.
Maps © 2012 by Avalon Travel.
All rights reserved.

Some photos and illustrations are used by permission and are the property of the original copyright owners.

Printed in Canada by Friesens

All recommendations, including those for sights, activities, hotels, restaurants, and shops, are based on each author's individual judgment. We do not accept payment for inclusion in our travel guides, and our authors don't accept free goods or services in exchange for positive coverage.

KEEPING CURRENT

If you have a favorite gem you'd like to see included in the next edition, or see anything that needs updating, clarification, or correction, please drop us a line. Send your comments via email to feedback@moon.com, or use the address above.